T0138664

ARTIFICIAL INTELLIGENCE

CRITICAL CONCEPTS

ARTIFICIAL INTELLIGENCE

Critical Concepts

Edited by Ronald Chrisley
Editorial Assistant: Sander Begeer

Volume II

London and New York

First published 2000
by Routledge
11 New Fetter Lane, London EC4P 4EE

Simultaneously published in the USA and Canada
by Routledge
29 West 35th Street, New York, NY 10001

Routledge is an imprint of the Taylor & Francis Group

Typeset in Times by RefineCatch Limited, Bungay, Suffolk
Printed and bound in Great Britain by
TJ International Ltd, Padstow, Cornwall

British Library Cataloguing in Publication Data
A catalogue record for this book is available from the British Library

Library of Congress Cataloging in Publication Data
Artificial intelligence: critical concepts/edited by Ronald Chrisley with Sander Begeer.
p.   cm.
Includes bibliographical references.
ISBN 0–415–19331–1 (set)—ISBN 0–415–19332–X (v. 1)—ISBN 0–415–19333–8 (v. 2)
—ISBN 0–415–19334–6 (v. 3)—ISBN 0–415–19335–4 (v. 4)
1. Artificial intelligence.   I. Chrisley, Ronald.   II. Begeer, Sander.

Q335.55.A7825 2000
006.3—dc21   00–062568

ISBN 0–415–19331–1 (set)
ISBN 0–415–19333–8 (volume 2)

The publishers have made every effort to contact authors/copyright
holders of works reprinted in *Artificial Intelligence: Critical Concepts*.
This has not been possible in every case, however, and we would
welcome correspondence from those individuals/companies whom we
have been unable to trace.

References within each chapter are as they appeared in the original complete work.

CONTENTS

v

CONTENTS

Part I

APPROACHES: SYMBOLIC ARTIFICIAL INTELLIGENCE

INTRODUCTION
Intelligence As Symbol Processing

Ronald Chrisley

1 Foundational texts

Alan Newell acknowledges a broad connection between symbol and mind, mentioning the writings of Jung, Cassirier (*sic*, presumably referring to Ernst Cassirer) and Susanne Langer, but quoting at length the earlier work of Whitehead:

> After this preliminary explanation we must start with a definition of symbolism: The human mind is functioning symbolically when some components of its experience elicit consciousness, beliefs, emotions, and usages, respecting other components of its experience. The former set of components are the "symbols", and the latter set constitute the "meaning" of the symbols. The organic functioning whereby there is transition from the symbol to the meaning will be called "symbolic reference".
>
> (Whitehead 1927: 7–8, quoted in Newell 1980: 137)

It is true that symbolic artificial intelligence embraces the passage from Whitehead, but only after insisting on dropping the scare quotes. The fact is, Jung's archetypes, Cassirer's Kantian cultural "symbolic forms", and Langer's aesthetic "presentational symbols" have little to do with the notion of symbol that was to play such an explosive role in the development of modern artificial intelligence. It is true that the Kantian intellectual lineage supports the first premises of the syllogism: "the mind is made of symbols; symbols are the objects of computation; so the mind is computational". But reasoning in this way from Kant to LISP is fallacious, trading as it does on an equivocation between the cultural notion of a symbol in the first premises and the physical, mechanical, computational notion of a symbol in the second. Much confusion has resulted from a failure to distinguish between *communicative* representations, which typically acquire their meaning from (communities of) sentient interpreters, and *cognitive* representations, which, when properly manipulated, might *constitute* rather than *require* sentience. It

3

is the latter kind of representation which is central to the aspirations of symbolic artificial intelligence.

It is difficult to overstate the importance of Alan Turing in the development of artificial intelligence; it is not an altogether arbitrary choice that places his 1950 paper as the first entry in a section on the symbolic approach to artificial intelligence. In this paper, Turing considers the question: can machines think? He agrees that this requires definitions of the terms, but claims that if one were to try to do so by appealing to what is normally meant by the terms, then the answer to the question should be sought in a Gallup poll. This is not entirely correct: appealing to normal use would determine the meanings, but then conceptual reasoning and/or empirical enquiry into machines would be required to determine the answer to the question so stated. Nevertheless, Turing instead proposes that the question be replaced by another: "Could a machine win at the imitation game?", the now-familiar challenge in which a person attempts to distinguish the responses of a human from those of a machine. But it is unclear what sense of "replacing" the original question he has in mind. Is it that an answer to the latter question is an answer to the former? Or is it that an answer to the latter will take away the need for an answer to the former? As is seen later (in section 3 of Volume IV, Part I), this ambiguity was to have a lasting effect. Concerning his replacement question, Turing does ask: is it worthy of investigation? Rather than answer this, he offers two advantages of pursuing the second question (a move which resembles the proverbial looking for one's keys where there is light, rather than where one lost them). First, it draws a sharp line between physical and intellectual capacities; looking like a human (*a fortiori* being beautiful), sounding like a human, being charming, strong or heroic – none of these are seen to be relevant to being intelligent. Second, the question and answer method allows any topic to be introduced. It is doubtless that Turing saw this as an advantage, but with hindsight we can wonder if this makes the imitation game a test for education rather than intelligence. Or if it is insisted that it is intelligence which is being tested, then it must be that intelligence is not being taken to be some kind of raw potential, but a practical capacity to operate in a particular culture. Turing admits that passing this test is not required for a machine to be intelligent (a point which many future discussants would forget); but it is implied that it is sufficient.

Turing explicitly allows the machines under consideration to be such that we do not understand how they operate. But then a familiar problem with the concept of artificial intelligence (see the general introduction) raises itself: if we include as artificially intelligent machines which we do not design, then on what grounds do we exclude child-rearing from what we take to be artificial intelligence research? Turing explicitly performs the exclusion, but gives no justification. Likewise, he does not justify the exclusion of genetic engineering (e.g. test-tube babies), except to say that contemporary interest in the question has been because of digital computers. He argues that a restriction to such machines is not drastic, since it will only hinder answering the question at hand if digital computers cannot do well in the imitation game. Furthermore, Turing makes it clear that he is interested in whether there are *imaginable* computers which could do well at this game.

In explicating the notion of a digital computer, Turing draws a correspondence between parts of the digital computer and parts of a human computer. So the store, for example, corresponds to human memory. Yet "the executive unit is the part which carries out the individual operations involved in a calculation". But surely this is what the human is doing in the case of human computation – so perhaps a better mapping would be between the human as a whole, and a part or parts of the digital computer. Given this, perhaps it is easier to excuse Searle, in his Chinese Room thought experiment, for making the oft-noted (in various versions of the "system reply") mistake of taking himself to be instantiating the computer as a whole, when in fact he is only instantiating the executive. Even so, there are disanalogies here: in the machine, the instructions are necessarily followed by the executive, whereas a human may decide to stop following the program. Perhaps it is understandable that Turing might have elided over this difference, since he could very well have been using as his model of human computation the recent code-breaking activities at Bletchley Park. This was a situation in which, in some sense, the humans performing computations did not have a choice to stop following the program, given the militaristic structure of discipline, and the survival, ethical, familial and legal imperatives to comply with what one was ordered to do.

Another point of interest is his crediting Babbage with designing the digital computer. Since Babbage's machines were not electronic, the significance of Babbage is that he demonstrates that there is nothing special about the fact that both the human nervous system and actual digital computers use electricity: it is only a superficial similarity, the deep similarities having to do with "mathematical analogies of function".

Chaos theory is anticipated when Turing considers the predictability of digital computers. He acknowledges that the world is non-linear, appealing to a kind of "butterfly principle". Given the paper's topic of artificial intelligence, his conclusion is odd: machines must be built such that their non-linearity is minimised, so that they are predictable. An opposing view would be that we do not deem computers intelligent until they become complex enough so as to be unpredictable from a simple mechanistic stance, that adhering to the restrictions Turing proposes would forever render computers unintelligent.

Turing observes that a digital computer can mimic (simulate) the behaviour of any discrete state machine; digital computers are universal. Specifically, the machine and the simulating computer could not be distinguished by the imitation game; thus, nothing is lost by restricting the question of the imitation game to the case of digital computers. What is often ignored is that this is only true in general if one takes simulation to be predicting what the simulated machine will do, not actually doing the same thing as that machine. (Harnad (1991) responds to this limitation by generalising the Turing Test (TT) to yield the Total Turing Test (TTT), which requires fooling an observer with respect to all, not just symbolic, behaviour.) Put another way, what is simulated are the formal or symbolic properties of the behaviour of the machine, not the full behaviour itself. Any universal Turing machine can simulate the formal properties of a drinks machine, but not every universal Turing machine can go so far as to dispense cans of drink! (Searle makes the point by saying that a computer simulation of a rainstorm will not leave us all drenched – see the panel discussion in Volume III, article 57.) It is perhaps understandable that the distinction was ignored, given that Turing had in mind primarily linguistic/symbolic behaviour, which is a special case of behaviour in that simulating it does seem thereby to reproduce it. Or perhaps the explanation runs the other way: that Turing focused upon the case of symbolic behaviour precisely because it was the kind of behaviour for which simulation entails replication (see also his remarks concerning differential analysers, a kind of analogue computer). In any case, there is another problem with Turing's claim concerning universality: he is assuming here that all discrete state machines have a finite table, which has not been shown, and seems false. Furthermore, the appellation "universal machine" seems misleading when one remembers that it does not cover non-discrete state machines, which Turing acknowledges the existence of in this paper: there are machines for which there is no proof that there exists a Turing machine which can simulate them.

Turing's paper contains his famous prediction about the possibilities for artificial intelligence in the year 2000, the year of the publication of this set:

> I believe that in about 50 years' time it will be possible to programme computers, with a storage capacity of about 10^9 [about 1.25 gigabytes – ed.], to make them play the imitation game so well that an average interrogator will not have more than 70 per cent chance of making the right identification after five minutes of questioning . . . One will be able to speak of machines thinking without expecting to be contradicted.

As for the former claim, a program written by Dr David Hamill of the University of Surrey participated in an experiment in 1999 involving 13,000 people, fooling just over 24% of people interacting with it into thinking it was human (a similar 2000 experiment appears to have reached the 29% mark, although its form does not match exactly that of the Turing Test). But as is examined by Block and Whitby in Volume IV, Part I, section 3, there are many doubts as to the relevance of this benchmark. And as for Turing's latter claim, it seems that there are many, philosopher and layman alike, who would still balk at talk of machines thinking.

Turing considerably strengthens his case by collecting in one place nine different kinds of objections to artificial intelligence, and persuasively rebutting them. It is particularly valuable to see his response to what he calls "The Mathematical Objection", based on diagonalisation (see Volume III, Part I, section 1), since his own work concerning the uncomputability of the halting problem is often cited as establishing that computers could never do as much as humans can. Turing seems to think that it is relevant that there will be some questions in the imitation game (questions such as "is your answer to this question 'no'?") which a computer cannot answer correctly. But it is hard to see what this has to do with intelligence, since the inability to answer such questions correctly would not provide any way for the player of the game to distinguish the human from the computer. Whatever response the human gives, the computer obviously also can give, whether it is true or not. It is particularly odd that Turing does not see this, given what he says later about the possibility of machines making mistakes, even in the context of the imitation game:

> The machine (programmed for playing the game) would not attempt to give the *right* answers to the arithmetic problems. It would deliberately introduce mistakes in a manner calculated to confuse the interrogator.

In his response to "The Argument from Consciousness" Turing employs scepticism about other minds in general to disarm scepticism about machine minds. In this, as in several other of his responses, we see the tension between what might be deemed external and internal criteria for intelligence, where the spatial notions are not to be taken literally, but as a metaphorical distinction between what can be known from a third-person perspective about an agent and what can only be known from the first-person perspective. This tension would culminate in Searle's Chinese Room thought experiment (see the panel discussion in Volume III, article 57): even though a computer might pass the Turing Test (even the Total Turing Test), it cannot by virtue of that fact alone (or even by virtue of achieving that behaviour by implementing a particular program) be said to be intelligent, understand, have a mind, etc. With Turing we see an explicit decision to be uninterested in this first-person aspect of intelligence, a decision which was also made by most artificial intelligence researchers that followed, symbolic or otherwise. Turing's two responses to Lady Lovelace's Objection are weak. First, he tries to make little of the notion of origination, questioning whether anyone can really be said to originate anything. This is not persuasive, since even if there are always casual antecedents of our activities that lie outside of us, we still have use for the distinction between what is original and what is not. Turing is employing an extreme form of creativity that requires the created work to be *ex nihilo*, a view which receives convincing refutation by Boden (see Volume

IV, Part II, section 1). Perhaps in anticipation of the reader not finding his unattainable notion of creativity a plausible one, he then goes to the other extreme by analysing origination as "being able to surprise". Of course, a machine will be able to do this in some sense, but that does not seem sufficient to overturn Lovelace's claim.

Although Turing's remarks about ESP have had comparatively little effect on artificial intelligence, it is disturbing to note that he does not consider the presence of telepathy in humans and the absence of it in machines to count against the possibility of artificial intelligence. Rather, he redefines the imitation game, *ad hoc*, explicitly to disallow the use of telepathy! Once again the trivialisation of artificial intelligence threatens, via defining intelligence to be whatever we can get mechanism to do.

In the final section of his paper, Turing turns to the idea of machine learning. He proposes that if one is to try to get a machine to win at the imitation game, then a good strategy might be to emulate the human condition by having the program start with a restricted number of abilities, which include the ability to acquire the rest through experience or education. (The reference Turing makes to a "child-machine" with which he has done experiments refers to the P-type machine, discussed in the paper by Copeland and Proudfoot (Volume II, Part II, section 1).) Here he lays down the groundwork for much of what is to come, be it McCarthy's Advice Taker program, expert systems, or Lenat and Feigenbaum's CYC. Here also we have two separate passages presaging the idea of genetic algorithms, a view of machine learning as search, and consideration of the idea of reinforcement learning for machines (though unfortunately Turing cites none of the work that had already been done in this area). The disembodied and atemporal view of intelligence that the symbolic approach was to adopt is put in graphic terms when a machine without "legs, eyes, etc." is likened to Helen Keller. The fact is that not only did Helen Keller have a body (including legs!), and the senses of touch, taste and smell, but she also had vision and hearing from birth (which she lost due to a high fever when very young). In her autobiography she credits her "awakening" at the well to the tapping into these earlier experiences. So Helen Keller is not a good illustration of the idea Turing appropriates her for: the idea that a mere symbolic link between teacher and machine pupil is sufficient for learning and intelligence.

The analogical implications of the first of Turing's two "recitations tending to produce belief" are a little disturbing: unintelligent machine is to creative machine as subcritical mass is to supercritical mass as unwashed masses are to intellectual elite. This adds to a similar unease caused by the original formulation of the imitation game in terms of a man and a woman, and Turing's discussion of the "idiocy" of trying to get a machine to enjoy strawberries and cream. The only drawback of not conferring this ability on machines, Turing says, is that it prevents "the same kind of friendliness occurring between man and machine as between white man and white man, or between black man and black man". But as far as intelligence is concerned, the right result is obtained, since Turing is claiming that machines (and, presumably, all humans) *can* be intelligent despite the lack of "friendliness" between them and others.

Twice in Turing's paper we see a manifestation of a view of the mind that dates back at least as far as Plato: the analogy between the soul and the state, and more specifically the identification of social norms with internal, mechanistic rules. First, there is the quite self-conscious move between "rules of conduct" and "laws regulating behaviour". But more striking is his resolution of the paradox of how the rules of operation of a machine might change, by offering an analogy with the US Constitution. The connection with Plato, though it should not be strained, is a little deeper than just the mere recognition of a correspondence; there is a shared emphasis on reason as what should rule both nation and mind:

> "Must we not then infer that the individual is wise in the same way, and in virtue of the same quality which makes the State wise? Certainly." [*The Republic*, 441c (Cornford division)]

> "And ought not the rational principle, which is wise, and has the care of the whole soul, to rule, and the passionate or spirited principle to be the subject and ally? Certainly." [*The Republic*, 441e (Cornford division)]

Much is said elsewhere concerning the 1956 Dartmouth conference, but the *Proposal for the Dartmouth Summer Research Project on Artificial Intelligence* deserves a few words as well. Its first sentence contains what is widely believed to be the first written usage of the phrase "artificial intelligence" (see, e.g., footnote 4 of Torrance's paper in Volume IV, Part II, section 2). In its second sentence, the proposal makes explicit an important aspect of the symbolic approach: the methodology of first describing intelligence, and then turning this description into instructions for a machine in order to get it to behave intelligently. Much else of the document expresses ideas that would come to prominence in the years ahead in one form or another. But it is also interesting to see ideas that are not usually associated with this conference that is generally agreed to have been the genesis of the field of symbolic artificial intelligence. Neural networks have a prominent place in the proposal. Shannon's statement explicitly rejects the focus, which seems to have already become a default, on high-level intelligence such as proving theorems and playing chess, in favour of a bottom-up approach. Less contentiously, Rochester's proposal contains an interesting argument in favour of random search as a way of minimising the need for communication in parallel systems. Finally, although the proposal talks of a report that was to come out of the project, no such report was written.

McCarthy's "Programs with Common Sense" was presented at the Teddington Conference on the Mechanization of Thought Processes in December 1958 and printed in the proceedings of that conference. It details his proposed, yet unrealised, advice taker program. The idea was to give programs the ability to learn from their experience in abstract ways, e.g. by being told, an approach that was in opposition to the relatively connectionist approach to learning of Samuel and Rosenblatt. McCarthy argues that the learning of abstractions requires that the abstraction be represented in a simple way. It is interesting that he argues against search over low-level, connectionist representations by using an analogy with genetic variation, a move which is only a few words away from encapsulating the idea of genetic algorithms. What follows is a proposal that launches the ideas of logic programming, the separation of heuristic from program, and knowledge engineering, to name a few. The discussion of the paper is provocative and lively, with McCarthy's ideas on machine epistemology and Lady Lovelace's Objection, among others, getting a look-in.

Much is said elsewhere about the General Problem Solver of Newell, Shaw and Simon, which grew out of their Logic Theorist program. The major feature of GPS in the development of the symbolic approach was that it architecturally separated knowledge from problem-solving techniques (means–end analysis and planning) in order to increase generality. A modest effort at learning was embodied in the activity of associating differences with operators.

Margaret Boden has stressed the importance of Miller, Galanter and Pribram's book, *Plans and the Structure of Behaviour* to the development of cognitive science and, to a lesser extent, the field of artificial intelligence. Its main contributions are: a critique of behaviourism, a description of the TOTE (Test Operate Test Exit) computational unit, a generalised version of a general problem solver, and an emphasis on the importance of meaning-based explanation in psychology. The authors portrayed psychology as the study of computational procedures. The chapter selected for inclusion here is primarily a historical recap of the major conceptual developments in psychology, culminating in an extension, via Turing's results, of Vaucanson's and Hull's idea of explaining intelligence through replication – except that replication is replaced by simulation. Unlike Turing, who bridged the replication/simulation divide by considering behaviour for which simulation *was* replication, the authors handle the problem by giving up on replication altogether: "Since it is necessary to simulate only the record of the animal's behaviour, not the animal itself, the big, fast digital computers that began to evolve after World War II could be used – they did not need to scurry around the room like a rat in a maze or resemble the three pints of brain matter they were supposed to imitate". The benefits of this approach were not only to make psychological theories more precise and testable, but also to show that one could discharge the homunculus from cognitivist (non-behaviourist) explanations. Finally, there is an explicit acknowledgement of the distinction between the artificial intelligence goal of reproducing human behaviour by any means available versus the psychological goal of reproducing (or simulating) human behaviour by the same means as humans.

The view of intelligence as efficient search through a space of possibilities became a central aspect of the symbolic approach, and Minsky's "Steps Towards Artificial Intelligence" constituted a significant development of this idea. The paper takes the form of a synthetic overview of then-current research. Even while acknowledging that "a computer can do, in a sense, only what it is told to do", Minsky responds to the Lovelace point by offering search as a way of getting a machine to find a solution to a problem that we cannot solve. Intelligence, then, is the capacity to reduce the number of possibilities that need to be searched, without eliminating the solution (or all solutions). Minsky explicates four ways of reducing search spaces: pattern recognition (including mention of Selfridge, Rosenblatt and multi-layer Perceptrons), learning, planning and induction. In this latter section we find an early statement of Minsky's relativist notion of intelligence: "To me 'intelligence' seems to denote little more than the complex of performances which we happen to respect, but do not understand" – a notion which is relative both to our knowledge and our interests.

2 Developments

In 1985 Boden denied that there had been much (or any) intellectual development in artificial intelligence in the preceding ten years (see the Bobrow and Hayes item, below). This is in a very important sense true, but it need not be a criticism: by the very nature of scientific enterprise, there comes a point in a discipline's development where progress is not measured in intellectual, conceptual advances, but in the refinement and elaboration of a pre-given framework. Thus, most of the development of the concept of artificial intelligence was to occur in communities outside, or on the fringe, of symbolic work; hence the existence of Volume II, Part II and Volume III, Part I in this set. But some exceptions to this view are worthy of documentation – between 1975 and the 1990s there were conceptual advances that further illuminated and developed the symbolic approach.

The title of Newell and Simon's 1976 paper, in that it mentions computer science and not artificial intelligence, belies the fact that it is, among other things, a conscious attempt to characterise the foundations of the symbolic approach to artificial intelligence. The authors' notion of intelligence, stated early on, is behavioural: "we measure the intelligence of a system by its ability to achieve stated ends in the face of variations, difficulties and complexities posed by the task environment". Their Physical-Symbol System Hypothesis then becomes a proposed law of qualitative structure, an empirical proposal as to the nature of all the systems that exhibit intelligence as defined behaviourally: "a physical-symbol system has the necessary and sufficient means for general intelligent action". The notion of a physical-symbol system is explicated, although not necessarily in the clearest terms: For example, central to their characterisation of such systems is the notion of designation. But do expressions designate objects in the world, as well as processes that the system can carry out, as well as other expressions? Are all three of these relations really the same, or do we need to distinguish, e.g. the EVAL relation between the LISP expressions CAR(JACKIE ADRIAN LESLIE) and JACKIE, from the referential relation between JACKIE and Jackie the person?

Next, Newell and Simon give a brief account of the historical development of their hypothesis, citing its roots in work in formal logic (formal non-semantic symbol manipulation) and computability/computers (automatic formal symbol manipulation). The idea of a stored program added to this the idea that a "system's own data can be interpreted". But it was not until the advent of list-processing in 1956 that the contents of the data-structures in machines were actually symbols, were "patterns that designated, that had referents".

Empirical evidence for the truth of the physical-symbol system hypothesis is then provided. The authors claim that they are providing evidence for both the sufficiency and necessity of the physical-symbol system for intelligence, but the "evidence" they cite for the latter, that human intelligence can be explained in terms of symbol systems, does not support a necessity claim at all.

Another law of qualitative structure, that intelligence is heuristic search, is offered. To exercise intelligence is to generate and modify symbol structures until a structure designating a solution is reached. Here we have symbolism perhaps in its most extreme form. The idea of search is claimed to answer Plato's worry, in the *Meno*, of how we could pose a problem and recognise a solution unless we already had the solution all along. But the authors later acknowledge that intelligence need not be search itself, but can also be any aspect of the system which reduces or eliminates the need for search, a reasonable concession which dramatically de-radicalises their position.

At the time of its 15th anniversary in 1985, the journal *Artificial Intelligence*, which had become the central resource of its kind for work in academic artificial intelligence, commissioned Bobrow and Hayes to present a survey of ten questions to key thinkers in the field, including Amarel, Boden, Berliner, Dennett, Dreyfus, Feldman, Longuet-Higgins, McCarthy, McCorduck, Meltzer, Michie, Newell, Nilsson, Schank, Seeley Brown, Sloman, and Winograd. Their responses give a good snapshot of artificial intelligence's self-image at the time, although the diversity of the responses prevents a single, coherent picture from developing and makes any kind of substantial summary here impossible.

The spirit of Plato's *Republic* finds its most thorough and explicit expression in artificial intelligence through Minsky's "Society of Mind" work in the 1980s. Although symbolic in nature, the ideas Minsky sketched incorporated some elements that were more familiar to other approaches to artificial intelligence: emergence, collections of simple units acting in parallel, etc. The eponymous book from which the included extracts were taken was a daring attempt to match content and form: each page was itself a "module" or "agent" contributing to the whole in a plurality of criss-cross-referencing ways. Minsky's methodology can be seen as philosophical, with his insights coming from *a priori* reflection, as long as one acknowledges (1) that this was reflection informed by thirty years of experience in attempting to create an intelligent machine; and (2) the reflections, unlike philosophical conclusions, were empirical: they were hypotheses as to how to go about building a mind. Many criticised the book as being too abstract or insufficiently technical and rigorous, but it is arguable that at the time, what symbolic artificial intelligence needed was a comprehensive "big picture" of intelligence, a picture that was complex enough to do that topic justice. No more simple equations: "intelligence is heuristic search". Rather, intelligence was the end result of a bewildering array of architectural and organisational forms of (primarily symbolic) activity. Minsky's final chapter in this volume (article 45) compares and contrasts the Society of Mind approach with connectionism.

Between 1960 and 1990, the logic branch of symbolic artificial intelligence got a better idea of what characterised its approach. McCarthy identifies four "levels" on which logical formalism applies to intelligence: intentional descriptions ("Much more can be said about ascribing mental qualities to machine, but that is not what AI is mainly concerned with today"), belief representation without logical inference, belief representation with logical inference (which is less practical since techniques for controlling reasoning are insufficiently developed), and program-independent knowledge representation ("still a goal", i.e. not much work has been done on it). This last level requires extensions to mathematical logic which are non-monotonic in that the set of models which satisfy a database of sentences may increase when another sentence is added to the database. McCarthy's favoured extension employs circumscription; the idea is that common sense reasoning is achieved by inferring what would be true in some minimal preferred model of what is already known to be true. McCarthy concludes with a discussion of what philosophy can offer the field of artificial intelligence – and vice versa.

After the focus on domain-specific, expert knowledge during the 1970s and 1980s, a return to the idea of creating general intelligence appeared in perhaps its most explicit form in the SOAR project. The SOAR methodology follows on from and further develops, Newell and Simon's hypothesised laws of qualitative structure and the idea of submitting them to the empirical test. But rather than being restricted to the role of testing *a priori* conjectures, experiments, on humans and machines, are used in order to formulate the architectural principles themselves. The three levels of SOAR are long-term memory (a production system containing both procedural and declarative elements), decisions (a level which first accesses memory "repeatedly, in parallel until quiescence is reached", and then applies a fixed decision procedure to the elements then in working memory) and goals (which are created whenever a decision cannot be reached, and thus create a new context and focus for reasoning). Intelligence is seen as the ability to solve problems, and this is done by the selection of an appropriate pre-given problem space and a search for the correct sequence of operators to apply to that problem space. Provision is not made for a kind of intelligence which creates new problem spaces. SOAR proposes that only one mechanism of learning – chunking – is required for intelligence in general and human intelligence in particular. SOAR is doubly bold in attempting to account for intelligence in general, with a single, uniform architecture. Further discussion of SOAR appears in the paper by Adam (article 82, Volume IV).

Quite a different understanding of intelligence underlies the CYC project, which like SOAR and the Society of Mind emphasises general, domain-independent intelligence, but follows in the tradition of expert systems in locating intelligence in (symbolically encoded) knowledge. CYC constitutes a brute-force approach to solving the problem of artificial intelligence: just keep adding knowledge frames, and eventually intelligence will emerge. The idea here is that one cannot properly judge a knowledge-based approach to intelligence unless it is attempted on a large enough scale (i.e. one million frames). The daunting task of hand-coding the data frames which will constitute this knowledge is made more tractable by adopting the Turing-esque proposal of just coding enough to give the system the ability to understand (or learn to understand?) natural language, and then letting the system teach itself thereafter by reading and communicating. Roots of CYC can be found in McCarthy's Advice Taker, but by relaxing the demand for global consistency, CYC rejects a logic-based approach. The paper included has too many more ideas and hypotheses to do justice here, but there is a substantial amount of (critical) analysis of CYC in the papers by Smith (article 49, Volume III), Dreyfus (article 61, Volume III) and Adam (article 82, Volume IV).

References

Harnad, S. (1991) "Other bodies other minds: A machine incarnation of an old philosophical problem", *Minds and Machines* 1: 43–54.

Highfield, R. (2000) "Are you smarter than a robot?", *The Electronic Telegraph*, March 9th, 2000.

Newell, A. (1980) "Physical Symbol Systems", *Cognitive Science* 4: 135–83.

Plato (1871) *The Republic*. Translated by Jowett, B., edited to reflect modern spelling and usage, and divided into the units suggested by Francis Cornford in his translation, *The Republic of Plato* (Oxford 1945).

Whitehead, A. N. (1927) *Symbolism: Its Meaning & Effect*, New York: Macmillan.

Section 1.1: Foundational Texts

COMPUTING MACHINERY AND INTELLIGENCE

A. M. Turing

Source: *Mind* LIX(236), Oct. 1950: 433–60.

1 The imitation game

I propose to consider the question, 'Can machines think?' This should begin with definitions of the meaning of the terms 'machine' and 'think'. The definitions might be framed so as to reflect so far as possible the normal use of the words, but this attitude is dangerous. If the meaning of the words 'machine' and 'think' are to be found by examining how they are commonly used it is difficult to escape the conclusion that the meaning and the answer to the question, 'Can machines think?' is to be sought in a statistical survey such as a Gallup poll. But this is absurd. Instead of attempting such a definition I shall replace the question by another, which is closely related to it and is expressed in relatively unambiguous words.

The new form of the problem can be described in terms of a game which we call the 'imitation game'. It is played with three people, a man (A), a woman (B), and an interrogator (C) who may be of either sex. The interrogator stays in a room apart from the other two. The object of the game for the interrogator is to determine which of the other two is the man and which is the woman. He knows them by labels X and Y, and at the end of the game he says either 'X is A and Y is B' or 'X is B and Y is A'. The interrogator is allowed to put questions to A and B thus:

C: Will X please tell me the length of his or her hair?

Now suppose X is actually A, then A must answer. It is A's object in the game to try and cause C to make the wrong identification. His answer might therefore be

'My hair is shingled, and the longest strands are about nine inches long.'

In order that tones of voice may not help the interrogator the answers should be written, or better still, typewritten. The ideal arrangement is to have a teleprinter communicating between the two rooms. Alternatively the question and answers can be repeated by an intermediary. The object of the game for the third player (B) is to help the interrogator. The best strategy for her is probably to give truthful answers. She can add such things as 'I am the woman, don't listen to him!' to her answers, but it will avail nothing as the man can make similar remarks.

We now ask the question, 'What will happen when a machine takes the part of A in this game?' Will the interrogator decide wrongly as often when the game is played like this as he does when the game is played between a man and a woman? These questions replace our original, 'Can machines think?'

2 Critique of the new problem

As well as asking, 'What is the answer to this new form of the question', one may ask, 'Is this new question a worthy one to investigate?' This latter question we investigate without further ado, thereby cutting short an infinite regress.

The new problem has the advantage of drawing a fairly sharp line between the physical and the intellectual capacities of a man. No engineer or chemist claims to be able to produce a material which is indistinguishable from the human skin. It is possible that at some time this might be done, but even supposing this invention available we should feel there was little point in trying to make a 'thinking machine' more human by dressing it up in such artificial flesh. The form in which we have set the problem reflects this fact in the condition which prevents the interrogator from seeing or touching the other competitors, or hearing their voices. Some other advantages of the proposed criterion may be shown up by specimen questions and answers. Thus:

Q: Please write me a sonnet on the subject of the Forth Bridge.
A: Count me out on this one. I never could write poetry.
Q: Add 34957 to 70764.
A: (Pause about 30 seconds and then give as answer) 105621.
Q: Do you play chess?
A: Yes.
Q: I have K at my K1, and no other pieces. You have only K at K6 and R at R1. It is your move. What do you play?
A: (After a pause of 15 seconds) R-R8 mate.

The question and answer method seems to be suitable for introducing almost any one of the fields of human endeavour that we wish to include. We do not wish to penalise the machine for its inability to shine in beauty competitions, nor to penalise a man for losing in a race against an aeroplane. The conditions of our game make these disabilities irrelevant. The 'witnesses' can brag, if they consider it advisable, as much as they please about their charms, strength or heroism, but the interrogator cannot demand practical demonstrations.

The game may perhaps be criticised on the ground that the odds are weighted too heavily against the machine. If the man were to try and pretend to be the machine he would clearly make a very poor showing. He would be given away at once by slowness and inaccuracy in arithmetic. May not machines carry out something which ought to be described as thinking but which is very different from what a man does? This objection is a very strong one, but at least we can say that if, nevertheless, a machine can be constructed to play the imitation game satisfactorily, we need not be troubled by this objection.

It might be urged that when playing the 'imitation game' the best strategy for the machine may possibly be something other than imitation of the behaviour of a man. This may be, but I think it is unlikely that there is any great effect of this kind. In any case there is no intention to investigate here the theory of the game, and it will be assumed that the best strategy is to try to provide answers that would naturally be given by a man.

3 The machines concerned in the game

The question which we put in §1 will not be quite definite until we have specified what we mean by the word 'machine'. It is natural that we should wish to permit every kind of engineering technique to be used in our machines. We also wish to allow the possibility that an engineer or team of engineers may construct a machine which works, but whose manner of operation cannot be satisfactorily described by its constructors because they have applied a method which is largely experimental. Finally, we wish to exclude from the machines men born in the usual manner. It is difficult to frame the definitions so as to satisfy these three conditions. One might for instance insist that the team of engineers should be all of one sex, but this would not really be satisfactory, for it is probably possible to rear a complete individual from a single cell of the skin (say) of a man. To do so would be a feat of biological technique deserving of the very highest praise, but we would not be inclined to regard it as a case of 'constructing a thinking machine'. This prompts us to abandon the requirement that every kind of technique should be permitted. We are the more ready to do so in view of the fact that the present interest in 'thinking machines' has been aroused by a particular kind of machine, usually called an 'electronic computer' or 'digital computer'. Following this suggestion we only permit digital computers to take part in our game.

This restriction appears at first sight to be a very drastic one. I shall attempt to show that it is not so in reality. To do this necessitates a short account of the nature and properties of these computers.

It may also be said that this identification of machines with digital computers, like our criterion for 'thinking', will only be unsatisfactory if (contrary to my belief), it turns out that digital computers are unable to give a good showing in the game.

There are already a number of digital computers in working order, and it may be asked, 'Why not try the experiment straight away? It would be easy to satisfy the conditions of the game. A number of interrogators could be used, and statistics compiled to show how often the right identification was given.' The short answer is that we are not asking whether all digital computers would do well in the game nor whether the computers at present available would do well, but whether there are imaginable computers which would do well. But this is only the short answer. We shall see this question in a different light later.

4 Digital computers

The idea behind digital computers may be explained by saying that these machines are intended to carry out any operations which could be done by a human computer. The human computer is supposed to be following fixed rules; he has no authority to deviate from them in any detail. We may suppose that these rules are supplied in a book, which is altered whenever he is put on to a new job. He has also an unlimited supply of paper on which he does his calculations. He may also do his multiplications and additions on a 'desk machine', but this is not important.

If we use the above explanation as a definition we shall be in danger of circularity of argument. We avoid this by giving an outline of the means by which the desired effect is achieved. A digital computer can usually be regarded as consisting of three parts:

  (i) Store.
 (ii) Executive unit.
(iii) Control.

The store is a store of information, and corresponds to the human computer's paper, whether this is the paper on which he does his calculations or that on which his book of rules is printed. In so far as the human computer does calculations in his head a part of the store will correspond to his memory.

The executive unit is the part which carries out the various individual operations involved in a calculation. What these individual operations are will vary from machine to machine. Usually fairly lengthy operations can be done such as 'Multiply 3540675445 by 7076345687' but in some machines only very simple ones such as 'Write down 0' are possible.

We have mentioned that the 'book of rules' supplied to the computer is

22

replaced in the machine by a part of the store. It is then called the 'table of instructions'. It is the duty of the control to see that these instructions are obeyed correctly and in the right order. The control is so constructed that this necessarily happens.

The information in the store is usually broken up into packets of moderately small size. In one machine, for instance, a packet might consist of ten decimal digits. Numbers are assigned to the parts of the store in which the various packets of information are stored, in some systematic manner. A typical instruction might say—

'Add the number stored in position 6809 to that in 4302 and put the result back into the latter storage position'.

Needless to say it would not occur in the machine expressed in English. It would more likely be coded in a form such as 6809430217. Here 17 says which of various possible operations is to be performed on the two numbers. In this case the operation is that described above, *viz.* 'Add the number. . . .' It will be noticed that the instruction takes up 10 digits and so forms one packet of information, very conveniently. The control will normally take the instructions to be obeyed in the order of the positions in which they are stored, but occasionally an instruction such as

'Now obey the instruction stored in position 5606, and continue from there' may be encountered, or again

'If position 4505 contains 0 obey next the instruction stored in 6707, otherwise continue straight on.'

Instructions of these latter types are very important because they make it possible for a sequence of operations to be repeated over and over again until some condition is fulfilled, but in doing so to obey, not fresh instructions on each repetition, but the same ones over and over again. To take a domestic analogy. Suppose Mother wants Tommy to call at the cobbler's every morning on his way to school to see if her shoes are done, she can ask him afresh every morning. Alternatively she can stick up a notice once and for all in the hall which he will see when he leaves for school and which tells him to call for the shoes, and also to destroy the notice when he comes back if he has the shoes with him.

The reader must accept it as a fact that digital computers can be constructed, and indeed have been constructed, according to the principles we have described, and that they can in fact mimic the actions of a human computer very closely.

The book of rules which we have described our human computer as using is of course a convenient fiction. Actual human computers really remember what they have got to do. If one wants to make a machine mimic the behaviour of the human computer in some complex operation one has to ask him how it is done, and then translate the answer into the form of an instruction table. Constructing instruction tables is usually described as 'programming'. To 'programme a machine to carry out the operation A' means to put the appropriate instruction table into the machine so that it will do A.

An interesting variant on the idea of a digital computer is a 'digital computer with a random element'. These have instructions involving the throwing of a die or some equivalent electronic process; one such instruction might for instance be, 'Throw the die and put the resulting number into store 1000'. Sometimes such a machine is described as having free will (though I would not use this phrase myself). It is not normally possible to determine from observing a machine whether it has a random element, for a similar effect can be produced by such devices as making the choices depend on the digits of the decimal for π.

Most actual digital computers have only a finite store. There is no theoretical difficulty in the idea of a computer with an unlimited store. Of course only a finite part can have been used at any one time. Likewise only a finite amount can have been constructed, but we can imagine more and more being added as required. Such computers have special theoretical interest and will be called infinitive capacity computers.

The idea of a digital computer is an old one. Charles Babbage, Lucasian Professor of Mathematics at Cambridge from 1828 to 1839, planned such a machine, called the Analytical Engine, but it was never completed. Although Babbage had all the essential ideas, his machine was not at that time such a very attractive prospect. The speed which would have been available would be definitely faster than a human computer but something like 100 times slower than the Manchester machine, itself one of the slower of the modern machines. The storage was to be purely mechanical, using wheels and cards.

The fact that Babbage's Analytical Engine was to be entirely mechanical will help us to rid ourselves of a superstition. Importance is often attached to the fact that modern digital computers are electrical, and that the nervous system also is electrical. Since Babbage's machine was not electrical, and since all digital computers are in a sense equivalent, we see that this use of electricity cannot be of theoretical importance. Of course electricity usually comes in where fast signalling is concerned, so that it is not surprising that we find it in both these connections. In the nervous system chemical phenomena are at least as important as electrical. In certain computers the storage system is mainly acoustic. The feature of using electricity is thus seen to be only a very superficial similarity. If we wish to find such similarities we should look rather for mathematical analogies of function.

5 Universality of digital computers

The digital computers considered in the last section may be classified amongst the 'discrete state machines'. These are the machines which move by sudden jumps or clicks from one quite definite state to another. These states are sufficiently different for the possibility of confusion between them to be ignored. Strictly speaking there are no such machines. Everything really moves continuously. But there are many kinds of machine which can profitably be *thought of* as being discrete state machines. For instance in considering the switches for a lighting system it is a convenient fiction that each switch must be definitely on or definitely off. There must be intermediate positions, but for most purposes we can forget about them. As an example of a discrete state machine we might consider a wheel which clicks round through 120° once a second, but may be stopped by a lever which can be operated from outside; in addition a lamp is to light in one of the positions of the wheel. This machine could be described abstractly as follows. The internal state of the machine (which is described by the position of the wheel) may be q_1, q_2 or q_3. There is an input signal i_0 or i_1 (position of lever). The internal state at any moment is determined by the last state and input signal according to the table

		Last State	
	q_1	q_2	q_3
i_0	q_2	q_3	q_1
i_1	q_1	q_2	q_3

Input is indicated at the left with i_0 and i_1.

The output signals, the only externally visible indication of the internal state (the light) are described by the table

State	q_1	q_2	q_3
Output	o_0	o_0	o_1

This example is typical of discrete state machines. They can be described by such tables provided they have only a finite number of possible states.

It will seem that given the initial state of the machine and the input signals it is always possible to predict all future states. This is reminiscent of Laplace's view that from the complete state of the universe at one moment of time, as described by the positions and velocities of all particles, it should be possible to predict all future states. The prediction which we are considering is, however, rather nearer to practicability than that considered by Laplace. The system of the 'universe as a whole' is such that quite small errors in the initial conditions can have an overwhelming effect at a later time. The displacement of a single electron by a billionth of a centimetre at one moment might make the difference between a man being killed by an avalanche a year later, or escaping. It is an essential property of the mechanical systems which we have called 'discrete state machines' that this phenomenon does not occur. Even when we consider the actual physical machines instead of the idealised machines, reasonably accurate knowledge of the state at one moment yields reasonably accurate knowledge any number of steps later.

As we have mentioned, digital computers fall within the class of discrete state machines. But the number of states of which such a machine is capable is usually enormously large. For instance, the number for the machine now working at Manchester it about $2^{165,000}$, *i.e.* about $10^{50,000}$. Compare this with our example of the clicking wheel described above, which had three states. It is not difficult to see why the number of states should be so immense. The computer includes a store corresponding to the paper used by a human computer. It must be possible to write into the store any one of the combinations of symbols which might have been written on the paper. For simplicity suppose that only digits from 0 to 9 are used as symbols. Variations in handwriting are ignored. Suppose the computer is allowed 100 sheets of paper each containing 50 lines each with room for 30 digits. Then the number of states is $10^{100 \times 50 \times 30}$, *i.e.* $10^{150,000}$. This is about the number of states of three Manchester machines put together. The logarithm to the base two of the number of states is usually called the 'storage capacity' of the machine. Thus the Manchester machine has a storage capacity of about 165,000 and the wheel machine of our example about 1·6. If two machines are put together their capacities must be added to obtain the capacity of the resultant machine. This leads to the possibility of statements such as 'The Manchester machine contains 64 magnetic tracks each with a capacity of 2560, eight electronic tubes with a capacity of 1280. Miscellaneous storage amounts to about 300 making a total of 174,380.'

Given the table corresponding to a discrete state machine it is possible to predict what it will do. There is no reason why this calculation should not be carried out by means of a digital computer. Provided it could be carried out sufficiently quickly the digital computer could mimic the behaviour of any discrete state machine. The imitation game could then be played with the machine in question (as B) and the mimicking digital computer (as A) and the interrogator would be unable to distinguish them. Of course the digital computer must have an adequate storage capacity as well as working sufficiently fast. Moreover, it must be programmed afresh for each new machine which it is desired to mimic.

This special property of digital computers, that they can mimic any discrete state machine, is described by saying that they are *universal* machines. The existence of machines with this property has the important consequence that, considerations of speed apart, it is unnecessary to design various new machines to do various computing processes. They can all be done with one digital computer, suitably programmed for each case. It will be seen that as a consequence of this all digital computers are in a sense equivalent.

We may now consider again the point raised at the end of §3. It was suggested tentatively that the question, 'Can machines think?' should be replaced by 'Are there imaginable digital computers which would do well in the imitation game?' If we wish we can make this superficially more general and ask 'Are there discrete state machines which would do well?' But in view of the universality property we see that either of these questions is equivalent to this, 'Let us fix our attention on one particular digital computer C. Is it true that by modifying this computer to have an adequate storage, suitably increasing its speed of action, and providing it with an appropriate programme, C can be made to play satisfactorily the part of A in the imitation game, the part of B being taken by a man?'

6 Contrary views on the main question

We may now consider the ground to have been cleared and we are ready to proceed to the debate on our question, 'Can machines think?' and the variant of it quoted at the end of the last section. We cannot altogether abandon the original form of the problem, for opinions will differ as to the appropriateness of the substitution and we must at least listen to what has to be said in this connexion.

It will simplify matters for the reader if I explain first my own beliefs in the matter. Consider first the more accurate form of the question. I believe that in about fifty years' time it will be possible to programme computers, with a storage capacity of about 10^9, to make them play the imitation game so well that an average interrogator will not have more than 70 per cent. chance of making the right identification after five minutes of questioning. The original question, 'Can machines think?' I believe to be too meaningless to deserve discussion. Nevertheless I believe that at the end of the century the use of words and general educated opinion will have altered so much that one will be able to speak of machines thinking without expecting to be contradicted. I believe further that no useful purpose is served by concealing these beliefs. The popular view that scientists proceed inexorably from well-established fact to well-established fact, never being influenced by any unproved conjecture, is quite mistaken. Provided it is made clear which are proved facts and which are conjectures, no harm can result. Conjectures are of great importance since they suggest useful lines of research.

I now proceed to consider opinions opposed to my own.

(1) *The theological objection*

Thinking is a function of man's immortal soul. God has given an immortal soul to every man and woman, but not to any other animal or to machines. Hence no animal or machine can think.[1]

I am unable to accept any part of this, but will attempt to reply in theological terms. I should find the argument more convincing if animals were classed with men, for there is a greater difference, to my mind, between the typical animate and the inanimate than there is between man and the other animals. The arbitrary character of the orthodox view becomes clearer if we consider how it might appear to a member of some other religious community. How do Christians regard the Moslem view that women have no souls? But let us leave this point aside and return to the main argument. It appears to me that the argument quoted above implies a serious restriction of the omnipotence of the Almighty. It is admitted that there are certain things that He cannot do such as making one equal to two, but should we not believe that He has freedom to confer a soul on an elephant if He sees fit? We might expect that He would only exercise this power in conjunction with a mutation which provided the elephant with an appropriately improved brain to minister to the needs of this soul. An argument of exactly similar form may be made for the case of machines. It may seem different because it is more difficult to 'swallow'. But this really only means that we think it would be less likely that He would consider the circumstances suitable for conferring a soul. The circumstances in question are discussed in the rest of this paper. In attempting to construct such machines we should not be irreverently usurping His power of creating souls, any more than we are in the procreation of children: rather we are, in either case, instruments of His will providing mansions for the souls that He creates.

However, this is mere speculation. I am not very impressed with theological arguments whatever they may be used to support. Such arguments have often been found unsatisfactory in the past. In the time of Galileo it was argued that the texts, 'And the sun stood still . . . and hasted not to go down about a whole day' (Joshua x. 13) and 'He laid the foundations of the earth, that it should not move at any time' (Psalm cv. 5)* were an adequate refutation of the Copernican theory. With our present knowledge such an argument appears futile. When that knowledge was not available it made a quite different impression.

(2) *The 'Heads in the Sand' objection*

'The consequences of machines thinking would be too dreadful. Let us hope and believe that they cannot do so.'

This argument is seldom expressed quite so openly as in the form above. But it affects most of us who think about it at all. We like to believe that Man is in some subtle way superior to the rest of creation. It is best if he can be shown to be *necessarily* superior, for then there is no danger of him losing his commanding position. The popularity of the theological argument is clearly connected with this feeling. It is likely to be quite strong in intellectual

---

* The original text, and at least some reprintings of the paper (e.g. Boden 1990) have the incorrect reference Psalm cv. 5. [Ed.]

people, since they value the power of thinking more highly than others, and are more inclined to base their belief in the superiority of Man on this power.

I do not think that this argument is sufficiently substantial to require refutation. Consolation would be more appropriate: perhaps this should be sought in the transmigration of souls.

(3) *The mathematical objection*

There are a number of results of mathematical logic which can be used to show that there are limitations to the powers of discrete-state machines. The best known of these results is known as Gödel's theorem,[2] and shows that in any sufficiently powerful logical system statements can be formulated which can neither be proved nor disproved within the system, unless possibly the system itself is inconsistent. There are other, in some respects similar, results due to *Church, Kleene, Rosser*, and *Turing*. The latter result is the most convenient to consider, since it refers directly to machines, whereas the others can only be used in a comparatively indirect argument: for instance if Gödel's theorem is to be used we need in addition to have some means of describing logical systems in terms of machines, and machines in terms of logical systems. The result in question refers to a type of machine which is essentially a digital computer with an infinite capacity. It states that there are certain things that such a machine cannot do. If it is rigged up to give answers to questions as in the imitation game, there will be some questions to which it will either give a wrong answer, or fail to give an answer at all however much time is allowed for a reply. There may, of course, be many such questions, and questions which cannot be answered by one machine may be satisfactorily answered by another. We are of course supposing for the present that the questions are of the kind to which an answer 'Yes' or 'No' is appropriate, rather than questions such as 'What do you think of Picasso?' The questions that we know the machines must fail on are of this type, 'Consider the machine specified as follows. . . . Will this machine ever answer "Yes" to any question?' The dots are to be replaced by a description of some machine in a standard form, which could be something like that used in §5. When the machine described bears a certain comparatively simple relation to the machine which is under interrogation, it can be shown that the answer is either wrong or not forthcoming. This is the mathematical result: it is argued that it proves a disability of machines to which the human intellect is not subject.

The short answer to this argument is that although it is established that there are limitations to the powers of any particular machine, it has only been stated, without any sort of proof, that no such limitations apply to the human intellect. But I do not think this view can be dismissed quite so lightly. Whenever one of these machines is asked the appropriate critical question, and gives a definite answer, we know that this answer must be wrong, and this gives us a certain feeling of superiority. Is this feeling illusory? It is no doubt quite genuine, but I do not think too much importance should be attached to it. We too often give wrong answers to questions ourselves to be justified in being very pleased at such evidence of fallibility on the part of the machines. Further, our superiority can only be felt on such an occasion in relation to the one machine over which we have scored our petty triumph. There would be no question of triumphing simultaneously over *all* machines. In short, then, there might be men cleverer than any given machine, but then again there might be other machines cleverer again, and so on.

Those who hold to the mathematical argument would, I think, mostly be willing to accept the imitation game as a basis for discussion. Those who believe in the two previous objections would probably not be interested in any criteria.

(4) *The argument from consciousness*

This argument is very well expressed in *Professor Jefferson's* Lister Oration for 1949, from which I quote. 'Not until a machine can write a sonnet or compose a concerto because of thoughts and emotions felt, and not by the chance fall of symbols, could we agree that machine equals brain—that is, not only write it but know that it had written it. No mechanism could feel (and not merely artificially signal, an easy contrivance) pleasure at its successes, grief when its valves fuse, be warmed by flattery, be made miserable by its mistakes, be charmed by sex, be angry or depressed when it cannot get what it wants.'

This argument appears to be a denial of the validity of our test. According to the most extreme form of this view the only way by which one could be sure that a machine thinks is to *be* the machine and to feel oneself thinking. One could then describe these feelings to the world, but of course no one would be justified in taking any notice. Likewise according to this view the only way to know that a *man* thinks is to be that particular man. It is in fact the solipsist point of view. It may be the most logical view to hold but it makes communication of ideas difficult. A is liable to believe 'A thinks but B does not' whilst B believes 'B thinks but A does not'. Instead of arguing continually over this point it is usual to have the polite convention that everyone thinks.

I am sure that Professor Jefferson does not wish to adopt the extreme and solipsist point of view. Probably he would be quite willing to accept the imitation game as a test. The game (with the player B omitted) is frequently used in practice under the name of *viva voce* to discover whether some one really understands something or has 'learnt it parrot fashion'. Let us listen in to a part of such a *viva voce*:

Interrogator: In the first line of your sonnet which reads 'Shall I compare thee to a summer's day', would not 'a spring day' do as well or better?

Witness: It wouldn't scan.

Interrogator: How about 'a winter's day' That would scan all right.

Witness: Yes, but nobody wants to be compared to a winter's day.

Interrogator: Would you say Mr. Pickwick reminded you of Christmas?

Witness: In a way.

Interrogator: Yet Christmas is a winter's day, and I do not think Mr. Pickwick would mind the comparison.

Witness: I don't think you're serious. By a winter's day one means a typical winter's day, rather than a special one like Christmas.

And so on. What would Professor Jefferson say if the sonnet-writing machine was able to answer like this in the *viva voce*? I do not know whether he would regard the machine as 'merely artificially signalling' these answers, but if the answers were as satisfactory and sustained as in the above passage I do not think he would describe it as 'an easy contrivance'. This phrase is, I think, intended to cover such devices as the inclusion in the machine of a record of someone reading a sonnet, with appropriate switching to turn it on from time to time.

In short then, I think that most of those who support the argument from consciousness could be persuaded to abandon it rather than be forced into the solipsist position. They will then probably be willing to accept our test.

I do not wish to give the impression that I think there is no mystery about consciousness. There is, for instance, something of a paradox connected with any attempt to localise it. But I do not think these mysteries necessarily need to be solved before we can answer the question with which we are concerned in this paper.

(5) *Arguments from various disabilities*

These arguments take the form, 'I grant you that you can make machines do all the things you have mentioned but you will never be able to make one to do X'. Numerous features X are suggested in this connexion. I offer a selection:

> Be kind, resourceful, beautiful, friendly (p. 448), have initiative, have a sense of humour, tell right from wrong, make mistakes (p. 448), fall in love, enjoy strawberries and cream (p. 448), make some one fall in love with it, learn from experience (pp. 456 f.), use words properly, be the subject of its own thought (p. 449), have as much diversity of behaviour as a man, do something really new (p. 450). (Some of these disabilities are given special consideration as indicated by the page numbers.)

No support is usually offered for these statements. I believe they are mostly founded on the principle of scientific induction. A man has seen thousands of machines in his lifetime. From what he sees of them he draws a number of general conclusions. They are ugly, each is designed for a very limited purpose, when required for a minutely different purpose they are useless, the variety of behaviour of any one of them is very small, etc., etc. Naturally he concludes that these are necessary properties of machines in general. Many of these limitations are associated with the very small storage capacity of most machines. (I am assuming that the idea of storage capacity is extended in some way to cover machines other than discrete-state machines. The exact definition does not matter as no mathematical accuracy is claimed in the present discussion.) A few years ago, when very little had been heard of digital computers, it was possible to elicit much incredulity concerning them, if one mentioned their properties without describing their construction. That was presumably due to a similar application of the principle of scientific induction. These applications of the principle are of course largely unconscious. When a burnt child fears the fire and shows that he fears it by avoiding it, I should say that he was applying scientific induction. (I could of course also describe his behaviour in many other ways.) The works and customs of mankind do not seem to be very suitable material to which to apply scientific induction. A very large part of space-time must be investigated, if reliable results are to be obtained. Otherwise we may (as most English children do) decide that everybody speaks English, and that it is silly to learn French.

There are, however, special remarks to be made about many of the disabilities that have been mentioned. The inability to enjoy strawberries and cream may have struck the reader as frivolous. Possibly a machine might be made to enjoy this delicious dish, but any attempt to make one do so would be idiotic. What is important about this disability is that it contributes to some of the other disabilities, *e.g.* to the difficulty of the same kind of friendliness occurring between man and machine as between white man and white man, or between black man and black man.

The claim that 'machines cannot make mistakes' seems a curious one. One is tempted to retort, 'Are they any the worse for that?' But let us adopt a more sympathetic attitude, and try to see what is really meant. I think this criticism can be explained in terms of the imitation game. It is claimed that the interrogator could distinguish the machine from the man simply by setting them a number of problems in arithmetic. The machine would be unmasked because of its deadly accuracy. The reply to this is simple. The machine (programmed for playing the game) would not attempt to give the *right* answers to the arithmetic problems. It would deliberately introduce mistakes in a manner calculated to confuse the interrogator. A mechanical fault would probably show itself through an unsuitable decision as to what sort of a mistake to make in the arithmetic. Even this interpretation of the criticism is not sufficiently sympathetic. But we cannot afford the space to go into it much further. It seems to me that this criticism depends on a confusion between two kinds of mistake. We may call them 'errors of functioning' and 'errors of conclusion'. Errors of functioning are due to some mechanical or electrical fault which causes the machine to behave otherwise than it was designed to do. In philosophical discussions one likes to ignore the possibility of such errors; one is therefore discussing 'abstract machines'. These abstract machines are mathematical fictions rather than physical objects. By definition they are incapable of errors of functioning. In this sense we can truly say that 'machines can never make mistakes'. Errors of conclusion can only arise when some meaning is attached to the output signals from the machine. The machine might, for instance, type out mathematical equations, or sentences in English. When a false proposition is typed we say that the machine has committed an error of conclusion. There is clearly no reason at all for saying that a machine cannot make this kind of mistake. It might do nothing but type out repeatedly '0 = 1'. To take a less perverse example, it might have some method for drawing conclusions by scientific induction. We must expect such a method to lead occasionally to erroneous results.

The claim that a machine cannot be the subject of its own thought can of course only be answered if it can be shown that the machine has *some* thought with *some* subject matter. Nevertheless, 'the subject matter of a machine's operations' does seem to mean something, at least to the people who deal with it. If, for instance, the machine was trying to find a solution of the equation $x^2 - 40x - 11 = 0$ one would be tempted to describe this equation as part of the machine's subject matter at that moment. In this sort of sense a machine undoubtedly can be its own subject matter. It may be used to help in making up its own programmes, or to predict the effect of alterations in its own structure. By observing the results of its own behaviour it can modify its own programmes so as to achieve some purpose more effectively. These are possibilities of the near future, rather than Utopian dreams.

The criticism that a machine cannot have much diversity of behaviour is just a way of saying that it cannot have much storage capacity. Until fairly recently a storage capacity of even a thousand digits was very rare.

The criticisms that we are considering here are often disguised forms of the argument from consciousness. Usually if one maintains that a machine *can* do one of these things, and describes the kind of method that the machine could use, one will not make much of an impression. It is thought that the method (whatever it may be, for it must be mechanical) is really rather base. Compare the parenthesis in Jefferson's statement quoted on p. 30.

(6) *Lady Lovelace's objection*

Our most detailed information of Babbage's Analytical Engine comes from a memoir by *Lady Lovelace*. In it she states, 'The Analytical Engine has no pretensions to *originate* anything. It can do *whatever we know how to order it to perform*' (her italics). This statement is quoted by *Hartree* (p. 70) who adds: 'This does not imply that it may not be possible to construct electronic equipment which will "think for itself", or in which, in biological terms, one could set up a conditioned reflex, which would serve as a basis for "learning". Whether this is possible in principle or not is a stimulating and exciting question, suggested by some of these recent developments. But it did not seem that the machines constructed or projected at the time had this property'.

I am in thorough agreement with Hartree over this. It will be noticed that he does not assert that the machines in question had not got the property, but rather that the evidence available to Lady Lovelace did not encourage her to believe that they had it. It is quite possible that the machines in question had in a sense got this property. For suppose that some discrete-state machine has the property. The Analytical Engine was a universal digital computer, so that, if its storage capacity and speed were adequate, it could by suitable programming be made to mimic the machine in question. Probably this argument did not occur to the Countess or to Babbage. In any case there was no obligation on them to claim all that could be claimed.

This whole question will be considered again under the heading of learning machines.

A variant of Lady Lovelace's objection states that a machine can 'never do anything really new'. This may be parried for a moment with the saw, 'There is nothing new under the sun'. Who can be certain that 'original work' that he has done was not simply the growth of the seed planted in him by teaching, or the effect of following well-known general principles. A better variant of the objection says that a machine can never 'take us by surprise'. This statement is a more direct challenge and can be met directly. Machines take me by surprise with great frequency. This is largely because I do not do sufficient calculation to decide what to expect them to do, or rather because, although I do a calculation, I do it in a hurried, slipshod fashion, taking risks. Perhaps I say to myself, 'I suppose the voltage here ought to be the same as there: anyway let's assume it is'. Naturally I am often wrong, and the result is a surprise for me for by the time the experiment is done these assumptions have been forgotten. These admissions lay me open to lectures on the subject of my vicious ways, but do not throw any doubt on my credibility when I testify to the surprises I experience.

I do not expect this reply to silence my critic. He will probably say that such surprises are due to some creative mental act on my part, and reflect no credit on the machine. This leads us back to the argument from consciousness, and far from the idea of surprise. It is a line of argument we must consider closed, but it is perhaps worth remarking that the appreciation of something as surprising requires as much of a 'creative mental act' whether the surprising event originates from a man, a book, a machine or anything else.

The view that machines cannot give rise to surprises is due, I believe, to a fallacy to which philosophers and mathematicians are particularly subject. This is the assumption that as soon as a fact is presented to a mind all consequences of that fact spring into the mind simultaneously with it. It is a very useful assumption under many circumstances, but one too easily forgets that it is false. A natural consequence of doing so is that one then assumes that there is no virtue in the mere working out of consequences from data and general principles.

(7) *Argument from continuity in the nervous system*

The nervous system is certainly not a discrete-state machine. A small error in the information about the size of a nervous impulse impinging on a neuron, may make a large difference to the size of the outgoing impulse. It may be argued that, this being so, one cannot expect to be able to mimic the behaviour of the nervous system with a discrete-state system.

It is true that a discrete-state machine must be different from a continuous machine. But if we adhere to the conditions of the imitation game, the interrogator will not be able to take any advantage of this difference. The situation can be made clearer if we consider some other simpler continuous machine. A differential analyser will do very well. (A differential analyser is a certain kind of machine not of the discrete-state type used for some kinds of calculation.) Some of these provide their answers in a typed form, and so are suitable for taking part in the game. It would not be possible for a digital computer to predict exactly what answers the differential analyser would give to a problem, but it would be quite capable of giving the right sort of answer. For instance, if asked to give the value of π (actually about 3·1416) it would be reasonable to choose at random between the values 3·12, 3·13, 3·14, 3·15, 3·16 with the probabilities of 0·05, 0·15, 0·55, 0·19, 0·06 (say). Under these circumstances it would be very difficult for the interrogator to distinguish the differential analyser from the digital computer.

(8) *The argument from informality of behaviour*

It is not possible to produce a set of rules purporting to describe what a man should do in every conceivable set of circumstances. One might for instance have a rule that one is to stop when one sees a red traffic light, and to go if one sees a green one, but what if by some fault both appear together? One may perhaps decide that it is safest to stop. But some further difficulty may well arise from this decision later. To attempt to provide rules of conduct to cover every eventuality, even those arising from traffic lights, appears to be impossible. With all this I agree.

From this it is argued that we cannot be machines. I shall try to reproduce the argument, but I fear I shall hardly do it justice. It seems to run something like this. 'If each man had a definite set of rules of conduct by which he regulated his life he would be no better than a machine. But there are no such rules, so men cannot be machines.' The undistributed middle is glaring. I do not think the argument is ever put quite like this, but I believe this is the argument used nevertheless. There may however be a certain confusion between 'rules of conduct' and 'laws of behaviour' to cloud the issue. By 'rules of conduct' I mean precepts such as 'Stop if you see red lights', on which one can act, and of which one can be conscious. By 'laws of behaviour' I mean laws of nature as applied to a man's body such as 'if you pinch him he will squeak'. If we substitute 'laws of behaviour which regulated his life' for 'laws of conduct by which he regulates his life' in the argument quoted the undistributed middle is no longer insuperable.* For we believe that it is not only true that being regulated by laws of behaviour implies being some sort of machine (though not necessarily a discrete-state machine), but that conversely being such a machine implies being regulated by such laws. However, we cannot so easily convince ourselves of the absence of complete laws of behaviour as of complete rules of conduct. The only way we know of for finding such laws is scientific observation, and we certainly know of no circumstances under which we could say, 'We have searched enough. There are no such laws.'

We can demonstrate more forcibly that any such statement would be unjustified. For suppose we could be sure of finding such laws if they existed. Then given a discrete-state machine it should certainly be possible to discover by observation sufficient about it to predict its future behaviour, and this within a reasonable time, say a thousand years. But this does not seem to be the case. I have set up on the Manchester computer a small programme using only 1000 units of storage, whereby the machine supplied with one sixteen figure number replies with another within two seconds. I would defy anyone to learn from these replies sufficient about the programme to be able to predict any replies to untried values.

(9) *The argument from extra-sensory perception*

I assume that the reader is familiar with the idea of extra-sensory perception, and the meaning of the four items of it, *viz.* telepathy, clairvoyance, precognition and psycho-kinesis. These disturbing phenomena seem to deny all our usual scientific ideas. How we should like to discredit them! Unfortunately the statistical evidence, at least for telepathy, is overwhelming.

---

* Clearly Turing must have meant to say 'If we substitute "laws of behaviour which regulated his life" for "rules of conduct by which he regulated his life" . . .' [Ed.]

It is very difficult to rearrange one's ideas so as to fit these new facts in. Once one has accepted them it does not seem a very big step to believe in ghosts and bogies. The idea that our bodies move simply according to the known laws of physics, together with some others not yet discovered but somewhat similar, would be one of the first to go.

This argument is to my mind quite a strong one. One can say in reply that many scientific theories seem to remain workable in practice, in spite of clashing with E.S.P.; that in fact one can get along very nicely if one forgets about it. This is rather cold comfort, and one fears that thinking is just the kind of phenomenon where E.S.P. may be especially relevant.

A more specific argument based on E.S.P. might run as follows: 'Let us play the imitation game, using as witnesses a man who is good as a telepathic receiver, and a digital computer. The interrogator can ask such questions as "What suit does the card in my right hand belong to?" The man by telepathy or clairvoyance gives the right answer 130 times out of 400 cards. The machine can only guess at random, and perhaps gets 104 right, so the interrogator makes the right identification.' There is an interesting possibility which opens here. Suppose the digital computer contains a random number generator. Then it will be natural to use this to decide what answer to give. But then the random number generator will be subject to the psycho-kinetic powers of the interrogator. Perhaps this psycho-kinesis might cause the machine to guess right more often than would be expected on a probability calculation, so that the interrogator might still be unable to make the right identification. On the other hand, he might be able to guess right without any questioning, by clairvoyance. With E.S.P. anything may happen.

If telepathy is admitted it will be necessary to tighten our test up. The situation could be regarded as analogous to that which would occur if the interrogator were talking to himself and one of the competitors was listening with his ear to the wall. To put the competitors into a 'telepathy-proof room' would satisfy all requirements.

7 Learning machines

The reader will have anticipated that I have no very convincing arguments of a positive nature to support my views. If I had I should not have taken such pains to point out the fallacies in contrary views. Such evidence as I have I shall now give.

Let us return for a moment to Lady Lovelace's objection, which stated that the machine can only do what we tell it to do. One could say that a man can 'inject' an idea into the machine, and that it will respond to a certain extent and then drop into quiescence, like a piano string struck by a hammer. Another simile would be an atomic pile of less than critical size: an injected idea is to correspond to a neutron entering the pile from without. Each such neutron will cause a certain disturbance which eventually dies away. If, however, the size of the pile is sufficiently increased, the disturbance caused by such an incoming neutron will very likely go on and on increasing until the whole pile is destroyed. Is there a corresponding phenomenon for minds, and is there one for machines? There does seem to be one for the human mind. The majority of them seem to be 'sub-critical', *i.e.* to correspond in this analogy to piles of sub-critical size. An idea presented to such a mind will on average give rise to less than one idea in reply. A smallish proportion are super-critical. An idea presented to such a mind may give rise to a whole 'theory' consisting of secondary, tertiary and more remote ideas. Animals' minds seem to be very definitely sub-critical. Adhering to this analogy we ask, 'Can a machine be made to be super-critical?'

The 'skin of an onion' analogy is also helpful. In considering the functions of the mind or the brain we find certain operations which we can explain in purely mechanical terms. This we say does not correspond to the real mind: it is a sort of skin which we must strip off if we are to find the real mind. But then in what remains we find a further skin to be stripped off, and so on. Proceeding in this way do we ever come to the 'real' mind or do we eventually come to the skin which has nothing in it? (In the latter case the whole mind is mechanical. It would not be a discrete state machine however. We have discussed this.)

These last two paragraphs do not claim to be convincing arguments. They should rather be described as 'recitations tending to produce belief'.

The only really satisfactory support that can be given for the view expressed at the beginning of §6, will be that provided by waiting for the end of the century and then doing the experiment described. But what can we say in the meantime? What steps should be taken now if the experiment is to be successful?

As I have explained, the problem is mainly one of programming. Advances in engineering will have to be made too, but it seems unlikely that these will not be adequate for the requirements. Estimates of the storage capacity of the brain vary from 10^{10} to 10^{15} binary digits. I incline to the lower values and believe that only a very small fraction is used for the higher types of thinking. Most of it is probably used for the retention of visual impressions. I should be surprised if more than 10^9 was required for satisfactory playing of the imitation game, at any rate against a blind man. (Note—The capacity of the *Encyclopaedia Britannica*, 11th edition, is 2×10^9.) A storage capacity of 10^7 would be a very practicable possibility even by present techniques. It is probably not necessary to increase the speed of operations of the machines at all. Parts of modern machines which can be regarded as analogues of nerve cells work about a thousand times faster than the latter. This should provide a 'margin of safety' which could cover losses of speed arising in many ways. Our problem then is to find out how to programme these machines to play the game. At my present rate of working I produce about a thousand digits of programme a day, so that about sixty workers, working steadily through the fifty years might accomplish the job, if nothing went into the waste-paper basket. Some more expeditious method seems desirable.

In the process of trying to imitate an adult human mind we are bound to think a good deal about the process which has brought it to the state that it is in. We may notice three components,

(*a*) The initial state of the mind, say at birth,
(*b*) The education to which it has been subjected,
(*c*) Other experience, not to be described as education, to which it has been subjected.

Instead of trying to produce a programme to simulate the adult mind, why not rather try to produce one which simulates the child's? If this were then subjected to an appropriate course of education one would obtain the adult brain. Presumably the child-brain is something like a note-book as one buys it from the stationers. Rather little mechanism, and lots of blank sheets. (Mechanism and writing are from our point of view almost synonymous.) Our hope is that there is so little mechanism in the child-brain that something like it can be easily programmed. The amount of work in the education we can assume, as a first approximation, to be much the same as for the human child.

We have thus divided our problem into two parts. The child-programme and the education process. These two remain very closely connected. We cannot expect to find a good child-machine at the first attempt. One must experiment with teaching one such machine and see how well it learns. One can then try another and see if it is better or worse. There is an obvious connection between this process and evolution, by the identifications

Structure of the child machine = Hereditary material
Changes   ,,   ,,   = Mutations
Natural selection   = Judgment of the experimenter

One may hope, however, that this process will be more expeditious than evolution. The survival of the fittest is a slow method for measuring advantages. The experimenter, by the exercise of intelligence, should be able to speed it up. Equally important is the fact that he is not restricted to random mutations. If he can trace a cause for some weakness he can probably think of the kind of mutation which will improve it.

It will not be possible to apply exactly the same teaching process to the machine as to a normal child. It will not, for instance, be provided with legs, so that it could not be asked to go out and fill the coal scuttle. Possibly it might not have eyes. But however well these deficiencies might be overcome by clever engineering, one could not send the creature to school without the other children making excessive fun of it. It must be given some tuition. We need not be too concerned about the legs, eyes, etc. The example of Miss *Helen Keller* shows that education can take place provided that communication in both directions between teacher and pupil can take place by some means or other.

We normally associate punishments and rewards with the teaching process. Some simple child-machines can be constructed or programmed on this sort of principle. The machine has to be so constructed that events which shortly preceded the occurrence of a punishment-signal are unlikely to be repeated, whereas a reward-signal increased the probability of repetition of the events which led up to it. These definitions do not presuppose any feelings on the part of the machine. I have done some experiments with one such child-machine, and succeeded in teaching it a few things, but the teaching method was too unorthodox for the experiment to be considered really successful.

The use of punishments and rewards can at best be a part of the teaching process. Roughly speaking, if the teacher has no other means of communicating to the pupil, the amount of information which can reach him does not exceed the total number of rewards and punishments applied. By the time a child has learnt to repeat 'Casabianca' he would probably feel very sore indeed, if the text could only be discovered by a 'Twenty Questions' technique, every 'NO' taking the form of a blow. It is necessary therefore to have some other 'unemotional' channels of communication. If these are available it is possible to teach a machine by punishments and rewards to obey orders given in some language, *e.g.* a symbolic language. These orders are to be transmitted through the 'unemotional' channels. The use of this language will diminish greatly the number of punishments and rewards required.

Opinions may vary as to the complexity which is suitable in the child-machine. One might try to make it as simple as possible consistently with the general principles. Alternatively one might have a complete system of logical inference 'built in'.[3] In the latter case the store would be largely occupied with definitions and propositions. The propositions would have various kinds of status, *e.g.* well-established facts, conjectures, mathematically proved theorems, statements given by an authority, expressions having the logical form of proposition but not belief-value. Certain propositions may be described as 'imperatives'. The machine should be so constructed that as soon as an imperative is classed as 'well-established' the appropriate action automatically takes place. To illustrate this, suppose the teacher says to the machine, 'Do your homework now'. This may cause 'Teacher says "Do your homework now"' to be included amongst the well-established facts. Another such fact might be, 'Everything that teacher says is true'. Combining these may eventually lead to the imperative, 'Do your homework now', being included amongst the well-established facts, and this, by the construction of the machine, will mean that the homework actually gets started, but the effect is very satisfactory. The processes of inference used by the machine need not be such as would satisfy the most exacting logicians. There might for instance be no hierarchy of types. But this need not mean that type fallacies will occur, any more than we are bound to fall over unfenced cliffs. Suitable imperatives (expressed *within* the systems, not forming part of the rules *of* the system) such as 'Do not use a class unless it is a subclass of one which has been mentioned by teacher' can have a similar effect to 'Do not go too near the edge'.

The imperatives that can be obeyed by a machine that has no limbs are bound to be of a rather intellectual character, as in the example (doing homework) given above. Important amongst such imperatives will be ones which regulate the order in which the rules of the logical system concerned are to be applied. For at each stage when one is using a logical system, there is a very large number of alternative steps, any of which one is permitted to apply, so far as obedience to the rules of the logical system is concerned. These choices make the difference between a brilliant and a footling reasoner, not the difference between a sound and a fallacious one. Propositions leading to imperatives of this kind might be 'When Socrates is mentioned, use the syllogism in Barbara' or 'If one method has been proved to be quicker than another, do not use the slower method'. Some of these may be 'given by authority', but others may be produced by the machine itself, *e. g.* by scientific induction.

The idea of a learning machine may appear paradoxical to some readers. How can the rules of operation of the machine change? They should describe completely how the machine will react whatever its history might be, whatever changes it might undergo. The rules are thus quite time-invariant. This is quite true. The explanation of the paradox is that the rules which get change in the learning process are of a rather less pretentious kind, claiming only an ephemeral validity. The reader may draw a parallel with the Constitution of the United States.

An important feature of a learning machine is that its teacher will often be very largely ignorant of quite what is going on inside, although he may still be able to some extent to predict his pupil's behaviour. This should apply most strongly to the later education of a machine arising from a child-machine of well-tried design (or programme). This is in clear contrast with normal procedure when using a machine to do computations: one's object is then to have a clear mental picture of the state of the machine at each moment in the computations. This object can only be achieved with a struggle. The view that 'the machine can only do what we know how to order it to do',[4] appears strange in face of this. Most of the programmes which we can put into the machine will result in its doing something that we cannot make sense of at all, or which we regard as completely random behaviour. Intelligent behaviour presumably consists in a departure from the completely disciplined behaviour involved in computation, but a rather slight one, which does not give rise to random behaviour, or to pointless repetitive loops.

Another important result of preparing our machine for its part in the imitation game by a process of teaching and learning is that 'human fallibility' is likely to be omitted in a rather natural way, *i.e.* without special 'coaching'. (The reader should reconcile this with the point of view on pp. 32, 33.) Processes that are learnt do not produce a hundred per cent. certainty of result; if they did they could not be unlearnt.

It is probably wise to include a random element in a learning machine (see p. 24). A random element is rather useful when we are searching for a solution of some problem. Suppose for instance we wanted to find a number between 50 and 200 which was equal to the square of the sum of its digits, we might start at 51 then try 52 and go on until we got a number that worked. Alternatively we might choose numbers at random until we got a good one. This method has the advantage that it is unnecessary to keep track of the values that have been tried, but the disadvantage that one may try the same one twice, but this is not very important if there are several solutions. The systematic method has the disadvantage that there may be an enormous block without any solutions in the region which has to be investigated first. Now the learning process may be regarded as a search for a form of behaviour which will satisfy the teacher (or some other criterion). Since there is probably a very large number of satisfactory solutions the random method seems to be better than the systematic. It should be noticed that it is used in the analogous process of evolution. But there the systematic method is not possible. How could one keep track of the different genetical combinations that had been tried, so as to avoid trying them again?

We may hope that machines will eventually compete with men in all purely intellectual fields. But which are the best ones to start with? Even this is a difficult decision. Many people think that a very abstract activity, like the playing of chess, would be best. It can also be maintained that it is best to provide the machine with the best sense organs that money can buy, and then teach it to understand and speak English. This process could follow the normal teaching of a child. Things would be pointed out and named, etc. Again I do not know what the right answer is, but I think both approaches should be tried.

We can only see a short distance ahead, but we can see plenty there that needs to be done.

Notes

1 Possibly this view is heretical. St. Thomas Aquinas (*Summa Theologica*, quoted by Bertrand Russell, p. 480) states that God cannot make a man to have no soul. But this may not be a real restriction on His powers, but only a result of the fact that men's souls are immortal, and therefore indestructible.
2 Author's names in italics refer to the Bibliography.
3 Or rather 'programmed in' for our child-machine will be programmed in a digital computer. But the logical system will not have to be learnt.

4 Compare Lady Lovelace's statement (p. 34) which does not contain the word 'only'.

Bibliography

Samuel Butler, Erewhon, London, 1865. Chapters 23, 24, 25, *The Book of the Machines*.

Alonzo Church, 'An Unsolvable Problem of Elementary Number Theory', *American J. of Math.*, 58 (1936), 345–363.

K. Gödel, 'Über formal unentscheidbare Sätze der Principia Mathematica und verwandter Systeme, I', *Monatshefte für Math. und Phys.* (1931), 173–189.

D. R. Hartree, *Calculating Instruments and Machines*, New York, 1949.

S. C. Kleene, 'General Recursive Functions of Natural Numbers', *American J. of Math.*, 57 (1935), 153–173 and 219–244.

G. Jefferson, 'The Mind of Mechanical Man'. Lister Oration for 1949. *British Medical Journal*, vol. i (1949), 1105–1121.

Countess of Lovelace, 'Translator's notes to an article on Babbage's Analytical Engine', *Scientific Memoirs* (ed. by R. Taylor), vol. 3 (1842), 691–731.

Bertrand Russell, *History of Western Philosophy*, London, 1940.

A. M. Turing, 'On Computable Numbers, with an Application to the Entscheidungsproblem', *Proc. London Math. Soc.* (2), 42 (1937), 230–265.

26

A PROPOSAL FOR THE DARTMOUTH SUMMER RESEARCH PROJECT ON ARTIFICIAL INTELLIGENCE

J. McCarthy, M. L. Minsky, N. Rochester and C. E. Shannon

Source: J. McCarthy, M. L. Minsky, N. Rochester and C. E. Shannon (A Proposal for the Dartmouth Summer Research Project on Artificial Intelligence), 1955

We propose that a 2 month, 10 man study of artificial intelligence be carried out during the summer of 1956 at Dartmouth College in Hanover, New Hampshire. The study is to proceed on the basis of the conjecture that every aspect of learning or any other feature of intelligence can in principle be so precisely described that a machine can be made to simulate it. An attempt will be made to find how to make machines use language, form abstractions and concepts, solve kinds of problems now reserved for humans, and improve themselves. We think that a significant advance can be made in one or more of these problems if a carefully selected group of scientists work on it together for a summer.

The following are some aspects of the artificial intelligence problem:

1. *Automatic Computers*
   If a machine can do a job, then an automatic calculator can be programmed to simulate the machine. The speeds and memory capacities of present computers may be insufficient to simulate many of the higher functions of the human brain, but the major obstacle is not lack of machine capacity, but our inability to write programs taking full advantage of what we have.
2. *How Can a Computer be Programmed to Use a Language*
   It may be speculated that a large part of human thought consists of manipulating words according to rules of reasoning and rules of conjecture. From this point of view, forming a generalization consists of

admitting a new word and some rules whereby sentences containing it imply and are implied by others. This idea has never been very precisely formulated nor have examples been worked out.

3. *Neuron Nets*

How can a set of (hypothetical) neurons be arranged so as to form concepts. Considerable theoretical and experimental work has been done on this problem by Uttley, Rashevsky and his group, Farley and Clark, Pitts and McCulloch, Minsky, Rochester and Holland, and others. Partial results have been obtained but the problem needs more theoretical work.

4. *Theory of the Size of a Calculation*

If we are given a well-defined problem (one for which it is possible to test mechanically whether or not a proposed answer is a valid answer) one way of solving it is to try all possible answers in order. This method is inefficient, and to exclude it one must have some criterion for efficiency of calculation. Some consideration will show that to get a measure of the efficiency of a calculation it is necessary to have on hand a method of measuring the complexity of calculating devices which in turn can be done if one has a theory of the complexity of functions. Some partial results on this problem have been obtained by Shannon, and also by McCarthy.

5. *Self-Improvement*

Probably a truly intelligent machine will carry out activities which may best be described as self-improvement. Some schemes for doing this have been proposed and are worth further study. It seems likely that this question can be studied abstractly as well.

6. *Abstractions*

A number of types of "abstraction" can be distinctly defined and several others less distinctly. A direct attempt to classify these and to describe machine methods of forming abstractions from sensory and other data would seem worthwhile.

7. *Randomness and Creativity*

A fairly attractive and yet clearly incomplete conjecture is that the difference between creative thinking and unimaginative competent thinking lies in the injection of some randomness. The randomness must be guided by intuition to be efficient. In other words, the educated guess or the hunch include controlled randomness in otherwise orderly thinking.

In addition to the above collectively formulated problems for study, we have asked the individuals taking part to describe what they will work on. Statements by the four originators of the project are attached.

We propose to organize the work of the group as follows.

Potential participants will be sent copies of this proposal and asked if they would like to work on the artificial intelligence problem in the group and if so what they would like to work on. The invitations will be made by the organizing committee on the basis of its estimate of the individual's potential contribution to the work of the group. The members will circulate their previous work and their ideas for the problems to be attacked during the months preceding the working period of the group.

During the meeting there will be regular research seminars and opportunity for the members to work individually and in informal small groups.

The originators of this proposal are:

1. **C. E. Shannon**, Mathematician, Bell Telephone Laboratories. Shannon developed the statistical theory of information, the application of propositional calculus to switching circuits, and has results on the efficient synthesis of switching circuits, the design of machines that learn, cryptography, and the theory of Turing machines. He and J. McCarthy are co-editing an Annals of Mathematics Study on "The Theory of Automata".
2. **M. L. Minsky**, Harvard Junior Fellow in Mathematics and Neurology. Minsky has built a machine for simulating learning by nerve nets and has written a Princeton PhD thesis in mathematics entitled, "Neural Nets and the Brain Model Problem" which includes results in learning theory and the theory of random neural nets.
3. **N. Rochester**, Manager of Information Research, IBM Corporation, Poughkeepsie, New York. Rochester was concerned with the development of radar for seven years and computing machinery for seven years. He and another engineer were jointly responsible for the design of the IBM Type 701 which is a large scale automatic computer in wide use today. He worked out some of the automatic programming techniques which are in wide use today and has been concerned with problems of how to get machines to do tasks which previously could be done only by people. He has also worked on simulation of nerve nets with particular emphasis on using computers to test theories in neurophysiology.
4. **J. McCarthy**, Assistant Professor of Mathematics, Dartmouth College. McCarthy has worked on a number of questions connected with the mathematical nature of the thought process including the theory of Turing machines, the speed of computers, the relation of a brain model to its environment, and the use of languages by machines. Some results of this work are included in the forthcoming "Annals Study" edited by Shannon and McCarthy. McCarthy's other work has been in the field of differential equations.

The Rockefeller Foundation is being asked to provide financial support for the project on the following basis:

1. Salaries of $1200 for each faculty level participant who is not being supported by his own organization. It is expected, for example, that the participants from Bell Laboratories and IBM Corporation will be

supported by these organizations while those from Dartmouth and Harvard will require foundation support.

2. Salaries of $700 for up to two graduate students.
3. Railway fare for participants coming from a distance.
4. Rent for people who are simultaneously renting elsewhere.
5. Secretarial expenses of $650, $500 for a secretary and $150 for duplicating expenses.
6. Organization expenses of $200. (Includes expense of reproducing preliminary work by participants and travel necessary for organization purposes.)
7. Expenses for two or three people visiting for a short time.

Estimated Expenses

6 salaries of 1200	$7200
2 salaries of 700	1400
8 traveling and rent expenses averaging 300	2400
Secretarial and organizational expense	850
Additional traveling expenses	600
Contingencies	550
	$13,500

Proposal for research by C. E. Shannon

I would like to devote my research to one or both of the topics listed below. While I hope to do so, it is possible that because of personal considerations I may not be able to attend for the entire two months. I, nevertheless, intend to be there for whatever time is possible.

1. Application of information theory concepts to computing machines and brain models. A basic problem in information theory is that of transmitting information reliably over a noisy channel. An analogous problem in computing machines is that of reliable computing using unreliable elements. This problem has been studied by von Neumann for Sheffer stroke elements and by Shannon and Moore for relays; but there are still many open questions. The problem for several elements, the development of concepts similar to channel capacity, the sharper analysis of upper and lower bounds on the required redundancy, etc. are among the important issues. Another question deals with the theory of information networks where information flows in many closed loops (as contrasted with the simple one-way channel usually considered in communication theory). Questions of delay become very important in the closed loop case, and a whole new approach seems necessary. This would probably involve concepts such as partial entropies when a part of the past history of a message ensemble is known.

2. The matched environment–brain model approach to automata. In

general a machine or animal can only adapt to or operate in a limited class of environments. Even the complex human brain first adapts to the simpler aspects of its environment, and gradually builds up to the more complex features. I propose to study the synthesis of brain models by the parallel development of a series of matched (theoretical) environments and corresponding brain models which adapt to them. The emphasis here is on clarifying the environmental model, and representing it as a mathematical structure. Often in discussing mechanized intelligence, we think of machines performing the most advanced human thought activities–proving theorems, writing music, or playing chess. I am proposing here to start at the simple and when the environment is neither hostile (merely indifferent) nor complex, and to work up through a series of easy stages in the direction of these advanced activities.

Proposal for research by M. L. Minsky

It is not difficult to design a machine which exhibits the following type of learning. The machine is provided with input and output channels and an internal means of providing varied output responses to inputs in such a way that the machine may be "trained" by a "trial and error" process to acquire one of a range of input-output functions. Such a machine, when placed in an appropriate environment and given a criterion of "success" or "failure" can be trained to exhibit "goal-seeking" behavior. Unless the machine is provided with, or is able to develop, a way of abstracting sensory material, it can progress through a complicated environment only through painfully slow steps, and in general will not reach a high level of behavior.

Now let the criterion of success be not merely the appearance of a desired activity pattern at the output channel of the machine, but rather the performance of a given manipulation in a given environment. Then in certain ways the motor situation appears to be a dual of the sensory situation, and progress can be reasonably fast only if the machine is equally capable of assembling an ensemble of "motor abstractions" relating its output activity to changes in the environment. Such "motor abstractions" can be valuable only if they relate to changes in the environment which can be detected by the machine as changes in the sensory situation, i.e., if they are related, through the structure of the environment, to the sensory abstractions that the machine is using.

I have been studying such systems for some time and feel that if a machine can be designed in which the sensory and motor abstractions, as they are formed, can be made to satisfy certain relations, a high order of behavior may result. These relations involve pairing, motor abstractions with sensory abstractions in such a way as to produce new sensory situations representing the changes in the environment that might be expected if the corresponding motor act actually took place.

The important result that would be looked for would be that the machine would tend to build up within itself an abstract model of the environment in which it is placed. If it were given a problem, it could first explore solutions within the internal abstract model of the environment and then attempt external experiments. Because of this preliminary internal study, these external experiments would appear to be rather clever, and the behavior would have to be regarded as rather "imaginative".

A very tentative proposal of how this might be done is described in my dissertation and I intend to do further work in this direction. I hope that by summer 1956 I will have a model of such a machine fairly close to the stage of programming in a computer.

Proposal for research by N. Rochester

Originality in machine performance

In writing a program for an automatic calculator, one ordinarily provides the machine with a set of rules to cover each contingency which may arise and confront the machine. One expects the machine to follow this set of rules slavishly and to exhibit no originality or common sense. Furthermore one is annoyed only at himself when the machine gets confused because the rules he has provided for the machine are slightly contradictory. Finally, in writing programs for machines, one sometimes must go at problems in a very laborious manner, whereas, if the machine had just a little intuition or could make reasonable guesses, the solution of the problem could be quite direct. This paper describes a conjecture as to how to make a machine behave in a somewhat more sophisticated manner in the general area suggested above. The paper discusses a problem on which I have been working sporadically for about five years and which I wish to pursue further in the Artificial Intelligence Project next summer.

The process of invention or discovery

Living in the environment of our culture provides us with procedures for solving many problems. Just how these procedures work is not yet clear but I shall discuss this aspect of the problem in terms of a model suggested by Craik.[1] He suggests that mental action consists basically of constructing little engines inside the brain which can simulate and thus predict abstractions relating to environment. Thus the solution of a problem which one already understands is done as follows:

1. The environment provides data from which certain abstractions are formed.
2. The abstractions together with certain internal habits or drives provide:

3. (a) A definition of a problem in terms of desired condition to be achieved in the future, a goal.
   (b) A suggested action to solve the problem.
   (c) Stimulation to arouse in the brain the engine which corresponds to this situation.

4. Then the engine operates to predict what this environmental situation and the proposed reaction will lead to.

5. If the prediction corresponds to the goal the individual proceeds to act as indicated.

The prediction will correspond to the goal if living in the environment of his culture has provided the individual with the solution to the problem. Regarding the individual as a stored program calculator, the program contains rules to cover this particular contingency.

For a more complex situation the rules might be more complicated. The rules might call for testing each of a set of possible actions to determine which provided the solution. A still more complex set of rules might provide for uncertainty about the environment, as for example in playing tic tac toe one must not only consider his next move but the various possible moves of the environment (his opponent).

Now consider a problem for which no individual in the culture has a solution and which has resisted efforts at solution. This might be a typical current unsolved scientific problem. The individual might try to solve it and find that every reasonable action led to failure. In other words the stored program contains rules for the solution of this problem but the rules are slightly wrong.

In order to solve this problem the individual will have to do something which is unreasonable or unexpected as judged by the heritage of wisdom accumulated by the culture. He could get such behavior by trying different things at random but such an approach would usually be too inefficient. There are usually too many possible courses of action of which only a tiny fraction are acceptable. The individual needs a hunch, something unexpected but not altogether reasonable. Some problems, often those which are fairly new and have not resisted much effort, need just a little randomness. Others, often those which have long resisted solution, need a really bizarre deviation from traditional methods. A problem whose solution requires originality could yield to a method of solution which involved randomness.

In terms of Craik's model, the engine which should simulate the environment at first fails to simulate correctly. Therefore, it is necessary to try various modifications of the engine until one is found that makes it do what is needed.

Instead of describing the problem in terms of an individual in his culture it could have been described in terms of the learning of an immature individual. When the individual is presented with a problem outside the scope of his experience he must surmount it in a similar manner.

So far the nearest practical approach using this method in machine solution of problems is an extension of the Monte Carlo method. In the usual problem which is appropriate for Monte Carlo there is a situation which is grossly misunderstood and which has too many possible factors and one is unable to decide which factors to ignore in working out analytical solutions. So the mathematician has the machine making a few thousand random experiments. The results of these experiments provide a rough guess as to what the answer may be. The extension of the Monte Carlo Method is to use these results as a guide to determine what to neglect in order to simplify the problem enough to obtain an approximate analytical solution.

It might be asked why the method should include randomness. Why shouldn't the method be to try each possibility in the order of the probability that the present state of knowledge would predict for its success? For the scientist surrounded by the environment provided by his culture, it may be that one scientist alone would be unlikely to solve the problem in his life so the efforts of many are needed. If they use randomness they could all work at once on it without complete duplication of effort. If they used system they would require impossibly detailed communication. For the individual maturing in competition with other individuals the requirements of mixed strategy (using game theory terminology) favor randomness. For the machine, randomness will probably be needed to overcome the shortsightedness and prejudices of the programmer. While the necessity for randomness has clearly not been proven, there is much evidence in its favor.

The machine with randomness

In order to write a program to make an automatic calculator use originality it will not do to introduce randomness without using forsight. If, for example, one wrote a program so that once in every 10,000 steps the calculator generated a random number and executed it as an instruction the result would probably be chaos. Then after a certain amount of chaos the machine would probably try something forbidden or execute a stop instruction and the experiment would be over.

Two approaches, however, appear to be reasonable. One of these is to find how the brain manages to do this sort of thing and copy it. The other is to take some class of real problems which require originality in their solution and attempt to find a way to write a program to solve them on an automatic calculator. Either of these approaches would probably eventually succeed. However, it is not clear which would be quicker nor how many years or generations it would take. Most of my effort along these lines has so far been on the former approach because I felt that it would be best to master all relevant scientific knowledge in order to work on such a hard problem, and I already was quite aware of the current state of calculators and the art of programming them.

The control mechanism of the brain is clearly very different from the control mechanism in today's calculators. One symptom of the difference is the manner of failure. A failure of a calculator characteristically produces something quite unreasonable. An error in memory or in data transmission is as likely to be in the most significant digit as in the least. An error in control can do nearly anything. It might execute the wrong instruction or operate a wrong input-output unit. On the other hand human errors in speech are apt to result in statements which almost make sense (consider someone who is almost asleep, slightly drunk, or slightly feverish). Perhaps the mechanism of the brain is such that a slight error in reasoning introduces randomness in just the right way. Perhaps the mechanism that controls serial order in behavior[2] guides the random factor so as to improve the efficiency of imaginative processes over pure randomness.

Some work has been done on simulating neuron nets on our automatic calculator. One purpose was to see if it would be thereby possible to introduce randomness in an appropriate fashion. It seems to have turned out that there are too many unknown links between the activity of neurons and problem solving for this approach to work quite yet. The results have cast some light on the behavior of nets and neurons, but have not yielded a way to solve problems requiring originality.

An important aspect of this work has been an effort to make the machine form and manipulate concepts, abstractions, generalizations, and names. An attempt was made to test a theory[3] of how the brain does it. The first set of experiments occasioned a revision of certain details of the theory. The second set of experiments is now in progress. By next summer this work will be finished and a final report will have been written.

My program is to try next to write a program to solve problems which are members of some limited class of problems that require originality in their solution. It is too early to predict just what stage I will be in next summer, or just how I will then define the immediate problem. However, the underlying problem which is described in this paper is what I intend to pursue. In a single sentence the problem is: how can I make a machine which will exhibit originality in its solution of problems?

Proposal for research by John McCarthy

During next year and during the Summer Research Project on Artificial Intelligence, I propose to study the relation of language to intelligence. It seems clear that the direct application of trial and error methods to the relation between sensory data and motor activity will not lead to any very complicated behavior. Rather it is necessary for the trial and error methods to be applied at a higher level of abstraction. The human mind apparently uses language as its means of handling complicated phenomena. The trial and error processes at a higher level frequently take the form of formulating conjectures and testing them. The English language has a number of properties which every formal language described so far lacks.

1. Arguments in English supplemented by informal mathematics can be concise.
2. English is universal in the sense that it can set up any other language within English and then use that language where it is appropriate.
3. The user of English can refer to himself in it and formulate statements regarding his progress in solving the problem he is working on.
4. In addition to rules of proof, English if completely formulated would have rules of conjecture. The logical languages so far formulated have either been instruction lists to make computers carry out calculations specified in advance or else formalization of parts of mathematics. The latter have been constructed so as:

   1 to be easily described in informal mathematics,
   2 to allow translation of statements from informal mathematics into the language,
   3 to make it easy to argue about whether proofs of (???). No attempt has been made to make proofs in artificial languages as short as informal proofs. It therefore seems to be desirable to attempt to construct an artificial language which a computer can be programmed to use on problems requiring conjecture and self-reference. It should correspond to English in the sense that short English statements about the given subject matter should have short correspondents in the language and so should short arguments or conjectural arguments. I hope to try to formulate a language having these properties and in addition to contain the notions of physical object, event, etc., with the hope that using this language it will be possible to program a machine to learn to play games well and do other tasks.

References to N. Rochester Proposal

1. K.J.W. Craik, *The Nature of Explanation*, Cambridge University Press, 1943 (reprinted 1952), p. 92.
2. K.S. Lashley, "The Problem of Serial Order in Behavior", in *Cerebral Mechanism in Behavior, the Hixon Symposium*, edited by L.A. Jeffress, John Wiley & Sons, New York, pp. 112–146, 1951.
3. D.O. Hebb, *The Organization of Behavior*, John Wiley & Sons, New York, 1949.

27

PROGRAMS WITH COMMON SENSE

John McCarthy

Source: *Proceedings of the Symposium on the Mechanization of Thought Processes*, National Physical Laboratory, HMSO, 1958: 77–91.

SUMMARY Interesting work is being done in programming computers to solve problems which require a high degree of intelligence in humans. However, certain elementary verbal reasoning processes so simple that they can be carried out by any non-feeble-minded human have yet to be simulated by machine programs.

This paper will discuss programs to manipulate in a suitable formal language (most likely a part of the predicate calculus) common instrumental statements. The basic program will draw immediate conclusions from a list of premises. These conclusions will be either declarative or imperative sentences. When an imperative sentence is deduced the program takes a corresponding action. These actions may include printing sentences, moving sentences on lists, and reinitiating the basic deduction process on these lists.

Facilities will be provided for communication with humans in the system via manual intervention and display devices connected to the computer.

The *advice taker* is a proposed program for solving problems by manipulating sentences in formal languages. The main difference between it and other programs or proposed programs for manipulating formal languages (the *Logic Theory Machine* of Newell, Simon and Shaw and the Geometry Program of Gelernter) is that in the previous programs the formal system was the subject matter but the heuristics were all embodied in the program. In this program the procedures will be described as much as possible in the language itself and, in particular, the heuristics are all so described.

The main advantages we expect the *advice taker* to have is that its behaviour will be improvable merely by making statements to it, telling it about its symbolic environment and what is wanted from it. To make these statements will require little if any knowledge of the program or the previous knowledge of the *advice taker*. One will be able to assume that the *advice taker* will have available to it a fairly wide class of immediate logical consequences of anything it is told and its previous knowledge. This property is expected to have much in common with what makes us describe certain humans as having *common sense*. We shall therefore say that *A program has common sense if it automatically deduces for itself a sufficiently wide class of immediate consequences of anything it is told and what it already knows.*

The design of this system will be a joint project with Marvin Minsky, but Minsky is not to be held responsible for the views expressed here.

Before describing the *advice taker* in any detail, I would like to describe more fully our motivation for proceeding in this direction. Our ultimate objective is to make programs that learn from their experience as effectively as humans do. It may not be realized how far we are presently from this objective. It is not hard to make machines learn from experience to make simple changes in their behaviour of a kind which has been anticipated by the programmer. For example, Samuel has included in his checker program facilities for improving the weights the machine assigns to various factors in evaluating positions. He has also included a scheme whereby the machine remembers games it has played previously and deviates from its previous play when it finds a position which it previously lost. Suppose, however, that we wanted an improvement in behavior corresponding, say, to the discovery by the machine of the principle of the opposition in checkers. No present or presently proposed schemes are capable of discovering phenomena as abstract as this.

If one wants a machine to be able to discover an abstraction, it seems most likely that the machine must be able to represent this abstraction in some relatively simple way.

There is one known way of making a machine capable of learning arbitrary behaviour; thus to anticipate every kind of behaviour. This is to make it possible for the machine to simulate arbitrary behaviours and try them out. These behaviours may be represented either by nerve nets (*ref. 2*), by Turing machines (*ref. 3*), or by calculator programs (*ref. 4*). The difficulty is twofold. First, in any of these representations the density of interesting behaviours is incredibly low. Second, and even more important, small interesting changes in behaviour expressed at a high level of abstraction do not have simple representations. It is as though the human genetic structure were represented by a set of blue-prints. Then a mutation would usually result in a wart or a failure of parts to meet, or even an ungrammatical blue-print which could not be translated into an animal at all. It is very difficult to see how the genetic representation scheme manages to be general enough to represent the great variety of animals observed and yet be such that so many interesting changes in the organism are represented by small genetic changes.

The problem of how such a representation controls the development of a fertilized egg into a mature animal is even more difficult.

In our opinion, a system which is to evolve intelligence of human order should have at least the following features:

1. All behaviours must be representable in the system. Therefore, the system should either be able to construct arbitrary automata or to program in some general purpose programming language.
2. Interesting changes in behaviour must be expressible in a simple way.
3. All aspects of behaviour except the most routine must be improvable. In particular, the improving mechanism should be improvable.
4. The machine must have or evolve concepts of partial success because on difficult problems decisive successes or failures come too infrequently.
5. The system must be able to create subroutines which can be included in procedures as units. The learning of subroutines is complicated by the fact that the effect of a subroutine is not usually good or bad in itself. Therefore, the mechanism that selects subroutines should have concepts of an interesting or powerful subroutine whose application may be good under suitable conditions.

Of the 5 points mentioned above, our work concentrates mainly on the second. We base ourselves on the idea that: *In order for a program to be capable of learning something it must first be capable of being told it.* In fact, in the early versions we shall concentrate entirely on this point and attempt to achieve a system which can be told to make a specific improvement in its behaviour with no more knowledge of its internal structure or previous knowledge than is required in order to instruct a human. Once this is achieved, we may be able to tell the *advice taker* how to learn from experience.

The main distinction between the way one programs a computer and modifies the program and the way one instructs a human or will instruct the *advice taker* is this: A machine is instructed mainly in the form of a sequence of imperative sentences; while a human is instructed mainly in declarative sentences describing the situation in which action is required together with a few imperatives that say what is wanted. We shall list the advantages of the two methods of instruction.

Advantages of Imperative Sentences

1. A procedure described in imperatives is already laid out and is carried out faster.
2. One starts with a machine in a basic state and does not assume previous knowledge on the part of the machine.

Advantages of Declarative Sentences

1. Advantage can be taken of previous knowledge.
2. Declarative sentences have logical consequences and it can be arranged that the machine will have available sufficiently simple logical consequences of what it is told and what it previously knew.
3. The meaning of declaratives is much less dependent on their order than is the case with imperatives. This makes it easier to have after-thoughts.
4. The effect of a declarative is less dependent on the previous state of the system so that less knowledge of this state is required on the part of the instructor.

The only way we know of expressing abstractions (such as the previous example of the opposition in checkers) is in language. That is why we have decided to program a system which reasons verbally.

The construction of the advice taker

The *advice taker* system has the following main features:

1. There is a method of representing expressions in the computer. These expressions are defined recursively as follows: A class of entities called terms is defined and a term is an expression. A sequence of expressions is an expression. These expressions are represented in the machine by list structures (*ref. 1*).

2. Certain of these expressions may be regarded as declarative sentences in a certain logical system which will be analogous to a universal Post canonical system. The particular system chosen will depend on programming considerations but will probably have a single rule of inference which will combine substitution for variables with modus ponens. The purpose of the combination is to avoid choking the machine with special cases of general proposition already deduced.

3. There is an *immediate deduction routine* which when given a set of premises will deduce a set of immediate conclusions. Initially, the immediate deduction routine will simply write down all one-step consequences of the premises. Later, this may be elaborated so that the routine will produce some other conclusions which may be of interest. However, this routine will not use semantic heuristics; i.e. heuristics which depend on the subject matter under discussion.

The intelligence, if any, of the advice taker will not be embodied in the immediate deduction routine. This intelligence will be embodied in the procedures which choose the lists of premises to which the immediate deduction routine is to be applied. Of course, the program should never attempt to apply the immediate deduction routine simultaneously to the list of everything it knows. This would make the deduction routine take too long.

4. Not all expressions are interpreted by the system as declarative sentences. Some are the names of entities of various kinds. Certain formulas represent *objects*. For our purposes, an entity is an object if we have something to say about it other than the things which may be deduced from the form of its name. For example, to most people, the number 3812 is not an object: they have nothing to say about it except what can be deduced from its structure. On the other hand, to most Americans the number 1778 is an object because they have filed somewhere the fact that it represents the year when the American Revolution started. In the *advice taker* each object has a *property list* in which are listed the specific things we have to say about it. Some things which can be deduced from the name of the object may be included in the property list anyhow if the deduction was actually carried out and was difficult enough so that the system does not want to carry it out again.

5. Entities other than declarative sentences which can be represented by formulas in the system are individuals, functions, and programs.

6. The program is intended to operate cyclically as follows. The immediate deduction routine is applied to a list of premises and a list of individuals. Some of the conclusions have the form of imperative sentences. These are obeyed. Included in the set of imperatives which may be obeyed is the routine which deduces and obeys.

We shall illustrate the way the *advice taker* is supposed to act by means of an example. Assume that I am seated at my desk at home and I wish to go to the airport. My car is at my home also. The solution of the problem is to walk to the car and drive the car to the airport. First, we shall give a formal statement of the premises the *advice taker* uses to draw the conclusions. Then we shall discuss the heuristics which cause the *advice taker* to assemble these premises from the totality of facts it has available. The premises come in groups, and we shall explain the interpretation of each group.

1. First, we have a predicate "*at*", "*at(x,y)*" is a formalization of "*x is at y*". Under this heading we have the premises

1. *at (I, desk)*
2. *at (desk, home)*
3. *at (car, home)*
4. *at (home, county)*
5. *at (airport, county)*

We shall need the fact that the relation "*at*" is transitive which might be written directly as

6. *at (x,y), at (y,z) → at (x,z)*

or alternatively we might instead use the more abstract premises

6'. *transitive (at)*

and

7'. *transitive (u)* $\rightarrow$ $(u(x,y), u(yz,z) \rightarrow u(x,z))$

from which 6. can be deduced.

2. There are two rules concerning the feasibility of walking and driving.

8. *walkable(x), at(y,x), at(z,x), at(I,y)* $\rightarrow$ *can(go(y,z, walking))*
9. *drivable(x), at(y,x), at(z,x), at(car,y), at(I,car)* $\rightarrow$ *can(go(y,z, driving))*

There are also two specific facts

10. *walkable (home)*
11. *drivable (county)*

3. Next we have a rule concerned with the properties of going.

12. *did(go(x,y,z))* $\rightarrow$ *at(I,y)*

4. The problem itself is posed by the premise:

13. *want (at(I, airport))*

5. The above are all the premises concerned with the particular problem. The last group of premises are common to almost all problems of this sort. They are:

14. $(x \rightarrow can(y))$, $(did(y) \rightarrow z) \rightarrow canachult(x,y,z)$

The predicate "*canachult(x,y,z)*" means that in a situation to which x applies, the action y can be performed and brings about a situation to which z applies. A sort of transitivity is described by

15. *canachult(x,y,z), canachult(z,u,v)* $\rightarrow$ *canachult(x,prog(y,u),v).*

Here *prog(u,v)* is the program of first carrying out u and then v. (Some kind of identification of a single action u with the one step program *prog(u)* is obviously required, but the details of how this will fit into the formalism have not yet been worked out).
   The final premise is the one which causes action to be taken.

59

16. x, $canachult(x, prog(y,z),w)$, $want(w) \rightarrow do(y)$

The argument the *advice taker* must produce in order to solve the problem deduces the following propositions in more or less the following order:

1. $at(I,desk) \rightarrow can(go(desk,car,walking))$
2. $at(I,car) \rightarrow can(go(home,airport,driving))$
3. $did(go(desk,car,walking)) \rightarrow at(I,car)$
4. $did(go(home,airport,driving)) \rightarrow at(I,airport)$
5. $canachult(at(I,desk), go(desk,car,walking), at(I,car))$
6. $canachult (at(I,car), go(home,airport,driving), at(I,airport))$
7. $canachult(at(I,desk), program(go(desk,car,walking), go(home,airport, driving)), \rightarrow at(I,airport))$
8. $do(go(desk,car,walking))$

The deduction of the last proposition initiates action.

The above proposed reasoning raises two major questions of heuristic. The first is that of how the 16 premises are collected, and the second is that of how the deduction proceeds once they are found. We cannot give complete answers to either question in the present paper; they are obviously not completely separate since some of the deductions might be made before some of the premises are collected. Let us first consider the question of where the 16 premises come from.

First of all, we assert that except for the 13th premise (*want(at(I, airport)*)) which sets the goal) and the 1st premise (*at(I,desk)* which we shall get from a routine which answers the question "where am I"), *all the premises can reasonably be expected to be specifically present in the memory* of a machine which has competence of human order in finding its way around. That is, none of them are so specific to the problem at hand that assuming their presence in memory constitutes an anticipation of this particular problem or of a class of problems narrower than those which any human can expect to have previously solved. We must impose this requirement if we are to be able to say that the *advice taker* exhibits *common sense*.

On the other hand, while we may reasonably assume that the premises are in memory, we still have to describe how they are assembled into a list by themselves to which the deduction routine may be applied. Tentatively, we expect the *advice taker* to proceed as follows: initially, the sentence "*want (at(I,airport))*" is on a certain list L, called the main list, all by itself. The program begins with an observation routine which looks at the main list and puts certain statements about the contents of this list on a list called "observations of the main list". We shall not specify at present what all the possible outputs of this observation routine are but merely say that in this case it will observe that "the only statement on L has the form '*want(u(x))*'." (We write this out in English because we have not yet settled on a formalism for representing statements of this kind). The "deduce and obey" routine is then applied to the combination of the "observations of the main list" list, and a list called the "standing orders list". This list is rather small and is never changed, or at least is only changed in major changes of the advice taker. The contents of the "standing orders" list has not been worked out, but what must be deduced is the extraction of certain statements from property lists. Namely, the program first looks at "*want(at(I,airport))*" and attempts to copy the statements on its property list. Let us assume that it fails in this attempt because "*want(at(I,airport))*" does not have the status of an object and hence has no property list. (One might expect that if the problem of going to the airport had arisen before, "*want(at(I,airport))*" would be an object, but this might depend on whether there were routines for generalizing previous experience that would allow something of general use to be filed under that heading). Next in order of increasing generality the machine would see if anything were filed under "*want(at(I,x))*" which would deal with the general problem of getting somewhere. One would expect that premises 6, (or 6′ and 7′), 8, 9, 12, would be so filed. There would also be the formula

$$want(at(I,x)) \rightarrow do(observe(where\ am\ I))$$

which would give us premise 1. There would also be a reference to the next higher level of abstraction in the goal statement which would cause a look at the property list of "*want(x)*". This would give us 14, 15, and 16.

We shall not try to follow the solution further except to remark that "*want-(at(I,x))*" there would be a rule that starts with the premises "*at(I,y)*" and "*want(I,x)*" and has as conclusion a search for the property list of "*go(y,x,z)*". This would presumably fail, and then there would have to be heuristics that would initiate a search for a *y* such that "*at(I,y)*" and "*at(air-port,y)*". This would be done by looking on the property lists of the origin and the destination and working up. Then premise 9 would be found which has as one of its premises *at(I,car)*. A repetition of the above would find premise 8, which would complete the set of premises since the other "*at*" premises would have been found as by-products of previous searches.

We hope that the presence of the heuristic rules mentioned on the property lists where we have put them will seem plausible to the reader. It should be noticed that on the higher level of abstraction many of the statements are of the stimulus-response form. One might conjecture that division in man between conscious and unconscious thought occurs at the boundary between stimulus-response heuristics which do not have to be reasoned about but only obeyed, and the others which have to serve as premises in deductions.

We hope to formalize the heuristics in another paper before we start programming the system.

References

1. Newell, A. and Simon, H. A. Empirical Explorations of the Logic Theory Machine. A Case Study in Heuristic. *Proceedings of the Western Joint Computer Conference*, p. 218 (February, 1957).
2. Minsky, M. L. Heuristic Aspects of the Artificial Intelligence Problem. *Lincoln Laboratory Report, 34–55.* (December, 1956). (See also his paper for this conference and his Princeton Ph.D. thesis).
3. McCarthy, J. Inversion of Functions Defined by Turing Machines. In Automata Studies, *Annals of Mathematics Study Number*.
4. Friedberg, R. A Learning Machine, Part I. *IBM Journal of Research and Development*, 1958, 2, No. 1.

DISCUSSION ON THE PAPER BY DR. J. McCARTHY

PROF. Y. BAR-HILLEL: Dr. McCarthy's paper belongs in the Journal of Half-Baked Ideas, the creation of which was recently proposed by Dr. I. J. Good. Dr. McCarthy will probably be the first to admit this. Before he goes on to bake his ideas fully, it might be well to give him some advice and raise some objections. He himself mentions some possible objections, but I do not think that he treats them with the full consideration they deserve; there are others he does not mention.

For lack of time, I shall not go into the first part of his paper, although I think that it contains a lot of highly unclear philosophical, or pseudo-philosophical assumptions. I shall rather spend my time in commenting on the example he works out in his paper at some length. Before I start, let me voice my protest against the general assumption of Dr. McCarthy – slightly caricatured – that a machine, if only its programme is specified with a sufficient degree of carelessness, will be able to carry out satisfactorily even rather difficult tasks.

Consider the assumption that the relation he designates by "*at*" is transitive (page 58). However, since he takes both "*at(I, desk)*" and "*at(desk, home)*" as premises, I presume – though this is never made quite clear – that "*at*" means something like being-a-physical-part-or-in-the-immediate-spatial-neighborhood-of. But then the relation is clearly not transitive. If A is in the immediate spatial neighborhood of B and B in the immediate spatial neighborhood of C, then A need not be in the immediate spatial neighborhood of C. Otherwise, everything would turn out to be in the immediate spatial neighborhood of everything, which is surely not Dr. McCarthy's intention. Of course, starting from false premises, one can still arrive at right conclusions. We do such things quite often, and a machine could do it. But it would probably be bad advice to allow a machine to do such things consistently.

Many of the other 23 steps in Dr. McCarthy's argument are equally or more questionable, but I don't think we should spend our time showing this in detail. My major question is the following: On page 60 McCarthy states that a machine which has a competence of human order in finding its way around will have almost all the premises of the argument stored in its memory. I am at a complete loss to understand the point of this remark. If Dr. McCarthy wants to say no more than that a machine, in order to behave like a human being, must have the knowledge of a human being, then this is surely not a very important remark to make. But if not, what was the intention of this remark?

The decisive question how a machine, even assuming that it will have somehow countless millions of facts stored in its memory, will be able to pick out those facts which will serve as premises for its deduction is promised to receive its treatment in another paper, which is quite alright for a half-baked idea.

It sounds rather incredible that the machine could have arrived at its conclusion – which, in plain English, is "Walk from your desk to your car!" – by sound deduction. This conclusion surely could not possibly follow from the premises in any serious sense. Might it not be occasionally cheaper to call a taxi and have it take you over to the airport: Couldn't you decide to cancel your flight or to do a hundred other things? I don't think it would be wise to develop a programme language so powerful as to make a machine arrive at the conclusion Dr. McCarthy apparently intends it to make.

Let me also point out that in the example the time factor has never been mentioned, probably for the sake of simplicity. But clearly this factor is here so important that it could not possibly be disregarded without distorting the whole argument. Does not the solution depend, among thousands of other things, also upon the time of my being at my desk, the time at which I have to be at the airport, the distance from the airport, the speed of my car, etc.?

To make the argument deductively sound, its complexity will have to be increased by many orders of magnitude. So long as this is not realized, any discussions of machines able to perform the deductive – and inductive! – operations necessary for treating problems of the kind brought forward by Dr. McCarthy is totally pointless. The gap between Dr. McCarthy's general programme (with which I have little quarrel, after discounting its "philosophical" features) and its execution even in such a simple case as the one discussed seems to me so enormous that much more has to be done to persuade me that even the first step in bridging this gap has already been taken.

DR. O. G. SELFRIDGE: I have a question which I think applies to this. It seems to me in much of that work, the old absolutist Prof. Bar-Hillel has really put his finger on something; he is really worried about the deduction actually made. He seemed really to worry that the system is not consistent, and he made a remark that conclusions should not be drawn from false premises. In my experience those are the only conclusions that have ever been drawn. I have never yet heard of someone drawing correct conclusions from correct premises. I mean this seriously. This, I think, is Dr. Minsky's point this morning. What this leads to is that the notion of deductive logic being something sitting there sacred which you can borrow for particularly sacred uses and producing inviolable results is a lot of nonsense. Deductive logic is inferred as much as anything else. Most women have never inferred it, but they get on perfectly well, marrying happy husbands, raising happy children, without ever using deductive logic at all. My feeling is that my criticism of Dr. McCarthy is the other way. He assumes deductive logic, whereas in fact that is something to be concocted.

This is another important point which I think Prof. Bar-Hillel ignores in this, the criticism of the programme should not be as to whether it is logically consistent, but only will he be able to wave it around saying "this in fact works the way I want it". Dr. McCarthy would be the first to admit that his programme is not now working, so it has to be changed. Then, can you make the changes in the programme to make it work? That has nothing to do with logic. Can he amend it in such a way that it includes the logic as well as the little details of the programme? Can he manage in such a way that it works the way he does? He said at the beginning of his talk that when he makes an arbitrary change in the programme it will not work usually, and you try to fix that so that it will. He has produced at least some evidence, to me at least, that small changes in his programme will not obviously not make the programme work and might even improve it. His next point is whether he can make small changes that in fact make it work. That is what we do not know yet.

PROF. Y. BAR-HILLEL: May I ask whether you could thrash this out with Dr. McCarthy? It was my impression that Dr. McCarthy's advice taker was meant to be able, among other things, to arrive at a certain conclusion from appropriate premises by faultless deductive reasoning. If this is still his programme, then I think your defence is totally beside the point.

DR. O. G. SELFRIDGE: I am not defending this programme, I am only defending him.

DR. J. McCARTHY: Are you using the word "programme" in the technical sense of a bunch of cards or in the sense of a project that you get money for?

PROF. Y. BAR-HILLEL: When I uttered my doubts that a machine working under the programme outlined by Dr. McCarthy would be able to do what he expects it to do, I was using "programme" in the technical sense.

DR. O. G. SELFRIDGE: In that case your criticisms are not so much philosophical as technical.

PROF. Y. BAR-HILLEL: They are purely technical. I said that I shall not make any philosophical criticisms, for lack of time.

DR. O. G. SELFRIDGE: A technical objection does not make ideas half-baked.

PROF. Y. BAR-HILLEL: A deductive argument, where you have first to find out what are the relevant premises, is something which many humans are not always able to carry out successfully. I do not see the slightest reason to believe that at present machines should be able to perform things that humans find trouble in doing. I do not think there could possibly exist a programme which would, given any problem, divide all facts in the universe into those which are and those which are not relevant for that problem. Developing such a programme seems to me to be by 10^{10} orders of magnitude more difficult than, say, the Newell-Simon problem of developing a heuristic for deduction in the propositional calculus. This cavalier way of jumping over orders of magnitude only tends to becloud the issue and throw doubt on ways of thinking for which I have a great deal of respect. By developing a powerful programme language you may have paved the way for the first step in solving problems of the kind treated in your example, but the claim of being well on the way towards their solution is a gross exaggeration. This was the major point of my objections.

DR. L. C. PAYNE: First a quick comment on the remark of no woman having ever brought up a child by means of deductive logic, the point surely is obvious. The feedback is very close: if she drops the baby in a disastrous way, she does not get another chance or she gets a great yelp. She learns very quickly by crude techniques of how to achieve precise control. There is direct feedback: If she is trying to win a spouse and tries a move which does not get the right response, she quickly changes her tack. Computer-wise, we have yet to develop an input (sensory system) and data-processing technique that can give even a gesture of such resourcefulness: It is a real-time trial and error process utilizing every bit of every nuance, quickly adapting and re-adapting.

A computer can deal with only a very small amount of information compared with the human brain, and therefore attention has to be concentrated on the efficiency with which this limited amount of information is handled. This is where one may usefully turn to deductive logic, because it will be appreciated that if a person is to benefit from all the studies and knowledge of many people in different places and epochs then synthesis of some sort is essential. Science in general is just this: its laws subsume with great economy the mechanisms of diverse processes. For example the application of deductive logic to Newton's three laws allows us to treat of a multitude of practical applications. Hence if a computer is to have any range of activity, it must be fed with explicit rules, so that by rapid deductions or transformations of data, it can evolve a host of ramifications from a limited amount of information.

The Countess of Lovelace remarked that "a machine can originate nothing: it can only do what we order it to perform". The essence of my contention is that we can only order to perform by means of transformations of data having as their basis existing logical systems. Because of this it might be well to summarize, perhaps boldly before an audience like this, what I think is a summary of existing logics. The first is Formal Logic and consists of statements of the form. If all A are B and C is A, then certainly C is B – the syllogistic type of statement by which one can establish direct connections. This sort of logic is reversible; that is, if you start from a given complex of consistent propositions, then it is possible to take some selection of a derivative statements and from them as a starting complex, derive propositions of the original set. If the original set contains a contradiction then all other contradictions are implied latently. The best example I know of this is one recently cited by Sir Ronald Fisher, which is said to stem from the high table at Trinity College, Cambridge. The late Professor G. H. Hardy was asked, "Do you mean to say, Hardy, that you can prove any contradiction whatsoever if you have got one contradiction?". Hardy replied, "Yes, that is so". The questioner went on, "Well, four equals five, you prove that McTaggart is the Pope". Hardy rejoined at once saying, "If four equals five, then by subtracting three from each, one equals two. McTaggart and the Pope are two, therefore McTaggart and the Pope are one":

The other important logic is Probability Theory. This consists of statements, that if some well defined proportion of A are B, and if C is A, then only an uncertain inference in the form of a probability statement, can be made about C being B. One has to be especially careful in statements of this kind to see that the total reference set is well defined and also the sub-set having some specified attribute. This kind of consideration, treated very carefully by Sir Ronald Fisher in his "Statistical Methods and Scientific Inference", nullifies the casual attitude which, to instance an example, can remark that, "statistics means that if you take enough inaccurate statements and put them together then a more accurate statement can be made". The well defined nature of the statistical mode of reasoning, if it is respected, means you can be as logically precise as with Formal Logic, but that the kind of statement you can be logically precise about is less certain, that is, it is a probability statement.

A more restricted logic can be based on what Sir Ronald Fisher calls "mathematical likelihood". This allows quantitative statements to be made on the fullest information available; it is discussed in the reference already given.

Beyond these systems one is very suspicious of the play with random exercises which purport to produce something out of nothing. It seems to me that computers can do nothing beyond applying the existing logics to effect transformations of data, since these are the limits within which exercises can be prescribed explicitly. These limits in fact are very wide and circumscribe most of the rational procedures used by human beings. They are not limited by pure mathematics, where one is constrained to using limited class functions which lend themselves to analysis. Numerical solutions can certainly explore regions which would bog down a more ponderous mathematical attack. In my opinion higher mathematics can be logically precise and very penetrating only about a very small class of entities, ones that are very abstract in content. Statistics allows one to deal with a wider class with less certainty, and so on down the scale until you reach common sense, where one may be rational about fairly concrete entities. Between common sense and high mathematics one has the whole range of human rationality, but for each refinement in logic one must pay the price of dealing with more restricted classes of entities which become progressively more abstract.

DR. J. McCARTHY (in reply): Prof. Bar-Hillel has correctly observed that my paper is based on unstated philosophical assumptions although what he means by "pseudo-philosophical" is unclear. Whenever we program a computer to learn from experience we build into the programme a sort of epistemology. It might be argued that this epistemology should be made explicit before one writes the programme, but epistemology is in a foggier state than computer programming even in the present half-baked state of the latter. I hope that once we have succeeded in making computer programs reason about the world, we will be able to reformulate epistemology as a branch of applied mathematics no more mysterious or controversial than physics.

On re-reading my paper I can't see how Prof. Bar-Hillel could see in it a proposal to specify a computer programme carelessly. Since other people have proposed this as a device for achieving "creativity", I can only conclude that he had some other paper in mind.

In his criticism of my use of the symbol "*at*", Prof. Bar-Hillel seems to have misunderstood the intent of the example. First of all, I was not trying to formalize the sentence form. A is at B as it is used in English. "*at*" merely was intended to serve as a convenient mnemonic for the relation between a place and a sub-place. Second I was not proposing a practical problem for the program to solve but rather an example intended to allow us to think about the kinds of reasoning involved and how a machine may be made to perform them.

Prof. Bar-Hillel's major point concerns my statement that the premises listed could be assumed to be in memory. The intention of this statement is to explain why I have not included formalizations of statements like, "it is possible to drive from my home to the airport" among my premises. If there were n known places in the country there would be $n(n - 1)/2$ such sentences and, since we are quite sure that we do not have each of them in our memories, it would be cheating to allow the machine to start with them.

The rest of Prof. Bar-Hillel's criticisms concern ways in which the model mentioned does not reflect the real world; I have already explained that this was not my intention. He is certainly right that the complexity of the model will have to be increased for it to deal with practical problems. What we disagree on is my contention that the conceptual difficulties arise at the present level of complexity and that solving them will allow us to increase the complexity of the model easily.

With regard to the discussion between Prof. Bar-Hillel and Oliver Selfridge – The logic is intended to be faultless although its premises cannot be guaranteed. The intended conclusion is "*do(go(desk,car,walking))*" not, of course, "*at(I,airport)*". The model oversimplifies but is not intended to oversimplify to the extent of allowing one to deduce one's way to the airport.

Dr. Payne's summary of formal logic does not seem to be based on much acquaintance with it and I think he underestimates the possibilities of applying it to making machines behave intelligently.

28

REPORT ON A GENERAL PROBLEM-SOLVING PROGRAM

A. Newell, J. C. Shaw and H. Simon

Source: *Proceedings of the International Conference on Information Processing*, 13–23 June 1959, UNESCO House, Paris, France, 1960: 256–64.

This paper reports on a computer program, called General Problem Solving Program I (GPS-I). Construction and investigation of this program is part of a research effort by the authors to understand the information processes that underlie human intellectual, adaptive, and creative abilities. The approach is synthetic—to construct computer programs that can solve problems requiring intelligence and adaptation, and to discover which varieties of these programs can be matched to data on human problem-solving.

GPS-I grew out of an earlier program, the Logic Theorist, and is an attempt to fit the recorded behavior of college students trying to discover proofs. The purpose of this paper is not to relate the program to human behavior, but to describe its main characteristics and to assess its capacities as a problem-solving mechanism. The program should be seen as an attempt to advance our basic knowledge of intellectual activity and should not be assessed on whether it offers an economical solution to a significant class of problems.

The major features of the program that are worthy of discussion are:

1) The recursive nature of its problem-solving activity;
2) The separation of problem content from problem-solving technique as a way of increasing the generality of the program;
3) The two general problem-solving techniques that now constitute its repertoire: means-ends analysis, and planning;
4) The memory and program organization used to mechanize the program.

1 Introduction

This paper deals with the theory of problem solving. It describes a program for a digital computer, called General Problem Solver I (GPS), which is part of an investigation into the extremely complex processes that are involved in intelligent, adaptive, and creative behavior. Our principal means of investigation is synthesis: programming large digital computers to exhibit intelligent behavior, studying the structure of these computer programs, and examining the problem-solving and other adaptive behaviors that the programs produce.

A *problem* exists whenever a problem solver desires some outcome or state of affairs that he does not immediately know how to attain. Imperfect knowledge about how to proceed is at the core of the genuinely problematic. Of course, some initial information is always available. A genuine problem-solving process involves the repeated use of available information to initiate exploration, which discloses, in turn, more information until a way to attain the solution is finally discovered.

Many kinds of information can aid in solving problems: information may suggest the order in which possible solutions should be examined; it may rule out a whole class of solutions previously thought possible; it may provide a cheap test to distinguish likely from unlikely possibilities; and so on. All these kinds of information are *heuristics*—things that aid discovery. Heuristics seldom provide infallible guidance; they give practical knowledge, possessing only empirical validity. Often they "work", but the results are variable and success is seldom guaranteed.

The theory of problem solving is concerned with discovering and understanding systems of heuristics. What kinds are there? How do very general injunctions ("Draw a figure" or "Simplify") exert their effects? What heuristics do humans actually use? How are new heuristics discovered? And so on. GPS, the program described in this paper, contributes to the theory of problem-solving by embodying two very general systems of heuristics—*means-ends analysis* and *planning*—within an organization that allows them to be applied to varying subject matters.

GPS grew out of an earlier computer program, the Logic Theorist [5, 8], which discovered proofs to theorems in the sentential calculus of Whitehead and Russell. It exhibited considerable problem-solving ability. Its heuristics were largely based on the introspections of its designers, and were closely tied to the subject matter of symbolic logic. The effectiveness of the Logic Theorist led to revised programs aimed at simulating in detail the problem-solving behavior of human subjects in the psychological laboratory. The human data were obtained by asking college sophomores to solve problems in symbolic logic, "thinking aloud" as much as possible while they worked. GPS is the program we constructed to describe as closely as possible the behavior of the laboratory subjects as revealed in their oral comments and in the steps they wrote down in working the problems. How far it is successful in simulating the subjects' behavior—its usefulness as a psychological theory of human thinking—will be reported elsewhere [7].

We shall first describe the overall structure of GPS, and the kinds of problems it can tackle. Then we shall describe two important systems of heuristics it employs. The first is the heuristic of means-ends analysis, which we shall illustrate with the tasks of proving theorems in symbolic logic and proving simple trigonometric identities. The second is the heuristic of constructing general plans of solutions, which we shall illustrate, again, with symbolic logic.

2 The executive program and the task environment

GPS operates on problems that can be formulated in terms of objects and operators. An operator is something that can be applied to certain objects to produce different objects (as a saw applied to logs produces boards). The objects can be characterized by the features they possess, and by the differences that can be observed between pairs of objects. Operators may be restricted to apply to only certain kinds of objects; and there may be operators that are applied to several objects as inputs, producing one or more objects as output (as the operation of adding two numbers produces a third number, their sum).

Various problems can be formulated in a task environment containing objects and operators: to find a way to transform a given object into another; to find an object possessing a given feature; to modify an object so that a given operator may be applied to it; and so on. In chess, for example, if we take chess positions as the objects and legal moves as the operators, then moves produce new positions (objects) from old. Not every move can be made in every position. The problem in chess is to get from a given object— the current position—to an object having a specified feature (a position in which the opponent's King is checkmated).

The problem of proving theorems in a formal mathematical system is readily put in the same form. Here the objects are theorems, while the operators are the admissible rules of inference. To prove a theorem is to transform some initial objects—the axioms—into a specified object—the desired theorem. Similarly, in integrating functions in closed form, the objects are the mathematical expressions; the operators are the operations of algebra, together with formulas to define special functions like sine and cosine. Integration closed form is an operation that does not apply directly to every object—if it did, there would be no problem. Integration involves transforming a given object into an equivalent object that is integrable, where equivalence is confined by the set of operations that can be applied.

Constructing a computer program can also be described as a problem in these same terms. Here, the objects are possible contents of the computer memory; the operators are computer instructions that alter the memory content. A program is a sequence of operators that transforms one state of memory into another; the programming problem is to find such a sequence when certain features of the initial and terminal states are specified.

To operate generally within a task environment characterized by objects and operators, GPS needs several main components:

1) A vocabulary for talking about the task environment containing terms like: object, operator, different feature, Object 34, Operator 7.
2) A vocabulary dealing with the organization of the problem-solving processes, containing terms like: goal type, method, evaluation, Goal Type 2, Method 1, Goal 14.
3) A set of programs defining the terms of the problem-solving vocabulary by terms on the vocabulary or describing the task environment. (We shall provide a number of examples presently.)
4) A set of programs (correlative definitions) applying the terms of the task-environment vocabulary to a particular environment: symbolic logic, trigonometry, algebra, integral calculus. (These will also be illustrated some detail.)

Items 2 and 3 of the above list, together with the common nouns (but not the proper nouns) of item 1 constitute GPS properly speaking. Item 4 and the proper nouns of item 1 are required in order to give GPS the capacity to solve problems relating to a specified subject matter. Speaking broadly, the core of GPS consists of some general, but fairly powerful, problem-solving heuristics. To apply these heuristics to a particular problem domain, GPS must be augmented by the definitions and rules of mathematics or logic that describe that domain, and then must be given a problem or series of problems to solve. The justification for calling GPS "general" lies in this separation of problem-solving heuristics from subject matter, and its ability to use the same heuristics to deal with different subjects.

Let us look more closely at the problem-solving vocabulary and heuristics. To specify problems and subproblems, GPS has a discrete set of *goal types*. We shall introduce two of these initially:

Goal Type 1: Find a way to transform object a into object b. (The objects, a and b, may be any objects defined in specifying the task environment. The phrase "way to transform" implies "by applying a sequence of operators from the task environment.")

Goal Type 2: Apply operator q to object a (or to an object obtained from a by admissible transformations).

Finding a proof of a theorem (object b) from axioms (object a) is an example of a Type 1 goal; integrating (operator q) an expression (object a) is an example of a Type 2 goal.

The executive organization of GPS, shown in fig. 1, is very simple. With each goal type is associated a set of *methods* related to achieving goals of that type. When an attempt is made to achieve a goal, it is first evaluated to see whether it is worthwhile achieving and whether achievement seems likely. If so, one of the methods is selected and executed. This either leads to success or to a repetition of the loop.

The principal heuristics of GPS are imbedded in the methods. All the heuristics apply the following general principle:

The principle of subgoal reduction: Make progress by substituting for the achievement of a goal the achievement of a set of easier goals.

This is, indeed, only a heuristic principle, and it is not as self-evident as it may appear. For example, none of the programs so far written for chess or checkers makes essential use of the principle [1, 3, 6].

The constant use of this principle makes GPS a highly recursive program, for the attempt to achieve one goal leads to other goals, and these, in turn, to still other goals. Thus, identical goal types and methods are used many times

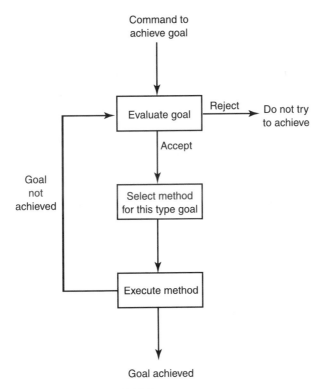

Figure 1 Executive organization of GPS

successively at various levels in the goal structure in solving a single problem. Application of the principle also combines the goals and methods into organized systems of heuristics, rather than establishing each method as an independent heuristic. We shall provide examples of two such systems in this paper.

3 Functional or means-ends analysis

3.1 Means-ends analysis, one of the most frequently used problem-solving heuristics, is typified by the following kind of common sense argument:

I want to take my son to nursery school. What's the difference between what I have and what I want? One of distance. What changes distance? My automobile. My automobile won't work. What's needed to make it work? A new battery. What has new batteries? An auto repair shop. I want the repair shop to put in a new battery; but the shop doesn't know I need one. What is the difficulty? One of communication. What allows communication? A telephone . . . And so on.

This kind of analysis—classifying things in terms of the functions they serve, and oscillating among ends, functions required, and means that perform them—forms the basic system of heuristic of GPS. More precisely, this means-ends system of heuristic assumes the following:

1) If an object is given that is not the desired one, differences will be detectable between the available object and the desired object.
2) Operators affect some features of their operands and leave others unchanged. Hence operators can be characterized by the changes they produce and can be used to try to eliminate differences between the objects to which they are applied and the desired objects.
3) Some differences will prove more difficult to effect than others. It is profitable, therefore, to try to eliminate "difficult" differences, even at the cost of introducing new differences of lesser difficulty. This process can be repeated as long as progress is being made toward eliminating the more difficult differences.

To incorporate this heuristic in GPS, we expand the vocabulary of goal types to include:

Goal Type 3: Reduce the difference, d, between object a and object b by modifying a.

The core of the system of functional analysis is given by three methods, one associated with each of the three goal types, as shown in fig. 2. Method 1, associated with Goal Type 1, consists in: (a) matching the objects a and b to find a difference, d, between them; (b) setting up the Type 3 subgoal of reducing d, which if successful produces a new transformed object c; (c) setting up the Type 1 subgoal of transforming c into b. If this last goal is achieved, the original Type 1 goal is achieved. The match in step (a) tests for the more important differences first. It also automatically makes substitutions for free variables.

Method 2, for achieving a Type 2 goal, consists in: (a) determining if the operator can be applied by setting up a Type 1 goal for transforming a into $C(q)$, the input form of q; (b) if successful, the output object is produced

Goal type 1: Transform object a into object b

Method 1:

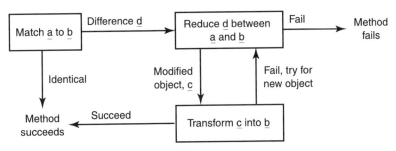

Goal type 2: Apply operator q to object a

Method 2

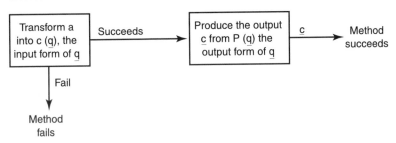

Goal type 3: Reduce the difference, d, between object a and object b

Method 3

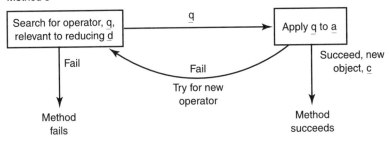

Figure 2 Methods for means-ends analysis

from P(q), the output form of q. This method is appropriate where the operator is given by two forms, one describing the input, or conditions, and the other the output, or product. The examples given in this paper have operators of this kind. Variants of this method exist for an operator given by a program, defined iteratively, or defined recursively.

Method 3, for achieving a Type 3 goal, consists in: (a) searching for an operator that is relevant to reducing the difference, d; (b) if one is found, setting up the Type 2 goal of applying the operator, which if successful produces the modified object.

3.2 *Application to symbolic logic.* This system of heuristics already gives GPS some problem-solving ability. We can apply GPS to a simple problem in symbolic logic. To do so we must provide correlative definitions for objects, operators, and differences. These are summarized in fig. 3. We must also associate with each difference the operators that are relevant to modifying it. For logic this is accomplished explicitly by the table of connections in fig. 3. These connections are given to GPS, but it is not difficult to write a program that will permit GPS itself to infer the connections from the lists of operators and differences. (E.g., comparing the right side of R1 with its left side, we find they have the difference ΔP, for the symbols A and B appear in opposite orders on the two sides; hence, there is a connection between ΔP and R1.) Finally, we provide criteria of progress, in terms of a list of the differences in order of difficulty.

An illustrative logic problem and its solution are shown in fig. 4. The object, L1, is given, and GPS is required to derive the object, L0. The problem is stated to GPS in the form of a Type 1 goal; (Goal 1) Find a way to transform L1 into L0. By fig. 2, this goal type calls for Method 1. Comparison of L1 and L0 shows that they have the difference, ΔP; for the "R" is on the left end of L1, but on the right end of L0. GPS now erects the Type 3 goal: (Goal 2) Reduce ΔP between L1 and L0. Goal Type 3 calls for application of Method 3. Since the table of connections (fig. 3) shows that R1 is relevant to reducing ΔP, GPS erects the Type 2 goal: (Goal 3) Apply operator R1 to L1. The reader can follow the remaining steps that lead to the solution from fig. 4. The resulting derivation may be summarized:

Object	*Operator*
L1 = R · (−P ⊃ Q)	
L2 = (−P ⊃ Q) · R	Apply R1 to L1
L3 = (P ∨ Q) · R	Apply R6 to left side of L2
L4 = (Q ∨ P) · R	Apply R1 to left side of L3
L4 is identical with L0	Q.E.D.

GPS can solve problems a good deal more difficult than the simple one illustrated. To make full use of the twelve operators, an additional method is added to the Type 3 goal that searches the available objects for the additional input required in rules R10, R11, and R12.

3.3 *Application to Trigonometry*. GPS is a general problem solver to the extent that its heuristics can be applied to varying subject matters, given the appropriate correlative definitions. Elementary algebra and trigonometry provides a subject matter distinct from logic, and fig. 5 shows the fragment of this task environment necessary for GPS to try to prove some simple trigonometric identities. The objects are now algebraic and trigonometric expressions; and the operators perform factorization, algebraic simplification, and trigonometric transformation. The differences are the same as in logic, except for two omissions, which are related to the associative and commutative laws. In logic these must be performed explicitly, whereas in ordinary algebra a notation is used that makes these laws implicit and their operation automatic. The connections between differences and operators is not made via a simple table, as in logic, but requires a comparison of the object with the output form of the operator. The criteria of progress remain the same as for logic.

GPS can now attempt to prove a trigonometric identity such as:

$$(\tan x + \cot x) \sin x \cos x = 1.$$

This is given as the problem of transforming the left side, which becomes L1, into the right side, L0. The process of solving the problem, which involves 33 goals and subgoals, is shown in fig. 6, which is to be interpreted in exactly the same way as fig. 4, with the help of fig. 2 and 5, except that the methods are not mentioned explicitly.

4 Planning as a problem-solving technique

The second system of heuristic used by GPS is a form of planning that allows GPS to construct a proposed solution in general terms before working out the details. It acts as an antidote to the limitation of means-ends analysis in seeing only one step ahead. It also provides an example of the use of an auxiliary problem in a different task environment to aid in the solution of a problem.* Planning is incorporated in GPS by adding a new method, Method 4, to the repertoire of the Type 1 goal.

This *Planning Method* (see fig. 7) consists in (a) *abstracting* by omitting certain details of the original objects and operators, (b) forming the corresponding problem in the abstract task environment, (c) when the abstract

---

* See the work of H. Gelernter and N. Rochester on theorem proving programs for plane geometry [2], where the geometric diagram provides an example of a *very powerful* auxiliary problem space.

Objects. Expressions are built up recursively from variables, P, Q, R, . . ., three binary connectives, ·, ⊃, ∨, and the unary prefix, —, called tilde. Examples of objects: P, —Q, P ∨ Q, (—R · P) ⊃ —Q. Double tildes cancel as in ordinary algebra: — —Q = Q.

Operators. There are twelve operators, given in the form C (q) → P (q), where C (q) is the input form, and P (q) is the output form. Thus anything of the form at the tail of an arrow can be transformed into the corresponding expression at the head of the arrow. A double arrow means the transformation works both ways. The abstracted operators (para. 4), used in the planning method, are given in the right hand column opposite the operator.

Operators		Abstracted Operators
R1	A ∨ B → B ∨ A, A · B → B · A	Identity
R2	A ⊃ B → — B ⊃ —A	Identity
R3	A ∨ A ↔ A, A · A ↔ A	(AA) ↔ A
R4	A ∨ (B ∨ C) ↔ (A ∨ B) ∨ C, A · (B · C) ↔ (A · A · B) · C	A (BC) ↔ (AB) C
R5	A ∨ B ↔ —(—A · —B)	Identity
R6	A ⊃ B ↔ —A ∨ B	Identity
R7	A ∨ (B · C) ↔ (A ∨ B) · (A ∨ C), A · (B ∨ C) ↔ (A · B) ∨ (A · C)	A (BC) ↔ (AB) (AC)
R8	A · B → A, A · B → B	(AB) → A
R9	A → A ∨ X (X is an expression.)	A → (AX)
R10	[A, B] → A · B (Two expressions input.)	[A, B] ↔ (AB)
R11	[A ⊃ B, A] → B (Two expressions input.)	[(AB), A] → B
R12	[A ⊃ B, B ⊃ C] → A ⊃ C (Two expressions input.)	[(AB), (BC)] → (AC)

Differences. The differences apply to subexpressions as well as total expressions, and several differences may exist simultaneously for the same expressions.

ΔV   A variable appears in one expression that does not in the other. E.g., P∨P differs by +V from P∨Q, since it needs a Q; P⊃R differs by —V from R, since it needs to lose the P.

ΔN   A variable occurs different numbers of times in the two expressions. E.g., P·Q differs from (P·Q)⊃Q by +N, since it needs another Q; P∨P differs from P by —N, since it needs to reduce the number of P's.

ΔT   There is a difference in the "sign" of the two expressions; e.g., Q versus —Q, or —(P∨R) versus P∨R.

ΔC   There is a difference in binary connective; e.g., P⊃Q versus P∨Q.

ΔG   There is a difference in grouping; e.g., P∨(Q∨R) versus (P∨Q)∨R.

ΔP   There is a position difference in the components of the two expressions; e.g., P⊃(Q∨R) versus (Q∨R)⊃P.

Connections between Differences and Operators. A +, —, or x in a cell means that the operator in the column of the cell affects the difference in the row of the cell. + in the first row means +V, — means —V, etc. The stars show the differences and operators that remain after abstracting, and thus mark the reduced table of connections used in the abstract task environment for planning (para. 4).

	R1	R2	R3	R4	R5	R6	R7	R8	R9	R10	R11	R12
			*	*			*	*	*	*	*	*
*ΔV								—	+	+	—	x
*ΔN								—	+	+	—	x
ΔT			x		x	x	x					
ΔC					x	x	x					
*ΔG				x								
ΔP	x	x										

Criteria of progress. All differences in subexpressions are less important than differences in expressions. For a pair of expressions the differences are ranked: +V, —V, +N, —N, ΔT, ΔC, ΔG, ΔP, from most important to least. E.g. ΔT is more important in —(P∨Q) versus P∨Q, but ΔC is more important in —P∨Q versus P⊃Q.

Figure 3 Symbolic logic task environment

Given: L1 = R · (— P ⊃ Q)
Obtain: L0 = (Q ∨ P) · R

Goal 1: Transform L1 into L0.
    Match produces position difference (ΔP).
    Goal 2: Reduce ΔP between L1 and L0.
        First operator found is R1.
        Goal 3: Apply R1 to L1.
            Goal 4: Transform L1 into C (R1).
                Match succeeds with A = R and B = — P ⊃ Q.
            Produce new object:

                L2 = (— P ⊃ Q) · R

Goal 5: Transform L2 into L0.
    Match produces connective difference (ΔC) in left subexpression.
    Goal 6: Reduce ΔC between left of L2 and left of L0.
        First operator found is R5.
        Goal 7: Apply R5 to left of L2.
            Goal 8: Transform left of L2 into C (R5).
                Match produces connective difference (ΔC) in left subexpression.
                Goal 9: Reduce ΔC between left of L2 and C (R5).
                    Goal rejected: difference is no easier than difference in Goal 6.
        Second operator found is R6.
        Goal 10: Apply R6 to left of L2.
            Goal 11: Transform left of L2 into C (R6).
                Match succeeds with A = — P and B = Q.
            Produce new object:

                L3 = (P ∨ Q) · R

Goal 12: Transform L3 into L0.
    Match produces position difference (ΔP) in left subexpression.
    Goal 13: Reduce ΔP between left of L3 and left of L0.
        First operator found is R1.
        Goal 14: Apply R1 to left of L3.
            Goal 15: Transform left of L3 into C (R1).
                Match succeeds with A = P and B = Q.
            Produce new object:

                L4 = (Q ∨ P) · R

Goal 16; Transform L4 into L0.
    Match shows L4 is identical with L0, QED.

Figure 4 Example of means-ends analysis in logic

problem has been solved, using its solution to provide a plan for solving the original problem, (d) translating the plan back into the original task environment and executing it. The power of the method rests on two facts. First, the entire machinery of GPS can be used to solve the abstract problem in its appropriate task environment; and, because of the suppression of

Objects. Ordinary algebraic expressions, including the trigonometric functions. The associative and commutative laws are implicit in the notation: the program can select freely which terms to use in an expression like $(x + y + z)$.

Operators

A0   Combine: recursively defined to apply the following elementary identities from the innermost subexpressions to the main expression:

$A + (B + C) \rightarrow A + B + C, A (BC) \rightarrow ABC$
$A + 0 \rightarrow A, A + A \rightarrow 2A, A - A \rightarrow 0$
$A0 \rightarrow 0, A1 \rightarrow A, AA \rightarrow A^2, A^B A^C \rightarrow A^{B+C}$
$A^0 \rightarrow 1, 0^A \rightarrow 0, A^1 \rightarrow A, (A^B)^C \rightarrow A^{BC}$

A1 $(A - B) (A + B) \leftrightarrow A^2 - B^2$
A2 $(A + B)^2 \leftrightarrow A^2 + 2AB + B^2$
A3 $A (B + C) \leftrightarrow AB + AC$
T1 $\tan x \leftrightarrow 1/\cot x$
T2 $(\tan x) (\cot x) \leftrightarrow 1$
T3 $\tan x \leftrightarrow \sin x/\cos x$
T4 $\cot x \leftrightarrow \cos x/\sin x$
T5 $\sin^2 x + \cos^2 x \leftrightarrow 1$

Differences. $\Delta V, \Delta N, \Delta C, \Delta T$, defined as in logic. ΔG and ΔP do not occur in algebra, since associativity and commutativity are built into the programs for handling expressions. The trigonometric functions are detected by ΔV and ΔN.

Connections between Differences and Operators. A $+$, $-$, or x in a cell means that the operator in the column of the cell affects the difference in the row of the cell. A t means that the test defined at the bottom is applied.

	A0	A1	A2	A3	T1	T2	T3	T4	T5
ΔV	—				t	t	t	t	t
ΔC	x	x	x	x					
ΔN	—	x	x	x	t	t	t	t	t
ΔT	x								

Test t: accept if other functions in output form already occur in expression.

Criteria of progress. Defined as in logic, but with ΔC more important than ΔN or ΔT.

Figure 5 Trigonometry task environment

detail, this is usually a simpler problem (having fewer steps) than the original one. Second, the subproblems that make up the plan are severally simpler (each having few steps) than the original problem. Since the exploration required to solve a problem generally increases exponentially with the number of steps in the solution, replacement of a single large problem with several smaller problems, the sum of whose lengths is about equal to the length of the original problem, may reduce very significantly the problem difficulty by whole orders of magnitude.

Fig. 8 shows the Planning Method applied to a problem of symbolic logic.

Given:　L1 = (tan x + cot x) sin x cos x
Obtain:　L0 = 1

Goal 1: Transform L1 into L0.
Goal 2: reduce —V between L1 and L0 (tan).
Goal 3: Apply A0 (combine) to L0 [no change produced].
Goal 4: Apply T1 to L1.
Goal 5: Transform L1 into C(T1) [succeeds]

$$L2 = [(1/\cot x) + \cot x] \sin x \cos x$$

Goal 6: Transform L2 into L0.
Goal 7: Reduce —V between L2 and L0 (cot).
Goal 8: Apply A0 to L2 [no change produced].
Goal 9: Apply T4 to L2.
Goal 10: Transform L2 into C(T4) [succeeds].

$$L3 = [(1/(\cos x/\sin x)) + (\cos x/\sin x)] \sin x \cos x$$

Goal 11: Transform L3 into L0.
Goal 12: Reduce —V between L3 and L0 (cos).
Goal 13: Apply A0 to L3:

$$L4 = [(\sin x/\cos x) + (\cos x/\sin x)] \sin x \cos x$$

Goal 14: Transform L4 into L0.
Goal 15: Reduce —V between L4 and L0 (sin).
Goal 16: Apply A0 to L4 [no change produced].
Goal 17: Apply T5 to L4.
Goal 18: Transform L4 into C(T5).
Goal 19: Reduce ΔC between L4 and C(T5) (· to +).
Goal 20: Apply A0 to L4 [no change produced].
Goal 21: Apply A1 to L4.
Goal 22: Transform L4 into C(A1).
Goal 23: Reduce ΔC between L4 and C(A1) [reject].
Goal 24: Apply A3 to L4.
Goal 25: Transform L4 into C(A3) [succeeds].

$$L5 = [\sin x/\cos x] \sin x \cos x + [\cos x/\sin x] \sin x \cos x$$

Goal 26: Transform L5 into C(T5).
Goal 27: Reduce ΔC between left of L5 and left of C(T5).
Goal 28: Apply A0 to left of L5:

$$L6 = \sin^2 x + [\cos x/\sin x] \sin x \cos x$$

Goal 29: Transform L6 into C(T5).
Goal 30: Reduce ΔC between right of L6 and right of C(T5).
Goal 31: Apply A0 to right of L6:

$$L7 = \sin^2 x = \cos^2 x$$

Goal 32: Transform L7 into C(T5) [succeeds].

$$L8 = 1$$

Goal 33: Transform L8 into L0 [identical], Q.E.D.

Figure 6 Example of means-ends analysis in trigonometry

Goal type 1: Transform object a into object b

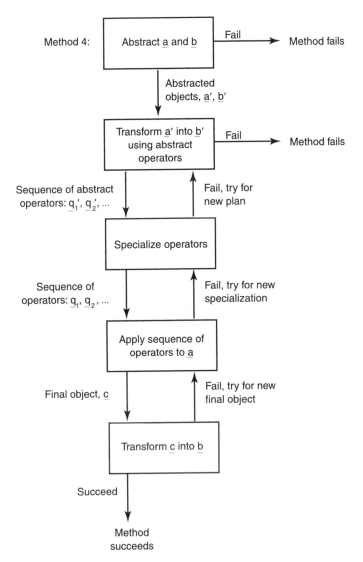

Figure 7 Planning method

The particular abstraction scheme that is illustrated ignores differences among connectives, signs and in the order of symbols (ΔC, ΔT and ΔP), replacing, for example, "(R $\supset$ –P) · (–R $\supset$ Q)" with "(PR) (QR)". The operators are similarly abstracted, so that "A $\vee$ B $\rightarrow$ B $\vee$ A" becomes "(AB) $\rightarrow$ (AB)"—i.e., the identity operator—and "A · B $\rightarrow$ A" becomes "(AB) $\rightarrow$ A",

Given: L1 = (R ⊃ −P) · (−R ⊃ Q)
Obtain; L0 = −(−Q · P)

Goal 1: Transform L1 into L0
[Method 1 fails; now Method 4 is tried].
Abstract L1 and L0:
    A1 = (PR) (QR)
    A0 = (PQ)

Goal 2: Transform A1 into A0 [using abstracted operators].

Several plans are generated [details are omitted]:

P1 = R8, R11, R12.
P2 = R8, R8, R12.
P3 = ...

Goal 3: Apply P1 to L1 [fails, details are omitted].

Goal 4: Apply P2 to L1.

Goal 5: Apply R8 to L1.

Goal 6: Transform L1 into C(R8) [succeeds].

    L2 = R ⊃ −P

Goal 7: Apply R8 to L1.

Goal 8: Transform L1 into C(R8) [succeeds].

    L3 = −R ⊃ Q

Goal 9: Apply R12 to L2 and L3.

Goal 10: Transform L2 and L3 into C(R12) [L2 fits B ⊃ C].

Goal 11: Reduce ∆P between L3 and C(R12) (A ⊃ B with B = R).

Goal 12: Apply R2 to L3.

Goal 13: Transform L3 into C(R2) [succeeds].

    L4 = −Q ⊃ R

Goal 14: Transform L2 and L4 into C(R12) [succeeds].

    L5 = −Q ⊃ −P

Goal 15: Transform L5 into L0.

Goal 16: Reduce ∆T between L5 and L0.

Goal 17: Apply R2 to L5 [fails, details omitted].

Goal 18: Apply R5 to L5.

Goal 19: Transform L5 into C(R5).

Goal 20: Reduce ∆C between L5 and C(R5).

Goal 21: Apply R5 to L5 [reject].

Goal 22: Apply R6 to L5.

Goal 23: Transform L6 into C(R6) [succeeds].

    L6 = −Q ∨ −P

Goal 24: Transform L5 into C(R5) [succeeds].

    L7 = −(−Q · P)

Goal 25: Transform L7 into L0 [identical], Q.E.D.

Figure 8 Example of planning in logic

as shown in fig. 3. The abstracted problem, Transform A1 into A0, has several solutions in the abstracted task environment. One of these may be summarized:

	Object	*Operation*
A1	(PR) (QR)	
A2	(PR)	Apply R8 to get left side of A1
A3	(QR)	Apply R8 to get right side of A1
	(PQ)	Apply R12 to A2 and A3
But	(PQ) is identical	
	with A0	Q.E.D.

Transforming A1 into A0 is the abstract equivalent of the problem of transforming L1 into L0. The former is solved by applying the abstracted operators corresponding to R8, R8, and R12 in sequence. Hence (fig. 8, goal 4) a plan for solving the original problem is to try to apply R8 to L1 (obtaining a new object whose abstract equivalent is (PR)), applying R8 to the other side of L1 (obtaining an object corresponding to (QR), applying R12 to the objects thus obtained, and finally, transforming this new object (which should be an abstract equivalent of L0) into L0. Each of the first three parts of this plan constitutes a Type 2 goal in the original task environment—that is, it requires the application of a specified operator to a specified expression. These three Type 2 goals are goals 5, 7, and 9, respectively, in fig. 8. The first two are achieved almost trivially, and the third requires only five subgoals. The result is the expression, L5, which is to be transformed to L0, as indicated, by a Type 1 goal (goal 15). Note that achieving the plan only involves operators that become the identity operator upon abstraction.

Like the other heuristics, the planning heuristic offers no guarantees that it will always work. It may generate no plan, a single plan, or several plans. More serious, a plan may turn out to be illusory—it may prove impossible to carry it out. The first plan generated in the illustrative problem, for example—R8, R11, R12—does not provide a basis for a valid derivation when it is translated back to the concrete task environment. The time wasted in fruitless efforts to execute invalid plans must be counted in evaluating the planning heuristic, but even when allowance is made for this cost, the heuristic remains a very powerful one.

5 Conclusion

We have now described the principal heuristics that are used by GPS, and have shown how these heuristics enable it to solve problems. Although limitations of space prevent full discussion, we would like to conclude by mentioning several aspects of GPS that have received inadequate treatment in this paper.

1) GPS requires additional goals and methods, and we have investigated a number of these to varying degrees. For example, in many problems features of objects come to play a larger role than differences between objects—e.g., control of center in chess. A goal and methods similar to Type 3 are needed to handle features. Solving single equations in one variable also requires a new goal and new methods, embodying such heuristics as operating on both sides of an equation to isolate the variable. This goal is already needed in trigonometry to recognize that $(\sin^4 - \cos^4 x)$ is of the form $(y^2 - z^2)$, so that it can be factorised. Already GPS can handle algebraic simplification with its present repertoire, and integration of relatively simple expressions with the aid of a table of integrals. There is some hope, as the example introducing means-ends analysis indicates, that GPS may be capable of the common sense thinking that gets most humans through the details of each day's living.

2) GPS is given very little information about a task environment, and deals with the most general features of it. Beyond a point, most of the heuristics of GPS will be devoted to discovering special systems of heuristics for particular subject matters. In trigonometry, for example, GPS needs to be able to learn such heuristics as "reduce everything to sines and cosines," and "follow a trigonometric step with an algebraic step." In fact it followed these roughly in the example given, but only in a cumbersome fashion. The one narrow piece of learning we have mentioned—associating differences with operators—is a start in this direction.

3) Realizing programs with GPS on a computer is a major programming task. Much of our research effort has gone into the design of programming languages (information processing languages) that make the writing of such programs practicable. We must refer the reader to other publications for a description of this work [4, 9]. However, we should like to emphasize that our description of GPS in this paper ignores all information handling problems; how to keep track of the goals; how to associate with them the necessary information, and retrieve this information; how to add methods to an already running system; and so on. These technical problems form a large part of the problem of creating intelligent programs.

4) In this paper we have also underemphasized the role of the evaluation step—the opportunity to reject a goal before any effort is spent upon it. The methods are generative, producing possible solutions. They are only heuristic, and so will produce many more possibilities than can be explored. The evaluation applies additional heuristics to select the more profitable paths, and strongly affects the problem-solving ability of GPS. The means-ends analysis is a general heuristic because progress can be evaluated in the same general terms as for the methods. More specific evaluations will again require learning.

5) Limitations of space have forced our examples to focus on the correct solution path. They do not convey properly the amount of selection, and trial and error. This is particularly unfortunate, since viewed dramatically, problem-solving is the battle of selection techniques against a space of possibilities that keeps expanding exponentionally [5, 7].

6 References

[1] Bernstein, A., et al.: *A chess-playing program for the IBM 704.* Proceedings of the 1958 Western Joint Computer Conference, May 1958.

[2] Kister, J., et al.: *Experiments in chess.* J. Assoc. for Computing Machinery, 4, 2, April 1957.

[3] Gelernter, H. L., and N. Rochester: *Intelligent behavior in problem-solving machines.* IBM Journal of Research and Development, 2, 4, October 1958.

[4] Newell, A., and J. C. Shaw: *Programming the Logic Theory Machine.* Proceedings of the 1957 Western Joint Computer Conference, February 1957.

[5] Newell, A., J. C. Shaw, and H. A. Simon: *Empirical explorations of the Logic Theory Machine.* Proceedings of the 1957 Western Joint Computer Conference, February 1957.

[6] Newell, A., J. C. Shaw, and H. A. Simon: *Chess playing programs and the problem of complexity.* IBM Journal of Research and Development, 2, 4, October 1958.

[7] Newell, A., J. C. Shaw, and H. A. Simon: *The processes of creative thinking.* P-1320, The RAND Corporation, Santa Monica, California, August 1958.

[8] Newell, A., and H. A. Simon: *The Logic Theory Machine.* Transactions on Information Theory, IT-2, No. 3, September 1956.

[9] Shaw, J. C., et al.: *A command structure for complex information processing.* Proceedings of the 1958 Western Joint Computer Conference, May 1958.

29

THE SIMULATION OF
PSYCHOLOGICAL PROCESSES

G. A. Miller, E. Galanter and K. H. Pribram

Source: G. A. Miller, E. Galanter and K. H. Pribram, *Plans and the Structure of Behavior*, Harcourt Brace, 1960, 41–57.

A reflex theorist who is asked to abandon his palpable *S*'s and *R*'s, to surrender his network of *S-R* connections modeled after a telephone switchboard, and to replace it all by ghostly Images and intangible Plans, is likely to feel he has been asked to walk on air. "How," he grumbles, "can a tough-minded scientist make sense out of such cognitive moonshine?" For years the reflex theorist's stock in trade has been his accusation that the cognitive theorist was at heart a vitalist who could never produce a believable mechanism that would accomplish what he claimed for the living brain. "Everyone recognizes," he would say, "that comparing the brain to a map control room is only a metaphor. If we were to take it seriously, we would have to assume that there is a little man inside the head, a homunculus who can read maps and make decisions."[1] At least since the time of Descartes, who invented reflex theory as part of his thesis that the body is just a machine, reflex theorists have been winning arguments by insisting on mechanical models for living systems.

Today, suddenly, the argument has lost its force. Now at long last there are machines complicated enough to do everything that cognitive theorists have been talking about. Descartes was impressed by the clockwork figures that jumped out of the shrubbery to startle a stroller; think how much more impressed he would be by a modern electronic computer that spins out calculations at lightning speeds. Leibnitz dreamed of such a machine and tried to describe a thought-calculus it might use to compute answers to problems that require thinking. Today such machines are operating in hundreds of laboratories. The reflex theorist is no longer the only psychologist who can summon up a tangible mechanism to make his claims sound more reasonable. Today a cognitive theorist is also free to become a materialist in good standing—if that is what he wants.

Typical of the new freedom deriving from a deeper conception of what machines can be and do was the discovery that machines can behave purposively. In 1943 Rosenblueth, Wiener, and Bigelow shocked many psychologists by putting their very tough-minded reputations behind the assertion that machines with negative feedback were teleological mechanisms.[2] At that time psychologists generally regarded "teleological" and "unscientific" as synonymous, and it was therefore surprising to realize that machines could strive toward goals, could collect information about the difference between their intentions and their performance and then work to reduce that difference. If entelechy was compatible with mechanism, then entelechy could be admitted as a respectable concept in psychology. Wiener stated the argument this way:

It is my thesis that the physical functioning of the living individual and the operation of some of the newer communication machines are precisely parallel in their analogous attempts to control entropy through feedback. Both of them have sensory receptors as one stage of their cycle of operation: that is, in both of them there exists a special apparatus for collecting information from the outer world at low energy levels, and for making it available in the operation of the individual or of the machine. In both cases these external messages are not taken *neat*, but through the internal transforming powers of the apparatus, whether it be alive or dead. The information is then turned into a new form available for the further stages of performance. In both the animal and the machine this performance is made to be effective on the outer world. In both of them, their *performed* action on the outer world, and not merely their *intended* action, is reported back to the central regulatory apparatus.[3]

Such declarations seemed remarkable at first. Given a little time to reflect, however, psychologists realized that these purposive machines were quite familiar, though the language used to discuss them was somewhat new. As early as 1896 the philosopher-psychologist John Dewey had described in much detail the servomechanism involved in reaching toward a candle flame and then jerking away. "The fact is," he said, "that stimulus and response are not distinctions of existence, but teleological distinctions, that is, distinctions of function, or part played, with reference to reaching or maintaining an end."[4] The new terms and explicit analysis supplied by the engineering development were needed, however, before the importance of Dewey's insight could be fully appreciated. Once a teleological mechanism could be built out of metal and glass, psychologists recognized that it was scientifically respectable to admit they had known it all along. They had known, for example, of the homeostatic mechanisms studied by Walter B. Cannon and his associates during the 1920's. They had known about L. T. Troland, who in 1928 introduced the term "retroflex" to name the sensory feedback.[5] They had known about the "circular reflexes" that E. B. Holt revived and elaborated in 1931.[6] And they had known about Edward Tolman, who anticipated the new respectability of teleology by at least two decades and who, in 1939, had described a perfectly respectable feedback mechanism that he called the "schematic sowbug."[7] Even in 1939, however, Tolman could claim no priority, for he had borrowed the central idea from the mechanistic biologist Jacques Loeb. That was something else the psychologists had known all along. Loeb's theory of tropisms was, in 1890, one of the earliest descriptions of a machine that would exhibit purposive, taxic behavior.[8] The idea of the biological servomechanism had been there all along—but the mechanical actualization of the idea in inorganic hardware provided the kind of demonstration that could no longer be ignored. Today we can, almost as a matter of course, propose teleological arrangements such as the TOTE unit discussed in the preceding chapter—the particular realization of the unit in tissue or in metal need not deter us, for we know now that it can be accomplished in a variety of ways.

What is the source of this remarkable increase in confidence that psychologists experience when their ideas can be translated into machinery? Clark Hull has suggested that designing robots is a "prophylaxis? against anthropomorphic subjectivism," and he recommends the following to his readers:

> Regard ... the behaving organism as a completely self-maintaining robot, constructed of materials as unlike ourselves as may be. In doing this it is not necessary to attempt the solution of the detailed engineering problems connected with the design of such a creature. It is a wholesome and revealing exercise, however, to consider the various general problems in behavior dynamics which must be solved in the design of a truly self-maintaining robot. ... The temptation to introduce an entelechy, soul, spirit, or daemon into a robot is slight; it is relatively easy to realize that *the introduction of an entelechy would not really solve the problem of design of a robot because there would still remain the problem of designing the entelechy itself, which is the core of the original problem all over again.* The robot approach thus aids us in avoiding the very natural but childish tendency to choose easy though false solutions to our problems, by removing all excuses for not facing them squarely and without evasion.[9]

Passages such as this suggest that nothing less than the construction of a teleological machine would convince an experimental psychologist that there is not something occult implied by the terms "goal," "purpose," "expectation," "entelechy."

Surely there is something more to a psychologist's feeling of materialistic satisfaction and confidence than just his triumph over subjectivism. Machines are not the only way he has of facing his problems "squarely and without evasion." Indeed, psychologists are most likely to construct machines for just those functions whose objective character is least in doubt, where the threat of subjectivism is most remote. The conditioned reflex, for example, is seldom considered an example of "anthropomorphic subjectivism," yet numerous machines have been designed and built to demonstrate the phenomenon of conditioning or of conditioning aided by the law of effect.[10] They were not designed to perform any mentalistic function but merely to display the rather mechanical fact that a new connection was being formed.

It seems to the present authors that the attempts to simulate psychological processes with machines are motivated in large measure by the desire to test—or to demonstrate—the designer's understanding of the theory he espouses. History suggests that man can create almost anything he can visualize clearly. The creation of a model is proof of the clarity of the vision. If you understand how a thing works well enough to build your own, then your understanding must be nearly perfect.

The germ of wisdom behind this intuition was made explicit by the mathematician A. M. Turing in 1937.[11] The import of Turing's work for psychologists was that if they could describe exactly and unambiguously anything that a living organism did, then a computing machine could be built that would exhibit the same behavior with sufficient exactitude to confuse the observer. The existence of the machine would be the test of the accuracy of the description.

One consequence of taking Turing's theorem seriously is that it directs attention toward the electronic computer as the right kind of machine to simulate human behavior. But many psychologists, impressed by the haphazard unpredictability of behavior generally, feel intuitively that models based on random processes offer better prospects than the computers do, and so the two kinds of machines, deterministic and stochastic, seem to compete with each other for the psychologist's attention. Kochen and Galanter, however, argue that computer models are more appropriate than stochastic models for describing human choice behavior:

> Ignoring the question of whether or not a "conscious" plan guides the decision-making procedure at each trial, it is assumed that the choices are made according to a plan. Such a plan shall be called a *strategy*. It differs mainly in degree from a relatively "stochastic decision-making procedure," as might be observed in the behavior of rats in a T-maze. The latter type of behavior seems best described by certain kinds of stochastic processes, whereas a computerlike mechanism in which random elements play a secondary role seems a more fruitful model for "planned" behavior.[12]

Although the work on stochastic models is being actively pursued by mathematical psychologists, it will not be reviewed here; since we are concerned here primarily with planned behavior, we shall concentrate on deterministic automata.

Another thing that Turing's theorem did—or should have done—was to focus attention on the adequacy of the description of behavior. A machine cannot be expected to simulate something that has never been described—it can be held responsible only for those aspects of behavior that an observer has recorded. No simulation is complete and no simulation preserves all the characteristics of behavior. If in building a machine to simulate the behavior of a moth flying toward a light we use wheels so that the machine rolls rather than flies, the simulation is considered adequate up to transformations of locomotion. In a sense, we say that we do not care how the beast gets there so long as its trajectory is "equivalent" to that of the moth. But even that is acceptable only when we allow a shift from three to two dimensions of movement.

A simulation is invariant with the behavior being simulated only up to some group of allowable transformations. The simulator and his critics must, for example, agree in advance on the aspects of the behavior that are to remain the same from organism to machine. This agreement is normally established by requiring the machine to simulate, not the behavior per se, but the psychologist's *record* of the behavior. A theorist is, therefore, at the mercy of the person who decides what aspects of the behavior are worth recording and simulating.

The extent to which an organism and a machine can be interchanged without altering specified aspects of the situation is the extent to which the simulation is successful. A successful model does not have to *look* like the organism it simulates—the fact that clever modelers can make a mechanical mouse look like a mouse, or a mechanical moth look like a turtle, is mere window dressing. A woman who broke a valuable vase took the pieces to a potter, asked him to make an "exact duplicate"—and was rightfully distressed when he duplicated every chip and shard.

The situation is most familiar, perhaps, in the concept of synonymy. We say that "bachelor" and "unmarried man" are synonymous because they are interchangeable in (nearly) all contexts without alteration of the truth value of the propositions in which they occur. In that case, it is the truth value that must remain invariant. In the case of a successful model, the thing that must remain invariant is the aspect of the organism's behavior that the experimenter chose to record.

Since it is necessary to simulate only the record of the animal's behavior, not the animal itself, the big, fast digital computers that began to evolve after World War II could be used—they did not need to scurry around the room like a rat in a maze or resemble the three pints of brain matter they were supposed to imitate. The computer did not even need to observe the same time scale. The computer's task was merely to simulate—to compute—those aspects of the experimental situation that students of human behavior were interested in. A theorist could embody his ideas in a program of instructions, the program could be stored in the "memory" of the computer, and when "stimuli" were presented the computer would, like an organism, operate upon the input information according to the instructions it had been given in order to generate a "response." In principle, it sounds very simple.

For several years, however, there was a good deal more talk than work. Writing the kind of complicated programs that are necessary in order to simulate a human being requires a tremendous investment of time and ingenuity. While the computers and the programming art were expanding, the theorists discussed how best to use them, eventually, for simulation. The first direction these discussions took was toward neurological, rather than psychological, simulation. This direction seemed especially promising because of a long list of analogies: the open-or-shut relay was analogous to the all-or-none neuron, the electrical pulses in the computer were analogous to the neural impulses, the mercury delay lines were analogous to the reverberating circuits in the nervous system, the memory circuits of the computer were analogous to the association areas of the brain, and so on and on. The neurological direction also seemed promising because McCulloch and Pitts had invented a formal representation of neural nets and used it to establish that any function that could be described logically, strictly, and unambiguously in a finite number of words could be realized by such nets.[13] That is to say, they showed that their neural nets comprised a Turing machine. This formalization made possible some very sophisticated analyses of neurological functions and properties even before they were simulated by computers. The speculations about neural nets were widely publicized and seem to have had a stimulating effect on neurology and neurophysiology. We have every reason to expect great strides forward in this field. It is not, however, the kind of theory we are interested in here.

Our present interest is in the use of computers as automata to illustrate the operation of various *psychological* theories. Efforts in this direction lagged somewhat behind the neurological and seem to have been of at least two different kinds. Some of the psychological theorizing aimed the computer at the Image, and some of it aimed the computer at the Plan. Not until late in the 1950's did these two lines grow together.

Consider the Image-inspired theories first. One of the early attempts to use computer simulation in order to understand psychological (rather than neurological) processes was made by the British psychologist Kenneth Craik, who was convinced that thought depends on images. But how was a computer to have an image? His answer was that an image is a form of symbol and that thought consists of building and modifying such symbols by processing the information from the sense organs; to the extent that a computer symbolizes and processes information, it is thinking. He says:

> My hypothesis then is that thought models, or parallels, reality—
> that its essential feature is not "the mind," "the self," "sense-data,"
> nor propositions but symbolism, and that this symbolism is largely
> of the same kind as that which is familiar to us in mechanical devices
> which aid thought and calculation.[14]

In the terms we have introduced here, Craik was struggling with the problem of how the Image could be represented in a computer.

Craik's untimely death prevented him from following up these ideas, and the work that pursued the problem of image formation and recognition by computers was largely cast in neurological rather than psychological terms.[15] However, Donald M. MacKay picked up the argument and carried it a step further when he pointed out that an Image could be constructed in a machine if the machine were able to remember the reactions it required to imitate its input.[16] The act of replication might be guided by feedback—the difference between the incoming configuration and the internal replication would represent an error signal for the machine to reduce. These acts of replication would then provide a basic "vocabulary" in terms of which the machine could describe its own experience (a notion not completely unlike Hebb's neurological "phase sequences").

These theories, clever as they were, did not seem to come to grips with the problem of motivation. It remained for Galanter and Gerstenhaber, in 1956, to point out the importance of motivation and to propose a theory for determining which Images would serve as models for thinking. Different evaluations do indeed modify a person's Image of his problem and so lead to different forms of behavior.[17]

Of all the work on machine imagery, however, the most impressive is that by Gelernter and Rochester.[18] They have programmed a computer to prove theorems in plane geometry and equipped the machine to draw diagrams experimentally, much as a student does. The diagrams simplify tremendously the process of searching for a proof. A more persuasive demonstration that Tolman's analogy to "a map control room" need not involve a homunculus to read the maps could hardly be imagined.

Psychologists seem to have been somewhat slower to recognize that the same kind of problems of pattern and organization exist at the behavioral level as at the level of the Image. Perhaps it was the interminable discussion of "trial-and-error" processes that fostered a general belief that relatively simple stochastic models would suffice as theories. In 1949 Miller and Frick tried to complicate this simple picture by using Markov processes to explain the sequential organization of behavior.[19] Their work represented a relatively obvious generalization of Claude Shannon's suggestion that Markov processes could be used to explain the sequential organization of messages.[20] Surely, sequential organization of behavior could nowhere be more important than for communication, so it seemed that if Markovian machines would generate grammatical English, they would be adequate for simulating all other forms of behavior as well. The actual creation of such a machine, however, was prohibited by the fantastically large number of internal states that would be required in the machine for even the crudest approximations to actual behavior. The crux of the problem was not clear, however, until Noam Chomsky proved that any machine that tries to generate all the grammatical strings of words by proceeding, as a Markovian machine would, from left to right, one word at a time in strict order, will need to have an infinite number of internal states.[21] Since the point of a theory is simplification, machines with infinitely many parameters cannot be considered seriously. The only alternative seems to be one that respects the hierarchical structure of the sequence—the kind of "parsing" machine that we have already mentioned in Chapter 1.

One reason that linguists have been motivated to express their description of language in terms congenial to communication theory and to modern computers has been their interest in the possibility of mechanical translation. The development of communication theory since 1948 has revolutionized our thinking in a dozen different fields, ranging all the way from electrical engineering to the social sciences.[22] Most of the implications of that work lie outside the scope of the present book, but the attempt to use computers to translate messages from one language into another is particularly relevant to this discussion.[23] The first step in this direction, of course, is to use a computer as an automatic dictionary, to exploit its high speeds to accomplish the humdrum task of searching through the vocabulary to find the possible equivalents in the target language. But word-for-word substitutions, even between closely related languages, do not produce grammatical or even intelligible translations. The machine must know something about the grammar as well as the vocabulary of the languages it is translating. Or, more precisely, it must have a set of instructions for deciding among alternative translations, for recognizing idioms, for rearranging the order of the words, for detaching or supplying affixes to roots, etc. In principle, there is no reason we cannot store a two-language dictionary and several hundred coded rules of grammar in a computer and get a usable output. But in practice, the actual coding of the dictionary and the efficient phrasing of the rules pose many tedious and perplexing puzzles. They will probably be overcome, but at the present writing, mechanical translation is still not proceeding as a routine business anywhere in the United States.

The current state of the world makes translation an important problem for the survival of our society, and we must hope the linguists and their programmers will soon succeed. Even without success, however, there are certain lessons that we can draw from their experience that have enlightening implications for psychologists and linguists.

In the first place, the very large amount of information that has to be encoded for the computer has comprised, until very recently, one of the major bottlenecks in the implementation of the scheme. There just is not enough room in a computer for it to contain a full vocabulary and still be able to retrieve items from the memory as rapidly as they would be needed for, say, ordinary speech rates. In the terms of our present discussion, the Image of the average, well-educated European or American adult must contain an amazing amount of knowledge all organized for fast access to attention. In some respects, apparently, our brains are still a great deal more complicated than the biggest computer ever built.

In the second place, it becomes obvious that there are two very different attitudes one can take toward the job. In one attitude, the programmer says, "I want to make it work any way I can, but the simpler it is, the better." In the other attitude, he says, "I want to make the computer do it the same way people do it, even though it may not look like the most efficient method." As citizens we should applaud the former attitude, but as psychologists, linguists, neurologists—as students of the human being—we are bound to be more interested in the latter. It has been suggested that the attempt to discover an efficient way for the computer to do the task should be called a problem in "artificial intelligence," whereas the attempt to imitate the human being should be called a problem in "simulation." To date, little effort has been made to approach the translation problem with the intent of simulating a human translator.

And, finally, there is nothing but a distressingly vague criterion for determining when the computer has succeeded and when it has failed.[24] A translation is multi-dimensional, and who can say how much better one dimension must be in order to counterbalance an inferiority in some other dimension? Probably the evaluation should be based upon the comparison of the machine's output with a professional translator's output, but exactly how the comparison is to be made is quite difficult to say. In the most successful branches of science we have learned how to measure the discrepancies between our observations and our theories, but with the kind of simulations now possible, criteria for the goodness of fit have yet to be devised.

Mechanical translation illustrates a general class of non-numerical problems toward which the computer has been directed. The inspiration for the work did not arise from an attempt to understand or develop any new theories in neurology or psychology, but from the translation problem itself and from a desire to see just how good our computers really are. It has been principally the computer engineers, plus a few mathematicians, who have tried to make computers play chess,[25] or prove theorems in logic,[26] or wrestle with some branch of mathematics.[27] Inasmuch as most of the efforts have been on problems of "artificial intelligence" rather than in the simulation of human beings, they contribute little but context to the psychological problem. However, the tasks that the engineers and mathematicians have selected to explore on the computer are, in some sense not easily defined, about the right "size" for present-day machines to tackle. The Image that a computer must have in order to play chess, or to do problems in the propositional calculus, is quite restricted and reasonably determinate, and therefore does not overload the computer. Yet at the same time these tasks are large and complicated enough to be interesting and to enable a machine to surprise us by its successes.[28] They are good problems. But what is needed, from the psychologist's point of view, is an attempt to *simulate* the human chess-player or logician, not just to replace him or defeat him.

The first intensive effort to meet this need was the work of Newell, Shaw, and Simon, who have advanced the business of psychological simulation further and with greater success than anyone else.[29] Later, particularly in Chapter 13, we discuss their ideas in more detail. For the present, however, we shall comment simply that they have created an information-processing language that enables them to use the computer in a non-numerical manner. Their language systematically exploits a hierarchical (list structure) system of organization that is uniquely suitable for writing heuristic programs for problem solving, programs that enable a computer to simulate the information processing done by human subjects who are given the same task to solve.[30] Newell, Shaw, and Simon have used their techniques to simulate human problem solving in logic, chess, and trigonometry and have evolved a set of principles, applicable to a wide variety of situations, that they feel are characteristic of the ways human beings solve problems in general. Their accomplishments have influenced the present authors in many ways—not merely in terms of their specific solutions to innumerable technical problems but generally by their demonstration that what so many had so long described was finally coming to pass.

It is impressive to see, and to experience, the increase in confidence that comes from the concrete actualization of an abstract idea—the kind of confidence a reflex theorist must have felt in the 1930's when he saw a machine that could be conditioned like a dog. Today, however, that confidence is no longer reserved exclusively for reflex theorists. Perhaps some of the more fanciful conjectures of the "mentalists" should now be seriously reconsidered. Psychologists have been issued a new license to conjecture. What will they do with it? Will the new ideas be incorporated into existing theory? Or will it be easier to begin afresh?

A major impetus behind the writing of this book has been the conviction that these new ideas *are* compatible with, and provide extensions of, familiar and established psychological principles. In the pages that follow the attempt will be made to show what these principles are and how they can be revised and elaborated in the light of recent developments in our understanding of man viewed as a system for processing information.

Notes

1 It is amusing that so many psychologists who abhor subjectivism and anthropo-morphism unhesitatingly put telephone switchboards inside our heads. In 1943, for example, Clark Hull, in his *Principles of Behavior* (New York: Appleton-Century-Crofts), could take it as self-evident that the brain "acts as a kind of automatic switchboard" (p. 18, repeated on p. 384). However, the important adjec-tive, "automatic," is a recent accomplishment. The telephone engineers who had to build and maintain those early switchboards that reflex theorists loved so well were dissatisfied with them because they required a human operator to make the connections. Eventually, of course, the operator was replaced by more elaborate machinery, thus rendering reflex theory scientifically impeccable at last. But in 1892, when Karl Pearson wrote *The Grammar of Science*, he unblushingly pro-vided a "clerk" who carried on the same valuable services in the brain as he would in a central telephone exchange.

2 Arturo Rosenblueth, Norbert Wiener, and Julian Bigelow, Behavior, purpose, and teleology, *Philosophy of Science*, 1943, 10, 18–24. W. Ross Ashby had also intro-duced the feedback mechanism as early as 1940 in his paper, Adaptiveness and equilibrium, *Journal of Mental Science*, 1940, 86, 478–483. Priorities are uncertain because the ideas were part of the development of servomechanisms and were subject to security restrictions during the war.

3 Norbert Wiener, *The Human Use of Human Beings* (Boston: Houghton Mifflin, 1954), pp. 26–27.

4 John Dewey, The reflex arc concept in psychology, *Psychological Review*, 1896, 3, 357–370. This remarkable paper, one of the cornerstones of American functional psychology, an anticipation of Gestalt psychology, and a criticism in advance of behaviorism, has been reprinted in Wayne Dennis, ed., *Readings in the History of Psychology* (New York: Appleton-Century-Crofts, 1948).

5 L. T. Troland, *The Fundamentals of Human Motivation* (New York: Van Nostrand, 1928).

6 Edwin B. Holt, *Animal Drive and the Learning Process* (New York: Holt, 1931). For the history of the circular reflexes, see Wayne Dennis, A note on the circular response hypothesis, *Psychological Review*, 1954, 61, 334–338. Dennis traces the circular response back to David Hartley in 1749.

7 E. C. Tolman, Prediction of vicarious trial and error by means of the schematic sowbug, *Psychological Review*, 1939, 46, 318–336.

8 W. J. Crozier, The study of living organisms, in C. Murchison, ed., *The Founda-tions of Experimental Psychology* (Worcester: Clark University Press, 1929), pp. 45–127. Another biologist who provided a clear and significant precybernetic account of teleological mechanisms was Alfred J. Lotka. See his *Elements of Physical Biology* (Baltimore: Williams & Wilkins, 1925). (Reissued in 1956 by Dover Press as *Elements of Mathematical Biology*.) Lotka illustrates his argument by the operation of a mechanical beetle that was able to avoid falling off table edges; and he expresses his scorn for thinkers who call a system teleological only so long as they are ignorant of its workings.

9 Hull, *Principles of Behavior*, pp. 27–28. This passage expresses Hull's distaste for nineteenth-century vitalism in general, and particularly for that purposeful, organ-izing, vital principle that Hans Driesch named "entelechy." In the twentieth cen-tury it has become clear that Hans Driesch was wrong, but not for the reason Hull gives. Hull thought that the vitalistic distinction between animals and robots failed because animals, being nothing but machines, could not operate purposefully. In fact, however, the distinction failed because *both* organisms and machines can demonstrate the operation of a purposeful entelechy. Designing an entelechy is no

trick at all for an electrical engineer. In spite of this resounding failure, however, vitalism is not dead. It has merely retreated. In order to find something distinctive about biological systems, the modern vitalists have retreated from purpose to memory, an alternative first suggested by Henri Bergson. The current contention is that the stability of genetic and personal memory is—according to the laws of quantum mechanics—incompatible with the microscopic sizes of the gene and the synapse. Therefore, the stability of memory requires some nonphysical explanation. For a sophisticated defense of the idea that maintaining information in an organism is not, in general, accomplished by mechanistic means, see Walter M. Elsasser, *The Physical Foundation of Biology* (New York: Pergamon, 1958). According to Elsasser's view, a self-maintaining robot that behaved like an organism would prove nothing unless its component parts were reduced to the extremely small size characteristic of biological systems.

10 In 1946 E. G. Boring, in Mind and mechanism, *American Journal of Psychology*, 1946, 59, 173–192, listed the following attempts to design robots that would learn: J. M. Stephens, A mechanical explanation of the law of effect, *American Journal of Psychology*, 1929, 41, 422–431; A. Walton, Conditioning illustrated by an automatic mechanical device, *American Journal of Psychology*, 1930, 42, 110 f.; H. D. Baernstein and C. L. Hull, A mechanical model of the conditioned reflex, *Journal of General Psychology*, 1931, 5, 99–106; R. G. Kreuger and C. L. Hull, An electrochemical parallel to the conditioned reflex, *Journal of General Psychology*, 1931, 5, 262–269; G. K. Bennett and L. B. Ward, A model of the synthesis of conditioned reflexes, *American Journal of Psychology*, 1933, 45, 339–342; D. G. Ellson, A mechanical synthesis of trial-and-error learning, *Journal of General Psychol.*, 1935, 13, 212–218; H. Bradner, A new mechanical "learner," *Journal of General Psychology*, 1937, 17, 414–419; T. Ross, The synthesis of intelligence—its implications, *Psychological Review*, 1938, 45, 185–189. The frequency with which these toys were described in the journals (and no one can guess how many more vanished unreported) bears eloquent testimony to the importance psychologists attach to having a credible mechanism to support their theoretical speculations.

11 An excellent introduction to Turing machines will be found in Martin Davis, *Computability and Unsolvability* (New York: McGraw-Hill, 1958).

12 Manfred Kochen and Eugene H. Galanter, The acquisition and utilization of information in problem solving and thinking, *Information and Control*, 1958, 1, 267–288. Of course, an electronic computer can be used to study stochastic models as well as deterministic ones; see, for example, Saul Gorn, On the mechanical stimulation of habit-forming and learning, *Information and Control*, 1959, 2, 226–259.

13 Warren S. McCulloch and Walter Pitts, A logical calculus of the ideas immanent in nervous activity, *Bulletin of Mathematical Biophysics*, 1943, 5, 115–133. For some of the earlier work, see Nicholas Rashevsky, *Mathematical Biophysics* (Chicago: University of Chicago Press, 1938). For some of the more recent work, see M. L. Minsky, *Neural-Analog Networks and the Brain-Model Problem*, Ph.D. thesis, Princeton University, 1954; see also the several selections in C. E. Shannon and J. McCarthy, eds., *Automata Studies* (Princeton: Princeton University Press, 1956). And for perspective, see John von Neumann, *The Computer and the Brain* (New Haven: Yale University Press, 1958).

14 K. J. W. Craik, *The Nature of Explanation* (Cambridge: Cambridge University Press, 1943), p. 57.

15 Some of the relevant contributions to a neurological theory of perception were: W. Pitts and W. S. McCulloch, How we know universals: The perception of auditory and visual forms, *Bulletin of Mathematical Biophysics*, 1947, 9, 127–147; D. O.

Hebb, *The Organization of Behavior* (New York: Wiley, 1949); W. A. Clark and B. G. Farley, Generalization of pattern recognition in a self-organizing system, *Proceedings of the Western Joint Computer Conference*, Los Angeles, March 1955, pp. 86–91; O. G. Selfridge, Pattern recognition and modern computers, *ibid.*, pp. 91–93; G. P. Dinneen, Programming pattern recognition, *ibid.*, pp. 94–100; N. Rochester, J. H. Holland, L. H. Haibt, and W. L. Duda, Test on a cell assembly theory of the action of the brain, using a large digital computer, *IRE Transactions on Information Theory*, 1956, Vol. PGIT-2, No. 3, 80–93; P. M. Milner, The cell assembly: Mark II, *Psychological Review*, 1957, 64, 242–252; F. Rosenblatt, The perception: A probabilistic model for information storage and organization in the brain, *Psychological Review*, 1958, 65, 386–408. This list is far from complete. The fact that we are in this book more interested in the Plan than in the Image deprives us of an excuse to summarize these valuable and interesting contributions to perceptual theory, but we mention them as part of the accumulating evidence that computer simulation will play an increasingly important role in the future development of both neurological and psychological theory.

16 D. M. MacKay, Mindlike behavior in artefacts, *British Journal for the Philosophy of Science*, 1951, 2, 105–121.

17 Eugene Galanter and Murray Gerstenhaber, On thought: The extrinsic theory, *Psychological Review*, 1956, 63, 218–227. Eugene Galanter and W. A. S. Smith, Some experiments on a simple thought-problem, *American Journal of Psychology*, 1958, 71, 359–366.

18 H. L. Gelernter and N. Rochester, Intelligent behavior in problem-solving machines, *IBM Journal of Research and Development*, 1958, 2, 336–345. H. L. Gelernter, Realization of a geometry proving machine. *Proceedings of the International Conference on Information Processing*, Paris, 1959 (in press).

19 George A. Miller and Frederick C. Frick, Statistical behavioristics and sequences of responses, *Psychological Review*, 1949, 56, 311–324. See also F. C. Frick and G. A. Miller, A statistical description of operant conditioning, *American Journal of Psychology*, 1951, 64, 20–36, and G. A. Miller, Finite Markov processes in psychology, *Psychometrika*, 1952, 17, 149–167.

20 Claude E. Shannon, A mathematical theory of communication, *Bell System Technical Journal*, 1948, 27, 379–423. Actually, Markov himself had used his ideas to describe written texts.

21 Noam Chomsky, Three models for the description of language, *IRE Transactions on Information Theory*, 1956, Vol. IT-2, 113–124. However, the difficulties involved in applying stochastic theory to sequences of responses that are patterned in a hierarchy of units had been noted earlier by John B. Carroll, *The Study of Language* (Cambridge: Harvard University Press, 1953, p. 107).

22 Cf. George A. Miller, *Language and Communication* (New York: McGraw-Hill, 1951).

23 An introduction to the problem can be found in W. N. Locke and A. D. Boothe, eds., *Machine Translation of Languages* (New York: Wiley, 1955). There is a journal devoted exclusively to the subject: *Mechanical Translation*, Massachusetts Institute of Technology, Cambridge, Mass. But see also R. A. Brower, ed., *On Translation* (Cambridge: Harvard University Press, 1959).

24 George A. Miller and J. G. Beebe-Center, Some psychological methods for evaluating the quality of translations, *Mechanical Translation*, 1956, 3, 73–80.

25 Some of the publications on this task, whose attractiveness is not solely a matter of showmanship, are C. E. Shannon, Programming a computer for playing chess, *Philosophical Magazine*, 1950, 41, 256–275; A. Newell, The chess machine, an example of dealing with a complex task by adaptation, *Proceedings of the Western*

Joint Computer Conference, Los Angeles, March 1955, pp. 101–108; J. Kister, P. Stein, S. Ulam, W. Walden, and M. Wells, Experiments in chess, *Journal of the Association for Computing Machinery*, 1957, 4, 174–177; A. Bernstein and M. de V. Roberts, Computer versus chess player, *Scientific American*, June 1958, 198, 96–105; A. Newell, J. C. Shaw, and H. A. Simon, Chess-playing programs and the problem of complexity, *IBM Journal of Research and Development*, 1958, 2, 320–335. See also A. L. Samuel, Some studies in machine learning using the game of checkers, *IBM Journal of Research and Development*, 1959, 3, 210–229.

26 Seven centuries of work on mechanical methods to solve problems in logic are reviewed by Martin Gardner, *Logic Machines and Diagrams* (New York: McGraw-Hill, 1958).

27 Cf. Gelernter and Rochester, *op. cit.*, and Allen Newell, J. C. Shaw, and Herbert A. Simon, *Report on a general problem solving program, Proceedings of the International Conference on Information Processing* (Paris, 1959, in press).

28 For a broad, imaginative, though highly condensed survey of the artificial intelligence problem, see M. L. Minsky, *Heuristic Aspects of the Artificial Intelligence Problem*, Group Report 34–55, Lincoln Laboratory, Massachusetts Institute of Technology, 17 December 1956. Minsky's psychology is generally quite sophisticated.

29 Cf. footnotes 10, 12, 13 in Chapter 1.

30 Since the development by Newell, Shaw, and Simon of their information-processing language (IPL), two other new programming languages have been created around the idea of list structures: At the Massachusetts Institute of Technology, John McCarthy has developed LISP, and at International Business Machines, H. L. Gelernter has developed FLPL. At the time this is written, however, neither of these newer programming languages has been described in publications.

30

STEPS TOWARD ARTIFICIAL INTELLIGENCE

Marvin Minsky

Source: *Proceedings of the IRE* 49(1), 1961: 8–30.

Summary—The problems of heuristic programming—of making computers solve really difficult problems—are divided into five main areas: Search, Pattern-Recognition, Learning, Planning, and Induction.

A computer can do, in a sense, only what it is told to do. But even when we do not know how to solve a certain problem, we may program a machine (computer) to *Search* through some large space of solution attempts. Unfortunately, this usually leads to an enormously inefficient process. With *Pattern-Recognition* techniques, efficiency can often be improved, by restricting the application of the machine's methods to appropriate problems. Pattern-Recognition, together with *Learning*, can be used to exploit generalizations based on accumulated experience, further reducing search. By analyzing the situation, using *Planning* methods, we may obtain a fundamental improvement by replacing the given search with a much smaller, more appropriate exploration. To manage broad classes of problems, machines will need to construct models of their environments, using some scheme for *Induction*.

Wherever appropriate, the discussion is supported by extensive citation of the literature and by descriptions of a few of the most successful heuristic (problem-solving) programs constructed to date.

Introduction

A visitor to our planet might be puzzled about the role of computers in our technology. On the one hand, he would read and hear all about wonderful "mechanical brains" baffling their creators with prodigious intellectual performance. And he (or it) would be warned that these machines must be restrained, lest they overwhelm us by might, persuasion, or even by the revelation of truths too terrible to be borne. On the other hand, our visitor would find the machines being denounced, on all sides, for their slavish obedience, unimaginative literal interpretations, and incapacity for innovation or initiative; in short, for their inhuman dullness.

Our visitor might remain puzzled if he set out to find, and judge for himself, these monsters. For he would find only a few machines (mostly "general-purpose" computers, programmed for the moment to behave according to some specification) doing things that might claim any real intellectual status. Some would be proving mathematical theorems of rather undistinguished character. A few machines might be playing certain games, occasionally defeating their designers. Some might be distinguishing between hand-printed letters. Is this enough to justify so much interest, let alone deep concern? I believe that it is; that we are on the threshold of an era that will be strongly influenced, and quite possibly dominated, by intelligent problem-solving machines. But our purpose is not to guess about what the future may bring; it is only to try to describe and explain what seem now to be our first steps toward the construction of "artificial intelligence."

Along with the development of general-purpose computers, the past few years have seen an increase in effort toward the discovery and mechanization of problem-solving processes. Quite a number of papers have appeared describing theories or actual computer programs concerned with game-playing, theorem-proving, pattern-recognition, and other domains which would seem to require some intelligence. The literature does not include any general discussion of the outstanding problems of this field.

In this article, an attempt will be made to separate out, analyze, and find the relations between some of these problems. Analysis will be supported with enough examples from the literature to serve the introductory function of a review article, but there remains much relevant work not described here. This paper is highly compressed, and therefore, cannot begin to discuss all these matters in the available space.

There is, of course, no generally accepted theory of "intelligence"; the analysis is our own and may be controversial. We regret that we cannot give full personal acknowledgements here—suffice it to say that we have discussed these matters with almost every one of the cited authors.

It is convenient to divide the problems into five main areas: Search, Pattern-Recognition, Learning, Planning, and Induction; these comprise the main divisions of the paper. Let us summarize the entire argument very briefly:

A computer can do, in a sense, only what it is told to do. But even when we do not know exactly how to solve a certain problem, we may program a machine to *Search* through some large space of solution attempts. Unfortunately, when we write a straightforward program for such a search, we usually find the resulting process to be enormously inefficient. With

Pattern-Recognition techniques, efficiency can be greatly improved by restricting the machine to use its methods only on the kind of attempts for which they are appropriate. And with *Learning*, efficiency is further improved by directing Search in accord with earlier experiences. By actually analyzing the situation, using what we call *Planning* methods, the machine may obtain a really fundamental improvement by replacing the originally given Search by a much smaller, more appropriate exploration. Finally, in the section on *Induction*, we consider some rather more global concepts of how one might obtain intelligent machine behavior.

I The problem of search[1]

Summary—If, for a given problem, we have a means for checking a proposed solution, then we can solve the problem by testing all possible answers. But this always takes much too long to be of practical interest. Any device that can reduce this search may be of value. If we can detect relative improvement, then "hill-climbing" (Section I-B) may be feasible, but its use requires some structural knowledge of the search space. And unless this structure meets certain conditions, hill-climbing may do more harm than good.

When we talk of problem-solving in what follows we will usually suppose that all the problems to be solved are initially *well defined* [1]. By this we mean that with each problem we are given some systematic way to decide when a proposed solution is acceptable. Most of the experimental work discussed here is concerned with such well-defined problems as are met in theorem-proving, or in games with precise rules for play and scoring.

In one sense all such problems are trivial. For if there exists a solution to such a problem, that solution can be found eventually by any blind exhaustive process which searches through all possibilities. And it is usually not difficult to mechanize or program such a search.

But for any problem worthy of the name, the search through all possibilities will be too inefficient for practical use. And on the other hand, systems like chess, or nontrivial parts of mathematics, are too complicated for complete analysis. Without complete analysis, there must always remain some core of search, or "trial and error." So we need to find techniques through which the results of *incomplete analysis* can be used to make the search more efficient. The necessity for this is simply overwhelming: a search of all the paths through the game of checkers involves some 10^{40} move choices [2]; in chess, some 10^{120} [3]. If we organized all the particles in our galaxy into some kind of parallel computer operating at the frequency of hard cosmic rays, the latter computation would still take impossibly long; we cannot expect improvements in "hardware" alone to solve all our problems!

Certainly we must use whatever we know in advance to guide the trial generator. And we must also be able to make use of results obtained along the way.[2,3]

A Relative improvement, hill-climbing, and heuristic connections

A problem can hardly come to interest us if we have no background of information about it. We usually have some basis, however flimsy, for detecting *improvement*; some trials will be judged more successful than others. Suppose, for example, that we have a *comparator* which selects as the better, one from any pair of trial outcomes. Now the comparator cannot, alone, serve to make a problem well-defined. No goal is defined. But if the comparator-defined relation between trials is "transitive" (*i.e.*, if *A dominates B* and *B dominates C* implies that *A dominates C*), then we can at least define "progress," and ask our machine, given a time limit, to do the best it can.

But it is essential to observe that a comparator by itself, however shrewd, cannot alone give any improvement over exhaustive search. The comparator gives us information about partial success, to be sure. But we need also some way of using this information to direct the pattern of search in promising directions; to select new trial points which are in some sense "like," or "similar to," or "in the same direction as" those which have given the best previous results. To do this we need some additional structure on the search space. This structure need not bear much resemblance to the ordinary spatial notion of direction, or that of distance, but it must somehow tie together points which are heuristically related.

We will call such a structure a *heuristic connection*. We introduce this term for informal use only—that is why our definition is itself so informal. But we need it. Many publications have been marred by the misuse, for this purpose, of precise mathematical terms, *e.g.*, *metric* and *topological*. The term "connection," with its variety of dictionary meanings, seems just the word to designate a relation without commitment as to the exact nature of the relation.

An important and simple kind of heuristic connection is that defined when a space has coordinates (or parameters) and there is also defined a numerical "success-function" E which is a reasonably smooth function of the coordinates. Here we can use local optimization or *hill-climbing* methods.

B Hill-climbing

Suppose that we are given a black-box machine with inputs $\lambda_1, \ldots, \lambda_n$ and an output $E(\lambda_1, \ldots, \lambda_n)$. We wish to maximize E by adjusting the input values. But we are not given any mathematical description of the function E; hence we cannot use differentiation or related methods. The obvious approach is to explore locally about a point, finding the direction of steepest

ARTICIAL INTELLIGENCE

ascent. One moves a certain distance in that direction and repeats the process until improvement ceases. If the hill is smooth this may be done,
approximately, by estimating the gradient component $\partial E/\partial \lambda_i$ separately for
each coordinate λ_i. There are more sophisticated approaches (one may use
noise added to each variable, and correlate the output with each input, see
Fig. 1), but this is the general idea. It is a fundamental technique, and we
see it always in the background of far more complex systems. Heuristically,
its great virtue is this: the sampling effort (for determining the direction of
the gradient) grows, in a sense, only linearly with the number of parameters.
So if we can solve, by such a method, a certain kind of problem involving
many parameters, then the addition of more parameters of the same kind
ought not cause an inordinate increase in difficulty. We are particularly
interested in problem-solving methods which can be so extended to more
difficult problems. Alas, most interesting systems which involve combin-
ational operations usually grow exponentially more difficult as we add
variables.

A great variety of hill-climbing systems have been studied under the names
of "adaptive" or "self-optimizing" servomechanisms.

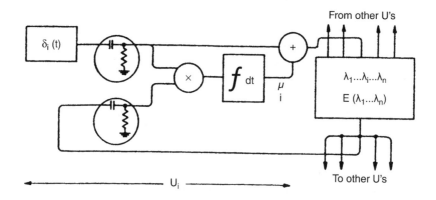

Figure 1 "Multiple simultaneous optimizers" search for a (local) maximum value of
some function $E(\lambda_1, \ldots, \lambda_n)$ of several parameters. Each unit U_i independently "jitters" its parameter λ_i, perhaps randomly, by adding a variation $\delta_i(t)$
to a current mean value μ_i. The changes in the quantities δ_i and E are correlated, and the result is used to (slowly) change μ_i. The filters are to remove dc
components. This simultaneous technique, really a form of coherent detection, usually has an advantage over methods dealing separately and sequentially with each parameter. (Cf. the discussion of "informative feedback" in
Wiener [11], p. 133 ff.)

106

C Troubles with hill-climbing

Obviously, the gradient-following hill-climber would be trapped if it should reach a *local peak* which is not a true or satisfactory optimum. It must then be forced to try larger steps or changes.

It is often supposed that this false-peak problem is the chief obstacle to machine learning by this method. This certainly can be troublesome. But for really difficult problems, it seems to us that usually the more fundamental problem lies in finding any significant peak at all. Unfortunately the known E functions for difficult problems often exhibit what we have called [7] the "*Mesa Phenomenon*" in which a small change in a parameter usually leads to either no change in performance or to a large change in performance. The space is thus composed primarily of flat regions or "mesas." Any tendency of the trial generator to make small steps then results in much aimless wandering without compensating information gains. A profitable search in such a space requires steps so large that hill-climbing is essentially ruled out. The problem-solver must find other methods; hill-climbing might still be feasible with a different heuristic connection.

Certainly, in our own intellectual behavior we rarely solve a tricky problem by a steady climb toward success. I doubt that in any one simple mechanism, *e.g.*, hill-climbing, will we find the means to build an efficient and general problem-solving machine. Probably, an intelligent machine will require a variety of different mechanisms. These will be arranged in hierarchies, and in even more complex, perhaps recursive, structures. And perhaps what amounts to straightforward hill-climbing on one level may sometimes appear (on a lower level) as the sudden jumps of "insight."

II The problem of pattern recognition

Summary—In order not to try all possibilities, a resourceful machine must classify problem situations into categories associated with the domains of effectiveness of the machine's different methods. These pattern-recognition methods must extract the heuristically significant features of the objects in question. The simplest methods simply match the objects against standards or prototypes. More powerful "property-list" methods subject each object to a sequence of tests, each detecting some *property* of heuristic importance. These properties have to be invariant under commonly encountered forms of distortion. Two important problems arise here—inventing new useful properties, and combining many properties to form a recognition system. For complex problems, such methods will have to be augmented by facilities for subdividing complex objects and describing the complex relations between their parts.

Any powerful heuristic program is bound to contain a variety of different methods and techniques. At each step of the problem-solving process the machine will have to decide what aspect of the problem to work on, and then which method to use. A choice must be made, for we usually cannot afford to try all the possibilities. In order to deal with a goal or a problem, that is, to choose an appropriate method, we have to recognize what kind of thing it is. Thus the need to choose among actions compels us to provide the machine with classification techniques, or means of evolving them. It is of overwhelming importance that the machine have classification techniques which are realistic. But "realistic" can be defined only with respect to the environments to be encountered by the machine, and with respect to the methods available to it. Distinctions which cannot be exploited are not worth recognizing. And methods are usually worthless without classification schemes which can help decide when they are applicable.

A Teleological requirements of classification

The useful classifications are those which match the goals and methods of the machine. The objects grouped together in the classifications should have something of heuristic value in common: they should be "similar" in a useful sense; they should depend on relevant or essential features. We should not be surprised, then, to find ourselves using inverse or teleological expressions to define the classes. We really do want to have a grip on "the class of objects which can be transformed into a result of form Y," that is, the class of objects which will satisfy some goal. One should be wary of the familiar injunction against using teleological language in science. While it is true that talking of goals in some contexts may dispose us towards certain kinds of animistic explanations, this need not be a bad thing in the field of problem-solving; it is hard to see how one can solve problems without thoughts of purposes. The real difficulty with teleological definitions is technical, not philosophical, and arises when they have to be used and not just mentioned. One obviously cannot afford to use for classification a method which actually requires waiting for some remote outcome, if one needs the classification precisely for deciding whether to try out that method. So, in practice, the ideal teleological definitions often have to be replaced by practical approximations, usually with some risk of error; that is, the definitions have to be made *heuristically effective*, or economically usable. This is of great importance. (We can think of "heuristic effectiveness" as contrasted to the ordinary mathematical notion of "effectiveness" which distinguishes those definitions which can be realized at all by machine, regardless of efficiency.)

B Patterns and descriptions

It is usually necessary to have ways of assigning *names*—symbolic expressions—to the defined classes. The structure of the names will have a crucial influence on the mental world of the machine, for it determines what kinds of things can be conveniently thought about. There are a variety of ways to assign names. The simplest schemes use what we will call *conventional* (or *proper*) names; here, arbitrary symbols are assigned to classes. But we will also want to use complex *descriptions* or *computed names*; these are constructed for classes by processes which *depend on the class definitions*. To be useful, these should reflect some of the structure of the things they designate, abstracted in a manner relevant to the problem area. The notion of description merges smoothly into the more complex notion of *model*; as we think of it, a model is a sort of active description. It is a thing whose form reflects some of the structure of the thing represented, but which also has some of the character of a working machine.

In Section III we will consider "learning" systems. The behavior of those systems can be made to change in reasonable ways depending on what happened to them in the past. But by themselves, the simple learning systems are useful only in recurrent situations; they cannot cope with any significant novelty. Nontrivial performance is obtained only when learning systems are supplemented with classification or pattern-recognition methods of some inductive ability. For the variety of objects encountered in a nontrivial search is so enormous that we cannot depend on recurrence, and the mere accumulation of records of past experience can have only limited value. Pattern-Recognition, by providing a heuristic connection which links the old to the new, can make learning broadly useful.

What is a "pattern"? We often use the term teleologically to mean a set of objects which can in some (useful) way be treated alike. For each problem area we must ask, "What patterns would be useful for a machine working on such problems?"

The problems of *visual* pattern-recognition have received much attention in recent years and most of our examples are from this area.

C Prototype-derived patterns

The problem of reading *printed* characters is a clearcut instance of a situation in which the classification is based ultimately on a fixed set of "prototypes"—*e.g.*, the dies from which the type font was made. The individual marks on the printed page may show the results of many distortions. Some distortions are rather systematic: change in size, position, orientation. Some are of the nature of noise: blurring, grain, low contrast, etc.

If the noise is not too severe, we may be able to manage the identification by what we call a *normalization and template-matching* process. We first remove the differences related to size and position—that is, we *normalize* the input figure. One may do this, for example, by constructing a similar figure inscribed in a certain fixed triangle (see Fig. 2); or one may transform the figure to obtain a certain fixed center of gravity and a unit second central moment. (There is an additional problem with rotational equivalence where it is not easy to avoid all ambiguities. One does not want to equate "6" and "9". For that matter, one does not want to equate $(0,o)$, or (X, x) or the o's in x_o and x^o, so that there may be context-dependency involved.) Once normalized, the unknown figure can be compared with *templates* for the prototypes and, by means of some measure of *matching*, choose the best fitting template. Each "matching criterion" will be sensitive to particular forms of noise and distortion, and so will each normalization procedure. The inscribing or boxing method may be sensitive to small specks, while the moment method will be especially sensitive to smearing, at least for thin-line figures, etc. The choice of a matching criterion must depend on the kinds of noise and transformations commonly encountered. Still, for many problems we may get acceptable results by using straightforward correlation methods.

When the class of equivalence transformations is very large, *e.g.*, when local stretching and distortion are present, there will be difficulty in finding a uniform normalization method. Instead, one may have to consider a process of adjusting locally for best fit to the template. (While measuring the matching, one could "jitter" the figure locally; if an improvement were found the process could be repeated using a slightly different change, etc.) There is usually no practical possibility of applying to the figure *all* of the admissible transformations. And to recognize the *topological* equivalence of pairs such as those in Fig. 3 is likely beyond any practical kind of iterative

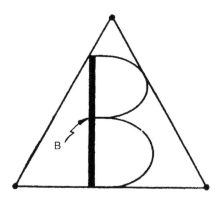

Figure 2 A simple normalization technique. If an object is expanded uniformly, without rotation, until it touches all three sides of a triangle, the resulting figure will be unique, and pattern-recognition can proceed without concern about relative size and position

110

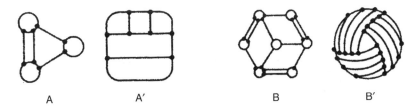

Figure 3 The figures *A, A′* and *B, B′* are topologically equivalent pairs. Lengths have been distorted in an arbitrary manner, but the connectivity relations between corresponding points have been preserved. In Sherman [8] and Haller [39] we find computer programs which can deal with such equivalences

local-improvement or hill-climbing matching procedure. (Such recognitions can be mechanized, though, by methods which follow lines, detect vertices, and build up a *description* in the form, say, of a vertex-connection table.)

The template matching scheme, with its normalization and direct comparison and matching criterion, is just too limited in conception to be of much use in more difficult problems. If the transformation set is large, normalization, or "fitting," may be impractical, especially if there is no adequate heuristic connection on the space of transformations. Furthermore, for each defined pattern, the system has to be presented with a prototype. But if one has in mind a fairly abstract class, one may simply be unable to represent its essential features with one or a very few concrete examples. How could one represent with a single prototype the class of figures which have an even number of disconnected parts? Clearly, the template system has negligible descriptive power. The property-list system frees us from some of these limitations.

D Property lists and "characters"

We define a *property* to be a two-valued function which divides figures into two classes; a figure is said to have or not have the property according to whether the function's value is 1 or 0. Given a number N of distinction properties, we could define as many as 2^n subclasses by their set intersections and, hence, as many as 2^{2^n} *patterns* by combining the properties with AND's and OR's. Thus, if we have three properties, *rectilinear*, *connected*, and *cyclic*, there are eight subclasses (and 256 patterns) defined by their intersections (see Fig. 4).

If the given properties are placed in a fixed order then we can represent any of these elementary regions by a vector, or string of digits. The vector so assigned to each figure will be called the *Character* of that figure (with respect to the sequence of properties in question). (In [9] we use the term *characteristic* for a property without restriction to 2 values.) Thus a square

111

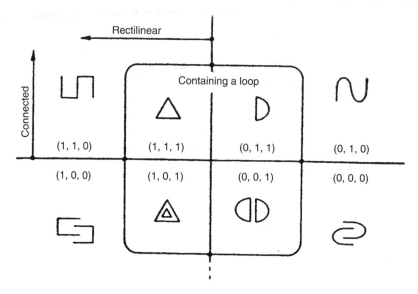

Figure 4 The eight regions represent all the possible configurations of values of the three properties "rectilinear," "connected," "containing a loop." Each region contains a representative figure, and its associated binary "Character" sequence

has the Character (1, 1, 1) and a circle the Character (0, 1, 1) for the given sequence of properties.

For many problems one can use such Characters as names for categories and as primitive elements with which to define an adequate set of patterns. Characters are more than conventional names. They are instead very rudimentary forms of *description* (having the form of the simplest symbolic expression—the *list*) whose structure provides some information about the designated classes. This is a step, albeit a small one, beyond the template method: the Characters are not simple instances of the patterns, and the properties may themselves be very abstract. Finding a good set of properties is the major concern of many heuristic programs.

E Invariant properties

One of the prime requirements of a good property is that it be invariant under the commonly encountered equivalence transformations. Thus for visual Pattern-Recognition we would usually want the object identification to be independent of uniform changes in size and position. In their pioneering paper Pitts and McCulloch [10] describe a general technique for forming invariant properties from noninvariant ones, assuming that the transformation space has a certain (group) structure. The idea behind their mathematical argument is this: suppose that we have a function P of figures, and suppose that for a given figure F we define $[F] = \{F_1, F_2, \dots\}$ to be the set of all figures equivalent to F under the given set of transformations; further, define $P[F]$ to be the set $\{P(F_1), P(F_2), \dots\}$ of values of P on those figures. Finally, define $P*[F]$ to be AVERAGE $(P[F])$. Then we have a new property $P*$ whose values are independent of the selection of F from an equivalence class defined by the transformations. We have to be sure that when different representatives are chosen from a class the collection $[F]$ will always be the same in each case. In the case of continuous transformation spaces, there will have to be a *measure* or the equivalent associated with the set $[F]$ with respect to which the operation AVERAGE is defined, say, as an integration.[4]

This method is proposed [10] as a neurophysiological model for pitch-invariant hearing and size-invariant visual recognition (supplemented with visual centering mechanisms). This model is discussed also by Wiener.[5] Practical application is probably limited to one-dimensional groups and analog scanning devices.

In much recent work this problem is avoided by using properties already invariant under these transformations. Thus a property might count the number of connected components in a picture—this is invariant under size and position. Or a property may count the number of vertical lines in a picture—this is invariant under size and position (but not rotation).

F Generating properties

The problem of generating useful properties has been discussed by Selfridge [12]; we shall summarize his approach. The machine is given, at the start, a few basic transformations $A_1, \dots, A_n$, each of which transforms, in some significant way, each figure into another figure. A_1 might, for example, remove all points *not on a boundary* of a solid region; A_2 might leave only *vertex* points; A_3 might *fill up hollow regions*, etc. (see Fig. 5). Each sequence $A_{i_1}, A_{i_2}, \dots A_{i_k}$ of these forms a new transformation, so that there is available an infinite variety. We provide the machine also with one or more "terminal" operations which convert a picture into a number, so that any sequence of the elementary transformations, followed by a terminal operation, defines a property. (Dineen [13] describes how these processes were programmed in a digital computer.) We can start with a few short sequences, perhaps chosen randomly. Selfridge describes how the machine might learn new useful properties.

> We now feed the machine A's and O's telling the machine each time which letter it is. Beside each sequence under the two letters, the machine builds up distribution functions from the results of applying the sequences to the image. Now, since the sequences were chosen

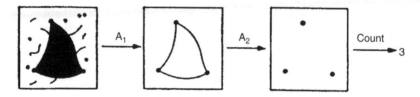

Figure 5 An arbitrary sequence of picture-transformations, followed by a numerical-valued function, can be used as a *property* function for pictures. A_1 removes all points which are not at the edge of a solid region. A_2 leaves only vertex points—at which an arc suddenly changes direction. The function C simply counts the number of points remaining in the picture. All remarks in the text could be generalized to apply to properties, like A_1A_2C, which can have more than two values

completely randomly, it may well be that most of the sequences have very flat distribution functions: that is, they [provide] no information, and the sequences are therefore [by definition] not significant. Let it discard these and pick some others. Sooner or later, however, some sequences will prove significant; that is, their distribution functions will peak up somewhere. What the machine does now is to build up new sequences *like* the significant ones. This is the important point. If it merely chose sequences at random it might take a very long while indeed to find the best sequences. But with some successful sequences, or partly successful ones, to guide it, we hope that the process will be much quicker. The crucial question remains: how do we build up sequences "like" other sequences, but not identical? As of now we think we shall merely build sequences from the transition frequencies of the significant sequences. We shall build up a matrix of transition frequencies from the significant ones, and use those as transition probabilities with which to choose new sequences.

We do not claim that this method is necessarily a very good way of choosing sequences—only that it should do better than not using at all the knowledge of what kind of sequences has worked. It has seemed to us that this is the crucial point of learning.[6]

It would indeed be remarkable if this failed to yield properties more useful than would be obtained from completely random sequence selection. The generating problem is discussed further in Minsky [14]. Newell, Shaw, and Simon [15] describe more deliberate, less statistical, techniques that might be used to discover sets of properties appropriate to a given problem area. One may think of the Selfridge proposal as a system which uses a finite-state language to describe its properties. Solomonoff [55], [18] proposes some techniques for discovering common features of a set of expressions, *e.g.*, of the descriptions of those properties of already established utility; the methods can then be applied to generate new properties with the same common features. I consider the lines of attack in [12], [15], [18] and [55], although still incomplete, to be of the greatest importance.

G Combining properties

One cannot expect easily to find a *small* set of properties which will be just right for a problem area. It is usually much easier to find a large set of properties each of which provides a little useful information. Then one is faced with the problem of finding a way to combine them to make the desired distinctions. The simplest method is to choose, for each class, a typical character (a particular sequence of property values) and then to use some matching procedure, *e.g.*, counting the numbers of agreements and disagreements, to compare an unknown with these chosen "Character prototypes." The linear weighting scheme described just below is a slight generalization on this. Such methods treat the properties as more or less independent evidence for and against propositions; more general procedures (about which we have yet little practical information) must account also for nonlinear relations between properties, *i.e.*, must contain weighting terms for joint subsets of property values.

1) *"Bayes nets" for combining independent properties:* We consider a single experiment in which an object is placed in front of a property-list machine. Each property E_i will have a value, 0 or 1. Suppose that there has been defined some set of "object classes" F_j, and that we want to use the outcome of this experiment to decide in which of these classes the object belongs.

Assume that the situation is basically probabilistic, and that we know the probability p_{ij} that, if the object is in class F_j then the ith property E_i will have value 1. Assume further that these properties are independent; that is, even given F_j, knowledge of the value of E_i tells us nothing more about the value of a different E_i in the same experiment. (This is a strong condition—see below.) Let ϕ_j be the absolute probability that an object is in class F_j. Finally, for this experiment define V to be the particular set of i's for which the E_i's are 1. Then this V represents the Character of the object. From the definition of conditional probability, we have

$$\Pr(F_j, V) = \Pr(V) \cdot \Pr(F_j \mid V) = \Pr(F_j) \cdot \Pr(V \mid F_j).$$

Given the Character V, we want to guess which F_j has occurred (with the least chance of being wrong—the so-called *maximum likelihood* estimate); that is, for which j is $\Pr(F_j \mid V)$ the largest? Since in the above $\Pr(V)$ does not depend on j, we have only to calculate for which j is $\Pr(F_j) \cdot \Pr(V \mid F_j) = \phi_j \Pr(V \mid F_j)$ the largest. Hence, by our independence hypothesis, we have to maximize

$$\phi \cdot \prod_{i \in V} p_{ij} \cdot \prod_{i \in \bar{V}} q_{ij} = \phi_j \prod_{i \in V} \frac{p_{ij}}{q_{ij}} \cdot \prod_{\text{all } i} q_{ij}. \tag{1}$$

These "maximum likelihood" decisions can be made (Fig. 6) by a simple network device.[7]

These nets resemble the general schematic diagrams proposed in the "Pandemonium" model of Selfridge [19] (see his Fig. 3). It is proposed there that some intellectual processes might be carried out by a hierarchy of simultaneously functioning submachines suggestively called "demons." Each unit is set to detect certain patterns in the activity of others and the output of each unit announces the degree of confidence of that unit that it sees what it is looking for. Our E_i units are Selfridge's "data demons." Our units F_j are his

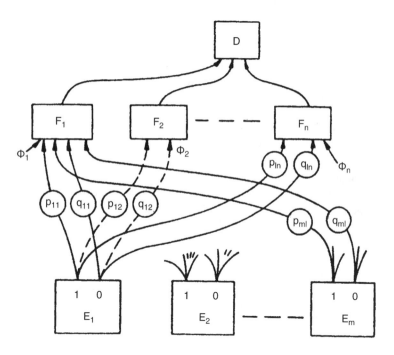

Figure 6 "Net" model for maximum-likelihood decisions based on linear weightings of property values. The input data are examined by each "property filter" E_i. Each E_i has "0" and "1" output channels, one of which is excited by each input. These outputs are weighted by the corresponding p_{ij}'s, as shown in the text. The resulting signals are multiplied in the F_j units, each of which "collects evidence" for a particular figure class. (We could have used here $\log(p_{ij})$, and *added* at the F_j units.) The final decision is made by the topmost unit D, who merely chooses that F_j with the largest score. Note that the logarithm of the coefficient p_{ij}/q_{ij} in the second expression of (1) can be construed as the "weight of the evidence" of E_i in favor of F_j. (See also [21] and [22])

116

"cognitive demons"; each collects from the abstracted data evidence for a specific proposition. The topmost "decision demon" D responds to that one in the multitude below it whose shriek is the loudest.[8]

It is quite easy to add to this "Bayes network model" a mechanism which will enable it to *learn* the optimal connection weightings. Imagine that, after each event, the machine is told which F_j has occurred; we could implement this by sending back a signal along the connections leading to that F_j unit. Suppose that the connection for p_{ij} (or q_{ij}) contains a two-terminal device (or "synapse") which stores a number w_{ij}. Whenever the joint event $(F_j, E_i = 1)$ occurs, we modify w_{ij} by replacing it by $(w_{ij} + 1)\theta$, where θ is a factor slightly less than unity. And when the joint event $(F_j, E_i = 0)$ occurs, we decrement w_{ij} by replacing it with $(w_{ij})\theta$. It is not difficult to show that the expected values of the w_{ij}'s will become proportional to the p_{ij}'s [and in fact, approach $p_{ij} [\theta/(1 - \theta)]$. Hence, the machine tends to learn the optimal weighting on the basis of experience. (One must put in a similar mechanism for estimating the ϕ_i's.) The variance of the normalized weight $w_{ij}[(1 - \theta)/\theta]$ approaches $[(1 - \theta)/(1 + \theta)]p_{ij}q_{ij}$. Thus a small value for θ means rapid learning but is associated with a large variance, hence, with low reliability. Choosing θ close to unity means slow, but reliable, learning. θ is really a sort of memory decay constant, and its choice must be determined by the noise and stability of the environment—much noise requires long averaging times, while a changing environment requires fast adaptation. The two requirements are, of course, incompatible and the decision has to be based on an economic compromise.[9]

2) *Possibilities of using random nets for Bayes decisions:* The nets of Fig. 6 are very orderly in structure. Is all this structure necessary? Certainly if there were a great many properties, *each of which provided very little marginal information*, some of them would not be missed. Then one might expect good results with a mere sampling of all the possible connection paths w_{ij}. And one might thus, *in this special situation*, use a random connection net.

The two-layer nets here resemble those of the "perceptron" proposal of Rosenblatt [22]. In the latter, there is an additional level of connections coming directly from randomly selected points of a "retina." Here the properties, the devices which abstract the visual input data, are simple functions which add some inputs, subtract others, and detect whether the result exceeds a threshold. Eq. (1), we think, illustrates what is of value in this scheme. It does seem clear that a maximum-likelihood type of analysis of the output of the property functions can be handled by such nets. But these nets, with their simple, randomly generated, connections can probably never achieve recognition of such patterns as "the class of figures having two separated parts," and they cannot even achieve the effect of template recognition without size and position normalization (unless sample figures have been presented previously in essentially all sizes and positions). For the chances are extremely small of finding, by random methods, enough properties usefully correlated with patterns appreciably more abstract than those of the prototype-derived

117

kind. And these networks can really only separate out (by weighting) information in the individual input properties: they cannot extract further information present in nonaddictive form. The "perceptron" class of machines have facilities neither for obtaining better-than-chance properties nor for assembling better-than-additive combinations of those it gets from random construction.[10]

For recognizing *normalized* printed or hand-printed characters, single-point properties do surprisingly well [23]: this amounts to just "averaging" many samples. Bledsoe and Browning [24] claim good results with point-pair properties. Roberts [25] describes a series of experiments in this general area. Doyle [26] without normalization but with quite sophisticated properties obtains excellent results; his properties are already substantially size- and position-invariant. A general review of Doyle's work and other pattern-recognition experiments will be found in Selfridge and Neisser [20].

For the complex discrimination, *e.g.*, between one and two connected objects, the property problem is very serious, especially for long wiggly objects such as are handled by Kirsch [27]. Here some kind of recursive processing is required and combinations of simple properties would almost certainly fail even with large nets and long training.

We should not leave the discussion of some decision net models without noting their important limitations. The hypothesis that, for given j, the p_{ij} represent independent events, is a very strong condition indeed. Without this hypothesis we could still construct maximum-likelihood nets, but we would need an additional layer of cells to represent all of the joint events V: that is, we would need to know all the $\Pr(F_j \mid V)$. This gives a general (but trivial) solution, but requires 2^n cells for n properties, which is completely impractical for large systems. What is required is a system which computes some sampling of all the joint conditional probabilities, and uses these to estimate others when needed. The work of Uttley [28], [29], bears on this problem, but his proposed and experimental devices do not yet clearly show how to avoid exponential growth.[11]

H Articulation and attention—limitations of the property-list method

Because of its fixed size, the property-list scheme is limited (for any given set of properties) in the detail of the distinctions it can make. Its ability to deal with a compound scene containing several objects is critically weak, and its direct extensions are unwieldy and unnatural. If a machine can recognize a chair and a table, it surely should be able to tell us that "there is a chair and a table." To an extent, we can invent properties which allow some capacity for superposition of object Characters.[12] But there is no way to escape the information limit.

What is required is clearly 1) a *list (of whatever length is necessary)* of the primitive objects in the scene and 2) a statement about the relations among them. Thus we say of Fig. 7(a), "A rectangle (1) contains two subfigures disposed horizontally. The part on the left is a rectangle (2) which contains two subfigures disposed vertically; the upper a circle (3) and the lower a triangle (4). The part on the right ... etc." Such a description entails an ability to separate or "articulate" the scene into parts. (Note that in this example the articulation is essentially *recursive*; the figure is first divided into two parts; then each part is described using the same machinery.) We can formalize this kind of description in an expression language whose fundamental grammatical form is a pair (R, L) whose first member R names a *relation* and whose second member L is an *ordered list* $(x_1, x_2, \ldots, x_n)$ of the objects or subfigures which bear that relation to one another. We obtain the required flexibility by allowing the members of the list L to contain not only the names of "elementary" figures but also "subexpressions" of the form (R, L) designating complex subfigures. Then our scene above may be described by the expression

$$[\odot, (\square, \rightarrow, (\{\odot, (\square, (\downarrow, (\bigcirc, \triangle)))), (\odot, (\bigcirc, (\nabla, (\bigcirc, \bigcirc, \bigcirc))))\}))]$$

where $(\odot, (x, y))$ means that y is contained in x; $(\rightarrow, (x, y))$ means that y is to the right of x; $(\downarrow, (x, y))$ means that y is below x, and $(\nabla, (x, y, z))$ means that y is to the right of x and z is underneath and between them. The symbols $\square$, $\bigcirc$, and $\triangle$ represent the indicated kinds of primitive geometric objects. This expression-pair description language may be regarded as a simple kind of "list-structure" language. Powerful computer techniques have been developed, originally by Newell, Shaw and Simon, for manipulating

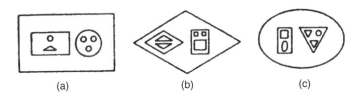

(a)   (b)   (c)

Figure 7 The picture 4(a) is first described verbally in the text. Then, by introducing notation for the relations "inside of," "to the left of" and "above," we construct a symbolic description. Such descriptions can be formed and manipulated by machines. By abstracting out the complex relation between the parts of the figure we can use the same formula to describe the related pictures 4(b) and 4(c), changing only the list of primitive parts. It is up to the programmer to decide at just what level of complexity a part of a picture should be considered "primitive"; this will depend on what the description is to be used for. We could further divide the drawings into vertices, lines, and arcs. Obviously, for some applications the relations would need more metrical information, *e.g.*, specification of lengths or angles

symbolic expressions in such languages for purposes of heuristic programming. (See the remarks at the end of Section IV. If some of the members of a list are themselves lists, they must be surrounded by exterior parentheses, and this accounts for the accumulation of parentheses.)

It may be desirable to construct descriptions in which the complex relation is extracted, *e.g.*, so that we have an expression of the form *FG* where *F* is an expression which at once denotes the composite relation between all the primitive parts listed in *G*. A complication arises in connection with the "binding" of variables, *i.e.*, in specifying the manner in which the elements of *G* participate in the relation *F*. This can be handled in general by the "λ" notation [32] but here we can just use integers to order the variables.

For the given example, we could describe the relational part *F* by an expression

$$\odot(1, \rightarrow (\odot(2, \downarrow (3, 4)), \odot(5, \triangledown(6, 7, 8))))$$

in which we now use a "functional notation"; "$(\odot, (x, y))$" is replaced by "$\odot$ (x, y)," etc., making for better readability. To obtain the desired description, this expression has to be applied to an ordered list of primitive objects, which in this case is ($\square$, $\square$, $\bigcirc$, $\triangle$, $\bigcirc$, $\bigcirc$, $\bigcirc$, $\bigcirc$). This composite functional form allows us to abstract the composite relation. By changing only the object list we can obtain descriptions also of the objects in Fig. 7(b) and 7(c).

The important thing about such "articular" descriptions is that they can be obtained by *repeated application of a fixed set of pattern-recognition techniques*. Thus we can obtain *arbitrarily complex* descriptions from a fixed complexity classification-mechanism. The new element required in the mechanism (beside the capacity to manipulate the list-structures) is the ability to articulate—to "attend fully" to a selected part of the picture and bring all one's resources to bear on that part. In efficient problem-solving programs, we will not usually complete such a description in a single operation. Instead, the depth or detail of description will be under the control of other processes. These will reach deeper, or look more carefully, only when they have to, *e.g.*, when the presently available description is inadequate for a current goal. The author, together with L. Hodes, is working on pattern-recognition schemes using articular descriptions. By manipulating the formal descriptions we can deal with overlapping and incomplete figures, and several other problems of the "Gestalt" type.

It seems likely that as machines are turned toward more difficult problem areas, *passive* classification systems will become less adequate, and we may have to turn toward schemes which are based more on internally-generated hypotheses, perhaps "error-controlled" along the lines proposed by MacKay [89].

Space requires us to terminate this discussion of pattern-recognition and description. Among the important works not reviewed here should be mentioned those of Bomba [33] and Grimsdale, *et al.* [34], which involve elements of description, Unger [35] and Holland [36] for parallel processing schemes, Hebb [37] who is concerned with physiological description models, and the work of the Gestalt psychologists, notably Kohler [38] who have certainly raised, if not solved, a number of important questions. Sherman [8], Haller [39] and others have completed programs using line-tracing operations for topological classification. The papers of Selfridge [12], [43], have been a major influence on work in this general area.

See also Kirsch, *et al.* [27], for discussion of a number of interesting computer image-processing techniques, and see Minot [40] and Stevens [41] for reviews of the reading machine and related problems. One should also examine some biological work, *e.g.*, Tinbergen [42] to see instances in which some discriminations which seem, at first glance very complicated are explained on the basis of a few apparently simple properties arranged in simple decision trees.

III Learning systems

Summary—In order to solve a new problem, one should first try using methods similar to those that have worked on similar problems. To implement this "basic learning heuristic" one must generalize on past experience, and one way to do this is to use success-reinforced decision models. These learning systems are shown to be averaging devices. Using devices which learn also which events are associated with reinforcement, *i.e.*, reward, we can build more autonomous "secondary reinforcement" systems. In applying such methods to complex problems, one encounters a serious difficulty—in distributing credit for success of a complex strategy among the many decisions that were involved. This problem can be managed by arranging for local reinforcement of partial goals within a hierachy, and by grading the training sequence of problems to parallel a process of maturation of the machine's resources.

In order to solve a new problem one uses what might be called the basic learning heuristic—first try using methods similar to those which have worked, in the past, on similar problems. We want our machines, too, to benefit from their past experience. Since we cannot expect new situations to be precisely the same as old ones, any useful learning will have to involve generalization techniques. There are too many notions associated with "learning" to justify defining the term precisely. But we may be sure that any useful learning system will have to use records of the past as *evidence for more general propositions*; it must thus entail some commitment or other about "inductive inference." (See Section V-B.) Perhaps the simplest way of generalizing about a set of entities is through constructing a new one which is an "ideal," or rather, a typical member of that set; the usual way to do this is to smooth away variation by some sort of averaging technique. And indeed we find that most of the *simple* learning devices do incorporate some averaging technique—often that of averaging some sort of product, thus obtaining a sort of correlation. We shall discuss this family of devices here, and some more abstract schemes in Section V.

A Reinforcement

A reinforcement process is one in which some aspects of the behavior of a system are caused to become more (or less) prominent in the future as a consequence of the application of a "reinforcement operator" Z. This operator is required to affect only those aspects of behavior for which instances have actually occurred recently.

The analogy is with "reward" or "extinction" (not punishment) in animal behavior. The important thing about this kind of process is that it is "operant" (a term of Skinner [44]); the reinforcement operator does not initiate behavior, but merely selects that which the Trainer likes from that which has occurred. Such a system must then contain a device M which generates a variety of behavior (say, in interacting with some environment) and a Trainer who makes critical judgments in applying the available reinforcement operators. (See Fig. 8.)

Let us consider a very simple reinforcement model. Suppose that on each presentation of a stimulus S an animal has to make a choice, *e.g.*, to turn left or right, and that its probability of turning right, at the nth trial, is p_n.

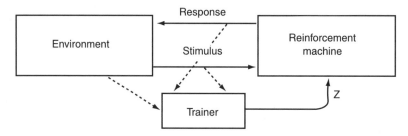

Figure 8 Parts of an "operant reinforcement" learning system. In response to a stimulus from the environment, the machine makes one of several possible responses. It remembers what decisions were made in choosing this response. Shortly thereafter, the Trainer sends to the machine positive or negative reinforcement (reward) signal: this increases or decreases the tendency to make the same decisions in the future. Note that the Trainer need not know how to solve problems, but only how to detect success or failure, or relative improvement; his function is selective. The Trainer might be connected to observe the actual stimulus-response activity or, in a more interesting kind of system, just some function of the state of the environment

Suppose that *we* want it to turn right. Whenever it does this we might "reward" it by applying the operator Z_+:

$$p_{n+1} = Z_+(p_n) = \theta p_n + (1 - \theta) \quad 0 < \theta < 1$$

which moves p a fraction $(1 - \theta)$ of the way towards unity.[13] If we dislike what it does we apply negative reinforcement,

$$p_{n+1} = Z_-(p_n) = \theta p_n$$

moving p the same fraction of the way toward 0. Some theory of such "linear" learning operators, generalized to several stimuli and responses, will be found in Bush and Mosteller [45]. We can show that the learning result is an average weighted by an exponentially-decaying time factor: Let Z_n be ± 1 according to whether the nth event is rewarded or extinguished and replace p_n by $c_n = 2p_n - 1$ so that $-1 \leq c_n \leq 1$, as for a correlation coefficient. Then (with $c_n = 0$) we obtain by induction

$$c_{n+1} = (1 - \theta) \sum_{i=0}^{n} \theta^{n-i} Z_i,$$

and since

$$1/(1 - \theta) \approx \sum_{0}^{n} \theta^{n-i},$$

we can write this as

$$c_{n+1} \approx \frac{\sum \theta^{n-i} Z_i}{\sum \theta^{n-i}}. \tag{1}$$

If the term Z_i is regarded as a product of i) how the creature responded and ii) which kind of reinforcement was given, then c_n is a kind of correlation function (with the decay weighting) of the joint behavior of these quantities. The ordinary, uniformly-weighted average has the same general form but with time-dependent θ:

$$c_{n+1} = \left(1 - \frac{1}{N}\right)c_n + \frac{1}{N}Z_n. \tag{2}$$

In (1) we have again the situation described in Section II-G, 1; a small value of θ gives fast learning, and the possibility of quick adaptation to a changing environment. A near-unity value of θ gives slow learning, but also smooths away uncertainties due to noise. As noted in Section II-G, 1, the response distribution comes to approximate the probabilities of rewards of the alternative responses. (The importance of this phenomenon has, I think, been overrated; it is certainly not an especially rational strategy. One reasonable alternative is that of computing the numbers p_{ij} as indicated, but actually playing at each trial the "most likely" choice. Except in the presence of a hostile opponent, there is usually no reason to play a "mixed" strategy.[14])

In Samuel's coefficient-optimizing program [2] [see Section III-C, 1)], there is a most ingenious compromise between the exponential and the uniform averaging methods: the value of N in (2) above begins at 16 and so remains until $n = 16$, then N is 32 until $n = 32$, and so on until $n = 256$. Thereafter N remains fixed at 256. This nicely prevents violent fluctuations in c_n at the start, approaches the uniform weighting for a while, and finally approaches the exponentially-weighted correlation, all in a manner that requires very little computation effort! Samuel's program is at present the outstanding example of a game-playing program which matches average human ability, and its success (in real time) is attributed to a wealth of such elegancies, both in heuristics and in programming.

The problem of extinction or "unlearning" is especially critical for complex, hierarchical, learning. For, once a generalization about the past has been made, one is likely to build upon it. Thus, one may come to select certain properties as important and begin to use them in the characterization of experience, perhaps storing one's memories in terms of them. If later it is discovered that some other properties would serve better, then one must face the problem of translating, or abandoning, the records based on the older system. This may be a very high price to pay. One does not easily give up an old way of looking at things, if the better one demands much effort and experience to be useful. Thus the *training sequences* on which our machines will spend their infancies, so to speak, must be chosen very shrewdly to insure that early abstractions will provide a good foundation for later difficult problems.

Incidentally, in spite of the space given here for their exposition, I am not convinced that such "incremental" or "statistical" learning schemes should play a central role in our models. They will certainly continue to appear as components of our programs but, I think, mainly by default. The more intelligent one is, the more often he should be able to learn from an experience something rather definite; *e.g.*, to reject or accept a hypothesis, or to change a goal. (The obvious exception is that of a truly statistical environment in which averaging is inescapable. But the heart of problem-solving is always, we think, the combinatorial part that gives rise to searches, and we should usually be able to regard the complexities caused by "noise" as mere annoyances, however irritating they may be.) In this connection we can refer to the discussion of memory in Miller, Galanter and Pribram [46].[15] This seems to be the first major work in Psychology to show the influence of work in the artificial intelligence area, and its programme is generally quite sophisticated.

B Secondary reinforcement and expectation models

The simple reinforcement system is limited by its dependence on the Trainer. If the Trainer can detect only the *solution* of a problem, then we may encounter "mesa" phenomena which will limit performance on difficult problems. (See Section I-C.) One way to escape this is to have the machine learn to generalize on what the Trainer does. Then, in difficult problems, it may be able to give itself partial reinforcements along the way, *e.g.*, upon the solution of relevant subproblems. The machine in Fig. 9 has some such ability. The new unit U is a device that learns which external stimuli are strongly correlated with the various reinforcement signals, and responds to such stimuli by reproducing the corresponding reinforcement signals. (The device U is *not* itself a reinforcement learning device; it is more like a "Pavlovian" conditioning device, treating the Z signals as "unconditioned" stimuli and the S signals as conditioned stimuli.) The heuristic idea is that any signal from the

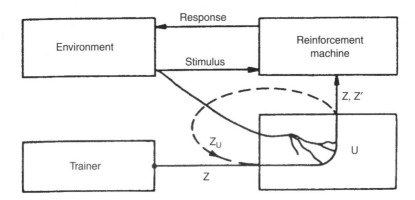

Figure 9 An additional device U gives the machine of Fig. 8 the ability to learn which signals from the environment have been associated with reinforcement. The primary reinforcement signals Z are routed through U. By a Pavlovian conditioning process (not described here), external signals come to produce reinforcement signals like those that have frequently succeeded them in the past. Such signals might be abstract, *e.g.*, verbal encouragement. If the "secondary reinforcement" signals are allowed, in turn, to acquire further external associations (through, *e.g.*, a channel Z_U, as shown) the machine might come to be able to handle chains of subproblems. But something must be done to stabilize the system against the positive symbolic feedback loop formed by the path Z_U. The profound difficulty presented by this stabilization problem may be reflected in the fact that, in lower animals, it is very difficult to demonstrate such chaining effects

environment which in the past has been well correlated with (say) positive reinforcement is likely to be an indication that something good has just happened. If the training on early problems was such that this is realistic, then the system eventually should be able to detach itself from the Trainer, and become autonomous. If we further permit "chaining" of the secondary reinforcers," e.g., by admitting the connection shown as a dotted line in Fig. 9, the scheme becomes quite powerful, in principle. There are obvious pitfalls in admitting such a degree of autonomy; the values of the system may drift to a "nonadaptive" condition.

C Prediction and expectation

The evaluation unit U is supposed to acquire an ability to tell whether a situation is good or bad. This evaluation could be applied to *imaginary* situations as well as to real ones. If we could estimate the consequences of a proposed action (without its actual execution), we could use U to evaluate the (estimated) resulting situation. This could help in reducing the effort in search, and we would have in effect a machine with some ability to look ahead, or *plan*. In order to do this we need an additional device P which, given the descriptions of a situation and an action, will predict a description of the likely result. (We will discuss schemes for doing this in Section IV-C.) The device P might be constructed along the lines of a reinforcement learning device. In such a system the required reinforcement signals would have a very attractive character. For the machine must reinforce P positively when the *actual outcome resembles that which was predicted*—accurate expectations are rewarded. If we could further add a premium to reinforcement of those predictions which have a novel aspect, we might expect to discern behavior motivated by a sort of curiosity. In the reinforcement of mechanisms for confirmed novel expectations (or new explanations) we may find the key to simulation of intellectual motivation.[16]

Samuel's Program for Checkers: In Samuel's "generalization learning" program for the game of checkers [2] we find a novel heuristic technique which could be regarded as a simple example of the "expectation reinforcement" notion. Let us review very briefly the situation in playing two-person board games of this kind. As noted by Shannon [3] such games are in principle finite, and a best strategy can be found by following out all possible continuations—if he goes there I can go there, or there, etc.—and then "backing-up" or "minimaxing" from the terminal positions, won, lost, or drawn. But in practice the full exploration of the resulting colossal "move-tree" is out of the question. No doubt, some exploration will always be necessary for such games. But the tree must be pruned. We might simply put a limit on depth of exploration—the number of moves and replies. We might also limit the number of alternatives explored from each position—this requires some heuristics for selection of "plausible moves."[17] Now, if the

126

backing-up technique is still to be used (with the incomplete move-tree) one has to substitute for the absolute "win, lose, or draw" criterion some other "static" way of evaluating nonterminal positions.[18] (See Fig. 10.) Perhaps the simplest scheme is to use a weighted sum of some selected set of "property" functions of the positions—mobility, advancement, center control, and the like. This is done in Samuel's program, and in most of its predecessors. Associated with this is a multiple-simultaneous-optimizer method for discovering a good coefficient assignment (using the correlation technique noted in Section III-A). But the source of reinforcement signals in [2] is novel. One cannot afford to play out one or more entire games for each single learning step. Samuel measures instead *for each more* the difference between what the evaluation function yields *directly* of a position and what it *predicts* on the basis of an extensive continuation exploration, *i.e.*, backing-up. The sign of this error, "Delta," is used for reinforcement: thus the system may learn something at *each move.*[19]

D The basic credit-assignment problem for complex reinforcement learning systems

In playing a complex game such as chess or checkers, or in writing a computer program, one has a definite success criterion—the game is won or lost. But in the course of play, each ultimate success (or failure) is associated with a vast number of internal decisions. If the run is successful, how can we assign credit for the success among the multitude of decisions? As Newell noted,

> It is extremely doubtful whether there is enough information in "win, lose, or draw" when referred to the whole play of the game to permit any learning at all over available time scales. . . . For learning to take place, each play of the game must yield much more information. This is . . . achieved by breaking the problem into components. The unit of success is the goal. If a goal is achieved, its subgoals are reinforced; if not they are inhibited. (Actually, what is reinforced is the transformation rule that provided the subgoal.) . . . This also is true of the other kinds of structure: every tactic that is created provides information about the success or failure of tactic search rules: every opponent's action provides information about success or failure of likelihood inferences; and so on. The amount of information relevant to learning increases directly with the number of mechanisms in the chess-playing machine.[20]

We are in complete agreement with Newell on this approach to the problem.[21]

It is my impression that many workers in the area of "self-organizing"

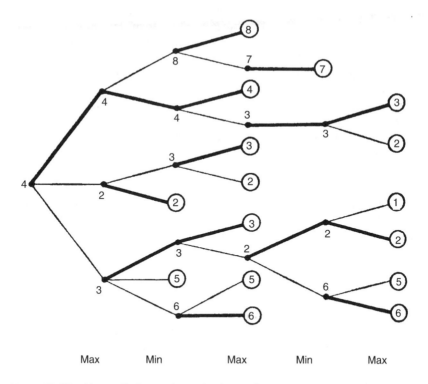

Max   Min   Max   Min   Max

Figure 10 "Backing-up" the static evaluations of proposed moves in a game-tree. From the vertex at the left, representing the present position in a board game, radiate three branches, representing the *player's* proposed moves. Each of these might be countered by a variety of *opponent* moves, and so on. According to some program, a finite tree is generated. Then the worth to the player of each terminal board position is estimated. (See test.) If the opponent has the same values, he will choose to minimize the score, while the player will always try to maximize. The heavy lines show how this minimaxing process backs up until a choice is determined for the present position.

The full tree for chess has the order of 10^{120} branches—beyond the reach of any man or computer. There is a fundamental heuristic exchange between the effectiveness of the evaluation function and the extent of the tree. A very weak evaluation (*e.g.*, one which just compares the players' values of pieces) would yield a devastating game if the machine could explore all continuations out to, say, 20 levels. But only 6 levels, roughly within range of our presently largest computers, would probably not give a brilliant game: less exhaustive strategies, perhaps along the lines of [49], would be more profitable systems and "random neural nets" do not feel the urgency of this problem. Suppose that one million decisions are involved in a complex task (such as winning a chess game). Could we assign to each decision element one-millionth of the credit for the completed task? In certain special situations we can do just this—e.g., in the machines of [22], [25] and [92], etc., where the connections being reinforced are to a sufficient degree independent. But the problem-solving ability is correspondingly weak.

For more complex problems, with decisions in hierarchies (rather than summed on the same level) and with increments small enough to assure probable convergence, the running times would become fantastic. For complex problems we will have to define "success" in some rich local sense. Some of the difficulty may be evaded by using carefully graded "training sequences" as described in the following section.

Friedberg's Program-Writing Program: An important example of comparative failure in this credit-assignment matter is provided by the program of Friedberg [53], [54] to solve program-writing problems. The problem here is to write programs for a (simulated) very simple digital computer. A simple problem is assigned, *e.g.,* "compute the AND of two bits in storage and put the result in an assigned location." A generating device produces a random (64-instruction) program. The program is run and its success or failure is noted. The success information is used to reinforce *individual instructions* (in fixed locations) so that each success tends to increase the chance that the instructions of successful programs will appear in later trials. (We lack space for details of how this is done.) Thus the program tries to find "good" instructions, more or less independently, for each location in program memory. The machine did learn to solve some extremely simple problems. But it took of the order of 1000 times longer than pure chance would expect. In part II of [54], this failure is discussed, and attributed in part to what we called (Section I-C) the "Mesa phenomena." In changing just one instruction at a time the machine had not taken large enough steps in its search through program space.

The second paper goes on to discuss a sequence of modifications in the program generator and its reinforcement operators. With these, and with some "priming" (starting the machine off on the right track with some useful instructions), the system came to be only a little worse than chance. The authors of [54] conclude that with these improvements "the generally superior performance of those machines with a success-number reinforcement mechanism over those without does serve to indicate that such a mechanism can provide a basis for constructing a learning machine." I disagree with this conclusion. It seems to me that each of the "improvements" can be interpreted as serving only to increase the step size of the search, that is, the randomness of the mechanism; this helps to avoid the Mesa phenomenon and thus approach chance behavior. But it certainly does not show that the "learning mechanism" is working—one would want at least to see some better-than-chance results before arguing this point. The trouble, it seems, is with credit-assignment. The credit for a working program can only be assigned to functional groups of instructions, *e.g.*, subroutines, and as these operate in hierarchies we should not expect individual instruction reinforcement to work well.[22] It seems surprising that it was not recognized in [54] that the doubts raised earlier were probably justified! In the last section of [54] we see some real success obtained by breaking the problem into parts and solving them sequentially. (This successful demonstration using division into subproblems does not use any reinforcement mechanism at all.) Some experiments of similar nature are reported in [94].

It is my conviction that no scheme for learning, or for pattern-recognition, can have very general utility unless there are provisions for recursive, or at least hierarchical, use of previous results. We cannot expect a learning system to come to handle very hard problems without preparing it with a reasonably graded sequence of problems of growing difficulty. The first problem must be one which can be solved in reasonable time with the initial resources. The next must be capable of solution in reasonable time by using reasonably simple and accessible combinations of methods developed in the first, and so on. The only alternatives to this use of an adequate "training sequence" are 1) advanced resources, given initially, or 2) the fantastic exploratory processes found perhaps only in the history on organs evolution.[23] And even there, if we accept the general view of Darlington [56] who emphasizes the heuristic aspects of genetic systems, we must have developed early (in, *e.g.*, the phenomena of meiosis and crossing-over) quite highly specialized mechanisms providing for the segregation of groupings related to solutions of subproblems. Recently, much effort has been devoted to the construction of training sequences in connection with programming "teaching machines." Naturally, the psychological literature abounds with theories of how complex behavior is built up from simpler. In our own area, perhaps the work of Solomonoff [55], while overly cryptic, shows the most thorough consideration of this dependency on *training sequences*.

IV Problem-solving and planning

Summary—The solution, by machine, of really complex problems will require a variety of administration facilities. During the course of solving a problem, one becomes involved with a large assembly of interrelated subproblems. From these, at each stage, a very few must be chosen for investigation. This decision must be based on 1) estimates of relative difficulties and 2) estimates of centrality of the different candidates for attention. Following subproblem selection (for which several heuristic methods are proposed), one must choose methods appropriate to the selected problems. But for really difficult problems, even these step-by-step heuristics for reducing search will fail, and the machine must have resources for analyzing the problem structure in the large—in short, for "planning." A number of schemes for planning are discussed, among them the use of models—analogous, semantic, and abstract. Certain abstract models, "Character Algebras," can be constructed by the machine itself, on the basis of experience or analysis. For concreteness, the discussion begins with a description of a simple but significant system (LT) which encounters some of these problems.

A The "Logic Theory" program of Newell, Shaw and Simon

It is not surprising that the testing grounds for early work on mechanical problem-solving have usually been areas of mathematics, or games, in which the rules are defined with absolute clarity. The "Logic Theory" machine of [57], [58], called "LT" below, was a first attempt to prove theorems in logic, by frankly heuristic methods. Although the program was not by human standards a brilliant success (and did not surpass its designers), it stands as a landmark both in heuristic programming and also in the development of modern automatic programming.

The problem domain here is that of discovering proofs in the Russell-Whitehead system for the propositional calculus. That system is given as a set of (five) axioms and (three) rules of inference: the latter specify how certain transformations can be applied to produce new theorems from old theorems and axioms.

The LT program is centered around the idea of "working backwards" to find a proof. Given a theorem T to be proved, LT searches among the axioms and previously established theorems for one from which T can be deduced by a single application of one of three simple "Methods" (which embody the given rules of inference). If one is found, the problem is solved. Or the search might fail completely. But finally, the search may yield one or more "problems" which are usually propositions from which T may be deduced directly. If one of these can, in turn, be proved a theorem the main problem will be solved. (The situation is actually slightly more complex.) Each such subproblem is adjoined to the "subproblem list" (after a limited preliminary attempt) and LT works around to it later. The full power of LT, such as it is, can be applied to each subproblem, for LT can use itself as a subroutine in a recursive fashion.

The heuristic technique of working backwards yields something of a teleological process, and LT is a forerunner of more complex systems which construct hierarchies of goals and subgoals. Even so, the basic administrative structure of the program is no more than a nested set of searches through lists in memory. We shall first outline this structure and then mention a few heuristics that were used in attempts to improve performance.

131

1 Take the next problem from problem list.
(If there are no more problems, EXIT with total failure.)
2 Choose the next of the three basic Methods.
(If no more methods, go to 1.)
3 Choose the next member of the list of axioms and previous theorems.
(If no more, go to 2.)
Then apply the Method to the problem, using the chosen theorem or axiom.
  If problem is solved, EXIT with complete proof.
  If no result, go to 3.
  If new subproblem arises, go to 4.
4 Try the special (substitution) Method on the subproblem.
  If problem is solved, EXIT with complete proof.
  If no result, put the subproblem *at the end* of the problem list and go to 3.

Among the heuristics that were studied were 1) a *similarity test* to reduce the work in step 4 (which includes another search through the theorem list), 2) a *simplicity test* to select apparently easier problems from the problem list, and 3) a *strong nonprovability test* to remove from the problem list expressions which are probably false and hence not provable. In a series of experiments "learning" was used to find which earlier theorems had been most useful and should be given priority in step 3. We cannot review the effects of these changes in detail. Of interest was the balance between the extra cost for administration of certain heuristics and the resultant search reduction: this balance was quite delicate in some cases when computer memory became saturated. The system seemed to be quite sensitive to the training sequence— the order in which problems were given. And some heuristics which gave no significant over-all improvement did nevertheless affect the class of solvable problems. Curiously enough, the general efficiency of LT was not greatly improved by any or all of these devices. But all this practical experience is reflected in the design of the much more sophisticated "GPS" system (described briefly in Section IV-D, 2).

Wang [59] has criticized the LT project on the grounds that there exist, as he and others have shown, mechanized proof methods which, for the particular run of problems considered, use far less machine effort than does LT and which have the advantage that they will ultimately find a proof for any provable proposition. (LT does not have this exhaustive "decision procedure" character and can fail ever to find proofs for some theorems.) The authors of [58], perhaps unaware of the existence of even moderately efficient exhaustive methods, supported their arguments by comparison with a particularly inefficient exhaustive procedure. Nevertheless, I feel that some of Wang's criticisms are misdirected. He does not seem to recognize that the authors of LT are not so much interested in proving these theorems as they are in the general problem of solving difficult problems. The combinatorial system of

Russell and Whitehead (with which LT deals) is far less simple and elegant than the system used by Wang.[24] (Note, *e.g.*, the emphasis in [49] and [60].) Wang's problems, while *logically* equivalent, are *formally* much simpler. His methods do not include any facilities for using previous results (hence they are sure to degrade rapidly at a certain level of problem complexity), while LT is fundamentally oriented around this problem. Finally, because of the very effectiveness of Wang's method on the *particular* set of theorems in question, he simply did not have to face the fundamental heuristic problem of *when to decide to give up on a line of attack.* Thus the formidable performance of his program [59] perhaps diverted his attention from heuristic problems that must again spring up when real mathematics is ultimately encountered.

This is not meant as a rejection of the importance of Wang's work and discussion. He and others working on "mechanical mathematics" have discovered that there are proof procedures which are much more efficient than has been suspected. Such work will unquestionably help in constructing intelligent machines, and these procedures will certainly be preferred, when available, to "unreliable heuristic methods." Wang, Davis and Putnam, and several others are now pushing these new techniques into the far more challenging domain of theorem-proving in the predicate calculus (for which exhaustive decision procedures are no longer available). We have no space to discuss this area,[25] but it seems clear that a program to solve real mathematical problems will have to combine the mathematical sophistication of Wang with the heuristic sophistication of Newell, Shaw and Simon.[26]

B Heuristics for subproblem selection

In designing a problem-solving system, the programmer often comes equipped with a set of more or less distinct "Methods"—his real task is to find an efficient way for the program to decide where and when the different methods are to be used.

Methods which do not dispose of a problem may still transform it to create new problems or subproblems. Hence, during the course of solving one problem we may become involved with a large assembly of interrelated subproblems. A "parallel" computer, yet to be conceived, might work on many at a time. But even the parallel machine must have procedures to allocate its resources because it cannot simultaneously apply all its methods to all the problems. We shall divide this administrative problem into two parts: the selection of those subproblem(s) which seem most critical, attractive, or otherwise immediate, and, in the next section, the choice of which method to apply to the selected problem.

In the basic program for LT (Section IV-A), subproblem selection is very simple. New problems are examined briefly and (if not solved at once) are placed at the end of the (linear) problem list. The main program proceeds along this list (step 1), attacking the problems in the order of their generation. More powerful systems will have to be more judicious (both in generation and selection of problems) for only thus can excessive branching be restrained.[27] In more complex systems we can expect to consider for each subproblem, at least these two aspects: 1) its apparent "centrality"—how will its solution promote the main goal, and 2) its apparent "difficulty"—how much effort is it liable to consume. We need heuristic methods to estimate each of these quantities and, further, to select accordingly one of the problems and allocate to it some reasonable quantity of effort.[28] Little enough is known about these matters, and so it is not entirely for lack of space that the following remarks are somewhat cryptic.

Imagine that the problems and their relations are arranged to form some kind of directed-graph structure [14], [57], [62]. The main problem is to establish a "valid" path between two initially distinguished nodes. Generation of new problems is represented by the addition of new, not-yet-valid paths, or by the insertion of new nodes in old paths. Then problems are represented by not-yet-valid paths, and "centrality" by location in the structure. Associate with each connection, quantities describing its current validity state (solved, plausible, doubtful, etc.) and its current estimated difficulty.

1) Global Methods: The most general problem selection methods are "global"—at each step they look over the entire structure. There is one such simple scheme which works well on at least one rather degenerate interpretation of our problem graph. This is based on an electrical analogy suggested to us by a machine designed by Shannon (related to one described in [63] which describes quite a variety of interesting gameplaying and learning machines) to play a variant of the game marketed as "Hex" (and known among mathematicians as "Nash"). The initial board position can be represented as a certain network of resistors. (See Fig. 11.) One player's goal is to construct a *short-circuit* path between two given boundaries; the opponent tries to open the circuit between them. Each move consists of shorting (or opening), irreversibly, one of the remaining resistors. Shannon's machine applies a potential between the boundaries and selects that resistor which carries the largest current. Very roughly speaking, this resistor is likely to be most critical because changing it will have the largest effect on the resistance of the net and, hence, in the goal direction of shorting (or opening) the circuit. And although this argument is not perfect, nor is this a perfect model of the real combinatorial situation, the machine does play extremely well. (It can make unsound moves in certain artificial situations, but no one seems to have been able to force this during a game.)

The use of such a global method for problem-selection requires that the available "difficulty estimates" for related subproblems be arranged to combine in roughly the manner of resistance values. Also, we could regard this machine as using an "analog model" for "planning." (See Section IV-D.)[29]

2) Local, and "Hereditary," Methods: The prospect of having to study at

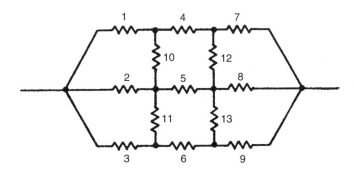

Figure 11 This board game (due to C. E. Shannon) is played on a network of equal
resistors. The first player's goal is to open the circuit between the endpoints;
the second player's goal is to short the circuit. A move consists of opening
or shorting a resistor. If the first player begins by opening resistor 1, the
second player might counter by shorting resistor 4, following the strategy
described in the text. The remaining move pairs (if *both* players use that
strategy) would be (5, 8) (9, 13) (6, 3) (12, 10 or 2) (2 or 10 *win*). In this game
the first player should be able to force a win, and the maximum-current
strategy seems always to do so, even on larger networks

each step the whole problem structure is discouraging, especially since the
structure usually changes only slightly after each attempt. One naturally
looks for methods which merely *update* or modify a small fragment of the
stored record. Between the extremes of the "first-come-first-served"
problem-list method and the full global-survey methods, lie a variety of
compromise techniques. Perhaps the most attractive of these are what we will
call the *Inheritance* methods—essentially recursive devices.

In an Inheritance method, the effort assigned to a subproblem is determined only by its immediate ancestry: at the time each problem is created it is
assigned a certain total quantity Q of time or effort. When a problem is later
split into subproblems, such quantities are assigned to them by some local
process which *depends only on their relative merits and on what remains of Q*.
Thus the centrality problem is managed implicitly. Such schemes are quite
easy to program, especially with the new programming systems such as IPL
[64] and LISP [32] (which are themselves based on certain hereditary or
recursive operations). Special cases of the inheritance method arise when one
can get along with a simple all-or-none Q, *e.g.*, a "stop condition"—this
yields the exploratory method called "back-tracking" by Golumb [65]. The
decoding procedure of Wozencraft [66] is another important variety of
Inheritance method.

In the complex exploration process proposed for chess by Newell, Shaw, and Simon [49] we have a form of Inheritance method with a *non-numerical stop-condition*. Here, the subproblems inherit *sets of goals to be achieved*. This teleological control has to be administered by an additional goal-selection system and is further complicated by a global (but reasonably simple) stop rule of the backing-up variety [Section III-C]. (Note: we are identifying here the move-tree-limitation problem with that of problem-selection.) Even though extensive experimental results are not yet available, we feel that the scheme of [49] deserves careful study by anyone planning serious work in this area. It shows only the beginning of the complexity sure to come in our development of intelligent machines.[30]

C "Character-method" machines

Once a problem is selected, we must decide which method to try first. This depends on our ability to classify or characterize problems. We first compute the Character of our problem (by using some pattern recognition technique) and then consult a "Character-Method" table or other device which is supposed to tell us which method(s) are most effective on problems of that Character. This information might be built up from experience, given initially by the programmer, deduced from "advice" [70], or obtained as the solution to some other problem, as suggested in the GPS proposal [68]. In any case, this part of the machine's behavior, regarded from the outside, can be treated as a sort of stimulus-response, or "table look-up," activity.

If the Characters (or descriptions) have too wide a variety of values, there will be a serious problem of filling a Character-Method table. One might then have to reduce the detail of information, *e.g.*, by using only a few important properties. Thus the *Differences* of GPS [see Section IV-D, 2] describe no more than is necessary to define a single goal, and a priority scheme selects just one of these to characterize the situation. Gelernter and Rochester [62] suggest using a property-weighting scheme, a special case of the "Bayes net" described in Section II-G.

D Planning

Ordinarily one can solve a complicated problem only by dividing it into a number of parts, each of which can be attacked by a smaller search (or be further divided). Generally speaking, a successful division will reduce the search time not by a mere fraction, but by a *fractional exponent*. In a graph with 10 branches descending from each node, a 20-step search might involve 10^{20} trials, which is out of the question, while the insertion of just four *lemmas* or *sequential subgoals* might reduce the search to only 5.10^4 trials, which is within reason for machine exploration. Thus it will be worth a relatively enormous effort to find such "islands" in the solution of complex problems.[31] Note that even if one encountered, say, 10^6 failures of such procedures before

136

success, one would still have gained a factor of perhaps 10^{10} in overall trial reduction! *Thus practically any ability at all to "plan," or "analyze," a problem will be profitable*, if the problem is difficult. It is safe to say that all simple, unitary, notions of how to build an intelligent machine will fail, rather sharply, for some modest level of problem difficulty. Only schemes which actively pursue an analysis toward obtaining a set of *sequential goals* can be expected to extend smoothly into increasingly complex problem domains.

Perhaps the most straightforward concept of planning is that of using a *simplified model* of the problem situation. Suppose that there is available, for a given problem, some other problem of "essentially the same character" but with less detail and complexity. Then we could proceed first to solve the simpler problem. Suppose, also, that this is done using a second set of methods, which are also simpler, but in some correspondence with those for the original. *The solution to the simpler problem can then be used as a "plan" for the harder one.* Perhaps each step will have to be expanded in detail. But the multiple searches will *add, not multiply*, in the total search time. The situation would be ideal if the model were, mathematically, a *homomorphism* of the original. But even without such perfection the model solution should be a valuable guide. In mathematics one's proof procedures usually run along these lines: one first assumes, *e.g.*, that integrals and limits always converge, in the planning stage. Once the outline is completed, in this simple-minded model of mathematics, then one goes back to try to "make rigorous" the steps of the proof, *i.e.*, to replace them by chains of argument using genuine rules of inference. And even if the plan fails, it may be possible to patch it by replacing just a few of its steps.

Another aid to planning is the *semantic*, as opposed to the homomorphic, model [14], [9]. Here we may have an *interpretation* of the current problem within another system, not necessarily simpler, but with which we are more familiar and have already more powerful methods. Thus, in connection with a plan for the proof of a theorem, we will want to know whether the proposed lemmas, or islands in the proof, are actually *true*; if not, the plan will surely fail. We can often easily tell if a proposition is true by looking at an interpretation. Thus the truth of a proposition from plane geometry can be supposed, at least with great reliability, by actual measurement of a few constructed drawings (or the analytic geometry equivalent). The geometry machine of Gelernter and Rochester [62], [69] uses such a semantic model with excellent results; it follows closely the lines proposed in [14].

1) The "Character-Algebra" Model: Planning with the aid of a model is of the greatest value in reducing search. Can we construct machines which find their own models? I believe the following will provide a general, straightforward way to construct certain kinds of useful abstract models. The critical requirement is that we be able to compile a "Character-Method Matrix" (in addition to the simple Character-Method table in Section IV-C). *The CM matrix is an array of entries which predict with some reliability what will hap-pen when methods are applied to problems.* Both of the matrix dimensions are indexed by problem Characters; if there is a method *which usually transforms problems of character* C_i *into problems of character* C_j then let the matrix entry C_{ij} be the name of that method (or a list of such methods). If there is no such method the corresponding entry is null.

Now suppose that there is no entry for C_{ij}—meaning that we have no *direct* way to transform a problem of type C_i into one of type C_j. Multiply the matrix by itself. If the new matrix has a non-null (i, j) entry then there must be a sequence of *two* methods which effects the desired transformation. If that fails, we may try higher powers. Note that [if we put unity for the (i, i) terms] we can reach the 2^n matrix power with just n multiplications. We don't need to define the symbolic multiplication operation; one may instead use arithmetic entries—putting *unity for any non-null entry* and zero for any null entry in the original matrix. This yields a simple connection, or flow dia-gram, matrix, and its nth power tells us something about its set of paths of length 2^n.[32] (Once a non-null entry is discovered, there exist efficient ways to find the corresponding sequences of methods. The problem is really just that of finding paths through a maze, and the method of Moore [71] would be quite efficient. Almost any problem can be converted into a problem of find-ing a chain between two terminal expressions in some formal system.) If the Characters are taken to be abstract representations of the problem expres-sions, this "Character-Algebra" model can be as abstract as are the available pattern-recognition facilities. See [14] and [9].

The critical problem in using the Character-Algebra model for planning is, of course, the *prediction-reliability of the matrix entries.* One cannot expect the Character of a result to be strictly determined by the Character of the original and the method used. And the reliability of the predictions will, in any case, deteriorate rapidly as the matrix power is raised. But, as we have noted, any plan at all is so much better than none that the system should do very much better than exhaustive search, even with quite poor prediction quality.

This matrix formulation is obviously only a special case of the character planning idea. More generally, one will have descriptions, rather than fixed characters, and one must then have more general methods to calculate from a description what is likely to happen when a method is applied.

2) Characters and Differences: In the GPS (General Problem Solver) pro-posal of Newell, Shaw, and Simon [68], [15], we find a slightly different framework: they use a notion of Difference between two problems (or expressions) where we speak of the Character of a single problem. These views are equivalent if we take our problems to be links or connections between expressions. But this notion of Difference (as the Character of a pair) does lend itself more smoothly to teleological reasoning. For what is the goal defined by a problem but to *reduce the "difference" between the present state and the desired state?* The underlying structure of GPS is pre-

138

cisely what we have called a "Character-Method Machine" in which each kind of Difference is associated in a table with one or more methods which are known to "reduce" that Difference. Since the characterization here depends always on 1) the current problem expression and 2) the desired end result, it is reasonable to think, as its authors suggest, of GPS as using "means-end" analysis.

To illustrate the use of Differences, we shall review an example [15]. The problem, in elementary propositional calculus, is to prove that from $S\wedge(-P \supset Q)$ we can deduce $(Q\vee P)\wedge S$. The program looks at both of these expressions with a recursive *matching* process which branches out from the main connectives. The first Difference it encounters is that S occurs on different sides of the main connective "$\wedge$". It therefore looks in the Difference-Method table under the heading "change position." It discovers there a method which uses the theorem $(A\wedge B) \equiv (B\wedge A)$ which is obviously useful for removing, or "reducing," differences of position. GPS applies this method, obtaining $(- P \supset Q)\wedge S$. GPS now asks what is the Difference between this new expression and the goal. This time the matching procedure gets down into the connectives inside the left-hand members and finds a Difference between the connectives "$\supset$" and "$\vee$". It now looks in the CM table under the heading "Change Connective" and discovers the appropriate method using $(- A \supset B) \equiv (A\vee B)$. It applies this method, obtaining $(P\vee Q)\wedge S$. In the final cycle, the difference-evaluating procedure discovers the need for a "change position" inside the left member, and applies a method using $(A\vee B) \equiv (B\vee A)$. This completes the solution of the problem.[33]

Evidently, the success of this "means-end" analysis in reducing general search will depend on the degree of specificity that can be written into the Difference-Method table—basically the same requirement for an effective Character-Algebra.

It may be possible to *plan* using Differences, as well.[33] One might imagine a "Difference-Algebra" in which the predictions have the form $D = D'D''$. One must construct accordingly a difference-factorization algebra for discovering longer chains $D = D_1 \ldots D_n$ and corresponding method plans. We should note that one *cannot* expect to use such planning methods with such primitive Differences as are discussed in [15]; for these cannot form an adequate Difference-Algebra (or Character Algebra). Unless the characterizing expressions have many levels of descriptive detail, the matrix powers will too swiftly become degenerate. This degeneracy will ultimately limit the capacity of any formal planning device.

One may think of the general planning heuristic as embodied in a recursive process of the following form. Suppose we have a problem P:

1   Form a plan for problem P.
2   Select first (next) step of the plan.
    (If no more steps, exit with "success.")

3   Try the suggested method(s):
      Success: return to b), *i.e.*, try next step in the plan.
      Failure: return to a), *i.e.*, form new plan, or perhaps change current plan to avoid this step.
      Problem judged too difficult: *Apply this entire procedure to the problem of the current step.*

Observe that such a program schema is essentially recursive; it uses itself as a subroutine (explicitly, in the last step) in such a way that its current state has to be stored, and restored when it returns control to itself.[34]

Miller, Galanter and Pribram[35] discuss possible analogies between human problem-solving and some heuristic planning schemes. It seems certain that, for at least a few years, there will be a close association between theories of human behavior and attempts to increase the intellectual capacities of machines. But, in the long run, we must be prepared to discover profitable lines of heuristic programming which do not deliberately imitate human characteristics.[36]

V Induction and models

A Intelligence

In all of this discussion we have not come to grips with anything we can isolate as "intelligence." We have discussed only heuristics, shortcuts, and classification techniques. Is there something missing? I am confident that sooner or later we will be able to assemble programs of great problem-solving ability from complex combinations of heuristic devices—multiple optimizers, pattern-recognition tricks, planning algebras, recursive administration procedures, and the like. In no one of these will we find the seat of intelligence. Should we ask what intelligence "really is"? My own view is that this is more of an esthetic question, or one of sense of dignity, than a technical matter! To me "intelligence" seems to denote little more than the complex of performances which we happen to respect, but do not understand. So it is, usually, with the question of "depth" in mathematics. Once the proof of a theorem is really understood its content seems to become trivial. (Still, there may remain a sense of wonder about how the proof was discovered.)

Programmers, too, know that there is never any "heart" in a program. There are high-level routines in each program, but all they do is dictate that "if such-and-such, then transfer to such-and-such a subroutine." And when we look at the low-level subroutines, which "actually do the work," we find senseless loops and sequences of trivial operations, merely carrying out the dictates of their superiors. The intelligence in such a system seems to be as intangible as becomes the meaning of a single common word when it is thoughtfully pronounced over and over again.

140

But we should not let our inability to discern a locus of intelligence lead us to conclude that programmed computers therefore cannot think. For it may be so with *man*, as with *machine*, that, when we understand finally the structure and program, the feeling of mystery (and self-approbation) will weaken.[37] We find similar views concerning "creativity" in [60]. The view expressed by Rosenbloom [73] that minds (or brains) can transcend machines is based, apparently, on an erroneous interpretation of the meaning of the "unsolvability theorems" of Godel.[38]

B Inductive inference

Let us pose now for our machines, a variety of problems more challenging than any ordinary game or mathematical puzzle. Suppose that we want a machine which, when embedded for a time in a complex environment or "universe," will essay to produce a description of that world—to discover its regularities or laws of nature. We might ask it to predict what will happen next. We might ask it to predict what would be the likely consequences of a certain action or experiment. Or we might ask it to formulate the laws governing some class of events. In any case, our task is to equip our machine with *inductive* ability—with methods which it can use to construct general statements about events beyond its recorded experience. Now, there can be no system for inductive inference that will work well in all possible universes. But given a universe, or an ensemble of universes, and a criterion of success, this (epistemological) problem for machines becomes technical rather than philosophical. There is quite a literature concerning this subject, but we shall discuss only one approach which currently seems to us the most promising; this is what we might call the "grammatical induction" schemes of Solomonoff [55], [16], [17], based partly on work of Chomsky and Miller [80], [81].

We will take *language* to mean the set of expressions formed from some given set of primitive symbols or expressions, by the repeated application of some given set of rules; the primitive expressions plus the rules is the *grammar* of the language. Most induction problems can be framed as problems in the *discovery of grammars*. Suppose, for instance, that a machine's prior experience is summarized by a large collection of statements, some labelled "good" and some "bad" by some critical device. How could we generate selectively more good statements? The trick is to find some relatively simple (formal) language in which the good statements are grammatical, and in which the bad ones are not. Given such a language, we can use it to generate more statements, and presumably these will tend to be more like the good ones. The heuristic argument is that if we can find a relatively simple way to separate the two sets, the discovered rule is likely to be useful beyond the immediate experience. If the extension fails to be consistent with new data, one might be able to make small changes in the rules and, generally, one may be able to use many ordinary problem-solving methods for this task.

The problem of finding an efficient grammar is much the same as that of finding efficient *encodings*, or programs, for machines; in each case, one needs to discover the important regularities in the data, and exploit the regularities by making shrewd *abbreviations*. The possible importance of Solomonoff's work [18] is that, despite some obvious defects, it may point the way toward systematic mathematical ways to explore this discovery problem. He considers the class of all programs (for a given general-purpose computer) which will produce a certain given output (the body of data in question). Most such programs, if allowed to continue, will add to that body of data. By properly weighting these programs, perhaps by length, we can obtain corresponding weights for the different possible continuations, and thus a basis for prediction. If this prediction is to be of any interest, it will be necessary to show some independence of the given computer; it is not yet clear precisely what form such a result will take.

C *Models of oneself*

If a creature can answer a question about a hypothetical experiment, without actually performing that experiment, then the answer must have been obtained from some submachine inside the creature. The output of that submachine (representing a correct answer) as well as the input (representing the question) must be coded descriptions of the corresponding external events or event classes. Seen through this pair of encoding and decoding channels, the internal submachine acts like the environment, and so it has the character of a "model." The inductive inference problem may then be regarded as the problem of constructing such a model.

To the extent that the creature's actions affect the environment, this internal model of the world will need to include some representation of the creature itself. If one asks the creature "why did you decide to do such and such" (or if it asks this of itself), any answer must come from the internal model. Thus the evidence of introspection itself is liable to be based ultimately on the processes used in constructing one's image of one's self. Speculation on the form of such a model leads to the amusing prediction that intelligent machines may be reluctant to believe that they are *just* machines. The argument is this: our own self-models have a substantially "dual" character; there is a part concerned with the physical or mechanical environment—with the behavior of inanimate objects—and there is a part concerned with social and psychological matters. It is precisely because we have not yet developed a satisfactory mechanical theory of mental activity that we have to keep these areas apart. We could not give up this division even if we wished to—until we find a unified model to replace it. Now, when we ask such a creature what sort of being it is, it cannot simply answer "directly;" it must inspect its model(s). And it must answer by saying that it seems to be a dual thing—which appears to have two parts—a "mind" and a

142

"body." Thus, even the robot, unless equipped with a satisfactory theory of artificial intelligence, would have to maintain a dualistic opinion on this matter.[39]

Conclusion

In attempting to combine a survey of work on "artificial intelligence" with a summary of our own views, we could not mention every relevant project and publication. Some important omissions are in the area of "brain models": the early work of Farley and Clark [92] (also Farley's paper in [D], often unknowingly duplicated, and the work of Rochester [82] and Milner [D]). The work of Lettvin, *et al.* [83] is related to the theories in [19]. We did not touch at all on the problems of logic and language, and of information retrieval, which must be faced when action is to be based on the contents of large memories; see, *e.g.*, McCarthy [70]. We have not discussed the basic results in mathematical logic which bear on the question of what can be done by machines. There are entire literatures we have hardly even sampled— the bold pioneering of Rashevsky (c. 1929) and his later co-workers [95]: Theories of Learning, *e.g.*, Gorn [84]; Theory of Games, *e.g.*, Shubik [85]; and Psychology, *e.g.*, Bruner, *et al.* [86]. And everyone should know the work of Polya [87] on how to solve problems. We can hope only to have transmitted the flavor of some of the more ambitious projects *directly* concerned with getting machines to take over a larger portion of problem-solving tasks.

One last remark: we have discussed here only work concerned with more or less self-contained problem-solving programs. But as this is written, we are at last beginning to see vigorous activity in the direction of constructing usable *time-sharing* or *multiprogramming* computing systems. With these systems, it will at last become economical to match human beings in real time with really large machines. This means that we can work toward programming what will be, in effect, "thinking aids." In the years to come, we expect that these man-machine systems will share, and perhaps for a time be dominant, in our advance towards the development of "artificial intelligence."

Notes

1 The adjective "heuristic," as used here and widely in the literature, means *related to improving problem-solving performance*; as a noun it is also used in regard to any method or trick used to improve the efficiency of a problem-solving system. A "heuristic program," to be considered successful, must work well on a variety of problems, and may often be excused if it fails on some. We often find it worthwhile to introduce a heuristic method which happens to cause occasional failures, if there is an over-all improvement in performance. But imperfect methods are not necessarily heuristic, nor vice versa. Hence "heuristic" should not be regarded as opposite to "foolproof"; this has caused some confusion in the literature.

2 McCarthy [1] has discussed the enumeration problem from a recursive-function theory point of view. This incomplete but suggestive paper proposes, among other things, that "the enumeration of partial recursive functions should give an early place to compositions of functions that have already appeared."

I regard this as an important notion, especially in the light of Shannon's results [4] on two-terminal switching circuits—that the "average" n-variable switching function requires about $2^n/n$ contacts. This disaster does not usually strike when we construct "interesting" large machines, presumably because they are based on composition of functions already found useful.

3 In [5] and especially in [6] Ashby has an excellent discussion of the search problem. (However, I am not convinced of the usefulness of his notion of "ultrastability," which seems to be little more than the property of a machine to search until something stops it.)

4 In the case studied in [10] the transformation space is a *group* with a uniquely defined measure: the set [F] can be computed without repetitions by *scanning* through the application of all the transforms T_a to the given figure so that the invariant property can be defined by

$$P^*(F) = \int_{a \in G} P(T_a(F))d\mu$$

where G is the group and μ the measure. By substituting $T_\beta(F)$ for F in this, one can see that the result is independent of choice of β since we obtain the same integral over $G\beta^{-1} = G$.

5 Seep, 160ff. of [11].

6 See p. 93 of [12].

7 At the cost of an additional network layer, we may also account for the possible cost g_{jk} that would be incurred if we were to assign to F_k a figure really in class F_j: in this case the minimum cost decision is given by the k for which

$$\sum_j g_{jk}\phi_j \prod_{i \in V} p_{ij} \prod_{i \in V} q_{ij}$$

is the least. V is the complement set to V_{iqij} is $(1 - p_{ij})$.

8 See also the report in [20].

9 See also [7] and [21].

10 See also Roberts [25], Papert [21], and Hawkins [22]. We can find nothing resembling an analysis [see (1) above] in [22] or subsequent publications of Rosenblatt.

11 See also Papert [21].

12 Cf. Mooers' technique of Zatocoding [30], [31].

13 Properly, the reinforcement functions should depend both on the p's and on the previous reaction—reward should *decrease* p if our animal has just turned to the left. The notation in the literature is also somewhat confusing in this regard.

14 The question of just how often one should play a strategy different from the estimated optimum, in order to gain information, is an underlying problem in many fields. See, *e.g.*, [85].

15 See especially ch. 10.

16 See also ch. 6 of [47].

17 See the discussion of Bernstein [48] and the more extensive review and discussion in the very suggestive paper of Newell, Shaw, and Simon [49]; one should not overlook the pioneering paper of Newell [50], and Samuel's discussion of the minimaxing process in [2].

18 In some problems the backing-up process can be handled in closed analytic form so that one may be able to use such methods as Bellman's "Dynamic Programming" [51]. Freimer [52] gives some examples for which limited "look-ahead" doesn't work.

19 It should be noted that [2] describes also a rather successful checker-playing program based on recording and retrieving information about positions encountered in the past, a less abstract way of exploiting past experience. Samuel's work is notable in the variety of experiments that were performed, with and without various heuristics. This gives an unusual opportunity to really find out how different heuristic methods compare. More workers should choose (other things being equal) problems for which such variations are practicable.

20 See p. 108 of [50].

21 See also the discussion in Samuel (p. 22 of [2]) on assigning credit for a change in "Delta."

22 See the introduction to [53] for a thoughtful discussion of the plausibility of the scheme.

23 It should, however, be possible to construct learning mechanisms which can select for themselves reasonably good training sequences (from an always complex environment) by pre-arranging a relatively slow development (or "maturation") of the system's facilities. This might be done by pre-arranging that the sequence of goals attempted by the primary Trainer match reasonably well, at each stage, the complexity of performance mechanically available to the pattern-recognition and other parts of the system. One might be able to do much of this by simply limiting the depth of hierarchical activity, perhaps only later permitting limited recursive activity.

24 Wang's procedure [59] too, works backwards, and can be regarded as a generalization of the method of "falsification" for deciding truth-functional tautology. In [93] and its unpublished sequel, Wang introduces more powerful methods (for much more difficult problems).

25 See [61] and [93].

26 All these efforts are directed toward the reduction of search effort. In that sense they are all heuristic programs. Since practically no one still uses "heuristic" in a sense opposed to "algorithmic," serious workers might do well to avoid pointless argument on this score. The real problem is to find methods which significantly delay the apparently inevitable exponential growth of search trees.

27 Note that the simple scheme of LT has the property that each generated problem will eventually get attention, even if several are created in a step 3. If one were to turn *full* attention to each problem, as generated, one might never return to alternate branches.

28 One will want to see if the considered problem is the same as one already considered, or very similar. See the discussion in [62]. This problem might be handled more generally by simply *remembering* the (Characters of) problems that have been attacked, and checking new ones against this memory, *e.g.*, by methods of [31], looking more closely if there seems to be a match.

29 A variety of combinatorial methods will be matched against the network-analogy opponent in a program being completed by R. Silver, Lincoln Lab., M.I.T., Lexington, Mass.

30 Some further discussion of this question may be found in Slagle [67].

31 See section 10 of [6].

32 See, *e.g.*, [88].

33 Compare this with the "matching" process described in [57]. The notions of "Character," "Character-Algebra," etc., originate in [14] but seem useful in

describing parts of the "GPS" system of [57] and [15]. Reference [15] contains much additional material we cannot survey here. Essentially, GPS is to be self-applied to the problem of discovering sets of Differences appropriate for given problem areas. This notion of "bootstrapping"—applying a problem-solving system to the task of improving some of its own methods—is old and familiar, but in [15] we find perhaps the first specific proposal about how such an advance might be realized.

34 This violates, for example, the restrictions on "DO loops" in programming systems such as FORTRAN. Convenient techniques for programming such processes were developed by Newell, Shaw, and Simon [64]; the program state-variables are stored in "push-down lists" and both the program and the data are stored in the form of "list-structures." Gelernter [69] extended FORTRAN to manage some of this. McCarthy has extended these notions in LISP [32] to permit *explicit* recursive definitions of programs in a language based on recursive functions of symbolic expressions; here the management of program-state variables is fully automatic. See also Orchard-Hays' article in this issue.

35 See chs. 12 and 13 of [46].

36 Limitations of space preclude detailed discussion here of theories of self-organizing neural nets, and other models based on brain analogies. (Several of these are described or cited in [C] and [D].) This omission is not too serious, I feel, in connection with the subject of heuristic programming, because the motivation and methods of the two areas seem so different. Up to the present time, at least, research on neural-net models has been concerned mainly with the attempt to show that certain rather simple heuristic processes, *e.g.*, reinforcement learning, or property-list pattern-recognition, can be realized or evolved by collections of simple elements without very highly organized interconnections. Work on heuristic programming is characterized quite differently by the search for new, more powerful heuristics for solving very complex problems, and by very little concern for what hardware (neuronal or otherwise) would minimally suffice for its realization. In short, the work on "nets" is concerned with how far one can get with a small initial endowment; the work on "artificial intelligence" is concerned with using all we know to build the most powerful systems that we can. It is my expectation that, in problem-solving power, the (allegedly brain-like) minimal-structure systems will never threaten to compete with their more deliberately designed contemporaries; nevertheless, their study should prove profitable in the development of component elements and subsystems to be used in the construction of the more systematically conceived machines.

37 See [14] and [9].

38 On problems of volition we are in general agreement with McCulloch [75] that our *freedom of will* "presumably means no more than that we can distinguish between what we intend [*i.e.*, our *plan*], and some intervention in our action." See also MacKay ([76] and its references); we are, however, unconvinced by his eulogization of "analogue" devices. Concerning the "mind-brain" problem, one should consider the arguments of Craik [77], Hayek [78] and Pask [79]. Among the active leaders in modern heuristic programming, perhaps only Samuel [91] has taken a strong position against the idea of machines thinking. His argument, based on the fact that reliable computers do only that which they are instructed to do, has a basic flaw; it does not follow that the programmer therefore has full knowledge (and therefore full responsibility and credit for) what will ensue. For certainly the programmer may set up an evolutionary system whose limitations are for him unclear and possibly incomprehensible. No better does the mathematician know all the consequences of a proposed set of axioms. Surely a machine

has to *be* in order to perform. But we cannot assign all the credit to its programmer if the operation of a system comes to reveal structures not recognizable or anticipated by the programmer. While we have not yet seen much in the way of intelligent activity in machines, Samuel's arguments in [91] (circular in that they are based on the presumption that machines do not have minds) do not assure us against this. Turing [72] gives a very knowledgeable discussion of such matters.

39 There is a certain problem of infinite regression in the notion of a machine having a *good* model of itself: of course, the nested models must lose detail and finally vanish. But the argument, *e.g.*, of Hayek (See 8.69 and 8.79 of [78]) that we cannot "fully comprehend the unitary order" (of our own minds) ignores the power of recursive description as well as Turing's demonstration that (with sufficient external writing space) a "general-purpose" machine can answer any question about a description of itself that any larger machine could answer.

40 *Bibliographic note:* Work in this area seems to be currently prominent in the following periodicals:

1   *IBM J. Res. & Dev.*
2   *Information and Control.*
3   *Proc. EJCC and WJCC* (EASTERN AND WESTERN JOINT COMPUTER CONFS.)
4   IRE NATIONAL CONVENTION RECORD.
5   *J. Assoc. Comp. Mach. (J. ACM).*
6   *Trans. Assoc. Comp. Mach.*
7   IRE TRANS. ON INFORMATION THEORY.

A more informative bibliography, compiled by the present author, should appear shortly in the IRE TRANS. ON HUMAN FACTORS IN ELECTRONICS.

Bibliography[40]

[1] J. McCarthy, "The inversion of functions defined by Turing machines," [B].
[2] A. L. Samuel, "Some studies in machine learning using the game of checkers," *IBM J. Res. & Dev.*, vol. 3, pp. 211–219; July, 1959.
[3] C. E. Shannon, "Programming a digital computer for playing chess," [K].
[4] C. E. Shannon, "Synthesis of two-terminal switching networks," *Bell Sys. Tech. J.*, vol. 28, pp. 59–98; 1949.
[5] W. R. Ashby, "Design for a Brain," John Wiley and Sons, Inc., New York, N. Y.; 1952.
[6] W. R. Ashby, "Design for an intelligence amplifier," [B].
[7] M. L. Minsky and O. G. Selfridge, "Learning in random nets," [H].
[8] H. Sherman, "A quasi-topological method for machine recognition of line patterns," [E].
[9] M. L. Minsky, "Some aspects of heuristic programming and artificial intelligence," [C].
[10] W. Pitts and W. S. McCulloch, "How we know universals," *Bull. Math. Biophys.*, vol. 9, pp. 127–147; 1947.
[11] N. Wiener, "Cybernetics," John Wiley and Sons, Inc., New York, N. Y.; 1948.
[12] O. G. Selfridge, "Pattern recognition and modern computers," [A].
[13] G. P. Dinneen, "Programming pattern recognition," [A].
[14] M. L. Minsky. "Heuristic Aspects of the Artificial Intelligence Problem,"

Lincoln Lab., M.I.T., Lexington, Mass., Group Rept. 34–55, ASTIA Doc. No. 236885; December, 1956. (M.I.T. Hayden Library No. H-58.)

[15] A. Newell, J. C. Shaw, and H. A. Simon, "A variety of intelligence learning in a general problem solver," [D].

[16] R. J. Solomonoff, "The Mechanization of Linguistic Learning." Zator Co., Cambridge, Mass., Zator Tech. Bull. No. 125, presented at the Second Internatl. Congress on Cybernetics, Namur, Belgium; September, 1958.

[17] R. J. Solomonoff, "A new method for discovering the grammars of phrase structure languages," [E].

[18] R. J. Solomonoff, "A Preliminary Report on a General Theory of Inductive Inference," Zator Co., Cambridge, Mass., Zator Tech. Bull. V-131; February, 1960.

[19] O. G. Selfridge, "Pandemonium: a paradigm for learning," [C].

[20] O. G. Selfridge and U. Neisser, "Pattern recognition by machine," *Sci. Am.*, vol. 203, pp. 60–68; August, 1960.

[21] S. Papert, "Some mathematical models of learning," [H].

[22] F. Rosenblatt, "The Perceptron," Cornell Aeronautical Lab., Inc., Ithaca, N. Y., Rept. No. VG-1196-G-1; January, 1958. See also the article of Hawkins in this issue.

[23] W. H. Highleyman and L. A. Kamentsky, "Comments on a character recognition method of Bledsoe and Browning" (Correspondence), IRE Trans. on Electronic Computers. vol. EC-9, p. 263; June, 1960.

[24] W. W. Bledsoe and I. Browning, "Pattern recognition and reading by machine," [F].

[25] L. G. Roberts, "Pattern recognition with an adaptive network," 1960 IRE International Convention Record, pt. 2, pp. 66–70.

[26] W. Doyle, "Recognition of Sloppy, Hand-Printed Characters," Lincoln Lab., M.I.T., Lexington, Mass, Group Rept. 54–12; December, 1959.

[27] R. A. Kirsch, C. Ray, L. Cahn, and G. H. Urban, "Experiments in Processing Pictorial Information with a Digital Computer," *Proc. EJCC*, Proc. IRE, pp. 221–229; December, 1957.

[28] A. M. Uttley, "Conditional probability machines," and "Temporal and spatial patterns in a conditional probability machine," [B].

[29] A. M. Uttley, "Conditional probability computing in a nervous system," [C].

[30] C. N. Mooers, "Information retrieval on structured content," [U].

[31] C. N. Mooers, "Zatocoding and developments in information retrieval," *Aslib Proc.*, vol. 8, pp. 3–22; February, 1956.

[32] J. McCarthy, "Recursive functions of symbolic expressions," [G].

[33] J. S. Bomba, "Alpha-numeric character recognition using local operations," [F].

[34] R. L. Grimsdale, *et al.*, "A system for the automatic recognition of patterns," *Proc. IEE*, vol. 106, pt. B: March, 1959.

[35] S. H. Unger, "Pattern detection and recognition," Proc. IRE, vol. 47, pp. 1737–1752; October, 1959.

[36] J. H. Holland, "On iterative circuit computers constructed of microelectronic components and systems." *Proc. WJCC*, pp. 259–265; 1960.

[37] D. O. Hebb, "The Organization of Behavior." John Wiley and Sons, Inc., New York, N. Y.; 1949.

[38] W. Kohler, "Gestalt Psychology," Mentor, No. MD 279; 1947.

[39] N. Haller, "Line Tracing for Character Recognition," M.S.E.E. thesis, M.I.T., Cambridge, Mass.; 1959.

[40] O. N. Minot, "Automatic Devices for Recognition of Visible Two-dimensional Patterns: A Survey of the Field," U. S. Naval Electronics Lab., San Diego, Calif., Tech. Memo. 364; June 25, 1959.

[41] M. E. Stevens, "A Survey of Automatic Reading Techniques," NBS, U. S. Dept. of Commerce, Washington, D. C., Rept. 5643: August, 1957.

[42] N. Tinbergen, "The Study of Instinct," Oxford University Press, New York, N. Y.: 1951.

[43] O. G. Selfridge, "Pattern recognition and learning," [J].

[44] B. F. Skinner, "Science and Human Behavior," The Macmillan Co., New York, N. Y.; 1953.

[45] R. R. Bush and F. Mosteller, "Stochastic Models For Learning," John Wiley and Sons, Inc., New York, N. Y.; 1955.

[46] G. A. Miller, E. Galanter, and K. H. Pribram, "Plans and the Structure of Behavior," Henry Holt and Co., Inc., New York, N. Y.; 1960.

[47] M. L. Minsky, "Neural Nets and the Brain Model Problem," Ph.D. dissertation, Princeton Univ., Princeton, N. J.; 1954. (University Microfilms, Ann Arbor.)

[48] A. Bernstein, *et al.*, "A chess playing program for the IBM 704," *Proc. WJCC*, pp. 157–159; 1958.

[49] A. Newell, J. C. Shaw, and H. A. Simon, "Chess-playing programs and the problem of complexity," *IBM J. Res. & Dev.*, vol. 2, p. 320 ff.; October, 1958.

[50] A. Newell, "The chess machine," [A].

[51] R. Bellman, "Dynamic Programming," Princeton University Press, Princeton, N. J.; 1957.

[52] M. Freimer, "Topics in Dynamic Programming II," Lincoln Lab., M.I.T., Lexington, Mass., Rept. 52-G-0020; April, 1960. (M.I.T. Hayden Library No. H-82). See especially sec. I–E.

[53] R. M. Friedberg, "A learning machine, part I," *IBM J. Res. & Dev.*, vol. 2, pp. 2–13; January, 1958.

[54] R. M. Friedberg, B. Dunham, and J. H. North, "A learning machine, part II." *IBM J. Res. & Dev.*, vol. 3, pp. 282–287; July, 1959.

[55] R. J. Solomonoff, "An inductive inference machine," 1957 IRE NATIONAL CONVENTION RECORD, pt. 2, pp. 56–62.

[56] C. D. Darlington, "The Evolution of Genetics," Basic Books, Inc., New York, N. Y.; 1958.

[57] A. Newell and H. A. Simon, "The logic theory machine," [L].

[58] A. Newell, J. C. Shaw, and H. A. Simon, "Empirical explorations of the logic theory machine," *Proc. WJCC*, pp. 218–230; 1957.

[59] H. Wang, "Toward mechanical mathematics," *IBM J. Res. & Dev.*, vol. 4, pp. 2–22; January, 1960.

[60] A. Newell, J. C. Shaw, and, H. A. Simon, "Elements of a theory of human problem solving," *Psych. Rev.* vol. 65, p. 151; March, 1958.

[61] M. Davis and H. Putnam, "A computing procedure for quantification theory," *J. ACM*, vol. 7, pp. 201–215: July, 1960.

[62] H. Gelernter and N. Rochester, "Intelligent behavior in problem-solving machines," *IBM J. Res. & Dev.*, vol. 2, p. 336 ff.: October, 1958.

[63] C. E. Shannon, "Game-playing machines," *J. Franklin Inst.*, vol. 206, pp. 447–453; December, 1955.

[64] A. Newell and F. Tonge, "Introduction to IPL-V," *Commun. ACM*, vol. 3; April, 1960.

[65] S. Golumb, "A mathematical theory of discrete classification," [H].

[66] J. Wozencraft and M. Horstein, "Coding for two-way channels," [H].

[67] J. Slagle, "A computer program for solving integration problems in 'Freshman Calculus'," thesis in preparation, M.I.T., Cambridge, Mass.

[68] A. Newell, J. C. Shaw, and H. A. Simon. "Report on a general problem-solving program," [E].

[69] H. L. Gelernter. "Realization of a geometry-proving machine," [E].

[70] J. McCarthy, "Programs with common sense," [C].

[71] E. F. Moore, "On the shortest path through a maze," *Proc. Internatl. Symp. on the Theory of Switching*, Harvard Univ., Cambridge, Mass.; 1959.

[72] A. M. Turing, "Can a machine think?," [K].

[73] P. Rosenbloom. "Elements of Mathematical Logic," Dover Publications, New York, N. Y.; 1951.

[74] H. Rogers, "Review of 'Gödel's Proof' by Newman and Nagel." *Am. Math. Monthly*, vol. 67, p. 98; January, 1960.

[75] W. S. McCulloch, "Through the den of the metaphysician," *Brit. J. Phil. Science*, vol. 5, pp. 18–34; 1954.

[76] D. M. MacKay. "Operational aspects of intellect," [C].

[77] K. J. W. Craik, "The Nature of Explanation," Cambridge Univ. Press. Cambridge, Eng.; 1952. Preface dated 1943.

[78] F. A. Hayek, "The Sensory Order," Routledge and Kegan Paul, London, Eng.; 1952.

[79] G. Pask, "Physical analogues to the growth of a concept," [C].

[80] A. N. Chomsky, "Syntactic Structures," Mouton, The Hague; 1957.

[81] N. Chomsky and G. A. Miller, "Finite state languages," *Inform. and Control*, vol 1, pp. 91–112; May, 1958.

[82] N. Rochester, *et al.*, "Tests on a cell assembly theory of the action of the brain, using a large digital computer," [L].

[83] J. Y. Lettvin, H. Maturana, W. S. McCulloch, and W. Pitts, "What the frog's eye tells the frog's brain," PROC. IRE, vol. 47, pp. 1940–1951; November, 1959.

[84] S. Gorn, "On the mechanical simulation of learning and habit-forming," *Inform. and Control*, vol. 2, pp. 226–259; September, 1959.

[85] M. Shubik, "Games, decisions and industrial organization," *Management Science*, vol. 6, pp. 455–474; July, 1960.

[86] J. S. Bruner, J. Goodnow, and G. Austin, "A Study of Thinking," John Wiley and Sons, Inc., New York, N. Y.; 1956.

[87] G. Polya, "How to Solve It," Princeton Univ. Press, Princeton, N. J.; 1945. Also, "Induction and Analogy in Mathematics," and "Patterns of Plausible Inference," 2 vols, Princeton Univ. Press, Princeton, N. J.; 1954. (Available in paperback.)

[88] F. E. Hohn, S. Seshu, and D. D. Aufenkamp, "The theory of nets," IRE TRANS ON ELECTRONIC COMPUTERS, vol. EC-6, pp. 154–161; September, 1957.

[89] D. M. MacKay. "The epistemological problem for automata," [B].

[90] I. J. Good, "Weight of evidence and false target probabilities," [H].

[91] A. Samuel, Letter to the Editor, *Science*, vol. 132, No. 3429; September 16, 1960. (Incorrectly labelled vol. 131 on cover.)

[92] B. G. Farley and W. A. Clark, "Simulation of self-organizing systems by digital computer," IRE TRANS. ON INFORMATION THEORY, vol. IT-4, pp. 76–84; September, 1954.

[93] H. Wang, "Proving theorems by pattern recognition, I," [G].

[94] T. Kilburn, R. L. Grimsdale, and F. H. Sumner, "Experiments in machine thinking and learning," [E].

[95] N. Rashevsky, "Mathematical Biophysics." Dover Publications, Inc., New York, N. Y., vol. 2; 1960.

Proceedings and collections containing more than one of the above references:

[A] *Proc. WJCC*; March, 1955.

[B] "Automata Studies," C. E. Shannon and J. McCarthy, Eds. Princeton Univ. Press, Princeton, N. J.; 1956.

[C] *Proc. Symp. on Mechanization of Thought Processes*, Her Majesty's Stationery Office, London, Eng.; 1959.

[D] "Self-Organizing Systems," M. T. Yovitts and S. Cameron, Eds., Pergamon Press. New York, N. Y.; 1960.

[E] *Proc. Internatl. Conf. on Information Processing*, UNESCO House, Paris, France; 1959.

[F] *Proc. EJCC*; December, 1959.

[G] *Commun. ACM*, vol. 3: April, 1960. (Preprints of *Conf. on Symbol Manipulation Programs.*)

[H] *Fourth London Symp. on Information Theory*, C. Cherry, Ed., to be published.

[J] *Third London Symp. on Information Theory*, C. Cherry, Ed., Academic Press, Inc., New York, N. Y.; 1956.

[K] "The World of Mathematics," Newman, Ed., Simon and Schuster, Inc., New York, N. Y., vol. 4; 1956.

[L] IRE TRANS. ON INFORMATION THEORY, vol. IF-2; September 1956.

Section 1.2: Developments

31

COMPUTER SCIENCE AS EMPIRICAL ENQUIRY:

Symbols and search

Allen Newell and Herbert A. Simon

Source: *Communications of the Association for Computing Machinery* 19 (1976): 105–32.

Computer science is the study of the phenomena surrounding computers. The founders of this society understood this very well when they called themselves the Association for Computing Machinery. The machine—not just the hardware, but the programmed living machine—is the organism we study.

This is the tenth Turing Lecture. The nine persons who preceded us on this platform have presented nine different views of computer science. For our organism, the machine, can be studied at many levels and from many sides. We are deeply honoured to appear here today and to present yet another view, the one that has permeated the scientific work for which we have been cited. We wish to speak of computer science as empirical enquiry.

Our view is only one of many; the previous lectures make that clear. However, even taken together the lectures fail to cover the whole scope of our science. Many fundamental aspects of it have not been represented in these ten awards. And if the time ever arrives, surely not soon, when the compass has been boxed, when computer science has been discussed from every side, it will be time to start the cycle again. For the hare as lecturer will have to make an annual sprint to overtake the cumulation of small, incremental gains that the tortoise of scientific and technical development has achieved in his steady march. Each year will create a new gap and call for a new sprint, for in science there is no final word.

Computer science is an empirical discipline. We would have called it an experimental science, but like astronomy, economics, and geology, some of its unique forms of observation and experience do not fit a narrow stereotype of the experimental method. Nonetheless, they are experiments. Each new machine that is built is an experiment. Actually constructing the machine poses a question to nature; and we listen for the answer by observing the machine in operation and analysing it by all analytical and measurement means available. Each new program that is built is an experiment. It poses a question to nature, and its behaviour offers clues to an answer. Neither machines nor programs are black boxes; they are artefacts that have been designed, both hardware and software, and we can open them up and look inside. We can relate their structure to their behaviour and draw many lessons from a single experiment. We don't have to build 100 copies of, say, a theorem prover, to demonstrate statistically that it has not overcome the combinatorial explosion of search in the way hoped for. Inspection of the program in the light of a few runs reveals the flaw and lets us proceed to the next attempt.

We build computers and programs for many reasons. We build them to serve society and as tools for carrying out the economic tasks of society. But as basic scientists we build machines and programs as a way of discovering new phenomena and analysing phenomena we already know about. Society often becomes confused about this, believing that computers and programs are to be constructed only for the economic use that can be made of them (or as intermediate items in a developmental sequence leading to such use). It needs to understand that the phenomena surrounding computers are deep and obscure, requiring much experimentation to assess their nature. It needs to understand that, as in any science, the gains that accrue from such experimentation and understanding pay off in the permanent acquisition of new techniques; and that it is these techniques that will create the instruments to help society in achieving its goals.

Our purpose here, however, is not to plead for understanding from an outside world. It is to examine one aspect of our science, the development of new basic understanding by empirical enquiry. This is best done by illustrations. We will be pardoned if, presuming upon the occasion, we choose our examples from the area of our own research. As will become apparent, these examples involve the whole development of artificial intelligence, especially in its early years. They rest on much more than our own personal contributions. And even where we have made direct contributions, this has been done in co-operation with others. Our collaborators have included especially Cliff Shaw, with whom we formed a team of three through the exciting period of the late fifties. But we have also worked with a great many colleagues and students at Carnegie-Mellon University.

Time permits taking up just two examples. The first is the development of the notion of a symbolic system. The second is the development of the notion of heuristic search. Both conceptions have deep significance for understanding how information is processed and how intelligence is achieved. However, they do not come close to exhausting the full scope of artificial intelligence, though they seem to us to be useful for exhibiting the nature of fundamental knowledge in this part of computer science.

1 Symbols and physical-symbol systems

One of the fundamental contributions to knowledge of computer science has been to explain, at a rather basic level, what symbols are. This explanation is a scientific proposition about Nature. It is empirically derived, with a long and gradual development.

Symbols lie at the root of intelligent action, which is, of course, the primary topic of artificial intelligence. For that matter, it is a primary question for all of computer science. For all information is processed by computers in the service of ends, and we measure the intelligence of a system by its ability to achieve stated ends in the face of variations, difficulties, and complexities posed by the task environment. This general investment of computer science in attaining intelligence is obscured when the tasks being accomplished are limited in scope, for then the full variations in the environment can be accurately foreseen. It becomes more obvious as we extend computers to more global, complex, and knowledge-intensive tasks—as we attempt to make them our agents, capable of handling on their own the full contingencies of the natural world.

Our understanding of the system's requirements for intelligent action emerges slowly. It is composite, for no single elementary thing accounts for intelligence in all its manifestations. There is no 'intelligence principle', just as there is no 'vital principle' that conveys by its very nature the essence of life. But the lack of a simple *deus ex machina* does not imply that there are no structural requirements for intelligence. One such requirement is the ability to store and manipulate symbols. To put the scientific question, we may paraphrase the title of a famous paper by Warren McCulloch (1961): What is a symbol, that intelligence may use it, and intelligence, that it may use a symbol?

Laws of qualitative structure

All sciences characterize the essential nature of the systems they study. These characterizations are invariably qualitative in nature, for they set the terms within which more detailed knowledge can be developed. Their essence can often be captured in very short, very general statements. One might judge these general laws, because of their limited specificity, as making relatively little contribution to the sum of a science, were it not for the historical evidence that shows them to be results of the greatest importance.

The cell doctrine in biology

A good example of a law of qualitative structure is the cell doctrine in biology, which states that the basic building block of all living organisms is the cell. Cells come in a large variety of forms, though they all have a nucleus surrounded by protoplasm, the whole encased by a membrane. But this internal structure was not, historically, part of the specification of the cell doctrine; it was subsequent specificity developed by intensive investigation. The cell doctrine can be conveyed almost entirely by the statement we gave above, along with some vague notions about what size a cell can be. The impact of this law on biology, however, has been tremendous, and the lost motion in the field prior to its gradual acceptance was considerable.

Plate tectonics in geology

Geology provides an interesting example of a qualitative structure law, interesting because it has gained acceptance in the last decade and so its rise in status is still fresh in our memory. The theory of plate tectonics asserts that the surface of the globe is a collection of huge plates—a few dozen in all—which move (at geological speeds) against, over, and under each other into the centre of the earth, where they lose their identity. The movements of the plates account for the shapes and relative locations of the continents and oceans, for the areas of volcanic and earthquake activity, for the deep sea ridges, and so on. With a few additional particulars as to speed and size, the essential theory has been specified. It was of course not accepted until it succeeded in explaining a number of details, all of which hung together (e.g. accounting for flora, fauna, and stratification agreements between West Africa and Northeast South America). The plate tectonics theory is highly qualitative. Now that it is accepted, the whole earth seems to offer evidence for it everywhere, for we see the world in its terms.

The germ theory of disease

It is little more than a century since Pasteur enunciated the germ theory of disease, a law of qualitative structure that produced a revolution in medicine. The theory proposes that most diseases are caused by the presence and multiplication in the body of tiny single-celled living organisms, and that contagion consists in the transmission of these organisms from one host to another. A large part of the elaboration of the theory consisted in identifying the organisms associated with specific diseases, describing them, and tracing their life histories. The fact that the law has many exceptions—that many diseases are not produced by germs—does not detract from its importance. The law tells us to look for a particular kind of cause; it does not insist that we will always find it.

The doctrine of atomism

The doctrine of atomism offers an interesting contrast to the three laws of qualitative structure we have just described. As it emerged from the work of Dalton and his demonstrations that the chemicals combined in fixed proportions, the law provided a typical example of qualitative structure: the elements are composed of small, uniform particles, differing from one element to another. But because the underlying species of atoms are so simple and limited in their variety, quantitative theories were soon formulated which assimilated all the general structure in the original qualitative hypothesis. With cells, tectonic plates, and germs, the variety of structure is so great that the underlying qualitative principle remains distinct, and its contribution to the total theory clearly discernible.

Conclusion

Laws of qualitative structure are seen everywhere in science. Some of our greatest scientific discoveries are to be found among them. As the examples illustrate, they often set the terms on which a whole science operates.

Physical-symbol systems

Let us return to the topic of symbols, and define a *physical-symbol system*. The adjective 'physical' denotes two important features:

1. Such systems clearly obey the laws of physics—they are realizable by engineered systems made of engineered components;
2. although our use of the term 'symbol' prefigures our intended interpretation, it is not restricted to human symbol systems.

A physical-symbol system consists of a set of entities, called symbols, which are physical patterns that can occur as components of another type of entity called an expression (or symbol structure). Thus a symbol structure is composed of a number of instances (or tokens) of symbols related in some physical way (such as one token being next to another). At any instant of time the system will contain a collection of these symbol structures. Besides these structures, the system also contains a collection of processes that operate on expressions to produce other expressions: processes of creation, modification, reproduction, and destruction. A physical-symbol system is a machine that produces through time an evolving collection of symbol structures. Such a system exists in a world of objects wider than just these symbolic expressions themselves.

Two notions are central to this structure of expressions, symbols, and objects: designation and interpretation.

Designation. An expression designates an object if, given the expression, the system can either affect the object itself or behave in ways depending on the object.

In either case, access to the object via the expression has been obtained, which is the essence of designation.

Interpretation. The system can interpret an expression if the expression designates a process and if, given the expression, the system can carry out the process.

Interpretation implies a special form of dependent action: given an expression, the system can perform the indicated process, which is to say, it can evoke and execute its own processes from expressions that designate them.

A system capable of designation and interpretation, in the sense just indicated, must also meet a number of additional requirements, of completeness and closure. We will have space only to mention these briefly; all of them are important and have far-reaching consequences.

1. A symbol may be used to designate any expression whatsoever. That is, given a symbol, it is not prescribed a priori what expressions it can designate. This arbitrariness pertains only to symbols: the symbol tokens and their mutual relations determine what object is designated by a complex expression.
2. There exist expressions that designate every process of which the machine is capable.
3. There exist processes for creating any expression and for modifying any expression in arbitrary ways.
4. Expressions are stable; once created, they will continue to exist until explicitly modified or deleted.
5. The number of expressions that the system can hold is essentially unbounded.

The type of system we have just defined is not unfamiliar to computer scientists. It bears a strong family resemblance to all general-purpose computers. If a symbol-manipulation language, such as LISP, is taken as defining a machine, then the kinship becomes truly brotherly. Our intent in laying out such a system is not to propose something new. Just the opposite: it is to show what is now known and hypothesized about systems that satisfy such a characterization.

We can now state a general scientific hypothesis—a law of qualitative structure for symbol systems:

The Physical-Symbol System Hypothesis. A physical-symbol system has the necessary and sufficient means for general intelligent action.

By 'necessary' we mean that any system that exhibits general intelligence will prove upon analysis to be a physical-symbol system. By 'sufficient' we mean that any physical-symbol system of sufficient size can be organized further to exhibit general intelligence. By 'general intelligent action' we wish to indicate the same scope of intelligence as we see in human action: that in any real situation behaviour appropriate to the ends of the system and adaptive to the demands of the environment can occur, within some limits of speed and complexity.

The Physical-Symbol System Hypothesis clearly is a law of qualitative structure. It specifies a general class of systems within which one will find those capable of intelligent action.

This is an empirical hypothesis. We have defined a class of systems; we wish to ask whether that class accounts for a set of phenomena we find in the real world. Intelligent action is everywhere around us in the biological world, mostly in human behaviour. It is a form of behaviour we can recognize by its effects whether it is performed by humans or not. The hypothesis could indeed be false. Intelligent behaviour is not so easy to produce that any system will exhibit it willy-nilly. Indeed, there are people whose analyses lead them to conclude either on philosophical or on scientific grounds that the hypothesis *is* false. Scientifically, one can attack or defend it only by bringing forth empirical evidence about the natural world.

We now need to trace the development of this hypothesis and look at the evidence for it.

Development of the symbol-system hypothesis

A physical-symbol system is an instance of a universal machine. Thus the symbol-system hypothesis implies that intelligence will be realized by a universal computer. However, the hypothesis goes far beyond the argument, often made on general grounds of physical determinism, that any computation that is realizable can be realized by a universal machine, provided that it is specified. For it asserts specifically that the intelligent machine is a symbol system, thus making a specific architectural assertion about the nature of intelligent systems. It is important to understand how this additional specificity arose.

Formal logic

The roots of the hypothesis go back to the program of Frege and of Whitehead and Russell for formalizing logic: capturing the basic conceptual notions of mathematics in logic and putting the notions of proof and deduction on a secure footing. This effort culminated in mathematical logic—our familiar propositional, first-order, and higher-order logics. It developed a characteristic view, often referred to as the 'symbol game'. Logic, and by incorporation all of mathematics, was a game played with meaningless tokens according to certain purely syntactic rules. All meaning had been purged. One had a mechanical, though permissive (we would now say non-deterministic), system about which various things could be proved. Thus progress was first made by walking away from all that seemed relevant to meaning and human symbols. We could call this the stage of formal symbol-manipulation.

This general attitude is well reflected in the development of information theory. It was pointed out time and again that Shannon had defined a system that was useful only for communication and selection, and which had nothing to do with meaning. Regrets were expressed that such a general name as 'information theory' had been given to the field, and attempts were made to rechristen it as 'the theory of selective information'—to no avail, of course.

Turing machines and the digital computer

The development of the first digital computers and of automata theory, starting with Turing's own work in the thirties, can be treated together. They agree in their view of what is essential. Let us use Turing's own model, for it shows the features well.

A Turing machine consists of two memories: an unbounded tape and a finite-state control. The tape holds data, i.e. the famous zeros and ones. The machine has a very small set of proper operations—read, write, and scan operations—on the tape. The read operation is not a data operation, but provides conditional branching to a control state as a function of the data under the read head. As we all know, this model contains the essentials of all computers, in terms of what they can do, though other computers with different memories and operations might carry out the same computations with different requirements of space and time. In particular, the model of a Turing machine contains within it the notions both of what cannot be computed and of universal machines—computers that can do anything that can be done by any machine.

We should marvel that two of our deepest insights into information processing were achieved in the thirties, before modern computers came into being. It is a tribute to the genius of Alan Turing. It is also a tribute to the development of mathematical logic at the time, and testimony to the depth of computer science's obligation to it. Concurrently with Turing's work appeared the work of the logicians Emil Post and (independently) Alonzo Church. Starting from independent notions of logistic systems (Post productions and recursive functions, respectively), they arrived at analogous results on undecidability and universality—results that were soon shown to imply that all three systems were equivalent. Indeed, the convergence of all these attempts to define the most general class of information-processing systems provides some of the force of our conviction that we have captured the essentials of information-processing in these models.

In none of these systems is there, on the surface, a concept of the symbol as something that *designates*. The data are regarded as just strings of zeros and ones—indeed that data be inert is essential to the reduction of computation to physical process. The finite-state control system was always viewed as a small controller, and logical games were played to see how small a state system could be used without destroying the universality of the machine. No games, as far as we can tell, were ever played to add new states dynamically to the finite control—to think of the control memory as holding the bulk of the system's knowledge. What was accomplished at this stage was half the principle of interpretation—showing that a machine could be run from a description. Thus this is the stage of automatic formal symbol-manipulation.

The stored program concept

With the development of the second generation of electronic machines in the mid-forties (after the Eniac) came the stored program concept. This was rightfully hailed as a milestone, both conceptually and practically. Programs now can be data, and can be operated on as data. This capability is, of course, already implicit in the model of Turing: the descriptions are on the very same tape as the data. Yet the idea was realized only when machines acquired enough memory to make it practicable to locate actual programs in some internal place. After all, the Eniac had only twenty registers.

The stored program concept embodies the second half of the interpretation principle, the part that says that the system's own data can be interpreted. But it does not yet contain the notion of designation—of the physical relation that underlies meaning.

List-processing

The next step, taken in 1956, was list-processing. The contents of the data-structures were now symbols, in the sense of our physical-symbol system: patterns that designated, that had referents. Lists held addresses which permitted access to other lists—thus the notion of list-structures. That this was a new view was demonstrated to us many times in the early days of list-processing when colleagues would ask where the data were—that is, which list finally held the collection of bits that were the content of the system. They found it strange that there were no such bits, there were only symbols that designated yet other symbol structures.

List-processing is simultaneously three things in the development of computer science.

1. It is the creation of a genuine dynamic memory structure in a machine

that had heretofore been perceived as having fixed structure. It added to our ensemble of operations those that built and modified structure in addition to those that replaced and changed content.

2. It was an early demonstration of the basic abstraction that a computer consists of a set of data types and a set of operations proper to these data types, so that a computational system should employ whatever data types are appropriate to the application, independent of the underlying machine.

3. List-processing produced a model of designation, thus defining symbol-manipulation in the sense in which we use this concept in computer science today.

As often occurs, the practice of the time already anticipated all the elements of list-processing: addresses are obviously used to gain access, the drum machines used linked programs (so-called one-plus-one addressing), and so on. But the conception of list-processing as an abstraction created a new world in which designation and dynamic symbolic structure were defining characteristics. The embedding of the early list-processing systems in languages (the IPLs, LISP) is often decried as having been a barrier to the diffusion of list-processing techniques throughout programming practice; but it was the vehicle that held the abstraction together.

LISP

One more step is worth noting: McCarthy's creation of LISP in 1959–60 (McCarthy 1960). It completed the act of abstraction, lifting list-structures out of their embedding in concrete machines, creating a new formal system with S-expressions, which could be shown to be equivalent to the other universal schemes of computation.

Conclusion

That the concept of the designating symbol and symbol-manipulation does not emerge until the mid-fifties does not mean that the earlier steps were either inessential or less important. The total concept is the join of computability, physical realizability (and by multiple technologies), universality, the symbolic representation of processes (i.e. interpretability), and, finally, symbolic structure and designation. Each of the steps provided an essential part of the whole.

The first step in this chain, authored by Turing, is theoretically motivated, but the others all have deep empirical roots. We have been led by the evolution of the computer itself. The stored program principle arose out of the experience with Eniac. List-processing arose out of the attempt to construct intelligent programs. It took its cue from the emergence of random access memories, which provided a clear physical realization of a designating symbol in the address. LISP arose out of the evolving experience with list-processing.

The evidence

We come now to the evidence for the hypothesis that physical-symbol systems are capable of intelligent action, and that general intelligent action calls for a physical-symbol system. The hypothesis is an empirical generalization and not a theorem. We know of no way of demonstrating the connection between symbol systems and intelligence on purely logical grounds. Lacking such a demonstration, we must look at the facts. Our central aim, however, is not to review the evidence in detail, but to use the example before us to illustrate the proposition that computer science is a field of empirical enquiry. Hence, we will only indicate what kinds of evidence there are, and the general nature of the testing process.

The notion of physical-symbol system had taken essentially its present form by the middle of the 1950s, and one can date from that time the growth of artificial intelligence as a coherent subfield of computer science. The twenty years of work since then has seen a continuous accumulation of empirical evidence of two main varieties. The first addresses itself to the *sufficiency* of physical-symbol systems for producing intelligence, attempting to construct and test specific systems that have such a capability. The second kind of evidence addresses itself to the *necessity* of having a physical-symbol system wherever intelligence is exhibited. It starts with Man, the intelligent system best known to us, and attempts to discover whether his cognitive activity can be explained as the working of a physical-symbol system. There are other forms of evidence, which we will comment upon briefly later, but these two are the important ones. We will consider them in turn. The first is generally called artificial intelligence, the second, research in cognitive psychology.

Constructing intelligent systems

The basic paradigm for the initial testing of the germ theory of disease was: identify a disease, then look for the germ. An analogous paradigm has inspired much of the research in artificial intelligence: identify a task-domain calling for intelligence, then construct a program for a digital computer that can handle tasks in that domain. The easy and well structured tasks were looked at first: puzzles and games, operations-research problems of scheduling and allocating resources, simple induction tasks. Scores, if not hundreds, of programs of these kinds have by now been constructed, each capable of some measure of intelligent action in the appropriate domain.

Of course intelligence is not an all-or-none matter, and there has been steady progress towards higher levels of performance in specific domains, as well as towards widening the range of those domains. Early chess programs, for example, were deemed successful if they could play the game legally and with some indication of purpose; a little later, they reached the level of human beginners; within ten or fifteen years, they began to compete with serious amateurs. Progress has been slow (and the total programming effort invested small) but continuous, and the paradigm of construct-and-test proceeds in a regular cycle—the whole research activity mimicking at a macroscopic level the basic generate-and-test cycle of many of the AI programs.

There is a steadily widening area within which intelligent action is attainable. From the original tasks, research has extended to building systems that handle and understand natural language in a variety of ways, systems for interpreting visual scenes, systems for hand–eye co-ordination, systems that design, systems that write computer programs, systems for speech understanding—the list is, if not endless, at least very long. If there are limits beyond which the hypothesis will not carry us, they have not yet become apparent. Up to the present, the rate of progress has been governed mainly by the rather modest quantity of scientific resources that have been applied and the inevitable requirement of a substantial system-building effort for each new major undertaking.

Much more has been going on, of course, than simply a piling up of examples of intelligent systems adapted to specific task-domains. It would be surprising and unappealing if it turned out that the AI programs performing these diverse tasks had nothing in common beyond their being instances of physical-symbol systems. Hence, there has been great interest in searching for mechanisms possessed of generality, and for common components among programs performing a variety of tasks. This search carries the theory beyond the initial symbol-system hypothesis to a more complete characterization of the particular kinds of symbol systems that are effective in artificial intelligence. In the second section of this paper, we will discuss one example of a hypothesis at this second level of specificity: the heuristic-search hypothesis.

The search for generality spawned a series of programs designed to separate out general problem-solving mechanisms from the requirements of particular task-domains. The General Problem Solver (GPS) was perhaps the first of these; while among its descendants are such contemporary systems as PLANNER and CONNIVER. The search for common components has led to generalized schemes of representation for goals and plans, methods for constructing discrimination nets, procedures for the control of tree search, pattern-matching mechanisms, and language-parsing systems. Experiments are at present under way to find convenient devices for representing sequences of time and tense, movement, causality, and the like. More and more, it becomes possible to assemble large intelligent systems in a modular way from such basic components.

We can gain some perspective on what is going on by turning, again, to the analogy of the germ theory. If the first burst of research stimulated by that theory consisted largely in finding the germ to go with each disease, subsequent effort turned to learning what a germ was—to building on the basic qualitative law a new level of structure. In artificial intelligence, an initial burst of activity aimed at building intelligent programs for a wide variety of almost randomly selected tasks is giving way to more sharply targeted research aimed at understanding the common mechanisms of such systems.

The modelling of human symbolic behaviour

The symbol-system hypothesis implies that the symbolic behaviour of man arises because he has the characteristics of a physical-symbol system. Hence, the results of efforts to model human behaviour with symbol systems become an important part of the evidence for the hypothesis, and research in artificial intelligence goes on in close collaboration with research in information-processing psychology, as it is usually called.

The search for explanations of man's intelligent behaviour in terms of symbol systems has had a large measure of success over the past twenty years; to the point where information-processing theory is the leading contemporary point of view in cognitive psychology. Especially in the areas of problem-solving, concept attainment, and long-term memory, symbol-manipulation models now dominate the scene.

Research in information-processing psychology involves two main kinds of empirical activity. The first is the conduct of observations and experiments of human behaviour in tasks requiring intelligence. The second, very similar to the parallel activity in artificial intelligence, is the programming of symbol systems to model the observed human behaviour. The psychological observations and experiments lead to the formulation of hypotheses about the symbolic processes the subjects are using, and these are an important source of the ideas that go into the construction of the programs. Thus many of the ideas for the basic mechanisms of GPS were derived from careful analysis of the protocols that human subjects produced while thinking aloud during the performance of a problem-solving task.

The empirical character of computer science is nowhere more evident than in this alliance with psychology. Not only are psychological experiments required to test the veridicality of the simulation models as explanations of the human behaviour, but out of the experiments come new ideas for the design and construction of physical-symbol systems.

Other evidence

The principal body of evidence for the symbol-system hypothesis that we have now considered is negative evidence: the absence of specific competing hypotheses as to how intelligent activity might be accomplished—whether by man or by machine. Most attempts to build such hypotheses have taken place within the field of psychology. Here we have had a continuum of theories from the points of view usually labelled 'behaviourism' to those usually labelled 'Gestalt theory'. Neither of these points of view stands as a real competitor to the symbol-system hypothesis, and for two reasons. First, neither behaviourism nor Gestalt theory has demonstrated, or even shown how to demonstrate, that the explanatory mechanisms it postulates are sufficient to account for intelligent behaviour in complex tasks. Second, neither theory has been formulated with anything like the specificity of artificial programs. As a matter of fact, the alternative theories are so vague that it is not terribly difficult to give them information-processing interpretations, and thereby assimilate them to the symbol-system hypothesis.

Conclusion

We have tried to use the example of the Physical-Symbol System Hypothesis to illustrate concretely that computer science is a scientific enterprise in the usual meaning of that term: it develops scientific hypotheses theses which it then seeks to verify by empirical enquiry. We had a second reason, however, for choosing this particular example to illustrate our point. The Physical-Symbol System Hypothesis is itself a substantial scientific hypothesis of the kind that we earlier dubbed 'laws of qualitative structure'. It represents an important discovery of computer science, which if borne out by the empirical evidence, as in fact appears to be occurring, will have major continuing impact on the field.

We turn now to a second example, the role of search in intelligence. This topic, and the particular hypothesis about it that we shall examine, have also played a central role in computer science, in general, and artificial intelligence, in particular.

2 Heuristic search

Knowing that physical-symbol systems provide the matrix for intelligent action does not tell us how they accomplish this. Our second example of a law of qualitative structure in computer science addresses this latter question, asserting that symbol systems solve problems by using the processes of heuristic search. This generalization, like the previous one, rests on empirical evidence, and has not been derived formally from other premises. We shall see in a moment, however, that it does have some logical connection with the symbol-system hypothesis, and perhaps we can expect to formalize the connection at some time in the future. Until that time arrives, our story must again be one of empirical enquiry. We will describe what is known about heuristic search and review the empirical findings that show how it enables action to be intelligent. We begin by stating this law of qualitative structure, the Heuristic Search Hypothesis.

> *Heuristic Search Hypothesis.* The solutions to problems are represented as symbol structures. A physical-symbol system exercises its intelligence in problem-solving by search—that is, by generating and progressively modifying symbol structures until it produces a solution structure.

Physical-symbol systems must use heuristic search to solve problems because such systems have limited processing resources; in a finite number of steps, and over a finite interval of time, they can execute only a finite number of processes. Of course that is not a very strong limitation, for all universal Turing machines suffer from it. We intend the limitation, however, in a stronger sense: we mean *practically* limited. We can conceive of systems that are not limited in a practical way but are capable, for example, of searching in parallel the nodes of an exponentially expanding tree at a constant rate for each unit advance in depth. We will not be concerned here with such systems, but with systems whose computing resources are scarce relative to the complexity of the situations with which they are confronted. The restriction will not exclude any real symbol systems, in computer or man, in the context of real tasks. The fact of limited resources allows us, for most purposes, to view a symbol system as though it were a serial, one-process-at-a-time device. If it can accomplish only a small amount of processing in any short time interval, then we might as well regard it as doing things one at a time. Thus 'limited resource symbol system' and 'serial symbol system' are practically synonymous. The problem of allocating a scarce resource from moment to moment can usually be treated, if the moment is short enough, as a problem of scheduling a serial machine.

Problem-solving

Since ability to solve problems is generally taken as a prime indicator that a system has intelligence, it is natural that much of the history of artificial intelligence is taken up with attempts to build and understand problem-solving systems. Problem-solving has been discussed by philosophers and psychologists for two millennia, in discourses dense with a feeling of mystery. If you think there is nothing problematic or mysterious about a symbol system solving problems, you are a child of today, whose views have been formed since mid-century. Plato (and, by his account, Socrates) found difficulty understanding even how problems could be *entertained*, much less how they could be solved. Let me remind you of how he posed the conundrum in the *Meno*:

MENO: And how will you inquire, Socrates, into that which you know not? What will you put forth as the subject of inquiry? And if you find what you want, how will you ever know that this is what you did not know?

To deal with this puzzle, Plato invented his famous theory of recollection: when you think you are discovering or learning something, you are really just recalling what you already knew in a previous existence. If you find this explanation preposterous, there is a much simpler one available today, based upon our understanding of symbol systems. An approximate statement of it is:

To state a problem is to designate (1) a *test* for a class of symbol structures (solutions of the problem), and (2) a *generator* of symbol structures (potential solutions). To solve a problem is to generate a structure, using (2), that satisfies the test of (1).

We have a problem if we know what we want to do (the test), and if we don't know immediately how to do it (our generator does not immediately produce a symbol structure satisfying the test). A symbol system can state and solve problems (sometimes) because it can generate and test.

If that is all there is to problem-solving, why not simply generate at once an expression that satisfies the test? This is, in fact, what we do when we wish and dream. 'If wishes were horses, beggars might ride.' But outside the world of dreams, it isn't possible. To know how we would test something, once constructed, does not mean that we know how to construct it—that we have any generator for doing so.

For example, it is well known what it means to 'solve' the problem of playing winning chess. A simple test exists for noticing winning positions, the test for checkmate of the enemy king. In the world of dreams one simply generates a strategy that leads to checkmate for all counter strategies of the opponent. Alas, no generator that will do this is known to existing symbol systems (man or machine). Instead, good moves in chess are sought by generating various alternatives, and painstakingly evaluating them with the use of approximate, and often erroneous, measures that are supposed to indicate the likelihood that a particular line of play is on the route to a winning position. Move generators there are; winning-move generators there are not.

Before there can be a move generator for a problem, there must be a problem space: a space of symbol structures in which problem situations, including the initial and goal situations, can be represented. Move generators are processes for modifying one situation in the problem space into another. The basic characteristics of physical-symbol systems guarantee that they can represent problem spaces and that they possess move generators. How, in any concrete situation they synthesize a problem space and move generators appropriate to that situation is a question that is still very much on the frontier of artificial intelligence research.

The task that a symbol system is faced with, then, when it is presented with a problem and a problem space, is to use its limited processing resources to generate possible solutions, one after another, until it finds one that satisfies the problem-defining test. If the system had some control over the order in which potential solutions were generated, then it would be desirable to arrange this order of generation so that actual solutions would have a high likelihood of appearing early. A symbol system would exhibit intelligence to the extent that it succeeded in doing this. Intelligence for a system with limited processing resources consists in making wise choices of what to do next.

Search in problem-solving

During the first decade or so of artificial intelligence research, the study of problem-solving was almost synonymous with the study of search processes. From our characterization of problems and problem-solving, it is easy to see why this was so. In fact, it might be asked whether it could be otherwise. But before we try to answer that question, we must explore further the nature of search processes as it revealed itself during that decade of activity.

Extracting information from the problem space

Consider a set of symbol structures, some small subset of which are solutions to a given problem. Suppose, further, that the solutions are distributed randomly through the entire set. By this we mean that no information exists that would enable any search generator to perform better than a random search. Then no symbol system could exhibit more intelligence (or less intelligence) than any other in solving the problem, although one might experience better luck than another.

A condition, then, for the appearance of intelligence is that the distribution of solutions be not entirely random, that the space of symbol structures exhibit at least some degree of order and pattern. A second condition is that pattern in the space of symbol structures be more or less detectable. A third condition is that the generator of potential solutions be able to behave differentially, depending on what pattern it detected. There must be information in the problem space, and the symbol system must be capable of extracting and using it. Let us look first at a very simple example, where the intelligence is easy to come by.

Consider the problem of solving a simple algebraic equation:

$$AX + B = CX + D$$

The test defines a solution as any expression of the form, $X = E$, such that $AE + B = CE + D$. Now one could use as generator any process that would produce numbers which could then be tested by substituting in the latter equation. We would not call this an intelligent generator.

Alternatively, one could use generators that would make use of the fact that the original equation can be modified—by adding or subtracting equal quantities from both sides, or multiplying or dividing both sides by the same quantity—without changing its solutions. But, of course, we can obtain even more information to guide the generator by comparing the original expression with the form of the solution, and making precisely those changes in the equation that leave its solution unchanged, while at the same time bringing it into the desired form. Such a generator could notice that there was an unwanted CX on the right-hand side of the original equation, subtract it from both sides, and collect terms again. It could then notice that there was an unwanted B on the left-hand side and subtract that. Finally, it could get rid of the unwanted coefficient $(A - C)$ on the left-hand side by dividing.

Thus by this procedure, which now exhibits considerable intelligence, the generator produces successive symbol structures, each obtained by modifying the previous one; and the modifications are aimed at reducing the differences between the form of the input structure and the form of the test expression, while maintaining the other conditions for a solution.

This simple example already illustrates many of the main mechanisms that are used by symbol systems for intelligent problem-solving. First, each successive expression is not generated independently, but is produced by modifying one produced previously. Second, the modifications are not haphazard, but depend upon two kinds of information. They depend on information that is constant over this whole class of algebra problems, and that is built into the structure of the generator itself: all modifications of expressions must leave the equation's solution unchanged. They also depend on information that changes at each step: detection of the differences in form that remain between the current expression and the desired expression. In effect, the generator incorporates some of the tests the solution must satisfy, so that expressions that don't meet these tests will never be generated. Using the first kind of information guarantees that only a tiny subset of all possible expressions is actually generated, but without losing the solution expression from this subset. Using the second kind of information arrives at the desired solution by a succession of approximations, employing a simple form of means-ends analysis to give direction to the search.

There is no mystery where the information that guided the search came from. We need not follow Plato in endowing the symbol system with a previous existence in which it already knew the solution. A moderately sophisticated generator-test system did the trick without invoking reincarnation.

Search trees

The simple algebra problem may seem an unusual, even pathological, example of search. It is certainly not trial-and-error search, for though there were a few trials, there was no error. We are more accustomed to thinking of problem-solving search as generating lushly branching trees of partial solution possibilities which may grow to thousands, or even millions, of branches, before they yield a solution. Thus, if from each expression it produces, the generator creates B new branches, then the tree will grow as B^D, where D is its depth. The tree grown for the algebra problem had the peculiarity that its branchiness, B, equalled unity.

Programs that play chess typically grow broad search trees, amounting in some cases to a million branches or more. Although this example will serve to illustrate our points about tree search, we should note that the purpose of search in chess is not to generate proposed solutions, but to evaluate (test) them. One line of research into game-playing programs has been centrally concerned with improving the representation of the chess board, and the processes for making moves on it, so as to speed up search and make it possible to search larger trees. The rationale for this direction, of course, is that the deeper the dynamic search, the more accurate should be the evaluations at the end of it. On the other hand, there is good empirical evidence that the strongest human players, grand masters, seldom explore trees of more than one hundred branches. This economy is achieved not so much by searching less deeply than do chess-playing programs, but by branching very sparsely and selectively at each node. This is only possible, without causing a deterioration of the evaluations, by having more of the selectivity built into the generator itself, so that it is able to select for generation only those branches which are very likely to yield important relevant information about the position.

The somewhat paradoxical-sounding conclusion to which this discussion leads is that search—successive generation of potential solution structures—is a fundamental aspect of a symbol system's exercise of intelligence in problem-solving but that amount of search is not a measure of the amount of intelligence being exhibited. What makes a problem a problem is not that a large amount of search is required for its solution, but that a large amount *would* be required if a requisite level of intelligence were not applied. When the symbolic system that is endeavouring to solve a problem knows enough about what to do, it simply proceeds directly towards its goal; but whenever its knowledge becomes inadequate, when it enters *terra incognita*, it is faced with the threat of going through large amounts of search before it finds its way again.

The potential for the exponential explosion of the search tree that is present in every scheme for generating problem solutions warns us against depending on the brute force of computers—even the biggest and fastest computers—as a compensation for the ignorance and unselectivity of their generators. The hope is still periodically ignited in some human breasts that a computer can be found that is fast enough, and that can be programmed cleverly enough, to play good chess by brute-force search. There is nothing known in theory about the game of chess that rules out this possibility. But empirical studies on the management of search in sizable trees with only modest results make this a much less promising direction than it was when chess was first chosen as an appropriate task for artificial intelligence. We must regard this as one of the important empirical findings of research with chess programs.

The forms of intelligence

The task of intelligence, then, is to avert the ever-present threat of the exponential explosion of search. How can this be accomplished? The first route, already illustrated by the algebra example and by chess programs that only generate 'plausible' moves for further analysis, is to build selectivity into the generator: to generate only structures that show promise of being solutions or of being along the path towards solutions. The usual consequence of doing this is to decrease the rate of branching, not to prevent it entirely. Ultimate exponential explosion is not avoided—save in exceptionally highly structured situations like the algebra example—but only postponed. Hence, an intelligent system generally needs to supplement the selectivity of its solution generator with other information-using techniques to guide search.

Twenty years of experience with managing tree search in a variety of task environments has produced a small kit of general techniques which is part of the equipment of every researcher in artificial intelligence today. Since these techniques have been described in general works like that of Nilsson (1971), they can be summarized very briefly here.

In serial heuristic search, the basic question always is: What shall be done next? In tree search, that question, in turn, has two components: (1) from what node in the tree shall we search next, and (2) what direction shall we take from that node? Information helpful in answering the first question may be interpreted as measuring the relative distance of different nodes from the goal. Best-first search calls for searching next from the node that appears closest to the goal. Information helpful in answering the second question—in what direction to search—is often obtained, as in the algebra example, by detecting specific differences between the current nodal structure and the goal structure described by the test of a solution, and selecting actions that are relevant to reducing these particular kinds of differences. This is the technique known as means-ends analysis, which plays a central role in the structure of the General Problem Solver.

The importance of empirical studies as a source of general ideas in AI research can be demonstrated clearly by tracing the history, through large numbers of problem-solving programs, of these two central ideas: best-first search and means-ends analysis. Rudiments of best-first search were already present, though unnamed, in the Logic Theorist in 1955. The General Problem Solver, embodying means-ends analysis, appeared about 1957—but combined it with modified depth-first search rather than best-first search. Chess programs were generally wedded, for reasons of economy of memory, to depth-first search, supplemented after about 1958 by the powerful alpha-beta pruning procedure. Each of these techniques appears to have been reinvented a number of times, and it is hard to find general, task-independent, theoretical discussions of problem-solving in terms of these concepts until the middle or late 1960s. The amount of formal buttressing they have received from mathematical theory is still minuscule: some theorems about the reduction in search that can be secured from using the alpha-beta heuristic, a couple of theorems (reviewed by Nilsson 1971) about shortest-path search, and some very recent theorems on best-first search with a probabilistic evaluation function.

'Weak' and 'strong' methods

The techniques we have been discussing are dedicated to the control of exponential expansion rather than its prevention. For this reason, they have been properly called 'weak methods'—methods to be used when the symbol system's knowledge or the amount of structure actually contained in the problem space are inadequate to permit search to be avoided entirely. It is instructive to contrast a highly structured situation, which can be formulated, say, as a linear-programming problem, with the less structured situations of combinatorial problems like the travelling salesman problem or scheduling problems. ('Less structured' here refers to the insufficiency or non-existence of relevant theory about the structure of the problem space.)

In solving linear-programming problems, a substantial amount of computation may be required, but the search does not branch. Every step is a step along the way to a solution. In solving combinatorial problems or in proving theorems, tree search can seldom be avoided, and success depends on heuristic search methods of the sort we have been describing.

Not all streams of AI problem-solving research have followed the path we have been outlining. An example of a somewhat different point is provided by the work on theorem-proving systems. Here, ideas imported from mathematics and logic have had a strong influence on the direction of enquiry. For example, the use of heuristics was resisted when properties of completeness could not be proved (a bit ironic, since most interesting mathematical systems are known to be undecidable). Since completeness can seldom be proved for best-first search heuristics, or for many kinds of selective generators, the effect of this requirement was rather inhibiting. When theorem-proving programs were continually incapacitated by the combinatorial explosion of their search trees, thought began to be given to selective heuristics, which in many cases proved to be analogues of heuristics used in general problem-solving programs. The set-of-support heuristic, for example, is a form of working backward, adapted to the resolution theorem-proving environment.

A summary of the experience

We have now described the workings of our second law of qualitative structure, which asserts that physical-symbol systems solve problems by means of heuristic search. Beyond that, we have examined some subsidiary characteristics of heuristic search, in particular the threat that it always faces of exponential explosion of the search tree, and some of the means it uses to avert that threat. Opinions differ as to how effective heuristic search has been as a problem-solving mechanism—the opinions depending on what task domains are considered and what criterion of adequacy is adopted. Success can be guaranteed by setting aspiration levels low—or failure by setting them high. The evidence might be summed up about as follows: few programs are solving problems at 'expert' professional levels. Samuel's checker program and Feigenbaum and Lederberg's DENDRAL are perhaps the best-known exceptions, but one could point also to a number of heuristic search programs for such operations-research problem domains as scheduling and integer programming. In a number of domains, programs perform at the level of competent amateurs: chess, some theorem-proving domains, many kinds of games and puzzles. Human levels have not yet been nearly reached by programs that have a complex perceptual 'front end': visual scene recognizers, speech understanders, robots that have to manœuvre in real space and time. Nevertheless, impressive progress has been made, and a large body of experience assembled about these difficult tasks.

We do not have deep theoretical explanations for the particular pattern of performance that has emerged. On empirical grounds, however, we might draw two conclusions. First, from what has been learned about human expert performance in tasks like chess, it is likely that any system capable of matching that performance will have to have access, in its memories, to very large stores of semantic information. Second, some part of the human superiority in tasks with a large perceptual component can be attributed to the special-purpose built-in parallel-processing structure of the human eye and ear.

In any case, the quality of performance must necessarily depend on the characteristics both of the problem domains and of the symbol systems used to tackle them. For most real-life domains in which we are interested, the domain structure has so far not proved sufficiently simple to yield theorems about complexity, or to tell us, other than empirically, how large real-world problems are in relation to the abilities of our symbol systems to solve them. That situation may change, but until it does, we must rely upon empirical explorations, using the best problem solvers we know how to build, as a principal source of knowledge about the magnitude and characteristics of problem difficulty. Even in highly structured areas like linear programming, theory has been much more useful in strengthening the heuristics that under-lie the most powerful solution algorithms than in providing a deep analysis of complexity.

Intelligence without much search

Our analysis of intelligence equated it with ability to extract and use information about the structure of the problem space, so as to enable a problem solution to be generated as quickly and directly as possible. New directions for improving the problem-solving capabilities of symbol systems can be equated, then, with new ways of extracting and using information. At least three such ways can be identified.

Non-local use of information

First, it has been noted by several investigators that information gathered in the course of tree search is usually only used *locally*, to help make decisions at the specific node where the information was generated. Information about a chess position, obtained by dynamic analysis of a subtree of continuations, is usually used to evaluate just that position, not to evaluate other positions that may contain many of the same features. Hence, the same facts have to be rediscovered repeatedly at different nodes of the search tree. Simply to take the information out of the context in which it arose and use it generally does not solve the problem, for the information may be valid only in a limited range of contexts. In recent years, a few exploratory efforts have been made to transport information from its context of origin to other appropriate contexts. While it is still too early to evaluate the power of this idea, or even exactly how it is to be achieved, it shows considerable promise. An important line of investigation that Berliner (1975) has been pursuing is to use causal analysis to determine the range over which a particular piece of information is valid. Thus if a weakness in a chess position can be traced back to the move that made it, then the same weakness can be expected in other positions descendant from the same move.

The HEARSAY speech-understanding system has taken another approach to making information globally available. That system seeks to recognize speech strings by pursuing a parallel search at a number of different levels: phonemic, lexical, syntactic, and semantic. As each of these searches provides and evaluates hypotheses, it supplies the information it has gained to a common 'blackboard' that can be read by all the sources. This shared information can be used, for example, to eliminate hypotheses, or even whole classes of hypotheses, that would otherwise have to be searched by one of the processes. Thus increasing our ability to use tree-search information non-locally offers promise for raising the intelligence of problem-solving systems.

Semantic recognition systems

A second active possibility for raising intelligence is to supply the symbol system with a rich body of semantic information about the task-domain it is dealing with. For example, empirical research on the skill of chess masters shows that a major source of the master's skill is stored information that enables him to recognize a large number of specific features and patterns of features on a chess board, and information that uses this recognition to propose actions appropriate to the features recognized. This general idea has, of course, been incorporated in chess programs almost from the beginning. What is new is the realization of the number of such patterns and associated information that may have to be stored for master-level play: something on the order of 50,000.

The possibility of substituting recognition for search arises because a particular, and especially a rare, pattern can contain an enormous amount of information, provided that it is closely linked to the structure of the problem space. When that structure is 'irregular', and not subject to simple mathematical description, then knowledge of a large number of relevant patterns may be the key to intelligent behaviour. Whether this is so in any particular task-domain is a question more easily settled by empirical investigation than by theory. Our experience with symbol systems richly endowed with semantic information and pattern-recognizing capabilities for accessing it is still extremely limited.

The discussion above refers specifically to semantic information associated with a recognition system. Of course, there is also a whole large area of AI research on semantic information processing and the organization of semantic memories that falls outside the scope of the topics we are discussing in this paper.

Selecting appropriate representations

A third line of enquiry is concerned with the possibility that search can be reduced or avoided by selecting an appropriate problem space. A standard example that illustrates this possibility dramatically is the mutilated chequer-board problem. A standard 64-square chequer-board can be covered exactly with 32 tiles, each a 1×2 rectangle covering exactly two squares. Suppose, now, that we cut off squares at two diagonally opposite corners of the chequer-board, leaving a total of 62 squares. Can this mutilated board be covered exactly with 31 tiles? With (literally) heavenly patience, the impossibility of achieving such a covering can be demonstrated by trying all possible arrangements. The alternative, for those with less patience and more intelligence, is to observe that the two diagonally opposite corners of a chequer-board are of the same colour. Hence, the mutilated chequer-board has two fewer squares of one colour than of the other. But each tile covers one square of one colour and one square of the other, and any set of tiles must cover the same number of squares of each colour. Hence, there is no solution. How can a symbol system discover this simple inductive argument as an alternative to a hopeless attempt to solve the problem by search among all possible coverings? We would award a system that found a solution high marks for intelligence.

Perhaps, however, in posing these problems we are not escaping from search processes. We have simply displaced the search from a space of possible problem solutions to a space of possible representations. In any event, the whole process of moving from one representation to another, and of discovering and evaluating representations, is largely unexplored territory in the domain of problem-solving research. The laws of qualitative structure governing representations remain to be discovered. The search for them is almost sure to receive considerable attention in the coming decade.

Conclusion

That is our account of symbol systems and intelligence. It has been a long road from Plato's *Meno* to the present, but it is perhaps encouraging that most of the progress along that road has been made since the turn of the twentieth century, and a large fraction of it since the mid-point of the century. Thought was still wholly intangible and ineffable until modern formal logic interpreted it as the manipulation of formal tokens. And it seemed still to inhabit mainly the heaven of Platonic ideals, or the equally obscure spaces of the human mind, until computers taught us how symbols could be processed by machines. A. M. Turing made his great contributions at the mid-century crossroads of these developments that led from modern logic to the computer.

Physical-symbol systems

The study of logic and computers has revealed to us that intelligence resides in physical-symbol systems. This is computer science's most basic law of qualitative structure.

Symbol systems are collections of patterns and processes, the latter being capable of producing, destroying, and modifying the former. The most important properties of patterns are that they can designate objects, processes, or other patterns, and that when they designate processes, they can be interpreted. Interpretation means carrying out the designated process. The two most significant classes of symbol systems with which we are acquainted are human beings and computers.

Our present understanding of symbol systems grew, as indicated earlier, through a sequence of stages. Formal logic familiarized us with symbols, treated syntactically, as the raw material of thought, and with the idea of manipulating them according to carefully defined formal processes. The Turing machine made the syntactic processing of symbols truly machinelike, and affirmed the potential universality of strictly defined symbol systems. The stored-program concept for computers reaffirmed the interpretability of symbols, already implicit in the Turing machine. List-processing brought to the forefront the denotational capacities of symbols, and defined symbol-processing in ways that allowed independence from the fixed structure of the underlying physical machine. By 1956 all of these concepts were available, together with hardware for implementing them. The study of the intelligence of symbol systems, the subject of artificial intelligence, could begin.

Heuristic search

A second law of qualitative structure for AI is that symbol systems solve problems by generating potential solutions and testing them—that is, by searching. Solutions are usually sought by creating symbolic expressions and modifying them sequentially until they satisfy the conditions for a solution. Hence, symbol systems solve problems by searching. Since they have finite resources, the search cannot be carried out all at once, but must be sequential. It leaves behind it either a single path from starting-point to goal or, if correction and backup are necessary, a whole tree of such paths.

Symbol systems cannot appear intelligent when they are surrounded by pure chaos. They exercise intelligence by extracting information from a problem domain and using that information to guide their search, avoiding wrong turns and circuitous bypaths. The problem domain must contain information—that is, some degree of order and structure—for the method to work. The paradox of the *Meno* is solved by the observation that information may be remembered, but new information may also be extracted from the domain that the symbols designate. In both cases, the ultimate source of the information is the task-domain.

The empirical base

Research on artificial intelligence is concerned with how symbol systems must be organized in order to behave intelligently. Twenty years of work in the area has accumulated a considerable body of knowledge, enough to fill several books (it already has), and most of it in the form of rather concrete experience about the behaviour of specific classes of symbol systems in specific task-domains. Out of this experience, however, there have also emerged some generalizations, cutting across task-domains and systems, about the general characteristics of intelligence and its methods of implementation.

We have tried to state some of these generalizations here. They are mostly qualitative rather than mathematical. They have more the flavour of geology or evolutionary biology than the flavour of theoretical physics. They are sufficiently strong to enable us today to design and build moderately intelligent systems for a considerable range of task domains, as well as to gain a rather deep understanding of how human intelligence works in many situations.

What next?

In our account we have mentioned open questions as well as settled ones; there are many of both. We see no abatement of the excitement of exploration that has surrounded this field over the past quarter century. Two resource limits will determine the rate of progress over the next such period. One is the amount of computing power that will be available. The second, and probably the more important, is the number of talented young computer scientists who will be attracted to this area of research as the most challenging they can tackle.

A. M. Turing concluded his famous paper 'Computing Machinery and Intelligence' with the words: 'We can only see a short distance ahead, but we can see plenty there that needs to be done.'

Many of the things Turing saw in 1950 that needed to be done have been done, but the agenda is as full as ever. Perhaps we read too much into his simple statement above, but we like to think that in it Turing recognized the fundamental truth that all computer scientists instinctively know. For all physical-symbol systems, condemned as we are to serial search of the problem environment, the critical question is always: What to do next?

References

Berliner, H. (1975). 'Chess as Problem Solving: The Development of a Tactics Analyzer.' Unpublished Ph.D. thesis. Carnegie-Mellon University.

McCarthy, J. (1960). 'Recursive Functions of Symbolic Expressions and their Computation by Machine.' *Commun. ACM* 3 (Apr.): 184–95.

McCulloch, W. S. (1961). 'What is a Number, that a Man may know it, and a Man that he may know a Number?' *General Semantics Bulletin* nos. 26–7: 7–18. Repr. in W. S. McCulloch, *Embodiments of Mind*, pp. 1–18. Cambridge, Mass.: MIT Press.

Nilsson, N. J. (1971). *Problem-Solving Methods in Artificial Intelligence*. New York: McGraw-Hill.

32

ARTIFICIAL INTELLIGENCE – WHERE ARE WE?

Daniel G. Bobrow and Patrick J. Hayes (Editors)

Source: *Artificial Intelligence* 25 (1985) 375–415.

The Artificial Intelligence Journal is 15 years old, and is publishing its 25th volume in 1985. From one volume of 300 pages to cover the field in 1970, we have grown to three volumes of over 1000 pages in 1984. The editors and publisher felt this was a good time to ask some of the people who have been in, or observers of, the field during these years to comment on where we have been, where we are and what the future might hold. To structure the responses, we constructed a set of 10 questions. Not all whom we sent them to responded, but those who did provide us with a varied view of the state of Artificial Intelligence. Some responded in long essays, some in direct but cryptic answers. We have tried to edit extracts from the responses into a coherent whole which reflects the pattern of views we received.

It seems best to begin with the answers to Question 5, which should obviously, in retrospect, have been the first question.

Question 5. It has been argued that there is no true coherence to AI, but that history will see the field as a miscellaneous collection of ideas to do with the application of nonnumerical computing to behavior which had until then required human levels of cognitive competence. Calling this a single discipline, it is argued, is like lumping together automobile engineering, classical dynamics and biomechanics because they are all concerned with movement. Is AI a single discipline? Is AI more or less coherent than it was 10 years ago? If not, what pieces are there? If so, what distinguishes it from other fields (problems, methods, theory, pretheoretical assumptions, methodology, . . .)?

Several respondents thought this was not an interesting issue at the present time, and that the field should not be burdened by methodological disputes.

[Saul Amarel]
"I would not be overly concerned at present with the 'nature of AI' and definitions of the discipline."

[Jerome Feldman]
"I don't think it matters at all whether or not AI is a discipline or where its boundaries might lie."

[Roger Schank]
"AI represents a small number of methodologies applied to a wide variety of disciplines. AI is the attempt to find process models that account for all kinds of human behaviors. Some day, I assume, academic disciplines will include on their faculties, AI people who are experts in application of AI methodologies to that discipline. Until that day, AI is best off left alone, pretending to be a single discipline."

And some saw AI as a broad inter- or cross-disciplinary mixture:

[Margaret Boden]
"AI suffers from some of the same problems as philosophy: it tackles the unanswered, or even the unanswerable, questions. As soon as it manages to find a fruitful way to answer one of them, the question gets hived off as a specialist sub-field. The special sciences started emerging from philosophy in the Renaissance. Specialist areas of study have been emerging from AI for only thirty years. But already we have distinctive sub-fields – such as pattern-recognition, image-processing, and rule-based systems. Their executors often speak of AI (if they speak of it at all) as something not quite respectable, something nasty in the woodshed that was once glimpsed but is better forgotten. What should not be forgotten is that the respectable topics were excluded from what people are prepared to call 'AI' as soon as they became 'respectable'."

[Christopher Longuet-Higgins]
"I sometimes wonder whether AI is a discipline at all, let along a single one!"

[Pamela McCorduck]
"AI is certainly a curious mixture of stuff right now, but so was medicine before the germ theory of disease, biology before the double helix."

[Nils Nilsson]
"AI, broadly conceived, is just too large to be a single discipline – mainly because intelligent perception and behavior touch so many aspects of computer science, control theory, and signal processing theory."

Nilsson goes on, however, to identify a part of AI, which we might call "classical" AI which does not have an inner coherence. Berliner, Dreyfus, Feldman, Newell and Winograd all identified essentially the same inner field, although they differed strongly on whether this was a promising paradigm, as shown later.

[Nils Nilsson]
"But, that part of AI based on reasoning with declaratively represented knowledge (e.g. logical formulas) with semantic attachment to specialized procedures and data structures is a coherent field. I think it will inherit the name AI and continue to develop as the core discipline underlying intelligent mechanisms."

[Aaron Sloman]
"If AI is a single discipline, it is more like Biology than like Neuro-biology. It is inherently multi-disciplinary, and the more AI is applied the more disciplines will be involved. There is a central coherent core of AI/Cognitive Science which is the systematic study of actual and possible intelligent systems. This seeks general principles, not just successful designs. Very few people are working on this. This is partly because it is the hardest part of AI, and has least short-term pay off.

Apart from this, people doing AI do not all have something in common apart from a concern with computation (compare low level vision and the study of non-monotonic reasoning). But there are lots of overlaps, as in Wittgenstein's analogy with family resemblances."

Several people felt that AI will become a coherent field, a science of intelligence or a science of information. Donald Michie draws an historical analogy with organic chemistry.

[John Seeley Brown]
"The study of mind is unquestionably a coherent discipline and if the Center for the Study of Language and Information is right, perhaps even the study of situated language and information will emerge as a discipline. AI surely encompasses both of these endeavours, and whether AI is more or less than these depends on one's interest in the construction of intelligent systems per se."

[Pamela McCorduck]
"I wouldn't be surprised if what is now called AI will eventually subsume most of computer science in general. The new field will be firmly based on a science of symbols, or information, or whatever we choose to call those artifacts then; moreover the new field will be as clear and orderly (or chaotic and frantic) as the biological sciences, with equivalents to the cell theory of organisms (which AI already has in the physical symbol hypothesis) and to molecular biology, and so forth. (Oh dear! Another outsider extrapolating wildly. Well, you asked.)"

[John McCarthy]
"I think there will be a unified AI methodology, but we don't have it yet."

[Donald Michie]
"The first point is that knowledge, rather than intelligence, is where today's action is. Note that I say 'action', not effort. The latter gets concentrated wherever academic fad or short-term corporate opportunism dictates. A historical analogy is with the first synthesis of an organic compound in 1828, when a trace of urea was made, previously believed impossible except by participation of living cells. At the recent private meeting of ISSEK in Bled, Yugoslavia, all present agreed that the present stage of AI is comparable. The first laboratory re-aggregation of primitive elements into new conceptualised structures has been achieved, and these structures are recognisable on a variety of tests as authentic human-type knowledge."

The view of AI as a science was best expressed by Newell:

[Alan Newell]
"One of the world's deepest mysteries – the nature of mind – is at the center of AI. It is our holy grail. Its discovery (which will no more be a single act than the discovery of the nature of life or the origins of the universe) will be a major chapter in the scientific advance of mankind. When it happens (i.e., as substantial progress becomes evident) there will be plenty of recognition that we have finally penetrated this mystery and in what that consists. There will be a coherent account of the nature of intelligence, knowledge, intention, desire, etc., and how it is possible for the phenomena that cluster under these names to occur in our physical universe.

Of course, the account can be coherent only if the phenomena are. We know enough about both mind and information processing by now, so that the possibility of fragmentation is hardly one of AI's more pressing issues. Intelligence (the aspect of mind currently most central in AI) will not turn out to be a doughnut-shaped phenomenon, quite empty in the center. At the center matters might turn out to be fundamentally simple, almost tautological. It can even be argued that such must be the case. But that will not make the center empty or remove any recognition of the profundity of the answer. The biological (Darwinian) theory of evolution provides a useful example. The basic theory is within a whisker of being completely transparent, yet we have no difficulty recognizing its transforming power in biology, along with the drama and glory of its scientific discovery.

But is AI coherent *now*? It seems so to me. Our foundation in symbolic and representational systems, the universal use of goal hierarchies, the pervasiveness of search and knowledge (and the way these articulate with each other), the grounding of AI's operational conceptions of knowledge in the classical developments in logic and theorem proving in formal systems, the large collections of problem-solving methods and memory organizations (and their fit into the larger framework) – all this adds up to sufficient coherency for the days thereof.

However, some special circumstances do pertain to AI's coherency as a discipline. One, noted above, is that AI is part of computer science, not an autonomous discipline. A second is that other disciplines, such as psychology, linguistics, anthropology and philosophy, share a concern with the mystery of mind and intelligence. A third is that for the moment AI and computer science combine basic science and applied science in one disciplinary matrix, rather than separating them out, as in physical science versus engineering, or biology versus medicine. All these keep AI from being a well-contained and tidy discipline. But they don't have much effect on the coherence of the core subject matter, only on the ferment of new unassimilated ideas.

Disciplines are human-formed institutions and only in part reflect the subject matter on which they stand. As good a definition as any is that a discipline is an inter-reading population of scientists (or whatever the participants are called). In these terms, the coherence of AI has recently gone down a little, because AI is expanding rapidly and has acquired many new recruits, diluting the extent to which we have all been reading the same literature over the last N years. But it is not intellectually less coherent than it was. That coherence will be assured by the text-book writers (the Elaine Rich's and Pat Winston's) who struggle to create a coherence that can be the basis for all to read. It will be helped by theoretical developments, but it is not dependent on them. Many extremely strong disciplines have existed and continue to exist with extremely weak theoretical structures (e.g., anthropology or geology before plate tectonics).

We should, by the way, be prepared for some radical, and perhaps surprising, transformations of the disciplinary structure of science (technology included) as information processing pervades it. In particular, as we become more aware of the detailed information processes that go on in doing science, the sciences will find themselves increasingly taking a metaposition, in which doing science (observing, experimenting, theorizing, testing, archiving . . .) will involve understanding these information processes, and building systems that do the object-level science. Then the boundaries between the enterprise of science as a whole (the acquisition and organization of the knowledge of the world) and AI (the understanding of how knowledge is acquired and organized) will become increasingly fuzzy. Disciplines will hardly fade away. The whole population can't all read the same literature, and other span-of-control issues exist as well. Most emphatically, AI (and computer science) will not become the new Queen of the Sciences. We live in too democratic an age for that. More likely is the diffusion into all of science of the scientific quest to understand the basic nature of intelligence and information processing. This is not so far-fetched if you consider the strong tendency of AI to accomplish its basic science in the context of real-world tasks. The bottom line must be that as mankind comes to understand its own intellectual (and other mental) processes in sufficient depth, their further understanding must become the central theme of intellectual endeavor throughout the whole academy and indeed the intelligentsia. Pope, with his 'The proper study of mankind is man', never had it more right."

In contrast, Winograd describes how he has come to have a more modest view of AI as a technology, an interesting but limited part of Computer Science.

[Terry Winograd]
"There are two quite different starting points to define AI – the dream and the technology. As a dream, there is a unified (if ill-defined) goal of duplicating human intelligence in its entirety. As a technology, there is a fairly coherent body of techniques (such as heuristic search and the use of propositional representations) that distinguish the field from others in computer science (Nilsson's Principles of Artificial Intelligence is a fairly comprehensive and integrated account of this material). In the end, this technological base will continue to be a unified area of study (like numerical analysis, or operations research) with its special methodology. We will recognize that it is not coextensive with the dream, but is only one (possibly small) piece.

My own work underwent a major change, as I moved away from the assumption that the way to make better and more useful computers (and interfaces) was to get them to be intelligent and use natural language. I recognized the depth of the difficulties in getting a machine to understand language in any but a superficial and misleading way, and am convinced that people will be much better served by machines that do well-defined and understandable things than those that appear to be like a person until something goes wrong (which won't take long), at which point there is only confusion."

This distinction between on the one hand AI as a science, essentially part of Cognitive Science, with its focus being theories of intelligence; and on the other AI as a technology, part of Computer Science, with its focus being the design of systems, ran through several responses. For example, two "technologists", Boden and Winograd, placed great emphasis on the fact that foreseeable AI systems don't have general intelligence; while two "scientists", Feldman and Newell, put the search for an architecture for general intelligence at the center of the subject.

Question 1. AI has developed rapidly in the last decade. What do you feel have been the most significant scientific and/or technological advances in that time scale? Has progress accelerated over previous

*decades, or are we seeing a damping effect of attacking harder prob-
lems? Simon has argued that good chess playing programs took longer
than expected because not enough students worked on these problems.
Are there other unsolved problems that you feel should have been
cracked?*

*Question 2. What do you think have been the most important advances
in your own work during the last decade? Are there any problems which
have seemed intractable, or on which progress has been slower than you
had expected?*

Not everyone agrees that AI has developed much in the last decade.

[Margaret Boden]
"The editor's first question to us begins: 'AI has developed rapidly within the
last decade.' I beg to differ.

AI has *grown* enormously in the last ten years, and the media – and the
money-men – have now discovered it. But growth need not imply development. With a few exceptions, what we have seen is 'more of the same' (or, at
most, 'better of the same'). The recent explosion of funding and publicity is
due to commercial and political factors, not to intellectual advances in the
field. The central problems of AI, and the theoretical basis of its achievements, have remained essentially the same. Most of the 'advance' has been in
technological efficiency, not scientific understanding."

[Aaron Sloman]
"I am not sure that 'AI has developed rapidly in the last decade' if that refers
to problems solved, concepts and theories tested successfully, etc., though the
number of people and the amount of money committed to AI have grown
rapidly. I am not sure that there is enough cumulative work yet."

[Hubert Dreyfus]
"Looking back over 25 years of AI the field seems to me a perfect example
of what Imre Lakatos has characterized as a degenerating research program.[1] AI began auspiciously with Newell and Simon's early work at RAND
showing that computers could be programmed to simulate certain forms of
human symbolic manipulations. In retrospect, I see I failed to appreciate the
importance of this early work. In those early days there were only a few
isolated initiates and believers, but by 1970 AI had turned into a flourishing
research program thanks to a series of micro-world successes such as Winograd's SHRDLU, Evan's Analogy Problem Program, Waltz's Scene Analysis
Program and Winston's program which learned concepts from examples.
The field soon had its own Ph.D. programs, journals, symposia, proceedings, gurus, etc. It looked like all one had to do was extend, combine, and
render more realistic the micro-worlds and one would have genuine artificial

intelligence. Minsky predicted that 'within a generation the problem of creating "artificial intelligence" will be substantially solved".[2]

Then, rather suddenly, the field ran into unexpected trouble. It started, as far as I can tell, with the failure of Charniak's attempt to program children's story understanding. It turned out to be much harder than one expected to formulate a theory of common-sense. It was not, as Minsky had hoped, just a question of cataloguing a few hundred thousand facts. The common-sense knowledge problem became the center of concern. A remark by Minsky reflects this change in mood: "the AI problem is one of the hardest science has ever undertaken".[3]

Related problems were also noted although not often seen as related. Cognitivists discovered the importance of images and prototypes in human understanding and computers turned out to be very poor at dealing with images and with seeing similarity of a given case to a prototypical one.[4] Learning also turned out to be much harder than anyone had expected."

[Terry Winograd]
"During the past ten years AI has entered a new phase. The technical ideas that fueled the early excitement have been pushed to the point where we are experiencing the limits of their applicability. It is not at all obvious that significant theoretical advances can be made by continuing in the same direction. At the same time, the revolution in hardware size and costs has made it possible to apply those techniques with economic effectiveness in a huge range of situations. As a result, the field has several major growth areas. One emphasizes applications and the resulting profits, with little pretense to theoretical advance; another leads to highly speculative and imprecise intuitions about learning, memory, etc., in an attempt to grasp at something that can get us beyond the limitations of the existing paradigm; another focusses on the design of better parallel (non-von-Neumann, etc.) hardware in hopes that the difficulties are in the end only those of scale."

[Bernard Meltzer]
"There is a widespread malaise among research workers in the field about the health of their subject. This has to do not only with logistic issues such as the drain of very good people from research into applications, or some of the gross inadequacies of structural and funding support by governments – but has to do with the very heart and methodology of the subject."

Others, while feeling that there is progress, admit that many problems are much harder than was thought.

[Saul Amarel]
"I believe there has been steady scientific progress in all areas of AI in the last decade. I cannot sense acceleration of progress over previous decades; certainly no spectacular advances in basic problems.

Important advances in my work: a better assessment of the nature, and the dimensions of complexity, of the problem of representations in problem solving; clarification of relationships between expertise acquisition in problem solving and theory formation; development of strategies for theory formation. I found that the problem of choosing a representation for a problem, and/or shifting a representation in an 'appropriate' direction, is harder than I thought. Also, progress has been slower than I expected in problems that have a strong 'formation' component, i.e., where there are many interdependent problem conditions, and the search for solution cannot receive strong a-priori guidance from these conditions."

[John McCarthy]
"The main scientific advance that I can identify is the formalization of nonmonotonic reasoning. Naturally this may be a prejudiced view. Perhaps the progress in learning amounts to a major advance.

Circumscription is my own best work. All the major problems of AI seem intractable."

[Roger Schank]
"The most significant advance in the last decade has been the appreciation of just how complex the nature of thinking is. We have come to understand what the issues are."

Others have a more optimistic view of how much progress has been made. Some see the field as in the process of becoming scientifically mature.

[John Seeley Brown]
"Given that much of AI is in a state of transition from a pretheoretic to a more mature endeavor, future progress may appear to be slower than in the past but will probably be more substantial. The actual contributions of a given piece of research (or system) will be less metaphorical but more precise; the principles of a given system will not only be articulated but also competitively argued; new techniques will not just be described but will also have their capabilities and boundary conditions characterized. Not only are the new problems under investigation more difficult – much of the cream has already been skimmed – but also the expectations of what constitutes interesting 'findings' are rising."

[Jerome Feldman]
"Progress has been greater and across a wider range of sub-disciplines than I would have guessed. The most striking thing is the increased scientific maturity of the field; the best work now has a firm basis both in past AI work and in the results of other disciplines."

[Alan Newell]

"I have the perception of steady progress, not just over the last decade but during the (almost) two decades prior to that. 'Steady progress' of course means exponential progress, because it goes pretty much as the number of scientists involved and the number of cycles available per scientist, both of which have been increasing exponentially. Looked at one way, that is acceleration; looked at another, it is just chugging along. One feature of progress in AI, which also holds for computer science as a whole, is the spreading out of application to new domains. This doesn't look like integrated science or like accumulation in depth, but it is an essential feature of our field and it counts as progress. In particular, it counts as scientific progress, because AI is in the game of understanding how to represent knowledge about the whole world, and we find this out only as AI gets applied to new aspects of the world."

Of the dozen or so specific topics which people thought were significant, only four were mentioned more than once: qualitative reasoning, learning, connectionism (or massive parallelism), and expert systems; and only the latter two were mentioned more than twice. Amarel, Berliner, Newell and Nilsson all find that the development of expert-system technology is one of the most significant developments of the decade, sometimes with a cautionary note. Nilsson, for example, while saying that "the realization that a practically useful amount of knowledge about various areas of expertise could be encoded in declarative form and made available in expert causality systems" is one of the "most significant" achievements, also cautions that "interest in applications has attracted a lot of attention to AI, but it has also shifted focus away from dealing with deep, conceptual problems. Most expert systems, for example, are based on ideas that were around ten years ago: they are not terribly profound."

[Saul Amarel]

"Progress has been excellent in methodologies and technologies for building expert systems. Interest in this area has grown enormously; it has been fueled by expectations of significant impact on practical problems. By now, we have impressive demonstrations of impact in some problems of engineering and medicine."

[Hans Berliner]

"At more than 30 years of age, AI is still a genuinely glorious enterprise that has achieved a great deal in the past. Not only have AI workers had significant impact on data structures for all of computer science, but the development and pushing of the 'symbol' hypothesis has had very important effects for understanding what intelligence is all about. This work appears to have found its present apex in the languages that support the building of expert systems, an activity that for the first time makes it possible for AI as a field to pay its own way in the scheme of things.

A great deal has already been said about this, so I will only add my voice to caution those that may expect too much. This generation of expert systems will not learn anything of significance, and as I will attempt to show below, I do not believe they will be able to intrude into the top 10% of experts in any chosen domain. This does not detract from their usefulness, but it does limit the research value of such systems."

[Alan Newell]
"There is no doubt, as far as I am concerned, that the development of expert systems is the major advance in the field during the last decade. I take the essence of this to be the knowledge-intensive, problem-solving-learn systems, such as *Mycin, Prospector, R1* and *Internist*. It makes no difference that these systems are extremely limited in many ways and do not incorporate much that is known in AI. Science advances by a sequence of approximating steps, and the important thing is that a next step get taken, not how limited each step is in itself. The emergence of expert systems has transformed the enterprise of AI, not only because it has been the main driver of the current wave of commercialization of AI, but because it has set the major scientific problems for AI for the next few years – namely, to assimilate expert systems into the general body of scientific knowledge in AI. (This process is already underway, but lots more input is arriving in the raft of new applied programs currently being built.)"

Boden, Feldman and Sloman all explicitly mention massively parallel or connectionist systems as an exciting recent idea with great promise. (We take up this again below in the answers to Question 7.)

[Margaret Boden]
"The one area where it seems that there may be a breakthrough is that of connectionist (massively parallel) machines. Very little is known, as yet, about the computational potential and limitations of such machines. But exploratory research should become possible within the next decade, as the first examples of connectionist hardware become available."

[Jerome Feldman]
"My own work has undergone a radical change in the last half-decade. I now believe that many of the core problems of AI, such as pattern matching, context sensitivity, representation of real world knowledge and plausible inference, are better approached on a non-symbolic computational basis. Massively parallel connection networks, spreading activation and evidential inference appear to be a natural scientific paradigm for exploring fundamental questions of intelligence. The surprising thing has been the rate of

progress along these lines and its close correspondence to evolving understanding in psychology and neuroscience."

Several people feel a central weakness is our inability to give computers a physical intuition. John Seeley Brown says he "would have expected more progress in our ability to provide our reasoning engines with better physical intuitions and common sense understanding of causality and causal mechanisms." Meltzer expresses this as a contrast between knowledge and experience, Sloman as a matter of good representation for shapes.

[Bernard Meltzer]
"Right from the start of the subject about 40 years ago John McCarthy emphasised, quite rightly, the centrality of the task of modelling commonsense reasoning and the knowledge required for it. In due course this led to intensive study and experimentation on ways of representing knowledge and modes of inference. I want however to point to a remarkable peculiarity of most of his work: the modelling of our notions of space and of time, which are basic to the commonsense view of the world, was hardly broached in any serious, principled way; at least until comparatively recently it was either ignored or dealt with in fragmentary and ad hoc ways. I don't know if others in the field have had the impression I have sometimes got, looking into the design of these programs – they seem to model a ghost, ethereal world in which not only there is no space or time but not even any physical objects: a solipsistic world insomma, as we say in Italy. Why this lacuna? I want to suggest that it is one symptom of the fact that the issue of knowledge became so dominant that it was allowed to push into the background the issue of experience."

[Aaron Sloman]
"Another major unsolved problem is how to represent shape. Work in image interpretation, and computer graphics has produced shape representations which are useful for a limited range of objects and a limited range of purposes. Humans and other animals seem to use much more powerful and general representations. I have tried elsewhere to characterise what it is we don't yet understand. For now I'll just remark that in my view we don't even know how to represent a straight line on a flat surface. This is because there is an enormous amount in common between the straight line and an arbitrary curve between the same two end points, and most of that is lost in the representations commonly used. E.g. is there any representation which captures our perception of all the neighbourhood relations between locations on the line and locations in the plane? I believe that when we know how to represent space, spatial structures and spatial relationships, many other areas of AI will benefit since spatial analogies and spatial modes of reasoning are so pervasive."

[Margaret Boden]

"The prime exception to my charge of intellectual stasis is low-level vision. A variety of mathematically sophisticated methods have been developed for 2D to 3D (and 3D to 4D) computation. These methods are not mutually independent, but are being developed within a coherent research programme based on detailed psychological optics. In the attempt to identify universal constraints on vision, for example, the 'smoothness' constraint has been replaced by the more general 'ordering' constraint. In this area, progress has accelerated considerably, and some significant applications have been made to robotics. (Presumably, similarly close attention to psychological acoustics could be useful in speech-analysis and synthesis: very recently, there has been some radical advance in the coding of the speech-signal.)

It remains to be seen whether the addition of model-driven methods can be done in a theoretically 'pretty' way. For instance, it seems highly implausible that the concept of generalized cylinders, despite its mathematical generality *in principle*, will be useful across the entire range of shape-recognition (as opposed to limited tasks in industrial robotics). Perhaps *no* primarily constructive, or generative, approach can be widely useful in real-time applications. Visual 'demons' are theoretically messy, but may be essential for many applications – and for the understanding of human vision."

[John Seeley Brown]

"I'm surprised that more effort hasn't been expended to theory formation systems a la Eurisko and that new paradigms of learning haven't been more explored.

I had [also] hoped that by now we would have created more significant bridges between symbolic and numeric computation schemes where each leverages the other."

[Christopher Longuet-Higgins]

"In my own work I would mention 3 worthwhile achievements.

(a) A theory of the perception of metrical tonal music, embodied in a programme which accurately transcribes from the keyboard the Prelude to Act III of Tristan and Isolde (Longuet-Higgins, H.C., Perception of melodies, *Nature* 263, No. 5579 (1976) 646).

(b) A paper with Richard Power, describing a programme which acquires the grammars of the numeral systems of a wide variety of human languages, upon presentation of a succession of number/numeral pairs such as 21/vingt-et-un (Power, R.J.D. and Longuet-Higgins, H.C., Learning to count: a computational model of language acquisition, *Proc. Roy. Soc. Lond. B* 200 (1978) 391).

(c) An 8-point algorithm for reconstructing a scene from two perspective projections (Longuet-Higgins, H.C., A computer algorithm for reconstructing a scene from two projections, *Nature* 293, No. 5828 (1981) 133), and a specification of the class of degenerate configurations for which the algorithm fails."

[Alan Newell]
"The re-establishment of robotics has to be the second major advance. Its long-term import for AI far exceeds the work in expert systems, for it will force AI to cope with the real physical world. However, it will be some time before this impact is felt in a major way. Robotics still has a lot of ground work to do that is close to the physics before the integration of symbolic systems and continuous control systems can come to the fore, and initiate rethinking of central intelligent processes.

My third candidate is the development of an understanding of the instructional process. For those mostly in AI rather than cognitive science, this will be identified as intelligent tutoring systems, and will perhaps seem a slender reed. But concomitant major advances have occurred in psychology in understanding cognitive skills and how they are acquired, including the different representations employed by novices and experts. This area provides an exemplary integration of scientific knowledge from AI and cognitive psychology. I think it marks an important advance.

At a somewhat different level, I also think the involvement of philosophy in AI and cognitive science is an important advance. This has only occurred in the last decade. What will ultimately come of it is another matter, other than the enrichment of parts of philosophy and the general increased sophistication of cognitive scientists from understanding the ways philosophy has dealt with epistemology and the mind/body problem. Revealing my scientific provincialism, no doubt, I do not share the view that there is latent in the philosophical record major material for scientific advance, if only it could be ferreted out.

Without a doubt, the most important advance in my own work is the development of a new architecture for a general intelligent agent (called *Soar*), done jointly with John Laird of Xerox PARC and Paul Rosenbloom of Stanford. It is a (successful) synthesis of almost all of what I have come to understand about the requirements of intelligent action during the thirty years I've been pursuing the question – problem spaces, production systems, subgoaling, weak methods, learning by chunking, and more to come. It also expresses my conviction that a central problem of the current era of AI (perhaps even *the* central problem) is the nature of the architecture. However, I do not believe that this conviction is widely shared, although neither is it an outlier."

[Nils Nilsson]
"The establishment of first-order logic (or its various equivalents) as the 'lingua franca' of knowledge representation.

Extensions of first-order logic to deal with several important topics in commonsense reasoning – such as reasoning about knowledge and belief, non-monotonic reasoning, and probabilistic reasoning.

Importation of 'speech-act' theory into AI and its applications in natural language processing.

Development of various 'naive' and 'qualitative' theories (naive physics, psychology; qualitative physics).

Development of various 'logic programming' languages such as *Prolog*. (I don't really see this as part of AI, but it provides us with another important tool.)"

[Aaron Sloman]
"As far as I know very limited progress has been made with the problem of coping with natural language input which is *really* natural, that is, includes many kinds of slips, grammatical errors, incomplete sentences, etc. I have thought, for a long time, that an essential step forward would be to build on some generalisations of Becker's concept of a 'Phrasal Lexicon' described in TINLAP-1 conference proceedings. I have done some small (unpublished) experiments with a parser that learns new 'flat' rules from successful parsers and uses these to improve in speed and robustness. However, substantial parallelism would be required for a large working system. Perhaps that's one reason why there has been little progress along these lines, so far.

I don't think there has been any really satisfactory answer to John Searle's attack on 'Strong AI' in *Behavioural and Brain Sciences* Journal 1980. I organised a panel on meaning at IJCAI 1983 hoping to hear about new advances in dealing with Searle's main question "How can a machine understand"? But I was disappointed. (I have some half-baked ideas I shall try to develop on this.)

In my own work I think there has been some progress on the problem of understanding the global architecture of an intelligent system with the constraints described above, and with the related problem of characterising the space of possible intelligent systems. But progress has been slow. The problem of how to represent shapes has proved surprisingly intractable, though I think I am making progress in understanding what is required of a solution."

[Terry Winograd]
"We can expect advances in applications. There is no particular sign of fruitful new paradigms, but one never knows; and the hardware will be successful in its own terms but will not lead to major advances in capability."

Question 3. Which areas of AI are likely to see the most progress during the next decade? Prediction is always risky, of course, especially in an area as weird as this one, but do you think any breakthroughs are imminent? Alternatively, do you think we are close to limits in any areas?

Turning to the future, again, a wide variety of ideas. A few common themes emerge: Amarel, Newell and Nilsson all foresee progress in machine learning; Brown, Longuet-Higgins, and Sloman all mention speech recognition and transcription as a hopeful area, and Newell agrees that it should be.

[John Seeley Brown]
"During the next decade there may well be some significant breakthroughs in speech understanding."

[Christopher Longuet-Higgins]
"I tend to think that we shall have achieved phonetic transcription under reasonably favourable conditions."

[Alan Newell]
"Something needs to be said about speech recognition. Progress will be made in the next decade, I expect. But at best it will be barely enough to get us to the breakthrough point, namely, where automatic speech recognition can start to become a standard input device. When that happens, it will indeed produce a major transformation of the way we use computers, certainly as large as the shift to graphics and probably substantially larger. This seems so obvious to me that I simply stand in wonder at the computer industry and the research establishment for dawdling along on the problem in the way they have been doing for the last decade."

Several people raised the question of finding an appropriate architecture. Dreyfus and Sloman predicted that "neural" networks will become essential for implementing the associative memories which will be needed for the large databases of specific facts which planners and reasoners will have to have at their mental fingertips. Feldman is already working on such systems, and predicts a rapid growth in their importance. Newell and Sloman emphasize the need to develop a unified architecture for general intelligence:

[Alan Newell]
"I think the consolidation of expert systems into the mainstream of AI will be the central line of progress. By this I do not mean that expert systems are somehow to one side of the main stream. Rather, expert systems will acquire all the mechanisms for intelligence that are currently understood, and so will become indistinguishable from the best intelligent systems AI can build. Expert systems as a distinguishable category will not survive (though the name is likely to be with us for a long time). I think this progress will take place slowly, continuously and across the board, so it will not be marked by any special event. This of course agrees with my assessment above about the general nature of progress in AI.

I have other more special predictions, but these are sufficiently mixed with hope and my own research interests, to make them suspect. I would hope the next decade will see a convergence on many characteristics of the right archi-tecture for general intelligence. (Per the paragraph just above, I expect expert systems, however domain circumscribed, to use such an architecture.) I could be off by a decade, but I doubt it. I used to think this might happen in an event-like way, but I now believe it will happen gradually (like the evolution of expert systems above) in terms of consensus on one characteristic after another, with a plethora of architectures continuing to exist, displaying the full variety of remaining features.

With the concept of an appropriate architecture (it now appears), comes the notion of systems that can continually and automatically improve them-selves in (almost) whatever they do – just as humans (almost always) improve with practice. Such a development has the possibility of dramatic change, and it could happen within the decade. But this is right on my major research line on *Soar*, so is an especially subjective prediction."

[Aaron Sloman]

"Now that AI has become respectable, and suitable machines and languages are becoming more widely available, far more bright people are going to enter the field. I expect to see significant progress in speech analysis (in noise free environments), speech synthesis and low-level image interpretation. Per-haps the availability of large fast machines and VLSI techniques will make it possible to design more convincing architectures for visual systems. I expect planning, problem solving, and learning systems will soon hit a plateau (or bottleneck?). Advances will then require major new developments in inte-grating many different kinds of knowledge using a large and powerful associative memory mechanism, and methods of reasoning by analogy. Long learning sequences will be required to enable space to be traded for speed. (Proving or deriving things from general principles will always be too slow for working systems.) Maybe we'll see a breakthrough in the application of AI approaches to understanding biological systems.

Are we close to limits? It may be that some aspects of human and animal performance depend for their speed and flexibility, on an enormous richly interconnected neural net. I suspect that theoretical understanding of these and our ability to replicate them are so limited, that we may soon reach the limits of what can be done using available technology."

Several people emphasized the need to study primitive or subconscious mental mechanisms: several refer to low-level vision: Brown and others refer to "sensorimotor intelligence", the embedding of an organism in a natural, complex environment, the mechanism of human emotion, and to the work of Freud:

[Bernard Meltzer]
"With very few exceptions all of AI until now has been concerned with what

Freud termed the *secondary* processes of the mind, that is, those concerned with logical, rational, reflexive or potentially reflexive, commonsense thinking; it has neglected the primary processes, that is those concerned with apparently non-rational, non-reflexive thinking that results for instance in new metaphors, shafts of wit, jokes, dreams, poems, brain-waves, neuroses and psychoses. There has been an almost complete ignoring of the wealth of insight into such processes that Freud's investigations, based on hundreds of case-studies, provided."

Perhaps the most surprising idea in this direction comes from Sloman, who suggests that insects might embody simple but important cognitive mechanisms.

[Aaron Sloman]
"Another major problem, which I suppose is largely a problem for future research, is to understand the many forms of intelligence we see in nature apart from the intelligence of higher mammals. How do insects find their way about, mate, land on flowers, build their nests? How do spiders build such gorgeous webs in such varied circumstances? How do animal digestive systems achieve such a clever selection and distribution of suitable sub-structures in food ingested? How do cells of various sorts all derived from the same genetic material perform their various functions? How do seeds and embryos develop in such intricate, pre-determined ways? All these are clearly information processing problems. If the methods of AI are not applied to them, then I don't believe any other existing discipline is going to make substantial progress with them. (E.g. practitioners of other disciplines generally have no means of representing processes with any precision, apart from statistical techniques or the numerical mathematics developed by physicists.)"

Other predictions include:

[Saul Amarel]
"Areas of AI that are likely to see most progress in the next decade: Machine learning; problems of design and planning; reasoning under the guidance of several, qualitative and quantitative, models; theory formation and concept discovery; technologies for building and refining expert systems with knowledge bases of about 10K rules."

[Nils Nilsson]
"Connecting knowledge in procedures and specialized data structures to reasoning systems based on declarative knowledge through semantic attachment mechanisms.

Automatic compilation of procedures and specialized data structures from frequently used declarative knowledge and hooks for semantic attachment-learning.

Better understanding of the relationships between perception and reasoning.

Codification of a large and useful store of commonsense knowledge.

Significant progress on such conundra as the frame problem and nonmonotonic reasoning.

Large-scale systems (for example, robots) based on the 'belief-desire-intention' model of intelligent agents.

Useful natural language processing systems."

> *Sloman thinks that work on "planning and learning will soon reach a plateau". Dreyfus believes that the "common sense" problem will be the ultimate barrier to AI success, while Winograd feels that we need to find the right domains to apply AI techniques.*

[Hubert Dreyfus]

"Current AI is based on the idea which has been around in philosophy since Descartes, that all understanding consists in forming and using appropriate representations. Given the nature of computers, in AI these have to be formal representations. So common-sense understanding has to be understood as some vast body of propositions, rules, facts and procedures. AI's failure to come up with the appropriate formal representations is called the common-sense knowledge problem. As thus formulated this problem has so far turned out to be insoluble, and I predict it never will be solved.

What hides this impasse is the conviction that the common-sense knowledge problem must be solvable since human beings have obviously solved it. But human beings may not normally use common-sense *knowledge* at all. What common-sense *understanding* amounts to might well be *everyday-know-how*. By know-how I do not mean procedural rules, but knowing what to do in a whole lot of special cases.[5] For example, common-sense physics has turned out to be extremely hard to spell out in a set of facts and rules. When one tries, one either requires more common-sense to understand the facts and rules one finds or else one produces formulas of such complexity that it seems unlikely they are in a child's mind. Theoretical physics also requires background skills which may not be formalizable, but at least the domain itself seems to be describable by abstract laws that make no reference to specific cases. AI researchers assume that common-sense physics too must be expressible as a set of abstract principles. But it just may be that the problem of finding a theory of common-sense physics is insoluble because there is none. By playing almost endlessly with all sorts of liquids and solids for several years the child may simply have built up a repertory of typical cases of solids, liquids, etc. and typical skilled response to their typical behavior in typical circumstances. This is coupled with what seems to be an innate human ability, present even in small children, to recognize a case at hand as similar to a learned typical case without decomposition into features which are processed by rules. If so, there may be no *theory* of common-sense physics more simple than a list of all such typical cases and even such a list is useless without a similarity-recognition ability.

If this is indeed the case, and only further research will give us an answer, we could understand the initial success and eventual failure of AI. AI techniques will work to some extent in isolated domains but fail in areas such as natural language understanding, speech recognition, story understanding, and learning whose structure mirrors the structure of our everyday physical and social world.

Even expert systems, which work as well as they do precisely because they deal with isolated, specialized domains and so have been able to finesse common-sense understanding, can only deal with a domain in so far as it can be understood in terms of some sort of theory. Since most domains in which human beings acquire skills and achieve expertise might well be domains like everyday physics which cannot be described in terms of principles but only by listing exemplars, there is no reason to expect systems based on principles abstracted from experts or any other principles, to do as well as experts who, according to Feigenbaum, are never satisfied with general principles but prefer to think of their field of expertise as a huge set of special cases. Competent systems are certainly valuable, but by being misnamed and over-sold they may contribute to an impending computer backlash."

[Terry Winograd]
"Progress in the next decade will come in discovering those domains in which the assumptions and techniques of AI are appropriate. Much work on expert systems has this flavor – the secret of success isn't in building the right program, but in finding the right domain. We will also begin to find better ways to integrate the kind of deduction done by AI systems with the reasoning done by people within a background of experience. The result may not be 'intelligent machines', but intelligent uses of machine capabilities."

Finally, Newell, McCarthy and McCorduck predict an open ended future:

[Alan Newell]
"The talk about limits in AI seems to be a preoccupation with the field. It always strikes me as odd. But now that I think about it, when I was a kid everyone was fascinated with the 'sound barrier' and whether it was possible to fly faster than it – to 'break it' they always said. By its nature science explores outward from the known to the unknown. It can say nothing about what limits it, except on the basis of its current understanding. Indeed, the sound barrier could be perceived as a real limit because a lot was understood

about what happened as one approached it from below (all kinds of inhibitory things). In terms of analogues to the sound barrier, I know of nothing yet that provides any indication of limits, except that perfect intelligence is not possible in general for finite computational devices in finite time."

[Pamela McCorduck]
"In a forthcoming book, I predict that results in complexity will begin to influence AI research, despite the fact that complexity theory and AI rest on radically different models. Just a feeling in my bones at the moment, not calculated to endear me to practitioners in either field. I don't see evidence for, nor can I imagine, limits to research possibilities. And hooray for that."

[John McCarthy]
"I see no limits, but I can't predict where there will be the most progress, because I see the requirements as conceptual."

Question 4. AI is currently attracting a level of industrial sponsorship which would have been fantastic ten years ago. Is this the beginnings of a new industrial revolution which will fundamentally change our society, or will there soon be widespread disillusionment when laymen – especially those with their money in it – realize just how little can be done at present? Or both? Is the flight of workers to industrial organizations diminishing our ability to generate intellectual capital in the field?

People differed widely on this. Michie and Nilsson, taking a long perspective, foresee a new industrial revolution by the end of the century, while Brown, Feldman and Winograd see AI techniques supplying useful software tools, but nothing to revolutionize society. Newell makes a subtle distinction: the computer represents an industrial revolution, but AI itself is just part of computer science.

Michie continues his interesting analogy with organic chemistry in the 1830's:

[Donald Michie]
"It took a century or so after the first organic synthesis before serious agro-chemical and pharmaceutical industries were established and flourishing. An order-of-magnitude speed-up seems about right for events in information technology relative to the first industrial revolution. So how will things be in the advanced countries at the turn of the century?

A corrective to over-extrapolation is that we are speaking of only a half generation. Consequently most of the people who will then be influencing events are already adult, with moderately fixed attitudes and aspirations. Having said this, I still clearly see within the time-scale the start of a new civilisation, in the same sense that fifth-century Greece represented a new start after Homer's football players and Hesiod's hicks. The torrential out-pourings of the knowledge-foundries and skill-synthetics plants of 1999 AD will be eminently reinjectable and assimilable by the consumer. If a person wishes to master a new branch of knowledge, or a new aptitude of mind or body, to a level beyond today's professional standards, and to do it fast, and if he is not prevented by limits set by his constitutional capacities (if IQ < 90, then avoid algebraic topology; if limbs < 4 then leave polevault alone, etc.) then he will find ample means to do this. What sort of society will evolve under such conditions? No-one knows. Certainly one can forget about employment; it has not been a concern of any leisured and cultivated class of the past. We have to envisage such a class expanded to include the whole population, and at the same time the attainable quality of leisure and culture expanded upwards."

[Nils Nilsson]
"This is the beginning of a new industrial revolution, but it might not really get off the ground in the next decade. Probably it will stumble around a lot before taking off just before the turn of the century. I don't think industrial activity will diminish interest in basic research during the next decade – although I think it did in the last. The field is somewhat bigger now and has a devoted cadre of basic researchers."

[John Seeley Brown]
"Current industrial interest in AI may not be so much in AI per se but rather in the programming methodologies (e.g., exploratory programming) and tools that the AI community has been so instrumental in creating. Thus if AI is broken down, metaphorically, into the low, middle and high road approaches, it is the first two levels that are capturing industrial attention."

[Jerome Feldman]
"Expert systems are custom programs written in a particular style. The soft-ware industry can and will add this to its repertoire and the mystique will fade. It seems unlikely that there are enough practitioners to meet the inflated expectations. There will almost certainly be a backlash, but my guess is that scientific AI will be relatively unaffected. There is no question that the intellectual base has been weakened by commercialization, but the attendant mass publicity seems to be attracting very promising students to the field and the net result could well be positive."

[Terry Winograd]
"The wave of commercial enthusiasm for AI was fueled by the possibilities created by microcomputers. It will find a substantial niche, but one that is far from revolutionary. There are many applications for AI techniques in indus-try, but the net impact will be like that of the introduction of a new useful technology (e.g., plastics), not a fundamental change in the way things are

done. There is bound to be disillusionment, given the grandiose claims being made by many researchers, including a number of the recognized leaders in the field. The result won't be as total as it was, say with machine translation, since the criteria for success are much less well defined. But it is likely that in spite of successful applications in many specialized areas, the public mood in ten years will be one of "What they promised didn't happen", instead of "We're on the way." This is because the public has been led to expect machines that really think, understand language, etc., not controllers for industrial processes or programs to diagnose engine flaws."

[Alan Newell]

"The current commercialization of AI should not be separated from the general spread of the computer into every nook and cranny of our society. AI is simply part of computer science here. Many of the ways in which information processing will be used require substantial intelligence; such applications are associated with AI and derive mostly from prior work in AI. Many applications have different aspects of computer science at their core, e.g., storage of large archives, digital communications technology, graphic interfaces, scientific supercomputing, word processing, etc. But it is all one big revolution. Gradually, some amount of intelligent processing will become associated with almost all applications. However, everything will not thereby become an AI application; rather, the concept of computer application will come to incorporate explicitly notions of intelligence and expertise. Furthermore – and contrary to the maxim that AI cannot be successful because AI successes are no longer seen as AI – AI will come increasingly to be taken as a (central) part of computer science and the basic principles of intelligent systems will come to be a part of the basic computer-science curriculum.

That the computer revolution will change society in fundamental ways is by now completely evident. The changes will be so pervasive that we have no way to predict what will be the major transformations or to understand their impact in advance – all we can do is live them. As a part of this revolution, AI applications are no more in danger of failing than any other part. By this I do not mean to imply that there won't be failures and overselling. Such features are part of the warp (or is it the woof?) of a capitalistic industrial society. Observe that the South Sea Bubble did not stop real estate speculation nor did the Great Crash of 1929 kill the market for stock. AI in its wildest dreams cannot compete with these disasters of overselling and underdelivering. Those who think what is going on in AI is in anyway special should review the period of the first computer applications to industry, e.g., the first big payroll programs. The order of the day was great expectations, hype, continuous handwringing about overselling, predications of total failure, etc. Indeed, the first big efforts were pretty dismal – over on costs, under on performance, late on delivery. And people and organizations were hurt.

But it was part of the process. None of this says that the individuals and corporations involved shouldn't be as prudent as possible. Those who are not will (mostly) lose."

Sloman agrees with Brown and Winograd from a sensible European perspective on applications in the near future, predicting substantial practical benefits from the use of AI tools.

[Aaron Sloman]
"I suspect that there's an enormous amount that can be gained under two headings.

(a) Simple 'expert' systems. There are probably thousands of manuals which could be replaced by simple expert systems which either advise or train unskilled operators, or do work which used to be done by scarce skilled operators. The spread of small Prolog systems is making it easy at least in the UK for many business firms, manufacturers, etc. to exploit the new ideas, often doing in Prolog what they might otherwise have done anyway in Fortran, but with far greater ease, extendability, maintainability. I suspect the large American tools will not have this impact (a) because they are expensive (b) because they require large expensive machines (c) because they are much more difficult to use for simple tasks.

(b) Use of AI tools to build non-AI software. I believe that the rapid prototyping facilities of AI software development environments can have an enormous effect on software production and maintenance generally. However, I've noticed a considerable resistance to LISP among industrial programmers, because of its appearance. There is far less resistance to POP-11 because of its similarity in syntax to Pascal, though POP (like LISP) has far greater power. Consequently, a number of industrial purchasers of POPLOG are using POP-11 for a variety of non-AI applications, including VLSI design, graphics, text processing, etc. If we can improve our packaging of such tools, make it easier to link in Fortran libraries and the like, and provide tools for producing runnable small systems without the development environment included, then AI software tools can conquer the world, leaving the software engineers gasping. (For many years to come, rapid prototyping and incremental testing will provide a better guarantee of reliability and robustness than the use of formal specifications, since the specifications will often be bug-ridden.)

Yes, there will be disillusionment amongst those who expect really intelligent systems to come out of AI soon. But, as I've indicated, we can offer them substantial consolation."

Some think that there is dangerous oversell, and a backlash must follow. Roger Schank in particular is alarmed.

[Margaret Boden]

"The current financial excitement and media-hype (for which we in the field must bear some responsibility) may invite a backlash from disillusioned clients and funding-agencies. One can only hope that enough useful, non-trivial, technological applications will soon be achieved for this disappointment to be manageable. ('Sexy' names for commercially-available programs should be avoided, as they encourage inflated expectations.)"

[Roger Schank]

"The industrial sponsorship is likely to spell disaster for AI. With rare exception, businesses want results that can be profitable in a year or two. With everyone hopping on the AI bandwagon, we are bound to see numerous industrial labs staffed with poorly-trained personnel. These labs will not be capable of producing very much beyond simplistic expert systems. Soon, AI will be characterized in the mind of business and government leaders in terms of those systems. I, for one, would not like to bet the future of AI in the potential usefulness of expert system building tools or expert systems built with those tools at random toothpaste companies."

Amarel says "I expect a stabilization of expectations (views) of the discipline by the end of the eighties." But McCorduck disagrees:

[Pamela McCorduck]

"I don't believe AI need worry about industrial disillusionment. That isn't to say there won't be disillusioned industrialists: there will be, and they will complain to the media, and AI will be accused once more of making promises it can't deliver on. This too shall pass. I observe that nobody ever investigates *who* made the promises: aside from Simon's prehistorical predictions, and a few off-the-wall remarks by Minsky, the promises have been mainly made by outsiders extrapolating wildly. For better or worse, AI researchers themselves are public models of humility, modesty and decorum, dreary dull compared to, oh say, paleoanthropologists or genetic engineers."

There is a consensus that the research manpower shortage is a real and acute problem, and that not enough basic research is being done, and we need to find ways to encourage basic research. Brown expresses it well:

[John Seeley Brown]

"The flight of workers from universities to industry is probably as damaging as professors spending nearly all their time consulting on truly short term industrial 'opportunities'. Also, the failure of most industrial labs to support truly fundamental research in the informational sciences is hardly healthy. Perhaps the time is coming to explore radically new mechanisms for supporting basic research in the information sciences – mechanisms that bridge university/industrial settings."

> *Question 6. It seems likely that machines with processing power several orders of magnitude greater than current machines will soon be available (doesn't it?). What effects, if any, will this have on AI? Are there any problems which will be trivialized by the power of the new machines? Bear in mind that in 1957, a Fortran compiler was considered an exercise in AI by some.*
>
> *Longuet-Higgins and Amarel express the consensus, that the advent of this computing power is not crucial for the theory of AI. Many people cheered at the thought of removing computing bottlenecks for research explorations. Newell puts it in the context of current growth curves.*

[Christopher Longuet-Higgins]
"I predict that a limiting factor in the progress of AI will not be the power of machines, but the quality of human judgements as to what tasks to set them."

[Saul Amarel]
"I don't think that the availability of gigantic amounts of machine processing power will have a decisive effect on basic AI issues. It will facilitate experimental work, and it will enable the study of new phenomena, and these are certainly positive things. In addition, it will permit broad dissemination of existing AI concepts and technologies to application areas. But we need, in addition, good new ideas and theories to complement (indeed to guide) machine power."

[Alan Newell]
"It will have no effect at all. More precisely, the only effects would be the negative ones if these machines were not built. The development of these machines is exactly what is required to translate the basic developments in computer technology into appropriate forms for intelligent systems. It is what we need to continue the exponential improvement of the underlying power (and memory) base that we (and the rest of computer science) have been feeding off of all these years. So we cannot do without them. But when the smoke clears (and the time-averaging takes place over the years their full development will take), they will not be special up-blips on the power curve, but will be simply one of the contributions that have kept the power curve on its course.

The issue of trivialization is interesting. An argument can be made that in speech recognition the signal processing has already become all but trivialized. Ten years ago it dominated the design of a speech recognition system. Now other issues dominate. (We are a long way from a similar situation for vision, where the dimensionality of the input makes the signal processing aspects much more forbidding.) We face the intriguing prospect of ultimately sealing up large numbers of Mips (Bips?) in a small hardened box, so that we will entirely forget about the amount of processing being done inside and treat its function as an elementary transduction (e.g., the signal processing for speech perception, to use the above example)."

Question 7. There is a great deal of interest in highly ("massively") parallel architectures. Some people think that such machines are of fundamental scientific importance, drawing attention to the analogy with neurological wetware; on these views, much of the basic work in the field will need to be rethought in the light of these new architectural ideas. Is the serial/parallel distinction of central scientific importance for AI? If so, where is the most work needed?

There is violent disagreement on the importance of parallelism. On the one hand there are those who are essentially negative; for example, Nilsson does not "expect that the current interest in specialized machines will lead to new conceptual advances", or Winograd who believes that parallelism might be necessary but certainly not sufficient for new approaches. McCarthy and Schank are more forthright on the irrelevance of this to research, while John Seeley Brown points out that we may be able to use the technology in specialized ways to further our understanding in new ways as a tool. Amarel is cynical about the analogies with neuroscience.

[John McCarthy]
"I don't think the serial/parallel distinction will be of much importance in the theory of AI."

[Roger Schank]
"The serial/parallel distinction is basically a red herring. Every few years AI gets enamored with yet another problem that distracts us from our real goal. Usually this distraction takes the form of a new 'savior' programming language. (Each of PLANNER, KRL, and PROLOG had that role in their time.) Now that distraction is parallel processing. This is not to say that people are not parallel processors or that having such technology wouldn't be helpful. Indeed the above cited languages were interesting and helpful in their way. But the real issue in AI is how the mind works. That is, we need to know what kinds of things are processed, not whether they are processed in parallel. There is nothing wrong with this work except to the extent that it distracts from the real work. Every time we concern ourselves with efficiency considerations we tend to ignore content issues. AI has a long way to go towards establishing what the content that is

processed is like before it should worry how that content would be processed."

[John Seeley Brown]
"Given the advances in VLSI design methodologies, system kits and the promises of wafer scale integration, it may soon become reasonable to construct special purpose massively parallel systems that are in service of one problem as opposed to more general purpose machines whose complexity stems in part from having to handle multiple problems. By considering just one problem, the topology of information inherent in that problem can be analyzed and modelled directly in the architecture of the system, itself."

[Saul Amarel]
"It still remains to be seen what is the impact of massively parallel architectures on AI. I doubt that they will have major impact on the discipline. Certainly, they are well suited for handling some specialized problems in perception. We need arguments/demonstrations that go beyond the analogies with neurological wetware in order to make serious assessments in this area."

On the other hand we have people like Feldman who see parallelism as a key new technology. Berliner expands on this theme by tying it to the problem of handling inexactitude. Sloman categorizes different types of parallelism relevant to AI, and feels that the serial/parallel distinction is of great importance conceptually, even while admitting that parallelism could in principle be simulated by a serial machine. Finally, Newell talks of this work as of "fundamental importance" in building bridges to neurobiology, and understanding the architecture of the mind.

[Jerome Feldman]
"I believe that massively parallel computational models are more appropriate for much of AI, independent of the existence of any particular hardware. It turns out, however, that the most practical known way to achieve high performance computers is with many (hundreds to thousands of) processors. There is a natural fit of massively parallel models onto these parallel machines and connectionist networks may be the best way to program them. This could be a coincidence but it also might be related to the fact that intelligence evolved on massively parallel systems."

[Hans Berliner]
"It seems that notions such as fuzziness, ranges, uncertainty, and probability distributions, are not only the equal of symbols, lists, slots, scripts, and plans, they far exceed these in importance. Symbolic constructions are just great when their presence can be determined with exactitude, and it is known how to use them.

However, **inexactitude** is a necessary fact of life in all other circumstances, which includes almost all of what there is. It is no accident that the creatures that have preceded the human race for the past billion years have had no symbol processing; they have not needed it. It is possible to get along just fine with simple evaluation functions that tell a creature where it is warmer, where the grass is higher, and a few 'drives' whose continuous valued output helps to encourage certain forms of behavior. In fact, such behavior is much more robust, and thus leads to much greater chances of surviving, than 'symbolic' behavior. The reason is that when you are wrong in estimating the value of a binary variable, then you are 'dead' wrong, while if you are wrong in estimating the value of a continuous variable, you will probably not be off by more than 15% or so, and could very well survive, though not optimally. That humans were able to build such a formidable hypothesizing and reasoning facility on top of this is very impressive, and certainly appears necessary to achieve the highest levels of the intellect. But, as the workers in robotics have now been made thoroughly aware, it is impossible to produce behavior from sensors by symbolic means alone.

The future for AI appears very much tied up in these notions. While it is difficult to point to a unifying theme for all the activities that go on under the AI umbrella, it seems to me that the ultimate distinguishing factor must be that our programs **learn**, while ordinary programs only **perform**. Unfortunately, only a small amount of progress has been made in this, and to the best of my knowledge there are no programs that are both **good** and **able to learn**. To get a general learner, which must be considered the task **par excellence** for AI, requires methods that can go smoothly from sensors to hypothesization. Even for more mundane things such as building a potential World Chess Champion, brute force methods that cannot examine their own workings in order to alter course appear to be reaching a limit. In fact, paradigms that are rigid in their approach can all be shown to have 'seams' or 'ridges' where a process without much understanding of itself will fall through, or become a ridge-follower forever. Although the answers are far from clear, it does appear that competence at the highest levels of intellect (and I mean this in contra-distinction to levels that correspond to [say] freshman college level knowledge) is dependent on knowing the bounds of uncertainty on almost everything that one knows, and knowing how to proceed to eliminate uncertainty in the case at hand.

It is difficult to point to exactly how these problems will be overcome, but it appears that 'massively parallel architectures' must have a role in this. Such an architecture, working bottom-up, can process literally millions of constructs, hypotheses, etc., by synthesizing the contributory factors of each, to see which has the greatest merit (measured in units of support).

A more 'symbolic' process, working top-down, can then notice patterns of 'lit' nodes and use this to produce new inputs based on such patterns, very much as productions finding matching left-hand sides. Such top-down, pattern matching processes will have great difficulty in explaining what was found, because it is not necessary (and very likely not even possible) for them to reach down all the way to the sensory input level in real time. Thus the verbal output that derives from such processes is usually little more than 'rationalization' and gives no reliable indication of what processes support the 'symbols' that have been noticed (I mean here to poke a little fun at verbal introspection experiments, which in the domains that I am familiar with show so little of what must really be going on).

However, I find it eminently plausible to believe that networks of neuron-like elements can percolate 'good' neuron-to-neuron connections upward in a knowledge structure, while an examining entity (like a production system) examines downward to explain what has happened and to sometimes recognize higher level 'patterns' that infuse new information based on past experience and in this way allow redirection of the process."

[Aaron Sloman]
"There are at least four sorts of parallelism relevant to AI.

(a) Parallel mechanisms for doing the same thing with many data – e.g. edge detection in low level vision. This will produce speed, but no major conceptual advances. (I could be wrong!)

(b) Parallel 'connectionist' machines of the kind being studied by Hinton, Ballard, Feldman and others. These will lead us to think about new ways of representing (compiling) knowledge, new ways of organising problem solving and in particular new ways of thinking about relatively low level perceptual and memory mechanisms. I won't be surprised if new ideas about robust and flexible parsers and planners emerge too. But I don't think we will ever want to embed *all* intelligent processing in such systems. E.g. some of the higher level human processes seem to require a different sort of virtual machine.

(c) Parallel decomposition of complex systems into independent cooperating modules of different sorts. This will achieve speed and modularity of design, improved reliability and maintenance, etc. It will not of itself provide terribly important theoretical advances, but will help to support the next sort of parallelism.

(d) Parallel organisation of monitoring and control. There are many ways in which having one process do something while another watches it and controls it can simplify design. I gave some examples in connection with counting in my book *The Computer Revolution in Philosophy*. For instance the 'doing' process can get on with its task without having to be constantly watching for new developments and taking decisions about how to react. This will simplify its programs, and enable it to be used unchanged in different conditions for different purposes, e.g. with different stopping conditions. This presupposes that the controlling process can 'send messages' which modify, suspend, or even abort the action. This simple idea, recursively applied, can, I believe, lead to a new understanding of requirements for the global architecture of intelligent systems (mentioned above). E.g. we can understand some forms of learning better in terms of programs *developed* in one processor where lots of monitoring and control processes can watch and influence behaviour, then *copied*(?) to other processes which run the programs more autonomously, but possibly faster. (Some have, wrongly in my view, used the distinction between interpreted and compiled programs here.)

To sum up: the serial/parallel distinction is of great importance conceptually (even though in principle any parallel machine can be simulated on a fast enough parallel one)."

[Alan Newell]

"I agree that massively parallel architectures are of fundamental importance, and especially those variants that reflect architectural considerations of the brain. My own view is rather simplistic. The history of biology and psychology reveals plainly the deep schism between what can be found out by studying the brain as a physical (biological) system and what can be found out by studying the behaviour of the organism. In general it is simply not possible to make good inferences across the gap in either direction. It is a scientific imperative that the gap be bridged. So we keep trying, from one side or the other. And we keep failing, nursing our wounds for a bit, and trying again.

Thus, psychology's stringent injunction against 'physiologizing' in the thirties and forties was a reaction to the size of the gap. Donald Hebb's book on the Organization of Behaviour in 1949 was an heroic attempt to bridge the gap, which at least made the effort seem legitimate again. The work on artificial neural nets in the fifties was another attempt (there was much more to this than just the Perceptron). The splitting of that work from the symbolic emphasis in AI in the sixties was an indication of how large the gap was, and how little of substance (as opposed to fascination) each side could speak to the other. The enthusiasm that greeted the discovery of split brains by Roger Sperry and Michael Gazzaniga shows the strength of the imperative (a bridge! a highway! but it turned out to be barely a ford). David Marr in the mid-seventies initiated one more renewed attempt to conceive how the bridge might be built. The hope engendered by his work is still alive and well. The recent work on massive parallelism draws on that and other advances as well. It is one more try.

Well, you've got to try to build the bridge. And, tautologically, all but the last attempt will fail, although such is the way of science that each attempt makes its contribution to the subsequent ones. So I am enthusiastic. That my own estimate of the chances on this time round remains fairly low is irrelevant to the enthusiasm. When it happens, whether from work in AI or more likely from some striking empirical discoveries in neuroscience, it will be like opening a floodgate. The floodgate metaphor is not very good, because enough is known on both sides so that the flood will flow in two directions. (Understanding the neural-structure implications of the mass of detailed microbehavioral results in experimental psychology, given the bridge of a few major connections, could produce a rush of neuroscientific understanding.) Certainly, the revolution and re-evaluation will extend to AI. Will symbols and symbolic processing become irrelevant? Will search disappear? Not a chance. Science doesn't operate like that. But we will surely understand it all in a much deeper way."

Question 8. It has been said that AI raises complex legal and moral issues; for example, the attribution of responsibility for medical decision, or ownership of software written by other software. Are there issues which will challenge our current legal system abilities? How?

The themes in these responses varied from the potential problem of deciding whether intelligent machines will have rights, whether people will be better off viewed as machines (see Nilsson below), to how will the legal system work. Saul Amarel claims that "AI technology is in a position to facilitate the handling of some of these issues because it can provide good means for analysis and tracing lines of reasoning, assumptions, etc. that underlie individual decisions." This contrasts with Terry Winograd who points out a danger from incorporating the machine into the system. Newell describes how handling such legal problems is a simple extrapolation of what is done now.

[Nils Nilsson]
"The next twenty years will be a period of great rethinking of many legal and philosophical issues. For example, will the agreements entered into by our 'intelligent agents' be binding upon us? – upon them?? AI will compel new views of 'man as mechanism'. This time, it is likely to be the whole man – not just parts of him – that are regarded as machines. My view is that we will find it much more humane to think of man as a machine than as a spiritual being. Far too much mischief and suffering have resulted from the latter view. Although future psychology will be based more on AI ideas than on Skinner's, we will be moving 'Beyond Freedom and Dignity'. "

[Terry Winograd]
"The legal and ethical issues are not different in kind from those raised by other complex systems that play a role in people's lives, but they are exacerbated by portraying the machine itself as being intelligent. Whenever a person or group of people set up a system of rules or patterns of behavior to be applied automatically (e.g., by a computer), there is the danger that the structure will later be applied in cases for which it is inappropriate, but that the accountability of the creators will be lost. It is hard to assign responsibility

for 'Who should have thought of that before it happened?' when the programming is done by groups, with high turnover, in institutions that are different from those in which the work is applied, etc. By calling something a 'knowledge base' we further obscure the fact that it is a collection of opinions entered by some specific people, with all of the foibles and flaws of what people say they believe. I believe that the practical considerations (i.e., lawsuits and their threat) will lead not to changes in the legal systems, but to changes in how we think of the programs. We will be pushed more into making the human origin of (and responsibility for) the behavior explicit, and moving away from selling systems purported to embody objective intelligence."

[Alan Newell]
"Computer science (AI included) is going to transform society. It will enter into almost everything good and bad, helpful and unhelpful, in our society. There is an old Anglo-Saxon tradition about how to deal with such issues. It is called case law, and it is fundamentally conservative. More sweeping approaches, ostensibly more principled and rational, seem to me to require substantial new knowledge about the structure of society and how to transform it. Such knowledge does not seem available yet. So you try locally to do the best you can, foreseeing and limiting the damage on the down side, enhancing the good things that can happen. The major dilemmas that wrack our society supporting health and fearing overpopulation, or supporting defense and fearing nuclear disaster do not automatically get transformed or even clarified by the saturation of society with information processing."

> *Question 9. Does AI provide opportunities for helping people, or present dangers of harming people, in new ways which concern you? What can be done about it if anything?*

> *There is general agreement that Artificial Intelligence, like any technology, has great potential for good and evil. Newell sees this as part and parcel of the way information processing is affecting society, and not specific to AI, and Nilsson and others point out that the political process that decides what is to be done with technology is the source of the problem and the solution. Dreyfus sees no harm in a degenerating research problem, and Terry Winograd speaks to an important worry shared by many.*

[Hubert Dreyfus]
"As to the moral question, if our leaders have any common-sense, I see no more danger from AI than there was once from alchemy. Of course, if our military, for example, is foolish enough to mistake competent systems for experts and rely on them, any sort of disaster is possible. Otherwise, as in the

days of alchemy, the only danger is that there may be a rather large waste of time and money and a few people may get burnt."

[Terry Winograd]
"One particular area of concern is the application of AI technology in weapons systems, especially those that could trigger nuclear war. The problems of over-expectation, loss of accountability, and unpredictability could all prove fatal if systems were assumed to embody sufficient intelligence to make life and death decisions. Computer Professionals for Social Responsibility is an organization created to study this kind of question and to educate the public (and the relevant leaders) about it. I believe this kind of education is the main thing to be done. The answer is not to stop the technology, but to have everyone understand its appropriate place and limitations."

An intriguing idea brought up by Michie in one form and John Seeley Brown in another is the idea that machines can be used to amplify our own capacities, both as individuals and as groups.

[John Seeley Brown]
"I believe one of the intriguing opportunities of AI is in constructing intelligent systems that help us help ourselves. An obvious but by no means encompassing example is in the field of intelligent tutoring systems aimed at enhancing experimental learning. Other kinds of examples include systems that enhance our abilities (and willingness) to engage in collaborative work – writing, problem-solving, etc. – as well as systems that enable us to reflect on our own problem-solving traces."

Michie focusses on the far future, and shows his faith that this work will reflect back to help human beings to a higher level.

[Donald Michie]
"We may envisage machine systems very much more intelligent and knowledgeable than man. But man may prove to be a moving target. On the one hand man (as he is) is augmentable simply by amplification of computer-mediated self-instruction and 're-injection' of synthetic knowledge. We cannot yet measure nor theoretically specify realistic limits to this form of augmentation. Beyond that there is a definite possibility of a more profound augmentation, namely via direct brain-computer communication: the subjective stream of consciousness incorporates processes of thought and memory-retrieval which are actually extrinsic although not so perceived. A crude start has been made in some US Air Force experiments in which pilots were able to summon data to cockpit displays by 'thought-power' (actually via computer monitoring of EEG patterns)."

A debate in the responses focusses on the potential for expert systems. Some, such as Sloman, focus on the potential positive benefits:

[Aaron Sloman]
"It may be possible, through widespread use of expert systems, to make ordinary people less dependent, and therefore less in the power of, expert advisors (e.g. doctors, lawyers, architects etc.) who don't necessarily have the client's interest at heart."

Dennett on the other hand, after noting that expert systems can do some good, worries about the effect this good can have on the receivers:

[Dan Dennett]
"I will mention a few paradigmatic possibilities each of which stands for a whole family of potential problems.

(1) Expert systems in medicine may indeed work miracles for raising the health care standards in the third world (by permitting cheaply trained paramedic types to serve vast rural areas expertly, etc.) but we should not expect the citizens of those nations to be particularly grateful, since the price they will pay for this better health care is a *widening* of the technology gap between us, the providers (trainers, designers, repairers) and them, the ever-more-dependent end users. They may commit their whole societal infra-structure to institutions that *cannot operate* without our expert systems (an intensification of such existing phenomena as dependence on oil, on tele-phone systems, etc.), and hence become technology junkies. Expert systems for the underdeveloped world are not just a mixed blessing; they are political dynamite (or, to continue the metaphor, political heroin).

(2) It has already been widely remarked that today's crop of engineers (aeronautical, civil, . . .) often *no longer know how to think* about problems their elders cut their teeth on. Why not? Because today you can just use trial and error and brute force, thanks to CAD/CAM and the like. Expert systems in such fields as engineering and medicine, where there has always been a very high pressure to *find shortcuts* will very likely lead to the withering away of some important diagnostic/design skills.

(3) Expert systems can be insidious Trojan Horses. Every student of ethics learns that '"ought" implies "can"' – you can't be obliged to do something that is simply not in your power. A vast increase in power thus opens the way for the *creation* of a new panoply of 'obligations'. Consider how the gov-ernment may now require institutions and businesses to maintain records that would have swamped them before computers. What will not be unreasonable for government to ask of us when we can be counted on to have expert systems at our disposal? "But what's the problem? We'll simply turn over these new tasks to our expert systems!" Right, and spend our days

216

putting our signatures on documents we get from these systems, without the faintest hope of knowing what we're committing ourselves to.

(4) Expert systems growth will no doubt be somewhat self-limiting (just as the growth of video-games and home computers has proven to be in the last year or so) as the limitations and compromises of their use become widely known. Their brittleness, the inability of even their designers to extrapolate reliably from their track record to their actual competence, and other such rude awakenings will stem the tide. What we had better hope for is a few 'Santa Barbara Channel oil slicks' – highly publicized but actually quite mild 'disasters' that will galvanize people and educate them to the risks. For the prospects of a truly catastrophic failure are too horrible to contemplate.

I think 'pure' academic AI also has attendant risks worth pausing to think carefully about. I agree with Joe Weizenbaum that the work on speech recognition, for instance, for all its theoretical importance and fascination as pure science, opens up the technology for vastly increased electronic surveillance. People working in the field should face that issue – and its kin – just as unblinkingly as the nuclear physicists and genetic engineers have faced their issues. The "I'm just a scientist; I can't help what they do with it" line should not sit comfortably on anyone's lips.

Would it not be a good idea to have a national or international workshop – on the lines of the Asilomar conference on genetic engineering hazards – to catalog and plan for the unintended but anticipatable effects of this research?"

Margaret Boden brings our attention to a way in which AI systems have potential for combatting one of the worst fears of people, 'dehumanization' by being forced into the mold of the computer.

[Margaret Boden]
"There is even a potential, if only we can exploit it, for helping humanity at its heart: for improving the interpersonal (as well as the intellectual) dimension of life. There are obvious possibilities for moving towards what I have called a 'Polynesian' culture, where there is time available for concentrating on social relations and rituals which confirm group-solidarity and release individual potential. In particular, men (even more than women) may benefit from this, if the expression of emotion – to friends as well as family – comes to be less alien to what is generally perceived as the masculine role. This may happen partly because of the extra time free for human pursuits, but it may be reinforced by the fact that most publicly available programs (produced to help solve problems of one sort or another) will be obviously *unemotional*. There's already evidence that the children of today's 'computer culture' emphasize feeling and emotionality as the crucial criteria of human beings, in contrast with computers.

However, one relevant prediction chills my blood: a social psychologist has forecast that our strong animistic tendencies, together with loneliness and social incompetence of various kinds, will (*will*, not *may*) lead to a society in which interactions with quasi-emotional – and sometimes even cuddly – commercially profitable AI-systems will loom large in many people's lives. I console myself with the thought that the writer concerned does not seem to realize just how technologically difficult the commercial production of such 'constant companions' would be.

Perhaps I shouldn't have mentioned the threat of AI-cuddlies – for it raises the question which, in my view, shouldn't be asked about AI. I think it is unprofitable to ask whether computers will *really* be intelligent, or *really* have purposes, and the like. The reason it is unprofitable is that it is ultimately not a question of fact, but of moral-political choice. If we agree that AI-systems will really merit such psychological predicates, then this means (*sic*) that we shall have admitted them into our moral universe. That is, their purposes (no scare-quotes) will be worthy of respect and attention just as a person's, or a squirrel's, are. We may decide to put our own (important) purposes first, just as we would run over a squirrel rather than swerve and run over a child. But there would be a *prima facie* obligation to respect their purposes and interests.

If such a situation ever arose, the technological feat mentioned in the previous paragraph would very likely have come about (otherwise we would not have convincing reasons for ascribing genuine purposes to AI-systems in the first place). Now, suppose Grandma Buggins has thought of popping out to see her neighbour (something she very rarely plucks up courage to do) – and her AI-cuddle says 'Won't you stay in tonight? I'd like to carry on our conversation'. (This is perfectly consistent with the sort of seemingly personal conversation which was being forecast.) Should she relent, and stay at home? Would you feel happy about that?

I don't think anything like this will actually happen, because I don't believe that such systems will ever exist. They aren't impossible in principle, in my view, but it won't be worth anyone's while to undertake the extraordinary efforts involved in producing them. Judging by some of the more sensational remarks coming from certain quarters, some AI-partisans do not agree. They relish the 'fact' that super-intelligent computers will one day worry about all the important social and political problems for us (*for* us, not *with* us). And they comfort us with the vision of 'personal immortality', achieved by having our individual fads and foibles preserved for ever in a computer program. Myself, I'd prefer Forest Lawns.

Pamela McCorduck expresses the faith implicit for many that if AI is a problem, it is also its own solution.

[Pamela McCorduck]
"In common with all important things, AI can both help and hurt people.

History presses down on us here: for the species, knowledge is better than ignorance. AI is a significant part of human knowledge (for my tastes, *la creme de la creme*). I see no choice but to go on with this project that, as I have argued tediously elsewhere, is probably *the* central project of the species, reproduction having been satisfied to a faretheewell. (Brian Oakley, head of Britain's Alvey Project, recently made fun of me in public for taking such a ridiculously lofty stand, arguing it's all a matter of the bottom line. While I'm not unmindful of the need to turn a buck, it doesn't seem a stimulating lifetime goal. Whereas AI . . .)

Yes, it will also hurt. Some of the injured will be innocents, who were misled, or never had a chance. I deal with one instance, the complicated question of AI in weapons – a place of great potential injury – in the forthcoming book. Another instance is work. If political fashions continue as they have recently in the United States, those innocents will have no remedy, no recourse, no mitigation of their pain. I cannot change that, only deplore it.

Yet paradoxically, by getting on with its tasks, AI can offer recourse and remedy, ease the pain; at last change minds, in the largest and best sense of that phrase."

Question 10. What questions shouldn't be asked about AI? What are the right questions?

Only Margaret Boden, above, and Terry Winograd thought there were questions which shouldn't be asked. These questions he felt obscured the appropriate ones:

[Terry Winograd]
"The wrong questions are 'Can computers be intelligent?' or 'Is that particular computer intelligent?' The right questions deal with what it is we do when we try to embody an area of human knowledge and practice into a formalized system, and how that determines both what the system can do and how we conduct our lives with it. I am just finishing (with Fernando Flores) a book titled Understanding Computers and Cognition (Ablex, 1985) dealing with these issues."

Aaron Sloman argued that even confused or misguided questions could be of value if one explored the implicit assumptions behind the question. Newell expresses below the feeling of most respondents that limits on questioning are inappropriate at best and dangerous at worst:

[Alan Newell]
"I have never been able to develop a model of the world where various domains of scientific knowledge should be placed out of bounds which is

what I take the question to be. There is no doubt that on occasion a little knowledge can be a dangerous thing. It happens all the time and the plots of many novels hinge on it. In fact, much garden-variety error can be seen in this light. Consider, as a simple example, the bad chess move, taken because you knew enough to capture the opponent's pawn, but turning into a disaster because you didn't know that the move put your own queen en prise. If only you had not asked what men could be captured, then you would have made a safe developing move and would have avoided the disaster. Therefore should asking about captures be off limits? Though the example may not be completely paradigmatic, it hints at the difficulties in limiting a priori the attempt to understand the world as best we can. Certainly, we need to tread carefully at decision time. That is what wise decision-making is all about; assessing the limits of knowledge, considering all the alternatives, constructing responses to the down-side failures of proposed actions, and so on. But the path of wisdom does not seem to lie in manipulating the decision process by restricting access to knowledge that is not yet available, hence whose implications cannot yet be known."

Margaret Boden argues strongly that people should be taught to ask the RIGHT questions about computer systems. Unwarranted extrapolation of surface abilities of a program (quasi-natural-language interaction or a modicum of common sense) may lead users to accept program outputs thinking all possibilities have been considered. Her suggestions seem a fitting way to end this 'state of the field' overview.

[Margaret Boden]
"To help avert this sort of over-enthusiastic misunderstanding by the user, we should actively encourage the sort of computer literacy which stresses the limitations as well as the potential of AI-systems (and computer programs in general). This could help to correct the currently popular belief that computers are *objective* systems. This is not merely false, but is a socially oppressive mystification – one which is sometimes deliberately fostered for questionable purposes (for example, by advertisements saying that because the computer chose a product as 'the best', you should choose it too).

A certain way of playing around with programs (which is already happening in some universities and schools) could help. For instance, if a person can play with a version of ELIZA, and can 'take the lid off' to see how the program works, they soon find out for themselves that it is not so clever as at first it seems, and that some of its faults *cannot* be rectified simply by adding a few more rules. After having had this experience, no-one could ever interact with a natural-language interface (or program) without wondering what its linguistic limitations were. They might not be able to find the answer, but the cautionary question would have been raised. At the least, they could never be fooled into thinking that the word-producing program must have the degree of understanding of its words that human beings have.

In general, everyone needs to understand that every program (just like every person) can, in principle, be challenged with respect to its data, its inferential rules, and its values or decision-criteria. This has nothing to do with the possibility of bugs or hardware faults, but with the fact that programs are *not* 'objective' systems (though many people today assume that they are). They are representations of the world, and ways of thinking about it, and as such are essentially open to question: some other representation (not excluding the one inside the user's head) might be preferable.

Accordingly, AI-programs (and/or interfaces) for public use should be written so as to remind the user that their data, reasoning, and decision-criteria are different from a human being's (and, for that matter, from other possible programs) – and, in principle, just as challengeable. Some very simple things might help: for example, reminding the user more than once during use (not just at login-time) that the program has been written by *X*, based on advice and data from *Y*, and following decision-criteria (the general priorities of which should ideally be indicated) approved by *Z*. In addition, the 'human window' (through which users can 'interrogate' a system) should not merely reveal how a certain conclusion has been generated: it should help the user to have some sense of what possibly relevant factors the system has *not* been able to consider. It may go against the grain to include such 'negative' or 'self-deprecatory' reminders in a system of which one is justly proud, and by means of which one may hope to become rich. But it is the responsible thing to do.

It may even happen that such reminders become legally necessary. Large sums of money will sometimes turn on the ascription of responsibility for a decision, or for the advice leading to that decision. In legal systems based on case-law, decisions are based on precedents arrived at in previous litigation. General principles are eventually laid down by the judges, but on the basis of specific cases. It might be helpful if some knowledgeable people were to think about these issues now, in an attempt to arrive at some systematic mapping of the sorts of issues that may be involved. I am unpersuaded by the argument (which I have heard) that such anticipatory discussion is a waste of time since the law will be laid down by the courts' decisions, and that will be that. At least the lawyers involved in the first cases would have the benefit of some prior disinterested discussion by informed persons."

Notes

1   Lakatos, I., in: J. Worrall (Ed.), *Philosophical Papers* (Cambridge University Press, New York, 1978).
2   Minsky, M.; *Computation: Finite and Infinite Machines* (Prentice-Hall, Englewood Cliffs, NJ, 1967) 2.

3 Kolata, G., How can computers get common sense?, *Science* 217 (24 September 1982) 1237.
4 Block, N., Mental pictures and cognitive science, *Philosophical Rev.* (October 1983). Carey, S., *Conceptual Change in Childhood* (MIT Press, Cambridge, MA, to appear).
5 In *Putting Computers in Their Place* (Free Press/Macmillan, New York, 1985), my brother, Stuart, and I argue that beginners in a domain are given principles which they know and use, but that experts can do much better than beginners because they know how to deal with thousands of special cases. Thus everyday expertise or know-how does not consist of the principles and rules of thumb thought to comprise common-sense knowledge. We fall back on procedures and principles only in situations which are so unlike any situation we have dealt with that our everyday skills fail us.

33

EXCERPTS FROM *THE SOCIETY OF MIND*

Marvin Minsky

Source: P. H. Winston and S. A. Shellard (eds), *Artificial Intelligence at MIT, Expanding Frontiers* Vol. 1, MIT Press, 1990, pp. 244–69.

In large human organizations, the members contribute to overall success according to their diverse points of view and diverse capabilities.

So it is with the little agents described in Marvin Minsky's seminal book, *The Society of Mind*. Intelligence emerges from the mutually compensating abilities of these little agents, no one of which is particularly intelligent by itself. Collectively, they form heterogeneous societies in which the inevitable weaknesses of each individual agent are compensated for by the limited talents of other members of the society.

This chapter introduces Minsky's thinking through a collection of representative excerpts drawn from *The Society of Mind*. In them, Minsky explains how societies of agents focus attention, solve problems, remember experience, and communicate with one another.

As you read through these excerpts, you may correctly conclude that many key ideas will require a generation or two of graduate students to work out in detail. Reading *The Society of Mind* is like poking around in a diamond mine, wondering which of the rocks, when polished, will become the most famous gems.

Noncompromise (3.2*)

To settle arguments, nations develop legal systems, corporations establish policies, and individuals may argue, fight, or compromise—or turn for help

---

* Section numbers in parenthesis after the section title refer to actual references in *The Society of Mind*.

to mediators that lie outside themselves. What happens when there are conflict inside minds?

Whenever several agents have to compete for the same resources, they are likely to get into conflicts. If those agents were left to themselves, the conflicts might persist indefinitely, and this would leave those agents paralyzed, unable to accomplish any goal. What happens then? We'll assume that those agents' supervisors, too, are under competitive pressure and likely to grow weak themselves whenever their subordinates are slow in achieving their goals, no matter whether because of conflicts between them, or because of individual incompetence.

> **The Principle of Non-Compromise.** The longer an internal conflict persists among an agent's subordinates, the weaker becomes that agent's status among its own competitors. If such internal problems aren't settled soon, other agents will take control and the agents formerly involved will be "dismissed."

So long as playing-with-blocks goes well, *Play* can maintain its strength and keep control. In the meantime, though, the child may also be growing hungry and sleepy, because other processes are arousing the agents *Eat* and *Sleep*. So long as *Eat* and *Sleep* are not yet strongly activated, *Play* can hold them both at bay. However, any conflict inside *Play* will weaken it and make it easier for *Eat* or *Sleep* to take over. Of course, *Eat* or *Sleep* must conquer in the end, since the longer they wait, the stronger they get.

We see this in our own experience. We all know how easy is it to fight off small distractions when things are going well. But once some trouble starts inside our work, we become increasingly impatient and irritable. Eventually we find it so hard to concentrate that the least disturbance can allow another, different, interest to take control. Now, when any of our agencies loses the power to control what other systems do, that doesn't mean it has to cease its own internal activity. An agency that has lost control can continue to work inside itself—and thus become prepared to seize a later opportunity. However, we're normally unaware of all those other activities proceeding deep inside our minds.

Where does it stop, this process of yielding control to other agencies? Must every mind contain some topmost center of control? Not necessarily. We sometimes settle conflicts by appealing to superiors, but other conflicts never end, and never cease to trouble us.

At first, our principle of non-compromise may seem too extreme. After all, good human supervisors plan ahead to avoid conflicts in the first place and—when they can't—they try to settle quarrels locally before appealing to superiors. But we should not try to find a close analogy between the low-level agents of a single mind and the members of a human community. Those tiny mental agents simply cannot know enough to be able to negotiate with one another, or to find effective ways to adjust to each other's interference. Only larger agencies could be resourceful enough to do such things. Inside an actual child, the agencies responsible for *Building* and *Wrecking* might indeed become versatile enough to negotiate by offering support for one another's goals. "Please, *Wrecker*, wait a moment more till *Builder* adds just one more block: it's worth it for a louder crash!"

B-Brains (6.4)

There *is* one way for a mind to watch itself, and still keep track of what's happening. Divide the brain into two parts, *A* and *B*. Connect the *A*-brain's inputs and outputs to the real world—so it can sense what happens there. But don't connect the *B*-brain to the outer world at all; instead, connect it so that the *A*-brain is the *B*-brain's world!

Now *A* can see and act upon what happens in the outside world—while *B* can "see" and influence what happens inside *A*. What uses could there be for such a *B*? Here are some *A*-activities that *B* might learn to recognize and influence.

This two-part arrangement could be a step toward having a more "reflective" mind-society. The *B*-brain could do experiments with the *A*-brain, just as the *A*-brain can experiment with the body, or with the objects and people surrounding it. And just as *A* can attempt to predict and control what happens in the outer world, *B* can try to predict and control what *A* will do. For example, the *B*-brain could supervise how the *A*-brain learns, either by making changes in *A* directly, or by influencing *A*'s own learning processes.

Even though *B* may have no concept of what *A*'s activities mean in relation to the outer world, it is still possible for *B* to be useful to *A*. This is because a *B*-brain could learn to play a role somewhat like that of a

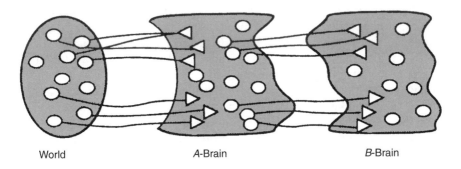

World   A-Brain   B-Brain

A seems disordered and confused.	Inhibit that activity.
A appears to be repeating itself.	Make *A* stop. Do something else.
A does something *B* considers good.	Make *A* remember this.
A is occupied with too much detail.	Make *A* take a higher-level view.
A is not being specific enough.	Focus *A* on lower-level details.

counselor, psychologist, or management consultant who can assess a client's mental strategy without having to understand all the details of that client's profession. Without having any idea of what A's goals are, B might be able to learn to tell when A is not accomplishing them, but only going around in circles, or wandering, confused because certain A-agents are repeating the same things over and over again. Then B might try some simple remedies, like suppressing some of those A-agents. To be sure, this could also result in B's activities becoming nuisances to A. For example, if A had the goal of adding up a long column of numbers, B might start to interfere with this because, from B's point of view, A appears to have become trapped in a repetitive loop. This could cause a person accustomed to more variety to find it difficult to concentrate on such a task, and complain of being bored.

To the extent that the B-brain knows what is happening in A, the entire system could be considered to be partly "self-aware." However, if we connect A and B to "watch" each other too closely, then anything could happen, and the entire system might become unstable. In any case, there is no reason to stop with only two levels; we could connect a C-brain to watch the B-brain, and so on.

Heads in the clouds (6.9)

What we call a mind is nothing but a heap or collection of different perceptions, united together by certain relations and suppos'd, tho' falsely, to be endow'd with a perfect simplicity and identity.
(David Hume)

We'll take the view that nothing can have meaning by itself, but only in relation to whatever other meanings we already know. One might complain that this has the quality of the old question, "Which came first, the chicken or the egg?" If each thing one knows depends on other things one knows, isn't that like castles built on air? What keeps them from all falling down, if none are tied to solid ground? Well, first, there's nothing basically wrong with the idea of a society in which each part lends meaning to the other parts. Some sets of thoughts are much like twisted ropes or woven cloths in which each strand holds others both together and apart. Consider all the music tunes you know. Among them you can surely find two tunes of which, you like each one the more because of how it's similar to or different from the other one. Besides, no human mind remains entirely afloat. Later we'll see how our conceptions of space and time can be based entirely on networks of relationships, yet can still reflect the structure of reality.

If every mind builds somewhat different things inside itself, how can any mind communicate with a different mind? In the end, surely, communication is a matter of degree but it is not always lamentable when different minds don't understand each other perfectly. For then, provided that *some* communication remains, we can still share the richness of each other's thoughts. What good would other people be if we were all identical? In any case, the situation is the same *inside* your mind—since even you, yourself, can never know precisely what *you* mean! How useless any thought would be if, afterward, your mind returned to the selfsame state. But that never happens, because every time we think about a certain thing, our thoughts go off in different ways.

> The secret of what anything means to us depends on how we've connected to other things we know. That's why it's almost always wrong to seek the "real meaning" of anything. A thing with just one meaning has scarcely any meaning at all.

An idea with a single sense can lead you only along one track. Then, if anything goes wrong, it just gets stuck—a thought which sits there in your mind with nowhere to go. That's why, when someone learns something "by rote"—that is, with no sensible connections—we say that they "don't really understand." Rich meaning-networks, however, give you many different ways to go: if you can't solve a problem one way, you can try another. True, too many indiscriminate connections will turn a mind to mush. But well-connected meaning-structures let you turn ideas around in your mind, to consider alternatives and envision things from many perspectives until you find one that works. And that's what we mean by thinking!

Internal communication (6.12)

If agents can't communicate, how is it that people can—in spite of having such different backgrounds, thoughts, and purposes? The answer is that we overestimate how much we actually communicate. Instead, despite those seemingly important differences, much of what we do is based on common knowledge and experience. So even though we can scarcely speak at all about what happens in our lower-level mental processes, we can exploit their common heritage. Although we can't express what we mean, we can often cite various examples to indicate how to connect structures we're sure must already exist inside the listener's mind. In short, we can often indicate which sorts of thoughts to think, even though we can't express how they operate.

The words and symbols we use to summarize our higher-level goals and plans are not the same as the signals used to control lower-level ones. So when our higher-level agencies attempt to probe into the fine details of the lower-level submachines that they exploit, they cannot understand what's happening. This must be why our language-agencies cannot express such facts from memory. We find it particularly hard to use our language skills to talk about the parts of the mind that learned such skills as balancing, seeing and remembering, before we started to learn to speak.

227

"Meaning" itself is relative to size and scale: it makes sense to talk about a meaning only in a system large enough to have many meanings. For smaller systems, that concept seems vacant and superfluous. For example, *Builder's* agents require no sense of meaning to do their work; *Add* merely had to turn on *Get* and *Put*. Then *Get* and *Put* do not need any subtle sense of what those turn-on signals "mean"—because they're wired up to do only what they're wired up to do. In general, the smaller an agency is, the harder it will be for other agencies to comprehend its tiny "language."

> The smaller two languages are, the harder it will be to translate between them. This is not because there are too many meanings, but because there are too few. The fewer things an agent does, the less likely that what another agent does will correspond to any of those things. And if two agents have nothing in common, no translation is conceivable.

In the more familiar difficulty of translating between human languages, each word has many meanings, and the main problem is to narrow them down to something they share. But in the case of communication between unrelated agents, narrowing down cannot help if the agents have nothing from the start.

Sensing similarities (11.5)

> *This difficulty [of making definitions] is increased by the necessity of explaining the words in the same language, for there is often only one word for one idea; and though it may be easy to translate words like bright, sweet, salt, bitter, into another language, it is not easy to explain them.*
> (Samuel Johnson)

Our ways to think depend in part on how we're raised. But at the start, much more depends upon the wiring in our brains. How do those microscopic features work to influence what happens in our mental worlds? The answer is, *our thoughts are largely shaped by which things seem most similar*. Which colors seem the most alike? Which forms and shapes, which smells and tastes, which timbres, pitches, aches and pains, which feelings and sensations seem most similar? Such judgments have a huge effect at every stage of mental growth—since *what we learn depends on how we classify*.

For example, a child who classified each fire just by the color of its light might learn to be afraid of everything of orange hue. Then we'd complain that the child had "generalized" too much. But if that child classified each flame, instead, by features which were never twice the same, that child would often be burned—and we'd complain that it hadn't generalized enough.

Our genes supply our bodies with many kinds of sensors—external event-detecting agents—each of which sends signals to the nervous system when it detects certain physical conditions. We have sensory agents in our eyes, ears, nose and mouth that discern light, sound, odors, and tastes; we have agents in the skin that sense pressure, touch, vibration, heat, and cold; we have internal agents that sense tensions in our muscles, tendons, and ligaments; and we have many other sensors of which we're normally unaware, such as those that detect the direction of gravity and sense the amounts of various chemicals in different parts of the body.

The agents that sense the colors of light in human eyes are much more complex than the "redness agents" of our toy machine. But this is not the reason that simple machines can't grasp what *Redness* means to us—for neither can the sense-detectors in our human eyes. For, just as there is nothing to say about a single point, there's nothing to be said about an isolated sensory signal. When our *Redness*, *Touch*, or *Toothache* agents send their signals to our brains, each by itself can only say "I'm here." The rest of what such signals "mean" to us depends on how they're linked to all our other agencies.

In other words, the "qualities" of signals sent to brains depend only on relationships—the same as with the shapeless points of space. This is the problem Dr. Johnson faced, when creating definitions for his dictionary: each separate word like "bitter," "bright," "salt," or "sweet" attempts to speak about a quality of a sensory signal. But all that a separate signal can do is to announce its own activity—perhaps with some expression of intensity. Your *tooth* can't ache it can only send signals; only *you* can ache, once your higher level agencies interpret those signals. Beyond the raw distinctiveness of every separate stimulus, all other aspects of its character or quality—be it of touch, taste, sound, or light—depend entirely on its relationships to the other agents of your mind.

The functions of structures (12.5)

Many things that we regard as physical are actually psychological. To see why this is so, let's try to say what we mean by "chair." At first it seems enough to say,

"A chair is a thing with legs and back and seat."

But when we look more carefully at what we recognize as chairs, we find that many of them do not fit this description, because they don't divide into those separate parts. When all is done, there's little we can find in common to all chairs—except for their intended use.

"A chair is something you can sit upon."

But, that too, seems inadequate: it makes it seem as though a chair were as insubstantial as a wish. The solution is that we need to combine at least two different kinds of descriptions. On one side, we need structural descriptions for recognizing chairs when we see them. On the other side we need functional descriptions in order to know what we can *do* with chairs. We can capture more of what we mean by interweaving both ideas. But it's not enough to merely propose a vague association, because in order for it to have some use, we need more intimate details about *how* those chair-parts actually help a person to sit. To catch the proper meaning, we need connections between parts of the chair-structure and the requirements of the human body that those parts are supposed to serve. Our network needs details like these:

Without such knowledge, we might just crawl under the chair or try to wear it on your head. But with that knowledge we can do amazing things, like applying the concept of a chair to see how we could sit on a box, even though it has no legs or back!

Uniframes that include structures like this can be powerful. For example, such knowledge about relations between structure, comfort, and posture could be used to understand when a box could serve as a chair: that is, only

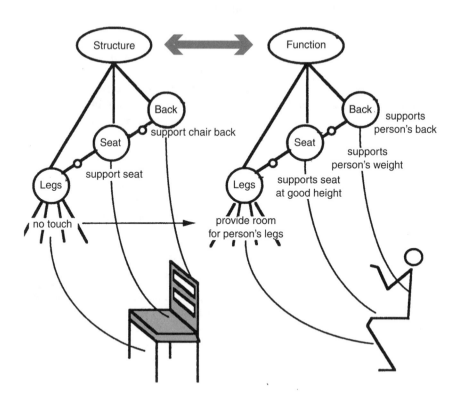

when it is of suitable height for a person who does not require a back-rest or room to bend the knees. To be sure, such clever reasoning requires special mental skills with which to re-describe or "re-formulate" the descriptions of both box and chair so that they "match" despite their differences. Until we learn to make old descriptions fit new circumstances, our old knowledge can be applied only to the circumstances in which it was learned. And that would scarcely ever work, since circumstances never repeat themselves perfectly.

Meaning and definition (12.12)

mean'ing. n. 1. that which exists in the mind, view, or contemplation as a settled aim or purpose; that which is meant or intended to be done; intent; purpose; aim; object. 2. that which is intended to be, or in fact is, conveyed, denoted, signified, or understood by acts or language; the sense, signification, or import of words; significance; force.

(Webster's Unabridged Dictionary)

What is a meaning? Sometimes we're told a definition of a word and suddenly, we know a way to use that word. But definitions do not often work so well. Suppose you had to explain what "game" means. You could start like this:

> **Game.** An activity in which two teams compete to make a ball do something that results in a winning score.

This fits a certain range of games—but what of games which just use words, or keep no scores, or lack the element of competition? We can capture the nature of more kinds of games by using other definitions, but nothing seems to catch them all. We simply cannot find much in common to everything we call a game. Yet one still feels there is a certain unity which underlies the idea of a game. For example, we feel that we could recognize new games, and that "game" is more than an arbitrary accumulation.

But now let's turn our attention away from the physical aspects of games and focus on the *psychological purposes* that games can serve. Then it is much easier to find some qualities that are common to most adult games:

> **Game.** An activity that is engaging and diverting, deliberately detached from real life.

This second kind of definition treats a game not as a kind of object-thing but as a process in the mind. At first this might seem somewhat strange, but really it is nothing new—even our first definition already contained psychological elements concealed in the words "competing" and "winning." When seen this way, different kinds of games seem much more similar. This is because they all serve common purposes—despite the great diversity of their physical appearances. After all, there is virtually no limit to the variety of physical objects or structures that could be used to accomplish the same psychological purpose—in this case, to make an activity diverting (whatever that might mean). Naturally, then, it would be hard to specify the range of all possible physical forms of games.

Of course, it is no great surprise to find that "game" has a more psychological character than does "brick," which we can define in physical terms without referring to our goals. But most ideas lie in between. We saw this in the case of "chair," which we cannot describe without referring both to a physical structure and to a psychological function.

Bridge-definitions (12.13)

At last we're coming close to capturing the meanings of things like chairs and games. We found that structural descriptions are useful, but they always seem too specific. Most chairs have legs, and most games have scores—but there are always exceptions. We also found purposeful descriptions to be useful, but they never seemed specific enough. "*Thing you can sit upon*" is too general to specify a chair, since you can sit on almost anything. "*Diverting activity*" is too broad for game—since there are many other ways to turn our minds from serious things. In general, a single definition rarely works.

> Purposeful definitions are usually too loose.
> > *They include many things which we do not intend.*
> Structural definitions are usually too tight.
> > *They reject many things that we want to include.*

But we can often capture an idea by squeezing in from several sides at once, to get exactly what we need by using two or more different kinds of descriptions at the same time.

> Our best ideas are often those that bridge between two different worlds!

I don't insist that every definition combine just these particular ingredients of structure and purpose. But that specific mixture does have a peculiar virtue: it helps us bridge between the "ends" we seek and the "means" we have. That is, it helps us connect things we can describe (or, make, find, do, or think) to problems we want to solve. It would be of little use to know that X's "exist," without some way to find and use them.

When we discussed accumulation, we saw that the concepts of "furniture" and "money" have reasonably compact functional definitions but accumulate many structural descriptions. Conversely, the concepts of "square" or "circle" have compact structural definitions, but accumulate endless collections of possible uses.

To learn to use a new or unfamiliar word, you start by taking it to be a sign that there exists, inside some other person's mind, a structure you could use. But no matter how carefully it is explained, you must still rebuild that thought yourself, from materials already in your own mind. It helps to be given a good definition, but still you must mold and shape each new idea to suit your existing skills—hoping to make it work for you the way it seems to work for those from whom you learn.

What people call "meanings" do not usually correspond to particular and definite structures, but to connections among and across fragments of the great, interlocking networks of connections and constraints among our agencies. Because these networks are constantly growing and changing, meanings are rarely sharp, and we cannot always expect to be able to "define" them in terms of compact sequences of words. Verbal explanations serve only as partial hints; we also have to learn from watching, working, playing—and thinking.

Learning a script (13.5)

An expert is one who does not have to think. He knows.
(Frank Lloyd Wright)

What will our portrait-drawing child try next? Some children keep working to improve their person pictures. But most of them go on to put their new-found skills to work at drawing more ambitious scenes in which two or more picture-people interact. This involves wonderful problems about how to depict social interactions and relationships—and these more ambitious projects lead the child away from being concerned with making the pictures of the individual more elaborate and realistic. When this happens, the parent may feel disappointed at what seems to be a lack of progress. But we should try to appreciate the changing character of our children's ambitions and recognize that their new problems may be even more challenging.

This doesn't mean that drawing learning stops. Even as those children cease to make their person pictures more elaborate, the speed at which they draw them keeps increasing, and with seemingly less effort. How and why does this happen? In everyday life, we take it for granted that "practice makes perfect," and that repeating and rehearsing a skill will, somehow, automatically cause it to become faster and more dependable. But when you come to think of it, this really is quite curious. You might expect, instead, that the more you learned, the *slower* you would get—from having more knowledge from which to choose! *How does practice speed things up?*

Perhaps, when we practice skills we can already perform, we engage a special kind of learning, in the course of which the original performance process is replaced or "bridged-across" by new and simpler processes. The "program" below shows the many steps our novice portrait drawer had to take in order to draw each childish body-face. The "script" to the right shows only those steps that actually produce the lines of the drawing; this script has only half as many steps.

The people we call "experts" seem to exercise their special skills with scarcely any thought at all—as though they were simply reading pre-assembled scripts. Perhaps when we "practice" to improve our skills, we're mainly building simpler scripts that don't engage so many agencies. This lets us do old things with much less "thought" and gives us more time to think of other things. The less the child had to think of where to put each arm and leg, the more time remains to represent what that picture-person is actually doing.

Parts and holes (14.7)

As an example of reformulation, we'll represent the concept of a box in the form of a machine that has a goal. We can use this to understand the *Hand-Change* phenomenon. What makes a *Block-Arch* trap a person's arm so that there's no way to escape except to withdraw? One way to explain this is to imagine the arch as made of four potential obstacles—that is, if we include the floor.

An obstacle is an object that interferes with the goal of moving in a certain direction. To be trapped is to be unable to move in any acceptable direction. Why does the *Block-Arch* form a trap? The simplest explanation is that each of its four sides is a separate obstacle that keeps us from escaping in a certain direction. (For our present purposes, we'll regard moving the hand forward or backward as unacceptable.) Therefore we're trapped, since there are only four acceptable directions—up, down, left, or right—and each of them is separately blocked. Psychologically, however, there's something missing in that explanation: it doesn't quite describe our sense of being trapped. When

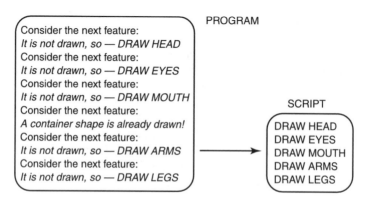

you're caught inside a box, you feel as though something is trying to keep you there. The box seems more than just its separate sides: you don't feel trapped by any particular side. It seems more like a conspiracy in which each obstacle is made more effective because of how all the other obstacles work together to keep you from going around it. In the next section we'll assemble an agency that represents this active sense of frustration by showing how those obstacles cooperate to keep you in.

In order to represent this concept of trap or enclosure, we'll first need a way to represent the idea of a container. To simplify matters, instead of trying to deal with a genuine, six-sided, three-dimensional boxlike container, we'll consider only a two-dimensional, four-sided rectangle. This will let us continue to use our *Block-Arch* uniframe, together with that extra side to represent the floor.

Why focus so sharply on the concept of a container? Because without that concept, we could scarcely understand the structure of the spatial world. Indeed, every normal child spends a great deal of time learning about space-surrounding shapes—as physical implements for containing, protecting, or imprisoning objects. But the same idea is also important not only physically, but psychologically, as a mental implement for envisioning and understanding other, more complicated structures. This is because the idea of a set of "all possible directions" is one of the great, coherent, cross-realm correspondences that can be used in many different realms of thought.

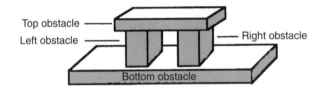

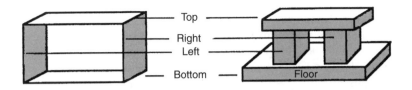

The power of negative thinking (14.8)

*When life walls us in, our intelligence cuts an opening, for,
though there be no remedy for an unrequited love, one can win
release from suffering, even if only by drawing from the
lessons it has to teach. The intelligence does not recognize in
life any closed situations without an outlet.*

(Marcel Proust)

How do boxes keep things in? Geometry is a fine tool for understanding shapes, but alone, it can't explain the *Hand-Change* mystery. For that, you also have to know how *moving* works! Suppose that you pushed a car through that *Block-Arch*. Your arm will be imprisoned until you pull it out. How can you comprehend the cause of this? The diagram below depicts an agency that represents the several ways an arm can move inside a rectangle. The top-level agent *Move* has four subagents: *Move-Left, Move-Right, Move-Up,* and *Move-Down*. (As before, we'll ignore the possibility of moving in and out, in three dimensions). If we connect each of these subagents to the corresponding side of our four-sided box-frame, each agent will be able to test whether the arm can move in the corresponding direction (by seeing whether there is an obstacle there). Then, if every direction is blocked, the arm can't move at all—and that's what we mean by being "trapped."

The "—o" symbol indicates that each box-frame agent is connected to *inhibit* the corresponding subagent of *Move*. An obstacle to the left puts *Move-Left* into a can't-move state. If all four obstacles are present, then all four box-frame agents will be activated; this will inhibit all of *Move's* agents—which will leave *Move* itself in a can't-move state—and we'll know that the trap is complete. However, if we saw a *Topless-Arch*, then the *Move-Up* agent would not be inhibited, and *Move* would not be paralyzed! This suggests an interesting way to find an escape from a *Topless-Arch*. First you *imagine* being trapped inside a box-frame—from which you know there's no escape. Then, since the top block is actually missing, when your vision system looks for actual obstacles, there will be no signal to inhibit the *Move-Up* agent. Accordingly *Move* can activate that agent, and your arm will move upward automatically to escape!

This method has a paradoxical quality. It begins by assuming that escaping is impossible. Then this pessimistic mental act—imagining that one's arm is trapped—leads directly to finding a way out. We usually expect to solve our problems in more positive, goal-directed ways, by comparing what we have with what we wish—and then removing the differences. But here we've done quite the opposite. We compared our plight, not with what we want, but with a situation even worse—the least desirable anti-goal. Yet even that can actually help, by showing how the present situation fails to match that hopeless state. Which strategy is best to use? Both depend on recognizing differences and on knowing which actions affect those differences. The optimistic strategy makes sense when one sees several ways to go—and merely has to choose the best. The pessimistic strategy should be reserved for when one sees no way at all, when things seem really desperate.

The recursion principle (15.11)

Let's consider one last time how a mind could juggle non-existent furniture inside an imaginary room. To compare different arrangements, we must somehow maintain at least two different descriptions in the mind at once. Can we store them in different agencies, both active at the same time? That would mean splitting our space-arranging-agency into two different smaller portions, each working on one of those descriptions. On the surface, there's nothing clearly wrong with that. However, if of those smaller agencies because involved with similar jobs then they, in turn, would also have to split in two. And then, we'd have to do each of those jobs with but one quarter of a mind! If we had to divide agencies into smaller and smaller fragments, each job would end up with no mind at all!

At first, this might seem to be an unusual situation. But it really is very common. The best way to solve a hard problem is always to break it into several simpler ones, and break those into even simpler ones. Then we face the same issue of mental fragmentation. Happily, there is another way. We can work on the various parts of a problem in serial order, one after another, using the same agency over and over again. Of course, this takes more time. But it has one absolutely fundamental advantage: each agency can apply its full power to every sub-problem!

> **The Recursion Principle.** When a problem splits into smaller parts, then unless one can apply the mind's full power to each such subjob, one's intellect will get dispersed, and leave less cleverness for each new task.

Indeed, our minds don't usually shatter into helpless fragments when problems split into parts. We *can* imagine how to pack a jewelry-box without forgetting where it will fit into a suitcase. This suggests that we can apply our full space-arranging resources to each problem in turn. But how, then, do we get back to the first problem, after we thought about the other ones, without having to start all over again? To common sense, the answer seems clear: we simply *"remember where we were."* But this means that we must have some way to store, and later re-create, the states of interrupted agencies. Behind the scenes, we need machinery to keep track of all the incomplete accomplishments, to remember what was learned along the way, to compare different results, and to measure progress in order to decide what to do next. All this must go on in accord with larger, sometimes changing plans.

The need to recall our recent states is why our "short term memories" *are* short term memories! In order to do their complex jobs so quickly and effect-ively, each micro-memory device must be a substantial system of machinery, with many intricate and specialized connections. If so, our brains cannot afford to make too many duplicate copies of that machinery, so we must re-use what we have for different jobs. Each time we reuse a micromemory-device, the information stored inside must be erased—or moved to another, less costly place. But that would also take some time and interrupt the flow of thought. Our short term memories must work too fast to have any time for consciousness.

Closing the ring (19.10)

Something amazing happens when you go around a loop like this! Suppose you were to imagine three properties of an apple—for example, its substance, taste, and thin-peeled structure. Then, even if there were no apple on the scene—and even if you had not yet thought of the word "apple"—the recognition-agent on the left will be aroused enough to excite your "apple"—polyneme. (This is because I used the number three for the required sum in the apple polyneme's recognizer instead of demanding that all five properties be present.) That agent can then arouse the K-lines in other agencies, like those for color and shape—and thus evoke your memories of other apple properties! In other words, if you start with enough clues to arouse one of your apple-nemes, it will automatically arouse memories of the other properties and qualities of apples and create a more complete impression,

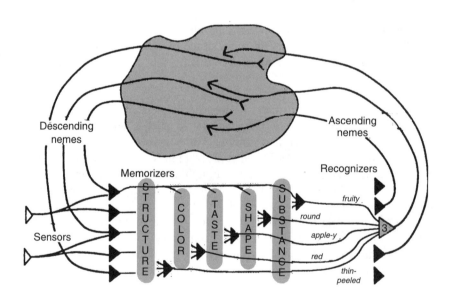

"stimulus," or hallucination of the experience of seeing, feeling, and even of eating an apple. This way, a simple loop machine can reconstruct a larger whole from clues about only certain of its parts!

Many thinkers have assumed that such abilities lie beyond the reach of all machines. Yet here we see that retrieving the whole from a few of its parts requires no magic leap past logic and necessity, but only simple societies of agents that "recognize" when certain requirements are met. If something is red and round and has the right size and shape for an apple, but some other round, red, fruit, such as a tomato or a pomegranate. Any such process leads only to guesses—and frequently these will be wrong. Nonetheless, to think effectively, we often have to turn aside from certainty—to take some chance of being wrong. Our memory systems are powerful *because* they're not constrained to be perfect!

Verbal expression (22.10)

How easily we people can communicate. We listen and speak without the slightest sense of what's involved! One of us expresses an idea, the other understands it, and neither thinks anything complicated has happened; it seems as natural to talk as it is to walk. Yet both simplicities are illusions. To walk, you must engage a vast array of agencies to move your body down the street. To talk, you must engage a vast array of agencies to build new structures in another person's mind. But *how* do you know just what to say, to affect the other person's agencies?

Let's suppose that Mary wants to tell Jack something. This means that there is a certain structure p, somewhere inside the network of Mary's agencies—and that Mary's language-agency must construct a similar structure inside Jack's mind. To do this, Mary will need to speak words that will activate appropriate activities inside Jack's agencies, then correctly link them together. How can she do that? Here is what we'll call the *"re-duplication"* theory of how we formulate what we say:

> *Mary proceeds, step by step, to construct a new version of p—call it q—inside her own mind.* In doing this, she will apply various memory-control operations to activate certain isonomes and polynemes.

> *As Mary performs each internal operation, her speech-agency selects certain corresponding verbal expressions—and these cause similar operations to occur inside Jack.* As a result, Jack builds a structure similar to q.

> *To be able to do that, Mary must have learned at least one expressive technique that corresponds to each frequently used mental operation.* And Jack must have learned to recognize those expressive

techniques—we'll call them *grammar-tactics*—and to use them to activate some corresponding isonomes and polynemes.

To build her new version of p, Mary could employ a goal-achieving scheme: she keeps comparing p with the latest version of q and, whenever she senses a significant difference, she applies some operation to q that removes or reduces that difference. For example, if Mary notices that p has an *Origin* pronome where q lacks one, her memory-control system will focus on p's *Origin*. In this case, if p itself is a motionframe, the usual speech-tactic is to use the word "*from.*" Next she must describe the substructure attached to p's *Origin* pronome. If this were a simple polyneme like "Boston," Mary's speech-agency could simply pronounce the corresponding word. But if that pronome is assigned to some more complicated structure, such as an entire frame, Mary's language-agency must interrupt itself to copy *that*. This is expressed, as we have seen, by using words like "who" or "which." In any case, Mary continues this difference-duplication process until she senses no significant discrepancies between q and p. Of course, what Mary finds "significant" depends on what she "wants to say."

This "re-duplication" theory of speech describes only the first stages of how we use language. In later stages, the mental operations we use to construct q are not always immediately applied to pronouncing words. Instead, we learn techniques for storing sequences of grammar-tactics, temporarily; this makes it possible to modify and rearrange our words and sentences before we say them. Learning these arts takes a long time: most children need a decade or more to complete their language systems, and many keep learning, throughout their lives, to sense new sorts of discrepancies and to discover ways to express them.

Creative expression (22.11)

There is a wonderful capacity that comes along with the ability to "express" ideas. Whatever we may want to say, we probably won't say exactly *that*. But in exchange, there is a chance of saying something else that is both good and new! After all, the "thing we want to say"—the structure p we're trying to describe—is not always a definite, fixed structure that our language-agents can easily read and copy. If p exists at all, it's likely to be a rapidly changing network involving several agencies. If so, then the language-agency may only be able to make guesses and hypotheses about p, and try to confirm or refute them by performing experiments. Even if p were well-defined in the first place, this very process is liable to change it, so that the final version q won't be the same as the original structure p. Sometimes we call this process "thinking in words."

In other words, whether or not what you "meant" to say actually existed before you spoke, your language-agencies are likely either to *reformulate* what did exist, or create something new and different from anything you had before. Whenever you try to express with words any complicated mental state, you're forced to oversimplify—and that can cause both loss and gain. On the losing side, no word description of a mental state can ever be complete; some nuances are always lost. But in exchange, when you're forced to try to separate the essences from accidents, you gain the opportunity to make reformulations. For example, when stuck on a problem, you may "say to yourself" things like, "*Now, let's see—just what was I really trying to accomplish?*" Then, since your language agency knows so little about the actual state of those other agencies, it must answer such questions by making theories about them, and these may well leave you in a state that is simpler, clearer, and better suited to solving your problem.

When we try to explain what we think we know, we're likely to end up with something new. All teachers know how often we understand something for the first time only after trying to explain it to someone else. Our abilities to make language descriptions can engage all our other abilities to think and to solve problems. If speaking involves thinking, then one must ask, "*How much of ordinary thought involves the use of words?*" Surely many of our most effective thinking-methods scarcely engage our language-agencies at all. Perhaps we turn to words only when other methods fail. But then, the use of language can open entirely new worlds of thought. This is because, once we can represent things in terms of strings of words, it becomes possible to use them in a boundless variety of ways to change and rearrange what happens in our other agencies. Of course, we never realize we're doing this; instead we refer to such activities by names like *paraphrase* or *change of emphasis* as though we weren't changing what we're trying to describe. The crucial thing is that during the moments in which those word-strings are detached from their "meanings," they are no longer subject to the constraints and limitations of other agencies, and the language-systems can do what they want with them. Then we can transmit, from one person's brain to another, the strings of words our grammar-tactics produce, and every individual can gain access to the most successful formulations that others can articulate. This is what we call culture—the conceptual treasures our communities accumulate through history.

Differences and duplicates (23.2)

It is important for us to be able to notice differences. But this seemingly innocent requirement poses a problem whose importance has never been recognized in psychology. To see the difficulty, let's return to the subject of mental rearrangements. Let's first assume that the problem is to compare two room-arrangement descriptions represented in two different agencies: agency *A* represents a room that contains a couch and a chair; agency *Z* represents the same room, but with the couch and chair exchanged.

Now if both agencies are to represent furniture-arrangements in ways that some third agency D can compare, then the "difference-detecting" agency D must receive two sets of inputs that match almost perfectly. Otherwise, every other, irrelevant difference between the outputs of A and Z would appear to D to be differences in those rooms—and D would perceive so many spurious differences that the real ones would be indiscernible!

The Duplication Problem. The states of two different agencies cannot be compared unless those agencies themselves are virtually identical.

But this is only the tip of the iceberg, for it is not enough that the descriptions to be compared emerge from two almost identical agencies. Those agencies must, in turn, receive inputs of near identical character. And for *that* to come about, each of their subagencies must also fulfill that same constraint. The only way to meet all these conditions is for both agencies— *and all the subagencies upon which they depend*—to be identical. *Unless we find another way, we'll need an endless host of duplicated brains!*

This duplication problem comes up all the time. What happens when you hear that *Mary bought John's house?* Must you have separate agencies to keep both Mary and John in your mind at once? Even that would not suffice, for unless both person-representing agencies had similar connections to all your other agencies, those two representations of "persons" would not have similar implications. The same kind of problem must arise when you compare your present situation with some recollection or experience—that is, when you compare how you react to those two different partial states of mind. But to compare those two reactions, what kind of simultaneous machinery would be needed to maintain both momentary personalities? How could a single mind hold room for two—one person old, the other new?

Time-blinking (23.3)

Fortunately, there is a way to get around the duplication problem entirely. Let's take a cue from how a perfume makes a strong impression first, but then appears to fade away, or how, when you put your hand in water that is very hot or very cold, the sensation is intense at first—but soon will almost disappear entirely. As we say, we "get used to" those sensations. Because *our senses react mainly to how things change in time.* This is true even for the sensors in our eyes—though, normally, we're unaware of it because our eyes are always moving imperceptibly. Most of the sensory agents that inform our brains about the world are sensitive *only* to various sorts of time-changes— and that surely is also true of most of the agents *inside* the brain.

Any agent that is sensitive to changes in time can also be used to detect differences. For whenever we expose such an agent, first to a situation A and then to a situation B, any output from that agent will signify some difference between A and B.

This suggests a way to solve the duplication problem. Since most agents can be made to serve as difference-agents, *we can compare two descriptions simply by presenting them to the same agency at different times.* This is easily done if that agency is equipped with a pair of high-speed, temporary K-line memories. Then we need only load the two descriptions into those memories and compare them by activating first one and then the other.

> Store the first description in pronome p.
> Store the second description in pronome q.
> Activate p and q in rapid succession.
> Then any changes in the agents' outputs represent differences between A and B!

We can use this trick to implement the scheme we described for escaping from a topless-arch. Suppose that p describes the present situation and q describes a box that permits no escape. Each *Move* agent is designed to detect the appearance of a wall. If we simply "blink" from the present situation to the box frame, one of these agents will announce the appearance of any box wall that was not already apparent in the present situation. Thus, automatically, this scheme will find all the directions that are not closed off. If the outputs of the *Move* agents were connected to cause you to move in the corresponding direction, this agency would lead you to escape!

The method of time-blinking can also be used to simplify our difference-engine scheme for composing verbal expressions, since now the speaker can maintain both p and q inside the selfsame agency. If not for this, each speaker would need what would amount to a duplicate society of mind, in order to simulate the listener's state. Although the method of time-blinking is powerful and efficient, it has some limitations; for example it cannot directly recognize relations among more than two things at a time. I suspect that people share this limitation, too—and this may be why we have relatively few language-forms, like "between" and "middle," for expressing three-way comparisons and relationships.

Several thoughts at once (29.2)

To see that we can think in several mental realms at once, consider the role of the word "give" in this simple sentence:

> "Mary gives Jack the kite."

We can see at least three distinct meanings here. First, we could represent the

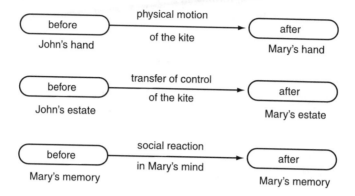

idea of the kite's motion through physical space by using a *Trans*-frame whose *Trajectory* begins at Mary's hand and ends at Jack's.

But quite beyond that realm of space, we also find a different significance in what Mary did—in another realm that we'll call "estates." This involves a different sense of "give," in which the object need not actually move at all! Instead, what happens is the transfer of its *ownership*.

Each of us has an "estate"—the collection of possessions we control. And this "realm of estate" is more important than it might seem, because it lies between the realms of objects and ideas. In order to carry out our plans, it is not enough only to know what things or ideas are required, and how to adapt them to our purposes. We must also be able to take possession of those objects or ideas, either by right or by might.

> Possession plays essential roles in all our plans, because we can't use any materials, tools, or ideas, until we gain control of them.

We can also interpret Mary's act within a social realm, in which we understand that giving gifts involves yet other kinds of relationships. No sooner do you hear of Mary's gift, than certain parts of your mind become concerned with why she was so generous, and how this involved her affections and obligations.

How can all these different thoughts proceed at the same time, without interfering with one another? I suspect that it is for the same reason that we have no trouble imagining an apple as both round and red at the same time: in that case, the processes for color and shape use agents that do not compete. Similarly, the different processes involved with ideas like "give" may operate in agencies so different they rarely need to compete for the same resources.

Paranomes (29.3)

What enables us to comprehend *"Mary gives Jack the kite"* in so many ways at once? Different meanings don't conflict when they apply to separate realms—but that can't be quite what's happening here, since the physical, social, and mental realms are closely linked in many ways. So now I'll argue just the opposite, that *these meanings are so similar that they don't conflict!* Here is my hypothesis about what holds together all these aspects of our thoughts.

> Many of our higher level conceptual-frames are really parallel arrays
> of analogous frames, each active in a different realm.

Consider all the different roles played by the *Actor* pronome of our sentence. In the physical realm, the *Origin* of *give* is Mary's hand. In the possessional realm of "give and take," that *Origin* is in Mary's estate—since Mary can only give Jack what she owns. Similarly, in the physical realm, it is the kite itself that moves from Mary's hand to Jack's; however, in the realm of estates, the kite's *ownership* is what "changes hands."

This suggests that certain pronomes can operate in several different realms at once. Let's call them "paranomes" to emphasize their parallel activities. When the language-agency activates some polynemes and paranomes, these agents run cross-wise through the agencies of various realms to arouse several processes and frames at the same time; these correspond to different interpretations, in different realms, of the same phrase or sentence. Then, because each major agency contains its own memory-control system, the agencies within each realm can simultaneously apply their own methods for dealing with the corresponding aspect of the common topic of concern. In this way, a single language-phrase can at the same time evoke different processes involved with social dispositions, spatial images, poetical fancies, musical themes, mathematical structures—or any other

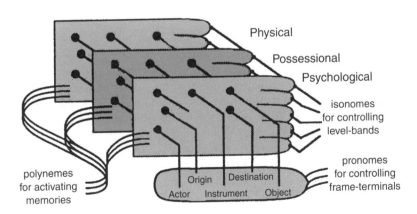

assortment of types of thought that don't interfere too much with one another.

This is not to say that all these different modes of thought will proceed independently of one another. Whenever any process gains momentary control over a paranome, many other processes can be affected. For example, one agency's memory-control process might thus cause the agencies in several other realms simultaneously to "blink" on and off their *Origin* and *Destination* paranomes. This would force the agencies active in each of those realms to focus upon whichever types of differences they then discern; then, in between such episodes, each agency can apply its own way of thinking to the corresponding topic, difference, or relationship. By using these cross-connecting polynemes and paranomes, the activity in each realm can proceed sometimes independently, yet at other times influence and be affected by what happens in the other realms.

Cross-realm correspondences (29.4)

We often describe the things we like as *"elevated," "lofty,"* or *"heavenly."* Why do we see such things in terms of altitude in space? We often speak of time itself in spatial terms, as though the future were "ahead" of us, while the past remains behind. We think of problems as "obstacles" to go around, and turn to using diagrams to represent things that don't have shapes at all. What enables us to turn so many skills to so many other purposes? These tendencies reflect the systematic "cross-realm correspondences" embodied in our families of polynemes and paranomes.

> At each instant, several realms may be engaged in active processing. Each has separate processes, but must compete for control of the ascending nemes that lead into the language-agency. Which polyneme will play the role of *Origin* in the next sentence-frame? Will it be Mary's physical arm or hand, or Mary's social role as party-guest? It sometimes seems as though the language-agency can focus on only one realm at a time.

This could be one reason why language-scientists find it hard to classify the roles words play in sentence-frames. No sooner does a language agency assign some polynemes and isonomes to a phrase, than various mind-divisions proceed to alter how they're used inside each different realm. Every shift of control from one realm to another affects which particular nemes will be next to influence the language agency. This causes moment-to-moment changes in the apparent meaning of a phrase.

> At one moment, control over language may reside in the realm of thought that is working most successfully; at the next moment, it

246

may be the one experiencing the most difficulty. Each shift in attention affects how the various expressions will be interpreted, and this in turn can affect which realm will next take center stage.

For example, the sentence, "*Mary gives Jack the kite*," might start by arousing a listener's concern with Mary's social role as party-guest. That would cause the pronomes of a social frame to represent Mary's obligation to bring a present. But then the listener's possession realm might become concerned with Mary's ownership of that gift, or with how she got control of it. This shift from social to possessional concern could then affect the processing of future sentences. For example, it will influence whether a phrase like "Jack's kite" is interpreted to refer to the kite that Jack happens to be holding or to a different kite that Jack happens to own.

Every mental realm accumulates its own abilities, but also discovers, from time to time, how to exploit the skills of other realms. Thus the mind as a whole can learn to exploit the frames developed in the realm of space both for representing events in time, and for thinking about social relationships. Perhaps our chaining skills are the best example of this; no matter which realm or realms they originate in, we eventually learn to apply them to any collection of entities, events, or ideas (in any realm whatever) that we can arrange into sequences. Then chains assume their myriad forms, such as spatial order, psychological causality, or social dominance.

Reference

Minsky, Marvin [1987], this chapter is a collection of excerpts from *The Society of Mind*, Simon and Schuster.

34

MATHEMATICAL LOGIC IN ARTIFICIAL INTELLIGENCE

John McCarthy

Source: *Daedalus: Journal of the American Academy of Arts and Sciences* 117(1) (1988): 297–311.

This article concerns computer programs that represent information about their problem domains in mathematical logical languages and use logical inference to decide what actions are appropriate to achieve their goals.

Mathematical logic is not a single language. There are many kinds of mathematical logic, and even choosing a kind does not specify the language. The language is determined by declaring what nonlogical symbols will be used and what sentences will be taken as axioms. The nonlogical symbols are those that concern the concrete subject matter to be stored in a computer's data base – for example, information about objects and their locations and motions.

Whatever the choice of symbols, all kinds of mathematical logic share two ideas. First, it must be mathematically definite what strings of symbols are considered formulas of the logic. Second, it must be mathematically definite what inferences of new formulas from old ones are allowed. These ideas permit the writing of computer programs that decide what combinations of symbols are sentences and what inferences are allowed in a particular logical language.

Mathematical logic has become an important branch of mathematics, and most logicians work on problems arising from the internal development of the subject. Mathematical logic has also been applied to studying the foundations of mathematics, and there it has had its greatest success. Its founders, Aristotle, Leibniz, Boole, and Frege, also wished to apply it to making reasoning about human affairs more rigorous. Indeed, Leibniz was explicit about his goal of replacing argument with calculation. However, expressing knowledge and reasoning about the commonsense world in mathematical logic has entailed difficulties that seem to require extensions of the basic concepts of logic, and these extensions are only beginning to develop.

If a computer is to store facts about the world and reason with them, it needs a precise language. The program must be based on a precise idea of what reasoning is allowed – that is, how new formulas may be derived from old. It was natural in the beginning to try to use mathematical logical language to express what an intelligent computer program "knows" that is relevant to the problems we want it to solve and to make the program use logical inference in order to decide what to do. The first proposal to use logic in artificial intelligence for expressing what a program knows and how it should reason was in a paper I wrote in 1960. The problem of proving logical formulas as a domain for AI had already been studied. In this paper I said:

> The *advice taker* is a proposed program for solving problems by manipulating sentences in formal languages. The main difference between it and other programs or proposed programs for manipulating formal languages (the *Logic Theory Machine* of Newell, Simon and Shaw and the Geometry Program of Herbert Gelernter) is that in the previous programs the formal system was the subject matter but the heuristics were all embodied in the program. In this program the procedures will be described as much as possible in the language itself and, in particular, the heuristics are all so described.
>
> The main advantage we expect the *advice taker* to have is that its behavior will be improvable merely by making statements to it, telling it about its symbolic environment and what is wanted from it. To make these statements will require little if any knowledge of the program or the previous knowledge of the *advice taker*. One will be able to assume that the *advice taker* will have available to it a fairly wide class of immediate logical consequences of anything it is told and its previous knowledge. This property is expected to have much in common with what makes us describe certain humans as having *common sense*. We shall therefore say that *a program has common sense if it automatically deduces for itself a sufficiently wide class of immediate consequences of anything it is told and what it already knows.*[1]

The advice taker prospectus, ambitious in 1960, would be considered ambitious even today and is still far from being immediately realizable. Mathematical logic is especially far from the goal of expressing the heuristics in the same language in which are expressed the facts the heuristics must act on. Yet the main reasons for using logical sentences extensively in AI are better understood by researchers today than in 1960. Expressing information in declarative sentences is far more flexible than expressing it in segments of computer program or in tables. Sentences can be true in much wider contexts than specific programs can be useful. The supplier of a fact does not have to understand much about how the receiver functions or about how or whether the receiver will use it. The same fact can be used for many purposes; the logical consequences of collections of facts can be made available.

Existing computer programs come more or less close to this goal, depending on the extent to which they use the formalisms of logic. I shall begin by describing four levels of their use.

1. A machine on the lowest level uses no logical sentences. It merely executes the commands of its program. All its "beliefs" are implicit in its state. Nevertheless, it is often appropriate to ascribe beliefs and goals to the program. A missile may believe its target is friendly and abandon the goal of hitting it. One can often usefully say that a certain machine does what it thinks will achieve its goals. Daniel Dennett, Allen Newell, and I have all discussed ascription of mental qualities to machines.[2] The intent of the machine's designers and the way it can be expected to behave may be more readily described in terms of intention than with a purely physical description.

    The relation between the physical and the intentional descriptions of a machine is most easy to understand in simple systems that admit readily understandable descriptions of both kinds. Take a thermostat as an example. We might say that when it believes the temperature is too hot, it turns on the cooling system in order to achieve its goal of getting the right temperature. Some finicky philosophers object to such ascription. Unless a system has a full human mind, they contend, it should not be regarded as having any mental qualities at all. This restriction is like omitting zero and one from the number system on the grounds that numbers are not required to count sets with no elements or with one element. Of course, ascribing beliefs to machines (and people) is more important when our physical knowledge is inadequate to explain or predict behaviour. Much more can be said about ascribing mental qualities to machines, but that is not what AI is mainly concerned with today.

2. The next level of logic use involves computer programs that put sentences in machine memory to represent their beliefs but use rules other than ordinary logical inference to reach conclusions. New sentences are often obtained from the old ones by *ad hoc* programs. Moreover, the sentences that appear in memory are from a program-dependent subset of the logical language being used. Adding certain true sentences in the language may even spoil the functioning of the program. Logic is used at this second level in "expert systems," programs that consist of knowledge bases (e.g., lists of disease symptoms in medical expert systems) and inference engines (which contain rules, in the form of explicit instructions to the machine, on how to manipulate the information in the knowledge base). In comparison with the languages of first-order logic, languages used at this level are often rather unexpressive. For example, they may not admit quantified sentences (i.e., sentences including "for all" or "there exists"), and they may represent general rules in a separate notation. Often, rules cannot be consequences of a program's action;

they must all be put in by a "knowledge engineer." Sometimes the reason programs have this form is just ignorance, but the usual reason for the restriction is the practical one of making the program run fast and deduce just the kinds of conclusions its designer anticipates. Most often, the rules are implications used in just one direction (in other words, the contrapositive of an implication is not used). I believe the need for such specialized inference will turn out to be temporary and will be reduced or eliminated by improved ways of controlling general inference – for example, by allowing the heuristic rules to be expressed also as sentences, as advocated in the preceding extract from my 1960 paper.

3. The third level uses first-order logic as well as logical deduction. Usually the sentences are represented as clauses, and the deduction methods are based on J. Allen Robinson's method of resolution.[3] A fact in one such program's data base might be:

> (for all (x) (if (and (inst x vegetable) (color x purple))
> (inst x eggplant)))

Translated into more common language, the fact reads: "All purple vegetables are eggplants." Its structure is typical of if-then clauses in logical data bases: given any x, if x satisfies the stated conditions, then x ensures a certain result – (for all (x) (if (conditions) then (result))).

In the example, x must satisfy two conditions: (inst x vegetable) and (color x purple). The first condition means that x must be a specific instance of the class of vegetables, and the second means that the color of x must be purple. The result, (inst x eggplant), means that x is an instance of an eggplant. Armed with this fact, the program might seem ready to take on this task:

> (inst Gertrude vegetable)
> (color Gertrude purple)
> (SHOW: (inst Gertrude eggplant))

Translated, the task is: Given the fact that Gertrude is a purple vegetable, show that Gertrude is an eggplant. But with just the logical fact, the program can do nothing with the task. It needs a method for reasoning from general statements about nondescript x's to specific statements about Gertrude. The reasoning of Robinson's resolution method prescribes a way to substitute Gertrude for x and thereby unify the clauses in the data base with those in the task.

Examples of such programs used commercially are "expert system shells" (ART, KEE, OPS-5) – computer programs that create generic expert systems. You tell the program what facts you want in the data base; the program converts the facts into logical statements and then follows the heuristics in its own inference engine to create an inference engine tailored to the facts you put into the program.

The third level of logic is less used for practical purposes than is level two because techniques for controlling the reasoning are still insufficiently developed and it is common for a program to generate many useless conclusions before it reaches a desired solution. Indeed, unsuccessful experience with this method[4] has led to more restricted uses of logic (for example, the STRIPS system of Richard Fikes and Nils Nilsson[5]).

In this connection it is important to mention logic programming, first introduced in Microplanner[6] and approached from different points of view by Robert Kowalski and Alain Colmerauer in the 1970s.[7] Microplanner was a rather unsystematic collection of tools, unlike Prolog, a computer language that relies almost entirely on one mathematically tractable kind of logic programming,[8] but the main idea is the same. If one uses a restricted class of sentences, the so-called Horn clauses, then it is possible to use a restricted form of logical deduction. This eases the control problem and makes it possible for the programmer to anticipate the course the deduction will take. The problem is that only certain kinds of facts are conveniently expressed as Horn clauses. Nevertheless, expressibility in Horn clauses is an important property of a set of facts, and logic programming has been successfully used for many applications (although it seems unlikely to dominate AI programming, as certain of its advocates hope).

Although they express both facts and rules as logical sentences, third-level systems are still rather specialized. The axioms with which the programs begin are not general truths about the world but sentences whose meaning and truth are limited to the narrow domain in which the program has to act. For this reason, the facts of one program usually cannot be used in a data base for other programs.

4. The fourth level is still a goal. It involves representing general facts about the world as logical sentences. Once put in a data base, the facts can be used by any program. The facts would have the neutrality of purpose characteristic of much human information. The supplier of information would not have to understand the goals of the potential user or how his mind works. The present ways of "teaching" computer programs amount to education by brain surgery.

A major difficulty is that fourth-level systems require extensions to mathematical logic. One kind of extension is nonmonotonic reasoning, first proposed in the late 1970s.[9] Traditional logic is monotonic in the following sense. If a sentence p is inferred from a collection A of sentences, and if B is a more inclusive set of sentences, then p can be inferred from B. For example, let collection A be these sentences: All bachelors are unmarried; John is a bachelor. Let collection B be these sentences: All bachelors are unmarried; John has no girlfriends; John is a bachelor. From both sets of questions, you can infer sentence p: John is unmarried. The set of sentences A is a model of the set: All x are y; w is x. If "w is y" is true in all models of this general set, then it will be true in all models of the general form of set B. So we see that the monotonic character of traditional logic does not depend on the details of the logical system, but is quite fundamental.

While much human reasoning corresponds to that of traditional logic, some important human commonsense reasoning is not monotonic. We reach conclusions from certain premises that we would not reach if certain other sentences were included in our premises. For example, learning that I own a car, you conclude that it is appropriate on a certain occasion to ask me for a ride; but when you learn the further fact that the car is in the garage being fixed, you no longer draw that conclusion. Some people think it is possible to try to save monotonicity by saying that what was in your mind was not a general rule about asking for a ride from car owners but a probabilistic rule – something like "On 70 percent of occasions it is appropriate for you to ask for a ride if I own a car." So far it has not proved possible to work out the detailed epistemology of this approach – that is, to determine exactly what probabilistic sentences should be used. Instead, AI has moved to directly formalizing nonmonotonic logical reasoning.

Formalized nonmonotonic reasoning is under rapid development, and many kinds of systems have been proposed. I shall concentrate on an approach called "circumscription" because I know it, and because it has met with wide acceptance and is perhaps the most actively pursued approach at present. The idea is to single out, from among the models of the collection of sentences being assumed, some "preferred," or "standard," models. The preferred models are those that satisfy a certain minimum principle. What is to be minimized is not yet decided in complete generality, but many domains that have been studied yield quite general theories using minimizations of abnormality or of the set of some kind of entity. The idea is not entirely unfamiliar. For example, Occam's razor, "Do not multiply entities beyond necessity," is such a minimum principle.

Minimization in logic is another example of an area of mathematics being discovered in connection with applications rather than through the normal internal development of mathematics. Of course, the reverse is happening on an even larger scale; many logical concepts developed for purely mathematical reasons turn out to have importance for AI.

As a more concrete example of nonmonotonic reasoning, consider the conditions under which a boat may be used to cross a river. Now consider things that might be wrong with a boat. It might have a leak. It might have no oars, no motor, or no sails, depending on what kind of a boat it is. It would be reasonably convenient to list some of these things in a set of axioms. However, besides those obstacles that we can expect to list in advance, human reasoning will admit still others should they arise, but it cannot be expected to think of them all in advance (e.g., a fence down the middle of the river). One can handle this difficulty by using circumscription to minimize the set of things that prevent the boat from crossing the river – that is, the set of obstacles to be overcome. If the reasoner knows of none in a particular case, he will conjecture that the boat can be used, but if he learns of one, he will get a different result when he minimizes.

This illustration shows that nonmonotonic reasoning is conjectural rather than rigorous. Indeed, it has been shown that certain mathematical logical systems cannot be rigorously extended, that they have a certain kind of completeness.

It is as misleading to conduct a discussion of this kind entirely without formulas as it would be to discuss the foundations of physics without formulas. Unfortunately, many people are unable to follow the mathematics. So I discuss instead a formalization by Vladimir Lifschitz of a simple example called "the Yale shooting problem."[10] Drew McDermott, who has become discouraged about the use of logic in AI and especially about nonmonotonic formalisms, devised the problem as a challenge.[11] Lifschitz's method works well here, but I think it will require further modification.

In this problem there is initially an unloaded gun and a person, Fred. The gun is then loaded. There is a wait, and then the gun is pointed at Fred and fired. The desired conclusion is that Fred dies. Informally, the rules are (1) that a living person remains alive until something happens to him, (2) that loading causes a gun to become loaded, (3) that a loaded gun remains loaded until something unloads it, (4) that shooting unloads a gun, and (5) that shooting a loaded gun at a person kills him. We are intended to reason as follows: Fred will remain alive until the gun is fired because nothing can be inferred to happen to him; the gun will remain loaded until it is fired because nothing can be inferred to happen to it; Fred will then die when the gun is fired. The nonmonotonic part of the reasoning is minimizing the things that happen or assuming that nothing happens without a reason.

The logical sentences are intended to express these five premises, but they do not explicitly say that no other phenomenon occurs. For example, there is no assertion that Fred is not wearing a bulletproof vest, nor are any properties of bulletproof vests mentioned. Nevertheless, a person will conclude that unless some unmentioned aspect of the situation is present to prevent Fred's death, he will die. The difficulty is that the sentences admit an "unintended minimal model," to use the terminology of mathematical logic. Namely, it may happen that for some unspecified reason the gun becomes unloaded during the wait, so that Fred remains alive. The way nonmonotonic formalisms (e.g., circumscription and R. A. Reiter's logic of defaults) were used to formulate the problem, minimizing "abnormality" results in two possibilities, not one. The unintended possibility is that the gun mysteriously becomes unloaded.

It seems likely that introducing nonmonotonic reasoning will not be the only modification of logic that will be required in order to give machines human capability for commonsense reasoning. To make programs that reason about their own knowledge and belief (i.e., programs that have even rudimentary consciousness), it is necessary to formalize many intensional notions (e.g., knowledge and belief). One can formalize some of them in first-order logic by introducing propositions and concepts as individuals.[12] Complicating such efforts are the paradoxes discovered by Richard Montague.[13] To avoid them, it will be necessary to weaken the axioms suitably, but a good way of doing so has yet to be found. It also seems necessary to formalize the notion of context, but this is in a very preliminary state of investigation.[14]

AI and philosophy

Artificial intelligence cannot avoid philosophy. If a computer program is to behave intelligently in the real world, it must be provided with some kind of framework into which to fit particular facts it is told or discovers. This amounts to at least a fragment of some kind of philosophy, however naive. Here I agree with philosophers who advocate the study of philosophy and claim that one who purports to ignore it is merely condemning himself to a naive philosophy.

Because it is still far behind the intellectual performance of people who are philosophically naive, AI could probably make do with a naive philosophy for a long time. Unfortunately, it has not been possible to say what a naive philosophy is, and philosophers offer little guidance.

The next plausible alternative might be to build our programs to seek and represent knowledge in accordance with the tenets of one of the philosophies that have been proposed by philosophers. This also has not been possible. Either no one in AI (including retreaded philosophers) understands philosophical theories well enough to program a computer in accordance with their tenets, or the philosophers have not even come close to the required precision. Actually, some of the empiricist philosophies appear to be precise enough, but they turn out to be inadequate when one attempts to use them in the most modest of computer programs. Therefore, we AI researchers have found ourselves on our own when it comes to providing a program with a basic intellectual structure. Here is some of what we think this would require:

Ontology. I adopt Willard Quine's idea that our ontology is defined by the range of bound variables.[15] With this idea, we need to specify what kinds of entities are to be assumed, that is, what the robot's beliefs are to be about. His nominalism would further suggest, it seems to me, that variables take only material objects as values. This theory promptly proves inadequate because, for example, it doesn't permit the robot's designer to inform it about what properties of objects are preserved when certain kinds of events take place.

Quine tells us that "there is no place in science for ideas," and argues for this view with examples of the difficulty of defining what it means for two people to have the same idea.[16] However, if a program is to search for a good idea by generating lots of ideas and then testing them, it needs some criteria for deciding when it has already tested a certain idea. Thus, ideas as objects seem to be required, but how to avoid the difficulty Quine cites has not yet been discovered. Present AI systems cannot enumerate ideas.

Free will. The robots we plan to build are entirely deterministic systems. However, a sophisticated robot must decide what to do by considering the various things it *can* do and choosing which has the best consequences in view of the goals it has been given. To do so, it must be able to represent "I can do *A* and I can do *B*, but *B* seems better, so while I can do *A*, I won't." What does it mean for a robot to believe "I can, but I won't"? It is a deterministic system, so either it will do *A* or it won't. Patrick J. Hayes and I have offered some proposals for resolving the problem of free will for robots.[17]

Nonmonotonic reasoning. AI programs require ways of jumping to conclusions on the basis of insufficient evidence.

AI researchers' attempts to determine an intellectual framework precise enough for programming AI systems have already led to certain philosophical views – both to taking sides in some ancient philosophical controversies and to proposals that we regard as new. I will discuss two points:

1. *Incrementalism, or modesty.* The facts about the effects of actions and other events that have been put into the data bases of AI programs are not very general. They are not even as general as what questioning would elicit from naive people, let alone general enough to satisfy people familiar with the philosophical literature. However, they suffice in certain cases to determine the appropriate action to achieve a goal. Observing the limitations of these cases leads to further advance. This is a useful methodology even when the objectives are philosophical. One can design formalisms that can be used in working systems and improve them when their defects become apparent.

   The philosopher might claim that the working systems are too trivial to be of interest to him. He would be wrong, because it turns out that the philosophical investigations of action have missed important phenomena that arise as soon as one tries to design systems that plan actions. Here are two examples. First, the ideas on association, dating at least from Mill and going through the behaviorists, are too vague to be programmed at all. Second, philosophers have missed most of the nonmonotonic character of the reasoning involved in everyday decision making. For AI it is important not only that the researcher be able to revise his ideas, but also that the program be able to improve its behavior incrementally, either by accepting advice from the user or by learning from experience, and such improvement requires new languages for expressing knowledge. For example, a baby first considers the word *mother* a proper name, then a general name for adult women, and still later a designation of a relation. I think that before we can have computer programs with the general intelligence and linguistic flexibility of a human child, AI researchers must develop languages with "elaboration tolerance." For example, such a language would allow the usage of the word *mother* to develop as described above without losing older information. Elaboration tolerance is a current AI research topic.

2. *Objectivity*. Regardless of one's ultimate view of reality, in designing robots we need to make the robot view the world as an external reality about which it has and can obtain only partial knowledge. We will not be successful if we design the robot to regard the world as merely a structure built on the robot's sensory information. There needs to be a theory (it could be called metaepistemology) relating the structure of a world, a knowledge-seeker in that world, the interaction channel between the knowledge-seeker and the rest of the world, the knowledge-seeker's rules for deciding what assertions about the world are meaningful, and the knowledge-seeker's rules for accepting evidence about the world and what the knowledge-seeker can discover. If the rules are too restrictive (as perhaps they are in some operationalist philosophies of science), the knowledge-seeker, regarding the assertions as insufficiently operational to be meaningful, will be unable to discover basic facts about the world.

Remarks

Much of what I want to say involves stating a position on issues that are controversial even within AI.

I believe, for example, that artificial intelligence is best regarded as a branch of computer science rather than as a branch of psychology. AI is concerned with methods of achieving goals in situations in which the information available has a certain complex character. The methods that have to be used are related to the problem presented by the situation and are similar whether the problem solver is human, a Martian, or a computer program.

Initially, some people were overoptimistic about how long it would take to achieve human-level intelligence. Optimism was natural because only a few of the difficulties had been identified. Enough difficulties have been identified by now to establish AI as one of the more difficult sciences. Maybe it will take five years to achieve human-level intelligence, and maybe it will take five hundred.

It is still not clear how to characterize situations in which intelligence is required. Evidently, they are open-ended. Even in a game like chess, where the rules are fixed, the methods for deciding on a move are open-ended in character – new ways of thinking about chess positions are invented all the time.

AI has so far identified certain methods of pattern matching, heuristic searching of trees of possibilities, and representation of information by rules and learning. Other methods are still to be characterized, especially methods of representing problems as collections of subproblems that can be examined separately to get results that can then be used in studying their interactions.

Approaching AI through logic is not the only strategy that may lead to success. For example, approaches more closely tied to biology may succeed eventually, even though most of the biology-motivated approaches that have been tried since the 1950s have dried up.

Much controversy surrounds AI's implications for philosophy, a subject about which there are strong views. AI tends to support rationalist and realist views of philosophical problems rather than empiricist, phenomenological, or idealist views. It encourages a piecemeal approach to the philosophy of mind, in which mental qualities are considered separately rather than as part of a grand package. This is because some systems have important, but rather limited, mental qualities.

There are many problems in formalizing common sense, and many approaches to solving them await exploration. Two thousand years of philosophy have only limited relevance in this regard. In my opinion, the proper discussion of these problems is unavoidably mostly technical, involving the actual logical formalisms being used. The situation calculus used has important known limitations. The *result* (*e, s*) formalism, used in AI to express the consequences of actions and other events, has to be modified to handle continuous time. A quite different formalism is needed to express facts about concurrent events. Robert Kowalski and Mark Sergot's "event calculus" is a candidate for meeting both of these requirements.[18]

The study of AI may lead to a mathematical metaepistemology analogous to metamathematics – to a study of the relation between a knower's rules for accepting evidence and a world in which he is embedded. This study could result in mathematical theorems about whether certain intellectual strategies can lead to the discovery of certain facts about the world. I think this possibility will eventually revolutionize philosophy.

Endnotes

1 John McCarthy, "Programs with Common Sense," in *Proceedings of the Teddington Conference on the Mechanization of Thought Processes* (London: Her Majesty's Stationery Office, 1960), 77–84.

2 Daniel C. Dennett, "Intentional Systems," *Journal of Philosophy* 68 (4) (25 February 1971):25; Allen Newell, "The Knowledge Level," *AI Magazine* 2 (2) (1981):87–106; and John McCarthy, "Ascribing Mental Qualities to Machines," in *Philosophical Perspectives in Artificial Intelligence*, ed. Martin Ringle (Brighton, Sussex: Harvester Press, 1979), 1–20.

3 J. Allen Robinson, "A Machine-oriented Logic Based on the Resolution Principle," *Journal of the Association for Computing Machinery* 12 (1) (1965):23–41.

4 Cordell Green, "Application of Theorem Proving to Problem Solving," *International Joint Conference on Artificial Intelligence* 1 (1969):219–39.

5 Richard Fikes and Nils Nilsson, "STRIPS: A New Approach to the Application of Theorem Proving to Problem Solving," *Artificial Intelligence* 2 (3,4) (January 1971):189–208.

6 Gerald J. Sussman, Terry Winograd, and Eugene Charniak, "Micro-planner Reference Manual," Report AIM-203A (Cambridge: Artificial Intelligence Laboratory, Massachusetts Institute of Technology, 1971).

7 Robert Kowalski, *Logic for Problem Solving* (Amsterdam: North-Holland, 1979); the first implementation of Prolog was developed by Alain Colmerauer of the University of Marseilles in 1971, but this is described only in the internal documents of his group.

8 A recent text on logic programming is Leon Sterling and Ehud Shapiro, *The Art of Prolog* (Cambridge: MIT Press, 1986).

9 John McCarthy, "Epistemological Problems of Artificial Intelligence," in *Proceedings of the Fifth International Joint Conference on Artificial Intelligence* (Cambridge: Massachusetts Institute of Technology, 1977); McCarthy, "Circumscription – A Form of Non-Monotonic Reasoning," *Artificial Intelligence* 13 (1,2) (1980):27–39; McCarthy, "Applications of Circumscription to Formalizing Common Sense Knowledge," *Artificial Intelligence* 28 (1) (1986):89–116. See also Raymond A. Reiter, "A Logic for Default Reasoning," *Artificial Intelligence* 13 (1,2) (1980):81–132; and Drew McDermott and Jon Doyle, "Non-Monotonic Logic I," *Artificial Intelligence* 13 (1) (1980):41–72.

10 Vladimir Lifschitz, "Formal Theories of Action," a preliminary report in vol. 2 of *Proceedings of the International Joint Conference on Artificial Intelligence* (Los Altos, Calif.: Morgan-Kaufmann, 1977), 966–72.

11 Drew McDermott, "A Critique of Pure Reason," *Computational Intelligence* (forthcoming, 1988).

12 John McCarthy, "First Order Theories of Individual Concepts and Propositions," in *Machine Intelligence 9*, ed. Donald Michie (Edinburgh: University of Edinburgh Press, 1979), 129–48.

13 Richard Montague, "Syntactical Treatments of Modality, with Corollaries on Reflexion Principles and Finite Axiomatizability," *Acta Philosophica Fennica* 16 (1963):153–67, reprinted in Richard Montague, *Formal Philosophy* (New Haven: Yale University Press, 1974).

14 Michael Genesereth and Nils Nilsson have written the best general text on the logic approach to AI, *The Logical Foundations of Artificial Intelligence* (Los Altos, Calif.: Morgan-Kaufmann, 1987).

15 Willard V. Quine, *Quiddities* (Cambridge: Harvard University Press, 1987).

16 Ibid.

17 John McCarthy and Patrick J. Hayes, "Some Philosophical Problems from the Standpoint of Artificial Intelligence," in *Machine Intelligence 4*, ed. Donald Michie (New York: American Elsevier, 1969).

18 Robert Kowalski and Sergot Marek, *A Logic-based Calculus of Events* (London: Department of Computing, Imperial College, 1985).

35

A PRELIMINARY ANALYSIS OF THE SOAR ARCHITECTURE AS A BASIS FOR GENERAL INTELLIGENCE

Paul S. Rosenbloom, John E. Laird, Allen Newell and Robert McCarl

Source: *Artificial Intelligence* 47 (1991): 289–325.

Abstract Rosenbloom, P.S., J.E. Laird, A. Newell and R. McCarl, A primary analysis of the Soar architecture as a basis for general intelligence, Artificial Intelligence 47 (1991) 289–325.

In this article we take a step towards providing an analysis of the Soar architecture as a basis for general intelligence. Included are discussions of the basic assumptions underlying the development of Soar, a description of Soar cast in terms of the theoretical idea of multiple levels of description, an example of Soar performing multi-column subtraction, and three analyses of Soar: its natural tasks, the sources of its power, and its scope and limits

Introduction

The central scientific problem of artificial intelligence (AI) is to understand what constitutes intelligent action and what processing organizations are capable of such action. Human intelligence—which stands before us like a holy grail—shows to first observation what can only be termed *general intelligence*. A single human exhibits a bewildering diversity of intelligent behavior. The types of goals that humans can set for themselves or accept from the environment seem boundless. Further observation, of course, shows limits to this capacity in any individual—problems range from easy to hard, and problems can always be found that are too hard to be solved. But the general point is still compelling.

Work in AI has already contributed substantially to our knowledge of what functions are required to produce general intelligence. There is substantial, though certainly not unanimous, agreement about some functions that need to be supported: symbols and goal structures, for example. Less agreement exists about what mechanisms are appropriate to support these functions, in large part because such matters depend strongly on the rest of the system and on cost-benefit tradeoffs. Much of this work has been done under the rubric of AI tools and languages, rather than AI systems themselves. However, it takes only a slight shift of viewpoint to change from what is an aid for the programmer to what is structure for the intelligent system itself. Not all features survive this transformation, but enough do to make the development of AI languages as much substantive research as tool building. These proposals provide substantial ground on which to build.

The Soar project has been building on this foundation in an attempt to understand the functionality required to support general intelligence. Our current understanding is embodied in the Soar architecture [22, 26]. This article represents an attempt at describing and analyzing the structure of the Soar system. We will take a particular point of view—the description of Soar as a hierarchy of levels—in an attempt to bring coherence to this discussion.

The idea of analyzing systems in terms of multiple levels of description is a familiar one in computer science. In one version, computer systems are described as a sequence of levels that starts at the bottom with the device level and works up through the circuit level, the logic level, and then one or more program levels. Each level provides a description of the system at some level of abstraction. The sequence is built up by defining each higher level in terms of the structure provided at the lower levels. This idea has also recently been used to analyze human cognition in terms of levels of description [38]. Each level corresponds to a particular time scale, such as ~100 msec. and ~1 sec., with a new level occurring for each new order of magnitude. The four levels between ~10 msec. and ~10 sec. comprise the cognitive band (Fig. 1). The lowest cognitive level—at ~10 msec.—is the symbol-accessing level, where the knowledge referred to by symbols is retrievable. The second cognitive level—at ~100 msec.—is the level at which elementary deliberate operations occur; that is, the level at which encoded knowledge is brought to bear, and the most elementary choices are made. The third and fourth cognitive levels—at ~1 sec. and ~10 sec.—are the simple-operator-composition and

Rational Band	. . .	
	~10 sec.	Goal attainment
Cognitive Band	~1 sec.	Simple operator composition
	~100 msec.	Elementary deliberate operations
	~10 msec.	Symbol accessing
Neural Band	. . .	

Figure 1 Partial hierarchy of time scales in human cognition

goal-attainment levels. At these levels, sequences of deliberations can be composed to achieve goals. Above the cognitive band is the rational band, at which the system can be described as being goal oriented, knowledge-based, and strongly adaptive. Below the cognitive band is the neural band.

In Section 2 we describe Soar as a sequence of three cognitive levels: the memory level, at which symbol accessing occurs; the decision level, at which elementary deliberate operations occur; and the goal level, at which goals are set and achieved via sequences of decisions. The goal level is an amalgamation of the top two cognitive levels from the analysis of human cognition.

In this description we will often have call to describe mechanisms that are built into the architecture of Soar. The architecture consists of all of the fixed structure of the Soar system. According to the levels analysis, the correct view to be taken of this fixed structure is that it comprises the set of mechanisms provided by the levels underneath the cognitive band. For human cognition this is the neural band. For artificial cognition, this may be a connectionist band, though it need not be. This view notwithstanding, it should be remembered that it is the Soar architecture which is primary in our research. The use of the levels viewpoint is simply an attempt at imposing a particular, hopefully illuminating, theoretical structure on top of the existing architecture.

In the remainder of this paper we describe the methodological assumptions underlying Soar, the structure of Soar, an illustrative example of Soar's performance on the task of multi-column subtraction, and a set of preliminary analyses of Soar as an architecture for general intelligence.

1 Methodological assumptions

The development of Soar is driven by four methodological assumptions. It is not expected that these assumptions will be shared by all researchers in the field. However, the assumptions do help explain why the Soar system and project have the shapes that they do.

The first assumption is the utility of focusing on the cognitive band, as opposed to the neural or rational bands. This is a view that has traditionally been shared by a large segment of the cognitive science community; it is not, however, shared by the connectionist community, which focuses on the neural band (plus the lower levels of the cognitive band), or by the logicist and expert-systems communities, which focus on the rational band. This assumption is not meant to be exclusionary, as a complete understanding of general intelligence requires the understanding of all of these descriptive bands.[1] Instead the assumption is that there is important work to be done by focusing on the cognitive band. One reason is that, as just mentioned, a complete model of general intelligence will require a model of the cognitive band. A second reason is that an understanding of the cognitive band can constrain models of the neural and rational bands. A third, more applied reason, is that a model of the cognitive band is required in order to be able to build practical intelligent systems. Neural-band models need the higher levels of organization that are provided by the cognitive band in order to reach complex task performance. Rational-band models need the heuristic adequacy provided by the cognitive band in order to be computationally feasible. A fourth reason is that there is a wealth of both psychological and AI data about the cognitive band that can be used as the basis for elucidating the structure of its levels. This data can help us understand what type of symbolic architecture is required to support general intelligence.

The second assumption is that general intelligence can most usefully be studied by not making a distinction between human and artificial intelligence. The advantage of this assumption is that it allows wider ranges of research methodologies and data to be brought to bear to mutually constrain the structure of the system. Our research methodology includes a mixture of experimental data, theoretical justifications, and comparative studies in both artificial intelligence and cognitive psychology. Human experiments provide data about performance universals and limitations that may reflect the structure of the architecture. For example, the ubiquitous power law of practice—the time to perform a task is a power-law function of the number of times the task has been performed—was used to generate a model of human practice [39, 55], which was later converted into a proposal for a general artificial learning mechanism [27, 28, 61]. Artificial experiments—the application of implemented systems to a variety of tasks requiring intelligence—provide sufficiency feedback about the mechanisms embodied in the architecture and their interactions [16, 51, 60, 62, 73]. Theoretical justifications attempt to provide an abstract analysis of the requirements of intelligence, and of how various architectural mechanisms fulfill those requirements [38, 40, 49, 54, 56]. Comparative studies, pitting one system against another, provide an evaluation of how well the respective systems perform, as well as insight about how the capabilities of one of the systems can be incorporated in the other [6, 50].

The third assumption is that the architecture should consist of a small set of orthogonal mechanisms. All intelligent behaviors should involve all, or nearly all, of these basic mechanisms. This assumption biases the development of Soar strongly in the direction of uniformity and simplicity, and away from modularity [10] and toolkit approaches. When attempting to achieve a new functionality in Soar, the first step is to determine in what ways the existing mechanisms can already provide the functionality. This can force the development of new solutions to old problems, and reveal new connections—through the common underlying mechanisms—among previously distinct capabilities [53]. Only if there is no appropriate way to achieve the new functionality are new mechanisms considered.

The fourth assumption is that architectures should be pushed to the extreme to evaluate how much of general intelligence they can cover. A serious attempt at evaluating the coverage of an architecture involves a long-term commitment by an extensive research group. Much of the research involves the apparently mundane activity of replicating classical results within the architecture. Sometimes these demonstrations will by necessity be strict replications, but often the architecture will reveal novel approaches, provide a deeper understanding of the result and its relationship to other results, or provide the means of going beyond what was done in the classical work. As these results accumulate over time, along with other more novel results, the system gradually approaches the ultimate goal of general intelligence.

2 Structure of Soar

In this section we build up much of Soar's structure in levels, starting at the bottom with memory and proceeding up to decisions and goals. We then describe how learning and perceptual-motor behavior fit into this picture, and wrap up with a discussion of the default knowledge that has been incorporated into the system.

2.1 Level 1: memory

A general intelligence requires a memory with a large capacity for the storage of knowledge. A variety of types of knowledge must be stored, including declarative knowledge (facts about the world, including facts about actions that can be performed), procedural knowledge (facts about how to perform actions, and control knowledge about which actions to perform when), and episodic knowledge (which actions were done when). Any particular task will require some subset of the knowledge stored in the memory. Memory access is the process by which this subset is retrieved for use in task performance.

The lowest level of the Soar architecture is the level at which these memory phenomena occur. All of Soar's long-term knowledge is stored in a single production memory. Whether a piece of knowledge represents procedural, declarative, or episodic knowledge, it is stored in one or more productions. Each production is a condition-action structure that performs its actions when its conditions are met. Memory access consists of the execution of these productions. During the execution of a production, variables in its actions are instantiated with values. Action variables that existed in the conditions are instantiated with the values bound in the conditions. Action variables that did not exist in the conditions act as generators of new symbols.

The result of memory access is the retrieval of information into a global working memory. The working memory is a temporary memory that contains all of Soar's short-term processing context. Working memory consists of an interrelated set of objects with attribute-value pairs. For example, an object representing a green cat named Fred might look like (object o025 ˆ name fred ˆ type cat ˆ color green). The symbol o025 is the identifier of the object, a short-term symbol for the object that exists only as long as the object is in working memory. Objects are related by using the identifiers of some objects as attributes and values of other objects.

There is one special type of working memory structure, the preference. Preferences encode control knowledge about the acceptability and desirability of actions, according to a fixed semantics of preference types. Acceptability preferences determine which actions should be considered as candidates. Desirability preferences define a partial ordering on the candidate actions. For example, a better (or alternatively, worse) preference can be used to represent the knowledge that one action is more (or less) desirable than another action, and a best (or worst) preference can be used to represent the knowledge that an action is at least as good (or as bad) as every other action.

In a traditional production-system architecture, each production is a problem-solving operator (see, for example, [42]). The right-hand side of the production represents some action to be performed, and the left-hand side represents the preconditions for correct application of the action (plus possibly some desirability conditions). One consequence of this view of productions is that the productions must also be the locus of behavioral control. If productions are going to act, it must be possible to control which one executes at each moment; a process known as conflict resolution. In a logic architecture, each production is a logical implication. The meaning of such a production is that if the left-hand side (the antecedent) is true, then so is the right-hand side (the consequent).[2] Soar's productions are neither operators nor implications. Instead, Soar's productions perform (parallel) memory retrieval. Each production is a retrieval structure for an item in long-term memory. The right-hand side of the rule represents a long-term datum, and the left-hand side represents the situations in which it is appropriate to retrieve that datum into working memory. The traditional production-system and logic notions of action, control, and truth are not directly applicable to Soar's productions. All control in Soar is performed at the decision level. Thus, there is no conflict resolution process in the Soar production system, and all productions execute in parallel. This all flows directly from the production system being a long-term memory. Soar separates the retrieval of long-term information from the control of which act to perform next.

Of course it is possible to encode knowledge of operators and logical implications in the production memory. For example, the knowledge about how to implement a typical operator can be stored procedurally as a set of productions which retrieve the state resulting from the operator's application. The productions' conditions determine when the state is to be retrieved—for example, when the operator is being applied and its preconditions are met. An alternative way to store operator implementation knowledge is declaratively as a set of structures that are completely contained in the actions of one or more productions. The structures describe not only the results of the operator, but also its preconditions. The productions' conditions determine when to retrieve this declarative operator description into working memory. A retrieved operator description must be interpreted by other productions to actually have an affect.

In general, there are these two distinct ways to encode knowledge in the production memory: procedurally and declaratively. If the knowledge is procedurally encoded, then the execution of the production reflects the knowledge, but does not actually retrieve it into working memory—it only retrieves the structures encoded in the actions. On the other hand, if a piece of knowledge is encoded declaratively in the actions of a production, then it is retrievable in its entirety. This distinction between procedural and declarative *encodings* of knowledge is distinct from whether the knowledge is declarative (represents facts about the world) or procedural (represents facts about procedures). Moreover, each production can be viewed in either way, either as a procedure which implicitly represents conditional information, or as the indexed storage of declarative structures.

2.2 *Level 2: decisions*

In addition to a memory, a general intelligence requires the ability to generate and/or select a course of action that is responsive to the current situation. The second level of the Soar architecture, the decision level, is the level at which this processing is performed. The decision level is based on the memory level plus an architecturally provided, fixed, decision procedure. The decision level proceeds in a two phase elaborate-decide cycle. During elaboration, the memory is accessed repeatedly, in parallel, until quiescence is reached; that is, until no more productions can execute. This results in the retrieval into working memory of all of the accessible knowledge that is relevant to the current decision. This may include a variety of types of information, but of most direct relevance here is knowledge about actions that can be performed and preference knowledge about what actions are acceptable and desirable. After quiescence has occurred, the decision procedure selects one of the retrieved actions based on the preferences that were retrieved into working memory and their fixed semantics.

The decision level is open both with respect to the consideration of arbitrary actions, and with respect to the utilization of arbitrary knowledge in making a selection. This openness allows Soar to behave in both plan-following and reactive fashions. Soar is following a plan when a decision is primarily based on previously generated knowledge about what to do. Soar is being reactive when a decision is based primarily on knowledge about the current situation (as reflected in the working memory).

2.3 Level 3: goals

In addition to being able to make decisions, a general intelligence must also be able to direct this behavior towards some end; that is, it must be able to set and work towards goals. The third level of the Soar architecture, the goal level, is the level at which goals are processed. This level is based on the decision level. Goals are set whenever a decision cannot be made; that is, when the decision procedure reaches an impasse. Impasses occur when there are no alternatives that can be selected (*no-change* and *rejection* impasses) or when there are multiple alternatives that can be selected, but insufficient discriminating preferences exist to allow a choice to be made among them (*tie* and *conflict* impasses). Whenever an impasse occurs, the architecture generates the goal of resolving the impasse. Along with this goal, a new *performance context* is created. The creation of a new context allows decisions to continue to be made in the service of achieving the goal of resolving the impasse—nothing can be done in the original context because it is at an impasse. If an impasse now occurs in this subgoal, another new subgoal and performance context are created. This leads to a goal (and context) stack in which the top-level goal is to perform some task, and lower-level goals are to resolve impasses in problem solving. A subgoal is terminated when either its impasse is resolved, or some higher impasse in the stack is resolved (making the subgoal superfluous).

In Soar, all symbolic goal-oriented tasks are formulated in problem spaces. A problem space consists of a set of states and a set of operators. The states represent situations, and the operators represent actions which when applied to states yield other states. Each performance context consists of a goal, plus roles for a problem state, a state, and an operator. Problem solving is driven by decisions that result in the selection of problem spaces, states, and operators for their respective context roles. Given a goal, a problem space should be selected in which goal achievement can be pursued. Then an initial state should be selected that represents the initial situation. Then an operator should be selected for application to the initial state. Then another state should be selected (most likely the result of applying the operator to the previous state). This process continues until a sequence of operators has been discovered that transforms the initial state into a state in which the goal has been achieved. One subtle consequence of the use of problem spaces is that each one implicitly defines a set of constraints on how the task is to be performed. For example, if the Eight Puzzle is attempted in a problem space containing only a slide-tile operator, all solution paths maintain the constraint that the tiles are never picked up off of the board. Thus, such conditions need not be tested for explicitly in desired states.

Each problem solving decision—the selection of a problem space, a state, or an operator—is based on the knowledge accessible in the production memory. If the knowledge is both correct and sufficient, Soar exhibits highly controlled behavior; at each decision point the right alternative is selected. Such behavior is accurately described as being algorithmic or knowledge-intensive. However, for a general intelligence faced with a broad array of unpredictable tasks, situations will arise—inevitably and indeed frequently—in which the accessible knowledge is either incorrect or insufficient. It is possible that correct decisions will fortuitously be made, but it is more likely that either incorrect decisions will be made or that impasses will occur. Under such circumstances search is the likely outcome. If an incorrect decision is made, the system must eventually recover and get itself back on a path to the goal, for example, by backtracking. If instead an impasse occurs, the system must execute a sequence of problem space operators in the resulting subgoal to find (or generate) the information that will allow a decision to be made. This processing may itself be highly algorithmic, if enough control knowledge is available to uniquely determine what to do, or it may involve a large amount of further search.

As described earlier, operator implementation knowledge can be represented procedurally in the production memory, enabling operator implementation to be performed directly by memory retrieval. When the operator is selected, a set of productions execute that collectively build up the representation of the result state by combining data from long-term memory and the previous state. This type of implementation is comparable to the conventional implementation of an operator as a fixed piece of code. However, if operator implementation knowledge is stored, then a subgoal occurs, and the operator must be implemented by the execution of a sequence of problem space operators in the subgoal. If a declarative description of the to-be-implemented operator is available, then these lower operators may implement the operator by interpreting its declarative description (as was demonstrated in work on task acquisition in Soar [61]). Otherwise the operator can be implemented by decomposing it into a set of simpler operators for which operator implementation knowledge is available, or which can in turn be decomposed further.

When an operator is implemented in a subgoal, the combination of the operator and the subgoal correspond to the type of deliberately created subgoal common in AI problem solvers. The operator specifies a task to be performed, while the subgoal indicates that accomplishing the task should be treated as a goal for further problem solving. In complex problems, like computer configuration, it is common for there to be complex high-level operators, such as **Configure-computer** which are implemented by selecting problem spaces in which they can be decomposed into simpler tasks. Many of the traditional goal management issues—such as conjunction, conflict, and selection—show up as operator management issues in Soar. For example, a set of conjunctive subgoals can be ordered by ordering operators that later lead to impasses (and subgoals).

As described in [54], a subgoal not only represents a subtask to be performed, but it also represents an introspective act that allows unlimited amounts of meta-level problem-space processing to be performed. The entire working memory—the goal stack and all information linked to it—is available for examination and augmentation in a subgoal. At any time a production can examine and augment any part of the goal stack. Likewise, a decision can be made at any time for any of the goals in the hierarchy. This allows subgoal problem solving to analyze the situation that led to the impasse, and even to change the subgoal, should it be appropriate. One not uncommon occurrence is for information to be generated within a subgoal that instead of satisfying the subgoal, causes the subgoal to become irrelevant and consequently to disappear. Processing tends to focus on the bottom-most goal because all of the others have reached impasses. However, the processing is completely opportunistic, so that when appropriate information becomes available at a higher level, processing at that level continues immediately and all lower subgoals are terminated.

2.4 Learning

All learning occurs by the acquisition of chunks—productions that summarize the problem solving that occurs in subgoals [28]. The actions of a chunk represent the knowledge generated during the subgoal; that is, the results of the subgoal. The conditions of the chunk represent an access path to this knowledge, consisting of those elements of the parent goals upon which the results depended. The results of the subgoal are determined by finding the elements generated in the subgoal that are available for use in subgoals—an element is a result of a subgoal precisely because it is available to processes outside of the subgoal. The access path is computed by analyzing the traces of the productions that fired in the subgoal—each production trace effectively states that its actions depended on its conditions. This dependency analysis yields a set of conditions that have been implicitly generalized to ignore irrelevant aspects of the situation. The resulting generality allows chunks to transfer to situations other than the one in which it was learned. The primary system-wide effect of chunking is to move Soar along the space-time trade-off by allowing relevantly similar future decisions to be based on direct retrieval of information from memory rather than on problem solving within a subgoal. If the chunk is used, an impasse will not occur, because the required information is already available.

Care must be taken to not confuse the power of chunking as a learning mechanism with the power of Soar as a learning system. Chunking is a simple goal-based, dependency-tracing, caching scheme, analogous to explanation-based learning [4, 36, 50] and a variety of other schemes [55]. What allows Soar to exhibit a wide variety of learning behaviors are the variations in the types of subgoals that are chunked; the types of problem solving, in conjunction with the types and sources of knowledge, used in the subgoals; and the ways the chunks are used in later problem solving. The role that a chunk will play is determined by the type of subgoal for which it was learned. State-no-change, operator-tie, and operator-no-change subgoals lead respectively to state augmentation, operator selection, and operator implementation productions. The content of a chunk is determined by the types of problem solving and knowledge used in the subgoal. A chunk can lead to skill acquisition if it is used as a more efficient means of generating an already generatable result. A chunk can lead to knowledge acquisition (or knowledge level learning [5]) if it is used to make old/new judgments; that is, to distinguish what has been learned from what has not been learned [52, 53, 56].

2.5 Perception and motor control

One of the most recent functional additions to the Soar architecture is a perceptual-motor interface [75, 76]. All perceptual and motor behavior is mediated through working memory; specifically, through the state in the top problem solving context. Each distinct perceptual field has a designated attribute of this state to which it adds its information. Likewise, each distinct motor field has a designated attribute of the state from which it takes its commands. The perceptual and motor systems are autonomous with respect to each other and the cognitive system.

Encoding and decoding productions can be used to convert between the high-level structures used by the cognitive system, and the low-level structures used by the perceptual and motor systems. These productions are like ordinary productions, except that they examine only the perceptual and motor fields, and not any of the rest of the context stack. This autonomy from the context stack is critical, because it allows the decision procedure to proceed without waiting for quiescence among the encoding and decoding productions, which may never happen in a rapidly changing environment.

2.6 Default knowledge

Soar has a set of productions (55 in all) that provide default responses to each of the possible impasses that can arise, and thus prevent the system from dropping into a bottomless pit in which it generates an unbounded number of content-free performance contexts. Figure 2 shows the default production that allows the system to continue if it has no idea how to resolve

---

If there is an impasse because of an operator conflict
    and there are no candidate problem spaces available
then reject the conflicting operators.

Figure 2 A default production

270

a conflict impasse among a set of operators. When the production executes, it rejects all of the conflicting operators. This allows another candidate operator to be selected, if there is one, or for a different impasse to arise if there are no additional candidates. This default response, as with all of them, can be overridden by additional knowledge if it is available.

One large part of the default knowledge (10 productions) is responsible for setting up operator subgoaling as the default response to no-change impasses on operators. That is, it attempts to find some other state in the problem space to which the selected operators can be applied. This is accomplished by generating acceptable and worst preferences in the subgoal for the parent problem space. If another problem space is suggested, possibly for implementing the operator, it will be selected. Otherwise, the selection of the parent problem space in the subgoal enables operator subgoaling. A sequence of operators is then applied in the subgoal until a state is generated that satisfies the preconditions of an operator higher in the goal stack.

Another large part of the default knowledge (33 productions) is responsible for setting up lookahead search as the default response to tie impasses. This is accomplished by generating acceptable and worst preferences for the *selection* problem space. The selection problem space consists of operators that evaluate the tied alternatives. Based on the evaluations produced by these operators, default productions create preferences that break the tie and resolve the impasse. In order to apply the evaluation operators, domain knowledge must exist that can create an evaluation. If no such knowledge is available, a second impasse arises—a no-change on the evaluation operator. As mentioned earlier, the default response to an operator no-change impasse is to perform operator subgoaling. However, for a no-change impasse on an evaluation operator this is overridden and a lookahead search is performed instead. The results of the lookahead search are used to evaluate the tied alternatives.

As Soar is developed, it is expected that more and more knowledge will be included as part of the basic system about how to deal with a variety of situations. For example, one area on which we are currently working is the provision of Soar with a basic arithmetical capability, including problem spaces for addition, multiplication, subtraction, division, and comparison. One way of looking at the existing default knowledge is as the tip of this large iceberg of background knowledge. However, another way to look at the default knowledge is as part of the architecture itself. Some of the default knowledge—how much is still unclear—must be innate rather than learned. The rest of the system's knowledge, such as the arithmetic spaces, should then be learnable from there.

3 Example: multi-column subtraction

Multi-column subtraction is the task we will use to demonstrate Soar. This task has three advantages. First, it is a familiar and simple task. This allows the details of Soar not to be lost in the complexities of understanding the task. Second, previous work has been done on modeling human learning of subtraction in the Sierra architecture [71]. Our implementation is inspired by the Sierra framework. Third, this task appears to be quite different from many standard search-intensive tasks common in AI. On the surface, it appears difficult to cast subtraction within the problem-space framework of Soar—it is, after all, a procedure. One might also think that chunking could not learn such a procedure. However, in this example, we will demonstrate that multi-column subtraction can be performed by Soar and that important parts of the procedure can be learned through chunking.

There exist many different procedures for performing multi-column subtraction. Different procedures result in different behaviors, both in the order in which scratch marks—such as borrowing notations—are made and in the type of mistakes that might be generated while learning [72]. For simplicity, we will demonstrate the implementation of just one of the many possible procedures. This procedure uses a borrowing technique that recursively borrows from a higher-order column into a lower-order column when the top number in the lower-order column is less than the bottom number.

3.1 A hierarchical subtraction procedure

One way to implement this procedure is via the processing of a goal hierarchy that encodes what must be done. Figure 3 shows a subtraction goal hierarchy that is similar to the one learned by Sierra.[3] Under each goal are shown the subgoals that may be generated while trying to achieve it. This Sierra goal hierarchy is mapped onto a hierarchy of operators and problem spaces in Soar (as described in Section 2). The boxed goals map onto operators and the unboxed goals map onto problem spaces. Each problem space consists of the operators linked to it from below in the figure. Operators that have problem spaces below them are implemented by problem solving in those problem spaces. The other operators are implemented directly at the memory level by productions (except for multiple-column and regroup, which are recursive). These are the primitive acts of subtraction, such as writing numbers or subtracting digits.

The states in these problem spaces contain symbolic representations of the subtraction problem and the scratch marks made on the page during problem solving. The representation is very simple and direct, being based on the spatial relationships among the digits as they would appear on a page. The state consists of a set of columns. Each column has pointers to its top and bottom digits. Additional pointers are generated when an answer for a column is produced, or when a scratch mark is made as the result of borrowing. The physical orientation of the columns on the page is represented by having "left" and "right" pointers from columns to their left and right neighbors. There is no inherent notion of multi-digit numbers except for these left and right relations between columns. This representation is consistent with the operators, which treat the problem symbolically and never manipulate multi-digit numbers as a whole.

Using this implementation of the subtraction procedure, Soar is able to solve all multi-column subtraction problems that result in positive answers. Unfortunately, there is little role for learning. Most of the control knowledge is already embedded in the productions that select problem spaces and operators. Within each problem space there are only a few operators from which to select. The preconditions of the few operators in each problem space are sufficient for perfect behavior. Therefore, goals arise only to implement operators. Chunking these goals produces productions that are able to compute answers without the intermediate subgoals.[4]

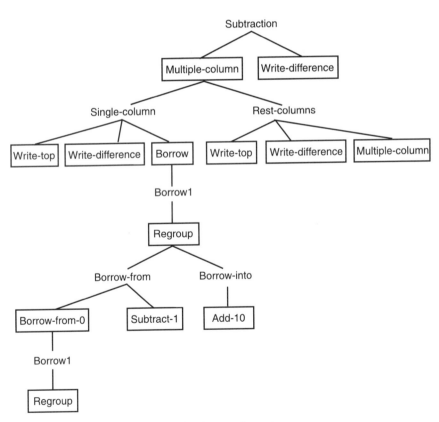

Figure 3 A goal hierarchy for multi-column subtraction

3.2 A single-space approach

One way to loosen up the strict control provided by the detailed problem-space/operator hierarchy in Fig. 3, and thus to enable the learning of the control knowledge underlying the subtraction procedure, is to have only a single subtraction problem space that contains all of the primitive acts (writing results, changing columns, and so on). Figure 4 contains a description of the problem space operators and the goal test used in this second implementation. The operators can be grouped into four classes: the basic acts of writing answers to a single column problem (write-difference, write-top); borrow actions on the upper digits (borrow-into, borrow-from); moving from one column to the next (move-left, move-borrow-left); and performing very simple arithmetic computations (subtract-two-digits, subtract-1, add-10). With this simple problem space. Soar must learn the subtraction procedure by acquiring control knowledge that correctly selects operators.

Every operator in the subtraction problem space is considered for every state in the space. This is accomplished by having a production for each operator that generates an acceptable preference for it. The conditions of the production only test that the appropriate problem space (subtraction) is selected. Similar productions existed in the original implementation, except that those productions also contained additional tests which ensured that the operators would only be considered when they were the appropriate ones to apply.

- *Operators:*
    Write-difference: If the difference between the top digit and the bottom digit of the current column is known, then write the difference as an answer to the current column.
    Write-top: if the lower digit of the current column is blank, then write the top digit as the answer to the current column.
    Borrow-into: If the result of adding 10 to the top digit of the current column is known, and the digit to the left of it has a scratch mark on it, then replace the top digit with the result.
    Borrow-from: If the result of subtracting 1 from the top digit in the current column is known, then replace that top digit with the result, augment it with a scratch mark and shift the current column to the right.
    Move-left: If the current column has an answer in it, shift the current column left.
    Move-borrow-left: If the current column does not have a scratch mark in it, shift the current column left.
    Subtract-two-digits: If the top digit is greater than or equal to the lower digit, then produce a result that is the difference.
    Subtract-1: If the top digit is not zero, then produce a result that is the top digit minus one.
    Add 10: Produce a result that is the top digit plus ten.
- *Goal Test:* If each column has an answer, then succeed.

Figure 4 Primitive subtraction problem space

In addition to productions which generate acceptable preferences, each operator has one or more productions which implement it. Although every operator is made acceptable for every state, an operator will actually be applied only if all of the conditions in the productions that implement it are satisfied. For example, write-difference will only apply if the difference between the top and bottom numbers is known. If an operator is selected, but the conditions of the productions that implement it are not satisfied, an impasse arises. As described in Section 2, the default response to this type of impasse is to perform operator subgoaling.

Figure 5 shows a trace of Soar's problem solving as it performs a simple two-column subtraction problem, after the learning of control knowledge has been completed. Because Soar's performance prior to learning on this problem is considerably more complicated, it is described after this simpler case. The top goal in this figure is to have the result of subtracting 3 from 22. Problem solving in the top goal proceeds from left to right, diving to a lower level whenever a subgoal is created in response to an impasse. Each state is a partially solved subtraction problem, consisting of the statement of the subtraction problem, a * designating the current column, and possibly column results and/or scratch marks for borrowing. Operator applications are represented by arrows going from left to right. The only impasses that occur in this trace are a result of the failure of operator preconditions—a form of operator no-change impasse. These impasses are designated by circles disrupting the operator-application arrows, and are labeled in the order they arise (A and B). For example, impasse A arises because write-difference cannot apply unless the lower digit in the current column (3) is less than the top digit (2).

For impasse A, operator subgoaling occurs when the subtraction problem space is selected in the subgoal. The preconditions of the write-difference

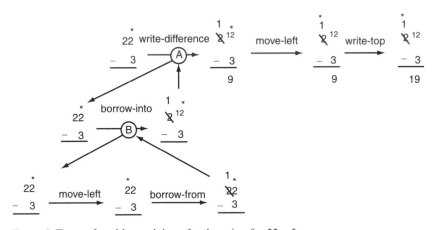

Figure 5 Trace of problem solving after learning for 22 – 3

275

operator are met when a state has been generated whose top digit has been changed from 2 to 12 (by borrowing). Once this occurs, the subgoal terminates and the operator applies, in this case writing the difference between 12 and 3. In this implementation of subtraction, operator subgoaling dynamically creates a goal hierarchy that is similar to the one programmed into the original implementation.

3.3 Performance prior to learning

Prior to learning, Soar's problem solving on this task is considerably more complicated. This added complexity arises because of an initial lack of knowledge about the results of simple arithmetic computations and a lack of knowledge about which operators should be selected for which states. Figure 6 shows a partial trace of Soar's pre-learning problem solving. Although many of the subgoals are missing, this small snapshot of the problem solving is characteristic of the impasses and subgoals that arise at all levels.

As before, the problem solving starts at the upper left with the initial state. As soon as the initial state is selected, a tie impasse (A) arises because all of the operators are acceptable and there are no additional preferences that distinguish between them. Default productions cause the selection space to be selected for this impasse. Within this space, operators are created to evaluate the tied operators. This example assumes that evaluate-object(write-difference) is selected, possibly based on advice from a teacher. Then, because there is no knowledge available about how to evaluate the subtraction operators, a no-change impasse (B) occurs for the evaluation operator. More default productions lead to a lookahead search by suggesting

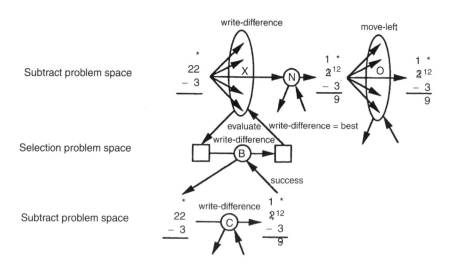

Figure 6 Trace of problem solving before learning for 22 − 3

276

the original problem space (subtraction) and state and then selecting the operator that is being evaluated. The operator then applies, if it can, creating a new state. In this example, an operator subgoal impasse (C) arises when the attempt is made to apply the write-difference operator—its preconditions are not satisfied. Problem solving continues in this subgoal, requiring many additional impasses, until the write-difference operator can finally be applied. The lookahead search then continues until an evaluation is generated for the write-difference operator. Here, this happens shortly after impasse C is resolved. The system was given the knowledge that a state containing an answer for the current column is a (partial) success—such states are on the path to the goal. This state evaluation is then converted by default productions into an evaluation of "success" for the operator, and from there into a best preference for the operator. The creation of this preference breaks the operator tie, terminating the subgoals, and leading to the selection of the preferred operator (write-difference). The overall behavior of the system during this lookahead search is that of depth-first search—where backtracking occurs by subgoal termination—intertwined with operator subgoaling. Once this search is completed, further impasses (N) arise to actually apply the selected operator, but eventually, a solution is found.

One way in which multi-column subtraction differs from the classic AI search tasks is that the goal test is underspecified. As shown in Fig. 4, the goal test used here is that a result has been generated for each column of the problem. This determines whether some answer has been given for the problem, but is inadequate to determine whether the correct answer has been generated. The reason for this is that when solving a subtraction problem, the answer is in general not already available. It is theoretically (and practically) possible to use an addition procedure to test whether the subtraction procedure has generated the correct result. However, that corresponds to a deliberate strategy of "checking your work", rather than to the normal procedural goal test of determining whether the sequence of steps has been completed.

One consequence of having an underspecified goal test is that the combination of the problem space and goal test are not sufficient to ensure correct performance. Additional knowledge—the control knowledge which underlies the subtraction procedure—must also be provided in some form. VanLehn provided Sierra with worked-out examples which included the order in which the primitive external actions were to be performed [71]. The approach that we have taken is to provide advice to Soar [12] about which task operators it should evaluate first in the selection problem space. This ensures that the first answer generated during the lookahead search is the correct one.

3.4 Learning in subtraction

When chunking is used during subtraction problem solving, productions are created which reproduce the results of the subgoals in similar future situations: For the subgoals created because of tie impasses, the chunks create best preferences for the operators that led to the solution. These chunks essentially cache the results of the lookahead searches. A set of such chunks corresponds to a plan (or procedure)—they determine at every step what should be done—thus chunking converts Soar's behavior from search into plan (or procedure) following. When Soar is rerun on the same problem, the tie impasses do not arise and the solution is found directly, as in Fig. 5.

One important issue concerning the chunked productions is their generality. Does Soar only learn chunks that can apply to the exact same problem, or are the chunks general enough so that advice is no longer needed after a few subtraction problems have been completed? The answer is that the learned control chunks are quite general—so general that only one or two are required per operator. Once these chunks are acquired, Soar is able to solve perfectly all multi-column subtraction problems that have a positive answer. One sample control chunk for the borrow-into operator is shown in Fig. 7. Similar chunks are learned for each of the other major operators.

One reason for this generality is that operator subgoaling leads to a fine-grained goal hierarchy. There are a large number of relatively simple goals having to do with satisfying the preconditions of an operator. Because the problem solving for these goals is relatively minimal, the resulting chunks are quite general. A second reason for the generality of the learning is that the control chunks do not test for the specific digits used in the problems—if such tests were included, the chunks would transfer to many fewer problems.[5]

Though the control chunks that are learned are quite general, many specialized implementation chunks are also learned for the simple arithmetic operators. For example, the set of chunks that are eventually learned for the subtract-two-digits operator comprise a partial subtraction table for one- and two-digit numbers. Conceivably, these chunks could have been learned before multi-column subtraction is ever attempted—one may imagine that most of these simple digit manipulations are learned during earlier lessons on addition and single-column subtraction. Alternatively, these chunks can continue to be acquired as more multi-column subtraction problems are solved. The control chunks would all be acquired after a few trials, but learning of arithmetic knowledge would continue through later problems.

If the super-operator is write-difference,
   and the bottom digit is greater than the top digit,
then make a best preference for borrow-into.

Figure 7 A control chunk for borrow-into

4 Analysis of Soar

There are a variety of analyses that could be performed for Soar. In this section we take our cue from the issues provided by the organizers of the 1987 Workshop on the Foundations of Artificial Intelligence [14]. We examine the set of tasks that are natural for Soar, the sources of its power, and its scope and limits.

4.1 Natural tasks

What does it mean for a task to be natural for an architecture? To answer this question we first must understand what a task is, and then what it means for such a task to be natural. By "task" we will mean any identifiable function, whether externally specified, or completely internal to the system. Computer configuration and maneuvering through an obstacle course are both tasks, and so are inheritance and skill acquisition. One way to define the idea of naturalness for a combination of a task and architecture is to say that a task is natural for an architecture if the task can be performed within the architecture without adding an extra level of interpretation within the software. This definition is appealing because it allows a distinction to be made between the tasks that the architecture can perform directly and those that can be done, but for which the architecture does not provide direct support. However, applying this definition is not without its problems. One problem is that, for any particular task, it is possible to replace the combination of an interpreter and its interpreted structures with a procedure that has the same effect. Some forms of learning—chunking, for example—do exactly this, by compiling interpreted structures into the structure of the interpreter. This has the effect of converting an unnatural task implementation into a natural one. Such a capability causes problems for the definition of naturalness— naturalness cannot be a fixed property of the combination of a task and an architecture—but it is actually a point in favor of architectures that can do such learning.

A second problem is that in a system that is itself built up in levels, as is Soar, different tasks will be performed at different levels. In Soar, tasks can be performed directly by the architecture, by memory retrieval, by a decision, or by goal-based problem solving. A task is implemented at a particular level if that level and all lower levels are involved, but the higher levels are not. For example, consider the task of inheritance. Inheritance is not directly implemented by the Soar architecture, but it can be implemented at the memory level by the firing of productions. This implementation involves the memory level plus the architecture (which implements the memory level), but not the decision or goal levels. Alternatively, inheritance could be implemented at the decision level, or even higher up at goal level. As the level of implementation increases, performance becomes more interpretive, but the model of computation explicitly includes all of these levels as natural for the system.

One way out of this problem is to have pre-theoretic notions about the level at which a particular task ought to be performable. The system is then natural for the task if it can be performed at that level, and unnatural if it must be implemented at a higher level. If, for example, the way inheritance works should be a function of the knowledge in the system, then the natural level for the capability is at the memory level (or higher).

In the remainder of this section we describe the major types of tasks that appear to us to be natural in Soar. Lacking any fundamental ways of partitioning the set of all tasks into principled categories, we will use a categorization based on four of the major functional capabilities of Soar: search-based tasks, knowledge-based tasks, learning tasks, and robotic tasks. The naturalness judgments for these task types are always based on assumptions about the natural level of implementation for a variety of subtasks within each type of task. We will try to be as clear as possible about the levels at which the subtasks are being performed, so that others may also be able to make these judgments for themselves.

4.1.1 Search-based tasks

Soar performs search in two qualitatively different ways: within context and across context. Within-context search occurs when Soar "knows" what to do at every step, and thus selects a sequence of operators and states without going into a subgoal. If it needs to backtrack in within-context search, and the states in the problem space are internal (rather than states of the outside world), it can do so by reselecting a previously visited state. Within-context search corresponds to doing the task, without lookahead, and recovering if anything goes wrong. Across-context search occurs when the system doesn't know what to do, and impasses arise. Successive states in the search show up in successively lower contexts. Backtracking occurs by terminating subgoals. Across-context search corresponds to lookahead search, hypothetical scenario generation, or simulation.

Various versions of Soar have been demonstrated to be able to perform over 30 different search methods [21, 25, 26]. Soar can also exhibit hybrid methods—such as a combination of hill-climbing and depth-first search or of operator subgoaling and depth-first search—and use different search methods for different problem spaces within the same problem.

Search methods are represented in Soar as method increments—productions that contain a small chunk of knowledge about some aspect of a task and its action consequences. For example, a method increment might include knowledge about how to compute an evaluation function for a task, along with the knowledge that states with better evaluations should be preferred. Such an increment leads to a form of hill climbing. Other increments lead to other search methods. Combinations of increments lead to mixed methods.

The basic search abilities of making choices and generating subgoals are provided by the architecture. Individual method increments are at the memory level, but control occurs at the decision level, where the results of all of the method increments can be integrated into a single choice. Some search knowledge, such as the selection problem space, exists at the goal level.

4.1.2 Knowledge-based tasks

Knowledge-based tasks are represented in Soar as a collection of interacting problem spaces (as are all symbolic goal-oriented tasks). Each problem space is responsible for a part of the task. Problem spaces interact according to the different goal-subgoal relationships that can exist in Soar. Within each problem space, the knowledge is further decomposed into a set of problem space components, such as goal testing, state initialization, and operator proposal [77]. These components, along with additional communication constructs, can then be encoded directly as productions, or can be described in a high-level problem space language called TAQL [77], which is then compiled down into productions. Within this overall problem space organization, other forms of organization—such as object hierarchies with inheritance—are implementable at the memory level by multiple memory accesses. Task performance is represented at the goal level as search in problem spaces.

Several knowledge-based tasks have been implemented in Soar, including the R1-Soar computer configuration system [51], the Cypress-Soar and Designer-Soar algorithm design systems [60, 62], the Neomycin-Soar medical diagnosis system [73], and the Merl-Soar job-shop scheduling system [16].

These five knowledge-based systems cover a variety of forms of both construction and classification tasks. Construction tasks involve assembling an object from pieces. R1-Soar—in which the task is to construct a computer configuration—is a good example of a construction task. Classification tasks involve selecting from among a set of objects. Neomycin-Soar—in which the task is to diagnose an illness—is a good example of a classification task.[6] In their simplest forms, both construction and classification occur at the decision level. In fact, they both occur to some extent within every decision in Soar—alternatives must be assembled in working-memory and then selected. These capabilities can require trivial amounts of processing, as when an object is constructed by instantiating and retrieving it from memory. They can also involve arbitrary amounts of problem solving and knowledge, as when the process of operator-implementation (or, equivalently, state-construction) is performed via problem solving in a subgoal.

4.1.3 Learning tasks

The architecture directly supports a form of experiential learning in which chunking compiles goal-level problem solving into memory-level productions. Execution of the productions should have the same effect as the problem solving would have had, just more quickly. The varieties of subgoals for which chunks are learned lead to varieties in types of productions learned: problem space creation and selection; state creation and selection; and operator creation, selection, and execution. An alternative classification for this same set of behaviors is that it covers procedural, episodic and declarative knowledge [56]. The variations in goal outcomes lead to both learning from success and learning from failure. The ability to learn about all subgoal results leads to learning about important intermediate results, in addition to learning about goal success and failure. The implicit generalization of chunks leads to transfer of learned knowledge to other subtasks within the same problem (within-trial transfer), other instances of the same problem (across-trial transfer), and other problems (across-task transfer). Variations in the types of problems performed in Soar lead to chunking in knowledge-based tasks, search-based, and robotic tasks. Variations in sources of knowledge lead to learning from both internal and external knowledge sources. A summary of many of the types of learning that have so far been demonstrated in Soar can be found in [61].

The apparent naturalness of these various forms of learning depends primarily on the appropriateness of the required problem solving. Towards the natural end of the spectrum is the acquisition of operator selection productions, in which the problem solving consists simply of a search with the set of operators for which selection knowledge is to be learned. Towards the unnatural end of the spectrum is the acquisition of new declarative knowledge from the outside environment. Many systems employ a simple store command for such learning, effectively placing the capability at the memory level. In Soar, the capability is situated two levels further up, at the goal level. This occurs because the knowledge must be stored by chunking, which can only happen if the knowledge is used in subgoal-based problem solving. The naturalness of this learning in Soar thus depends on whether this extra level of interpretation is appropriate or not. It turns out that the problem solving that enables declarative learning in Soar takes the form of an understanding process that relates the new knowledge to what is already known. The chunking of this understanding process yields the chunks that encode the new knowledge. If it is assumed that new knowledge should always be understood to be learned, then Soar's approach starts to look more natural, and verbatim storage starts to look more inappropriate.

4.1.4 Robotic tasks

Robotic tasks are performed in Soar via its perceptual-motor interface. Sensors autonomously generate working memory structures representing what is being sensed, and motor systems autonomously take commands from working memory and execute them. The work on robotics in Soar is still very much in its infancy; however, in Robo-Soar [30], Soar has been successfully hooked up to the combination of a camera and a Puma arm, and then applied to several simple blocks-world tasks.[7] Low-level software converts the camera signal into information about the positions, orientations and identifying characteristics of the blocks. This perceptual information is then input to working memory, and further interpreted by encoding productions. Decoding productions convert the high-level robot commands generated by the cognitive system to the low-level commands that are directly understood by the controller for the robot arm. These low-level commands are then executed through Soar's motor interface.

Given a set of operators which generate motor commands, and knowledge about how to simulate the operators and about the expected positions of blocks following the actions, Robo-Soar is able to successfully solve simple blocks-world problems and to learn from its own behavior and from externally provided advice. It also can make use of a general scheme for recovering from incorrect knowledge [23] to recover when the unexpected occurs—such as when the system fails in its attempt to pick up a triangular prism—and to learn to avoid the failure in the future. Robo-Soar thus mixes planning (lookahead search with chunking), plan execution and monitoring, reactivity, and error recovery (with replanning). This performance depends on all of the major components of the architecture, plus general background knowledge—such as how to do lookahead search and how to recover from errors—and specific problem spaces for the task.

4.2 Where the power resides

Soar's power and flexibility arise from at least four identifiable sources. The first source of power is the universality of the architecture. While it may seem that this should go without saying, it is in fact a crucial factor, and thus important to mention explicitly. Universality provides the primitive capability to perform any computable task, but does not by itself explain why Soar is more appropriate than any other universal architecture for knowledge-based, search-based, learning, and robotic tasks.

The second source of power is the uniformity of the architecture. Having only one type of long-term memory structure allows a single, relatively simple, learning mechanism to behave as a general learning mechanism. Having only one type of task representation (problem spaces) allows Soar to move continuously from one extreme of brute-force search to the other extreme of knowledge-intensive (or procedural) behavior without having to make any representational decisions. Having only one type of decision procedure allows a single, relatively simple, subgoal mechanism to generate all of the types of subgoals needed by the system.

The traditional downside of uniformity is weakness and inefficiency. If instead the system were built up as a set of specialized modules or agents, as proposed in [10, 34], then each of the modules could be optimized for its own narrow task. Our approach to this issue in Soar has been to go strongly with uniformity—for all of the benefits listed above—but to achieve efficiency (power) through the addition of knowledge. This knowledge can either be added by hand (programming) or by chunking.

The third source of power is the specific mechanisms incorporated into the architecture. The production memory provides pattern-directed access to large amounts of knowledge; provides the ability to use strong problem solving methods; and provides a memory structure with a small-grained modularity. The working memory allows global access to processing state. The decision procedure provides an open control loop that can react immediately to new situations and knowledge; contributes to the modularity of the memory by allowing memory access to proceed in an uncontrolled fashion (conflict resolution was a major source of nonmodularity in earlier production systems); provides a flexible control language (preferences); and provides a notion of impasse that is used as the basis for the generation of subgoals. Subgoals focus the system's resources on situations where the accessible knowledge is inadequate; and allow flexible meta-level processing. Problem spaces separate control from action, allowing them (control and action) to be reasoned about independently; provide a constrained context within which the search for a desired state can occur; provide the ability to use weak problem solving methods; and provide for straightforward responses to uncertainty and error (search and backtracking). Chunking acquires long-term knowledge from experience; compiles interpreted procedures into non-interpreted ones; and provides generalization and transfer. The perceptual-motor system provides the ability to observe and affect the external world in parallel with the cognitive activity.

The fourth source of power is the interaction effects that result from the integration of all of the capabilities within a single system. The most compelling results generated so far come about from these interactions. One example comes from the mixture of weak methods, strong methods, and learning that is found in systems like R1-Soar. Strong methods are based on having knowledge about what to do at each step. Because strong methods tend to be efficient and to produce high-quality solutions, they should be used whenever possible. Weak methods are based on searching to make up for a lack of knowledge about what should be done. Such methods contribute robustness and scope by providing the system with a fall-back approach for situations in which the available strong methods do not work. Learning results in the addition of knowledge, turning weak methods into strong ones. For example, in R1-Soar it was demonstrated how computer configuration could be cast as a search problem, how strong methods (knowledge) could be used to reduce search, how weak methods (subgoals and search) could be used to make up for a lack of knowledge, and how learning could add knowledge as the result of search.

Another interesting interaction effect comes from work on abstraction planning, in which a difficult problem is solved by first learning a plan for an abstract version of the problem, and then using the abstract plan to aid in finding a plan for the full problem [41, 57, 69, 70]. Chunking helps the abstraction planning process by recording the abstract plan as a set of operator-selection productions, and by acquiring other productions that reduce the amount of search required in generating a plan. Abstraction helps the learning process by allowing chunks to be learned more quickly— abstract searches tend to be shorter than normal ones. Abstraction also helps learning by enabling chunks to be more general than they would otherwise be—the chunks ignore the details that were abstracted away—thus allowing more transfer and potentially decreasing the cost of matching the chunks (because there are now fewer conditions).

4.3 Scope and limits

The original work on Soar demonstrated its capabilities as a general problem solver that could use any of the weak methods when appropriate, across a wide range of tasks. Later, we came to understand how to use Soar as the basis for knowledge-based systems, and how to incorporate appropriate learning and perceptual-motor capabilities into the architecture. These developments increased Soar's scope considerably beyond its origins as a weak-method problem solver. Our ultimate goal has always been to develop the system to the point where its scope includes everything required of a general intelligence. In this section we examine how far Soar has come from its relatively limited initial demonstrations towards its relatively unlimited goal. This discussion is divided up according to the major components of the Soar architecture, as presented in Section 2: memory, decisions, goals, learning, and perception and motor control.

4.3.1 Level 1: memory

The scope of Soar's memory level can be evaluated in terms of the amount of knowledge that can be stored, the types of knowledge that can be represented, and the organization of the knowledge.

Amount of knowledge. Using current technology, Soar's production memory can support the storage of thousands of independent chunks of knowledge. The size is primarily limited by the cost of processing larger numbers of productions. Faster machines, improved match algorithms and parallel implementations [13, 65, 66] may raise this effective limit by several orders of magnitude over the next few years.

Types of knowledge. The representation of procedural and propositional declarative knowledge is well developed in Soar. However, we don't have well worked-out approaches to many other knowledge representation problems, such as the representation of quantified, uncertain, temporal, and episodic knowledge. The critical question is whether architectural support is required to adequately represent these types of knowledge, or whether such knowledge can be adequately treated as additional objects and/or attributes. Preliminary work on quantified [43] and episodic [56] knowledge is looking promising.

Memory organization. An issue which often gets raised with respect to the organization of Soar's memory, and with respect to the organization of production memories in general, is the apparent lack of a higher-order memory organization. There are no scripts [59], frames [33], or schemes [1] to tie fragments of related memory together. Nor are there any obvious hierarchical structures which limit what sets of knowledge will be retrieved at any point in time. However, Soar's memory does have an organization, which is derived from the structure of productions, objects, and working memory (especially the context hierarchy).

What corresponds to a schema in Soar is an object, or a structured collection of objects. Such a structure can be stored entirely in the actions of a single production, or it can be stored in a piecemeal fashion across multiple productions. If multiple productions are used, the schema as a unit only comes into existence when the pieces are all retrieved contemporaneously into working memory. The advantage of this approach is that it allows novel schemes to be created from fragments of separately learned ones. The disadvantage is that it may not be possible to determine whether a set of fragments all originated from a single schema.

What corresponds to a hierarchy of retrieval contexts in Soar are the production conditions. Each combination of conditions implicitly defines a retrieval context, with a hierarchical structure induced by the subset relationship among the combinations. The contents of working memory determines which retrieval contexts are currently in force. For example, problem spaces are used extensively as retrieval contexts. Whenever there is a problem solving context that has a particular problem space selected within it, productions that test for other problem space names are not eligible to fire in that context. This approach has worked quite well for procedural knowledge, where it is clear when the knowledge is needed. We have just begun to work on appropriate organizational schemes for episodic and declarative knowledge, where it is much less clear when the knowledge should be retrieved. Our initial approach has been based on the incremental construction, via chunking, of multi-production discrimination networks [53, 56]. Though this work is too premature for a thorough evaluation in the context of Soar, the effectiveness of discrimination networks in systems like Epam [7] and Cyrus [19] bodes well.

4.3.2 Level 2: decisions

The scope of Soar's decision level can be evaluated in terms of its speed, the knowledge brought to bear, and the language of control.

Speed. Soar currently runs at approximately 10 decisions/second on current workstations such as a Sun4/280. This is adequate for most of the types of tasks we currently implement, but is too slow for tasks requiring large amounts of search or very large knowledge bases (the number of decisions per second would get even smaller than it is now). The principal bottleneck is the speed of memory access, which is a function of two factors: the cost of processing individually expensive productions (the *expensive chunks* problem) [67], and the cost of processing a large number of productions (the *average growth effect* problem) [64]. We now have a solution to the problem of expensive chunks which can guarantee that all productions will be cheap—the match cost of a production is at worst linear in the number of conditions [68]—and are working on other potential solutions. Parallelism looks to be an effective solution to the average growth effect problem [64].

Bringing knowledge to bear. Iterated, parallel, indexed access to the contents of long-term memory has proven to be an effective means of bringing knowledge to bear on the decision process. The limited power provided by this process is offset by the ability to use subgoals when the accessible knowledge is inadequate. The issue of devising good access paths for episodic and declarative knowledge is also relevant here.

Control language. Preferences have proven to be a flexible means of specifying a partial order among contending objects. However, we cannot yet state with certainty that the set of preference types embodied in Soar is complete with respect to all the types of information which ultimately may need to be communicated to the decision procedure.

4.3.3 Level 3: goals

The scope of Soar's goal level can be evaluated in terms of the types of goals that can be generated and the types of problem solving that can be performed in goals. Soar's subgoaling mechanism has been demonstrated to be able to create subgoals for all of the types of difficulties that can arise in problem solving in problem spaces [21]. This leaves three areas open. The first area is how top-level goals are generated; that is, how the top-level task is picked. Currently this is done by the programmer, but a general intelligence must clearly have grounds—that is, motivations—for selecting tasks on its own. The second area is how goal interactions are handled. Goal interactions show up in Soar as operator interactions, and are normally dealt with by adding explicit knowledge to avoid them, or by backtracking (with learning) when they happen. It is not yet clear the extent to which Soar could easily make use of more sophisticated approaches, such as non-linear planning [2]. The third area is the sufficiency of impasse-driven subgoaling as a means for determining when meta-level processing is needed. Two of the activities that might fall under this area are goal tests and monitoring. Both of these activities can be performed at the memory or decision level, but when they are complicated activities it may be necessary to perform them by problem solving at the goal level. Either activity can be called for explicitly by selecting a "monitor" or "goal-test" operator, which can then lead to the generation of a subgoal. However, goals for these tasks do not arise automatically, without deliberation. Should they? It is not completely clear.

The scope of the problem solving that can be performed in goals can itself be evaluated in terms of whether problem spaces cover all of the types of performance required, the limits on the ability of subgoal-based problem solving to access and modify aspects of the system, and whether parallelism is possible. These points are addressed in the next three paragraphs.

Problem space scope. Problem spaces are a very general performance model. They have been hypothesized to underlie all human, symbolic, goal-oriented behavior [37]. The breadth of tasks that have so far been represented in problem spaces over the whole field of AI attests to this generality. One way of pushing this evaluation further is to ask how well problem spaces account for the types of problem solving performed by two of the principal competing paradigms: planning [2] and case-based reasoning [20].[8] Both of these paradigms involve the creation (or retrieval) and use of a data structure that represents a sequence of actions. In planning, the data structure represents the sequence of actions that the system expects to use for the current problem. In case-based reasoning, the data structure represents the sequence of actions used on some previous, presumably related, problem. In both, the data structure is used to decide what sequence of actions to perform in the current problem. Soar straightforwardly performs procedural analogues of these two processes. When it performs a lookahead search to determine what operator to apply to a particular state, it acquires (by chunking) a set of search control productions which collectively tell it which operator should be applied to each subsequent state. This set of chunks forms a procedural plan for the current problem. When a search control chunk transfers between tasks, a form of procedural case-based reasoning is occurring.

Simple forms of declarative planning and case-based reasoning have also been demonstrated in Soar in the context of an expert system that designs floor systems [47]. When this system discovers, via lookahead search, a sequence of operators that achieves a goal, it creates a declarative structure representing the sequence and returns it as a subgoal result (plan creation). This plan can then be used interpretively to guide performance on the immediate problem (plan following). The plan can also be retrieved during later problems and used to guide the selection of operators (case-based reasoning). This research does not demonstrate the variety of operations one could conceivably use to modify a partial or complete plan, but it does demonstrate the basics.

Meta-level access. Subgoal-based problem solving has access to all of the information in working memory—including the goal stack, problem spaces, states, operators, preferences, and other facts that have been retrieved or generated—plus any of the other knowledge in long-term memory that it can access. It does not have direct access to the productions, or to any of the data structures internal to the architecture. Nonetheless, it should be able to indirectly examine the contents of any productions that were acquired by chunking, which in the long run should be just about all of them. The idea is to reconstruct the contents of the production by going down into a subgoal and retracing the problem solving that was done when the chunk was learned. In this way it should be possible to determine what knowledge the production cached. This idea has not yet been explicitly demonstrated in Soar, but research on the recovery from incorrect knowledge has used a closely related approach [23].

The effects of problem solving are limited to the addition of information to working memory. Deletion of working memory elements is accomplished by a garbage collector provided by the architecture. Productions are added by chunking, rather than by problem solving, and are never deleted by the system. The limitation on production creation—that it only occurs via chunking—is dealt with by varying the nature of the problem solving over which chunking occurs [56]. The limitation on production deletion is dealt with by learning new productions which overcome the effects of old ones [23].

Parallelism. Two principal sources of parallelism in Soar are at the memory level: production match and execution. On each cycle of elaboration, all productions are matched in parallel to the working memory, and then all of the successful instantiations are executed in parallel. This lets tasks that can be performed at the memory level proceed in parallel, but not so for decision-level and goal-level tasks.

Another principal source of parallelism is provided by the motor systems. All motor systems behave in parallel with respect to each other, and with respect to the cognitive system. This enables one form of task-level parallelism in which non-interfering external tasks can be performed in parallel. To enable further research on task-level parallelism we have added the experimental ability to simultaneously select multiple problem space operators within a single problem solving context. Each of these operators can then proceed to execute in parallel, yielding parallel subgoals, and ultimately an entire tree of problem solving contexts in which all of the branches are being processed in parallel. We do not yet have enough experience with this capability to evaluate its scope and limits.

Despite all of these forms of parallelism embodied in Soar, most implementations of the architecture have been on serial machines, with the parallelism being simulated. However, there is an active research effort to implement Soar on parallel computers. A parallelized version of the production match has been successfully implemented on an Encore Multimax, which has a small number (2–20) of large-grained processors [66], and unsuccessfully implemented on a Connection Machine [15], which has a large number (16 K–64 K) of small-grained processors [9]. The Connection Machine Implementation failed primarily because a complete parallelization of the current match algorithm can lead to exponential space requirements. Research on restricted match algorithms may fix this problem in the future. Work is also in progress towards implementing Soar on message-passing computers [65].

4.3.4 Learning

In [61] we broke down the problem of evaluating the scope of Soar's learning capabilities into four parts: when can the architecture learn; from what can the architecture learn; what can the architecture learn; and when can the architecture apply learned knowledge. These points are discussed in Section 4.1, and need not be elaborated further here.

One important additional issue is whether Soar acquires knowledge that is at the appropriate level of generalization or specialization. Chunking provides a level of generality that is determined by a combination of the representation used and the problem solving performed. Under varying circumstances, this can lead to both overgeneralization [29] and overspecialization. The acquisition of overgeneral knowledge implies that the system must be able to recover from any errors caused by its use. One solution to this problem that has been implemented in Soar involves detecting that a performance error has occurred, determining what should have been done instead, and acquiring a new chunk which leads to correct performance in the future [23]. This is accomplished without examining or modifying the overgeneral production; instead it goes back down into the subgoals for which the overgeneral productions were learned.

One way to deal with overspecialization is to patch the resulting knowledge gaps with additional knowledge. This is what Soar does constantly—if a production is overspecialized, it doesn't fire in circumstances when it should, causing an impasse to occur, and providing the opportunity to learn an additional chunk that covers the missing case (plus possibly other cases). Another way to deal with overspecialized knowledge is to work towards acquiring more general productions. A standard approach is to induce general rules from a sequence of positive and negative examples [35, 45]. This form of generalization must occur in Soar by search in problem spaces, and though there has been some initial work on doing this [48, 58], we have not yet provided Soar with a set of problem spaces that will allow it to generate appropriate generalizations from a variety of sets of examples. So, Soar cannot yet be described as a system of choice for doing induction from multiple examples. On the other hand, Soar does generalize quite naturally and effectively when abstraction occurs [69]. The learned rules reflect whatever abstraction was made during problem solving.

Learning behaviors that have not yet been attempted in Soar include the construction of a model of the environment from experimentation in it [46], scientific discovery and theory formation [31], and conceptual clustering [8].

4.3.5 Perception and motor control

The scope of Soar's perception and motor control can be evaluated in terms of both its low-level I/O mechanisms and its high-level language capabilities. Both of these capabilities are quite new, so the evaluation must be even more tentative than for the preceding components.

At the low-level, Soar can be hooked up to multiple perceptual modalities (and multiple fields within each modality) and can control multiple effectors. The critical low-level aspects of perception and motor control are currently done in a standard procedural language outside of the cognitive system. The resulting system appears to be an effective testbed for research on high-level aspects of perception and motor-control. It also appears to be an effective testbed for research on the interactions of perception and motor control with other cognitive capabilities, such as memory, problem solving, and learning. However, it does finesse many of the hard issues in perception and motor control, such as selective attention, shape determination, object identification, and temporal coordination. Work is actively in progress on selective attention [74].

At the high end of I/O capabilities is the processing of natural language. An early attempt to implement a semantic grammar parser in Soar was only a limited success [44]. It worked, but did not appear to be the right long-term solution to language understanding in Soar. More recent work on NL-Soar has focused on the incremental construction of a model of the situation by applying comprehension operators to each incoming word [32]. Comprehension operators iteratively augment and refine the situation model, setting up expectations for the part of the utterance still to be seen, and satisfying earlier expectations. As a side effect of constructing the situation model, an utterance model is constructed to represent the linguistic structure of the sentence. This approach to language understanding has been successfully applied to acquiring task-specific problem spaces for three immediate reasoning tasks: relational reasoning [18], categorical syllogisms, and sentence verification [3]. It has also been used to process the input for these tasks as they are performed. Though NL-Soar is still far from providing a general linguistic capability, the approach has proven promising.

5 Conclusion

In this article we have taken a step towards providing an analysis of the Soar architecture as a basis for general intelligence. In order to increase understanding of the structure of the architecture we have provided a theoretical framework within which the architecture can be described, a discussion of methodological assumptions underlying the project and the system, and an illustrative example of its performance on a multi-column subtraction task. In order to facilitate comparisons between the capabilities of the current version of Soar and the capabilities required to achieve its ultimate goal as an architecture for general intelligence, we have described the natural tasks for the architecture, the sources of its power, and its scope and limits. If this article has succeeded, it should be clear that progress has been made, but that more work is still required. This applies equally to the tasks of developing Soar and analyzing it.

Acknowledgement

This research was sponsored by the Defense Advanced Research Projects Agency (DOD) under contract N00039-86-C-0133 and by the Sloan Foundation. Computer facilities were partially provided by NIH grant RR-00785 to Sumex-Aim. The views and conclusions contained in this document are those of the authors and should not be interpreted as representing the official policies, either expressed or implied, of the Defense Advanced Research Projects Agency, the US Government, the Sloan Foundation, or the National Institutes of Health.

We would like to thank Beth Adelson, David Kirsh, and David McAllester for their helpful comments on an earlier draft of this article.

Notes

1 Investigations of the relationship of Soar to the neural and rational bands can be found in [38, 49, 56].
2 The directionality of the implication is reversed in logic programming languages such as Prolog, but the point still holds.
3 Sierra learned a slightly more elaborate, but computationally equivalent, procedure.
4 This work on subtraction was done in an earlier version of Soar that did not have the perceptual-motor interface described in Section 2. In that version, these chunks caused Soar to write out all of the column results and scratch marks in parallel—not very realistic motor behavior. To work around this problem, chunking was disabled for goals in this task during which environmental interactions occurred.
5 Chunking would include tests for the digits if their specific values were examined during the lookahead searches. However, the actual manipulation of the numbers is performed by the simple arithmetic operators: add-10, subtract-1 and subtract-two-digits. Before an operator such as write-difference is applied, an operator

subgoal is created in which subtract-two-digits is selected and applied. The chunk for this subgoal reproduces the result whenever the same two digits are to be subtracted, eliminating the need for subtract-two-digits in such situations in the future. In the following lookahead searches, only pointers to the digits rather than the actual digits are ever tested, thereby leading to control chunks that are independent of the actual digits.

6   In a related development, as part of an effort to map the Generic Task approach to expert system construction onto Soar, the Generic Task for classification by establish-refine has been implemented in Soar as a general problem space [17].

7   The work on Robo-Soar has been done in the newest major release of Soar (version 5) [24, 63], which differs in a number of interesting ways from the earlier versions upon which the rest of the results in this article are based.

8   The work on Robo-Soar also reveals Soar's potential to exhibit reactive planning [11]. The current version of Soar still has problems with raw speed and with the unbounded nature of the production match (the expensive chunks problem), but it is expected that these problems will be solved in the near future.

References

[1] F.C. Bartlett, *Remembering: A Study in Experimental and Social Psychology* (Cambridge University Press, Cambridge, England, 1932).

[2] D. Chapman, Planning for conjunctive goals, *Artif. Intell.* 32 (1987) 333–377.

[3] H.H. Clark and W.G. Chase, On the process of comparing sentences against pictures, *Cogn. Psychol.* 3 (1972) 472–517.

[4] G. DeJong and R.J. Mooney, Explanation-based learning: an alternative view, *Mach. Learn.* 1 (1986) 145–176.

[5] T.G. Dietterich, Learning at the knowledge level. *Mach. Learn.* 1 (1986) 287–315.

[6] O. Etzioni and T.M. Mitchell, A comparative analysis of chunking and decision analytic control, in: *Proceedings AAAI Spring Symposium on Limited Rationality and AI*, Stanford, CA (1989).

[7] E.A. Feigenbaum and H.A. Simon, Epam-like models of recognition and learning, *Cogn. Sci.* 8 (1984) 305–336.

[8] D.H. Fisher and P. Langley, Approaches to conceptual clustering, in: *Proceedings IJCAI-85*, Los Angeles, CA (1985) 691–697.

[9] R. Flynn, Placing Soar on the connection machine, Prepared for and distributed at the AAAI Mini-Symposium "How Can Slow Components Think So Fast" (1988).

[10] J.A. Fodor, *The Modularity of Mind* (Bradford Books/MIT Press, Cambridge, MA, 1983).

[11] M.P. Georgeff and A.L. Lansky, Reactive reasoning and planning, in: *Proceedings AAAI-87*, Seattle, WA (1987) 677–682.

[12] A. Golding, P.S. Rosenbloom and J.E. Laird. Learning general search control from outside guidance, in: *Proceedings IJCAI-87*, Milan, Italy (1987).

[13] A. Gupta and M. Tambe, Suitability of message passing computers for implementing production systems, in: *Proceedings AAAI-88*, St. Paul, MN (1988) 687–692.

[14] C. Hewitt and D. Kirsh, Personal communication (1987).

[15] W.D. Hillis, *The Connection Machine* (MIT Press, Cambridge, MA, 1985).

[16] W. Hsu, M. Prietula and D. Steier, Merl-Soar: applying Soar to scheduling, in:

Proceedings Workshop on Artificial Intelligence Simulation, AAAI-88, St. Paul, MN (1988) 81–84.

[17] T.R. Johnson, J.W. Smith Jr and B. Chandrasekaran, Generic Tasks and Soar, in: *Working Notes AAAI Spring Symposium on Knowledge System Development Tools and Languages*, Stanford, CA (1989) 25–28.

[18] P.N. Johnson-Laird, Reasoning by rule or model? in: *Proceedings 10th Annual Conference of the Cognitive Science Society*, Montreal, Que. (1988) 765–771.

[19] J.L. Kolodner, Maintaining order in a dynamic long-term memory, *Cogn. Sci.* 7 (1983) 243–280.

[20] J.L. Kolodner, ed., *Proceedings DARPA Workshop on Case-Based Reasoning*, Clearwater Beach, FL (1988).

[21] J.E. Laird. Universal subgoaling, Ph.D. thesis, Carnegie-Mellon University, Pittsburgh, PA (1983); also in: J.E. Laird, P.S. Rosenbloom and A. Newell, *Universal Subgoaling and Chunking: The Automatic Generation and Learning of Goal Hierarchies* (Kluwer, Hingham, MA, 1986).

[22] J.E. Laird, Soar user's manual (version 4), Tech. Rept. ISL-15, Xerox Palo Alto Research Center, Palo Alto, CA (1986).

[23] J.E. Laird, Recovery from incorrect knowledge in Soar, in: *Proceedings AAAI-88*, St. Paul, MN (1988) 618–623.

[24] J.E. Laird and K.A. McMahon, Destructive state modification in Soar. Draft V, Department of EECS, University of Michigan, Ann Arbor, MI (1989).

[25] J.E. Laird and A. Newell. A universal weak method, Tech. Rept. 83-141, Department of Computer Science, Carnegie-Mellon University, Pittsburgh, PA (1983).

[26] J.E. Laird, A. Newell and P.S. Rosenbloom, SOAR: an architecture for general intelligence, *Artif. Intell.* 33 (1987) 1–64.

[27] J.E. Laird, P.S. Rosenbloom and A. Newell, Towards chunking as a general learning mechanism, in: *Proceedings AAAI-84*, Austin, TX (1984) 188–192.

[28] J.E. Laird, P.S. Rosenbloom and A. Newell, Chunking in Soar: the anatomy of a general learning mechanism. *Mach. Learn.* 1 (1986) 11–46.

[29] J.E. Laird, P.S. Rosenbloom and A. Newell, Overgeneralization during knowledge compilation in Soar, in: T.G. Dietterich, ed., *Proceedings Workshop on Knowledge Compilation*, Otter Crest, OR (1986).

[30] J.E. Laird, E.S. Yager, C.M. Tuck and M. Hucka, Learning in tele-autonomous systems using Soar, in: *Proceedings NASA Conference on Space Telerobotics*, Pasadena, CA (1989).

[31] P. Langley, H.A. Simon, G.L. Bradshaw and J.M. Zytkow, *Scientific Discovery: Computational Explorations of the Creative Processes* (MIT Press, Cambridge, MA, 1987).

[32] R.L. Lewis, A. Newell and T.A. Polk, Toward a Soar theory of taking instructions for immediate reasoning tasks, in: *Proceedings 11th Annual Conference of the Cognitive Science Society*, Ann Arbor, MI (1989).

[33] M. Minsky, A framework for the representation of knowledge, in: P. Winston, ed., *The Psychology of Computer Vision* (McGraw-Hill, New York, 1975).

[34] M. Minsky, *The Society of Mind* (Simon and Schuster, New York, 1986).

[35] T.M. Mitchell, Generalization as search, *Artif. Intell.* 18 (1982) 203–226.

[36] T.M. Mitchell, R.M. Keller and S.T. Kedar-Cabelli, Explanation-based generalization: a unifying view, *Mach. Learn.* 1 (1986) 47–80.

[37] A. Newell, Reasoning, problem solving and decision processes: the problem space as a fundamental category, in: R. Nickerson, ed., *Attention and performance* 8 (Erlbaum, Hillsdale, NJ, 1980).

[38] A. Newell, *Unified Theories of Cognition* (Harvard University Press, Cambridge, MA, 1990).

[39] A. Newell and P.S. Rosenbloom, Mechanisms of skill acquisition and the law of practice, in: J.R. Anderson, ed., *Cognitive Skills and Their Acquisition* (Erlbaum, Hillsdale, NJ, 1981) 1–55.

[40] A. Newell, P.S. Rosenbloom and J.E. Laird, Symbolic architectures for cognition, in: M.I. Posner, ed., *Foundations of Cognitive Science* (Bradford Books/MIT Press, Cambridge, MA, 1989).

[41] A. Newell and H.A. Simon, *Human Problem Solving* (Prentice-Hall, Englewood Cliffs, NJ, 1972).

[42] N.J. Nilsson, *Principles of Artificial Intelligence* (Tioga, Palo Alto, CA, 1980).

[43] T.A. Polk and A. Newell, Modeling human syllogistic reasoning in Soar, in: *Proceedings 10th Annual Conference of the Cognitive Science Society*, Montreal, Que. (1988) 181–187.

[44] L. Powell, Parsing the picnic problem with a Soar 3 implementation of Dypar-1, Department of Computer Science, Carnegie-Mellon University, Pittsburgh, PA (1984).

[45] J.R. Quinlan, Induction of decision trees, *Mach. Learn.* 1 (1986) 81–106.

[46] S. Rajamoney, G.F. DeJong, and B. Faltings, Towards a model of conceptual knowledge acquisition through directed experimentation, in: *Proceedings IJCAI-85*, Los Angeles, CA (1985) 688–690.

[47] Y. Reich, Learning plans as a weak method for design, Department of Civil Engineering. Carnegie-Mellon University, Pittsburgh, PA (1988).

[48] P.S. Rosenbloom, Beyond generalization as search: towards a unified framework for the acquisition of new knowledge, in: G.F. Dejong, ed., *Proceedings AAAI Symposium on Explanation-Based Learning*, Stanford, CA (1988) 17–21.

[49] P.S. Rosenbloom, A symbolic goal-oriented perspective on connectionism and Soar, In: R. Pfeifer, Z. Schreter, F. Fogelman-Soulie and L. Steels, eds., *Connectionism in Perspective* (Elsevier, Amsterdam, 1989).

[50] P.S. Rosenboom and J.E. Laird., Mapping explanation-based generalization onto Soar, in: *Proceedings AAAI-86*, Philadelphia, PA (1986) 561–567.

[51] P.S. Rosenbloom, J.E. Laird, J. McDermott, A. Newell and E. Orciuch, Rl-Soar: an experiment in knowledge-intensive programming in a problem-solving architecture, *IEEE Trans. Pattern Anal. Mach. Intell.* 7 (1985) 561–569.

[52] P.S. Rosenbloom, J.E. Laird and A. Newell, Knowledge level leaning in Soar, in: *Proceedings AAAI-87*, Seattle, WA (1987) 499–504.

[53] P.S. Rosenbloom, J.E. Laird and A. Newell. The chunking of skill and knowledge, in: B.A.G. Elsendoorn and H. Bouma, eds., *Working Models of Human Perception* (Academic Press, London, 1988) 391–410.

[54] P.S. Rosenbloom, J.E. Laird and A. Newell, Meta-levels in Soar, in: P. Maes and D. Nardi, eds., *Meta-Level Architectures and Reflection* (North-Holland, Amsterdam, 1988) 227–240.

[55] P.S. Rosenbloom and A. Newell. The chunking of goal hierarchies: a generalized model of practice, in: R.S. Michalski, J.G. Carbonnell and T.M. Mitchell, eds.,

Machine Learning: An Artificial Intelligence Approach 2 (Morgan Kaufmann, Los Altos, CA, 1986) 247–288.

[56] P.S. Rosenbloom, A. Newell and J.E. Laird, Towards the knowledge level in Soar: the role of the architecture in the use of knowledge, in: K. VanLehn, ed., *Architectures for Intelligence* (Erlbaum, Hillsdale, NJ, 1990).

[57] E.D. Sacerdoti, Planning in a hierarchy of abstraction spaces, *Artif. Intell.* 5 (1974) 115–135.

[58] R.H. Saul, A Soar2 implementation of version-space inductive learning, Department of Computer Science, Carnegie-Mellon University, Pittsburgh, PA (1984).

[59] R. Schank and R. Ableson, *Scripts, Plans, Goals and Understanding* (Erlbaum, Hillsdale, NJ, 1977).

[60] D. Steier, Cypress-Soar: a case study in search and learning in algorithm design, in: *Proceedings IJCAI-87*, Milan, Italy (1987) 327–330.

[61] D.M. Steier, J.E. Laird, A. Newell, P.S. Rosenbloom, R. Flynn, A. Golding, T.A. Polk, O.G. Shivers, A. Unruh and G.R. Yost, Varieties of learning in Soar: 1987, in: P. Langley, ed., *Proceedings Fourth International Workshop on Machine Learning*, Irvine, CA (1987) 300–311.

[62] D.M. Steier and A. Newell, Integrating multiple sources of knowledge in Designer-Soar: an automatic algorithm designer, in: *Proceedings AAAI-88*, St. Paul, MN (1988) 8–13.

[63] K.R. Swedlow and D.M. Steier, Soar 5.0 user's manual. School of Computer Science, Carnegie-Mellon University, Pittsburgh, PA (1989).

[64] M. Tambe, Speculations on the computational effects of chunking, Department of Computer Science, Carnegie-Mellon University, Pittsburgh, PA (1988).

[65] M. Tambe, A. Acharya and A. Gupta. Implementation of production systems on message passing computers: Simulation results and analysis, Tech. Rept. CMU-CS-89-129, School of Computer Science, Carnegie-Mellon University, Pittsburgh, PA (1989).

[66] M. Tambe, D. Kalp, A. Gupta, C.L. Forgy, B. Milnes and A. Newell, Soar/PSM-E: Investigating match parallelism in a learning production system, in: *Proceedings ACMI SIGPLAN Symposium on Parallel Programming: Experience with Applications, Languages, and Systems* (1988) 146–161.

[67] M. Tambe and A. Newell, Some chunks are expensive, in: J. Laird, ed., *Proceedings Fifth International Conference on Machine Learning*, Ann Arbor, MI (1988) 451–458.

[68] M. Tambe and P.S. Rosenbloom, Eliminating expensive chunks by restricting expressiveness, in: *Proceedings IJCAI-89*, Detroit, MI (1989).

[69] A. Unruh and P.S. Rosenbloom. Abstraction in problem solving and learning, in: *Proceedings IJCAI-89*, Detroit, MI (1989).

[70] A. Unruh, P.S. Rosenbloom and J.E. Laird, Dynamic abstraction problem solving in Soar, in: *Proceedings Third Annual Aerospace Applications of Artificial Intelligence Conference*, Dayton, OH (1987) 245–256.

[71] K. VanLehn, *Mind Bugs: The Origins of Procedural Misconceptions* (MIT Press, Cambridge, MA, 1990).

[72] K. VanLehn and W. Ball, Non-LIFO execution of cognitive procedures, *Cogn. Sci.* 13 (1989) 415–465.

[73] R. Washington and P.S. Rosenbloom. Applying problem solving and learning to diagnosis, Department of Computer Science, Stanford University, CA (1988).

[74] M. Wiesmeyer, Personal communication (1988).
[75] M. Wiesmeyer, Soar I/O reference manual, version 2, Department of EECS, University of Michigan, Ann Arbor, MI (1988).
[76] M. Wiesmeyer, New and improved Soar IO, Department of EECS, University of Michigan, Ann Arbor, MI (1989).
[77] G.R. Yost and A. Newell, A problem space approach to expert system specification, in: *Proceedings IJCAI-89*, Detroit, MI (1989).

36

ON THE THRESHOLDS OF KNOWLEDGE

Douglas Lenat and Edward A. Feigenbaum

Source: *Artificial Intelligence*, 47 (1991): 185–250.

Abstract Lenat, D.B. and E.A. Feigenbaum, On the thresholds of knowledge, Artificial Intelligence 47 (1991) 185–250.

We articulate the three major findings and hypotheses of AI to date:

(1) The Knowledge Principle: If a program is to perform a complex task well, it must know a great deal about the world in which it operates. In the absence of knowledge, all you have left is search and reasoning, and that isn't enough.

(2) The Breadth Hypothesis: To behave intelligently in unexpected situations, an agent must be capable of falling back on increasingly general knowledge and analogizing to specific but superficially far-flung knowledge. (This is an extension of the preceding principle.)

(3) AI as Empirical Inquiry: Premature mathematization, or focusing on toy problems, washes out details from reality that later turn out to be significant. Thus, we must test our ideas experimentally, *falsifiably*, on large problems.

We present evidence for these propositions, contrast them with other strategic approaches to AI, point out their scope and limitations, and discuss the future directions they mandate for the main enterprise of AI research.

1 Introduction

For over three decades, our field has pursued the dream of the computer that competently performs various difficult cognitive tasks. AI has tried many approaches to this goal and accumulated much empirical evidence. The evidence suggests the need for the computer to have and use domain-specific knowledge. We shall begin with our definition of intelligence:

Definition. *Intelligence* is the power to rapidly find an adequate solution in what appears a priori (to observers) to be an immense search space.

So, in those same terms, we can summarize the empirical evidence: "Knowledge is Power" or, more cynically "Intelligence is in the eye of the (uninformed) beholder". The *knowledge as power* hypothesis has received so much confirmation that we now assert it as:

Knowledge Principle (KP). A system exhibits intelligent understanding and action at a high level of competence primarily because of the *knowledge* that it can bring to bear: the concepts, facts, representations, methods, models, metaphors, and heuristics about its domain of endeavor.

The word *knowledge* in the KP is important. There is a tradeoff between knowledge and search; that is, often one can either memorize a lot of very detailed cases, or spend time applying very general rules. Neither strategy, carried to extremes, is optimal. On the one hand, *searching* is often costly, compared to the low cost of just not forgetting—of preserving the knowledge for future use. Our technological society would be impossible if everyone had to rediscover everything for themselves. On the other hand, even in a relatively narrow field, it's impractical if not impossible to have a pre-stored database of all the precise situations one will run into. Some at least moderately general knowledge is needed, rules which can be applied in a variety of circumstances. Since *knowledge* includes control strategies and inference methods, one might ask what is *excluded* by the KP. The answer is that we exclude unbalanced programs: those which do not contain, and draw power from, a mixture of explicit and compiled knowledge, and we advocate programs in which the balance is tipped toward the explicit, declarative side. Section 2 discusses the Knowledge Principle in more detail, and Section 3 provides experimental evidence for it.

The KP suggests that any system which is to perform intelligently incorporate both particular facts and heuristic rules. But how far-ranging must such knowledge be? Consider the brittleness of current knowledge-based systems. They have a plateau of competence, but the edges of that plateau are steep descents into complete incompetence. Evidence for how *people* cope with novelty is sparse and unreliable. Still, there is suggestive evidence supporting their reliance on general "commonsense" knowledge, and their reliance on partial or analogical matching. This leads us to a plausible extension of the Knowledge Principle:

Breadth Hypothesis (BH). Intelligent performance often requires the problem solver to fall back on increasingly general knowledge, and/or to analogize to specific knowledge from far-flung domains.

Are we, of all people, advocating the use of weak methods? Yes, but only in the presence of a breadth of knowledge far afield of the particular task at hand. We are adding to the KP here, not contradicting it. Much of the power still derives from a large body of task-specific expertise (cases and rules). We are adding to the KP a new speculation, namely that intelligent problem solvers cope with novel situations by analogizing and by drawing on "common sense". Section 4 examines the brittleness of current expert systems, and Section 5 presents evidence in support of the Breadth Hypothesis. That evidence comes from considering the limits of what AI can do today, in areas such as natural language understanding and machine learning.

The natural tendency of any search program is to slow down (often combinatorially explosively) as additional assertions are added and the search space therefore grows. All our real and imagined intelligent systems must, at some level, be *searching* as they locate and apply general rules and as they locate and perform analogical (partial) matches. Is it inevitable, then, that programs must become less intelligent in their previously-competent areas, as their KPs grow? We believe not. The key to avoiding excess search is to have a little meta-knowledge along to guide and constrain the search. Hence, the key to preserving effective intelligence of a growing program lies in judicious adding of meta-knowledge along with the addition of object-level knowledge. Some of this meta-knowledge is in the form of meta-rules, and some of it is encoded by the ontology of the KP; these are, respectively, the dynamic and static ways of effectively preserving whatever useful bundlings already existed in the KP. (Of course, meta-rules can and should be represented explicitly, declaratively, as well as having a procedural form. That way, meta-meta-knowledge can apply to *them*; and so on.) This is a prescription for one to gradually add and refine categories and predicates (types of slots) as one grows the KP. This is why we believe the KP works "in the large", why we can scale up a KP to immense size without succumbing to the combinatorial explosion.

There is an additional element in our paradigm of AI research, which says that intelligence is still so poorly understood that Nature still holds most of the important surprises in store for us. This leads, in Section 6, to our central *methodological* tenets:

Empirical Inquiry Hypothesis (EH). The most profitable way to investigate AI is to embody our hypotheses in programs, and gather data by running the programs. The surprises usually suggest revisions that start the cycle over again. Progress depends on these experiments being able to *falsify* our hypotheses. Falsification is the most common and yet most crucial of surprises. In particular, these programs must be capable of behavior not expected by the experimenter.

Difficult Problems Hypothesis. There are too many ways to solve simple problems. Raising the level and breadth of competence we demand of a system makes it *easier* to test—and raise—its intelligence.

The Knowledge Principle is a mandate for humanity to concretize the knowledge used in solving hard problems in various fields.[1] This *might* lead to faster training based on explicit knowledge rather than apprenticeships. It has *already* led to thousands of profitable expert systems.

The Breadth Hypothesis is a mandate to spend the resources necessary to construct one immense knowledge base spanning human consensus reality, to serve as scaffolding for specific clusters of expert knowledge.

The Empirical Inquiry Hypothesis is a mandate to actually try to build such systems, rather than theorize about them and about intelligence. AI is a science when we use computers the way Tycho Brahe used the telescope, or Michaelson the interferometer—as a tool for looking at Nature, trying to test some hypothesis, and quite possibly getting rudely surprised by finding out that the hypothesis is false. There is quite a distinction between using a tool to gather data about the world, and using tools to, shall we say, merely fabricate ever more beautiful crystalline scale models of a geocentric universe.

In Section 7, the various principles and hypotheses above combine to suggest a sweeping three-stage research program for the main enterprise of AI research:

(1) Slowly hand-code a large, broad knowledge base.
(2) When enough knowledge is present, it should be faster to acquire more from texts, databases, etc.
(3) To go beyond the frontier of human knowledge, the system will have to rely on learning by discovery, to expand its KP.

Some evidence is then presented that stages (1) and (2) may be accomplished in approximately this century; i.e., that artificial intelligence is within our grasp. Lenat's current work at MCC, on the CYC program [28], is a serious effort to carry out the first stage by the mid-1990s.

We are betting our professional lives—the few decades of useful research we have left in us—on KP, BH, and EH. That's a scary thought, but one has to place one's bets somewhere, in science. It's especially scary because:

(a) the hypotheses are not obvious to most AI researchers,
(b) they are unpalatable in many ways even to us, their advocates!

Why are they not obvious? Most AI research focuses on very small problems, attacking them with machinery (both hardware and search methods) that overpower them. The end result is a program that "succeeds" with very little knowledge, and so KP, BH, and EH *are irrelevant*. One is led to them only by tackling problems in difficult "real" areas, with the world able to surprise and falsify.

Why are our three hypotheses (KP, BH, EH) not particularly palatable? Because they are unaesthetic! And they entail person-centuries of hard knowledge-entry work. Until we are forced to them, Occam's Razor encourages us to try more elegant solutions, such as training a neutral net "from scratch"; or getting an infant-simulator and then "talking to it". Only as these fail do we turn, unhappily, to the "hand-craft a huge KP" tactic.

Section 8 summarizes the differences between our position and that of some other schools of thought on AI research. Section 9 lists several limitations and problems. We do not see any of them as insurmountable. Some of the problems seem at first blush to be "in-principle limitations", and some seem to be pragmatic engineering and usability problems. Yet we lump them side by side, because our methodology says to approach them all as symptoms of gaps in our (and our programs') knowledge, which can be identified and filled in incrementally, by in-context knowledge acquisition. Several of these problems have, in the two years since the first draft of this paper was prepared, been adequately "solved". The quote marks around "solved" mean that we have found adequate ways of handling them, typically by identifying a large collection of special-case solutions that cover the vast majority of occurrences in actuality.

The biggest hurdle of all has already been put well behind us: the enormous local maximum of building and using *explicit-knowledge-free* systems. On the far side of that hill we found a much larger payoff, namely expert systems. We have learned how to build intelligent artifacts that perform well, using knowledge, on specialized tasks within narrowly defined domains. An industry has been formed to put this technological understanding to work, and widespread transfer of this technology has been achieved. Many fields are making that transition, from data processing to knowledge processing.

And yet we see expert systems technology, too, as just a local maximum. AI is finally beginning to move on beyond that threshold. This paper presents what its authors glimpse on the far side of the expert systems local-maximum hill: the promise of a large, broad KP serving as the nucleus of crystallization for programs which respond sensibly to novel situations because they can reason more by analogy than by perfect matching, and, ultimately, because, like us, they understand the meanings of their terms.

2 The Knowledge Principle

There is a continuum between the power of already knowing and the power of being able to search for the solution. In between those two extremes lie, e.g., generalizing and analogizing and plain old observing (for instance, noticing that your opponent is Castling). Even in the case of having to search for a solution, the *method* to carry out the search may be something that you already know, or partial-match to get, or search for in some other way. This recursion bottoms out in things (facts, methods, etc.) that are *already known*. Though the knowledge/search tradeoff is often used to argue for the primacy of search, we see by this line of reasoning that it equally well argues for the primacy of knowledge.

2.1 Thresholds of competence

Before you can apply search *or* knowledge to solve some problem, though, you need to already know enough to at least state the problem in a well-formed fashion. For each task, there is some minimum knowledge needed for one to even formulate it—that is, so that one can recognize when one has solved the problem.

Beyond this bare minimum, today's expert systems also include enough knowledge to reach the level of a typical practitioner performing the task. Up to that "competence" level, the knowledge/search tradeoff is strongly tipped in favor of knowledge. That is, there is an ever greater "payoff" to adding each piece of knowledge, up to some level of competence (e.g., where a useful subset of the original KP-complete problem becomes polynomial). Some of the knowledge that competent practitioners have is the knowledge of which distinctions to make and which ones to ignore. As shown by Polya [39] and Amarel [2], the space one needs to search for a solution to a problem can become smaller and smaller as one incorporates more and more such knowledge into the representation.

Beyond that "practitioner" level is the "expert" level. Here, each piece of additional knowledge is only infrequently useful. Such knowledge deals with rare but not unheard-of cases. In this realm, the knowledge/search tradeoff is fairly evenly balanced. Sometimes it's worth knowing all those obscure cases, sometimes it's more cost-effective to have general models and "run" them.

Notice that we have not yet considered "the rest of human knowledge", all the facts, heuristics, models, etc., that are not known to be relevant to this particular task. This does not mean that all other knowledge is truly irrelevant and useless to the task; perhaps it will one day be seen to be relevant through new discoveries, perhaps it will be useful to analogize from (and thereby lead to a novel solution to some tough situation), etc. Of course, putting this into an expert system for just one particular task is even *less* cost-effective, per piece of knowledge added, so no one seriously considers doing it.

2.2 Why the Knowledge Principle works so frequently

The above arguments describe how the KP *might* work; but why *does* it work so frequently? In other words, why is building even conventional expert systems a powerful and useful thing to do?

(1) Many useful real-world tasks are sufficiently narrow that the "practitioner level" and even some degree of "expert level" can be achieved by a system containing only, say, several hundred if/then rules—hence requiring only a few person-years of effort.

(2) These systems often embody only the delta, the *difference* between expert and non-expert. MYCIN may outperform general practitioners at deciding which kind of meningitis a patient has, but that's because the GPs have to know about thousands of varieties of medical problems, and relatively rarely encounter meningitis, while the program can assume that the other 99% of medicine has been judged to be irrelevant, and is free to focus on how to differentiate one type of meningitis from another.

(3) Conventional programs that perform a similar task lack most of the "if" parts of the corresponding expert system's rules. That is, they have compiled away much of the knowledge, in order to gain efficiency. The price they pay for this, though, is the high cost of integrating a new piece of knowledge into their program once it exists. To put this the other way, you can never be sure, in advance, how the knowledge already in the system is going to be used, or added to, in the future. Therefore, much of the knowledge in an intelligent system needs to be represented explicitly, declaratively, although compiled forms of it may of course also be present. We might call this the "Explicit Knowledge Principle". In other words, the experts in a field often do not yet have all the required knowledge explicitly codified (otherwise anyone could be proficient, and there wouldn't *be* recognized experts). Therefore, standard software design methodology may fail to build a program "in one pass" to perform the task. However, as the developing expert system makes mistakes, the experts can correct them, and those corrections incrementally accrete the bulk of the hitherto unexplicated rules. In this manner, the system incrementally approaches competence, and even expertise, where no traditional software solution would work.

(4) There is another benefit that accrues when knowledge—including procedural knowledge—is represented declaratively, as explicit objects, following the "Explicit Knowledge Principle", above. Namely, *meta*-rules can apply to it, e.g., helping to acquire, check, or debug other rules. Structured objects that represent knowledge can be more easily

analogized to, and can enable generalizations to be structurally induced from them. So while we concede to procedural attachment (having opaque lumps of code here and there in the system) for efficiency reasons, we argue that there should be a declarative version of that also (i.e., a declarative structure containing the information which is encoded in the procedure).

2.3 Control in knowledge-based systems

What about the control structure of an intelligent system? Even granted that lots of knowledge is necessary, might we not need sophisticated as-yet-unknown reasoning methods?

Knowledge Is All There Is Hypothesis. No sophisticated, as-yet-unknown control structure is required for intelligent behavior.

On the one hand, we already understand deduction, induction, analogy, specialization, generalization, and so on, well enough to have *knowledge* be our bottleneck, not control strategies. This does not mean that we fully understand such processes, of course. To be sure, additional work still needs to be done there. But we have examined them enough to eliminate the gross inefficiencies in their execution, to devise data structures and algorithms for efficiently performing them in the most commonly occurring cases. (For instance, consider Stickel's non-clausal connection graph resolution theorem prover [44], which was a response to the known inefficiency of deduction.)

On the other hand, all such strategies and methods are themselves just pieces of knowledge. The control structure of the intelligent system can be *opportunistic*: select one strategy, apply it for a while, monitor progress, and perhaps decide to switch to another strategy (when some other piece of knowledge suggests it do so).

Carefully reading our wording in this section will reveal that we are making a pragmatic argument, involving choices for where to focus current AI research, rather than making a hypothesis we expect to hold true forever. We don't understand induction, analogy, etc., perfectly, but further progress on understanding them needs to be done in the context of a large knowledge base. So let's worry about getting that built, and then return to study these phenomena. Perhaps at that time we will see the need to develop some useful new control scheme.

2.4 The manner in which knowledge boosts competence

Can we be more specific about the manner in which knowledge boosts competence? Can we give, say, an equation for how to measure the effective power of the knowledge in a system, when it's applied to a problem P? It is premature to even attempt to do so—it may *never* be possible to do so. It may never even be possible to give precise definitions for terms like "useful" and "competence". Nevertheless, this section speculates on what some of the terms in that equation would be.

Factor 1. Consider a heuristic H; e.g., "Drive carefully late at night". It has a characteristic curve of how powerful or useful it is, as a function of what problem it's applied to. As detailed in [25], the area under this curve is often constant across heuristics. In simpler and more familiar terms, this is just the generality/power tradeoff: the more powerful a heuristic's "peak power" is, the narrower its domain of applicability is likely to be. A heuristic that only applies to driving on Saturday nights, in Austin, might be far more powerful than H, but its range of applicability is correspondingly narrower. As a first approximation to the power of the knowledge in the system, we might simply superpose all the "power curves" of the heuristics (and algorithms) that comprise the knowledge. That would give us an overall idea of the power of the system as a function of what problem it was applied to. If we're interested in applying the system to a particular problem P, we could then read off the value of this curve at point P. If we're going to apply the system to several problems, so that P is a large distribution, then we would weight the result by that distribution.

Factor 2. As a correction to this first rough guess, attempt to factor out some of the redundancy and dependence among the pieces of knowledge.

Factor 3. Weight each heuristic by how costly it is to run. "Cost" here includes literal CPU and memory resources used, and also includes the less tangible cost of asking questions of slow and busy human beings. Also included in this factor would be the downside risks of what might happen if the heuristic gave incorrect advice.

Factor 4. To be fair to the less-knowledge-based approaches, we should also deduct some amount which amortizes the effort we spent *acquiring* that rule or method.

Those represent just four of the factors in measuring the effective power of the knowledge in a system. We encourage further investigation in this direction. Recent work in nonmonotonic logic may bear on Factors 1 and 3; and [46] may bear on Factor 2.

3 Evidence for the Knowledge Principle

Half a century ago, before the modern era of computation began, Turing's theorems and abstract machines gave a hint of the fundamental idea that the computer could be used to model the symbol-manipulating processes that make up that most human of all behaviors: thinking.

Thirty years ago, following the 1956 Dartmouth Summer Conference on

AI, the work began in earnest. The founding principle of the AI research paradigm is really an article of faith, first concretized by Newell and Simon. (See [35] for more details.)

Physical Symbol System Hypothesis. The digital computer has sufficient means for intelligent action; to wit: representing real-world objects, actions, and relationship internally as interconnected structures of symbols, and applying symbol manipulation procedures to those structures.

The early dreaming included intelligent behavior at very high levels of competence. Turing speculated on wide-ranging conversations between people and machines, and also on expert-level chess playing programs. Newell and Simon also wrote about champion chess programs, and began working with Cliff Shaw toward that end. McCarthy wrote about the Advice Taking program. Gelernter, Moses, Samuel, and many others shared the dream.

Lederberg and Feigenbaum chose, in 1964, to pursue the AI dream by focusing on scientific reasoning tasks. With Buchanan and Djerassi, they built Dendral, a program that solved structure elucidation problems at a high level of competence. Many years of experimenting with Dendral led to some hypotheses about what its source of power might be, how it was able to solve chemical structure problems from spectral data. Namely, the program worked because it had enough knowledge of basic and spectral chemistry.

Table 1 shows that as each additional source of chemical knowledge was added, the Dendral program proposed fewer and fewer candidates (topologically plausible structures) to consider (see [7]). The fifth and final type of rule of thumb were rules for interpreting nuclear mass resonance (NMR) data. With all five types of rule in the program, many problems—such as the one illustrated—resulted in only a single candidate isomer being proposed as worth considering! Threatened by an a priori huge search space, Dendral managed to convert it into a tiny search space. That is, Dendral exhibited intelligence.

Table 1 Dendral at work: Finding all atom-bond graphs that could have the formula $C_{20}H_{43}N$. The sources given are cumulative; thus, the final "I" refers to Dendral with all five types of rules running in it

Information source	Number of structures generated
Topology (limits of 3D space)	47,867,912
Chemical topology (valences)	14,715,814
Mass spectrography (heuristics)	1,284,792
Chemistry (first principles)	1,074,648
NMR (interpretation rules)	1

When searching a space of size 1, it is not crucial in what order you expand the candidate nodes. If you want to speed up a blind search by a factor of 43 million, one could perhaps parallelize the problem and (say, by 1995) employ a 43-mega-processor; but even back in 1965 one could, alternatively, talk with the human experts who routinely solve such problems, and then encode the knowledge they bring to bear to avoid searching. There is a cost associated with making the generator "smarter" in this fashion (i.e., there is inferencing going on inside the generator, to utilize the knowledge it now contains) but that cost is insignificant compared to the seven orders of magnitude reduction in the size of the search space it permits.

Obvious? Perhaps, in retrospect. But at the time, the prevailing view in AI ascribed power to the reasoning processes, to the inference engine and not to the knowledge base. (E.g., consider LT and GPS and the flurry of work on resolution theorem provers.) The *knowledge as power* hypothesis, supported by Feigenbaum (Dendral), McCarthy (Advice Taker), and a few others, stood as a *contra*-hypothesis. It stood awaiting further empirical testing to either confirm it or falisfy it.

The 1970s were the time to start gathering evidence for or against the Knowledge Principle. Medical and scientific problem solving provided the springboard.

- Shortliffe's MYCIN program formed the prototype for a large suite of expert-level advisory systems which we now label "expert systems" [12]. Its reasoning system was simple (exhaustive backward chaining) and ad hoc in parts.

- DEC has been using and extending R I program (EXCON) since 1981; its control structure is also simple: exhaustive forward chaining [32].

- Over a period of two decades, Bledsoe was led to incorporate more and more heuristics into his theorem provers, ultimately rejecting resolution entirely and opting for knowledge-guided natural deduction [3, 4].

- The INTERNIST program [40] got underway at nearly the same time as MYCIN. By now it has grown to a KP of 572 diseases, 4500 manifestations, and many hundreds of thousands of links between them.

- The AM [9] and EURISKO [25] programs, 15 years old by now, demonstrated that several hundred heuristic rules, of varying levels of generality and power, could adequately begin to guide a search for plausible (and often interesting) new concepts in many domains, including set theory, number theory, naval wargaming tactics, physical device design, evolution, and programming. These experiments showed how scientific discovery—a very different sort of intelligent behavior from most expert systems' tasks—might be explained as rule-guided, knowledge-guided, search. Not all of the AM experiments were successful; indeed, the ultimate limitations of AM as it was run longer and longer finally led to

EURISKO, whose ultimate empirical limitations [27] led to CYC, of which more later.

In the past decade, thousands of expert systems have mushroomed in engineering, manufacturing, geology, molecular biology, financial services, machinery diagnosis and repair, signal processing, and in many other fields. From the very beginning, these expert systems could interact with professionals in the jargon of the specialty; could explain their line of reasoning by displaying annotated traces of rule-firings; and had subsystems (such as MYCIN'S TEIRESIAS [9] and XCON'S SALT [29]) which aided the acquisition of additional knowledge by guiding the expert to find and fix defects in the knowledge (rule) base.

Very little ties these areas together, other than that in each one, some technical problem solving is going on, guided by heuristics: experimental, qualitative rules of thumb—rules of good guessing. Their reasoning components are weak and simple; in their knowledge bases lies their power. The evidence for the various propositions we made in Section 2 lies in their details—in the details of their design, development, and performance.

In the 1980s, many other areas of AI research began making the shift over to the knowledge-based point of view. It is now common to hear that a program for understanding natural language must have extensive knowledge of its domain of discourse. Or, a vision program must have an understanding of the "world" it is intended to analyze scenes from. Or even, a machine learning program must start with a significant body of knowledge which it will expand, rather than trying to learn from scratch.

4 The Breadth Hypothesis

A limitation of past and current expert systems is their brittleness. They operate on a high plateau of knowledge and competence until they reach the extremity of their knowledge; then they fall off precipitously to levels of ultimate incompetence. People suffer the same difficulty, too, but their plateau is much broader and their slope is more gentle. Part of what cushions the fall are layer upon layer of weaker, more general models that underlie their specific knowledge.

For example, if engineers are diagnosing a faulty circuit they are unfamiliar with, they can bring to bear: circuit analysis techniques; their experiences with the other products manufactured by the same company, published handbook data for the individual components, and commonsense rules of thumb for water circuits (looking for leaks, or breaks), for electrical devices (turn it off and on a few times), and for mechanical devices in general (shake it or smack it a few times). Engineers might analogize to the last few times their automobile engine failed, or even to something as distant as a failed love affair. Naturally, the more different the causality of the thing they analogize to, the less likely it will be to apply in the electronic circuit diagnosis situation.

Domain-specific knowledge represents the distillation of experience in a field, nuggets of compiled hindsight. In a situation similar to the one in which they crystallized, they can powerfully guide search. But when confronted by a *novel* situation, human beings turn to reasoning strategies like generalizing and analogizing in real time and (even better) *already having* more general rules to fall back on. This leads to the Breadth Hypothesis (BH), which we stated in Section 1.

4.1 Falling back on increasingly general knowledge

Each of us has a vast storehouse of general knowledge, though we rarely talk about any of it explicitly to one another; we just assume that other people already know these things. If they're included in a conversation, or an article, they confuse more than they clarify. Some examples are:

- water flows downhill,
- living things get diseases,
- doing work requires energy,
- people live for a single, contiguous, finite interval of time,
- most cars today are riding on four tires,
- each tire a car is riding on is mounted on a wheel,
- if you fall asleep while driving, your car will start to head out of your lane pretty soon,
- if something big is between you and the thing you want, you probably will have to go around it.

It is *consensus reality* knowledge. Lacking these simple commonsense concepts, expert systems' mistakes often appear ridiculous in human terms. For instance, when a car loan authorization program approves a loan to a teen-ager who put down he'd worked at the same job for twenty years; or when a skin disease diagnosis program concludes that my rusted out decade-old Chevy has measles; or when a medical system prescribes an absurd dosage of a drug for a maternity patient whose weight (105) and age (35) were accidentally swapped during the case's type-in.

As we build increasingly complex programs, and invest them with increasing power, the humor quickly evaporates.

4.2 Reasoning by analogy

Reasoning by analogy involves *partial*-matching from your current situation to another one. There are two independent dimensions along which analogizing occurs, vertical (simplifying) and horizontal (cross-field) transformation.

310

- *Vertical:* When faced with a complex situation, we often analogize to a much simpler one. Of course simplification can be overdone: "the stock market is a seesaw"; "medication is a resource" (this leads many patients to overdose).
- *Horizontal:* Cross-field mapping is rarer but can pay off: "curing a disease is like fighting a battle" may help doctors devise new tactics to try (e.g., viruses employed to perform the analogue of propaganda) and may help soldiers devise new military tactics (e.g., choosing missions which function like vaccination).

Successful analogizing often involves components of both vertical and horizontal transformation. For instance, consider reifying a country as if it were an individual person: "Russia is angry". That accomplishes two things: it simplifies dealing with the other country, and it also enables our vast array of first-hand experiences (and lessons learned) about inter-personal relations to be applied to international relations.

Do not make the mistake we did, of thinking of this reasoning method as little more than a literary device, used for achieving some sort of emotional impact. It can be used to help discover solutions to problems, and to flesh out solutions; and it can be argued that analogy pervades human communication and perhaps almost all of human thought! (see [22]). Even conceding that analogy is powerful, and often applies, still two questions linger: "*Why* does such an unsound problem-solving method work well?", and "Why does it work so often?"

There is much common causality in the world; that leads to similar events *A* and *B*; people (with our limited perception) then notice a little bit of that shared structure; finally, since we *know* that human perception is often limited, people come to rely on the following rule of thumb:

> **Analogical Method.** If *A* and *B* appear to have some unexplained similarities, then it's worth your time to hunt for additional shared properties.

This rule is general but inefficient. There are many more specialized versions for successful analogizing in various task domains, in various user-modes (e.g., by someone in a hurry, or a child), among analogues with various epistemological statuses, depending on how much data there is about *A* and *B*, and so on. These are some of the *n* dimensions of analogy space; we can conceive having a special body of knowledge—an expert system—in each cell of that *n*-dimensional matrix, to handle just that sort of analogical reasoning.

Why focus on causality? If cause (*A*) and cause (*B*) have no specific common generalization, then similarities between *A* and *B* are more likely to be superficial coincidences, a metaphor useful perhaps as a literary device but not as a heuristic one.

Analogy in mathematics, where there is no clear notion of causality, operates similarly to "genuine" analogy, with the weaker relation of material implication substituting for causality. In that case, what one is often finding is a connection between two instances of a not-yet-conceptualized generalization. Also, much of analogizing in the doing of mathematics [39] is analogizing between the current problem-solving situation and a past one, i.e., between two search processes, not between two mathematical entities. And the act of trying to solve math problems is indeed fraught with causality and, hence, opportunities for the above sort of "genuine" analogizing.

The above paragraphs are really just a rationalization of how analogy *might* work. The reason this unsound reasoning method *frequently* succeeds has to do with three *moderation properties* that happen to hold in the real world:

(1) The moderate distribution of causes with respect to effects. If there were a vast number of unrelated kinds of causes, or if there were only one or two distinguishable causes, then analogy would be less useful.

(2) The moderately high frequency with which we must cope with novel situations, and the moderate degree of novelty they present. Lower frequency, or much higher (volatility of the world in which the problem solver must perform), would decrease the usefulness of trying to analogize. Why? In a world with essentially no surprises, memory is all you need; and in a volatile world, matching to past occurrences is more of a hindrance than a help.

(3) The obvious metric for locating relevant knowledge—namely, "closeness of subject matter"—is just a moderately good predictor of true relevance. Far-flung knowledge and imagery *can* be useful. If we already understood all the connections, we'd always know when X was relevant; and if we had no attributes of knowledge to match to, we'd have no idea of how to generate (let alone flesh out) an analogy.

Analogizing broadens the relevance of the entire knowledge base. It can be used to construct interesting and novel interpretations of situations and data; to retrieve knowledge that has not been stored the way that it is now needed; to guess values for attributes; to suggest methods that just might work; and as a device to help students learn and remember. It can provide access to powerful methods that might work in this case, but which might not otherwise be perceived as "relevant". E.g., Dirac analogized between quantum theory and group theory, and very gingerly brought the group theory results over into physics for the first time, with quite successful results.

Today, we suffer with laborious manual knowledge entry in building expert systems, carefully codifying knowledge and placing it in a data structure. Analogizing may be used in the future not only as an inference method inside a program, but also as an aid to adding new knowledge to it.

312

5 Evidence for the Breadth Hypothesis

If we had as much hard evidence about the BH as we do for the KP, we would be calling it the Breadth *Principle*. Still, the evidence is there, if we look closely at the limits of what AI programs can do today. Most of the current AI research we've read about is currently stalled. As Mark Stefik recently remarked in a note to us, "*Progress will be held back until a sufficient corpus of knowledge is available on which to base experiments.*" For brevity, we will focus on natural language understanding (NL) and machine learning (ML), but similar results are appearing in most other areas of AI as well.

5.1 The limits of natural language understanding

To understand sentences in a natural language, one must be able to disambiguate which meaning of a word is intended, what the referent of a pronoun probably is, what each ellipsis means, and so on. These are knowledge-intensive skills.

Consider the first sentence in Fig. 1. Who's flying, you or the statue? Clearly we aren't getting any clues from English to do that disambiguation; we must know about people, statues, passenger air travel, the size of cargo that is shipped by air, the size and location of the Statue of Liberty, the ease or difficulty of seeing objects from a distance, and numerous other consensus reality facts and heuristics. What if we'd said "I saw the Statue of Liberty standing in New York Harbor." It's not fair to say the verb (flying *versus* standing) decides it for you; consider, e.g., "I saw the Statue of Liberty standing at the top of the Empire State Building." See [45] for similar examples.

On line 2, in Fig. 1, the first "pen" is a corral, the other is a writing implement. But how do you know that? It has to do with storage of solids and liquids, of how big various objects are, with your ability to almost instantly and subconsciously consider *why* one might place a box in each kind of pen, *why* one might put ink inside each kind of pen, and choose the plausible interpretation in each case. This ability can of course be misled, as for example in one category of jokes.

On line 3, does "it" refer to the dog or the window? What if we'd said "She *smashed* it", or "She pressed her nose up against it"?

A program which *understood* line 4 should be able to answer "Did Wellington hear of Napoleon's death?" Often, we communicate by what *isn't* said, in

---

1. I saw the Statue of Liberty flying over New York.
2. The box is in the pen. The ink is in the pen.
3. Mary saw a dog in the window. She wanted it.
4. Napoleon died on St. Helena. Wellington was saddened.

Figure 1 Sentences presume world knowledge furiously.

313

between one sentence and the next one. And of course we should then be able to draw the obvious conclusions from those inferred assertions; e.g., being able to answer the question "Did Wellington outlive Napoleon?"

For any particular chosen text, an NL program can incorporate the small set of necessary twentieth century Americana, the few commonsense facts and scripts that are required for semantic disambiguation, question answering, anaphoric reference, and so on. But then one turns to a new page, and the new text requires more semantics (pragmatics) to be added.

In a sense, the NL researchers *have* cracked the language understanding problem. But to produce a general Turing-testable system, they would have to provide more and more domain-specific information, and the program's semantic component would more and more resemble the immense KP mandated by the Breadth Hypothesis. As Norvig [38] concludes: "the complexity [has been shifted] from the algorithm to the knowledge base, to handle examples that other systems could do only by introducing specialized algorithms."

Have we overstated the argument about how NL programs must ultimately have a large, real-world knowledge base to draw upon? Hardly; if anything we have drastically *under*stated it! Look at almost any newspaper story, e.g., and attend to how often a word or concept is used in a clearly metaphorical, non-literal sense. Once every few minutes, you might guess? No! Reality is full of surprises. The surprise here is that almost every sentence is packed with metaphors and analogies [22]. An unbiased sample: here is the first article we saw today (April 7, 1987), the lead story in the *Wall Street Journal* [50]:

> Texaco lost a major ruling in its legal battle with Pennzoil. The Supreme Court dismantled Texaco's protection against having to post a crippling $12 billion appeals bond, pushing Texaco to the brink of a Chapter 11 filing.

Lost? Major? Battle? Dismantled? Posting? Crippling? Pushing? Brink? The example drives home the point that, far from overinflating the need for real-world knowledge in language understanding, the usual arguments about disambiguation barely scratch the surface. (Drive? Home? The point? Far? Overinflating? Scratch? Surface? Oh no, I can't call a halt to this! (call? halt?)) These layers of analogy and metaphor eventually "bottom out" at physical—*somatic*—primitives: up, down, forward, back, pain, cold, inside, seeing, sleeping, tasting, growing, containing, moving, making noise, hearing, birth, death, strain, exhaustion, ... , and calling and halting.

NL researchers—and dictionaries—usually get around analogic usage by allowing several meanings to a word. Definition #1 for "war", say, is the literal one, and the other definitions are various common metaphorical uses of "war" (such as "an argument", "a commercial competition", "a search for a cure for", etc.).

There are many millions (perhaps a few hundred million) of things we authors can assume you readers know about the world: the number of tires an auto has; who Ronald Reagan is; what happens if you fall asleep when driving—what we called consensus reality. To use language effectively, we select the best consensus image to quickly evoke in the listener's mind the complex thought we want to convey. If our program doesn't already know most of those millions of shared concepts (experiences, objects, processes, patterns, . . .), it will be awkward for us to communicate with it in NL.

It is common for NL researchers to acknowledge the need for a large semantic component nowadays; Schank and others were saying similar things a decade ago! But the first serious efforts have only recently begun to try to actually build one: at MCC (in conjunction with CYC), and at EDR, the Japanese Electronic Dictionary Research project [10]. We shall have to wait a few more years until the evidence is in.

5.2 The limits of machine learning (induction)

Machine learning is a second area where research is stalled owing to insufficiently broad knowledge bases. We will pick on AM and EURISKO because they exemplify the extreme knowledge-rich end of the current ML spectrum. Many experiments in machine learning were performed on them. We had many surprises along the way, and gained an intuitive feel for how and why heuristics work, for the nature of their power and their brittleness. Lenat and Brown present many of those surprises in [27]; some are listed in Fig. 2.

Despite their relative knowledge-richness, the ultimate limitations of these programs derived from their small size. Not their small number of methods, which were probably adequate, but the small initial knowledge base they had to draw upon. One can analogize to a campfire that dies out because it was too small, and too well isolated from nearby trees, to start a major blaze. The heuristics, the representations chosen, etc., provide the kindling and the spark, but the real fuel must come from without.

In other words, AM and other machine learning programs "ran down" because of insufficient knowledge. EURISKO partially solved this, by having new heuristics be learned simultaneously with the object-level learning, but this merely delayed the inevitable. The point here is that one can only learn something—by discovery or by being told—if one almost knows it already. This leads to Piagetian stages in young children, courses of study in young adults, and suggests the need for large knowledge bases in AI programs.

Marvin Minsky cites a variant of this relationship in his afterword to *True Names* [49]: "The more you know, the more (and faster) you can learn." The inverse of this enabling relationship is a disabling one, and that's what ultimately doomed AM and EURISKO:

1. It works. several thousand concepts, including some novel concepts and heuristics, from several domains, were discovered.
2. Most of the interesting concepts could be discovered in several different ways.
3. Performing the top N tasks on the Agenda in simulated-parallel provided only about a factor of 3 speedup even when N grew as large as 100.
4. Progress slows down unless the program learns new heuristics (compiles its hindsight) often.
5. Similarly, progress slowed down partly because the programs could not competently learn to choose, switch, extend, or invent different representations.
6. These programs are sensitive to the assumptions woven into their representations' semantics; e.g., 'What does it *mean* for Jane to appear as the value on the spouse slot of the Fred frame?'
7. Some of their apparent power is illusory, only present in the mind of the intelligent observer who recognizes concepts which the program defines but does not properly appreciate.
8. Structural mutation works iff syntax mirrors semantics: represent heuristics using many small if- and many small then-parts, so the results of point mutation can be more meaningful.
9. In each new domain, there would be a flurry of plausible activities, resulting in several unexpected discoveries, followed by a period of decreased productivity, and finally lapsing into useless thrashing. The above techniques (e.g., 4, 5, 8) only delayed this decay.

Figure 2 Some of the major suprises of the "discovery guided by heuristic rules" experiments performed with the AM and EURISKO programs, during the decade 1975–1984

Knowledge Facilitates Learning (Catch 22). If you don't know very much to begin with, don't expect to learn a lot quickly.

This is the standard criticism of pure Baconian induction. As philosophers are wont to say, "To get ahead, get a theory." Without one, you'll be lost. It will be difficult (or time-consuming) to determine whether or not each new generalization is going to be useful. In hindsight, perhaps we shouldn't have been surprised at this. After all, learning can be considered a task; and, like other tasks, it is subject to the Knowledge Principle.

This theme (knowledge facilitates learning) is filtering into ML in the form of explanation-based generalization (EBG) and goal-based learning. Unfortunately, EBG requires well-defined theories (too strong a requirement) and works by logically deducing (too restrictive a process) the explanandum. Hence we would expect this method of getting machines to learn to have some—but limited—success, which seems to be empirically what ML researchers report. E.g., Mostow [34] concludes that "scaling up for harder learning problems . . . is likely to require integrating [additional] sources of knowledge."

Don't human beings violate this Catch, starting as we do "from nothing"? Maybe, but it's not clear *what* human infants start with. Evolution has produced not merely physically sophisticated structures, but also brains whose architecture make us well suited to learning many of the simple facts that are worth learning about the world. Other senses, e.g., vision, are carefully tuned as well, to supply the brain with data that is already filtered for meaning (edges, shapes, motion, etc.) in the world in which we do happen to live. The exploration of those issues is beyond the scope of this paper, and probably beyond the scope of twentieth century science, but one thing is clear: neonatal brains are far from *tabula rasae*.

Besides starting from well-prepared brain structures, humans also have to spend a lot of time learning. It is unclear what processes go on during infancy. Once the child begins to communicate by speaking, *then* we are into the symbolic sort of learning that AI has traditionally focused on. One theory of why it's difficult to remember one's infancy and young childhood is that we radically reorganize our knowledge once or twice during our early life, and the memory structures we built as infants are not interpretable by the retrieval and reasoning methods we use as an adult [33].

6 The Empirical Inquiry Hypothesis

We scientists have a view of ourselves as terribly creative, but compared to Nature we suffer from a poverty of the imagination; it is thus much easier for us to uncover than to invent. As we state elsewhere in this paper, experimentation must be hypothesis-driven; we are not advocating the random mixture of chemicals in the hope that lead transmutes to gold. But there is a difference between having theories as one's guide versus as one's master. Premature adherance to a theory keeps Nature's surprises hidden, washing out details that later turn out to be significant (i.e., either not perceiving them at all, or labeling them as anomalies [20] and then not attending to them). E.g., contrast the astonishing early empirical studies by Piaget (*Stages of Development*) with his subsequent five decades of barren attempts to mathematize them.

This attitude leads to our central methodological hypothesis, our paradigm for AI research: the Empirical Inquiry Hypothesis (EH). We stated it in Section 1, and repeat it here:

Empirical Inquiry Hypothesis (EH). Intelligence is still so poorly understood that Nature still holds most of the important surprises in store for us. So the most profitable way to investigate AI is to embody our hypotheses in programs, and gather data by running the programs. The surprises usually suggest revisions that start the cycle over again. Progress depends on these experiments being able to *falsify* our hypotheses. Falsification is the most common and yet most crucial of surprises! In particular, these programs must be capable of behavior not expected by the experimenter.

What do we mean by "a surprise"? Surely we wouldn't want to increase surprises by having more naive researchers, less careful thought and planning of experiments, sloppier coding, unreliable machines, etc. We have in mind astronomers getting surprised by what they see (and "see") through telescopes; i.e., things surprising to the professional. Early AI programs often surprised their builders in this fashion; e.g., Newell, Simon, and Shaw's LT program [36] and Gelernter's geometry program [15]. Then fascination with axiomatizing and proving set in, and surprises from "the real world" became rare.

We have no objection to experimentation and theorizing proceeding hand in hand, we object only to the nearly exclusive doing of one of those activities and ignoring the other. As Genesereth and Nilsson argue in the preface of [17], having a good understanding of the theoretical issues can enable one to be a better experimenter.

The inverse to the EH is cruel:

Inverse to the Empirical Inquiry Hypothesis. If one builds programs which cannot possibly surprise him/her, then one is using the computer either

(a) as an engineering workhorse, or
(b) as a fancy sort of word processor (to help articulate one's hypothesis), or
(c) as a (self-)deceptive device masquerading as an experiment.

Most expert systems work falls into the first category; DART's use of MRS exemplifies the middle [16]; PUP5 (by the young Lenat [24]) and HACKER (by the young Sussman [47]) exemplify the latter category.

6.1 PUP5: a bad example

To illustrate this point, we will use some of our own earlier work. The PUP5 program [24] used a community of about one hundred Beings (similar to what have since been called actors and blackboard knowledge sources) to cooperate and synthesize a long LISP program, namely a variant of the Arch-learning program that Patrick Winston had written for his thesis a few years earlier.

That was the program that PUP5 was built to synthesize, the target it was to hit. We chose that target first, and wrote a clean version of the program in INTERLISP. Next, we wrote down an English dialogue in which a user talked to an idealized automatic program synthesis program which then gradually wrote the target program. Next, we analyzed the script of that dialogue, writing down the specific knowledge needed on the part of the synthesizer to handle each and every line that the user typed in. Finally, we encoded each of those pieces of knowledge, and bundled up the related ones into little actors or Beings.

Given this methodology, it should come as no surprise that PUP5 was then able to carry on that exact dialogue with a user, and synthesize that exact Arch program. We still firmly believe in the paradigm of multiple cooperating knowledge sources, it's just that our methodology ensured that there wouldn't be any surprises when we ran PUP5. Why? All along the way, there were numerous chances to cut corners, to consciously or unconsciously put down knowledge in a very specific form: just the knowledge that was needed, and in just the form that it would be needed during the dialogue we know was going to be run. There wasn't much else PUP5 could do, therefore, besides hit its target, and there wasn't much that we learned about automatic programming or intelligence from that six-month exercise.

There was one crucial *meta*-level lesson we did learn: You can't do science if you just use a computer as a word processor, to illustrate your ideas rather than test them. That's the coarse form of the Empirical Inquiry Hypothesis. We resolved, in late 1974, to choose a task that eliminated or minimized the chance of building a wind-up toy like PUP5. We did not want a program whose target behavior was so narrow, so precisely defined, that it could "succeed" and yet teach us nothing. The AM program, written during 1975, was the direct result of Lenat's violent recoil from the PUP5 project.

There was no particular target behavior that AM was designed with; rather, it was an experiment: What would happen if a moderate-sized body of a few hundred math heuristics (about what were plausible directions to go in, about when something was and wasn't interesting) were applied in an agenda-managed best-first search, given an initial body of a hundred or so simple math concepts. In this sense, AM's task was less constrained than any program's had ever been: to explore areas of mathematics and do interesting things (gather data, notice regularities, etc.), with no preconceptions about what it might find or by what route it would find it. (Actually, we did have a few examples in mind for what AM might do, involving simple lattice theory and abstract algebra, but it never did those!)

Unlike PUP5, AM provided hundreds of surprises, including many experiments that led to the construction of EURISKO. EURISKO ran for several thousand CPU hours, in half a dozen varied domains (see Fig. 2, above). And again the ultimate limitation was not what we expected (CPU time), or hoped for (the need to learn new representations of knowledge), but rather something at once surprising and daunting: the need to have a large fraction of consensus reality already in the machine. In this case, the data led Lenat to the next project to work on—CYC—an undertaking we would have shied away from like the plague if the empirical evidence hadn't forced us to it. It has similarly led Feigenbaum to undertake his current line of research, namely building a large KP of engineering and scientific knowledge.

Thus, progress along our personal "paths of evolution" was due to running large experiments. As the Difficult Problems Hypothesis said in Section 1, *There are too many ways to solve simple problems. Raising the level and breadth of competence we demand of a system makes it easier to test and raise its intelligence.*

Much research in cognitive psychology, e.g., traditionally sidesteps hard-to-quantify phenomena such as scientific creativity or reading and comprehending a good book, in favor of very simple tasks such as remembering nonsense syllables. If a "messy" task *is* studied, then usually either (1) it is abstracted and simplified almost beyond recognition [23], or (2) the psychologist focuses on (and varies) one specific variable, so "respectable" statistical tests for significance can be run.

6.2 Paradigms for AI research

Much of the confusion about AI methodology may be due to our casual mixing together of two quite different things: AI *goals* and AI *strategies* for achieving those goals. The confusion arises because many entries appear on both lists. Almost any strategy can apply toward any goal. Consider just one example: (1) An *expert system strategy* for a *language understanding goal* might be to build a rule-based system containing rules like "If a person gets excited, they break more grammatical rules than usual." By contrast: (2) A *language understanding strategy* for an *expert system goal* might be to build a restricted-English front end that helps an expert enter and edit rules.

All scientific disciplines adopt a paradigm: a list of the problems that are acceptable and worthwhile to tackle, a list of the methods that can and should be tried, and the standards by which the results are judged. Adopting a paradigm is done for reasons of cognitive economy, but each paradigm is one narrow view. Adding to the confusion, some paradigms in AI have grown up both around the various goals *and* around the various strategies! See Appendix A for a more detailed look into AI goals and strategies.

Finer distinctions can be drawn, involving the *tactical* choices to be made, but this turns out to be misleading. In what way misleading? Tactics that appear to be superficially different may share a common source of power: E.g., predicate calculus and frames both rely on a judicious dividing up of the world. Much of the "scruffies'" recent work on plausible reasoning by heuristic rules overlaps (but with very little shared vocabulary!) the "neats'" recent work on nonmonotonic reasoning and circumscription.

The KP and BH and EH are all *strategic* statements. Each could be prefaced by the phrase "*Whichever of the ultimate goals for AI you are pursuing* ... ". The strategic level is, apparently, the level where one needs to take a stand. This is rarely stated explicitly, and it is rarely taken into account by news media or by conference organizers.

We have an abiding trust in our chosen paradigm—empirical inquiry—in doing science the same way as the early Piaget, Newell, Simon, and

Gelernter. The number of states that a brain or a computer can be in is immense; both those numbers are so huge as to be almost unimaginable. Turing's Hypothesis likens them to each other; the only other system we're familiar with with that degree of complexity is Nature itself. Mankind has made progress in studying natural phenomena only after centuries of empirically studying those phenomena; there is no reason to expect intelligence to be exempt. Eventually, many of the natural sciences advanced to the point that theory now often precedes experiment by years or decades, but we have far to go in AI before reaching that stage.

James Wilkinson was asked in 1974 why *he* was the first to discover the truncation errors of early twentieth century integration methods. After all, Wilkes at Cambridge, and others, had access to equal or better machines at the same time. He replied that at the National Physical Laboratory, the Pilot Ace machine was sitting out, available to all to use and to watch. He was fascinated by the rows of blinking lights, and often stood mesmerized by them while his programs ran. Soon he began to recognize patterns in the lights—patterns where there should *not* have been patterns! By contrast, the Cambridge computer was screened off from its users, who got one-day turn-around on their card decks, but who were denied access to the phenomenon that Wilkinson was allowed to observe.

The point is that while having a theory is essential, it is equally important to examine data and be driven by exceptions and anomalies to revise, criticize, and if necessary reject one's theory. To take one last example: a computer-simulated Newtonian world really would *be* Newtonian; only by hooking up actual telescopes and interferometers and such (or the data from them) can the non-Newtonian nature be perceived.

7 A mandate for AI research: mapping the human menome

AI must somehow get to that stage where—as called for by KP and BH—learning begins to accelerate due to the amount already known. Induction will not be an effective means to get to that stage, unfortunately; we shall have to hand-craft that large "seed" KP one piece at a time. In terms of the graph in Fig. 3, all the programs that have ever been written, including AM and EURISKO, lie so far toward the left edge of the x-axis that the learning rate is more or less zero. Several of the more successful recent additions to the suite of ML techniques can be interpreted as pushes in the direction of adding more knowledge from which to begin the learning.

The graph in Fig. 3 shows learning by induction (DISCOVERY) constantly accelerating: the more one knows, the faster one can discover still more. Once you speak fluently, learning by talking with other people (LANGUAGE) is more efficient than rediscovery, until you cross the frontier of what humanity already knows (the vertical line at $x = F$), at which point there is no one to tell you the next piece of knowledge.

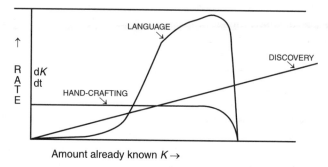

Figure 3 The rate at which one can learn new knowledge. One can also integrate these three curves with respect to time, to see how the total amount known might grow over time

"Learning by discovery" is meant to include not only scientific research (e.g., cancer research), but also the many smaller-scale events in which someone formulates a hypothesis, gathers data to test it, and uses the results to adjust their "theory". That small-scale case can occur in a (good) classroom; or just by driving the same route to work over various different times of the day (and hypothesizing on rush hour patterns). It involves defining new concepts (at least in principle), formulating new heuristics, and even adjusting or changing one's representation of knowledge. Figure 3 illustrates two more things. Learning by discovery is much *slower* than other forms of learning—such as being told something in natural language—but it is the chief method that extends the boundary F of human knowledge.

By contrast, the rate of hand-coding of knowledge is fairly constant, though it, too, drops to zero once we cross the boundary of what is already known by humanity. The hand-coding rate may slope down a bit, since the time to find related concepts will increase perhaps as the log of the size of the KP. Or, instead, the hand-coding rate may slope *up* a bit, since copy and edit is a powerful technique for knowledge entry, and, as the KP grows, there will be more chance that some very similar concept is already present.

This is an example of EH (the Empirical Inquiry Hypothesis which was presented in Section 1): Only by trying to hand-code the KP will we see which of those two counteracting factors outweighs the other, and by how much. Only by continued work on NL and ML will we determine whether or not there is a region, near where all three curves meet, where ML temporarily surpasses NL as a way to grow the KP. And only much further in the future, after our program crosses the frontier F will we find out if the discovery curve begins to slope up or down.

Figure 3 suggests a sweeping three-stage research program for the coming three decades of AI research:

- Slowly hand-code a large, broad knowledge base.
- When enough knowledge is present, it will be faster to acquire more through reading, assimilating databases, etc.
- To go beyond the frontier of human knowledge, the system will have to rely on learning by discovery, carrying out research and development projects to expand its KP.

Three decades? What are the scales on the axes of Fig. 3? Why do we think it's not a three-*century* or three-*millennia* program? Even if the vague shapes of the curves are correct, and even if we are near the left edge, how far over to the right is that place where language understanding meets and then surpasses the hand-coding level? Might we need a trillion things in our knowledge base, in order to get analogy and generalization to pay off? The usefulness and timeliness of the Breadth Hypothesis rest on the following quantitative assumption:

> **Breadth Is within Our Grasp.** A KP of about a million "frames" will provide a significant performance increase, due to generalization and analogy; this will consume ~ 2 person-centuries of time, ~ $50 million, and ~ 1 decade. Why such a "small size"? That's about all that people know!

"Just one million 'frames'! Where did that number come from? What an insult!" you may say. "You just argued that the world is a complicated place. Surely we human beings each know an effectively infinite number of things! It's hopeless to try to represent an appreciable fraction of that, so we may as well settle on writing programs that know only 10–1000 specific things."

What goes on during the 200,000 hours between birth and age 21? Certainly most of it is spent gathering experiences, building up long-term memories; some conscious time (and perhaps some sleep time) is spent generalizing and organizing one's memories. Much of what we're learning is quite specific to ourselves, our home, our family, our friends, and our culture. The result of thrusting someone into a different culture is often tragic or comic; consider, e.g., Crocodile Dundee, A Connecticut Yankee, The Beverly Hillbillies, and The Gods Must Be Crazy.

Three recent estimates of the number of concepts (frames) needed for full breadth of knowledge all came up with a figure of approximately one million:

(1) Alan Kay: 30,000 articles × 30 frames per article.[2]
(2) EDR: 200k words × 1 frame for each of a few languages.[3]
(3) Marvin Minsky: 4 LTM entries/hour from birth to adulthood.[4]

Two other ways for bounding the "bits" a human brain can store lead to much larger numbers: (1) counting neurons and synapses; but it's unclear how memories are stored in them; (2) counting pixels in our "mental images"; but controversy rages in cognitive psychology over whether mental imagery is just an illusion caused by the consistency and regularity in the world that lets us fill in missing pieces of memories—and of dynamic sensory experiences—with default values (see, e.g., [13]). And humans who are blind from birth are not particularly less intelligent for want of those terabytes of stored mental images. So it's unclear what those larger numbers signify. (Also, though it's clearly an over-simplification, having a million entries means that there can be a trillion one-step inferences involving pairs of them. And it would surprise no one to discover that one-step inference is going on unconsciously in our minds constantly.)

Here again is a situation in which one should apply the EH. Various theories give various estimates, and the way to settle the issue—and, perhaps, much more importantly, achieve the goal of having the KP we want—is to go off and try to build the large KP. Along the way, it will no doubt become clear how big it is growing and what the actual obstacles are that must be overcome.

Lenat started the CYC project in late 1984 for this very purpose. It is now halfway through its ten-year time frame, and, most surprisingly, it is still on schedule. A book describing the project and its philosophy has been published [28], and the interested reader is referred there for details. Here, we shall just very briefly list a few of the surprises that actually trying to build this immense KP has engendered:

(1) The need for more formality, for a more principled representation language. In a typical expert system application, much of the meaning of an entry on a slot of a frame can be idiosyncratic to that particular application; but CYC, which might be used for any application, cannot afford such sloppiness. E.g., consider placing "IceCream" on the "likes" slot of the "Fred" frame. Does this mean that that's all he likes? Does he like all ice cream? In what sense does he like it? Has he liked it from birth onward (and does it mean he'll like it until he dies), or is there some temporal sub-abstraction of Fred that likes it? etc.

(2) The search for a use-neutral control structure and use-neutral representation is not unlike the search for a single universal carpenter's tool. The pragmatic global *effect* of use-neutrality arises by having a large set of tools that complement each other (and sometimes overlap) and easily work together to get most common jobs done. On very, very rare occasions, a new tool may have to get invented; use the existing ones to fabricate it then.

(3) In the case of control structure, CYC has by now amassed two dozen separate inference engines: inheritance, inverse slots, automatic classification, Horn clause rules, transfersThrough, etc. One lesson is that it is

cost-effective to write and fine-tune a separate truth (actually, justifica-tion) maintenance system (TMS) for each feature, rather than relying on any one general (but of necessity inefficient) TMS algorithm.

(4) In the case of representation, besides frames, we now have numerous other "tools". One of them is a powerful constraint language which is essentially predicate calculus. This is because much of the knowledge in the system is inherently constraint-like. Consider "The number of chil-dren that Joe and Sam have are equal." We could define a new slot same-NumberOfChildrenAs, and such tactics might well get us through any one application, but that's hardly a scalable solution. In general, though, we wanted, needed, and developed a general constraint language. The constraint language is superficially second-order; in almost all real uses, any quantification over predicates (slot names) can be mechanically reduced to first-order. Several dozen of the most common sorts of constraints (e.g., the domain and range of slots) have been "slotized"; i.e., special slots (in this case, makesSenseFor and entryIsA) have been created and optimized, but still the general language is there to fall back on when needed. From time to time, when numerous constraints of the same form have been entered, we "slotize" that form by defining a new slot. For instance, we could create sameNumberOfChildrenAs if there were really heavy use of that sort of constraint.

(5) There are almost ten times as many "frames" required as we had origin-ally expected; luckily, our rate of knowledge entry is also that much faster, so we still hope to "finish" by 1994. In the search for eliminating ambiguity, the knowledge being entered must be more precise than we are used to being in everyday conversation. E.g., the meaning of "Japan" or "water" varies depending on the context of the conversation. Each separate meaning (e.g., political Japan during the 1890s) has its own frame, which is why there are more than we expected. But balancing that, it is relatively easy to build a knowledge entry tool which assists the user in copying and editing an entire cluster of related frames at once. So the two order-of-magnitude increases are not unrelated. By the way, "finishing by 1994" means approaching the crossover point (see Fig. 3), where it will be more cost-effective to continue building CYC's KP by having it read online material, and ask questions about it, than to con-tinue the sort of manual "brain-surgery" approach we are currently employing.

8 Differences with other positions

8.1 Our position regarding the aesthetes

There is a *methodological* difference between our "scruffy" way of doing AI and the aesthetes' "neat" way. This in turn stems from a difference of opinion about whether the world must admit an elegant and simple formalization of intelligence.

If only there were a *secret ingredient* for intelligence—Maxwell's equations of thought. If only we could axiomatize the world in a small set of axioms, and deduce everything. If only our learning program could start from scratch. If only our neural nets were big or cerebellar or hyperlinear enough. If only the world were like that. But it isn't. The *evidence indicates* that almost all the power is in the bulk knowledge. As Whitehead remarked, "God is in the details."

Following the Difficult Problems Hypothesis, we are firmly convinced that the AI researcher must make a major time commitment to the domain(s) in which his/her programs are to be competent; e.g., the two years that Stefik and Friedland spent to learn about molecular biology before doing MOLGEN [14]; the decade-long time frame for CYC. This is in contrast to, e.g., research that uses the Fifteen Puzzle, or cryptarithmetic, as its domain. Even in physics, where Nature so far *has* been remarkably elegant, it is still strongly cost-effective to expend the enormous time and money to build and use a SLAC or a CERN or a superconducting super-collider.

We may be exhausting the range of potent experimental AI theses that can be carried out in two years, by a student starting more or less from scratch; witness the trend to give the Computers and Thought Award to increasingly less recent graduates. The presence of a large, widely-accessible "tested" KP should enable a new round of important theses.

People do prefer—and *should* prefer—the simplest consistent hypothesis about any phenomenon. That doesn't make the hypotheses correct, of course [20]. A few examples:

- Early astronomers with poor instruments had no problem with a geocentric model. When one friend of Wittgenstein's ridiculed them for making this error, he replied "Ah, yes, how foolish. But I wonder what it would have looked like if the sun *did* go around the earth?"
- Biologists, who are unable to perform experiments on evolution, or even get precise data on it, can still believe it operates so quickly as it does, using nothing more than random mutation, random generate-and-test—a simple, elegant, appealing, but (as we in AI found out empirically) woefully inadequate problem-solving method.
- James Wilkinson, a fellow of the Royal Society and one of the world's leading numerical analysts, spoke at Stanford in 1974 about bugs in early twentieth century methods of numerical integration. These algorithms had "proofs", and were used (to a couple of iterations only) by human beings armed only with pencil and paper. Those people, by the way, were called "computers". The introduction of the high-speed electronic digital computer provided the next round of "criticism"—namely, truncation

errors made the algorithms unstable—which led to the next round of improvement in that field.

- Lakatos [21] presents the historical series of mathematicians' retreats from the initial form of the Euler–Descartes conjecture to increasingly longer, less elegant versions, with more and more terms getting added to take obscure cases and exceptions into account.

A quarter century ago, Simon provided the spectacular image of an ant on a beach: though its path is complex, that is due to the complexity of the beach, not the ant. It is a beautiful hypothesis that thinking might be based on such simple mechanisms; i.e., that the apparent complexity of the human mind is an illusion, reflecting a very simple, very general problem solver thrust into a complex environment. With apologies to Wittgenstein, and to Newell and Simon, we reply, "Ah, yes, but I wonder what it would look like if the mind *were* filled with—and dependent upon—knowledge?"

Eventually, we *will* want layers of increasing "neatness". E.g., in physics, students learn each year that last year's equations were a special case. We always try to reason at the highest, most superficial, most efficient level at which we can, and delve down one level deeper when we are forced to. But devoting so much effort to the attempt at "neatness" today just drains time and intellectual energy away from the prime enterprise of the field.

Many AI researchers quest for an elegant solution in a desperate desire for scientific respectability. The name of our field—artificial intelligence—invites everyone to instantly form an opinion. Too bad it wasn't called quantum cognodynamics. But perhaps, by interposing a layer of mathematical formalism, we can come to be accepted as hard scientists. Hence the physics-envy!

Formalizing has never driven any early science along. In designing new drug molecules, the biochemist knows it's too inefficient to apply Schrödinger's wave equation to compute the energy minimizations, hence from his/her point of view the fact that such a deep understanding even exists is *irrelevant* to the task at hand. S/he relies on crude design heuristics, and the drug companies using this methodology occasionally are enriched. As Minsky remarked about the A* algorithm in 1970: "Just because it's mathematical doesn't mean it deserves to be taught."

There are actually three separate extreme "aesthete" positions we are arguing against here! In caricature, the first one is the CMU "Soar" (and MIT Robotics) school of letting simple mechanisms give rise to slightly less simple behavior, and then claiming that that will scale up and eventually give rise to human-level intelligence. In that world view, one does not need to assemble a large knowledge base, the machine learner will acquire it automatically. Rod Brooks at MIT goes one step further, denying that one needs even a representation scheme for knowledge [6].

Again in caricature, the second one is the Stanford (and elsewhere) Logic

Group school of formalizing some aspect of reasoning (e.g., analogy), programming it to run on a few simple examples, and claiming that that will scale up, that that obviates the need for a huge KP, and besides the important thing is the theorems isn't it? Actually, to be fair, several of these researchers, such as John McCarthy, Mike Genesereth, and Pat Hayes, have been strong advocates of the need for a large KP eventually; they just believe that there are various tools required to build it which we don't have at present, formal tools which they are researching.

The third, increasingly popular type of aestheticism is the trend to highly parallel (e.g., connectionistic) and ever faster devices. The trouble is that most difficult tasks in knowledge-rich areas can't be highly parallelized. If we were to set a billion people to work trying to find a cure for cancer, we wouldn't find one in 0.2 seconds. Each cancer experiment takes months or years to perform, and there are only a moderate number of promising experiments to do at any one time; their *results* will determine what the next round of promising experiments should be.

Parallelism is useful at one extreme for implementing very carefully engineered algorithms (e.g., systolic algorithms), and at the other extreme for allowing a community of meaningfully-individuated agents act independently, asynchronously. For most technical tasks, until we understand the task very well, the size of such an actor community that we can design is typically only ~100.

The time to perform a task often increases exponentially with its size (e.g., looking ahead n moves in chess). Taking a microcoding approach or a parallelizing approach cuts off a constant factor; taking a knowledge-based approach may add a constant overhead but more importantly, for the long run, it may chip at the *exponent*. On the other hand, it is worth remarking that there are some special tasks where the desired level of performance (x-coordinate) is fixed: just barely beating all humans at chess, just barely understanding spoken words in real time, tracking the space shuttle in real time, etc. In such a case, getting a large enough constant factor speedup really could solve the problem, with no need to apply the KP, BH, or EH. As our ambition to attack ever more difficult problems grows, though, the exponential nature of the search hurts worse.

8.2 *Our position regarding expert systems*

The KP underlies the current explosion of work on expert systems (ESs). Still, there are additional things our position argues for, that are not yet realized in today's ESs. Knowledge space *in toto* is not a homogeneous solid surface, but more like a set of self-supporting buttes, and one ought to be able to hop from one to its neighbors. But current ESs are too narrow, too independent, and too informal, as we discuss below.

One major power source for ESs, the reason they can be so readily constructed, is the synergistic additivity of many rules. Using a blackboard [11] or partitioned rule sets, it is possible to combine small packets of rules into mega-rules: knowledge sources for one large expert system.

The analogue at the next higher level would be to hook hundreds of large ESs together, and achieve even greater synergy. That dream repeatedly fails to materialize. Why? As we increase the domain of each "element" we are trying to couple together, the "semantic glue" we need gets to be larger and more sophisticated. The "gluing" or communicating is made all the more difficult by the unstated and often ambiguous semantics that typically exist in a single ES. We discussed, earlier, how the CYC project at MCC has been driven toward increased formality and precision as they have labored to build that large system. It seems to us that it will require the construction of such a system, as mandated by the Breadth Hypothesis, and built not haphazardly but with a clean and formalized semantics, before the true potential of ES technology will be realized.

Plateau-hopping requires breadth

To harness the power of a large number of disparate expert systems will require something approaching full consensus reality—the millions of abstractions, models, facts, rules of thumb, representations, etc., that we all possess and that we assume everyone else does. Moreover, the ESs will need to be coded in a clean, formal representation, and integrated into a global ontology of knowledge.

The INTERNIST program is carefully engineered to do a good job of diagnosing diseases from symptoms. But consider coupling it to a machine learning program, which tries to speculate on new disease mechanisms for epidemiology. The knowledge in INTERNIST isn't stored in "the right way", and much of the needed mechanism knowledge has *already* been compiled away, condensed into numeric correlations. Clancey encountered similar difficulties when he tried to adapt MYCIN's diagnostic KP to *teach* medical students [8].

As we try to combine ESs from various tasks, even somewhat related tasks, their particular simplifications and idiosyncrasies prevent synergy. The simplifying was done in the interests of highly efficient and competent problem solving; breadth was not one of the engineering goals.

This naturally results in each ES being a separate, simplified, knowledge universe. When you sit down to build an ES for a task—say scheduling machines on a factory floor—you talk to the experts and find out the compiled knowledge they use, the ways they finesse things. For instance, how do they avoid general reasoning about time and belief? Probably they have a very simple, very specialized data structure that captures just the bits of information about time and belief that they need to solve their task. How do they deal with the fact that this milling machine M has a precise location, relative to all the others; that its base plate is a solid slab of metal of such and such a size and orientation; that its operator is a human; that only one operator at a time can use it; etc.?

If someone accidentally drills a hole through the base plate, most human beings would realize that the machine can still be used for certain jobs but not for others—e.g., it's okay if you want to mill a very large part, but not a very small one that might fall through the hole! People can fluidly shift to the next more detailed grain size, to reason out the impact of the hole in the base plate, even if they've never thought of it happening before; but the typical ES would have had just one particular level built in to it, so it couldn't adapt to using the crippled milling machine.

Sometimes the ES's precipitous fall into incompetent behavior is obvious, but sometimes its explanations remain dangerously plausible. Meta-rules about the system's area of competence can guard against this accidental misuse, but that is just a patch. A true solution would be to provide a broad KP so that (1) the plateau sloped off gently on all sides, and (2) we could hop from one ES's plateau or butte to another.

This brings up a point which is appropriate both to ESs and to the aesthetes (Section 8.1) as well. Both positions tacitly assume a kind of global consistency in the knowledge base. Inconsistencies may exist for a short period, but they are errors and must be tracked down and corrected. We expect, however, that this is just an idealized, simplified view of what will be required for intelligent systems. Namely, we advocate:

> **The Local Consistency Hypothesis.** There is no need—and probably not even any possibility—of achieving a *global* consistent unification of several expert systems' KPs (or, equivalently, for one very large KP). Large systems need *local consistency*.

> **The Coherence Hypothesis.** Moreover, whenever two large internally consistent chunks C_1, C_2 are similar, their heuristics and analogies should *cohere*; e.g., if the "going up" metaphor usually means "getting better" for C_1, then it should again mean "getting better" for C_2, or else it should not apply at all there.

As regards local consistency, consider how physics advanced for many decades with inconsistent particle and wave models for light. Local consistency is what permits each knowledge-space butte to be independent of the others; as with large office buildings, independent supports should make it easier for the whole structure to weather tremors such as local anomalies. In a locally consistent system, inferring an inconsistency is only slightly more serious than the usual sort of "dead-end" a searcher runs into; the system should be able to back up a bit and continue on. Intelligent behavior derives not from the razor's edge of absolute true versus absolute false—from perfect matching—but rather is suggested by plausibility heuristics and supported by empirical evidence.

Coherence is what keeps one from getting disoriented in stepping from one KP butte to its neighbor. Having the metaphors line up coherently can make the hops so small that one is unaware they have hopped at all: "Her academic career, her mood, and her prospects were all going up." See [22] for many more examples, and a more detailed discussion of this phenomenon. Coherence applies at the conceptual level, not just at the word level. It is not so much the *words* "going up" as the concept, the *script* of moving upwards, that applies coherently in so many situations.

9 Problems and solutions

Problem 1. *Possible "in-principle" limitations.* There are several extremes that one can point to where the Knowledge Principle and Breadth Hypothesis might be inapplicable or even harmful: perceptual and motor tasks; certain tasks which must be performed in small pieces of real time; tasks that involve things we don't yet know how to represent well (the word "yet" is very important here); tasks for which an adequate algorithm exists; tasks so poorly understood that no one can do it well yet; and (until our proposed large KP becomes a reality) tasks involving large amounts of common sense.

Just as we believe that language faculties will require a large consensual reality KP, we expect it to be invaluable in most of the image understanding process (beyond retina-level edge detection and similar operations).

Our response—in principle and in CYC—is to describe perception, emotion, motion, etc., down to some level of detail that enables the system to understand humans doing those things, and/or to be able to reason simply about them. As discussed under Problem 2, below, we let a large body of examples dictate what sorts of knowledge, and to what depth, are required.

A similar answer applies to all the items which we don't yet know very clearly how to represent. In building CYC, e.g., a large amount of effort in the first five years was spent on capturing an adequate body of knowledge (including representations and problem-solving strategies) for time, space, belief, substances, and so on. We did not set out to do this, the effort was driven completely empirically, completely by need, as we examined snippets of encyclopedia and newspaper articles and had to develop machinery to represent them and answer questions about them. Our response is a tactical hypothesis, not a strategic one; we would find it interesting if it is falsified, but the effect would be negligible on our overall research strategy.

Tasks which can be done without knowledge, or which require some that no one yet possesses, should be shied away from. One does not use a hammer to type with.

The huge KP mandated by the Breadth Hypothesis is AI's "mattress in the road". Knowing that we can go around it one more time, AI researchers build a system in six months that will perform adequately on a narrow version of task X; they don't pause for a decade to pull the mattress away. This research opportunity is finally being pursued; but until CYC or a similar project succeeds, the knowledge-based approach must shy away from tasks that involve a great deal of wide-ranging common sense or analogy.

The remainder of the problems in this section are primarily pragmatic, engineering problems, dealing with the mechanics of constructing systems and making them more usable. As can be seen from our response to the in-principle limitations, we personally view Problem 1 in that very same category! That is a view based on the EH, of course.

> **Problem 2.** *How exactly do we get the knowledge?* Knowledge must be extracted from people, from databases, from the intelligent systems' KPs themselves (e.g., thinking up new analogies), and from Nature directly. Each source of knowledge requires its own special extraction methods.

In the case of the CYC project, the goal is to capture the full breadth of human knowledge. To drive that acquisition task, Lenat and his team examine pieces of text (chosen from encyclopediae, newspapers, advertisements, and so on), sentence by sentence. They aren't just entering the facts stated, but—much more importantly—are encoding what the writer of that sentence assumed the reader already knew about the world. These are the facts and heuristics and simplified models of the world which one would need in order to understand the sentence, things which would be insulting or confusing for the writer to have actually stated explicitly (e.g., if coke is commercially consumed to turn ore into metal, then coke and ore must both be worth less than metal). They also generalize each of these as much as possible (e.g., the products of commercial processes are more valuable than their inputs). Another useful place they focus is the inter-sentential gap: in a historical article, what actions should the reader infer have happened between each sentence and the next one? Yet another focus: what questions should anyone be able to answer having just read that article? These foci drive the extraction process. Eventually, CYC itself began helping to add knowledge, by proposing analogues, extending existing analogies, and noticing gaps in nearly symmetric structures.

This methodology will collect, e.g., all the facts and heuristics about "Water" that newspaper articles assume their readers already know. This is in contrast to, for instance, naive physics and other approaches that aim to somehow capture a deeper theory of "Water" in all its various forms.

> **Problem 3.** *How do we adequately represent it?* Human experts

choose or devise representations that enable the significant features of the problem to remain distinguished, for the relevant connections to be quickly found, etc. Thus, one can reduce this to a special case of Problem 2, and try to elicit appropriate representations from human experts. CYC takes a pragmatic approach: when something proves awkward to represent, add new kinds of slots to make it compactly representable. In extreme cases, add a whole new representation language to the toolkit. Besides frames and "rules" and our formal constraint language (described above), we use stored images and neural nets as representation schemes. Images are useful for users to point at; e.g., to say something about the strike plate of a door lock—if you don't happen to know what it's called, but you could pick it out instantly given a photo of a door lock. Statistical space partitioning (neural nets) may be useful for certain kinds of user modeling (e.g., gesture level), and the CYC group is currently training one on examples of good analogizing, so as to suggest promising "hunches" of new analogies to investigate, an activity which CYC will then do symbolically.

The quality of the solutions to many of these "Problems", including this one, depend on the quality of our system's emerging ontology. What category boundaries are drawn; what individuals get explicitly represented; what is the vocabulary of predicates (slots) with which to describe and interrelate them, etc.? Much of the 1984–89 work on CYC has been to get an adequate global ontology; i.e., has been worrying about ways to represent knowledge; most of the 1990–94 work will be actually representing knowledge, entering it into CYC. That is why we have "only" a million entries of CYC's KP today, but expect dozens of times that many in 1994.

Problem 4. *How will inference be done in CYC?* The representation chosen will of course impact on what inference methods are easy or difficult to implement. Our inclination was, once again, to apply EH: when we encountered some kind of operation that needed to be performed often, but it was very inefficient, then we adjusted the representation or the inference methods available, or both. As with Problem 3, there is a temptation to early specialization: it is a local optimum, like swerving around a mattress in the road. Pulling this mattress aside means assembling a large repertoire of reasoning methods, and heuristics for choosing, monitoring, and switching among them. When we first prepared this article, such a toolkit of methods was merely an expectation; today (as described earlier), we have two dozen such inference engines, each with its own optimized justification maintenance system (and each capable of running "forward" or "backward").

To illustrate one of those inference methods briefly, consider
"transfersThrough". If I tell you that Michael's last name is Douglas, and Michael's father is Kirk, then you infer that Kirk's last name
is Douglas. If you see a car with snazzy wire wheels, and I tell you
that Fred owns that car, then you infer that Fred owns those wheels.
One could represent such inferencing by general if-then rules; for
instance, "If x's last name is y, and x's father is z, then guess that z's
last name is y." So many such rules were added to CYC, though, that
we defined a new inference template (predicate, slot, ...) called
"transfersThrough". There is a frame representing the transfers-
Through relationship, and one of its slots contains a definition in our
constraint language, of the form:

$$(\text{ForAll slots s1, s2}) \; ((\text{transfersThrough s1 s2}) \Leftrightarrow$$
$$[(\text{ForAll x, y, z}) \; (\text{s 1 x y}) \text{ and } (\text{s2 x z}) \Rightarrow (\text{s1 x z})])$$

We're often asked how we expect to efficiently "index"—find relevant partial matches—as the KP grows larger and larger. The
implicit assumption behind that question is that the problem gets
worse and worse as the KP size grows. Our answer therefore often
appears startling at first glance: wait until our programs *are* finding
many, far-flung analogies, but inefficiently, i.e. only through large
searches. Then investigate what additional knowledge *people* bring to
bear, to eliminate large parts of the search space in those cases.
Codify the knowledge so extracted, and add it to the system. This is a
combined application of the Difficult Problems Hypothesis and the
EH. It is a claim that the true nature of the indexing problem will
only become apparent—and solvable—in the context of a large
problem running in an already very large KP.

Earlier, we sketched an opportunistic (nonmonolithic) control
structure which utilizes items in the control-strategy region of the
KP. As with partial matching, we expect that meta-level control
mechanism to be more, and more easily, fleshed out as the system
grows.

In other words, the large and increasing size of the KP makes
certain tasks less difficult, due to having a large and representative
sample of cases one ought to try to make efficient. That holds for
choosing specialized inference engines, for meta-level control, and
for partial matching.

Problem 5. *How can someone interact "naturally" with KP systems?*
Knowledge-based systems built so far share with their knowledge-
free predecessors an intolerant rigidity of stylistic expression,
vocabulary, and concepts. They rarely accept synonyms and

pronouns, never metaphors, and only acknowledge users willing to wear a rigid grammatical straitjacket. The coming few years should witness the emergence of systems which begin to overcome this problem. As is only fitting, they will overcome it with knowledge: knowledge of the user, of the system's domain, of discourse, of metaphor. They will employ pictures, gestures, and sound as well as text, as means of input and output. Many individual projects (such as CYC) and expert system tools (such as KEE) are already moving in this direction.

Problem 6. *How can you combine several enterers'/systems' knowledge?* One solution is to sequentialize the entry, but it's not a good solution. Many EMYCIN-based programs designated someone to be the knowledge base czar, with whom all the other experts would discuss the knowledge to be entered. EURISKO, built on RLL, tried *explicitly* enforced semantics. Each slot was given a description of its intended use, constraints that could be checked statically or dynamically (e.g., each rule's If-maybe-relevant slot should take less CPU time to execute than its If-truly-relevant slot). When someone enters rules that violate that constraint, the system can complain to them, to get everyone back on track using the same semantics again. CYC extends this to *implicitly* enforced semantics: having such a large existing KP that copy and edit is the clearly favourite way of entering new knowledge. When one copies and edits an existing frame, virtually all of its slots' semantics (and even most of their values!) carry right over.

We are not talking about just text-editing here, but rather a problem-solving process in its own right, which CYC should monitor and assist with. Already, CYC makes guesses about which "slots" will exist on the new "frame", which entries on the value will carry over, which will need to be changed, if they're to be changed then will the new entries be idiosyncratic (e.g., monarch) or predictable based on other information about this new frame (e.g., majorExports).

Although this discussion has assumed that inconsistency should be detected and stamped out, there is a much more fundamental long-range solution to the problem of inconsistent KPs: live with them! Problem 7 describes this position:

Problem 7. *How should the system cope with inconsistency?* View the knowledge space, and hence the KP, not as one rigid body, but rather as a set of independently supported buttes. Each butte should be locally consistent, and neighboring buttes should be maximally coherent. These terms are described in Section 8.2. The power of such systems should derive, then, not from perfect matching, but rather from partial matching, heuristic guidance, and (ultimately) confirming empirical evidence. Systems such as we are describing must encompass several points of view; they are "open" in the sense of Hewitt [18]. It should be possible for new knowledge to compatibly and safely flow among them. At a much more exotic level, one can imagine mental immune systems providing (in the background) constant cross-checking, healthy skepticism, advice, and criticism.

Problem 8. *How can the system builder, and the system user, not get lost?* "Getting lost" is probably the right metaphor to extend here, because what they need to do is to successfully navigate their way through knowledge space, to find and/or extend the relevant parts. Many systems, including CYC, are experimenting with various exploration metaphors and orientation tools: helicoptering through semantic nets; exploring a museum with Alician entry into display cases and posters, etc. Both of these are physical spatial metaphors, which allow us to use kinesthetic memory to some extent, as the enterer or user gets more and more familiar with the layout of the KP.

On a typical day in mid-1989, ten to thirty people are logged into CYC's Knowledge Server, all actively adding to its KP simultaneously. Thus, one's world sometimes changes out from under one a bit, adding to the relevance of the (dis)orientation metaphor. For more elaborately scripted interface metaphors, see *True Names* [49], *Riding the Torch* [42], or *Knoesphere* [26]. For instance, the latter suggests clip-on filters to shade or highlight certain aspects of what was seen; models of groups and each individual user; and simulated tour-guides with distinct personalities.

Problem 9. *How big a fraction of "consensus reality" do you need to represent, before the "crossover" occurs and language understanding is a better knowledge entry paradigm?* We believe the answer is around 30–50%. Why? When communicating with an intelligent entity, having chosen some concept X, we would expect the "listener" to be familiar with X; if it fails several times in a row—often!—then it is missing too much of consensus reality. A similar argument applies to analogizing, and to generalizing. Now to have a 30% chance for the chosen analogue to be already known by the listener, he/she/it might have to know 30% of the concepts that are analogized to. But how *uniformly* are good analogues distributed in concept space? Lacking more data, we assume that they are uniformly distributed, which means the system should embody 30% of the full corpus of consensus reality. The distribution is quite possibly *not* uniform, which is why (the EH again) we need to build the KP and see.

10 Conclusion: beyond local maxima

Our position includes the statements:

- One must include *domain-specific* knowledge to solve difficult problems effectively.
- One must also include both *very general* knowledge (to fall back on) and very *wide-ranging* knowledge (to analogize to), to cope with novel situations.
- We already have plenty of theories about mechanisms of intelligence; we need to proceed empirically: go off and build large testbeds for performing, analogizing, ML, NL, . . .
- Despite the progress in learning, language understanding, and other areas of AI, *hand-crafting* is still the fastest way to get the knowledge into the program for at least the next several years.
- With a large KP of facts, heuristics, and methods, the fastest way will, after some years, tip toward NL (reading online textual material), and then eventually toward ML (learning by discovery).
- The hand-crafting and language-based learning phases may each take about one decade, partially overlapping (ending in 1994 and 2001, respectively, although the second stage never quite "ends"), culminating in a system with human-level breadth and depth of knowledge.

Each of those statements is more strongly believed than the one following it. There is overwhelming evidence for the KP and EH. There is strong evidence in favor of the BH. There is a moderate basis for our three-stage program. And there is suggestive evidence that it may be possible to carry out the programs this century.

As a partial application of the Breadth Hypothesis, consider the task of building a knowledge-based system covering most of engineering design. Interestingly, this task was chosen independently by the Japanese EDR project, by Bob Kahn's fledgling National Research Institute, and by Feigenbaum at Stanford. All three see this task as a moderate-term (~ 1994) goal. It is certainly much broader than any single expert system, yet much narrower than the universal knowledge base mandated by the BH.

Slightly narrower "lawyers' workstations" or "botanists' workstations", etc., are similar sorts of compromises (partial applications of BH) worth working on. They would possess a crown of very general knowledge, plus their specific field's next level of generalities, useful representations, etc., and some detailed knowledge including, e.g., methods for extracting and using entries in that field's online databases. These have the nice side effect of enticing the experts to use them, and then modify them and expand them.

The impact of systems mandated by the KP and BH cannot be overestimated. Public education, e.g., is predicated on the *un*availability of an intelligent, competent tutor for each individual for each hour of their life. AI will change that. Our present entertainment industry is built largely on passive viewing; AI will turn "viewers" into "doers". What will happen to society as the cost of wisdom declines, and society routinely applies the best of what it knows? Will a *knowledge utility* arise, like the electric utility, and how might it (and other AI infrastructures) effect what will be economically affordable for personal use?

When we give talks on expert systems, on commonsense reasoning, or on AI in general, we are often asked about the ethical issues involved, the *mental* "environmental impact" it will have, so to speak, as well as the direct ways it will alter everyday life. We believe that this technology is the analogue of language. We cannot hold AI back any more than primitive man could have suppressed the spread of speaking. It is too powerful a technology for that. Language marks the start of what we think of as civilization; we look back on pre-linguistic cultures as uncivilized, as comprised of intelligent apes but not really human beings yet. Can we even imagine what it was like when people couldn't talk with each other? Minsky recently quipped that a century from now people might look back on us and wonder "Can you imagine when they used to have libraries where the books didn't talk to each other?" Our distant descendants may look back on the synergistic man–machine systems that emerge from AI, as the natural dividing line between "real human beings" and "animals". We stand, at the end of the 1980s, at the interstice between the first era of intelligent systems (competent, thanks to the KP, but quite brittle and incombinable) and the second era, the era in which the Breadth Hypothesis will finally come into play.

> **Man–Machine Synergy Prediction.** In that "second era" of knowledge systems, the "system" will be reconceptualized as a kind of colleagular relationship between intelligent computer agents and intelligent people. Each will perform the tasks that he/she/it does best, and the intelligence of the system will be an *emergent* of the collaboration.

The interaction may be sufficiently seamless and natural that it will hardly matter to anyone which skills, which knowledge, and which ideas resided where (in the head of the person or the knowledge structures of the computer). It would be inaccurate to identify Intelligence, then, as being "in the program". From such man–machine systems will emerge intelligence and competence surpassing the unaided human's. Beyond that threshold, in turn, lie wonders which we (as unaided humans) literally cannot today imagine.

Appendix A. Goals and strategies for AI research

In Section 6, we briefly touched on the common confusion between AI goals and AI strategies. The next two sections list nine of each. As we mentioned in the body of the paper, much confusion in our field stems from several entries appearing on both lists. If one researcher chooses, say, the ultimate goal of language understanding, then they could approach that strategically in several ways. E.g., humans first learn language by discovery, by imitating others' sounds, noting correlations and inducing simple vocabulary and grammar rules. Later, as we enter school, we further improve our language abilities by taking English classes, i.e., by discussing in natural language the fine points of English vocabulary and grammar and composition.

Scientific disciplines not only adopt a paradigm, in the early stages they are partitioned into subfields by paradigm. If more than one paradigm remains viable for any length of time, it will soon come to see itself as a different discipline altogether and split off; AI faced this around 1970 with cognitive psychology, and is facing this again now with robotics and vision. People can't mentally focus on too much at once, and paradigms provide some of the obligatory cognitive simplifying.

All 9×9 pairs of the form $\langle$goal, strategy$\rangle$ could in principle be separate paradigms. Today there are only a small fraction of that number, and the groupings that have developed are in many cases poorly matched; e.g., all pairs of the form $\langle x,$ Learning$\rangle$ unioned with $\langle$Learning, $x\rangle$, come together for machine learning workshops every year. This leads to confusion and mis-communication—often unrealized by both parties! Let's give an illustration of this phenomenon, still in the domain of machine learning. When they say they are working on analogy, they might mean either one of the following:

(1) They are using analogy as a strategy to pursue some other AI goal G. For instance, they might be building a program whose goal is to parse or disambiguate English sentences by analogy.
(2) They are using some other strategy S, such as knowledge engineering, as the power source in a program whose task is to discover and flesh out analogies. In that case their program's final output would be a data structure that humans somehow recognize as symbolizing an analogy; but that data structure might be built by a set of if-then rules, or a neutral net, or by talking with a human being, etc.

The trouble is that, today, they are equally likely to mean they're pursuing analogy as a strategy or as a goal.

A.1 Nine ultimate goals of AI

We share, or are sympathetic to, almost all of these:

- *Understand human cognition.* The goal is to understand how people think, not to have machine artifacts to put to work. Try for a deeper knowledge of human memory, problem-solving abilities, learning, decision making in general, etc.
- *Cost-effective automation.* The goal is to replace humans at various tasks requiring intelligence. This goal is met by programs that perform as well as the humans currently on the job; it doesn't matter if the programs think like people or not. The harder the problems it can solve, and the faster it solves them, the smarter it is.
- *Cost-effective intelligence amplification.* The goal is to build mental prostheses that help us think better, faster, deeper, more clearly, ... Science's goal—and measure of success—is how much it augments human being's leg muscles, immune system, vocal cords, and (in this case) brain. This goal further divides depending on whose performance is being so amplified: do we want to amplify the average person's ability to diagnose disease, or the average GP's ability, or the world's best diagnostician's?
- *Superhuman intelligence.* The goal is to build programs which exceed human performance. Crossing that particular threshold could lead to an explosion of progress: technological innovation in manufacturing, theoretical breakthroughs, superhuman teachers and researchers (including AI researchers), and so on.
- *General problem solving.* Be able to solve—or at least plausibly attack—a broad range of problems, including some from fields you've never even heard of before. It doesn't matter if the programs perfectly fit human performance data, nor does it matter if they are at an expert's level. The point is that intelligent creatures can get somewhere on almost any problem; intelligence is flexibility and breadth of mind, not depth in some narrow area.
- *Coherent discourse.* This is similar to the Turing test. The goal is to competently communicate with people, using complete sentences in some natural human language. A system is intelligent iff it can carry on a coherent dialogue.
- *Autonomy.* This goal holds that a system is intelligent iff it can, on its own initiative, do things in the real world. This is to be contrasted with, say, merely planning in some abstract space, or "performing" in a simulated world, or advising a human who then goes off and does things. The idea is that the real world is always so much more complex than our models of it, that it is the only fair test of the programs we claim to be intelligent.

- *Learning (induction).* This goal is to have a program that chooses what data to gather and how; gathers it; generalizes (or otherwise converts) its experiences into useful new beliefs, methods, heuristics and representations; and reasons analogically.
- *Information.* Having stored lots of facts about a wide range of topics. This is more of a "straw man" view than the others, as it could be satisfied by an online textual encyclopedia, or even by a hardcopy one! The other views all require the intelligent entity not merely possess information but also use it appropriately.

A.2 Broad strategies for achieving those goals

Most of these are not *our* strategies:

- *Duplicate low-level cognitive performance.* Get your program to duplicate even micro-level measurements that psychologists have gathered from human subjects, such as memory storage and recall times, STM size, forgetting rate, errors, etc. Hopefully, if you do that, then your program's internal mechanisms will be similar to humans', and your program will be able to scale up the same way that human low-level mechanisms scale up (even though we don't know how that is, we won't have to know if we get the lowest level built the same way). One variation is to use slightly less low-level mechanisms (such as Soar's chunking), but still the idea is that repeated application of simple IPS processes let intelligence emerge.
- *Duplicate low-level structure.* Mimicking the human brain's architecture will lead to mimicking its functionality. This strategy traditionally makes the further assumption that McCulloch–Pitts threshold logic is the right level at which to abstract brain cell structure (rather than, e.g., at the chemical and enzymatic levels). It gained attention as perceptrons, and now enjoys a renaissance due to the promise that VLSI technology holds for soon producing parallel neural nets of immense size.
- *Simulate a society of mind.* This is yet another variant on the "duplicate and hope" strategy, but this one is not so low-level as either of the previous two strategies. Build a program that consists of hundreds of specialized mental beings or actors—think of them as kludged knowledge sources—and marshall them to solve problems by cooperating and communicating among themselves. This is how Nature managed to evolve us, and it may be the easiest way for us to in turn evolve AI.
- *Knowledge engineering.* Talk with human experts who perform the task, and extract from them the facts, representations, methods, and rules of thumb that they employ in doing the task. Encode these in a running prototype system, and then extract more and more knowledge, as the program runs and makes mistakes which the expert can easily translate—in context—into additional pieces of knowledge that should have been

341

in the system all along. Have faith that this incremental knowledge acquisition will attain an adequate level of competence.

- *Natural language understanding.* Have a program talk with people, read articles, etc. People achieve intelligence that way; so can machines!
- *Learning (induction).* Build a program that can learn. Then let it. People get to be smart by learning, starting from a tabula rasa; so can machines.
- *Formalizing and advanced reasoning.* Marshall a toolkit of sophisticated deductive procedures for maintaining consistency and inferring new assertions. Having such a set of snazzy mechanisms will be necessary and sufficient. The strong version of this view says "It worked for physics; we must strive to find the 'Maxwell's equations of thought'." The mild version is more conservative: "As you formalize, you find the gaps in your understanding."
- *Intelligence amplification.* Build some intelligent interfaces that allow us to write programs more easily, or synthesize ideas more rapidly, etc. Then let these improved man–machine systems loose on the problem of achieving AI, whichever goal we choose to define it. In other words, instead of tackling the AI task right away, let's spend time getting prostheses that let us be smarter, then we'll come back to working on "real" AI.
- *Superhuman intelligence.* An extreme form of the previous strategy. Build a program that does AI research just slightly better than people do, and then go sit on a beach while it investigates low-level cognition, or language understanding, or whatever your chosen AI goal is.

Notes

This article was originally prepared in May 1987 for the MIY Workshop on Foundations of AI the following month, and issued then as MCC Technical Report AI-126-87. A very much shortened version was given as an invited paper at IJCAI-87 in Milan, August 1987. It was edited in 1989 in preparation for this publication.

1 Russell and others started a similar codification in the 1920s, but that movement was unfortunately led astray by Wittgenstein (see [41]).
2 Based on research performed at Atari Research Labs, in conjunction with *Encyclopaedia Britannica*, during 1983.
3 Reported at the First Workshop on Electronic Dictionaries, Tokyo, November 1988; proceedings available.
4 Back of the envelope calculation performed for Bob Kahn, at NRI planning meeting, 1985.

References

[1] G. Abrett and M.H. Burstein. The KREME knowledge editing environment, in: *Proceedings Workshop on Knowledge Acquisition for Knowledge-Based Systems*, Banff, Alta (1986).
[2] S. Amarel, On representations and modelling in problem solving and on future

directions for intelligent systems, RCA Labs Scientific Rept. No. 2, Princeton, NJ (1967).

[3] W.W. Bledsoe, Non-resolution theorem proving, *Artif. Intell.* **9** (1977) 1–35.

[4] W.W. Bledsoe, I had a dream: AAAI Presidential Address, *AI Mag.* **7** (1) (1986) 57–61.

[5] A. Borning and S. Weyer, A prototype electronic encyclopedia, *ACM Trans. Off. Inf. Syst.* **3** (1) (1985) 63–88.

[6] R.A. Brooks, Intelligence without representation, *Artif. Intell.* **47** (1991) 139–159, this volume.

[7] B.G. Buchanan, G. Sutherland and E.A. Feigenbaum, Heuristic Dendral: a program for generating explanatory hypotheses in organic chemistry; in: B. Meltzer and D. Michie, eds., *Machine Intelligence* **4** (American Elsevier, New York, 1969) 209–254.

[8] W.J. Clancey, Dialogue management for rule-based tutorials, in: *Proceedings IJCAI-79*, Tokyo (1979) 155–161.

[9] R. Davis and D.B. Lenat, *Knowledge Based Systems in Artificial Intelligence* (McGraw-Hill, New York, 1982).

[10] EDR (Japan Electronic Dictionary Research Institute, LTD), Tokyo, Japan, Personal communication (1987).

[11] L. Erman, F. Hayes-Roth, V. Lesser and D.R. Reddy, Hearsay-II speech understanding system, *Comput. Surv.* **12** (1980) 224–225.

[12] E.A. Feigenbaum. The art of artificial intelligence: themes and case studies in knowledge engineering, in: *Proceedings IJCAI-77*, Cambridge, MA (1977).

[13] J.A. Fodor and Z.W. Pylyshyn, How direct is visual perception? *Cognition* **9** (1981) 139–196.

[14] P. Friedland, Knowledge-based experiment design in molecular genetics, in: *Proceedings IJCAI-79*, Tokyo (1979) 285–287.

[15] H. Gelernter, J.R. Hansen and D.W. Loveland, Empirical exploration of the geometry theorem machine, in: *Proceedings Western Joint Computer Conference* (1960) 143–147.

[16] M.R. Genesereth, The use of design descriptions in automated diagnosis. *Artif. Intell.* **24** (1984) 411–436.

[17] M.R. Genesereth and N.J. Nilsson, *Logical Foundations of Artificial Intelligence* (Morgan Kaufmann, Los Altos, CA, 1987).

[18] C. Hewitt, Open systems, AI Memo 691, MIT, Cambridge, MA (1982).

[19] Japan Electronic Dictionary Research Institute, Concept dictionary, Tech. Rept. TR-009, EDR, Tokyo (1988).

[20] T.S. Kuhn, *The Structure of Scientific Revolutions* (University of Chicago Press, Chicago, IL, 2nd ed., 1970).

[21] I. Lakatos, *Proofs and Refutations* (Cambridge University Press, Cambridge, 1976).

[22] G. Lakoff and M. Johnson, *Metaphors We Live By* (University of Chicago Press, Chicago, IL, 1980).

[23] P. Langley, J. Zytkow, H.A. Simon and G. Bradshaw, The search for regularity: four aspects of scientific discovery, in: R.S. Michalski, J.G. Carbonell and T.M. Mitchell, eds., *Machine Learning* 2 (Tioga, Palo Alto, CA, 1985).

[24] D.B. Lenat, Beings: Knowledge as interacting experts, in: *Proceedings of IJCAI-75*. Tblisi, USSR (1975).

[25] D.B. Lenat, The nature of heuristics, *Artif. Intell.* **19** (1982) 189–249.

[26] D.B. Lenat, A. Borning, D. McDonald, C. Taylor and S. Weyer, Knoesphere: expert systems with encyclopedic knowledge, in: *Proceedings IJCAI-83*, Karlsruhe, FRG (1983).

[27] D.B. Lenat and J.S. Brown, Why AM and EURISKO appear to work, *Artif. Intell.* **23** (1983) 269–294.

[28] D.B. Lenat and R.V. Guha, *Building Large Knowledge-Based Systems: Representation and Inference in the CYC Project* (Addison-Wesley, Reading, MA, 1990); portions also available as: The world according to CYC, MCC Tech. Rept. ACA-AI-300-88, Austin, TX (1988).

[29] S. Marcus, J. McDermott and T. Wang, Knowledge acquisition for constructive systems, in: *Proceedings IJCAI-85*, Los Angeles, CA (1985).

[30] J. McCarthy, Programs with common sense, in: *Proceedings Symposium on Mechanisation of Thought Processes*, Teddington, England (H.M. Stationery Office, London, 1959); reprinted in: M. Minsky, ed., *Semantic Information Processing* (MIT Press, Cambridge, MA, 1968).

[31] J. McCarthy, We need better standards for AI research, *AI Mag.* **5** (3) (1984) 7–8.

[32] J. McDermott, RI: an expert in the computer systems domain, in: *Proceedings AAAI-80*, Stanford, CA (1980) 269–271.

[33] M. Minsky, *Society of Mind* (Simon and Schuster, New York, 1985).

[34] J. Mostow, Searching for operational concept descriptions in BAR, MetalEX, and EBG, in: *Proceedings Fourth International Workshop on Machine Learning*, Irvine, CA (1987) 376–382.

[35] A. Newell, The knowledge level, *AI Mag.* **1** (1) (1980).

[36] A. Newell and J.C. Shaw, Programming the logic theory machine, in: *Proceedings Western Joint Computer Conference* (1957) 230–240.

[37] A. Newell and H.A. Simon, *Human Problem Solving* (Prentice-Hall, Englewood Cliffs, NJ, 1972).

[38] P. Norvig, Inference in text understanding, in: *Proceedings AAAI-87*, Seattle, WA (1987) 561–565.

[39] G. Polya, *How to Solve It* (Princeton University Press, Princeton, NJ, 1957).

[40] H. Pople, Heuristic methods for imposing structure on ill-structured problems: the structuring of medical diagnosis, in: P. Szolovitz, ed., *Artificial Intelligence in Medicine* (Westview Press, Boulder, CO, 1982) 119–190.

[41] B. Russell, *Human Knowledge: Its Scope and Limitations* (Unwin, 1948).

[42] N. Spinrad, *Riding the Torch* (Bluejay Books, New York, 1984).

[43] M. Stefik, The knowledge medium, *AI Mag.* **7** (1) (1986) 34–46.

[44] M. Stickel, A non-clausal connection graph resolution theorem-proving program, in: *Proceedings AAAI-82*, Pittsburgh, PA (1982) 229–233.

[45] W. Strunk and E.B. White, *The Elements of Style* (Macmillan, New York, 3rd ed., 1979).

[46] D. Subramanian, A theory of justified reformulations, Ph.D. Thesis, Computer Science Department, Stanford University, Stanford, CA (1988).

[47] G.J. Sussman, *A Computer Model of Skill Acquisition* (American Elsevier, New York, 1975).

[48] A. Tversky, P. Slovic and D. Kahneman, eds., *Judgement under Uncertainty: Heuristics and Biases* (Cambridge University Press, Cambridge, 1982).

[49] V. Vinge, *True Names* (Bluejay, New York, 1984).

[50] What's News, *Wall Street J.* **LXXIX** (65) (April 7, 1987) 1.

Part II

APPROACHES: SUBSYMBOLIC ARTIFICIAL INTELLIGENCE

Section 2.1: Historical context
Section 2.2: Developments

INTRODUCTION

The Emergence of Connectionism

Ronald Chrisley

1 Historical context

As discussed in the Introduction to Part I of this volume, a substantial development in the concept of artificial intelligence found its apotheosis in the Physical-Symbol System Hypothesis of Newell and Simon. After seeing the strengths of the approach, it is not unreasonable to wonder: how could the hypothesis fail to be true? What could artificial intelligence be other than the construction of an adequate symbol-processing machine?

Connectionist artificial intelligence has gone a long way to answering that question, to showing how subsymbolic artificial intelligence is coherent and perhaps the only way to proceed. To be sure, there are many points of agreement between connectionism (the most influential form of subsymbolic artificial intelligence) and symbolic artificial intelligence – the emphasis on representations; on a distinction between inner (subject) and outer (object); the usual practice of modelling time, if at all, as a discrete sequence; conceiving intelligence as a process that occurs between (spatially and temporally) perception and action – points which are themselves questioned by the approaches covered in Part I next Volume. But the differences between the two are significant and numerous. Connectionism questions the idea that the way for a designer to get a machine to behave intelligently is to first analyse the behaviour into a sequence of steps, and then give a representation of this sequence to the machine, which then interprets the list and behaves accordingly. Instead, connectionism places an emphasis on the system learning for itself the best way to act or even represent the situation. Along with this goes the idea that a designer cannot anticipate every situation in which an aspiringly intelligent artefact may find itself, so the only way to provide for intelligence is to give the system adaptivity, rather than a static program. Defenders of symbolism would point out that symbolic artificial intelligence programs are not static: they allow learning in the form of new items being added to memory (e.g. a new chunk in SOAR, a new frame in CYC) or modifications being made to what is already there (e.g. a change of value for a slot in a frame). In order to see what is new about the adaptivity in connectionist artificial intelligence, one must see why it is *sub*symbolic. Hofstadter makes the point by claiming that the key to artificial intelligence is the processes that in humans occur "below the 100 millisecond level – the time it takes you to recognize your mother". But the sense in which connectionism is intended to be more fundamental than symbolism is not just temporal, but also semantic. The aspects of the world to which connectionist representations and operations correspond are not the everyday conceptual world of objects, properties and events. The semantic values are subconceptual because it is believed that the conceptual world can be recovered as particular combinations and manipulations of these finer-grained semantic features. One final underwriting of the "below" metaphor is the bottom-up connectionist methodology of making an intelligent artefact by trying to understand the physical basis of human intelligence (the brain), rather than proceeding with a top-level notion of human intelligence and trying to discover a mechanism that will realise it.

Aizawa's paper is a response to a well-known history of the rise of connectionism by the brothers Dreyfus (it is not included here because, *inter alia*, Dreyfus' views are given extensive coverage in Volume III, Part II, section 2, and Aizawa gives an extensive recapitulation). The upshot of the Dreyfus and Dreyfus account was that connectionism was not based on the Western philosophical tradition, but on neuroscience. Thus, it was not rooted in logic, rationalism or holism. Aizawa argues that this is incorrect on all counts. He gives an alternative history of connectionism which attempts to demonstrate connectionism's roots in the Western philosophical tradition. But he is at his strongest when he addresses the specific points of Dreyfus and Dreyfus. First, he shows that McCulloch and Pitts were patrons of logic, and points out the logical nature of their influential paper (included in Volume I, Part II). Aizawa claims that rationalism (defined in Dreyfus and Dreyfus as the view that "understanding a domain consists in having a theory of that domain") is implied by at least some connectionist accounts, such as interactive activation networks. But even non-localist networks with patterns distributed across hidden units do not support the Dreyfus brothers' position. The semantic features which these units represent are not everyday, invariant features, which classifies connectionism as holistic according to Dreyfus and Dreyfus' definition of the term, but Aizawa contends that holism, so defined, is not incompatible with the Western philosophical tradition: nowhere do Hobbes, Descartes and Leibniz insist that the atoms of thought be everyday or invariant. Finally, much connectionist work proceeds independently of neuroscience. Aizawa's positive account is that symbolic artificial intelligence (he just calls it "AI", as if there were no connectionist artificial intelligence) and connectionist artificial intelligence are best differentiated by their views on what counts as a cognitive process. He notes that although traditional AI is representationalist through and through, he constructs a thought experiment to show that this need not be the case. His speculations here seem to resonate strongly with the recent anti-representational rhetoric in mobile robotics, evolutionary and otherwise, though he oddly does not cite any of this work. The strangeness is acute in his choice of "G" as the name for a hypothetical program which allows a modeller to "generate a working AI program without having to understand the domain in terms of data structures and program code", since the "G" could very well stand for "genetic algorithm".

Another challenge to the generally accepted history of connectionism is made by Copeland and Proudfoot, who show that "Turing was probably the first person to consider building computing machines out of simple, neuron-like elements connected together into networks in a largely random manner". Rather than the simple "first McCulloch and Pitts, then Rosenblatt" account, Copeland and Proudfoot argue that a better history would be: Turing 1936, McCulloch and Pitts 1943, Turing 1948, Uttley 1956 (*inter alia*), and only then Rosenblatt 1957. Turing developed the now-familiar notion of "propagation" and "activation" rules, and his research was an advance on the McCulloch and Pitts networks in its investigation of learning, and use of thresholds and weighted connections, all notions definitive of connectionist artificial intelligence. Turing even envisaged the dominant connectionist practice of simulating the training of such networks using a conventional digital computer. There is further discussion of Turing's 1948 paper in the Brooks selection in Volume III, article 50.

The term "connectionist" was invented by Rosenblatt, the inventor of the Perceptron, a simple neuron-like pattern recognition unit that was to have great influence on the development of a non-symbolic approach to artificial intelligence. His paper locates the task of understanding (and therefore reproducing) what he calls "biological intelligence" with the task of understanding information: how and in what form it is stored, is remembered, and influences behaviour. He distinguishes representational from non-representational approaches to this task, placing his own work in the latter camp. This is at odds with more recent views of connectionism, which agree that it is at root representational. Rosenblatt chooses a statistical, rather than logical, formalism for the analysis of the Perceptron, seeing that ignorance of the precise structure of the system to be modelled left him no choice. He blames the limitations of similar, earlier work (such as McCulloch and Pitts, von Neumann and Minsky) on a failure to understand how biological systems actually work, and thus aligns himself with the work of Hebb, Hayek and Uttley. He proposes his "theory of statistical separability" as a way of overcoming these limitations. In particular, Rosenblatt shows that under certain conditions the Perceptron could learn to classify stimuli in a way that facilitated generalisation: the ability to correctly classify stimuli not previously encountered, a desideratum that would become a focus of connectionist research. He also emphasised the distributed nature of connectionist memory. Rosenblatt puts his work forward as being more parsimonious, verifiable, and as having more explanatory power than what had gone before. In particular, the variables and laws of the Perceptron are meant to correspond to entities "already present in the structure of physical and biological science", thus avoiding mere curve-fitting and explanatory circularity. But these are not central concerns for artificial intelligence.

Perceptrons were notoriously discredited in 1969 by Minsky and Papert when, in their eponymous book, they established a dilemma: interesting functions (those not linearly separable, such as exclusive disjunction) could not be computed by Perceptrons with no (in today's parlance) hidden layers. Although such functions can be computed by networks with hidden layers, at that time there was no known, provably effective learning algorithm for such Perceptrons. This limited the prospects for connectionist artificial intelligence: one could have either computational power, or learning, but not both. The discovery, in the early 1980s, of learning algorithms for networks with hidden layers was primarily responsible for the resurgence of interest in connectionist, and therefore subsymbolic, AI.

Selfridge's paper, on his influential Pandemonium system, is included not so much for being an intellectual advance in the concept of connectionist artificial intelligence, but because it provides a snapshot of what connectionist work was like after Rosenblatt but before its resurgence in the 1980s. That said, Pandemonium did incorporate a novel combination of standard connectionist ideas with a limited form of evolutionary learning: "demons" (independently active processing units) which are found to be "worthy" are mutated and reproduced; instead of mutation ("fission"), there is also a "conjugation" procedure which combines two worthy demons: an operation analogous to crossover in genetic algorithms. But selection is performed directly on the demons – there is no genotype/phenotype distinction. The subsymbolism of Pandemonium is illustrated in the application considered in the paper: Morse translation. Rather than starting with the symbolic primitives of dots and dashes, Selfridge focuses on the task of identifying these dots and dashes from real signals.

Boden emphasises the crucial role that McCulloch and Pitts played in the genesis of both symbolic and subsymbolic artificial intelligence. From this she concludes that in some sense (a sense which is not made entirely clear), GOFAI (good old-fashioned artificial intelligence, after Haugeland) and connectionism are the same. It would be a weak argument indeed if she only relied on the common origin of the two. But she further supports her claim by arguing that much connectionist work has been influenced by GOFAI. Unfortunately, the only detailed example she gives is the work of David Marr, who was not a paradigmatic connectionist in any sense, and particularly not someone who was doing work in subsymbolic artificial intelligence. Boden's discussion seems to make the "mistake" of comparing symbolic artificial intelligence with connectionism as an explanatory model in psychology – until one realises that for Boden, artificial intelligence is not as narrow a notion as it is being conceived in this book. For her, it embraces using computers not only in the attempt to create minds, but also in the attempt to understand human minds. So her contention that serial processors are needed in order to model higher aspects of human thought may be true, and yet irrelevant to the artificial intelligence researcher who is trying to create an artificial mind rather than explain existing ones. But some of her points do carry across to non-psychological artificial intelligence: How can a connectionist system exhibit the systematicity characteristic of intelligence? If we do not understand how a connectionist system is achieving some task, how can we make incremental alterations to our design, rather than having to start all over again and retrain the system from scratch? Boden expects that answering these questions will require further interaction between connectionism and GOFAI.

2 Developments

Hofstadter's subsymbolic manifesto starts by claiming that much of intelligence is perception, and by calling for a return to the toy domains of early work in the field of artificial intelligence. But his central claim is that the essence of intelligence is what might be termed subcognition: the processes which underlie conscious mental activity such as rule application. Cognition (and presumably intelligence) is a phenomenon which emerges out of the collective behaviour of active subsymbols, and therefore cannot be programmed directly – cognition is not computation (although presumably subcognition might be). The problem of symbolic artificial intelligence is that every low-level event has a high-level reason for its occurrence; this rules out the possibility of active subsymbols. Hofstadter concludes from this that "we cannot decide what we will next think of", but it seems that this is a mistake: the will may also be an emergent phenomenon, and thus should not be identified with conscious rule application either. Although he is not really a connectionist, and he sometimes is more concerned with understanding how humans in particular have intelligence, rather than understanding intelligence in general so that an artefact may have it, Hofstadter's critique of symbolic artificial intelligence is a clear and compelling call to subsymbolism. The postscript traces these ideas back to Poincaré (although his observations did not embrace the notion of an artificial mind), ties them in with the connectionist research that was blossoming at the time, argues against the requirement of embodiment for intelligence, and responds to a reply that Simon made to the main text.

The prevalence of a particular kind of hardware, that of conventional digital computers, has restricted the success of work in artificial intelligence, according to Waltz. This is for two reasons. On the one hand, von Neumann architecture has led to an undue emphasis on search, and it has contributed to the neglect of subsymbolic issues such as the organisation of memory. On the other hand, conventional hardware lacks the scalability and parallelism that is required for true intelligence. Waltz closes with some calculations concerning the hardware necessary to support human-level intelligence.

Perhaps the most articulate statement of subsymbolism is provided by Smolensky. Although he begins his discussion explicitly addressing the issue of connectionist artificial intelligence, true to connectionist form he soon slips into a discussion of the best account of human cognition. He notes that the demand for symbolic knowledge is a cultural phenomenon, leaving open the possibility that individual, "intuitive" processing is subsymbolic. He rejects the idea that the connectionist level is the neural level, instead seeing it as being in-between the neural and the conceptual. Smolensky's "connectionist dynamical system hypothesis" agrees with much of the viewpoint expressed in Volume III, Part I, section 2, and Smolensky defends it against some objections. He insists, however, that it is only by construing symbolism and subsymbolism semantically that one can see that a substantial issue is at stake. However, room is still left for a symbiosis between symbolism and subsymbolism, with each paradigm illuminating the other.

Another form of ecumenicism is proffered in Minsky's Japan prize lecture. He argues that artificial intelligence has held itself back by hoping for a simple, unitary architecture inspired by the mathematical foundations of physics. Instead, understanding intelligence is probably more like biology: complex and involving a host of diverse processes. Thus, we should not rely on just one representational scheme, but design systems that use multiple schemes and shift between them as needed (cf. Sloman 1985). Minsky then puts forward the Society of Mind approach to artificial intelligence (see article 33 in Part I of this Volume) as a way to steer this middle course between symbolism and connectionism. Accordingly, the paper takes the form of a discussion of how one might "augment symbolic systems with connectionist machinery", followed by a discussion of ways that connectionist systems would benefit from symbolic structure. However, the former section is brief, and does not really match its description; a call for the classification of objects according to how they are used, while welcome, is not exactly a call for connectionism. Rather, Minsky's real concerns are expressed in the section on the limitations of connectionism. He identifies two trade-offs that connectionism tends to respond to with non-optimal extremism: parallelism vs. distributed representation, and specialisation vs. flexibility. Minsky also notes the problems that connectionism has with binding features to objects, and with semantic opacity, which prevents knowledge from being used elsewhere. Although insightful, his writing here lacks an authoritative tone, since he fails to mention any specific connectionist work (or indeed, any work other than his own. For example, Minsky made the last point, about connectionist systems not reusing knowledge, during an informal discussion at the first International Conference on Neural Networks (San Diego, 1987), a discussion in which I participated. I countered that Minsky's claim was false;

I cited as an example Fukushima's Neocognitron work (Fukushima 1980), which copies successful weights from one part of the network to other modules. One reason why Minsky might be slow to recognise networks like this as answering his call is that he may be making a mistake common in artificial intelligence and cognitive science: confounding the artefact's conceptualisation of the world with the theorist's – not realising that the system's "take" on the world will almost certainly be different from his own (see the paper by Smith in Volume III, article 49). Thus, for Minsky, if a bit of artefact structure is semantically opaque *to him*, then duplicating it will not count as reusing knowledge, since *he* does not see it as knowledge. In this sense, symbolic artificial intelligence has an anti-realist streak: the only extant ways of seeing the world are the ones we (or I) can experience. A connectionist would be more of a realist, recognising the existence of ways of seeing the world which we ourselves do not (cannot?) experience. Thus, the mentioned duplication may be an instance of what Minsky is calling for (knowledge reuse) even if we cannot express in conceptual–linguistic terms what the content of the duplicated knowledge is. But even this view is not radical enough. A central idea of subsymbolism is that opacity applies to operations as well as representations – an operation may be one of "knowledge duplication" if that is its functional upshot – even if it is not a literal duplication of weight or activity patterns. Where Minsky is right is that few connectionists think of what they are doing in these terms, and yet they would benefit from doing so (a point which Smolensky also makes, as we have seen).

Minsky's paper also demonstrates the problematic role that introspection plays in modern artificial intelligence methodology: on the one hand, most of Minsky's statements concerning the nature of intelligence and what is required derive solely from his own awareness of what he is doing when he is thinking. And yet, when considering the possibility of sub-networks monitoring other sub-networks, he states that "the insights we gain from meditation and other forms of self-examination are genuine only infrequently".

The paper draws to a close with a number of interesting observations. Minsky anticipates the evolutionary approach of Volume III, Part I, section 3: "designing an artificial mind will be much like evolving an animal". Later he proposes an even more radical shift in methodology, from engineering to art:

> I expect that the future art of brain design will have to be more like sculpturing than our present craft of programming . . . ; perhaps this better resembles politics, sociology or management than present-day engineering.

This is significant in several ways, including the rejection of an individualist conception of the artificial intelligence project, since "no one will be able to keep track of all the details". So, while the design constraint is kept as a way of distinguishing natural from artificial intelligence creation, it is a de-individualised notion of design: for something to be an artificial intelligence, it need not have an architecture as envisaged by any one person.

Finally, we see again the notion of human intelligence as flawed and imperfect, implying the existence of some non-actualised norm of intelligence to which we aspire, and fail, but which an artificial intelligence, through our design, might better approximate: Minsky speaks of "suppressing the emergence of serious bugs", which apparently in humans include such phenomena as depression.

References

Dreyfus, H. and Dreyfus, S. (1988) "Making a Mind versus Modeling a Brain: Artificial Intelligence back at a branchpoint", *Daedalus: Journal of the American Academy of Arts and Sciences* 117(1): 15–44.

Fukushima, K. (1980) "Neocognitron: A Self-Organizing Neural Network Model for a Mechanism of Pattern Recognition Unaffected by Shift in Position", *Biological Cybernetics* 36(4): 193–202.

Minsky, M. and Papert, S. (1969) *Perceptrons*, Cambridge, MA: MIT Press.

Sloman, A. (1985) "Why we need many knowledge representation formalisms", in M. Bramer (ed.), *Research and Development in Expert Systems*, Cambridge: Cambridge University Press, pp. 163–83.

Section 2.1: Historical context

37

CONNECTIONISM AND ARTIFICIAL INTELLIGENCE

History and Philosophical Interpretation

Kenneth Aizawa

Source: *Journal of Experimental & Theoretical Artificial Intelligence* 4 (1992): 295–313.

Abstract. Hubert and Stuart Dreyfus have tried to place connectionism and artificial intelligence in a broader historical and intellectual context. This history associates connectionism with neuroscience, conceptual holism, and non-rationalism, and artificial intelligence with conceptual atomism, rationalism, and formal logic. The present paper argues that the Dreyfus account of connectionism and artificial intelligence is both historically and philosophically misleading.

Keywords: Dreyfus, connectionism, atomism, holism, rationalism, neuroscience

1 Introduction

Philosophers from time to time attempt to fit scientific ideas into a broader historical context so as to support a philosophical analysis of the significance of those scientific ideas. Hubert and Stuart Dreyfus (1988) have recently undertaken such an effort with regards to connectionism and classical artificial intelligence (AI). They argue that connectionism has historical and conceptual affiliations with what they call 'holism', 'non-rationalism', and neuroscience, where AI has historical and conceptual affinities to 'atomism', rationalism, logic, and traditional philosophy. Unfortunately, the Dreyfus brothers have brought forth a very selective history of connectionism in support of their bold philosophical contentions about connectionism and AI. The present paper seeks both to revise and refine the Dreyfus account. After a review of the somewhat impressionistic Dreyfus account in section 2, section 3 will present a more complete history of connectionism that loosens connectionism's ties to holism, non-rationalism, and even neuroscience. It follows from this that connectionism *per se* does not have any necessary conceptual ties with either holism, non-rationalism, or even neuroscience. Section 4 will consider the Dreyfus view from a more purely philosophical perspective. The principal concern of this section will be an examination of the relationship between AI and the rejection of holism. What we find is that the rejection or acceptance of holism is independent of the type of computational device thought to be instantiated by the brain. Instead, it depends on the possession of a particular conception of what is necessary for a process to count as cognitive.

2 The Dreyfus intellectual history

According to many contemporary accounts, the vigorous intellectual controversies surrounding connectionism and AI go beyond mere scientific questions of nodes, activation values, and weights, versus computer programs and data structures. At root, connectionism and AI embody distinct conceptions of the nature of the human mind and how the mind might best be investigated further. On the Dreyfus brothers' version of these deeper differences, classical AI is a contemporary version of 'atomist', 'rationalist' ideas about the mind taken from Western philosophy. It is bits and pieces of the 'traditional philosophy' of Socrates, Descartes, Leibniz, Locke, and Kant in computational form. In contrast, connectionism is a 'holistic', 'non-rationalist' theory of the mind based in neuroscientific conceptions, free from the misconceptions fostered by philosophical tradition.

The Dreyfus brothers build up this conception through an intellectual history of the development of connectionism and AI. On this account, one of the central planks of the classical AI platform was first articulated by Plato in his view of the nature of human understanding. This is the 'rationalist' view that

> understanding a domain consists in having a *theory* of that domain. A theory formulates the relationships among objective, *context-free*, elements (simples, primitives, features, attributes, factors, data points, cues, etc.) in terms of abstract principles (covering laws, rules, programs, etc.).
>
> (Dreyfus and Dreyfus 1988, p. 25)

So, for example, to understand the moral domain is to have the correct set of rules (abstract principles) that take into account the various aspects of moral situations (objective, context-free elements) so as to determine the morally right thing to do in that situation. The non-rationalist account is simply that understanding a domain does not involve having a theory of the domain.

Plato limited his rationalist theory of understanding to *a priori* disciplines, such as mathematics, and perhaps, ethics, but in the 17th century, Gottfried

Leibniz extended the theory to cover understanding in all domains. Thus, for Leibniz, understanding in mathematics, biology, physics, business, music, sculpture, and carpentry consists of having theories in those domains. An important aspect of this extension, for the Dreyfus brothers, was that it asserted that there could be theories not only of planets, the tides, and falling bodies, but also what the Dreyfus brothers call a theory of the everyday world, a theory of ordinary objects such as hammers and chairs. The 17th century brought with it some measure of empirical support for rationalism in the form of the scientific successes in analysing various physical phenomena in terms of simple mathematical relations between simple quantities such as gravity, mass, speed, velocity, and acceleration. If the understanding of mathematics and physics could be reduced to the grasp of simple principles operating on a few kinds of things, perhaps all understanding could be so reduced.

Yet another contribution of the Century of Genius was the second plank of classical AI: the doctrine of (psychological) 'atomism'. According to René Descartes, Thomas Hobbes, and Gottfried Leibniz, who developed this view, there exist formal, atomic mental representations from which can be constructed formal, complex mental representations. Furthermore, the composition and decomposition of these representations constitutes the dynamics of thought. In the late 19th and early 20th centuries, the revolutionary mathematical logic developed by Gottlob Frege, Bertrand Russell, and Alfred North Whitehead allowed for the refinement of the atomist plank of AI. With the ability to capture patterns of reasoning not amenable to the simpler Aristotelian syllogistic logic or the sentential logic of George Boole, the predicate logic of Frege, Russell, and Whitehead could capture many extremely important patterns of reasoning used in science. The early Wittgenstein, the Wittgenstein of the *Tractatus Logico-Philosophicus*, combined this logic with atomism and rationalism. To understand a domain was thus to have a formal logical mental language containing representations of the primitive objects and properties of the domain and of the principles governing those objects and properties.

By the middle of the 20th century, Alan Newell and Herbert Simon synthesized these planks found in the history of philosophy into the platform of 'symbolic information processing'. In the course of developing computer programs that could generate proofs (solve problems) in logic and geometry, Newell and Simon came to the view that the electronic digital computer is, at an appropriate level of abstraction, the sort of mechanism that could instantiate the atomism and rationalism found throughout traditional philosophy. To quote Dreyfus and Dreyfus,

> AI can be thought of as the attempt to find the primitive elements and logical relations in the subject (man or computer) that mirror the primitive objects and their relations that make up the world. Newell

and Simon's physical symbol system hypothesis in effect turns the Wittgensteinian vision (which is itself the culmination of the classical rationalist philosophical tradition) into an empirical claim and bases a research program on it.

(Dreyfus and Dreyfus 1988, p. 18)

It was not just Descartes and his descendants who stood behind symbolic information processing, but all of Western philosophy.

(Dreyfus and Dreyfus 1988, p. 24)

and

It was obvious that researchers such as Newell, Simon, and [Marvin] Minsky were the heirs to the philosophical tradition.

(Dreyfus and Dreyfus 1988, p. 26)

This history of AI will likely be news to anyone not familiar with the Dreyfus brothers' views, but the portion of the history of connectionism they rehearse is rather widely known. According to the Dreyfus brothers, 'The opposed [connectionist] intuition, that we should set about creating artificial intelligence by modeling the brain rather than the mind's symbolic representation of the world, drew its inspiration not from philosophy but from what was soon to be called neuroscience' (Dreyfus and Dreyfus 1988, p. 18). In 1949, the neuropsychologist D. O. Hebb published the *Organization of Behavior* in which he supposed there to be two principal neurophysiological processes underlying psychological processes. According to Hebb, the electrical activity found in neuronal action potentials is responsible for such cognitive processing as speech recognition, speech production, motor skills, perception, and memory recall. He also hypothesized that simultaneous or successive activity in adjacent neurons increases the effect that the electrical activity of one neuron will have on the other. This idea is now generally known as the 'Hebb rule'. The psychological correlate of this neurophysiological facilitation is learning or the formation of memories. The results of these developments in philosophy and neuroscience were that

In the early 1950's, . . ., two opposed visions of what computers could be . . . emerged and struggled for recognition. One faction saw computers as a system for manipulating mental symbols: the other, as a medium for modeling the brain. One sought to use computers to instantiate a formal representation of the world; the other, to simulate the interactions of neurons. One took problem solving as its paradigm of intelligence: the other, learning. One utilized logic; the other, statistics. One school was heir to the rationalist, reductionist

360

tradition in philosophy; the other viewed itself as idealized, holistic neuroscience.

(Dreyfus and Dreyfus 1988, pp. 15–16)

Through the 1950s and into the 1960s, classical AI and connectionism were close scientific rivals and both had enjoyed modest successes. Newell and Simon, on the one hand, had produced computer programs that could do geometric and logical proofs (see, for example, Newell and Simon 1956), while Frank Rosenblatt and others had found ways of teaching neural networks to perform various pattern recognition tasks (see, for example, Rosenblatt 1962). In addition, both faced the challenge of moving from small-scale 'toy' problems to larger, more recalcitrant 'real' problems. In other words, both had to face the facts of the combinatorial explosion implicit in the computational methods they used.

Despite the comparable standing of connectionism and AI during the 1960s, there was a dramatic change of fortunes during the 1970s. During the late 1960s, there was intense competition for research funds. At this time, Marvin Minsky and Seymour Papert circulated a manuscript that later became the book *Perceptrons* (1969). In this text, they showed the limitations of two-layer perceptrons; they proved that perceptrons could not compute the very large class of linearly inseparable functions. By most popular accounts, the mathematical limitations of perceptrons were the proximal cause of the collapse of perceptron research that left only a handful of dedicated and unappreciated connectionists, such as Steven Grossberg, Teuvo Kohonen, and John Anderson.

Dreyfus and Dreyfus believe that the popular accounts of the reason for the waning of connectionist research during the 1970s do not square with the significance of Minsky and Papert's mathematical results. Minsky and Papert's proofs concerned only two-layer networks, networks having only input and output nodes; they did not touch multi-layered nets. Why, then, the Dreyfuses ask, was the possibility of using multi-layered nets not widely and vigorously pursued during the 1970s? The Dreyfuses suggest that three factors, or better, three prejudices, were at work. Two of these reasons are relatively straightforward, but one requires a bit of exegetical analysis. The Dreyfuses suggest that the first prejudice hindering connectionism was the feeling that it was hard to get neural networks to do what they did, namely, pattern recognition, but easy to get computer programs to do what they did, namely, discover proofs in logic and geometry (Dreyfus and Dreyfus 1988, p. 24). In other words, it took clever people a long time to get nets to classify patterns correctly, but not so long for people to write computer programs that would generate proofs. Second, they suggest that scientists believed that the problem-solving tasks that occupied AI were more intellectually useful, or more theoretically important, than the pattern recognition tasks undertaken by neural networks (Dreyfus and Dreyfus 1988, p. 24).

The more problematic third suggestion is that scientists simply assumed Hobbesian–Cartesian–Leibnizian atomism (and rationalism?), so that they intuitively preferred the atomistic classical AI to 'holistic' connectionism (Dreyfus and Dreyfus 1988, pp. 23–24). In support of this interpretation, they cite a passage from Minsky and Papert's book on perceptrons:

> Both of the present authors (first independently and later together) became involved with a somewhat therapeutic compulsion: to dispel what we feared to be the first shadows of a 'holistic' or 'Gestalt' misconception that would threaten to haunt the fields of engineering and artificial intelligence as it had earlier haunted biology and psychology.
> (Minsky and Papert, p. 19, cited in Dreyfus and Dreyfus 1988, p. 22)

While Minsky and Papert do not define what they mean by 'holism', the Dreyfus brothers offer something of an analysis. They say that networks are holistic in the sense that

> [they] need not allow an interpretation of their hidden nodes in terms of features a human being could recognize and use to solve the problem. While neural network modeling itself is committed to neither view, it can be demonstrated that association does not *require* that the hidden nodes be interpretable.
> (Dreyfus and Dreyfus 1988, p. 22)

This passage is ambiguous. The first sentence suggests that networks are holistic if there is a conceptual interpretation of the individual hidden nodes in the network, provided that the interpretation does not have features a human being could recognize and use to solve the problem. Call this *weak holism*. The Dreyfus brothers suggest that networks display this form of holism when they assert that

> In one very limited sense, any successfully trained multilayer net can be interpreted in terms of features—not everyday features but what we shall call highly abstract features . . .
> The fact that intelligence . . . can always be accounted for in terms of relations among a number of highly abstract features of a skill domain does not, however, preserve the rationalist intuition . . .
> (Dreyfus and Dreyfus 1988, p. 36)

This form of holism, although also discussed in the connectionist literature, is evidently not inconsistent with Hobbesian–Cartesian–Leibnizian atomism. Hobbes, Descartes, and Leibniz never claimed that the mental atoms must be 'everyday features'. The second sentence quoted above suggests

something stronger than the first, namely, that there is no conceptual interpretation of the hidden nodes at all, not when taken individually and not
even when taken as a whole. Through their allusions to Ludwig Wittgenstein's later views, the Dreyfus brothers suggest that this is the sort of holism
they take networks to display. Compare this form of holism with a passage
from Wittgenstein:

> 608. No supposition seems to me more natural than that there is no
> process in the brain correlated with associating or with thinking; so
> that it would be impossible to read off thought-processes from brain-
> processes. I mean this: if I talk or write there is, I assume, a system of
> impulses going out from my brain and correlated with my spoken or
> written thoughts. But why should the *system* continue further in the
> direction of the centre? Why should this order not proceed, so to
> speak, out of chaos?
>
>   609. It is thus perfectly possible that certain psychological phe-
> nomena *cannot* be investigated physiologically, because physiologic-
> ally nothing corresponds to them.
>
>   (Wittgenstein 1981, p. 106, cited in Davies 1991, p. 230)

We might refer to this stronger form of holism as *Wittgensteinian* holism or
perhaps *radical holism*.

Despite the slump in connectionist research during the 1970s, connectionist research became more popular than ever during the 1980s. The Dreyfus
brothers offer a two-fold explanation for this dramatic reversal. First, connectionists, working under the rubric of 'parallel distributed processing'
(PDP), developed new types of holistic, non-rationalist networks that do not
have the computational limitations of perceptrons. Most notably, there is the
wealth of research on numerous variations of the so-called back-propagation
weight change procedure. This procedure directs the changes of weights in
multi-layer nets, permitting nets to learn, in principle, arbitrary boolean
functions (see, for example, Rumelhart *et al* 1986b). The Dreyfus brothers
contend that, in addition to being weakly holistic, these networks are
non-rationalist for the following reason:

> If the net were taught one more association of an input-output pair
> (where the input prior to training produced an output different from
> the one to be learned), the interpretation of at least some of the
> nodes would have to be changed. So the features that some of the
> nodes picked out before the last instance of training would turn out
> not to have been invariant structural features of the domain.
>
>   (Dreyfus and Dreyfus 1988, p. 36)

In other words, train a network on one input–output mapping and it will have one set of structural features represented in its hidden nodes, retrain the network with a new input–output mapping differing from the previous mapping only in one input–output pair, and the set of structural features will be different. This means that, contrary to rationalism, the features are not invariants of the domain. Note that here the Dreyfus attack on rationalism is inconsistent with claiming that networks are radically holistic, since there is mention of the conceptual interpretation of what are implicitly hidden nodes (cf. Dreyfus and Dreyfus 1988, p. 36).

The second source of strength for connectionism stemmed from the perception of weakness in the classical AI tradition. Following the initial successes of AI during the 1950s and early 1960s, there was a movement to develop computer programs that would work in isolated domains called 'microworlds'. A typical microworld might contain only a few colored blocks of various sizes that could be moved in limited ways and placed in a limited number of relations to each other. The hope of this research was that by producing programs that could function in these severely impoverished contexts, one might learn how to handle more complex contexts, those involving many possible transformations of many objects with a multitude of properties. While the 'microworlds' projects sustained AI for the decade from 1965 to 1975, there arose the perception that microworlds could not in fact be extended to more realistic worlds. Classical AI began to encounter difficulty with what is often referred to as the 'problem of common sense knowledge'. The problem, roughly, is to explain how people effortlessly know how to handle themselves in the almost endless number of contingencies that might arise in restaurants, shopping malls, and social occasions. While this may seem simple enough in description, computer programs have yet to become sophisticated enough to handle it.

The Dreyfus brothers now believe that the stage may be set to give connectionism a much deserved chance to fail as did AI. They suggest that just as humanity has proved to be too holistic and complicated to be captured by an AI computer program, so it may be that it is too holistic to be scrutinized even through the relatively holistic conceptual resources of contemporary connectionism.

3 Critique of the Dreyfus history of connectionism

From the preceding it is clear that the Dreyfus brothers have in mind both a philosophical and a historical analysis of connectionism and AI. Their philosophical interpretation is that the atomist, rationalist, logical tradition in philosophy leads (inexorably?) to the pursuit of AI (or perhaps vice versa); while holistic non-rationalist neuroscience (necessarily?) leads one to connectionism (or perhaps vice versa). In other words, AI is conceptually tied to the atomism, rationalism, and logic of traditional philosophy, whereas connectionism is bound up with holism, non-rationalism, and neuroscience.

Their historical analysis is supposed to testify to the truth of this analysis, since history reveals these clusterings of concepts.

Although the Dreyfus history of AI is sometimes a bit strained, it does not seem to be fundamentally flawed. In contrast, the history of connectionism, apparently gleaned from the introductory sections of papers in the contemporary PDP literature, makes for a most unrepresentative sample of what connectionism is about. For a more balanced understanding of the intellectual heritage of connectionism, we must return to the 18th century. Reviewing this history will be the first step in a revised philosophical understanding of connectionism and AI.

Early in the 18th century, the Hobbesian–Cartesian–Leibnizian atomism described by the Dreyfus brothers came to be assimilated into the psychological/philosophical tradition of associationism. Along with the hypothesis of atomic and molecular mental representations, associationism asserts a theory of learning, roughly, that the strength of association amongst ideas in the mind is determined by their frequency of co-occurrence in experience. In other words, objects and properties that frequently co-occur in the environment will cause an observing mind to join firmly together the ideas of those objects and properties. Dozens of versions of this basic plan of associationism were articulated through the course of the 18th and 19th century by such thinkers as John Locke, David Hume, John Gay, David Hartley, Joseph Priestley, Alexander Bain, James Mill, John Stuart Mill, and Herbert Spencer, just to name an illustrious few.

During the late 19th century, the psychological ideas of associationism were combined with a theory of the function of the nervous system. According to these late 19th century conceptions, the brain contributes two fundamentally distinct biological processes to the operations of the mind: (1) the passage of electrical activity in the nerves; and (2) physiological changes in the substrate of the brain that facilitate the flow of this electrical activity. Ideas in the mind, both simple and complex, correspond to the electrical fluxes; learning and the formation of memory correspond to the facilitations in those fluxes. Here we find functional analogies between the neurobiological views of the late 19th century and contemporary connectionist/PDP views concerning the neurobiological basis of cognition. The electrical activity of the late 19th century theories plays the same sort of functional role in cognition as does activation propagation in late 20th century PDP. The facilitation of the flow of the electrical activity in the late 19th century theories is comparable to synaptic modification and weight change in late 20th century connectionism. Further support for these analogies comes, as we shall see, from the evolution of these 19th century ideas into the ideas of the late 20th century.

The British Empiricist philosopher Herbert Spencer developed an extremely elaborate version of these late 19th century ideas in the massive third edition of his *Principles of Psychology*, published in 1872. On Spencer's scheme, the electrical activity in the nerves was the result of a 'polarizing' chemical chain reaction that propagated through a system of hollow nerve tubules. Spencer's metaphor for this process was the process that occurs when a domino in a line of dominoes falls thereby starting the fall of all the dominoes. On this metaphor, environmental stimulation would topple the first domino causing a chain reaction to propagate to the brain and ultimately to the motor nerves effecting a response. Ideas were thus occasions of these chemical chain reactions. The biological basis of learning and memory, on this scheme, was a facilitation in the speed and reliability of this chemical reaction. Spencer described this facilitation metaphorically as a matter of the dominoes coming into more perfect alignment with each other through repeated topplings.

We should emphasize here that Spencer understood behaviour as the product of environmentally-driven reflexes, a picture that emerged from 19th century physiological studies of spinal reflexes and which became common in subsequent connectionist analyses. On this view, the invertebrate organisms, such as starfish, insects, and worms, have very simple reflexes with few ganglia to regulate them. Moving up the scale of complexity to the vertebrates, we find more sophisticated systems of reflexes regulated by the spinal ganglia and a special enlarged ganglion, the brain. On this view, the brain is essentially a very sophisticated regulator belonging to the vertebrate reflex system. It is easy to see how this picture of the brain and cognition might be combined with connectionism, since connectionism apparently embraces all the anatomy and physiology one might think is necessary for this view.

For all the influence the Spencerian picture was to have on connectionism, Spencer's theory was not genuine connectionism. Spencer believed that the nervous system was an unbroken set of tubules. He did not believe in the existence of individual nerve cells with connections, or synapses, between them, hence, he could not suppose that learning involved synaptic modification. Synapses were discovered only around 1888, over 15 years after the initial publication of the third edition of the *Principles*. With the rather rapid scientific acceptance of synapses, however, there appeared numerous versions of genuine connectionism postulating electrical activity in neurons as the biological basis of ideas coupled with synaptic modification as the biological basis of learning and memory. These neuropsychological hypotheses, combined with associationist psychological principles and the analysis of behaviour as environmentally-driven reflex action, form what we might call 'classical connectionism'. Such a collection of ideas remained a powerful force in Anglo-American psychology through the first quarter of the century. It could be found regularly in issues of the *Psychological Review* during the 1920s, for example.

To avoid oversimplifying too much, we should note that not all connectionists were uniformly committed to associationism and reflexology, or environmentally driven psychological processes. In a work written in 1895, the *Project for a Scientific Psychology*, Sigmund Freud used the connectionist theory of the biological basis of psychological processes to articulate a theory of neuroses. In his version of connectionism, the electrical activity of nerves was described in terms of the flow of an unknown substance Q, while learning and memory formation were based on decreases in the thresholds of pressure-sensitive valves between neurons. Freud challenged the idea that behaviour is driven predominantly by environmental stimuli insofar as he maintained that internal sources of Q played a significant role in determining behaviour. Such internal sources he supposed to underlie sexual desire, thirst, and hunger.

For reasons we will not explore here, the 1930s was a period of relative decline in the popularity of neural network theories in neuroscience and psychology. Nevertheless, they became a topic of interest in mathematical biology. Nicolas Rashevsky, at the University of Chicago, began to build a mathematical biophysics that he hoped would rival the sophistication of mathematical physics and that would include a mathematical treatment of neural networks and psychology (Rashevsky 1938, pp. vii f). In essence, Rashevsky's work was the application of differential equations and linear algebra to neural networks and psychology. Among his more interesting ideas was a neural network theory of Pavlovian conditioning, a theory of shape perception that incorporates size and positional invariance, and the description of the behaviour of neural networks in terms of energy minimization (Rashevsky 1938, chapters XXIV, XXV, XXVII). It is especially interesting to note that, in explaining the concept of energy minimization, Rashevsky had recourse to the same metaphor as do contemporary advocates of PDP, namely, that of a ball rolling over a curved, smooth two-dimensional surface (Rashevsky 1938, chap. XXIV, cf. Hinton and Sejnowski 1986, pp. 287f).

The broader historical significance of Rashevsky's mathematical treatment of neural networks begins to become clear when we observe that it was Rashevsky's seminar on Mathematical Biology at the University of Chicago that in 1941 brought together Warren McCulloch, an Associate Professor of Psychiatry at the University of Illinois, and the 17-year-old student Walter Pitts. Within two years of their meeting, McCulloch and Pitts produced their seminal contribution to connectionism, 'A Logical Calculus of the Ideas Immanent in Nervous Activity'. This paper, published in Rashevsky's journal, the *Bulletin for Mathematical Biophysics*, is certainly among the most influential contributions to connectionism ever.

It should be noted that McCulloch and Pitts' views on the biological basis of memory departed from the classical connectionist conception. In 'A Logical Calculus' they treated memory in terms of electrical activity in closed neuronal loops, so that forming a memory was, at the neuronal level, the initiation of electrical activity in some loop with the memory surviving only as long as the reverberating electrical activity survived undisturbed. At the time, this view was not entirely unproblematic. It was known, for example, that epileptics do not suffer memory losses following epileptic fits that might be supposed to disrupt regular electrical reverberations. Moreover, in a lecture given in 1952, 'Finality and Form', McCulloch observes that memories survive sleep in which a great deal of electrical activity apparently ceases (McCulloch 1965, p. 262). Certainly many factors contributed to McCulloch and Pitts' support of the reverberatory theory of memory in the face of conflicting evidence, but we may mention just two. First, this was a natural theory for Pitts. Before he met McCulloch, Pitts had investigated Alston Householder's mathematical theory of closed nervous loops (cf. Householder 1941a, 1941b, 1941c, 1942, Pitts 1942a, 1942b, 1942c). A second factor may have been the sense that even if memory were truly a matter of 'synaptic growth', this could be treated mathematically as if it were reverberatory activity in a closed loop:

> However physically unlike, the two kinds of memory are *functionally equivalent* in this sense: Instead of the supposed change in the form of the synapse, we have but to imagine a circle of neurons in which a train of impulses is started by the conjunction of falls . . . Now any formal property of memory or learning, of the kind due to synaptic growth, is to be found in the circling of this train of impulses, due, that is, to an enduring figure of activity within the net.
>
> (cf. McCulloch 1965, p. 263, italics in original)

Here we find not an outright repudiation of synaptic modification, but an indifference toward it because of its apparent mathematical equivalence to reverberatory activity.

Despite this significant departure from classical connectionist doctrine, McCulloch and Pitts still provide a powerful illustration of the inadequacy of the Dreyfus historical account. What they interjected into the connectionist literature flatly contradicts what the Dreyfus brothers would have us expect. First, and most obviously, this chapter in connectionist history provides clear evidence that connectionism was influenced by the formal logic of Frege, Russell, and Whitehead. Among the central, and most widely known, achievements of 'A Logical Calculus' are proofs of how one might associate networks of binary threshold neurons with formulae in the first-order predicate calculus. Even a superficial glance at the paper reveals the characteristic Russell–Whitehead dot notation of the *Principia Mathematica*. A closer examination reveals that McCulloch and Pitts had provided an effective procedure for generating a member of a particular class of formulae in the predicate calculus to describe any given network, and a procedure for generating a network to be described by a selected member of that class of formulae. Biographical and autobiographical evidence also corroborates the significance of formal logic to the connectionist project. It was rather well known that, as a young man, McCulloch was quite interested in logic (McCulloch 1991, p. 28). Moreover, Pitts was a student of Rudolph Carnap, perhaps the greatest advocate of applying formal logic to philosophical problems ever. Jerome Lettvin, a friend and colleague of Pitts and McCulloch, wrote that 'Walter Pitts, who was companion, protege, and friend to Warren, had, for a long time, been convinced that the only way of understanding nature was by logic and logic alone. . . . Pitts had committed himself to logic as the key to the structure of the world in a way that no other person that I know had ever done' (Lettvin 1991, p. 12).

Biographical and autobiographical evidence also reveals that 'traditional philosophy' played an important part in McCulloch and Pitts' work. It is clear from an examination of McCulloch's career that, contrary to the Dreyfus caricature, McCulloch was not one to ignore 'traditional philosophy' and turn only to neurophysiology and neurology for his intellectual inspiration. Instead, he was a neuroscientist who combined his scientific views of the brain with philosophical views of mental representation taken from modern philosophy. McCulloch had studied Aristotle, Descartes, Leibniz, Locke, Berkeley, Hume and Kant as part of his major in philosophy at Yale (McCulloch 1991, pp. 21ff). After receiving his M.D. from Columbia in 1927, and holding various sundry medical positions, McCulloch returned to Yale to work in the Laboratory for Neurophysiology with J. G. Dusser de Barenne. There, from 1934 to 1941, he produced some 40 papers on neurophysiology, 32 in collaboration with Dusser de Barenne. His philosophical and scientific training certainly prepared him to infuse both 'traditional philosophical' views about the mind and neuroscience into his connectionism.

It is also clear that McCulloch endorsed his own idiosyncratic version of atomism. He tells us that, prior to having met Pitts:

> My object, as a psychologist, was to invent a kind of last psychic event, or 'psychon', that would have the following properties: First, it was to be so simple an event that it either happened or else it did not happen. Second, it was to happen only if its bound cause had happened . . . Third, it was to propose this to subsequent psychons. Fourth, these were to be compounded to produce the equivalents of more complicated propositions concerning their antecedents.
> (McCulloch 1991, p. 1233, cf. pp. 359, 1355)

Clearly McCulloch wanted to use traditional philosophical ideas about mental representation in his neuroscientifically-inspired understanding of the mind.

The groundbreaking work of Rashevsky, McCulloch, Pitts, and many others in the 1940s inspired enough interesting mathematical problems to sustain a connectionist research tradition independent of psychological and even neurobiological input. The result of this development was that, during the 1950s, there was not merely AI and connectionism; there was AI and roughly three types of connectionist research. This might be divided roughly into: (1) the mathematical/computational strain of connectionism following up the work begun by Rashevsky, McCulloch, and Pitts; (2) the neuro-psychological work by Hebb and his colleagues; and (3) the more purely neuroscientific work by, for example, Sir John Eccles. The mathematical/computational tradition gave rise to the connectionist work by Frank Rosen-blatt, Albert Uttley, Bernard Widrow, M. E. Hoff, and many others, as well as the study of finite state automata. The neuropsychological tradition stereotypically attempted to relate the properties of neural networks to the behaviour of rats and monkeys in various types of mazes and perceptual discrimination tasks. In the neuroscientific tradition, there were neuroscientists investigating biological questions about the structure and function of individual neurons and their pairwise interactions. An aspect of this research that was exceptionally exciting for the synaptic modification theory of the biological basis of memory concerned the phenomenon of *post-tetanic potentiation*. In experiments on the neuromuscular junction, it was observed that intense electrical stimulation of a nerve synapsing onto a muscle would cause the muscle to display increased sensitivity to subsequent nervous action potentials. In other words, intense electrical activity increased the effect of subsequent electrical activity. Sir John Eccles, and others, studied this neurophysiological facilitation process for over twenty years. (See, for example, Eccles 1953, and various contributions in Karczmar and Eccles 1972.)

Post-tetanic potentiation research declined during the 1970s, at about the same time as did perceptron research, although for independent reasons we shall not consider. Recall that the Dreyfus brothers suggested three reasons that might explain what they take to be the exaggerated response to Minsky and Papert's proofs of the limitations of perceptrons. These were, first, a prejudice against pattern recognition, second, the intuition that artificial neural networks were uninteresting because so much human effort was required to get them to perform pattern recognition, and third, a prejudice against the holism found in connectionism, but not in AI. While it may very well be true that these first two reasons were at work in the events of the 1970s, a prejudice against the sorts of holism the Dreyfus brothers suggest cannot be any part of the explanation. Suppose, first of all, that by 'holism' they mean the antithesis of Hobbesian–Cartesian–Leibnizian atomism, the view that there are no atomic mental representations from which more complex mental representations are constructed. This cannot be correct. Perceptrons were just as much committed to analysing a perceived environment into 'objective, *context-free*' atoms as were AI models. In perceptrons, the elements were the things represented by the input nodes. They were such things as 'Light at position x, y in the visual field'. Weak holism, the view that

370

individual hidden nodes do not have a conceptual interpretation in terms of features a human could recognize and use to solve a problem, and radical holism, the view that hidden nodes do not have a conceptual interpretation at all, also cannot explain the failure of perceptrons either, since perceptrons obviously had no hidden nodes. Of course, as the Dreyfus brothers noted, Minsky and Papert did describe nets as 'holistic'. It is not obvious exactly what they meant by this, but it cannot have been what the Dreyfuses suggest. One possibility is that, for Minsky and Papert, 'holistic' was merely a generic pejorative term for vague thinking, perhaps comparable to calling something 'metaphysical' or even 'philosophical'.

This brings us to the diversity of contemporary connectionist research. Consider contemporary PDP. This was the focus of the Dreyfus account, but it alone provides ample disproof of the Dreyfus analysis. First, we should note that various contemporary connectionist models admit of atomism and, apparently, rationalism. Interactive activation networks are backed with a theory of 'constraint satisfaction'. In these networks, each node stands for a hypothesis, such as 'There is a horizontal bar in the lower left corner', or 'There is a letter 'A' present', or 'The word being scanned is 'READ'' (McClelland and Rumelhart 1981). Presumably a human could recognize at least some of these concepts and use them to solve some cognitive task. The connections between these nodes are positively or negatively weighted, as determined by the consistency (mutual support) or inconsistency (lack of mutual support) of the hypotheses associated with the connected nodes. In these 'hand-wired' networks, the conceptual interpretation of the individual nodes must be fairly clear to allow the proper weighting of the connections, hence the inclination to propose any form of holism should be altogether removed. Moreover, one might well take a rationalist view of constraint satisfaction networks, that is, assume that the system of positive and negative weightings corresponds to a network's theory of the domain over which it computes. Exactly the same considerations about atomism and rationalism apply when we examine Hinton and Sejnowski's discussion of constraint satisfaction in Boltzmann machine networks (Hinton and Sejnowski 1986, pp. 286ff) and Smolensky's discussion of 'knowledge atoms' and their role in his theory of the dynamic construction of schemata (Smolensky 1986, pp. 201ff).

These observations suggest that we must consider a weaker interpretation of the Dreyfus view, namely, that all the Dreyfus brothers intended was to assert that *back-propagation* networks, rather than all artificial neural networks, are holistic and non-rationalist. Even this, however, is not entirely satisfactory. Consider holism. As we observed in section 2, the hidden nodes in back-propagation networks use 'highly abstract' structural features (Dreyfus and Dreyfus 1988, p. 36). This is inconsistent with what we have called radical Wittgensteinian holism, since there are some representations in the hidden nodes. This leaves weak holism, the thesis that back-propagation

371

networks do in fact use features that people could not recognize and use to solve a task. Whether the hidden nodes of a back-propagation network use such representations is, however, an open empirical question that the Dreyfus brothers do not address. Consider what the Dreyfus brothers say against rationalism. They evidently concede that semantic features represented by the hidden nodes of a back-propagation network constitute a theory of some domain, but they object that these features are not *invariant*. The meanings of the hidden nodes change as a network learns a new input–output mapping. Note, however, that the change of features constitutes a change of theories and that, while every rationalist will maintain that the features postulated by any particular theory are supposed by the theory to be invariants of the domain, no rationalist ever held that all theories must postulate the same set of invariant features. To harness rationalists with the view that all theoretical ontologies must be the same is outrageous.

Note as well that, while associationism has apparently exerted no direct influence on PDP, the attempt to combine it with connectionism is so seductive that associationism arises almost spontaneously in PDP. Recall once again that the associationist proposal is that learning involves having ideas in the mind come to occur in the combinations and in the frequency with which their causes occur in the environment. Suppose that an event in the external world occurs with a probability of 0.3. In their description of a Boltzmann machine 'generative model' of this environment, Hinton and Sejnowski (1986) would let such an event be represented as a pattern of activation on the visible nodes of the Boltzmann machine, say '01010101', and, like many early associationists, they would want learning to lead to the representation '01010101' occurring in the model with a probability of 0.3 (Hinton and Sejnowski 1986, p. 294). This is a more or less precise mathematical way to capture the associationist theory of learning.

In addition to connectionist research in the PDP tradition, there continue to be connectionist efforts in neurobiology and neuropsychology. As one example, the earlier study of Eccles' post-tetanic potentiation has given way to even greater interest in what is called 'long-term potentiation' (cf. Landfield and Deadwyler 1988). This phenomenon, or cluster of phenomena, has attracted tremendous interest for a number of reasons. For example, unlike post-tetanic potentiation, long-term potentiation occurs in a structure of the brain (the hippocampus) that is known to play an important role in memory, rather than at the neuromuscular junction. Second, it is more durable form of potentiation, lasting days or weeks, rather than minutes or hours. Third, long-term potentiation occurs in response to a much more biologically natural stimulation than that needed to induce post-tetanic potentiation.

Just as we should not overlook the neurobiological and neuropsychological connectionist research, we should not ignore the very large body of contemporary connectionist research that is pursued in almost complete isolation from neurobiology. Some of this neurobiologically isolated connectionist research takes the form of mathematical or computational studies of neural network behaviour as an interesting form of computation in its own right, independently of its application or relevance to psychology. Investigators in this tradition are concerned with understanding the properties of neural networks as an end in itself, not necessarily as a means to better understanding animal minds or minds in general. Discussions with practising connectionist cognitive psychologists also reveal another neurobiologically-indifferent strain of connectionism. Some of these investigators treat the nodes, connections, and weights of connectionist models as just another set of mathematical objects that are postulated and justified on the basis of their ability to account for psychological phenomena, independently of their relation to the anatomy and physiology of the brain. One might, for example, try to justify the interactive activation model of letter perception in this way. Cognitive psychologists interested in connectionism sometimes adopt this stance in response to the complaint that their networks are not neurobiologically plausible. In short, it is quite misleading to suggest that all of contemporary connectionism is neuroscientifically-inspired. In truth, some is and some is not.

Part of the purpose of these last observations has been to indicate the diversity of approaches to connectionism. As has been mentioned frequently, connectionism is of tremendous interest to cognitive psychologists, computer scientists, engineers, mathematicians, neuroscientists, neuropsychologists, and philosophers. Given this intellectual diversity, one should be suspicious of sweeping philosophical generalizations about what connectionism is all about. There is ample reason to fear that connectionism will likely prove to be different things to different investigators.

4 The philosophical interpretation of connectionism and AI

The Dreyfus brothers have suggested that as a matter of historical fact, AI has been tied to atomism and rationalism, as well as the logic of traditional philosophy, where connectionism has adopted holism and non-rationalism along with its neuroscientific inspiration. The preceding section argued that these claims about connectionism, both in the past and at present, are false. Around the turn of the century, connectionism was linked to atomism, rationalism, and traditional philosophical conceptions of the mind through associationism. During the 1930s and 1940s there emerged a mathematical tradition in neural network theory that was able to distance itself somewhat from neuroscience. During the 1940s and thereafter, McCulloch and Pitts combined connectionism with atomism, rationalism, the logic of Frege, Russell, and Whitehead, and traditional philosophical conceptions of the mind. Perceptron research also embodied atomism and rationalism. In contemporary PDP, various advocates have been quite sympathetic to holism and non-rationalism and have derived inspiration from neuroscience, but

PDP *per se* does not require holism or non-rationalism. In fact, some advocates of PDP have adopted atomism and rationalism. In addition, there continues to be a strain of connectionist theorizing that is indifferent to neuroscience.

These historical findings refute some of the philosophical claims about connectionism that one might have taken to be implicit in the Dreyfus analysis, namely, that neuroscience, holism, and non-rationalism lead (inexorably) to connectionism or that connectionism leads (inexorably) to a concern for neuroscience, holism, and non-rationalism. Presumably if it was historically possible to combine atomism, rationalism, and formal logic with connectionism, there is no logical contradiction or conceptual confusion in this combination. In essence, there is very little truth to the Dreyfus brothers' analysis of connectionism and its intellectual history and philosophical consequences. If, however, we turn to AI, the Dreyfus analysis is more accurate. Although it is misleading to suggest that AI cannot make use of neuroscientific facts (cf. Aizawa 1992), there is something to the claim that AI rejects holism and this merits further examination.

At the heart of AI is the hypothesis that cognition is computation, that cognitive processes are a species of computational process. According to AI, other processes in the brain may be computational as well, but insofar as they are not cognitive, they are not part of the project of developing artificial intelligence. In elaborating this picture, advocates of AI have frequently assumed that a necessary condition for a process being cognitive is that it manipulate representations. Processes that do not involve the manipulation of whole markers that represent objects, properties, and relations in the external world are, by this account, non-cognitive processes, hence not within the scope of AI. A process that manipulates only parts of representations are subcognitive, hence outside the scope of AI. Exactly how such an idea is fully and clearly articulated is somewhat open, but the consequences for Wittgensteinian holism are clear: the holistic non-representational processes from which behaviour and certain cognitive processes are supposed to emerge simply do not count as cognitive. State changes that do not involve changes in atomic or molecular representations are non-cognitive. A holistic theory of cognition is simply not a conceptual possibility. While this picture, or some version of it, enjoys rather broad support in AI, in the connectionist community, both within and without the PDP tradition, there has been more diversity of opinion. While some connectionists hold the view that *cognitive* processes are connectionist network processes, some hold the less controversial view that *brain (neuronal)* processes are connectionist processes. Here we see that there is some truth in what the Dreyfus brothers say, namely, that AI is concerned with making a mind, where connectionism attempts (at least sometimes (only?)) to model the brain. Given that some connectionists are concerned only with modelling neuronal processes, it is not surprising that they are less concerned to embrace the representationalist criterion for cognition.

374

According to this analysis of what is involved in the conflict between advocates of AI and advocates of connectionism, what separates AI from connectionism is not the type of computing devices that the respective investigators study—networks rather than production systems or LISP functions—but the theory of the mark of the cognitive they assume (or do not assume). In other words, there are really two separable questions that are at issue in contemporary AI-connectionist debates:

(1) What sorts of computational processes are cognitive processes?
(2) What must a process be like to be cognitive?

The former question has become more serious in recent years with the increased popularity of neural networks with their distinctly different computational 'flavour', while the latter is related to the traditional philosophical question about the mark of the mental. Distinguishing these two questions leaves us with four possible combinations of scientific and philosophical views. Connectionists will hold that brain processes are connectionist processes, but they may then go on to accept or reject the hypothesis that cognitive processes must be representational. If they accept the view, they must reject Wittgensteinian holism; if they reject it, then they are free to accept Wittgensteinian holism. Similarly, advocates of AI will begin with the hypothesis that cognitive processes are computational processes such as are found in production systems, Turing machines, etc., then go on either to accept or reject the further hypothesis that cognition must be representational. Traditional AI accepts the representationalist hypothesis, hence rejects Wittgensteinian holism; a revised AI would reject the representationalist hypothesis perhaps admitting Wittgensteinian holism.

In order to get the same sort of feel for holism in an AI that admits Wittgensteinian holism as a conceptual possibility as one may have for holism in back-propagation networks, a thought experiment is in order. First, recall what motivates the move to the various forms of holism associated with connectionism. When the back-propagation weight change procedure is applied to a multi-layered network, it is frequently difficult to specify 'natural' concepts for the activation values of individual hidden nodes. The radical response to this observation is to claim that the hidden nodes do not represent anything at all, not even as a whole. Contrast this situation with what happens in the AI enterprise using productions systems or LISP functions. In this context one always knows what the variables mean and what the routines and subroutines do. Suggestive variable names, documentation, and the block structuring of code help make these things clear. Indeed, one of the features of good code is that the programmer's understanding of the data structures and code is readily accessible to those other than the original programmer. To put this another way, in order to develop a connectionist model that does a passable job of, say, producing an encoding of phonemes from an encoding of certain types of English texts does not require that the modeller have an understanding of the conceptual role of the hidden nodes. Given the back-propagation procedure and an encoding of information in the input layer and the output layer, the modeller can ignore any conceptual interpretation of the hidden nodes. The back-propagation weight change procedure gives a modeller a type of procedure for generating networks for computing many desired input–output mappings. In contrast, there is no general means by which an AI modeller can generate a computer program for a given task with no more than an input–output description of the task, even when the task is known to be within the realm of the computable. The only way the AI modeller can proceed is through personally developing some understanding of the task domain in terms of 'atomistic' data structures and 'rationalist' program code. The short of it is that, in the typical AI context, there is none of the mystery that, in the connectionist design context, engenders the move to holism and non-rationalism.

Consider now what would happen if the styles of model generation were reversed. Suppose, first, that the only way one could generate a network with a set of weights that would perform a desired task would be to wire the network by hand. In such a case, a modeller would have to have some conceptual understanding of the domain, hence the sense of conceptual inscrutability of the network would be greatly diminished, if not completely eliminated. In fact, this is essentially the situation with models inspired by constraint satisfaction, such as interactive activation networks, where the modeller must know whether to put positive or negative connections between hypotheses based on their consistency or inconsistency. In such models, the meanings of the individual nodes must be open to scrutiny (or better, stipulation). Here holism gets no hold on the imagination. It should not, therefore, be surprising that the suggestions of holism appear in the context of back-propagation weight change and not in close proximity to discussions of constraint satisfaction and interactive activation.

Continue the thought experiment and suppose that AI programs were generated by some means other than that currently available. Suppose, counterfactually, that the AI modeller were to have a computer program G that could take an input–output specification of a task and generate a computer program that computes any desired computable input–output function. With the program G, the modeller could generate a working AI program without having to understand the domain in terms of data structures and program code. Using G, we might find that a conceptual interpretation of the variables, routines, and subroutines of the program generated by G is generally extremely difficult to find. G, we may suppose, does not choose 'helpful' variable, routine, and sub-routine names. It does not use block structure, but simply writes the code in a single, wraparound line. It does not add documentation. It does not even write the code in English characters. In such a case, as with the hidden nodes of a connectionist network, we might be tempted to suppose that there is no conceptual analysis of the code, except as a whole. One might be moved to claim that we can say no more about the code, its variables, and so forth, than that the program as a whole computes the desired input–output function. In other words, in such a circumstance, we might find the computer program to be a holistic program.

The argument of this section suggests a refinement or elaboration of part of the Dreyfus philosophical interpretation of contemporary AI and connectionism. The Dreyfus brothers are correct to point out that AI is traditionally committed to a rejection of holism, but we have argued that this commitment is based, not on the type of computational device AI supposes the brain to be, but on a theory of what is necessary for counting as cognitive. The present account also suggests, through a thought experiment, how it is that the phenomenon that moves many theorists to assert Wittgensteinian holism in the context of connectionism can be produced in more traditional AI computer programs.

5 Conclusion

The present paper has two principal objectives. First, to introduce some of the highlights of the history of connectionism, especially as they relate to the Dreyfus brothers' concepts of holism and non-rationalism. Second, on the philosophical front, we have seen that connectionism is logically independent of theses about atomism and rationalism. We have also examined what truth there is to the claim that AI rejects holism. We have indicated that this rejection of holism is conceptually independent of any views of the nature of the biological processes in the brain that give rise to cognition. AI's rejection of holism stems from a theory of the cognitive. Insofar as AI can reject the view that cognitive processes must be representational, then we might have AI that is conceptually independent of holism and rationalism. In other words, we might say that the conceptual differences between AI and connectionism do not have to do with the differences between atomism/rationalism and holism/ non-rationalism.

To tie the present investigations to more recent philosophical work, we should note that the present negative philosophical conclusion about connectionism, that it is does not involve any specific commitments concerning neuroscience, atomism, or rationalism, actually accords with a number of new philosophical efforts to detach connectionism from philosophical views of the nature of mind. For example, Ramsey and Stich (1991) have in effect argued that a difference over three conceptions of nativism does not separate connectionism and AI. Lycan (1991) has argued that AI and connectionism are equally at home with homuncular functionalism. Cummins (1991), in a paper quite similar in spirit to the present one, has very effectively argued that the nature of representation and learning are not issues that fundamentally separate connectionism and AI. Adams et al (1992), argue that the difference between using explicit rules and not using explicit rules does not fall along the connectionist/AI line. They also argue that the use of distributed versus localist representations, in many senses of these terms, does not fall along this line either. Aizawa (1992), challenges the neurobiological superiority of connectionism over AI. Although not all recent philosophical work on connectionism has this deflationary tenor (see, for example, van Gelder 1991), what the papers just mentioned share with the present work is the sense that, despite the tremendous changes connectionism has wrought in the problems addressed by practising cognitive psychologists, computer scientists, and engineers, and despite the numerous philosophical and cognitive scientific contentions to the contrary, it may yet turn out that connectionism will require fewer changes in our understanding of the nature of the mind than one might have expected. Part of what this means is that one cannot support one's favourite philosophical views about the nature of the mind simply by reference to the fact that those ideas may be found in the very popular connectionist movement. Such philosophical views must be given independent philosophical support.

References

Adams, F., Aizawa, K., and Fuller, G. (1992) Rules in programming languages and network. In J. Dinsmore (ed.) *The Symbolic and Connectionist Paradigms: Closing the Gap* (Hillsdale, NJ: Lawrence Erlbaum).

Aizawa, K. (1992) Biology and sufficiency in connectionist theory. In J. Dinsmore (ed.) *The Symbolic and Connectionist Paradigms: Closing the Gap* (Hillsdale, NJ: Lawrence Erlbaum).

Cummins, R. (1991) The role of representation in connectionist explanations of cognitive capacities. In W. Ramsey, S. Stich and D. Rumelhart (eds), *Philosophy and Connectionist Theory* (Hillsdale, NJ: Lawrence Erlbaum), 91–114.

Davies, M. (1991) Concepts, connectionism, and the language of thought. In W. Ramsey, S. Stich, and D. Rumelhart (eds), *Philosophy and Connectionist Theory* (Hillsdale, NJ: Lawrence Erlbaum), 229–257.

Dreyfus, H. and Dreyfus, S. (1988) Making a mind versus modelling the brain: artificial intelligence back at a branchpoint. In S. Graubard (ed.), *The Artificial Intelligence Debate: False Starts, Real Foundations* (Cambridge, MA: MIT Press).

Dreyfus, H. and Dreyfus, S. (1986) *Mind over Machine* (New York: Macmillan).

Eccles, J. C. (1953) *The Neurophysiological Basis of Mind* (Oxford: Clarendon Press).

Freud, S. (1966) Project for a scientific psychology. In J. Strachey (ed. and trans.), *The Standard Edition of the Complete Psychological Works of Sigmund Freud, vol. I* (London: Hogarth Press), 295–397. (Original work unpublished).

Hebb, D. O. (1949) *The Organization of Behavior* (New York: John Wiley).

Hinton, G. and Sejnowski, T. (1986) Learning and relearning in Boltzmann machines. In D. E. Rumelhart, J. L. McClelland, and the PDP Research Group. *Parallel Distributed Processing: Explorations in the Microstructure of Cognition*, vol. I (Cambridge, MA: MIT Press), 282–317.

Householder, A. (1941a) A theory of steady-state activity in nerve-fiber networks: I.

Definitions and preliminary lemmas. *Bulletin of Mathematical Biophysics*, **3**: 63–70.

Householder, A. (1941b) A theory of steady-state activity in nerve-fiber networks: II. The simple circuit. *Bulletin of Mathematical Biophysics*, **3**: 105–112.

Householder, A. (1941c) A theory of steady-state activity in nerve-fiber networks: III. The simple circuit in complete activity. *Bulletin of Mathematical Biophysics*, **3**: 137–140.

Householder, A. (1942) A theory of steady-state activity in nerve-fiber networks: IV. N circuits with a common synapse. *Bulletin of Mathematical Biophysics*, **4**: 7–14.

Karczmar, A. G., and Eccles, J. C. (1972) *Brain and Human Behavior* (Berlin: Springer-Verlag).

Landfield, P. and Deadwyler, S. (eds.) (1988) *Long-term Potentiation: From Biophysics to Behavior* (New York: Liss).

Lettvin, J. (1991) Introduction to Volume I of *The Collected Works of Warren S. McCulloch* (Salinas, CA: Intersystems Publications).

Lycan, W. (1991) Homuncular functionalism meets PDP. In W. Ramsay, S. Stich, and D. Rumelhart (eds), *Philosophy and Connectionist Theory* (Hillsdale, NJ: Lawrence Erlbaum), 259–286.

McClelland, J. and Rumelhart, D. (1981) An interactive activation model of context effects in letter perception: Part I. An account of basic findings. *Psychological Review*, **88**: 375–407.

McCulloch, W. (1965) *Embodiments of Mind* (Cambridge, MA: MIT Press).

McCulloch, W. (1991) *Collected Works of Warren S. McCulloch* (4 vols.) (Salinas, CA: Intersystems Publications).

McCulloch, W. and Pitts, W. (1943) A logical calculus of ideas immanent in nervous activity. *Bulletin of Mathematical Biophysics*, **5**: 115.

Minsky, M. and Papert, S. (1969) *Perceptrons* (Cambridge, MA: MIT Press).

Newell, A. and Simon, H. (1956) Empirical explorations with the logic theory machine. *Proceedings of the Western Joint Computer Conference*, 1957, **15**: 218–239.

Pitts, W. (1942a) Some observations on the simple neuron circuit. *Bulletin of Mathematical Biophysics*, **4**: 121–129.

Pitts, W. (1942b) The linear theory of neuron networks: The static problem. *Bulletin of Mathematical Biophysics*, **4**: 169–175.

Pitts, W. (1942c) The linear theory of neuron networks: The dynamic problem. *Bulletin of Mathematical Biophysics*, **5**: 23–31.

Pyle, W. H. (1924) A theory of learning. *Psychological Review*, **31**: 321–327.

Pylyshyn, Z. (1984) *Computation and Cognition* (Cambridge, MA: MIT Press).

Ramsey, W. and Stich, S. (1991) Connectionism and three levels of nativism. In W. Ramsey, S. Stich, and D. Rumelhart (eds), *Philosophy and Connectionist Theory* (Hillsdale, NJ: Lawrence Erlbaum), 287–310.

Rashevsky, N. (1938) *Mathematical Biophysics: Physicomathematical Foundations of Biology* (Chicago: University of Chicago Press).

Rosenblatt, F. (1958) The Perceptron, a probabilistic model for information storage and organization in the brain. *Psychological Review*, **62**: 386.

Rosenblatt, F. (1962) *Neurodynamics* (New York: Spartan).

Rumelhart, D., Hinton, G., and McClelland, J. (1986) A general framework for parallel distributed processing. In J. L. McClelland, D. E. Rumelhart, and the PDP

Research Group, *Parallel Distributed Processing: Explorations in the Microstructure of Cognition*, vol. 2 (Cambridge, MA: MIT Press), 45–76.

Rumelhart, D., Hinton, G. and Williams, R. (1986b) Learning representations by back-propagating errors. *Nature*, **323**: 533.

Smolensky, P. (1986) Information processing in dynamical systems: foundations of harmony theory. In D. E. Rumelhart, J. L. McClelland, and the PDP Research Group, *Parallel Distributed Processing: Explorations in the Microstructure of Cognition*, vol. 1 (Cambridge, MA: MIT Press), 194–281.

Smolensky, P. (1988) On the proper treatment of connectionism. *Behavioral and Brain Sciences*, **11**: 1–74.

Spencer, H. (1872) *Principles of Psychology*, 3rd edn (3 vols.) (New York: D. Appleton).

van Gelder, T. (1991) What is the 'D' in PDP?: A survey of the concept of distribution. In W. Ramsey, S. Stich, and D. Rumelhart (eds), *Philosophy and Connectionist Theory* (Hillsdale, NJ: Lawrence Erlbaum), 33–59.

Wittgenstein, L. (1981) *Zettel* (Oxford: Blackwell).

38

ON ALAN TURING'S ANTICIPATION OF CONNECTIONISM

B. Jack Copeland and Diane Proudfoot

Source: *Synthese* 108 (1996): 361–77.

In Memory of Robin Gandy

Abstract. It is not widely realised that Turing was probably the first person to consider building computing machines out of simple, neuron-like elements connected together into networks in a largely random manner. Turing called his networks 'unorganised machines'. By the application of what he described as 'appropriate interference, mimicking education' an unorganised machine can be trained to perform any task that a Turing machine can carry out, provided the number of 'neurons' is sufficient. Turing proposed simulating both the behaviour of the network and the training process by means of a computer program. We outline Turing's connectionist project of 1948.

1 Introduction

In a lecture given in London in 1947 Turing described the human brain as a 'digital computing machine' (Turing 1947, 111). When he spoke of digital computing machines he had in mind a range of architectures considerably wider than the class of (what we would now call) von Neumann machines and their near relatives.[1] Turing was probably the first person to consider building computing machines out of simple, neuron-like elements connected together into networks in a largely random manner. Turing called his networks 'unorganised machines'. His only published discussion of them occurs in a little-known report written in 1948 and entitled 'Intelligent Machinery'.

Turing describes three types of unorganised machine. A-type and B-type unorganised machines consist of randomly connected two-state 'neurons' whose operation is synchronised by means of a central digital clock. By the application of 'appropriate interference, mimicking education' a B-type machine can be trained to 'do any required job, given sufficient time and provided the number of units is sufficient' (Turing 1948, 14–15). His P-type unorganised machines, which are not neuron-like, have 'only two interfering inputs, one for "pleasure" or "reward" . . . and the other for "pain" or "punishment"' (Turing 1948, 17). Turing studied P-types in the hope of discovering training procedures 'analogous to the kind of process by which a child would really be taught' (Turing 1948, 20). It is a P-type machine that Turing was speaking of when, in the course of his famous discussion of strategies for building machines to pass the Turing Test, he said 'I have done some experiments with one such child-machine, and succeeded in teaching it a few things' (Turing 1950, 457). A-type, B-type and P-type machines are described more fully in what follows.

Turing had no doubts concerning the significance of his unorganised machines.

[M]achines of this character can behave in a very complicated manner when the number of units is large . . . A-type unorganised machines are of interest as being about the simplest model of a nervous system with a random arrangement of neurons. It would therefore be of very great interest to find out something about their behaviour.

(Turing 1948, 10)

He theorised that 'the cortex of the infant is an unorganised machine, which can be organised by suitable interfering training' (Turing 1948, 16). Turing found 'this picture of the cortex as an unorganised machine . . . very satisfactory from the point of view of evolution and genetics' (Turing 1948, 16–17).

The 1948 report was prepared for the National Physical Laboratory, London, where Turing was employed as chief architect of the proposed Automatic Computing Engine or ACE. (He resigned from the NPL in 1948 to take up the position of Deputy Director of the Computing Laboratory at Manchester University.) Nominally the report was an account of research undertaken by Turing during a year he spent at Cambridge on sabbatical from the NPL; in fact it is a wide-ranging and strikingly original survey of the prospects for machine intelligence. In it Turing anticipated many key developments in the field, including the theorem-proving approach to problem-solving (Turing 1948, 22). Also present is the idea, subsequently made popular by Newell and Simon (1957, 1961, 1976), that 'intellectual activity consists mainly of various kinds of search' (Turing 1948, 23). In 1968 the report appeared in an edited collection (Evans and Robertson 1968) and the following year in the journal *Machine Intelligence*, but unfortunately these reprintings attracted little discussion.[2] The report will become more widely known now that it is available in D. C. Ince's *Collected Works of A. M. Turing: Mechanical Intelligence*. It merits the same degree of attention that Turing's other major paper on artificial intelligence has attracted (Turing 1950).

2 Other early work on neuron-like computation

As a result of his lukewarm interest in publication Turing's work on neuron-like computation remained unknown to others working in the area. His unorganised machines are not mentioned by the other pioneers of neuron-like computation in Britain, Ashby, Beurle, Taylor, and Uttley (Ashby 1952, Beurle 1957, Taylor 1956, Uttley 1956a, 1956b, 1959). The situation was the same on the other side of the Atlantic. Rosenblatt—the inventor of the perceptron and first to use the term 'connectionist'—seems not to have heard of Turing's unorganised machines (Rosenblatt 1957, 1958a, 1958b, 1959, 1962 esp. pp. 5 and 12ff).[3] Nor is Turing's work mentioned in Hebb's influential book *The Organization of Behavior* (1949), the source of the so-called Hebbian approach to neural learning studied in connectionism today. Discussions of the history of connectionism by Rumelhart, McClelland et al. (1986) show no awareness of Turing's early contribution to the field (see for example pp. 41ff, 152ff, 424).

The pioneering work of Beurle, Taylor and Uttley has been neglected almost to the same extent as Turing's. According to connectionist folklore it was Rosenblatt, influenced by McCulloch, Pitts and Hebb, who originated the field of neuron-like computation. This is not the case. Rosenblatt records that the 'groundwork of perceptron theory was laid in 1957' (Rosenblatt 1962, 27). A series of memoranda by Uttley concerning his probabilistic approach to neuron-like computation survives from as early as 1954 (Uttley 1954a–d) and published accounts of the work of all three men appeared prior to 1957 (see the references given above).

In 1958 Rosenblatt travelled to London and unveiled the perceptron at a symposium held at the National Physical Laboratory. He rashly claimed that 'the only machine prior to the perceptron which has shown itself to be capable of *spontaneous* improvement (as opposed to learning under the tutelage of an experimenter) has been Ashby's homeostat' (Rosenblatt 1959, 424). In a frosty reply to Rosenblatt's paper Stafford Beer remarked:

> [T]here are tendencies to exaggerated claims to be found in the paper.
> . . . [O]ne which ought really to be mentioned is that, apart from the Homeostat, the perceptron is the first machine 'to show spontaneous improvement'. This is not so. But perhaps Dr. Rosenblatt rightly assumed that, after all, everyone here must certainly have heard of Dr. Uttley's work.
>
> (Rosenblatt 1959, Discussion, 463)

Subsequent to the symposium Rosenblatt wrote generously of Uttley's work, describing him, along with Hebb, Hayek and Ashby, as having 'elaborated [the position] . . . upon which the theory of the perceptron is based' (Rosenblatt 1958b, 388). Concerning Taylor's work Rosenblatt wrote:

> Clearly our neuron models are very similar . . . The one important difference which I see in our neuron models is in the choice of a suitable memory variable—in Dr. Taylor's case the threshold, and in my own case, the strength or 'value' of the output signal.
>
> (Rosenblatt 1959, 471)

Rosenblatt's work was also prefigured in the U.S. by that of Clark and Farley (Farley and Clark 1954, Clark and Farley 1955), who in 1954 simulated a network of threshold units with variable connection weights. The training algorithm, or 'modifier', that they employed to adjust the weights during learning is similar to the algorithms subsequently investigated by Rosenblatt. Rosenblatt acknowledged that 'the mechanism for pattern generalisation proposed by Clark and Farley is essentially identical to that found in simple perceptrons' (Rosenblatt 1962, 24).

3 Turing's unorganised machines

Turing introduces the idea of an unorganised machine by means of an example.

> A typical example of an unorganised machine would be as follows. The machine is made up from a rather large number N of similar units. Each unit has two input terminals, and has an output terminal which can be connected to the input terminals of (0 or more) other units. We may imagine that for each integer r, $1 \leq r \leq N$, two numbers $i(r)$ and $j(r)$ are chosen at random from $1 \ldots N$ and that we connect the inputs of unit r to the outputs of units $i(r)$ and $j(r)$. All of the units are connected to a central synchronizing unit from which synchronizing pulses are emitted at more or less equal intervals of time. The times when these pulses arrive will be called 'moments'. Each unit is capable of having two states at each moment. These states may be called 0 and 1.
>
> (1948, 9–10)

Turing then gives (what would now be called) a propagation rule and an activation rule for the network. A propagation rule calculates the net input into a unit, and an activation rule calculates what the new state of a unit is to be, given its net input.

PROPAGATION RULE. The net input into unit r at moment m, $\mathbf{net}(r, m)$, is the product of the state of $i(r)$ at $m - 1$ and the state of $j(r)$ at $m - 1$.

ACTIVATION RULE. The state of r at m is $1 - \mathbf{net}(r, m)$.

A network of the sort described whose behaviour is determined by these two rules is an A-type unorganised machine.

In modern terminology an A-type machine is a collection of NAND units ($P\text{NAND}Q$ is $\neg\,(P\&Q)$). The propagation rule in effect takes the conjunction of the values on the unit's two input lines, and the activation rule forms the negation of this value. Alternative choices of propagation rule and/or activation rule will cause the units to perform other Boolean operations. As is well known, NAND is more fundamental than certain other binary operators (including conjunction, material implication, material equivalence, and inclusive and exclusive disjunction) in the sense that any Boolean operation can be performed by a circuit consisting entirely of NAND units. Thus any such operation can be performed by an A-type machine.

When considering A-type circuits one has to take account of the fact that each unit introduces a delay of one moment into the circuit. Suppose, for example, that the job of some particular unit U in the circuit is to compute $X\text{NAND}Y$ for some pair of specific truth-functions X and Y. The sub-circuits that compute X and Y may deliver their outputs at different moments yet obviously the values of X and Y must reach U at the *same* moment. Turing does not mention how this is to be achieved. A nowadays familiar solution to this problem—which also arises in connection with cpu design—involves the concept of a 'cycle of operation' of n moments duration. Input to the machine is held constant, or 'clamped', throughout each cycle and output is not read until the end of a cycle. Provided n is large enough then by the end of a cycle the output signal will have the desired value.

4 Trainable Boolean networks

The most significant aspect of Turing's discussion of unorganised machines is undoubtedly his idea that an initially random network can be organised to perform a specified task by means of what he describes as 'interfering training' (Turing 1948, 16).

> Many unorganised machines have configurations such that if once that configuration is reached, and if the interference thereafter is appropriately restricted, the machine behaves as one organised for some definite purpose.
>
> (Turing 1948, 14–15)

Turing illustrates his idea by means of the circuit shown in Figure 1 (1948, 10–11). (He stresses that this particular circuit is employed 'for illustrative purposes' and not because it is 'of any great intrinsic importance'.) We will call a pair of units connected in the way shown an 'introverted pair'. By means of external interference the state of unit A may be set to either 0 or 1. The state selected will be referred to as the 'determining condition' of the pair. (Concerning specific interfering mechanisms for changing the state of A Turing remarks '[i]t is ... not difficult to think of appropriate methods by which this could be done' (1948, 15). He gives one simple example of such a mechanism.)

As the reader may verify, the signal produced in unit B's free output connection will be constant from moment to moment and the polarity of the signal will depend only upon the determining condition of the pair. Thus an introverted pair functions as an elementary memory.

Turing defines B-type machines in terms of a certain process of substitution applied to A-type machines: a B-type results if every unit-to-unit connection within an A-type machine is replaced by the device shown in Figure 2 (Turing 1948, 11). That is to say, what is in the A-type a simple connection between points D and E now passes via the depicted device. (Notice that all B-types are A-types.)

Depending on the polarity of the constant signal at C, the signal at E will either (i) be 1 if the signal at D is 0 and 0 if the signal at D is 1, or (ii) always be 1 no matter what the signal at D. If by means of interference the state of A is changed from moment to moment, the device will cycle through these two alternatives. (This interference may be supplied either from outside or from within the network.)

In the first of these cases the device functions as a negation module. In the second case the device in effect disables the connection to which it is attached. That is to say, a unit with the device attached to one of its input connections delivers an output that is a unary function of the signal arriving along its other input connection. (If the devices on both the unit's input connections are placed in disable mode then the unit's output is always 0.) By means of these devices an external agent can organise an initially random B-type machine by selectively disabling and enabling connections within it. This arrangement is functionally equivalent to one in which the stored information takes the form of new connections within the network.[4]

Turing claims that it is a 'general property of B-type machines ... that with suitable initial [i.e. determining] conditions they will do any required job, given sufficient time and provided the number of units is sufficient' (Turing 1948, 15). This follows from the more specific claim that given 'a B-type unorganised machine with sufficient units one can find initial conditions which will make it into a universal [Turing] machine with a given storage capacity' (Turing 1948, 15).

Concerning the latter claim Turing remarks: 'A formal proof to this effect

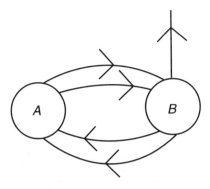

Figure 1

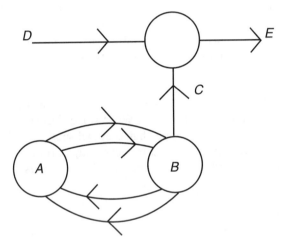

Figure 2

might be of some interest, or even a demonstration of it starting with a particular unorganized B-type machine, but I am not giving it as it lies rather too far outside the main argument' (Turing 1948, 15).[5] It is a pity that Turing does not give any details of the proof, for this might have cast some light on what appears to be an inconsistency in his paper. It is reasonably obvious that not all Boolean functions can be computed by B-type machines as defined and thus that each of the claims quoted in the preceding paragraph is false. (A good way to get a feel for the difficulty is to attempt to design a B-type circuit for computing exclusive disjunction.) The simplest remedy seems to be to modify the substitution in terms of which B-type machines are defined: a B-type results if every unit-to-unit connection within an A-type machine is replaced by *two* of the devices shown in Figure 2 linked in series.

That is to say, what is in the A-type a simple connection between two units now passes through two additional units each with its own introverted pair attached. It is trivially the case that if a function can be computed by some A-type machine then it can also be computed by some machine satisfying the modified definition of a B-type. However, Turing's paper contains no clues as to his own procedure.

As already indicated, the training process for a B-type unorganised machine consists in an external agent setting the determining condition of each introverted pair. In modern architectures repeated applications of a training algorithm—for example the back propagation algorithm—cause the encoding of the problem solution to 'evolve' gradually within the network during the training phase. Turing had no algorithm for training his B-types. He regarded the development of training algorithms for unorganised machines as a central problem and he envisaged the procedure—first implemented by Farley and Clark and nowadays used extensively by connectionists—of programming the training algorithm into a computer simulation of the unorganised machine. With characteristic farsightedness Turing ends his discussion of unorganised machines by sketching the research programme that connectionists are now pursuing:

> I feel that more should be done on these lines. I would like to investigate other types of unorganised machines . . . When some electronic machines are in actual operation I hope that they will make this more feasible. It should be easy to make a model of any particular machine that one wishes to work on within such a UPCM [universal practical computing machine] instead of having to work with a paper machine as at present. If also one decided on quite definite 'teaching policies' these could also be programmed into the machine. One would then allow the whole system to run for an appreciable period, and then break in as a kind of 'inspector of schools' and see what progress had been made.
>
> (1948, 20–21)

The importance that this project held for Turing may be gauged from a remark in a letter that he wrote to Ashby at about the same time:

> In working on the ACE I am more interested in the possibility of producing models of the action of the brain than in the practical applications to computing.[6]

Turing himself was unable to pursue his proposed research programme very far. It must be remembered that at the time he wrote, the only electronic stored-program computer in existence on either side of the Atlantic was a tiny pilot version of the Manchester Mark I.[7] (The pilot version of the ACE did not run its first program until 1950.) By the time he did have access to real computing power (at the University of Manchester) his interests had shifted and he devoted his time to modelling biological growth. It was not until the year of Turing's death that Farley and Clark, working at MIT, succeeded in running the first computer simulation of a small neural network (Farley and Clark 1954).

5 P-type unorganised machines

Turing's main purpose in studying P-type machines seems to have been to search for general training procedures. A P-type machine is not a neural network but a modified Turing machine. Chief among the modifications is the addition of two input lines: the pleasure (or reward) line and the pain (or punishment) line. (Turing considers other modifications, in particular sensory input lines and internal memory units; in the interest of simplicity we say nothing further concerning these.) Unlike standard Turing machines a P-type has no tape.

Initially the P-type machine is unorganised in the sense that its machine table is 'largely incomplete' (Turing 1948, 18). Application of either pleasure or pain by the trainer serves to alter an incomplete table to some successor table. After sufficient training a complete table will emerge.

As is well known the machine table of a standard Turing machine consists of quintuples of the form: (state, symbol under head, symbol to be written, new state, direction of movement). The P-types that Turing explicitly considers have machine tables consisting of triples. There follows an example of such a table. (This is a simplified version of Turing's own example on pp. 18–19.)

State	Control Symbol	External Action
1	U	A
2	D0	B
3	T1	B
4	U	A
5	D1	B

'U' means 'uncertain', 'T' means 'tentative' and 'D' means 'definite'. (It is unnecessary to specify the nature of the external actions.) This table is incomplete in that no control symbol at all is specified for states 1 and 4 and the control symbol 1 has been entered only tentatively in the line for state 3. Only in the case of states 2 and 5 are definite control symbols listed. The table is complete only when a definite control symbol has been specified for each state.

The control symbol determines the state the machine is to go into once it has performed the specified external action. The rules that Turing gives governing the state transitions are:

(a) If the control symbol is 1 (either definitely or tentatively) then **next state** is the remainder of (2 × **present state**) + 1 on division by the total number of states (in this case 5).

For example, if the machine is in state 3 then **next state** is 2.

(b) If the control symbol is 0 (again, either definitely or tentatively) then **next state** is the remainder of 2 × **present state** on division by the total number of states.

For example, if the machine is in state 2 then **next state** is 4.

Let us suppose that the machine is set in motion in state 2. It performs the external action B, shifts to state 4, and performs the action A. No control symbol is specified in state 4. In this case the machine selects a binary digit at random, say 0, and replaces U by T0. The choice of control symbol determines the next state, in this case 3.

The trainer may apply a pleasure or pain stimulus at any time, with the effect that '[w]hen a pain stimulus occurs all tentative entries are cancelled, and when a pleasure stimulus occurs they are all made permanent' (Turing 1948, 18). In other words pleasure replaces every T in the table by D and pain replaces all occurrences of T0 and T1 by U.

Turing suggests that 'it is probably possible to organise these P-type machines into universal machines' but warns that this 'is not easy' (Turing 1948, 19). He continues:

> If, however, we supply the P-type machine with a systematic external memory this organising becomes quite feasible. Such a memory could be provided in the form of a tape, and the [external actions] could include movement to right and left along the tape, and altering the symbol on the tape to 0 or 1 . . . I have succeeded in organising such a (paper) machine into a universal machine . . . This P-type machine with external memory has, it must be admitted, considerably more 'organisation' than say the A-type unorganised machine. Nevertheless the fact that it can be organised into a universal machine still remains interesting.
>
> (Turing 1948, 19–20)

As a search for 'teaching policies' Turing's experiments with P-types were not a success. The method he used to train the P-type with external memory required considerable intelligence on the part of the trainer and he describes it as 'perhaps a little disappointing', remarking that '[i]t is not sufficiently analogous to the kind of process by which a child would really be taught' (Turing 1948, 20).

The key to success in the search for training algorithms was the use of weighted connections or some equivalent device such as variable thresholds. During training the algorithm increments or decrements the values of the weights by some small fixed amount. The relatively small magnitude of the increment or decrement at each step makes possible a smooth convergence towards the desired configuration. In contrast there is nothing smooth about the atomic steps involved in training a B-type. Switching the determining condition of an introverted pair from 0 to 1 or vice versa is a savage all-or-nothing shift. Turing seems not to have considered employing weighted connections or variable thresholds.

6 McCulloch-Pitts networks

It is interesting that Turing makes no reference in the 1948 report to the work of McCulloch and Pitts, itself influenced by his own 1936 paper. Their 1943 article represents the first attempt to apply what they refer to as 'the Turing definition of computability' to the study of neuronal function (McCulloch and Pitts 1943, 129). McCulloch stressed the extent to which his and Pitts' work is indebted to Turing in the course of some autobiographical remarks made during the public discussion of a lecture given by von Neumann in 1948:

> I started at entirely the wrong angle . . . and it was not until I saw Turing's paper [Turing 1936] that I began to get going the right way around, and with Pitts' help formulated the required logical calculus. What we thought we were doing (and I think we succeeded fairly well) was treating the brain as a Turing machine.
>
> (Von Neumann 1961, 319)

Like Turing, McCulloch and Pitts consider Boolean nets of simple two-state 'neurons'. They show (i) that such a net augmented by an external tape can compute all and only numbers that can be computed by Turing machines, and (ii) that without the external tape some but not all of these numbers, and no other numbers, can be computed by nets (McCulloch and Pitts 1943). They give no discussion of universal machines.

McCulloch and Pitts make no use of weighted connections or variable thresholds. Part of the burden of their argument is to show that the behaviour of a net of binary units with variable thresholds can be exactly mimicked by a simple Boolean net without thresholds 'provided the exact time for impulses to pass through the whole net is not crucial' (McCulloch and Pitts 1943, 119, 123–4). They establish the same result in the case of various other phenomena associated with human neurons, in particular relative inhibition, extinction, temporal summation, and the formation of new synapses.

McCulloch and Pitts say that two nets are 'equivalent in the extended sense' when the one exactly mimics the input/output behaviour of the other save possibly for the exact time it takes impulses to pass through the net (1943, 119, 123). There are some differences between the Boolean architectures of Turing and McCulloch-Pitts but there is equivalence in the extended sense. For example, inhibitory synapses are a primitive feature of McCulloch-Pitts nets but not of A-types and B-types. (An input of 1 at an inhibitory synapse at moment m unconditionally sets the output of the unit to 0 at $m + 1$.) An inhibitory synapse can be mimicked by an arrangement consisting essentially of three introverted pairs, one modified in such a way that each unit of the pair has an external input. Working in the opposite direction, an introverted pair can be mimicked by one of the class of nets that McCulloch and Pitts call 'Nets with Circles'.

Turing had undoubtedly heard something of the work of McCulloch and Pitts. Wiener would almost certainly have mentioned McCulloch in the course of his 'talk over the fundamental ideas of cybernetics with Mr Turing' at the NPL in the spring of 1947 (Wiener 1948, 32). (Wiener and McCulloch were founding members of the cybernetics movement.) Moreover von Neumann mentions the McCulloch-Pitts article—albeit very briefly—in the 'First Draft of a Report on the EDVAC', which Turing read in 1945. (Von Neumann appears to have employed a modified version of their diagrammatic notation for neural nets in order to depict the EDVAC's logic gates. Turing went on to extend considerably the notation he found in the 'First Draft' (Carpenter and Doran 1986, 277; Hartree 1949, 97, 102).) Turing and McCulloch seem not to have met until 1949. After their meeting Turing spoke dismissively of McCulloch, referring to him as a charlatan.[8] It is an open question whether the work of McCulloch and Pitts had any influence whatsoever on the development of the ideas presented in the 1948 report.

Over the years a number of commentators on the history of electronic computing machinery, especially those whose primary concern has been with developments in the United States, have found Turing's contributions hard to place. It has often been falsely assumed that most of the early work done in Britain on logical and electronic design was derived from work carried out in the United States, via von Neumann's report on the EDVAC (1945) and the Moore School lecture series of 1946. Turing did read von Neumann's report before writing his 'Proposal for Development in the Mathematics Division of an Automatic Computing Engine (ACE)' but his design is strikingly different from von Neumann's (see Carpenter and Doran 1986, 1977; Huskey 1984). (Max Newman remarked in his obituary of Turing (*Manchester Guardian*, 11 June 1954) 'It was, perhaps, a defect of his qualities that he found it hard to accept the work of others, preferring to work things out for himself'.[9]) A fundamental difference between the machine that Turing proposed and both the EDVAC and its British derivative the EDSAC was that in Turing's design complex behaviour was to be achieved by complex programming rather than by complex equipment. We know of Turing's opinion of Maurice Wilkes' design for the EDSAC from a memo turing wrote in late 1946 or early 1947 to Womersley at the National Physical Laboratory: Wilkes' proposals are 'very contrary to the line of development here, and much more in the American tradition of solving one's difficulties by means of much equipment rather than by thought'.[10]

Turing followed his own path from the abstract machines of his 1936 paper to the idea of a high-speed stored-program computer and contemporaneous research in the United States meant little to him.[11] The same may well have been true in the case of his work on neuron-like computation.

Whatever the influences were on Turing at that time, there is no doubt that his work on neural nets goes importantly beyond the earlier work of McCulloch and Pitts. The latter give only a perfunctory discussion of learning, saying no more than that the mechanisms supposedly underlying learning in the brain—they specifically mention threshold change and the formation of new synapses—can be mimicked by means of nets whose connections and thresholds remain unaltered (McCulloch and Pitts 1943, 117, 124). Turing's idea of using supervised interference to train an initially random arrangement of units to compute a specified function is nowhere prefigured.[12]

Notes

1 That Turing anticipated connectionism was first suggested to us by Justin Leiber in correspondence. Leiber gives a brief discussion on pp. 117–18 and p. 158 of his (1991) and on p. 59 of his (1995). We cannot endorse Leiber's claim that Turing made use of weighted connections (Leiber 1991, 118).

2 We are grateful to Andrew Hodges for drawing our attention to the reprinting in Evans and Robertson 1968.

3 Rosenblatt introduces the term 'connectionist' in the following way: '[According to] theorists in the empiricist tradition . . . the stored information takes the form of new connections, or transmission channels in the nervous system (or the creation of conditions which are functionally equivalent to new connections) . . . The theory to be presented here takes the empiricist, or "connectionist" position . . . The theory has been developed for a hypothetical nervous system, or machine, called a *perceptron*' (Rosenblatt 1958b, 387).

4 See Note 3.

5 Such proofs have been given for a number of modern connectionist architectures, for example by Pollack (1987) and Siegelmann and Sontag (1992). The latter establish the existence of a network capable of simulating a finite-tape universal Turing machine in linear time. They are able to give an upper bound on the size of the network: at most 1058 units are required.

6 The letter is held in the NPL archive, Science Museum, South Kensington, London. It is undated but was written while Turing was working at the NPL.

7 Turing wrote the report during July and August of 1948 (Hodges 1983, 377). The prototype Manchester machine ran its first progam in June 1948 and the

Cambridge EDSAC not until May 1949 (Kilburn and Williams 1953, 120; Wilkes 1985, 142). The American ENIAC first went into operation in November 1945 but was not stored-program. It was not until September 1948 that the ENIAC began operating with program code stored in its function tables (Goldstine 1972, 233; Metropolis and Worlton 1980, 53–54). However, since the function tables were read-only, variable addressing was not possible and so the ENIAC was never stored-program in the full sense. The American BINAC, which was stored-program, was first tested in August 1949 (Stern 1979, 12–13). The IBM SSEC, which first ran in public in January 1948, was stored-program but was not fully electronic, being largely electromechanical (Bowden 1953, 174–5; Eckert 1948). Despite a widespread belief to the contrary, the ENIAC was not the first electronic computing machine. This distinction belongs to the Colossi, constructed at Bletchley Park, Buckinghamshire, from 1943 onwards for use against the German 'fish' codes. The Colossus was program-controlled rather than stored-program. It performed Boolean operations and had some arithmetical capability (Randell 1980). The Colossus was designed and built by Flowers and Newman with—according to Donald Michie, himself a junior member of Newman's team—some assistance from Turing. (Possibly Turing's contributions concerned the methods of search employed by the Colossus.) The existence of the Colossus was kept secret by the British government for a number of years after the war and so it was that von Neumann and others, in lectures and public addresses, told the world that the ENIAC was 'the first electronic computing machine' (von Neumann 1954, 238–9). (The Manchester firm Ferranti built a production version of the Manchester Mark I. The first was installed in February 1951, two months before the first UNIVAC (Lavington 1975, 20).)

8 This was Robin Gandy's recollection.
9 Quoted in Kleene 1987, 492.
10 The memo is reproduced in Huskey 1984, 354.
11 Turing's wartime involvement with electronics was no doubt the key link between his earlier theoretical work and the ACE: by means of this new technology the abstract stored-program machines of his 1936 paper could be turned into a reality. (Probably his wartime involvement with the Colossus at Bletchley Park was a particularly important influence in that respect.) Here is Turing's own statement of the relationship between the universal Turing machine and the ACE.

> Some years ago I was researching on what might now be described as an investigation of the theoretical possibilities and limitations of digital computing machines. I considered a type of machine which had a central mechanism, and an infinite memory which was contained on an infinite tape . . . Machines such as the ACE may be regarded as practical versions of this same type of machine.
>
> (Turing 1947, 106–7)

In the previously mentioned letter to Ashby Turing says:

> The ACE is in fact, analogous to the 'universal machine' described in my paper on computable [sic] numbers . . . [W]ithout altering the design of the machine itself, it can, in theory at any rate, be used as a model of any other machine, by making it remember a suitable set of instructions.

As Hodges suggests (1983, 556) Sara Turing was probably more or less quoting her son's own words when she wrote in connection with the ACE project that 'his aim [was] to see his logical theory of a universal machine, previously set out in his paper "Computable Numbers" [sic] . . . take concrete form in an actual machine' (Turing 1959, 78).

12 We are indebted to John Andreae, Sean Broadley, Nat Gilman, Simeon Lodge, Donald Michie, Seth Wagoner and Justin Zajac for discussion, and especially so to Craig Webster. John Andreae, Kevin Korb and Craig Webster commented helpfully on earlier versions of this paper. Craig and Bruce Webster wrote a B-type simulator for us.

References

Ashby, W. R.: 1952, *Design for a Brain*, Chapman and Hall, London.

Beurle, R. L.: 1957, 'Properties of a Mass of Cells Capable of Regenerating Pulses', *Philosophical Transactions of the Royal Society of London*, Series B, **240**, 55–94.

Bowden, B. V. (ed.): 1953, *Faster than Thought*, Pitman, London.

Carpenter, B. E. and R. W. Doran: 1977, 'The Other Turing Machine'. *Computer Journal* **20**, 269–79.

Carpenter, B. E. and R. W. Doran (eds): 1986, *A. M. Turing's* ACE *Report of 1946 and Other Papers*, MIT Press, Cambridge, Mass.

Clark, W. A. and B. G. Farley: 1955, 'Generalisation of Pattern Recognition in a Self-Organising System', *Proceedings of the Western Joint Computer Conference*, 86–91.

Eckert, W. J.: 1948, 'Electrons and Computation', reprinted in B. Randell (ed.): 1982, *The Origins of Digital Computers*, Springer-Verlag, Berlin, pp. 219–28.

Evans, C. R. and A. D. J. Robertson (eds): 1968, *Cybernetics: Key Papers*, Butterworths, London.

Farley, B. G. and W. A. Clark: 1954, 'Simulation of Self-Organising Systems by Digital Computer', *Institute of Radio Engineers Transactions on Information Theory* **4**, 76–84.

Goldstine, H. H.: 1972, *The Computer from Pascal to von Neumann*, Princeton University Press, Princeton.

Hartree, D. R.: 1949, *Calculating Instruments and Machines*, University of Illinois Press, Illinois.

Hebb, D. O.: 1949, *The Organization of Behavior: A Neuropsychological Theory*, John Wiley, New York.

Hodges, A.: 1983, *Alan Turing: The Enigma*, Burnett, London.

Huskey, H. D.: 1984, 'From ACE to the G-15', *Annals of the History of Computing* **6**, 350–71.

Ince, D. C. (ed.): 1992, *Collected Works of A.M. Turing: Mechanical Intelligence*, North Holland, Amsterdam.

Kilburn, T. and F. C. Williams: 1953, 'The University of Manchester Computing Machine', in Bowden 1953, pp. 117–29.

Kleene, S. C.: 1987, 'Reflections on Church's Thesis', *Notre Dame Journal of Formal Logic* **28**, 490–98.

Lavington, S. H.: 1975, *A History of Manchester Computers*, NCC Publications, Manchester.

Leiber, J.: 1991, *An Invitation to Cognitive Science*, Basil Blackwell, Oxford.

Leiber, J.: 1995, 'On *Turing's* Turing Test and Why the *Matter* Matters', *Synthese* **104**, 59–69.

McCulloch, W. S. and W. Pitts: 1943, 'A Logical Calculus of the Ideas Immanent in Nervous Activity', *Bulletin of Mathematical Biophysics* **5**, 115–33.

Minsky, M. L. and S. Papert: 1969, *Perceptrons: An Introduction to Computational Geometry*, MIT Press, Cambridge, Mass.

Metropolis, N. and J. Worlton: 1980, 'A Trilogy of Errors in the History of Computing', *Annals of the History of Computing* **2**, 49–59.

Newell, A., J. C. Shaw, and H. A. Simon: 1957, 'Empirical Explorations with the Logic Theory Machine: a Case Study in Heuristics', reprinted in E. A. Feigenbaum and J. Feldman (eds), *Computers and Thought*, McGraw-Hill, New York (1963), pp. 109–33.

Newell, A. and H. A. Simon: 1961, 'GPS, a Program that Simulates Human Thought', reprinted in E. A. Feigenbaum and J. Feldman (eds), *Computers and Thought*, McGraw-Hill, New York (1963), pp. 279–93.

Newell, A. and H. A. Simon: 1976, 'Computer Science as Empirical Inquiry: Symbols and Search', in J. Haugeland (ed.), *Mind Design: Philosophy, Psychology, Artificial Intelligence*, MIT Press, Cambridge, Mass. (1981), pp. 35–66.

Pollack, J. B.: 1987, *On Connectionist Models of Natural Language Processing*, Ph.D. Dissertation, University of Illinois, Urbana.

Randell, B.: 1980, 'The Colossus', in N. Metropolis, J. Howlett, and G. C. Rota (eds), *A History of Computing in the Twentieth Century*, Academic Press, New York, pp. 47–92.

Rosenblatt, F.: 1957, *The Perceptron, a Perceiving and Recognizing Automaton*, Cornell Aeronautical Laboratory Report No. 85-460-1.

Rosenblatt, F.: 1958a, *The Perceptron: a Theory of Statistical Separability in Cognitive Systems*, Cornell Aeronautical Laboratory Report No. VG-1196-G-1.

Rosenblatt, F.: 1958b, 'The Perceptron: a Probabilistic Model for Information Storage and Organisation in the Brain', *Psychological Review* **65**, 386–408.

Rosenblatt, F.: 1959, 'Two Theorems of Statistical Separability in the Perceptron', in *Mechanisation of Thought Processes*, Vol. 1, H.M. Stationery Office, London (1959), pp. 419–72.

Rosenblatt, F.: 1962, *Principles of Neurodynamics*, Spartan, Washington, D.C.

Rumelhart, D. E., J. L. McClelland, and the PDP Research Group: 1986, *Parallel Distributed Processing: Explorations in the Microstructure of Cognition*, Vol. 1: *Foundations*, MIT Press, Cambridge, Mass.

Siegelmann, H. T. and E. D. Sontag: 1992, 'On the Computational Power of Neural Nets', *Proceedings of the 5th Annual ACM Workshop on Computational Learning Theory*, 440–49.

Stern, N.: 1979, 'The BINAC: A Case Study in the History of Technology', *Annals of the History of Computing* **1**, 9–20.

Taylor, W. K.: 1956, 'Electrical Simulation of Some Nervous System Functional Activities', in C. Cherry (ed.), *Information Theory*, Butterworths, London (1956), pp. 314–28.

Turing, A. M.: 1936, 'On Computable Numbers, with an Application to the Entscheidungsproblem', *Proceedings of the London Mathematical Society*, Series 2, **42** (1936–37), 230–65.

Turing, A. M.: 1946, 'Proposal for Development in the Mathematics Division of an Automatic Computing Engine (ACE)', in Carpenter and Doran (eds), 1986, pp. 20–105.

Turing, A. M.: 1947, 'Lecture to the London Mathematical Society on 20 February 1947', in Carpenter and Doran (eds), 1986, pp. 106–24.

Turing, A. M.: 1948, 'Intelligent Machinery', National Physical Laboratory Report, in B. Meltzer and D. Michie (eds), *Machine Intelligence*, Vol. 5, Edinburgh University Press, Edinburgh (1969), pp. 3–23. Reproduced with the same pagination in Ince (1992). Also in Evans and Robertson (1968).

Turing, A. M.: 1950, 'Computing Machinery and Intelligence', *Mind* **59**, 433–60.

Turing, S.: 1959, *Alan M. Turing*, W. Heffer, Cambridge.

Uttley, A. M.: 1954a, 'Conditional Probability Machines and Conditioned Reflexes', Radar Research Establishment Memorandum No. 1045.

Uttley, A. M.: 1954b, 'The Classification of Signals in the Nervous System', R.R.E. Memorandum No. 1047.

Uttley, A. M.: 1954c, 'The Probability of Neural Connections', R.R.E. Memorandum No. 1048.

Uttley, A. M.: 1954d, 'The Stability of a Uniform Population of Neurons', R.R.E. Memorandum No. 1049.

Uttley, A. M.: 1956a, 'Conditional Probability Machines and Conditioned Reflexes', in C. E. Shannon and J. McCarthy (eds), *Automata Studies*, Princeton University Press, Princeton (1956), pp. 253–75.

Uttley, A. M.: 1956b, 'Temporal and Spatial Patterns in a Conditional Probability Machine', in C. E. Shannon and J. McCarthy (eds), *Automata Studies*, Princeton University Press, Princeton (1956), pp. 277–85.

Uttley, A. M.: 1959, 'Conditional Probability Computing in a Nervous System', in *Mechanisation of Thought Processes*, Vol. 1, H.M. Stationery Office, London (1959), pp. 121–47.

Von Neumann, J.: 1945, 'First Draft of a Report on the EDVAC'. An edited version appears in B. Randell (ed.), *The Origins of Digital Computers*, Springer-Verlag, Berlin (1982), pp. 383–92.

Von Neumann, J.: 1954, 'The NORC and Problems in High Speed Computing', in Taub, A. H. (ed.), *Collected Works of John von Neumann*, Vol. 5, Pergamon Press, Oxford (1961), pp. 238–47.

Wiener, N.: 1948, *Cybernetics*, John Wiley, New York.

Wilkes, M. V.: 1985, *Memoirs of a Computer Pioneer*, MIT Press, Cambridge, Mass.

39

THE PERCEPTRON

A Probabilistic Model for Information Storage and Organization in the Brain[1]

F. Rosenblatt

Source: *Psychological Review* 65(6) (1958): 386–408.

If we are eventually to understand the capability of higher organisms for perceptual recognition, generalization, recall, and thinking, we must first have answers to three fundamental questions:

1. How is information about the physical world sensed, or detected, by the biological system?
2. In what form is information stored, or remembered?
3. How does information contained in storage, or in memory, influence recognition and behavior?

The first of these questions is in the province of sensory physiology, and is the only one for which appreciable understanding has been achieved. This article will be concerned primarily with the second and third questions, which are still subject to a vast amount of speculation, and where the few relevant facts currently supplied by neurophysiology have not yet been integrated into an acceptable theory.

With regard to the second question, two alternative positions have been maintained. The first suggests that storage of sensory information is in the form of coded representations or images, with some sort of one-to-one mapping between the sensory stimulus and the stored pattern. According to this hypothesis, if one understood the code or "wiring diagram" of the nervous system, one should, in principle, be able to discover exactly what an organism remembers by reconstructing the original sensory patterns from the "memory traces" which they have left, much as we might develop a photographic negative, or translate the pattern of electrical charges in the "memory" of a digital computer. This hypothesis is appealing in its simplicity and ready intelligibility, and a large family of theoretical brain models has been developed around the idea of a coded, representational memory (2, 3, 9, 14). The alternative approach, which stems from the tradition of British empiricism, hazards the guess that the images of stimuli may never really be recorded at all, and that the central nervous system simply acts as an intricate switching network, where retention takes the form of new connections, or pathways, between centers of activity. In many of the more recent developments of this position (Hebb's "cell assembly," and Hull's "cortical anticipatory goal response," for example) the "responses" which are associated to stimuli may be entirely contained within the CNS itself. In this case the response represents an "idea" rather than an action. The important feature of this approach is that there is never any simple mapping of the stimulus into memory, according to some code which would permit its later reconstruction. Whatever information is retained must somehow be stored as a *preference for a particular response*; i.e., the information is contained in *connections* or *associations* rather than topographic representations. (The term *response*, for the remainder of this presentation, should be understood to mean any distinguishable state of the organism, which may or may not involve externally detectable muscular activity. The activation of some nucleus of cells in the central nervous system, for example, can constitute a response, according to this definition.)

Corresponding to these two positions on the method of information retention, there exist two hypotheses with regard to the third question, the manner in which stored information exerts its influence on current activity. The "coded memory theorists" are forced to conclude that recognition of any stimulus involves the matching or systematic comparison of the contents of storage with incoming sensory patterns, in order to determine whether the current stimulus has been seen before, and to determine the appropriate response from the organism. The theorists in the empiricist tradition, on the other hand, have essentially combined the answer to the third question with their answer to the second: since the stored information takes the form of new connections, or transmission channels in the nervous system (or the creation of conditions which are functionally equivalent to new connections), it follows that the new stimuli will make use of these new pathways which have been created, automatically activating the appropriate response without requiring any separate process for their recognition or identification.

The theory to be presented here takes the empiricist, or "connectionist" position with regard to these questions. The theory has been developed for a hypothetical nervous system, or machine, called a *perceptron*. The perceptron is designed to illustrate some of the fundamental properties of intelligent systems in general, without becoming too deeply enmeshed in the special, and frequently unknown, conditions which hold for particular biological organisms. The analogy between the perception and biological systems should be readily apparent to the reader.

During the last few decades, the development of symbolic logic, digital computers, and switching theory has impressed many theorists with the functional similarity between a neuron and the simple on-off units of which computers are constructed, and has provided the analytical methods necessary for representing highly complex logical functions in terms of such elements. The result has been a profusion of brain models which amount simply to logical contrivances for performing particular algorithms (representing "recall," stimulus comparison, transformation, and various kinds of analysis) in response to sequences of stimuli—e.g., Rashevsky (14), McCulloch (10), McCulloch & Pitts (11), Culbertson (2), Kleene (8), and Minsky (13). A relatively small number of theorists, like Ashby (1) and von Neumann (17, 18), have been concerned with the problems of how an imperfect neural network, containing many random connections, can be made to perform reliably those functions which might be represented by idealized wiring diagrams. Unfortunately, the language of symbolic logic and Boolean algebra is less well suited for such investigations. The need for a suitable language for the mathematical analysis of events in systems where only the gross organization can be characterized, and the precise structure is unknown, has led the author to formulate the current model in terms of probability theory rather than symbolic logic.

The theorists referred to above were chiefly concerned with the question of how such functions as perception and recall might be achieved by a deterministic physical system of any sort, rather than how this is actually done by the brain. The models which have been produced all fail in some important respects (absence of equipotentiality, lack of neuroeconomy, excessive specificity of connections and synchronization requirements, unrealistic specificity of stimuli sufficient for cell firing, postulation of variables or functional features with no known neurological correlates, etc.) to correspond to a biological system. The proponents of this line of approach have maintained that, once it has been shown how a physical system of any variety might be made to perceive and recognize stimuli, or perform other brainlike functions, it would require only a refinement or modification of existing principles to understand the working of a more realistic nervous system, and to eliminate the shortcomings mentioned above. The writer takes the position, on the other hand, that these shortcomings are such that a mere refinement or improvement of the principles already suggested can never account for biological intelligence: a *difference in principle* is clearly indicated. The theory of statistical separability (Cf. 15), which is to be summarized here, appears to offer a solution in principle to all of these difficulties.

Those theorists—Hebb (7), Milner (12), Eccles (4), Hayek (6)—who have been more directly concerned with the biological nervous system and its activity in a natural environment, rather than with formally analogous machines, have generally been less exact in their formulations and far from rigorous in their analysis, so that it is frequently hard to assess whether or not the systems that they describe could actually work in a realistic nervous system, and what the necessary and sufficient conditions might be. Here again, the lack of an analytic language comparable in proficiency to the Boolean algebra of the network analysts has been one of the main obstacles. The contributions of this group should perhaps be considered as suggestions of what to look for and investigate, rather than as finished theoretical systems in their own right. Seen from this viewpoint, the most suggestive work, from the standpoint of the following theory, is that of Hebb and Hayek.

The position, elaborated by Hebb (7), Hayek (6), Uttley (16), and Ashby (1), in particular, upon which the theory of the perceptron is based, can be summarized by the following assumptions:

1. The physical connections of the nervous system which are involved in learning and recognition are not identical from one organism to another. At birth, the construction of the most important networks is largely random, subject to a minimum number of genetic constraints.

2. The original system of connected cells is capable of a certain amount of plasticity; after a period of neural activity, the probability that a stimulus applied to one set of cells will cause a response in some other set is likely to change, due to some relatively long-lasting changes in the neurons themselves.

3. Through exposure to a large sample of stimuli, those which are most "similar" (in some sense which must be defined in terms of the particular physical system) will tend to form pathways to the same sets of responding cells. Those which are markedly "dissimilar" will tend to develop connections to different sets of responding cells.

4. The application of positive and/or negative reinforcement (or stimuli which serve this function) may facilitate or hinder whatever formation of connections is currently in progress.

5. *Similarity*, in such a system, is represented at some level of the nervous system by a tendency of similar stimuli to activate the same sets of cells. Similarity is not a necessary attribute of particular formal or geometrical classes of stimuli, but depends on the physical organization of the perceiving system, an organization which evolves through interaction with a given environment. The structure of the system, as well as the ecology of the stimulus-environment, will affect, and will largely determine, the classes of "things" into which the perceptual world is divided.

The organization of a perceptron

The organization of a typical photo-perceptron (a perceptron responding to optical patterns as stimuli) is shown in Fig. 1. The rules of its organization are as follows:

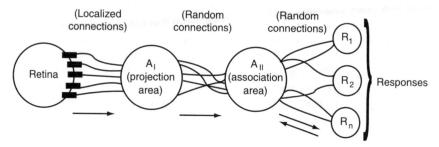

Figure 1 Organization of a perceptron

1. Stimuli impinge on a retina of sensory units (S-points), which are assumed to respond on an all-or-nothing basis, in some models, or with a pulse amplitude or frequency proportional to the stimulus intensity, in other models. In the models considered here, an all-or-nothing response will be assumed.

2. Impulses are transmitted to a set of association cells (A-units) in a "projection area" (A_I). This projection area may be omitted in some models, where the retina is connected directly to the association area (A_{II}). The cells in the projection area each receive a number of connections from the sensory points. The set of S-points transmitting impulses to a particular A-unit will be called the *origin points* of that A-unit. These origin points may be either *excitatory* or *inhibitory* in their effect on the A-unit. If the algebraic sum of excitatory and inhibitory impulse intensities is equal to or greater than the threshold (θ) of the A-unit, then the A-unit fires, again on an all-or-nothing basis (or, in some models, which will not be considered here, with a frequency which depends on the net value of the impulses received). The origin points of the A-units in the projection area tend to be clustered or focalized, about some central point, corresponding to each A-unit. The number of origin points falls off exponentially as the retinal distance from the central point for the A-unit in question increases. (Such a distribution seems to be supported by physiological evidence, and serves an important functional purpose in contour detection.)

3. Between the projection area and the association area (A_{II}), connections are assumed to be random. That is, each A-unit in the A_{II} set receives some number of fibers from origin points in the A_I set, but these origin points are scattered at random throughout the projection area. Apart from their con-nection distribution, the A_{II} units are identical with the A_I units, and respond under similar conditions.

4. The "responses," R_1, R_2, ..., R_n are cells (or sets of cells) which respond in much the same fashion as the A-units. Each response has a typic-ally large number of origin points located at random in the A_{II} set. The set of A-units transmitting impulses to a particular response will be called the

source-set for that response. (The source-set of a response is identical to its set of origin points in the A-system.) The arrows in Fig. 1 indicate the direction of transmission through the network. Note that up to A_{II} all connections are forward, and there is no feedback. When we come to the last set of connections, between A_{II} and the R-units, connections are established in both directions. The rule governing feedback connections, in most models of the perceptron, can be either of the following alternatives:

(a) Each response has excitatory feedback connections to the cells in its own source-set, or

(b) Each response has inhibitory feedback connections to the complement of its own source-set (i.e., it tends to prohibit activity in any association cells which do not transmit to it).

The first of these rules seems more plausible anatomically, since the R-units might be located in the same cortical area as their respective source-sets, making mutual excitation between the R-units and the A-units of the appropriate source-set highly probable. The alternative rule (b) leads to a more readily analyzed system, however, and will therefore be assumed for most of the systems to be evaluated here.

Figure 2 shows the organization of a simplified perceptron, which affords a convenient entry into the theory of statistical separability. After the theory has been developed for this simplified model, we will be in a better position

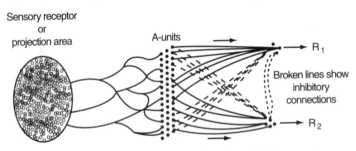

Figure 2A Schematic representation of connections in a simple perceptron

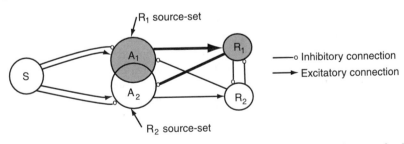

Figure 2B Venn diagram of the same perceptron (shading shows active sets for R_1 response)

to discuss the advantages of the system in Fig. 1. The feedback connections shown in Fig. 2 are inhibitory, and go to the complement of the source-set for the response from which they originate; consequently, this system is organized according to Rule *b*, above. The system shown here has only three stages, the first association stage having been eliminated. Each A-unit has a set of randomly located origin points in the retina. Such a system will form similarity concepts on the basis of *coincident areas* of stimuli, rather than by the similarity of contours or outlines. While such a system is at a disadvantage in many discrimination experiments, its capability is still quite impressive, as will be demonstrated presently. The system shown in Fig. 2 has only two responses, but there is clearly no limit on the number that might be included.

The responses in a system organized in this fashion are mutually exclusive. If R_1 occurs, it will tend to inhibit R_2, and will also inhibit the source-set for R_2. Likewise, if R_2 should occur, it will tend to inhibit R_1. If the total impulse received from all the A-units in one source-set is stronger or more frequent than the impulse received by the alternative (antagonistic) response, then the first response will tend to gain an advantage over the other, and will be the one which occurs. If such a system is to be capable of learning, then it must be possible to modify the A-units or their connections in such a way that stimuli of one class will tend to evoke a stronger impulse in the R_1 source-set than in the R_2 source-set, while stimuli of another (dissimilar) class will tend to evoke a stronger impulse in the R_2 source-set than in the R_1 source-set.

It will be assumed that the impulses delivered by each A-unit can be characterized by a value, V, which may be an amplitude, frequency, latency, or probability of completing transmission. If an A-unit has a high value, then all of its output impulses are considered to be more effective, more potent, or more likely to arrive at their endbulbs than impulses from an A-unit with a lower value. The value of an A-unit is considered to be a fairly stable characteristic, probably depending on the metabolic condition of the cell and the cell membrane, but it is not absolutely constant. It is assumed that, in general, periods of activity tend to increase a cell's value, while the value may decay (in some models) with inactivity. The most interesting models are those in which cells are assumed to complete for metabolic materials, the more active cells gaining at the expense of the less active cells. In such a system, if there is no activity, all cells will tend to remain in a relatively constant condition, and (regardless of activity) the net value of the system, taken in its entirety, will remain constant at all times. Three types of systems, which differ in their value dynamics, have been investigated quantitatively. Their principal logical features are compared in Table 1. In the alpha system, an active cell simply gains an increment of value for every impulse, and holds this gain indefinitely. In the beta system, each source-set is allowed a certain constant rate of gain, the increments being apportioned among the cells of

Table 1 Comparison of logical characteristics of α, β, and γ systems

	α-System (Uncompensated Gain System)	β-System (Constant Feed System)	γ-System (Parasitic Gain System)
Total value-gain of source set per reinforcement	N_{a_r}	K	0
ΔV for A-units active for 1 unit of time	+1	K/N_{a_r}	+1
ΔV for inactive A-units outside of dominant set	0	K/N_{A_r}	0
ΔV for inactive A-units of dominant set	0	0	$\dfrac{-N_{a_r}}{N_{A_r} - N_{a_r}}$
Mean value of A-system	Increases with number of reinforcements	Increases with time	Constant
Difference between mean values of source-sets	Proportional to differences of reinforcement frequency $(n_{s_{rl}} - n_{s_{rl}})$	0	0

Note: In the β and γ systems, the total value-change for any A-unit will be the sum of the ΔV's for all source-sets of which it is a member.

N_{a_r} = Number of active units in source-set
N_{A_r} = Total number of units in source-set
$n_{s_{rl}}$ = Number of stimuli associated to response r_j
K = Arbitrary constant

the source-set in proportion to their activity. In the gamma system, active cells gain in value at the expense of the inactive cells of their source-set, so that the total value of a source-set is always constant.

For purposes of analysis, it is convenient to distinguish two phases in the response of the system to a stimulus (Fig. 3). In the *predominant phase*, some proportion of A-units (represented by solid dots in the figure) responds to the stimulus, but the R-units are still inactive. This phase is transient, and quickly gives way to the *postdominant phase*, in which one of the responses becomes active, inhibiting activity in the complement of its own source-set, and thus preventing the occurrence of any alternative response. The response which happens to become dominant is initially random, but if the A-units are reinforced (i.e., if the active units are allowed to gain in value), then when the same stimulus is presented again at a later time, the same response will have a stronger tendency to recur, and learning can be said to have taken place.

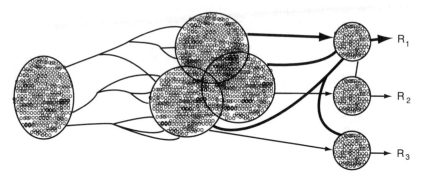

Figure 3A Predominant phase. Inhibitory connections are not shown. Solid black units are active

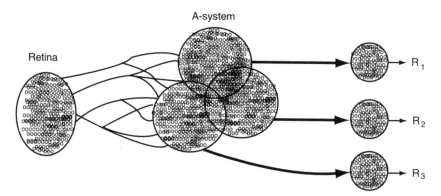

Figure 3B Postdominant phase. Dominant subset suppresses rival sets. Inhibitory connections shown only for R_1

Figure 3 Phases of response to a stimulus

Analysis of the predominant phase

The perceptrons considered here will always assume a fixed threshold, θ, for the activation of the A-units. Such a system will be called a *fixed-threshold model*, in contrast to a *continuous transducer model*, where the response of the A-unit is some continuous function of the impinging stimulus energy.

In order to predict the learning curves of a fixed-threshold perceptron, two variables have been found to be of primary importance. They are defined as follows:

P_a = the expected proportion of A-units activated by a stimulus of a given size,

P_c = the conditional probability that an A-unit which responds to a given stimulus, S_1, will also respond to another given stimulus, S_2.

It can be shown (Rosenblatt, 15) that as the size of the retina is increased, the number of S-points (N_s) quickly ceases to be a significant parameter, and the values of P_a and P_c approach the value that they would have for a retina with infinitely many points. For a large retina, therefore, the equations are as follows:

$$P_a = \sum_{e=0}^{x} \sum_{i=0}^{\substack{min \\ (y,\, e-1)}} P(e,i) \tag{1}$$

where

$$P(e,\, i) = \binom{x}{e} R^e (1 - R)^{x-e} \binom{y}{i} R^i (1 - R)^{y-i}$$

and

R = proportion of S-points activated by the stimulus
x = number of excitatory connections to each A-unit
y = number of inhibitory connections to each A-unit
θ = threshold of A-units.

(The quantities e and i are the excitatory and inhibitory components of the excitation received by the A-unit from the stimulus. If the algebraic sum $a = e + i$ is equal to or greater than θ, the A-unit is assumed to respond.)

$$P_c = \frac{1}{P_a} \sum_{e=0}^{x} \sum_{i=e-\theta}^{y} \sum_{l_e=0}^{e} \sum_{l_i=0}^{i} \sum_{g_e=0}^{x-e} \sum_{g_i=0}^{y-i} P(e,\, i,\, l_e,\, l_i,\, g_e,\, g_i) \tag{2}$$

$$(e - i - l_e + l_i + g_e - g_i \geq \theta)$$

where

$$P(e,\, i,\, l_e,\, l_i,\, g_e,\, g_i) = \binom{x}{e} R^e (1 - R)^{x-e} \binom{y}{i} R^i (1 - R)^{y-i} \binom{e}{l_e} L^{l_e} (1 - L)^{e - l_e}$$

$$\times \binom{i}{l_i} L^{l_i} (1 - L)^{i - l_i} \binom{x-e}{g_c} G^{g_e} (1 - G)^{x-e-g_e} \binom{y-i}{g_i} G^{g_i} (1 - G)^{y-i-g_i}$$

407

and

L = proportion of the S-points illuminated by the first stimulus, S_1, which are not illuminated by S_2

G = proportion of the residual S-set (left over from the first stimulus) which is included in the second stimulus (S_2).

The quantities R, L, and G specify the two stimuli and their retinal overlap. l_e and l_i are, respectively, the numbers of excitatory and inhibitory origin points "lost" by the A-unit when stimulus S_1 is replaced by S_2; g_e and g_i are the numbers of excitatory and inhibitory origin points "gained" when stimulus S_1 is replaced by S_2 The summations in Equation 2 are between the limits indicated, subject to the side condition $e - i - l_e + l_i + g_e - g_i \geq 0$.

Some of the most important characteristics of P_a are illustrated in Fig. 4, which shows P_a as a function of the retinal area illuminated (R). Note that P_a can be reduced in magnitude by either increasing the threshold, θ, or by increasing the proportion of inhibitory, connections (y). A comparison of Fig. 4b and 4c shows that if the excitation is about equal to the inhibition, the curves for P_a as a function of R are flattened out, so that there is little variation in P_a for stimuli of different sizes. This fact is of great importance

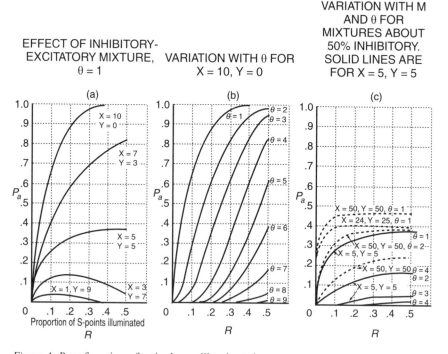

Figure 4 P_a as function of retinal area illuminated

for systems which require P_a to be close to an optimum value in order to perform properly.

The behavior of P_e is illustrated in Fig. 5 and 6. The curves in Fig. 5 can be compared with those for P_a in Fig. 4. Note that as the threshold is increased, there is an even sharper reduction in the value of P_c than was the case with P_a. P_c also decreases as the proportion of inhibitory connections increases, as does P_a. Fig. 5, which is calculated for nonoverlapping stimuli, illustrates the fact that P_c remains greater than zero even when the stimuli are completely disjunct, and illuminate no retinal points in common. In Fig. 6, the effect of varying amounts of overlap between the stimuli is shown. In all cases, the value of P_c goes to unity as the stimuli approach perfect identity. For smaller stimuli (broken line curves), the value of P_c is lower than for large stimuli. Similarly, the value is less for high thresholds than for low thresholds. The minimum value of P_c will be equal to

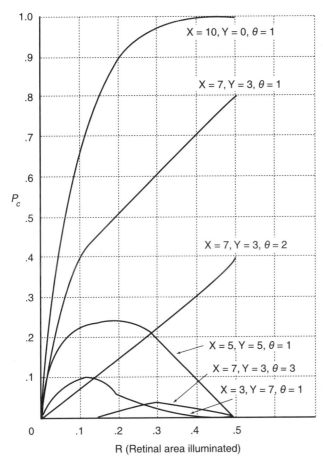

Figure 5 P_e as a function of R, for nonoverlapping stimuli

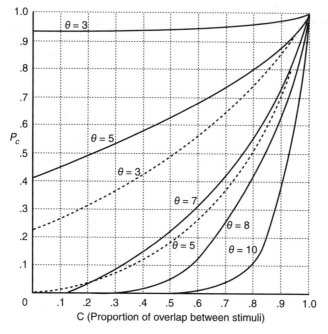

Figure 6 P_c as a function of C. $X = 10$, $Y = 0$. Solid lines; $R = .5$; broken lines: $R = .2$

$$P_{c_{min}} = (1 - L)^x(1 - G)^y. \tag{3}$$

In Fig. 6, $P_{c_{min}}$ corresponds to the curve for $\theta = 10$. Note that under these conditions the probability that the A-unit responds to both stimuli (P_c) is practically zero, except for stimuli which are quite close to identity. This condition can be of considerable help in discrimination learning.

Mathematical analysis of learning in the perceptron

The response of the perceptron in the predominant phase, where some fraction of the A-units (scattered throughout the system) responds to the stimulus, quickly gives way to the postdominant response, in which activity is limited to a single source-set, the other sets being suppressed. Two possible systems have been studied for the determination of the "dominant" response, in the postdominant phase. In one (the mean-discriminating system, or μ-system), the response whose inputs have the greatest mean value responds first, gaining a slight advantage over the others, so that it quickly becomes dominant. In the second case (the sum-discriminating system, or Σ-system), the response whose inputs have the greatest net value gains an advantage. In

410

most cases, systems which respond to mean values have an advantage over systems which respond to sums, since the means are less influenced by random variations in P_a from one source-set to another. In the case of the γ-system (see Table 1), however, the performance of the μ-system and Σ-system become identical.

We have indicated that the perceptron is expected to learn, or to form associations, as a result of the changes in value that occur as a result of the activity of the association cells. In evaluating this learning, one of two types of hypothetical experiments can be considered. In the first case, the perceptron is exposed to some series of stimulus patterns (which might be presented in random positions on the retina) and is "forced" to give the desired response in each case. (This forcing of responses is assumed to be a prerogative of the experimenter. In experiments intended to evaluate trial-and-error learning, with more sophisticated perceptrons, the experimenter does not force the system to respond in the desired fashion, but merely applies positive reinforcement when the response happens to be correct, and negative reinforcement when the response is wrong.) In evaluating the learning which has taken place during this "learning series," the perceptron is assumed to be "frozen" in its current condition, no further value changes being allowed, and the same series of stimuli is presented again in precisely the same fashion, so that the stimuli fall on identical positions on the retina. The probability that the perceptron will show a bias towards the "correct" response (the one which has been previously reinforced during the learning series) in preference to any given alternative response is called P_r, the probability of correct choice of response between two alternatives.

In the second type of experiment, a learning series is presented exactly as before, but instead of evaluating the perceptron's performance using the same series of stimuli which were shown before, a new series is presented, in which stimuli may be drawn from the same *classes* that were previously experienced, but are not necessarily identical. This new test series is assumed to be composed of stimuli projected onto random retinal positions, which are chosen independently of the positions selected for the learning series. The stimuli of the test series may also differ in size or rotational position from the stimuli which were previously experienced. In this case, we are interested in the probability that the perceptron will give the correct response for the *class* of stimuli which is represented, regardless of whether the particular stimulus has been seen before or not. This probability is called P_g, the probability of correct generalization. As with P_r, P_g is actually the probability that a bias will be found in favor of the proper response rather than any one alternative; only one pair of responses at a time is considered, and the fact that the response bias is correct in one pair does not mean that there may not be other pairs in which the bias favors the wrong response. The probability that the correct response will be preferred over *all* alternatives is designated P_R or P_G.

In all cases investigated, a single general equation gives a close approximation to P_r and P_g, if the appropriate constants are substituted. This equation is of the form:

$$P = P(N_{a_r} > 0) \cdot \varphi(Z) \tag{4}$$

where

$$P(N_{a_r} > 0) = 1 - (1 - P_a)^{N_e}$$

$\varphi(Z) = $ normal curve integral from $-\infty$ to Z

and

$$Z = \frac{c_1 n_{s_r} + c_2}{\sqrt{c_3 n_{s_r}^2 + c_4 n_{s_r}}} .$$

If R_1 is the "correct" response, and R_2 is the alternative response under consideration, Equation 4 is the probability that R_1 will be preferred over R_2 after n_{s_r} stimuli have been shown for each of the two responses, during the learning period. N_e is the number of "effective" A-units in each source-set; that is, the number of A-units in either source-set which are not connected in common to both responses. Those units which are connected in common contribute equally to both sides of the value balance, and consequently do not affect the net bias towards one response or the other. N_a is the number of active units in a source-set, which respond to the test stimulus, $S_t \cdot P(N_{a_r} > 0)$ is the probability that at least one of the N_e effective units in the source-set of the correct response (designated, by convention, as the R_1 response) will be activated by the test stimulus, S_t.

In the case of P_g, the constant c_2 is always equal to zero, the other three constants being the same as for P_r. The values of the four constants depend on the parameters of the physical nerve net (the perceptron) and also on the organization of the stimulus environment.

The simplest cases to analyze are those in which the perceptron is shown stimuli drawn from an "ideal environment," consisting of randomly placed points of illumination, where there is no attempt to classify stimuli according to intrinsic similarity. Thus, in a typical learning experiment, we might show the perceptron 1,000 stimuli made up of random collections of illuminated retinal points, and we might arbitrarily reinforce R_1 as the "correct" response for the first 500 of these, and R_2 for the remaining 500. This environment is "ideal" only in the sense that we speak of an ideal gas in physics; it is a convenient artifact for purposes of analysis, and does not lead to the best performance from the perceptron. In the ideal environment situation, the constant c_1 is always equal to zero, so that, in the case of P_g (where c_2 is also zero), the value of Z will be zero, and P_g can never be any better than the random expectation of 0.5. The evaluation of P_r for these conditions, however, throws some interesting light on the differences between the alpha, beta, and gamma systems (Table 1).

First consider the alpha system, which has the simplest dynamics of the three. In this system, whenever an A-unit is active for one unit of time, it gains one unit of value. We will assume an experiment, initially, in which N_{s_r} (the number of stimuli associated to each response) is constant for all responses. In this case, for the sum system,

$$
\left.
\begin{aligned}
c_1 &= 0 \\
c_2 &= (1 - P_a)N_e \\
c_3 &= 2P_a\omega \\
c_4 &\approx 0
\end{aligned}
\right\} \tag{5}
$$

where ω = the fraction of responses connected to each A-unit. If the source-sets are disjunct, $\omega = 1/N_R$, where N_R is the number of responses in the system. For the μ-system,

$$
\left.
\begin{aligned}
c_1 &= 0 \\
c_2 &= (1 - P_a)N_e \\
c_3 &= 0 \\
c_4 &= 2\omega
\end{aligned}
\right\} \tag{6}
$$

The reduction of c_3 to zero gives the μ-system a definite advantage over the Σ-system. Typical learning curves for these systems are compared in Fig. 7 and 8. Figure 9 shows the effect of variations in P_a upon the performance of the system.

If n_{s_r}, instead of being fixed, is treated as a random variable, so that the number of stimuli associated to each response is drawn separately from some distribution, then the performance of the a-system is considerably poorer than the above equations indicate. Under these conditions, the constants for the μ-system are

$$
\left.
\begin{aligned}
c_1 &= 0 \\
c_2 &= 1 - P_a \\
c_3 &= 2P_a^2 q^2 \left[\frac{(\omega N_R - 1)^2}{N_R - 2} + 1 \right] \\
c_4 &= \frac{2(1 - P_a)N_R}{(1 - \omega_c)N_A}
\end{aligned}
\right\} \tag{7}
$$

where

q = ratio of $\sigma_{n_{s_r}}$ to $\bar{n}_{s_r}$
N_R = number of responses in the system
N_A = number of A-units in the system
ω_c = proportion of A-units common to R_1 and R_2.

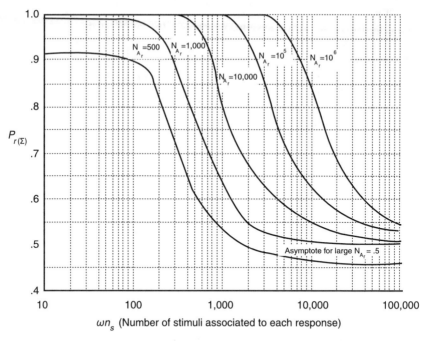

Figure 7 $P_{r(\Sigma)}$ as function of ωn_s, for discrete subsets. ($\omega_e = 0$, $P_a = .005$. Ideal environment assumed)

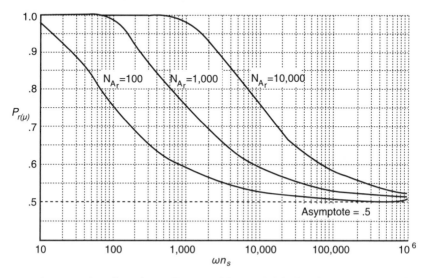

Figure 8 $P_{r(\mu)}$ as function of ωn_s. (For $P_a = .07$, $\omega_c = 0$. Ideal environment assumed)

414

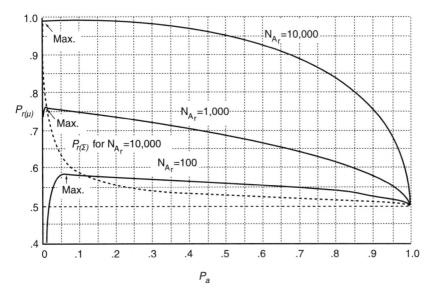

Figure 9 $P_{r(\mu)}$ as function of P_a. (For $n_{s_r} = 1,000$, $\omega_e = 0$. Ideal environment assumed)

For this equation (and any others in which n_{s_r} is treated as a random variable), it is necessary to define n_{s_r} in Equation 4 as the expected value of this variable, over the set of all responses.

For the β-system, there is an even greater deficit in performance, due to the fact that the net value continues to grow regardless of what happens to the system. The large net values of the subsets activated by a stimulus tend to amplify small statistical differences, causing an unreliable performance. The constants in this case (again for the μ-system) are

$$\left.\begin{array}{l} c_1 = 0 \\ c_2 = (1 - P_a)N_e \\ c_3 = 2(P_a N_e q \omega N_R^2)^2 \\ c_4 = 2(1 - P_a)\omega N_R N_e \end{array}\right\} \tag{8}$$

In both the alpha and beta systems, performance will be poorer for the sum-discriminating model than for the mean-discriminating case. In the gamma-system, however, it can be shown that $P_{r(\Sigma)} = P_{r(\mu)}$; i.e., it makes no difference in performance whether the Σ-system or μ-system is used. Moreover, the constants for the γ-system, with variable n_{s_r}, are identical to the constants for the alpha μ-system, with n_{s_r} fixed (Equation 6). The performance of the three systems is compared in Fig. 10, which clearly demonstrates the advantage of the γ-system.

Let us now replace the "ideal environment" assumptions with a model for a "differentiated environment," in which several distinguishable classes of

415

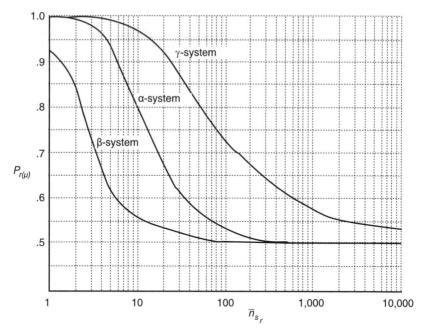

Figure 10 Comparison of a, β, and γ systems, for variable n_{s_r} ($N_R = 100$, $\sigma n_{r'} = .5\bar{n}_{s_r}$, $N_A = 10,000$, $P_a = .07$, $\omega = .2$)

stimuli are present (such as squares, circles, and triangles, or the letters of the alphabet). If we then design an experiment in which the stimuli associated to each response are drawn from a different class, then the learning curves of the perceptron are drastically altered. The most important difference is that the constant c_1 (the coefficient of n_{s_r} in the numerator of Z) is no longer equal to zero, so that Equation 4 now has a nonrandom asymptote. Moreover, in the form for P_g (the probability of correct generalization), where $c_2 = 0$, the quantity Z remains greater than zero, and P_g actually approaches the same asymptote as P_r. Thus the equation for the perceptron's performance after infinite experience with each class of stimuli is identical for P_r and P_g:

$$P_{r\infty} = P_{g\infty} = [1 - (1 - P_a)^{N_q}] \, \varphi\left(\frac{c_1}{\sqrt{c_3}}\right) \tag{9}$$

This means that *in the limit it makes no difference whether the perceptron has seen a particular test stimulus before or not; if the stimuli are drawn from a differentiated environment, the performance will be equally good in either case.*

In order to evaluate the performance of the system in a differentiated environment, it is necessary to define the quantity $P_{c_{aff}}$. This quantity is interpreted as the expected value of P_c between pairs of stimuli drawn at random from classes a and β. In particular, $P_{c_{11}}$ is the expected value of P_c between members of the same class, and $P_{c_{12}}$ is the expected value of P_c between an S_1 stimulus drawn from Class 1 and an S_2 stimulus drawn from Class 2. $P_{c_{1x}}$ is the expected value of P_c between members of Class 1 and stimuli drawn at random from all other classes in the environment.

If $P_{c_{11}} > P_a > P_{c_{12}}$, the limiting performance of the perceptron ($P_{g\infty}$) will be better than chance, and learning of some response, R_1, as the proper "generalization response" for members of Class 1 should eventually occur. If the above inequality is not met, then improvement over chance performance may not occur, and the Class 2 response is likely to occur instead. It can be shown (15) that for most simple geometrical forms, which we ordinarily regard as "similar," the required inequality can be met, if the parameters of the system are properly chosen.

The equation for P_r, for the sum-discriminating version of an a-perceptron, in a differentiated environment where n_{s_r} is fixed for all responses, will have the following expressions for the four coefficients:

$$
\left.
\begin{aligned}
c_1 &= P_a N_e \, (P_{c_{11}} - P_{c_{12}}) \\
c_2 &= P_a N_e \, (1 - P_{c_{11}}) \\
c_3 &= \sum_{r=1,2} P_a \, (1 - P_a) \, N_e \, [P_{c_{1r}}^2 + \sigma_3^2 \, (P_{c_{1r}}) + \sigma_j^2 \, (P_{c_{1r}}) + (\omega N_R - 1)^2 \\
&\qquad \times (P_{c_{1x}} + \sigma_s^2 \, (P_{c_{1x}}) + \sigma_j^2 \, (P_{c_{rx}}) + 2(\omega N_R - 1) \, (P_{c_{1r}} P_{c_{1x}})] + P_a^2 \, N_e^2 \, \} \\
&\qquad \times [\sigma_s^2 \, (P_{c_{1r}}) + (\omega N_R - 1)^2 \sigma_s^2 \, (P_{c_{1x}}) + 2(\omega N_R - 1)\varepsilon] \\
c_4 &= \sum_{r=1,2} P_a N_e \, [P_{c_{1r}} - P_{c_{1r}}^2 - \sigma_s^2 \, (P_{c_{1r}}) - \sigma_j^2 \, (P_{c_{1r}}) + (\omega N_R - 1) \\
&\qquad \times (P_{c_{1x}} - P_{c_{1x}}^2 - \sigma_j^2 \, (P_{c_{1x}}))]
\end{aligned}
\right\} \quad (10)
$$

where

$\sigma_s^2(P_{c_{1r}})$ and $\sigma_s^2(P_{c_{1x}})$ represent the variance of $P_{c_{1r}}$ and $P_{c_{1x}}$ measured over the set of possible test stimuli, S_t, and

$\sigma_j^2(P_{c_{1r}})$ and $\sigma_j^2(P_{c_{1x}})$ represent the variance of $P_{c_{1r}}$ and $P_{c_{1x}}$ measured over the set of all A-units, a_j.

ε = covariance of $P_{c_{1r}} P_{c_{1x}}$, which is assumed to be negligible.

The variances which appear in these expressions have not yielded, thus far, to a precise analysis, and can be treated as empirical variables to be determined for the classes of stimuli in question. If the sigma is set equal to half the expected value of the variable, in each case, a conservative estimate can be obtained. When the stimuli of a given class are all of the same shape, and uniformly distributed over the retina, the subscript s variances are equal to zero. $P_{g(\Sigma)}$ will be represented by the same set of coefficients, except for c_2, which is equal to zero, as usual.

For the mean-discriminating system, the coefficients are:

$$c_1 = (P_{c_{11}} - P_{c_{12}})$$

$$c_2 = (1 - P_{c_{11}})$$

$$c_3 = \sum_{r=1,2} \left[\frac{1}{P_a(N_e - 1)} - \frac{1}{N_e - 1} \right] [\sigma_j^2 \ (P_{c_{1r}}) + (\omega N_R - 1)^2$$

$$\times \sigma_j^2 \ (P_{c_{1x}})] + [\sigma_s^2(P_{c_{1r}}) + (\omega N_R - 1)^2 \sigma_s^2(P_{c_{1x}})]$$

$$c_4 = \sum_{r=1,2} \frac{1}{P_a N_e} [P_{c_{1r}} - P_{c_{1r}}^2 - \sigma_s^2 \ (P_{c_{1r}}) - \sigma_j^2 \ (P_{c_{1r}})$$

$$+ (\omega N_R - 1) \ (P_{c_{1x}} - P_{c_{1x}}^2 - \sigma_s^2 \ (P_{c_{1x}}) - \sigma_j^2 \ (P_{c_{1x}}))]$$

$$(11)$$

Some covariance terms, which are considered negligible, have been omitted here.

A set of typical learning curves for the differentiated environment model is shown in Fig. 11, for the mean-discriminating system. The parameters are based on measurements for a square-circle discrimination problem. Note that the curves for P_r and P_g both approach the same asymptotes, as predicted. The values of these asymptotes can be obtained by substituting the proper coefficients in Equation 9. As the number of association cells in the system increases, the asymptotic learning limit rapidly approaches unity, so that for a system of several thousand cells, the errors in performance should be negligible on a problem as simple as the one illustrated here.

As the number of responses in the system increases, the performance becomes progressively poorer, if every response is made mutually exclusive of all alternatives. One method of avoiding this deterioration (described in detail in Rosenblatt, 15) is through the binary coding of responses. In this case, instead of representing 100 different stimulus patterns by 100 distinct, mutually exclusive responses, a limited number of discriminating features is found, each of which can be independently recognized as being present or absent, and consequently can be represented by a single pair of mutually exclusive responses. Given an ideal set of binary characteristics (such as dark, light; tall, short; straight, curved; etc.), 100 stimulus classes could be distinguished by the proper configuration of only seven response pairs. In a further modification of the system, a single response is capable of denoting by its activity or inactivity the presence or absence of each binary characteristic. The efficiency of such coding depends on the number of independently recognizable "earmarks" that can be found to differentiate stimuli. If the

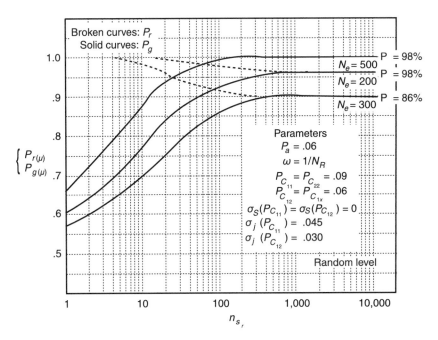

Figure 11 P_r and P_g as function of n_{s_r}. Parameters based on square-circle discrimination

stimulus can be identified only in its entirety and is not amenable to such analysis, then ultimately a separate binary response pair, or bit, is required to denote the presence or absence of each stimulus class (e.g., "dog" or "not dog"), and nothing has been gained over a system where all responses are mutually exclusive.

Bivalent systems

In all of the systems analyzed up to this point, the increments of value gained by an active A-unit, as a result of reinforcement or experience, have always been *positive*, in the sense that an active unit has always *gained* in its power to activate the responses to which it is connected. In the gamma-system, it is true that some units lose value, but these are always the *inactive units*, the active ones gaining in proportion to their rate of activity. In a *bivalent system*, two types of reinforcement are possible (positive and negative), and an active unit may either gain or lose in value, depending on the momentary state of affairs in the system. If the positive and negative reinforcement can be controlled by the application of external stimuli, they become essentially equivalent to "reward" and "punishment," and can be used in this sense by the experimenter. Under these conditions, a perceptron appears to be capable of trial-and-error learning. A bivalent system need not

419

necessarily involve the application of reward and punishment, however. If a binary-coded response system is so organized that there is a single response or response-pair to represent each "bit," or stimulus characteristic that is learned, with positive feedback to its own source-set if the response is "on," and negative feedback (in the sense that active A-units will lose rather than gain in value) if the response is "off," then the system is still bivalent in its characteristics. Such a bivalent system is particularly efficient in reducing some of the bias effects (preference for the wrong response due to greater size or frequency of its associated stimuli) which plague the alternative systems.

Several forms of bivalent systems have been considered (15, Chap. VII). The most efficient of these has the following logical characteristics.

If the system is under a state of positive reinforcement, then a positive ΔV is added to the values of all active A-units in the source-sets of "on" responses, while a negative ΔV is added to the active units in the source-sets of "off" responses. If the system is currently under negative reinforcement, then a negative ΔV is added to all active units in the source-set of an "on" response, and a positive ΔV is added to active units in an "off" source-set. If the source-sets are disjunct (which is essential for this system to work properly), the equation for a bivalent γ-system has the same coefficients as the monovalent a-system, for the μ-case (Equation 11).

The performance curves for this system are shown in Fig. 12, where the asymptotic generalization probability attainable by the system is plotted for the same stimulus parameters that were used in Fig. 11. This is the probability that all bits in an n-bit response pattern will be correct. Clearly, if a majority of correct responses is sufficient to identify a stimulus correctly, the performance will be better than these curves indicate.

In a form of bivalent system which utilizes more plausible biological assumptions, A-units may be either excitatory or inhibitory in their effect on connected responses. A positive ΔV in this system corresponds to the incrementing of an excitatory unit, while a negative ΔV corresponds to the incrementing of an inhibitory unit. Such a system performs similarly to the one considered above, but can be shown to be less efficient.

Bivalent systems similar to those illustrated in Fig. 12 have been simulated in detail in a series of experiments with the IBM 704 computer at the Cornell Aeronautical Laboratory. The results have borne out the theory in all of its main predictions, and will be reported separately at a later time.

Improved perceptrons and spontaneous organization

The quantitative analysis of perceptron performance in the preceding sections has omitted any consideration of *time* as a stimulus dimension. A perceptron which has no capability for temporal pattern recognition is referred to as a "momentary stimulus perceptron." It can be shown (15) that the same

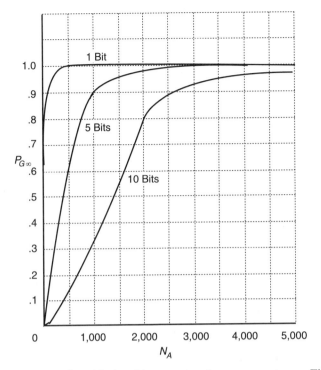

Figure 12 P_{G_∞} for a bivalent binary system (same parameters as Fig. 11)

principles of statistical separability will permit the perceptron to distinguish velocities, sound sequences, etc., provided the stimuli leave some temporarily persistent trace, such as an altered threshold, which causes the activity in the A-system at time t to depend to some degree on the activity at time $t-1$.

It has also been assumed that the origin points of A-units are completely random. It can be shown that by a suitable organization of origin points, in which the spatial distribution is constrained (as in the projection area origins shown in Fig. 1), the A-units will become particularly sensitive to the location of contours, and performance will be improved.

In a recent development, which we hope to report in detail in the near future, it has been proven that if the values of the A-units are allowed to decay at a rate proportional to their magnitude, a striking new property emerges: the perceptron becomes capable of "spontaneous" concept formation. That is to say, if the system is exposed to a random series of stimuli from two "dissimilar" classes, and all of its responses are automatically reinforced without any regard to whether they are "right" or "wrong," the system will tend towards a stable terminal condition in which (for each binary response) the response will be "1" for members of one stimulus class, and "0" for members of the other class; i.e., the perceptron will spontaneously recognize the difference between the two classes. This phenomenon has been successfully demonstrated in simulation experiments, with the 704 computer.

A perceptron, even with a single logical level of A-units and response units, can be shown to have a number of interesting properties in the field of selective recall and selective attention. These properties generally depend on the intersection of the source sets for different responses, and are elsewhere discussed in detail (15). By combining audio and photo inputs, it is possible to associate sounds, or auditory "names" to visual objects, and to get the perceptron to perform such selective responses as are designated by the command "Name the object on the left," or "Name the color of this stimulus."

The question may well be raised at this point of where the perceptron's capabilities actually stop. We have seen that the system described is sufficient for pattern recognition, associative learning, and such cognitive sets as are necessary for selective attention and selective recall. The system appears to be potentially capable of temporal pattern recognition, as well as spatial recognition, involving any sensory modality or combination of modalities. It can be shown that with proper reinforcement it will be capable of trial-and-error learning, and can learn to emit ordered sequences of responses, provided its own responses are fed back through sensory channels.

Does this mean that the perceptron is capable, without further modification in principle, of such higher order functions as are involved in human speech, communication, and thinking? Actually, the limit of the perceptron's capabilities seems to lie in the area of relative judgment, and the abstraction of relationships. In its "symbolic behavior," the perceptron shows some striking similarities to Goldstein's brain-damaged patients (5). Responses to definite, concrete stimuli can be learned, even when the proper response calls for the recognition of a number of simultaneous qualifying conditions (such as naming the color if the stimulus is on the left, the shape if it is on the right). As soon as the response calls for the recognition of a relationship between stimuli (such as "Name the object left of the square." or "Indicate the pattern that appeared before the circle."), however, the problem generally becomes excessively difficult for the perceptron. Statistical separability alone does not provide a sufficient basis for higher order abstraction. Some system, more advanced in principle than the perceptron, seems to be required at this point.

Conclusions and evaluation

The main conclusions of the theoretical study of the perceptron can be summarized as follows:

1. In an environment of random stimuli, a system consisting of randomly connected units, subject to the parametric constraints discussed above, can

learn to associate specific responses to specific stimuli. Even if many stimuli are associated to each response, they can still be recognized with a better-than-chance probability, although they may resemble one another closely and may activate many of the same sensory inputs to the system.

2. In such an "ideal environment," the probability of a correct response diminishes towards its original random level as the number of stimuli learned increases.

3. In such an environment, no basis for generalization exists.

4. In a "differentiated environment," where each response is associated to a distinct class of mutually correlated, or "similar" stimuli, the probability that a learned association of some specific stimulus will be correctly retained typically approaches a better-than-chance asymptote as the number of stimuli learned by the system increases. This asymptote can be made arbitrarily close to unity by increasing the number of association cells in the system.

5. In the differentiated environment, the probability that a stimulus *which has not been seen before* will be correctly recognized and associated to its appropriate class (the probability of correct generalization) approaches the same asymptote as the probability of a correct response to a previously reinforced stimulus. This asymptote will be better than chance if the inequality $P_{c_{12}} < P_a < P_{c_{11}}$ is met, for the stimulus classes in question.

6. The performance of the system can be improved by the use of a contour-sensitive projection area, and by the use of a binary response system, in which each response, or "bit," corresponds to some independent feature or attribute of the stimulus.

7. Trial-and-error learning is possible in bivalent reinforcement systems.

8. Temporal organizations of both stimulus patterns and responses can be learned by a system which uses only an extension of the original principles of statistical separability, without introducing any major complications in the organization of the system.

9. The memory of the perceptron is *distributed*, in the sense that any association may make use of a large proportion of the cells in the system, and the removal of a portion of the association system would not have an appreciable effect on the performance of any one discrimination or association, but would begin to show up as a general deficit in *all* learned associations.

10. Simple cognitive sets, selective recall, and spontaneous recognition of the classes present in a given environment are possible. The recognition of relationships in space and time, however, seems to represent a limit to the perceptron's ability to form cognitive abstractions.

Psychologists, and learning theorists in particular, may now ask: "What has the present theory accomplished, beyond what has already been done in the quantitative theories of Hull, Bush and Mosteller, etc., or physiological theories such as Hebb's?" The present theory is still too primitive, of course, to be considered as a full-fledged rival of existing theories of human learning. Nonetheless, as a first approximation, its chief accomplishment might be stated as follows:

For a given mode of organization (a, β, or γ; Σ or μ; monovalent or bivalent) the fundamental phenomena of *learning, perceptual discrimination, and generalization can be predicted entirely from six basic physical parameters*, namely:

> x: the number of excitatory connections per A-unit,
>
> y: the number of inhibitory connections per A-unit,
>
> θ: the expected threshold of an A-unit,
>
> ω: the proportion of R-units to which an A-unit is connected,
>
> N_A: the number of A-units in the system, and
>
> N_R: the number of R-units in the system.

N_s (the number of sensory units) becomes important if it is very small. It is assumed that the system begins with all units in a uniform state of value; otherwise the initial value distribution would also be required. *Each of the above parameters is a clearly defined physical variable, which is measurable in its own right, independently of the behavioral and perceptual phenomena which we are trying to predict.*

As a direct consequence of its foundation on physical variables, the present system goes far beyond existing learning and behavior theories in three main points: parsimony, verifiability, and explanatory power and generality. Let us consider each of these points in turn.

1. *Parsimony.* Essentially all of the basic variables and laws used in this system are already present in the structure of physical and biological science, so that we have found it necessary to postulate only one hypothetical variable (or construct) which we have called V, the "value" of an association cell; this is a variable which must conform to certain functional characteristics which can clearly be stated, and which is assumed to have a potentially measurable physical correlate.

2. *Verifiability.* Previous quantitative learning theories, apparently without exception, have had one important characteristic in common: they have all been based on measurements of *behavior*, in specified situations, using these measurements (after theoretical manipulation) to predict *behavior* in other situations. Such a procedure, in the last analysis, amounts to a process of curve fitting and extrapolation, in the hope that the constants which describe one set of curves will hold good for other curves in other situations. While such extrapolation is not necessarily circular, in the strict sense, it shares many of the logical difficulties of circularity, particularly when used as an "explanation" of behavior. Such extrapolation is difficult to justify in a new situation, and it has been shown that if the basic constants and parameters are to be derived anew for any situation in which they break down

empirically (such as change from white rats to humans), then the basic "theory" is essentially irrefutable, just as any successful curve-fitting equation is irrefutable. It has, in fact, been widely conceded by psychologists that there is little point in trying to "disprove" any of the major learning theories in use today, since by extension, or a change in parameters, they have all proved capable of adapting to any specific empirical data. This is epitomized in the increasingly common attitude that a choice of theoretical model is mostly a matter of personal aesthetic preference or prejudice, each scientist being entitled to a favorite model of his own. In considering this approach, one is reminded of a remark attributed to Kistiakowsky, that "given seven parameters, I could fit an elephant." This is clearly *not* the case with a system in which the independent variables, or parameters, can be measured *independently* of the predicted behavior. In such a system, it is not possible to "force" a fit to empirical data, if the parameters in current use should lead to improper results. In the current theory, a failure to fit a curve in a new situation would be a clear indication that either the theory or the empirical measurements are wrong. Consequently, if such a theory *does* hold up for repeated tests, we can be considerably more confident of its validity and of its generality than in the case of a theory which must be hand-tailored to meet each situation.

3. *Explanatory power and generality.* The present theory, being derived from basic physical variables, is not specific to any one organism or learning situation. It can be generalized in principle to cover any form of behavior in any system for which the physical parameters are known. A theory of learning, constructed on these foundations, should be considerably more powerful than any which has previously been proposed. It would not only tell us what behavior might occur in any known organism, but would permit the *synthesis* of behaving systems, to meet special requirements. Other learning theories tend to become increasingly qualitative as they are generalized. Thus a set of equations describing the effects of reward on T-maze learning in a white rat reduces simply to a statement that rewarded behavior tends to occur with increasing probability, when we attempt to generalize it from any species and any situation. The theory which has been presented here loses none of its precision through generality.

The theory proposed by Donald Hebb (7) attempts to avoid these difficulties of behavior-based models by showing how psychological functioning might be derived from neurophysiological theory. In his attempt to achieve this, Hebb's philosophy of approach seems close to our own, and his work has been a source of inspiration for much of what has been proposed here. Hebb, however, has never actually achieved a model by which behavior (or any psychological data) can be *predicted* from the physiological system. His physiology is more a suggestion as to the *sort* of organic substrate which might underlie behavior, and an attempt to show the plausibility of a bridge between biophysics and psychology.

425

The present theory represents the first actual completion of such a bridge. Through the use of the equations in the preceding sections, it is possible to predict learning curves from neurological variables, and likewise, to predict neurological variables from learning curves. How well this bridge stands up to repeated crossings remains to be seen. In the meantime, the theory reported here clearly demonstrates the feasibility and fruitfulness of a quantitative statistical approach to the organization of cognitive systems. By the study of systems such as the perceptron, it is hoped that those fundamental laws of organization which are common to all information handling systems, machines and men included, may eventually be understood.

Note

1   The development of this theory has been carried out at the Cornell Aeronautical Laboratory, Inc., under the sponsorship of the Office of Naval Research, Contract Nonr-2381(00). This article is primarily an adaptation of material reported in Ref. 15, which constitutes the first full report on the program.

References

1. Ashby, W. R. *Design for a brain*. New York: Wiley, 1952.
2. Culbertson, J. T. *Consciousness and behavior*. Dubuque, Iowa: Wm. C. Brown, 1950.
3. Culbertson, J. T. Some uneconomical robots. In C. E. Shannon & J. McCarthy (Eds.), *Automata studies*. Princeton: Princeton Univer. Press, 1956. Pp. 99–116.
4. Eccles, J. C. *The neurophysiological basis of mind*. Oxford: Clarendon, 1953.
5. Goldstein, K. *Human nature in the light of psychopathology*. Cambridge: Harvard Univer. Press, 1940.
6. Hayek, F. A. *The sensory order*. Chicago: Univer. Chicago Press, 1952.
7. Hebb, D. O. *The organization of behavior*. New York: Wiley, 1949.
8. Kleene, S. C. Representation of events in nerve nets and finite automata. In C. E. Shannon & J. McCarthy (Eds.), *Automata studies*. Princeton: Princeton Univer. Press, 1956. Pp. 3–41.
9. Köhler, W. Relational determination in perception. In L. A. Jeffress (Ed.), *Cerebral mechanisms in behavior*. New York: Wiley, 1951. Pp. 200–243.
10. McCulloch, W. S. Why the mind is in the head. In L. A. Jeffress (Ed.), *Cerebral mechanisms in behavior*. New York: Wiley, 1951. Pp. 42–111.
11. McCulloch, W. S., & Pitts, W. A. logical calculus of the ideas immanent in nervous activity. *Bull. math. Biophysics*, 1943, 5, 115–133.
12. Milner, P. M. The cell assembly: Mark II. *Psychol, Rev.*, 1957, 64, 242–252.
13. Minsky, M. L. Some universal elements for finite automata. In C. E. Shannon & J. McCarthy (Eds.), *Automata studies*. Princeton: Princeton Univer. Press, 1956. Pp. 117–128.
14. Rashevsky, N. *Mathematical biophysics*. Chicago: Univer. Chicago Press, 1938.
15. Rosenblatt, F. *The perceptron: A theory of statistical separability in cognitive systems*. Buffalo: Cornell Aeronautical Laboratory, Inc. Rep. No. VG-1196-G-1, 1958.
16. Uttley, A. M. Conditional probability machines and conditioned reflexes. In C. E.

Shannon & J. McCarthy (Eds.), *Automata studies*. Princeton: Princeton Univer. Press, 1956. Pp. 253–275.

17. von Neumann, J. The general and logical theory of automata. In L. A. Jeffress (Ed.), *Cerebral mechanisms in behavior*. New York: Wiley, 1951. Pp. 1–41.

18. von Neumann, J. Probabilistic logics and the synthesis of reliable organisms from unreliable components. In C. E. Shannon & J. McCarthy (Eds.), *Automata studies*. Princeton: Princeton Univer. Press, 1956. Pp. 43–98.

40

PANDEMONIUM

A Paradigm for Learning

O. G. Selfridge

Source: *Proceedings of the Symposium on Mechanisation of Thought Processes*, HMSO, 1959, pp. 513–31.

Introduction

We are proposing here a model of a process which we claim can adaptively improve itself to handle certain pattern recognition problems which cannot be adequately specified in advance. Such problems are usual when trying to build a machine to imitate any one of a very large class of human data processing techniques. A speech typewriter is a good example of something that very many people have been trying unsuccessfully to build for some time.

We do not suggest that we have proposed a model which can learn to typewrite from merely hearing speech. Pandemonium does not, however, seem on paper to have the same kinds of inherent restrictions or inflexibility that many previous proposals have had. The basic motif behind our model is the motion of parallel processing. This is suggested on two grounds: first, it is often easier to handle data in a parallel manner, and, indeed, it is usually the more 'natural' manner to handle it in; and, secondly, it is easier to modify an assembly of quasi-independent modules than a machine all of whose parts interact immediately and in a complex way.

We are not going to apologize for a frequent use of anthropomorphic or biomorphic terminology. They seem to be useful words to describe our notions.

What we are describing is a process, or, rather, a model of a process. We shall not describe all the reasons that led to its particular formulation, but we shall give some reasons for hoping that it does in fact possess the flexibility and adaptability that we ascribe to it.

428

The problem environment for learning

Pandemonium is a model which we hope can learn to recognize patterns which have not been specified. We mean that in the following sense: we present to the model examples of patterns taken from some set of them, each time informing the model which pattern we had just presented. Then, after some time the model guesses correctly which pattern has just been presented before we inform it. For a large class of pattern recognition ensembles there has never existed any adequate written or statable description of the distinctions between the patterns. The only requirement we can place on our model is that we want it to behave in the same way that men observably behave in. In an absolute sense this is a very unsatisfactory definition of any task, but it may be apparent that it is the way in which most tasks are defined for most men. Lucky is he whose job can be exactly specified in words without any ambiguity or necessary inferences. The example we shall illustrate in some detail is translating from manually keyed Morse code into, say, typewritten messages. Now it is true that when one learns Morse code one learns that a dash should be exactly three times the length of a dot and so on, but it turns out that this is really mostly irrelevant. What matters is only what the vast army of people who use Morse code and with whom one is going to have to communicate understand and practise when they use it. It turns out that this is nearly always very different from school book Morse.

In the same way the only adequate definition of the pattern of a spoken word, or one hand-written, must be in terms of the consensus of the people who are using it.

We use the term pattern recognition in a broad sense to include not only that data processing by which images are assigned to one or another pattern in some set of patterns, but also the processes by which the patterns and data processing are developed by the organism or machine; we generally call this latter 'learning'.

Pandemonium, idealized and practical

We first construct an idealized pandemonium (*fig. 1*). Each possible pattern of the set, represented by a demon in a box, computes his similarity with the image simultaneously on view to all of them, and gives an output depending monotonically on that similarity. The decision demon on top makes a choice of that pattern belonging to the demon whose output was the largest.[1]

Each demon may, for example, be assigned one letter of the alphabet, so that the task of the A-demon is to shout as loud of the amount of 'A-ness' that he sees in the image.[2] Now it will usually happen that with a reasonable collection of categories – like the letters of the alphabet – the computations performed by each of these ideal cognitive demons will be largely the same. In many instances a pattern is nearly equivalent to some logical function of a

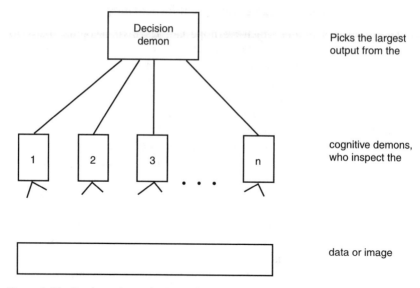

Picks the largest output from the

cognitive demons, who inspect the

data or image

Figure 1 Idealized pandemonium

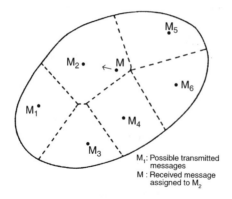

M_i: Possible transmitted messages
M : Received message assigned to M_2

Figure 2 Signal space

set of features, each of which is individually common to perhaps several patterns and whose absence is also common to several other patterns.[3]

We therefore amend our idealized Pandemonium. The amended version – *fig. 3* – has some profound advantages, chief among which is its susceptibility to that kind of adaptive self-improvement that I call learning.

The difference between *fig. 1* and *fig. 3* is that the common parts of the computations that each cognitive demon carries out in *fig. 1* have in *fig. 3* been assigned instead to a host of subdemons. At this stage the organization has four levels. At the bottom the data demons serve merely to store and pass

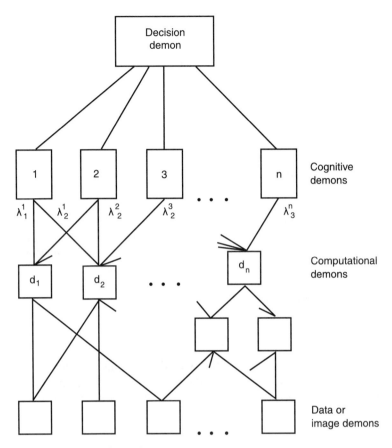

Figure 3 Amended Pandemonium

on the data. At the next level the computational demons or subdemons perform certain more or less complicated computations on the data and pass the results of these up to the next level, the cognitive demons who weigh the evidence, as it were. Each cognitive demon computes a shriek, and from all the shrieks the highest level demon of all, the decision demon, merely selects the loudest.

The conception of Pandemonium

We cannot ab initio know the ideal construction of our Pandemonium. We try to assure that it contains the seeds of self-improvement. Of the four levels in *fig. 3*, all but the third, the subdemons, which compute, are specified by the task. For the third level, therefore, we collect a large number of possible useful functions, eliminating a priori only those which could not conceivably be relevant, and make a reasonable selection of the others, being bound by economy and space. We then guess reasonable weights for them. The behaviour at this point may even be acceptably good, but usually it must be improved by means of the adaptive changes we are about to discuss.

The evolution of Pandemonium

There are several kinds of adaptive changes which we will discuss for our γ Pandemonium. They are all essentially very similar, but they may be pro-grammed and discussed separately. The first may be called 'Feature Weighting'.

Although we have not yet specified what the cognitive demons compute, the sole task at present is to add a weighted sum of the outputs of all the computational demons or subdemons; the weightings will of course differ for the different cognitive demons, but the weightings will be the only difference between them. Feature weighting consists of altering the weights assigned to the subdemons by the cognitive demons so as to maximize the score of the entire γ Pandemonium. How then can we do this?

The score

What we mean by the score here is how well the machine is doing the task we want it to do. This presumes that we are monitoring the machine and telling it when it makes an error and so on, and for the rest of the discussion we shall be assuming that we have available some such running score. Now at some point we shall be very interested in having the machine run without that kind of direct supervision, and the question naturally arises whether the machine can meaningfully monitor its own performance. We answer that question tentatively yes, but delay discussing it till a later section.

Feature weighting and hill-climbing

The output of any cognitive demon is

$$d_i = \sum \lambda_j^i d_j$$

so that the complete set of weights for all the cognitive demons over all the subdemons is a vector:

$$\Lambda = \left\{ \Lambda^i \right\} = \left\{ \lambda_1^1, \lambda_2^1 \ldots \lambda_1^2, \ldots \lambda_m^n \right\}$$

Now for some (unknown) set of weights Λ, the behaviour of this whole Pandemonium is optimum, and the problem of feature weighting is to find that set. This may be described as a hill-climbing problem. We have a space (of Λ) and a function on the space (the score), which we may consider an altitude, and which we wish to maximize by a proper search through Λ. One possible technique is to select weighting vectors at random, score them, and finally to select the vector that scored highest (see *fig. 4*). It will usually, however, turn out to be profitable to take advantage of the continuity properties of the space, which usually exist in some sense, in the following way: select vectors at random until you find one that scores perceptibly more than the others. From this point take small random steps in all directions (that is, add small random vectors) until you find a direction that improves your score. When you find such a step, take it and repeat the process. This is illustrated in *fig. 5*, and is the case of a blind man trying to climb a hill. There may be, of course, many false peaks on which one may find oneself trapped in such a procedure (*fig. 6*).

The problem of false peaks in searching techniques is an old and familiar one. In general, one may hope that in spaces of very high dimensionality the interdependence of the components and the score is so great as to make very unlikely the existence of false peaks completely isolated from the main or true peak. It must be realized, however, that this is a purely experimental question that has to be answered separately for every hill-climbing situation. It does turn out in hill-climbing situations that the choice of starting point is often very important. The main peak may be very prominent, but unless it

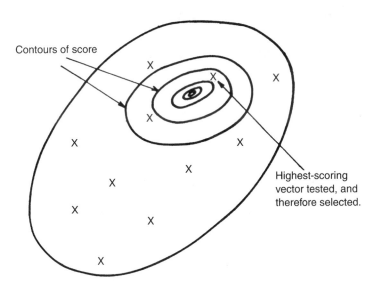

Figure 4 First hill-climbing technique: pick vectors at random (points in the space), score them, and select the one that scores highest

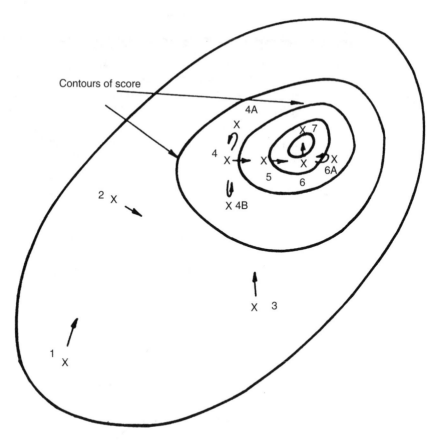

Figure 5 Second hill-climbing technique: pick vectors until one of them (Number 4) outscores the previous ones. Then take short random steps, retracing any that decrease the score

has wide-spread foot-hills it may take a very long time before we ever begin to gain altitude.

This may be described as one of the problems of training, namely, to encourage the machine or organism to get enough on the foot-hills so that small changes in his parameters will produce noticeable improvement in his altitude or score. One can describe learning situations where most of the difficulty of the task lies in finding any way of improving one's score, such as learning to ride a unicycle, where it takes longer to stay on for a second than it does to improve that one second to a minute; and others where it is easy to do a little well and very hard to do very well, such as learning to play chess. It is also true that often the main peak is a plateau rather than an isolated spike. That is to say, optimal behaviour of the mechanism, once reached, may be rather insensitive to the change of some of the parameters.

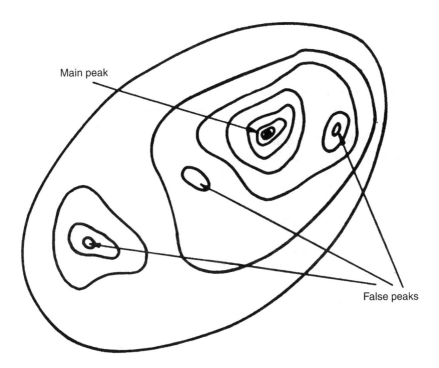

Main peak

False peaks

Figure 6 General space showing false peaks. One of the false peaks is quite isolated from the main or true peak

Subdemon selection

The second kind of adaptive change that we wish to incorporate into our Pandemonium is subdemon selection. At the conception of our demoniac assembly we collected somewhat arbitrarily a large number of subdemons which we guessed would be useful and assigned them weights also arbitrarily. The first adaptive change, feature weighting, optimized these weights, but we have no assurance at all that the particular subdemons we selected are good ones. Subdemon selection generates new subdemons for trial and eliminates inefficient ones, that is, ones that do not much help improve the score.

We propose to do this initially by two different techniques, which may be called 'mutated fission' and 'conjugation'. The first point to note is that it is possible to assign a worth to each of the subdemons. It may be done in several ways, and we may, for example, write the worth W_i of the ith demon

$$W_i = \sum_j |\lambda_i^j|,$$

435

so that the worthy demons are those whose outputs are likely to affect most strongly the decisions made.

We assume that feature weighting has already run so long that the behaviour of the machine has been approximately optimized, and that scores and worths of machine and its demons have been obtained. First we eliminate those subdemons with low worths. Next we generate new subdemons by mutating the survivors and reweighting the assembly. At present we plan to pick one subdemon and alter some of his parameters more or less at random. This will usually require that we reduce the subdemon himself to some canonical form so that the random changes we insert do not have the effect of rewriting the program so that it will not run or so that it will enter a closed loop without any hope of getting out of it.[4]

Besides mutated fission, we are proposing another method of subdemon improvement called 'conjugation'. Our purpose here is two-fold: first to provide a logical variety in the functions computed by the subdemons, and, secondly, to provide length and complexity in them.

What we do is this: given two 'useful' subdemons, we generate a new subdemon which is the continuous analogue of one of the ten non-trivial binary two-variable functions on them. For example, the product of two subdemon outputs, corresponding to the logical product, would suggest the simultaneous presence of two features. The ten non-trivial such functions are listed in *Table 1*.

Table 1 Non-trivial binary functions on two variables.

A. B	A_V B
A.~B	A_V~B
~A.~B	~A_V~B
~A. B	~A_V~B
A. B_V~A.~B	A.~B_V~A. B

Control adaptation

The first two levels of adaptation are directly concerned with immediate improvement of behaviour and the score. We should also like to improve the entire organization, and in the same way. We shall deal with this point somewhat cursorily, being reluctant to specify things too far in advance of experiment. In principle, we propose that the control operations should themselves be handled by demons subject to changes like feature weighting and subdemon selection. It is obviously a little more difficult and perhaps impossible here to define the usefulness or worth of a particular demon. It is also clear that it will sometimes take much longer to check the usefulness of some change in some control demon – for example, in one of those which control the mutations in subdemon selection. Furthermore, at this level, some of the demons, presumably, will be in a position to change themselves, for otherwise we should need another level of possible change, and so on. This raises the possibility of irreversible changes, and it is not obvious that *all* parts of the machine should be subject to adaptive change. But these are largely heuristic questions.

The evolutionary process

The adaptive changes mentioned above will tend, we hope, to promote a kind of evolution in our Pandemonium. The scheme sketched is really a natural selection on the processing demons. If they serve a useful function they survive, and perhaps are even the source for other subdemons who are themselves judged on their merits.

It is perfectly reasonable to conceive of this taking place on a broader scale – and in fact it takes place almost inevitably. Therefore, instead of having but one Pandemonium we might have some crowd of them, all fairly similarly constructed, and employ natural selection on the crowd of them. Eliminate the relatively poor and encourage the rest to generate new machines in their own images.

Unsupervised operation

So far all of the operation of the machine has been on the basis of constant monitoring by a person who is telling the machine when it makes an error. A very valid question is whether the machine can form any independent opinion of its own on how well it is doing. I suggest that it can in the following way: one criterion of correct decisions will be that they are fairly unequivocal, that is, that there is one and only one cognitive demon whose output far outshines the rest. Some running average of the degree to which this is so would presumably somewhat reflect the score of the machine. Note that it would be vital that the machine be trained first to do well enough before it is left to its own resources and supervision.

A real-life example: Morse translation

As we mentioned before, the entire notion of Pandemonium was conceived as a practical way of automatically improving data-processing for pattern recognition. Our initial model task is to distinguish dots and dashes in manually keyed Morse code, so that our Pandemonium can be illustrated in *fig. 7*. Note that the functions and behaviour of all demons have been specified except for the computing subdemons. We shall reiterate those specifications.

1   The decision demon's output is 'dot' or 'dash' according as the dot demon's output is greater or less than the dash demon's.

437

2   The cognitive demons, dot and dash, each compute a weighted sum of the outputs of some 150 computing subdemons. Initial weights we have assigned arbitrarily, but, we hope, reasonably.
3   The data-handling demons receive data in the form of durations, alternatively of marks and spaces, and they pass them down the line.

The computing subdemons are constructed from only a very few operational functions, which are carefully non-binary. For example the subdemons $d_0 = d_2$ and $d_0 d_2$ have their outputs shown in *fig. 8*. The operational functions follow:

1   ' = '. This function computes the degree of equality of some set of variables (see *fig. 8*).
2   ' ', ' ', compute the degree to which some variable is less than or is greater than some other variable (see *fig. 8*).
3   '*max*', '*max*', compute the degree to which some variable is the largest of an arbitrary set of variables or an arbitrary set of consecutive variables.
4   'O_i', 'A_i', store the degree to which the ith duration *has been* identified as a dot or dash.

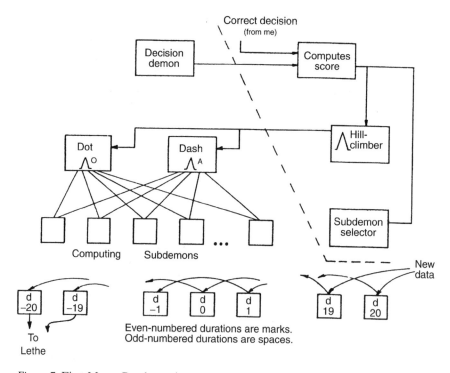

Figure 7 First Morse Pandemonium

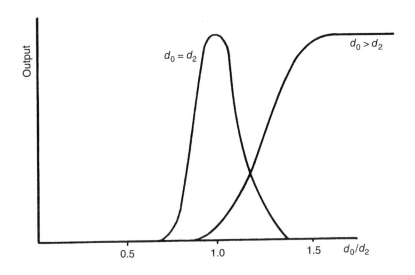

Figure 8 Operation of the subdemons $d_0 = d_2$, $d_0 > d_2$

5   '*Av*' computes an average of some set of variables.
6   '*M*' is a family of tracking means. For example, it might compute

$$M^\alpha(c) = \alpha M(i - 1) + (1 - \alpha)$$

7   '*Ox*', '*Ax*'. Ox_1 is the last duration identified as a dot. Ax_3 is the third last duration identified as a dash, etc.

The above is the present functional vocabulary of the computing operations for our subdemons. The subdemons themselves are built with a simple syntax. For the initial set, at conception, we merely select a set of operational functions and follow them with the numbers of some particular data demons.

Conclusion

What I shall present at the meeting in November will be the details of the progress of Pandemonium on the Morse code translation problem. The initial problem we have given the machine is to distinguish dots and dashes. When the behaviour of the machine has improved itself to the point where little further improvement seems to be occurring, we shall add three more cognitive demons, the symbol space, the letter space, and the word space. Presumably after some further time this new Pandemonium will settle down to some unimprovable state. Then we shall replace the senior

439

or decision-making demon with a row of some forty or so character demons with a new decision-making demon above them, letting the new cognitive demons for the character demons use all the inferior demons, cognitive and otherwise, for their inputs. It is probably also desirable that previous decisions be available for present decisions, so that a couple of new functional operations might be added. There need be little concern about logical circularity, because we have no requirement for logical consistency, but are merely seeking agreeable Morse translation.

How much of the whole program will have been run and tested by November I cannot be sure of. At the present (July) we have had some fair testing of hill-climbing procedures.

Acknowledgement

I should like to acknowledge the valuable contributions of discussions with many of my friends, including especially M. Minsky, U. Neisser, F. Frick and J. Lettvin.

Notes

1   This is an exact correlate of a communications system wherein given a received message $M(T)$ and a number of possible transmitted messages $M_i(T)$, that M_i is chosen, that is, deemed to have been transmitted, which minimizes $\int | M(T) - M_i(T) |^2 dT$. (Such a procedure is optimum under certain conditions). This integral is, as it were, the square of a distance in a signal phase space – *fig. 2* – and thus that transmitted message is selected that is most similar to the received one.

2   It is possible also to phrase it so that the A-demon is computing the distance in some phase of the image from some ideal A; it seems to me unnecessarily platonic to postulate the existence of 'ideal' representatives of patterns, and, indeed, there are often good reasons for not doing so.

3   See, for example, Jerome Bruner, 'A Study of Thinking',

4   We are at present running our Pandemonium on an IBM 704. The analogues for kinds of simulation are obvious.

Discussion on the paper by Dr. O. G. Selfridge

DR. J. W. BRAY: May I ask Dr. Selfridge what he thinks of this approach to his problem? Let x = duration of the last signal, which may be a dot or a dash, a signal space, letter space or word space. Let y = 2, if in fact it was a dash, 1 if dot, 0 if signal space, −1 if letter space and −2 if word space. To form the polynomial:

$$y = A_0 + A_1x + A_2x^2 + A_3x^3 \ldots \ldots$$

take a number of observations, as he suggests, and let the machine learn the code by determining the coefficients A_0 etc. by simple curvilinear regression. The duration of previous and subsequent signals and the interpretation given to previous signals could be added as further variables on the right hand side.

MR. C. STRACHEY: At the end of the paper you promise us some further information about the latest state of the programme. Could you let us know what this is?

DR. C. McCARTHY: I would like to speak briefly about some of the advantages of the pandemonium model as an actual model of conscious behaviour. In observing a brain, one should make a distinction between that aspect of the behaviour which is available consciously, and those behaviours, no doubt equally important, but which proceed unconsciously. If one conceives of the brain as a pandemonium – a collection of demons – perhaps what is going on within the demons can be regarded as the unconscious part of thought, and what the demons are publicly shouting for each other to hear, as the conscious part of thought.

DR. D. M. MACKAY: Dr. Selfridge's 'pandemonium' has a certain family resemblance to a class of mechanism considered in some earlier papers (*ref. 1*) (though I had never suspected its demonic implications!).

In one of these, (*ref. 2*) after discussing the general principle that you penalise the unsuccessful, I pointed out that the amount of information per 'kick' (to use Dr. Selfridge's metaphor) is very small unless the probability of success and failure are equal. If you have a system where there are a vast number of possibilities to be eliminated by rather feckless trial and error, then of course failure occurs much more often than success. The solution I suggested was to form a kind of syndicated learning process in which at first large numbers of elements, destined eventually for independence, should be coupled together so as to reduce the diversity of response. A hand, for example, might not at first have each finger separately controllable, but could work clumsily as a whole. In that way, you can greatly decrease the amount of groping which is necessary before a successful adaptive action is found, although of course the degree of success achieved may be less. On this principle, if pursued to the limit, even the earliest trials could have a non-negligible chance of success, (though success in a very small way).

Given this easy start, simple self-organising subroutines can build up fairly quickly. As they increase their number and their success, however, the idea is that the couplings between elements should gradually be dissolved to increase the complexity of the problem. If you keep the complexity increasing step by step with the degree of development of successful internal matching sub-routines, then fully adaptive behaviour can be enormously more quickly developed than if the system starts with the full repertoire to be explored. My question is why Dr. Selfridge has not incorporated this principle in his 'pandemonium', so that each 'kick' could have something nearer to one bit of information instead of an almost negligible fraction.

DR. P. C. PRICE (written contribution): This is a very interesting and stimulating paper. I have one comment to make, and that is on the discussion of 'Feature Weighting and Hill-Climbing'.

I think that in this discussion the author has not brought out one important distinction between types of 'hill-climbing' problems – that between determinate and stochastic problems. Whereas in a determinate problem the 'hill' is defined by a single function of many variables

$$f(x) \equiv f(x_1, \ldots x_n)$$

in a stochastic problem it is defined by the mean value of a number of functions:

$$f(x) \equiv f_\alpha(x)$$

when

$$f_\alpha(x) \equiv f(x_1, \ldots x_n; \alpha)$$

and α is a random variable whose value depends on the particular trial made.

Now I would have thought that most of the more interesting pattern recognition problems are essentially stochastic: the objective is to make a machine that will obtain as high a proportion as possible of correct answers to a series of questions 'what is this pattern?' referring to a random series of patterns.

The author has given an excellent account of some of the difficulties of determinate hill-climbing and of the techniques for overcoming them, but stochastic hill-climbing presents additional problems, and I think this may become very apparent when a pandemonium is built to deal with a practical task. In particular, two problems which will need investigation are:

(i) how large a sample of trial values $f_\alpha(x)$ and $f_\alpha(y)$, belonging to two points x and y in the vector space being explored, will be needed to obtain a satisfactory estimate of $[f(x) - f(y)]$ for the purposes of hill-climbing?

(ii) how much longer will a particular stochastic hill-climbing procedure take than the corresponding determinate procedure, and will this ratio prove to be too large, in some practical instances, to allow the evolutionary development of the pandemonium to take place?

I should be very interested to learn if the author has considered these problems and developed any solutions. The problem of stochastic hill-climbing is of practical interest outside the context of this paper, for instance in connection with the evolutionary operation of chemical processes.

DR. O. G. SELFRIDGE (in reply*): Since I have been working on Morse code, which I am doing in addition to working on learning, I have met probably 50 people and when I say that I am working on a machine to do manually keyed Morse code, they say 'I will tell you how to do that' and they then proceed to come up with some scheme. Actually, this is the first time I have heard this particular one, whereas I have come across the others many times, so Dr. Bray should be congratulated on a new scheme for solving Morse code. Let me assure him that it will not work; we have tried it. Morse code manually received is not that simple. The context necessary apparently extends at least 10 letters on *either* side – not just one side, both sides. In fact, the real question about doing this – why I chose Morse code – was exactly that it had had this kind of interactions with each other. You cannot do it by looking at binary functions of the durations, that is, expressing durations as binary digits and then looking on binary functions of lots of them. If I take 10 letters on either side, each has three marks, you should consider the spaces as well, but leaving those out, that is three times 20, which is 60 durations, and if we specify them to one part in 32, that is 300 bits, and binary functions of 300 bits cannot be picked at random. So the question is to take some steps in the right direction and then hope the steps are right enough so that you will get enough improvements, so that the following steps will get you even more so.

I maintain that there is some merit in studying self-improvement systems and if I am going to do that I am going to study systems where I know what I want, rather than more difficult problems, however attractive they may be to mathematicians. Mathematicians like to work on unsolved problems for the greater glory, and problems already solved like the prime number theorem are left to graduate students. I have a suspicion that John McCarthy might later bring up some important points about descriptions, and here I see my point about solving useful problems, because Morse code is a useful problem. The whole question is at what level you are going to deal with descriptions of your data. In most problems, especially in dealing with the amount of things which people do, binary functions are just not adequate. For one thing there is too much data, and one of the first questions you talk about in the conditioned reflex – remember that conditional probability assumes that you have already recognised the stimulus; if you know that the stimulus belongs to one of a small class of functions, it is pretty easy, as a man, but mostly in human problems you do not know this.

Dr. Mackay made some very kind remarks. I would go further back than he did, as he well knows, in crediting demonology. All of us have sinned in Adam, we have eaten of the tree of the knowledge of good and evil, and the demonological allegory is a very old one, indeed. As for his remarks about the syndicate approach, the evolution of diversative organisation, I think

* Edited version by the author was not available.

that is an extremely accurate and good point. One of the things a species learns is not only how to survive but to have exactly the right variants in its members. The reason horseshoe crabs have not changed much is not because they don't adapt; they can adapt, but there is no variation, so they can only adapt very little, and they are about as good as they can be; whereas there are all kinds of people.

In speed and information theory, I really consider that speed in the classic sense of computation is so completely irrelevant to this problem – the number of binary operations one does a second – that it does not interest me very much though it interests computer designers. I would rather like to see lots of operations which could conceivably be done in parallel, being done sequentially, because this is the only machine we have, and then I hope people will have machines which will work in parallel, so that when I want a machine to do twice as difficult a problem I merely build twice as big a machine, instead of letting one machine work twice as long.

Dr. Strachey asked about results, and they are roughly as I have indicated. Improvement does take place; the hill-climbing does work. The sub-demon selection in the programmes that we have did not do what we hoped, but the sub-demons were effectively thrown out, and the ones which were kept were largely concentrated around those demons which relate those ones very close. The most effective demon by itself, which worked 90 per cent. of the time, which was very surprising, was when a mark was the maximum, or within a just noticeable difference of the maximum of six demons clustered round zero from minus 3 to plus 3. I am afraid that that is as much as one can say fairly.

Notes

1   Mackay, D. M. Mentality in Machines. *Proc. Arist. Soc. Suppt.*, 1952, 61.
2   Mackay, D. M. The Epistemological Problem for Automata, ed. J. McCarthy and C. E. Shannan *Automata Studies, Princeton* (1955). See also *Brit. J. Psychol.*, 1956, 47, 30 and *Advancement of Science*, 1956, 392.

41

HORSES OF A DIFFERENT COLOR?

Margaret A. Boden

Source: W. H. Ramsey, S. P. Stich and D. E. Rumelhart, *Philosophy and Connectionist Theory*, Taylor & Francis, 1991, pp. 3–19.

One of the many memorable images in the film *The Wizard of Oz* is the horse whose coat changed from green to pink, to blue, to yellow. . . . The Wizard countered Dorothy's surprise by explaining: "That's a horse of a different color!" As was only to be expected, however, his explanation was bogus. Like the wizardly activities in the Palace, this equine inhabitant of the Emerald City was something of a cheat. Normally (that is, outside the Land of Oz), "a horse of a different color" distinguishes one thing from another, very different, thing—chalk and cheese, perhaps. But the pretty creature in the film was visibly the *same* horse, changing color as it trotted along. Moreover, the change was not one of essence but of accident: an effect of the lighting.

Still in the ambit of Hollywood, imagine a movie allegory depicting *The Story of AI*. The story line must reflect the fact that the theories of mental processing on offer from AI have varied over the years. Good Old-Fashioned AI (GOFAI; Haugeland, 1985) and connectionism must surely be portrayed. But should they be played as two different characters, or as a single person shown in different lights? (Perhaps neither: a casting manager with a nice sensitivity to the AI literature might hire several actors to play contrasting "connectionist" roles—including a current pop star as parallel distributed processing—PDP.) If cast as two characters, should they enjoy the camaraderie of Newman and Redford (respectively, no doubt) or suffer unrelenting antagonism? And if antagonism is the theme which is the hero and which is the anti-hero? Which is Tom, and which is Jerry?

In short, what are the relations between GOFAI and connectionism? Are they, as is sometimes claimed, two different paradigms? Are they respectively "False Starts and Real Foundations," as the subtitle of a recent collection of essays on AI (Graubard, 1988) would have it? Or are they complementary partners in a common intellectual enterprise? And if cooperation is in question, are they strange bedfellows who will never find real ease with each other? Or are they siblings sprung from the same intellectual roots, sadly separated in childhood but destined to be reunited? (Hankies out for the happy ending.)

Differences between GOFAI and connectionism

Those who see GOFAI and connectionism as two utterly different approaches often use the labels *symbolic paradigm* and *subsymbolic paradigm* to differentiate them. These labels remind us of two differences between (much) traditional and (most) connectionist AI, concerning what is computed on the one hand and how it is computed on the other.

Paul Smolensky (1987, 1988), for example, pointed out that the basic units of many connectionist systems compute "meanings" that are not recognizable as near-equivalents of everyday concepts. These computational units do not code the presence or absence of a feature corresponding to a single word, or even to a phrase made up of familiar words; that is, they do not represent the "thoughts" spoken of in folk psychology. Rather, each unit represents some tiny detail or microfeature, whose presence or absence *en masse* may correspond to a readily verbalizable idea but whose individual significance may be nigh-unintelligible. In a system-modeling stereopsis, for instance, there is no unit that computes the depth of the object being looked at. Rather, each unit codes a comparison between the light falling on corresponding points on the two retinae. By contrast, many GOFAI-models—the so-called "expert systems," for instance—compute inferential relations between recognizable concepts, or even entire propositions (patient has red spot/patient has measles).

As for the way in which depth is computed, this—with one important qualification, discussed later—is different from the methods used in GOFAI models. Features (like depth) that are symbolized by ordinary language, and contribute to the content of everyday thoughts, are embodied as the pattern of activity over the network as a whole. While the network is doing its computations (each of which involves only locally neighbouring units) in parallel, this pattern changes continually. Eventually, however, the system settles into a stable state that represents the recognizable concept or judgment in question. In a stereoptic system, for example, the distance of the object being viewed is represented as the activity pattern (at equilibrium) of all the abstract point comparisons. The process of equilibration is described not by sequences of symbol-manipulating instructions as used in GOFAI, but by differential equations like those used in physics.

The so-called subsymbolic paradigm, then, is exemplified by the PDP approach. Most of my discussion focuses on PDP examples. They are currently attracting the most attention, not to say hype (hence the pop star on the casting director's list). And they are even more different from GOFAI than some other connectionist approaches are, so invite even more curiosity about the nature of the explanations they offer (Clark, 1989, 1990). But they are only one among many types of connectionism.

Connectionist models in general are broadly reminiscent of—and, at least indirectly, specifically inspired by—the neural networks in the brain. They are parallel-processing systems, involving cooperative computations grounded in local interactions between connected units. But many different actual examples, and indefinitely many potential ones, fall under this bland description.

Each individual computation is relatively simple, as compared with, for example, a LISP-instruction within a program for a von Neumann machine. Even so, connectionist units and computations vary significantly, both in their semantic interpretation and in their basic function. Some connectionist units are interpreted as the truth values of entire (logically complex) propositional expressions. Others code the presence of familiar concepts, or features easily describable in English. Still others stand for microfeatures defined at a much more detailed level than everyday concepts or symbols. It is only the last of these three types of connectionism that can properly be termed *subsymbolic*.

PDP models themselves vary in important ways, not only in their learning rules (of which there are several types), but in their basic functioning too. For instance, the activity of the constituent units may be binary or continuous, determinist or stochastic, and based on a wide or a narrow range of (overlapping or nonoverlapping) "evidence." Each of these computational distinctions is mirrored somewhere in the nervous system. It was discovered in the 1950s, for instance, that—contrary to the Sherringtonian view—neurones sometimes fire spontaneously (Burns, 1968). That is, the cell sometimes behaves randomly with respect to the signals input from neighbouring neurones. Mathematical analysis of some of today's connectionist models suggests that this unpredictable behavior may be a positive advantage, not an example of "botched" evolutionary engineering.

In brief, all connectionist systems compute in a way that is different from the way in which a von Neumann machine computes, and some (such as PDP systems) consist of basic units that compute matters unlike anything that is dreamed of in folk psychology.

Whether GOFAI and connectionism are utterly distinct paradigms, implacable rivals in the race to understand the mind, is another matter.

The origins of connectionism

Whereas GOFAI was largely inspired by the belief that mental processes might be essentially similar to the information processes going on in von Neumann computers, connectionism was not. Donald Norman (1986), for example, said that PDP models can "in no way" be interpreted as growing from our metaphor of the modern computer. He continues: "Here, we are

talking about a new form of computation, one clearly based upon principles that have heretofore not had any counterpart in computers"
(p. 534).

Describing the computations concerned as "neurologically inspired,"
Norman quoted Frank Rosenblatt's (1962) perceptrons and Stephen Grossberg's (1982) mathematical analyses of brain function as important forerun-
ners. So, indeed, they were. But so too was the seminal work of Warren
McCulloch and Walter Pitts (1943), whose paper entitled "A Logical Calculus of the Ideas Immanent in Nervous Activity" first showed that networks
of simple computational units could in principle perform computations of
great complexity.

McCulloch and Pitts proved, for instance, that every function of propositional logic is realizable by some (fairly simple) net of all-or-none threshold units, and that every Turing-computable function can be computed by
some such net. And they suggested that learning, too (along with other psychological phenomena) could be achieved by neural nets. Indeed, they
claimed in this paper that the whole of psychology—"all that could be
achieved in that field"—boils down to the specification of nets capable of
computations of various kinds. As they put it, "If our nets are undefined,
our facts are undefined." Action, perception, reasoning, introspection,
motivation, value judgment: all may one day be understood. Mental processes are theoretically tractable, because they are physically realizable in
intelligible ways. Even in psychiatry, "'Mind' no longer goes 'more ghostly
than a ghost'."

McCulloch and Pitts' conviction that mind can be understood in computational terms of some sort was comparable to the insight that biology can be
based in chemistry of some sort. This insight, not the discovery of the genetic code (which led to the "new" science of molecular biology), was the truly
revolutionary moment in biology. Similarly, McCulloch and Pitts made it
possible to ask how mental processes can be understood as computations—
of various kinds.

Their equation of thinking with computation inspired early work in connectionist modeling. (Examples were described in *The Mechanization of
Thought Processes*, 1959.) Some of this pioneering research was influenced
also by other work of theirs (Pitts & McCulloch, 1947), in which they argued
that a neurophysiologically realistic theory must qualify their claim (of 1943)
that "the fundamental relations [in psychology] are those of two-valued
logic" (p. 38).

In principle, this claim was still true: Anything computable can be computed by some net of the type they had defined. (Even in practice, it has
some force: Most connectionist models, so far, are simulated on von
Neumann machines.) But an anatomically plausible theory of mental
process (as opposed to an "existence proof" of its physical realizability) cannot assume such neat and tidy connections, nor such constantly reliable

thresholds, as were posited in their earlier paper. Cerebral nets, unlike logic circuits, cannot be tailormade—still less, rigid—in every detail. As they put it:

> It is wise to construct . . . these nets so that their principal function is little perturbed by small perturbations in excitation, threshold, or details of connection within the same neighbourhood. Genes can only predetermine statistical order, and original chaos must reign over nets that learn, for learning builds new order according to a law of use.
>
> (p. 46)

In light of present-day concerns, it is interesting to note that Pitts and McCulloch's paper of 1947 developed a processing theory (of the visual reflex that controls the direction of gaze) in statistical terms. The theory focused on the identification of "weighted centres of gravity" of neural activity. They located this activity in anatomically specified groups of cells in the superior colliculus, arguing that these cells functioned as spatial maps of the visual input. And, in rebutting both Gestalt theories of brain-world isomorphism and what would now be called "grandmother-cell" neurological theories, they insisted: "That language in which information is communicated to the homunculus who sits always beyond any incomplete analysis of sensory mechanisms and before any analysis of motor ones neither needs to be nor is apt to be built on the plan of those languages men use toward one another" (p. 56).

McCulloch and Pitts were by no means the first to claim that "learning builds new order [in the brain] according to a law of use" (p. 46). This had been a common tenet of late British empiricism; in the mid-18th century, for example, David Hartley had explained sensory and motor learning in terms of the association of "medullary particles" and "vibratiuncles" in the brain. Over a century later, William James had suggested that the activation of one brain-cell by another increases the probability of such activation in the future, because of some physiological change at the synapse. But McCulloch and Pitts' logical proof that computations of indefinite complexity could be realized in nervous nets, and their mathematical definitions of neural functioning, inspired Donald Hebb to cast James' suggestion in more precise terms (Hebb, 1949).

Hebb's account of synaptic modification (which he himself described as "a form of connectionism") is the basis of most of the learning rules used in today's connectionist systems. Anyone who had sixpence for every reference in the current literature to "Hebbian" rules would be wealthy indeed. At the outset of *The Organization of Behavior*, Hebb commended McCulloch and Pitts' application of mathematics to the interaction of populations of neurones (and he drew also on McCulloch's neurophysiological work, in arguing for the empirical plausibility of his learning rule). In short, behind Hebb, McCulloch and Pitts are hovering.

So what? Surely, Norman's attempt to dissociate connectionism from GOFAI still stands? To identify another historical precursor, one even earlier than those he mentioned, is not to argue against him. And even McCulloch and Pitts theorized in a connectionist fashion when they had real brains in mind.

Granted. But the crucial point is that the McCulloch and Pitts paper of 1943 was just as much a precursor of GOFAI as it was of connectionism.

The dual role of McCulloch and Pitts

The preceding statement should come as no surprise. For McCulloch and Pitts' paper on the logical activity immanent in nervous nets is often seen as even more closely connected with GOFAI than with connectionism.

For instance, the paper was criticized 15 years later by Rosenblatt (1958), for engendering "a profusion of brain models which amount simply to logical contrivances for performing particular algorithms . . . in response to sequences of stimuli." He allowed that McCulloch and Pitts had been "chiefly concerned with the question of how [psychological functions] might be achieved by a deterministic physical system of any sort, rather than how this is actually done by the brain." But he denied their implicit assumption that it would require "only a refinement or modification of existing [logical] principles to understand the working of a more realistic nervous system." A fundamentally different approach was needed. Ignoring McCulloch and Pitts' paper of 1947, Rosenblatt said:

> A relatively small number of theorists, like Ashby and von Neumann, have been concerned with the problems of how an imperfect neural network, containing many random connections, can be made to perform reliably those functions which might be represented by idealized wiring diagrams. Unfortunately, the language of symbolic logic and Boolean algebra is less well suited [than a statistical theory] for such investigation.

The very earliest research on computers concentrated on number crunching, and was done without thought of the logical functions that might be instantiated in the brain. The use of computers in the war effort was then more to the point. But the potential relevance of McCulloch and Pitts' work for modeling thinking in general was soon recognized.

Norbert Wiener, for example, reported a conversation with Pitts in 1943:

> At that time Mr. Pitts was already thoroughly acquainted with mathematical logic and neurophysiology, but had not had the chance to make very many engineering contacts. In particular, he was not acquainted with Dr. Shannon's work, and he had not had much

experience of the possibilities of electronics. He was very much interested when I showed him examples of modern vacuum tubes and explained to him that these were ideal means for realizing in the metal the equivalents of his neuronic circuits and systems. From that time, it became clear to us that the ultra-rapid computing machine, depending as it does on consecutive switching devices, must represent an almost ideal model of the problems arising in the nervous system. The all-or-none character of the discharge of the neurons is precisely analogous to the single choice made in determining a digit on the binary scale, which more than one of us had already contemplated as the most satisfactory basis of computing-machine design.

(Wiener, 1948, p. 14)

With respect to "computing-machine design," the architecture of the electronic digital computer itself was influenced by the ideas of McCulloch and Pitts. Their neural-net specifications of logical functions (such as AND, OR, and NOT) were embodied in electronic circuitry as and-gates, or-gates, and the like. This embodiment, in effect, turned computers from mere number crunchers into general-purpose symbol-manipulating machines.

John von Neumann (1945) referred to them several times in an early report on computer design, commending, for example, their idea that neurones—or basic computational units—could be thought of as digital elements. He said:

Every digital computing device contains certain relay-like *elements*, with discrete equilibria. Such an element has two or more distinct states in which it can exist indefinitely . . . In existing digital computing devices various mechanical or electrical devices have been used as elements: [wheels, telegraph relays] . . . and finally there exists the plausible and tempting possibility of using vacuum tubes . . . It is worth mentioning, that the neurons of the higher animals are definitely elements in the above sense . . . Following Pitts and McCulloch [1943], we ignore the more complicated aspects of neuron functioning . . . It is easily seen, that these simplified neuron functions can be imitated by telegraph relays or by vacuum tubes.

A few paragraphs later, he pointed out that vacuum tubes used as current valves, or gates, are all-or-none devices, and continued:

Since these tube arrangements are to handle numbers by means of their digits, it is natural to use a system of arithmetic in which the digits are also two-valued. This suggests the use of the binary system. The analogs of human neurons, discussed [above] are equally all-or-none elements. It will appear that they are quite useful for all preliminary, orienting considerations on vacuum tube systems. It is

451

therefore satisfactory that here too, the natural arithmetical system to handle is the binary one.

(von Neumann, 1945, pp. 359–362)

Like McCulloch and Pitts themselves, von Neumann (1958, 1960) did not believe that "the logic of the brain" could be the same as the formal logic of the computer. He suggested statistical thermodynamics as a better analogy for cerebral processing.

As regards what the newly designed digital computer was soon to be used for, this too was strongly influenced by McCulloch and Pitts' 1943 paper. On the one hand, it was seen as an encouraging invitation to try to model psychological processes in physical mechanisms of some sort. On the other, the eponymous "logical activity," and the authors' remark that "the fundamental relations are those of two-valued logic," were seen as suggesting how this could actually be done.

At first, many researchers tried to work at the level of elementary logic circuits like those McCulloch and Pitts had defined. After a few years, however, it was realized that the thought processes that most interested psychologists could not readily be conceived of at the level of AND, OR, and NOT. Higher level descriptions (programming languages) were developed accordingly, although these were defined at base in logical terms. For instance, Allen Newell, Herbert Simon, and Clifford Shaw developed the first list-processing languages (the IPL family) so as to be able to represent symbolic manipulations more directly. IPL functioned as a *virtual* machine, an information-processing system conceptualized at a level above that of the logic circuits in which it was, ultimately, implemented. Where IPL went, LISP (and others) soon followed.

The pendulum in connectionist research

For a time, the two streams of computational modeling—statistical and logical—moved ahead side by side. However, the early successes of the logical approach (notably, Arthur Samuel's checkers player and the *Logic Theorist* and *General Problem Solver* of Newell, Simon, and Shaw; Feigenbaum & Feldman, 1963) were not matched by comparably impressive achievements on the other side. And in the late 1960s, Marvin Minsky (perhaps the first person to build a connectionist learning device) and Seymour Papert proved that simple networks have unexpected limitations, and suggested—without formal proof—that more complex, many-leveled, networks would likewise prove "sterile" (Minsky & Papert, 1969).

Despite Minsky and Papert's explicit statement that checking their intuitive judgment on this point was "an important research problem," the result was a catastrophic fall in the opportunities, and the funding, for connectionist research in AI. A few stubborn souls continued this approach to computational modeling. And a few scientists—neurophysiologists and physicists—unconnected with the AI-community developed mathematical theories of neural functioning or information-processing that were connectionist in temper, if not in title. (Rosenblatt and Grossberg, the precursors mentioned by Norman, fall into the first and second groups respectively.) Within mainstream AI, however, logic—not statistics—was the name of the game. The two streams of computational modeling that arose from McCulloch and Pitts' work had separated long since. Now, so far as the AI community was concerned, one had gone deep underground.

Only very recently has connectionism resurfaced in AI. And, according to some, with revival has come reversal: Seemingly, the tables have turned. Many people today can be heard announcing that GOFAI is utterly discredited.

Hubert Dreyfus, for example, described connectionism as a "devastating" challenge to traditional AI, of which he said: "the rationalist tradition had finally been put to an empirical test, and it had failed" (Dreyfus & Dreyfus, in press, 1988). The pithiest expression of this view was mentioned in the opening section: *False Starts, Real Foundations*. Appended as a subtitle to the book title *The AI Debate*, this puts the case for "reversal" in a nutshell. GOFAI was a waste of time; only connectionist theories can explain the mind—so, at least, we are told. But is this judgment fair?

The contribution of GOFAI

Such wholesale rejection of GOFAI, in favor of connectionism, is too quick and too easy. Far from being strange bedfellows, these two computational approaches have a common ancestry (both tracing their descent from McCulloch and Pitts). Moreover, although their relationship has been strained for many years, they have not been utterly estranged. There is reason, as we see later, for expecting further reconciliation in the future. But fruitful interchange has quietly been taking place for some time. In fact, connectionism already owes a lot to GOFAI.

The most ardent champions of connectionism (e.g., Dreyfus) suggest that this is true, if at all, only in a Popperian sense. The fathers of AI made a bold conjecture, and encountered an equally uncompromising refutation. The more historically minded may exempt McCulloch and Pitts (and von Neumann too), despite their responsibility for this conjecture's being made in the first place: Over 40 years ago, after all, they recommended statistical theories for explaining brain-embodied thought. But the AI community as a whole stands charged with delaying the advance of psychology for many years. Rarely has there been such an expensive blind alley. The only comfort to be drawn from nearly 40 years of AI research is that it has finally been shown to be a dead end. The abject failure of GOFAI has at least spurred the investigation of alternative computational approaches.

This negativistic evaluation of GOFAI has something to be said for it. Undoubtedly, GOFAI's failure in modeling common sense reasoning and flexible pattern matching, and its general inability to achieve graceful degradation, have recently spurred interest in connectionist systems.

But GOFAI can be judged also in much more positive terms. Sometimes, the computations involved in current connectionist models are essentially comparable with those already used in GOFAI models addressing similar problems. (The relevant GOFAI programs were often able to cope with "noise" of various kinds, contrary to the widespread belief that graceful degradation is available *only* in connectionist systems.) Even when they are not, they may be computations of a kind whose relevance was first realized because of work in the GOFAI tradition.

By this I mean not that their absence from GOFAI models caused deficiencies that (in Popperian mode) had to be met by different conjectures, but rather that GOFAI took the first positive steps in identifying their theoretical importance. Many computational constraints or heuristics initially identified by GOFAI are now implemented in connectionist systems (which add the advantages of parallelism and greater noise tolerance).

For instance, consider Marrian models of visual processing. These deal with such matters as stereopsis, the preliminary identification of line segments (in building the Primal Sketch), and the construction of the 2.5-D Sketch. David Marr's (1982) theoretical approach owes much to a general insight gained through over a decade of GOFAI work in scene analysis: namely, that a successful visual system requires (implicit or explicit) systematic knowledge about the detailed ways in which 2-D images can be projected within a 3-D world. It is indebted, too, to various specific insights gained from prior GOFAI vision research. One example is the notion of gradient space: a formal account of how surface orientation can be represented, given certain general constraints on image formation (Mackworth, 1973, 1983).

This should not surprise anyone who takes seriously Marr's emphasis on abstract task analysis (at what he called the "computational" level) in defining *what vision is*. This fundamental question is distinguishable from the processing-level question, *how vision is done* (and also from the hardware-level puzzle as to *what does it*). Because the concept of gradient space was developed with abstract constraints (on projective geometry) in mind, it was a theory that could be used by processing models of any type. As it happens, it was originally developed for use in sequential scene-analysis models. But there was no reason why it should not be used in parallel-processing models too. Indeed, it must feature in any successful processing model of vision, for it identifies basic constraints on 2-D to 3-D mapping.

Marr's theoretical approach—and, indirectly, his seminal treatment of stereopsis—was specifically seeded by Minsky, a fact that underlines the ambivalence of Minsky's role in the history of connectionist research.

In the late 1960s and early 1970s, Marr was using ideas about parallel processing to ask how the cerebellum, considered as a piece of biological hardware, comes to control skilled movement (Blomfield & Marr, 1970). He defined a connectionist algorithm whereby neural "contexts" (originating in cortical impulses, and mediated by the mossy and parallel fibres of the cerebellum) could be learned, and then reproduced, by the Purkinje cells. Although this algorithm was later proved to be faulty (it eventually leads to a state in which all the weights are at a maximum value; Sejnowski, 1977), it was an ancestor of some connectionist processes that are now current.

This work was done as an exercise in mathematical neurophysiology, and—although influenced by McCulloch and Pitts—owed nothing to AI. Marr did not need Minsky to make him a connectionist. But his shift to theorizing at what he later called the "computational" level occurred after he gave a seminar on his ideas about the cerebellum at MIT, at which Minsky remarked from the floor that we have to think about "the [abstract] problem of motor control" before we can ask the right questions about the cerebellar hardware. That is, unless we know what is being done we cannot ask fruitful questions about how it is being done, nor about what is doing it. Largely as a result of this interchange, Marr moved to Minsky's laboratory at MIT, where he decided to consider "the problem of *vision*" instead (Poggio, personal communication, August, 1988).

Throughout his time at MIT, Marr accepted the prevailing view that the abstract problem of 2-D to 3-D mapping was theoretically basic to the understanding of vision. This view had developed throughout a decade of AI work in scene analysis, and the physics of image formation was being elucidated by Berthold Horn. Marr's initial research reports cast scorn on GOFAI models of vision, many of which had been developed at MIT under Minsky's direction. But he later incorporated some of their theoretical ideas—not only gradient space, but top-down processing and object models too. From the start, however, he accepted the insight (hard won by work in scene analysis) that some general account of image projection must underlie a computational theory of vision.

Vision is not the only example where connectionist work has benefited from its GOFAI predecessors. Nor is it the only example where GOFAI modeling pioneered the computation of "subsymbolic" functions, undreamed of in folk psychology. Natural language processing, for instance, involves syntactic and semantic distinctions that are normally inaccessible to consciousness and are expressible only in highly technical language.

Accordingly, "False Starts" is a most ungenerous judgment. To a significant extent, the current achievements of connectionism rest on substantive insights gleaned from traditional AI research.

Continuing influence of GOFAI

As for the future achievements of connectionism, these too will very likely benefit from GOFAI. Indeed, sequential processing may be essential for some human thought processes, such as ordered problem solving or logical reasoning, generalized thinking involving variable binding, and perhaps certain structural aspects of language.

Prima facie, these phenomena pose a challenge to connectionism. It is not clear that the equilibration of multiple constraints, powerful though it may be for pattern matching, is well suited to model conscious planning or arithmetic. For the perception of similarity or analogy, "soft" constraints—which incline without necessitating—are ideal. But for logical deduction, or ordered contingency planning, they are not. The virtual machine that carries out such thinking is, apparently, more reminiscent of a digital computer than of a connectionist system: The brain sometimes seems to simulate a von Neumann machine. As Norman (1986) said, "people do seem to have at least two modes of operation, one rapid, efficient, subconscious, the other slow, serial, and conscious" (p. 534), and he allowed that the second mode might involve computations of a type used in GOFAI.

Some claim that there is no "might" about it. Theorists committed to a logicist approach to computational psychology have argued that sequential processes, and a compositional semantics, must underlie not only conscious deliberations but language-understanding too (Fodor & Pylyshyn, 1988; Pinker & Prince, 1988, in press). If so, then work in the GOFAI tradition is potentially relevant to psychology, and will need to be integrated with connectionist foundations.

Certain leading connectionists acknowledged this possibility several years ago. The theoretical challenge for connectionism, they said, is to show that "we succeed in solving logical problems not so much through the use of logic, but by making the problems we wish to solve conform to problems we are good at solving" (Rumelhart, Smolensky, McClelland, & Hinton, 1986, p. 44). In other words, connectionists must show that logical thought can be based on pattern recognition.

One suggestion about how this might be done is that the connectionist system could utilize *multi-level* networks that exploit our natural ability to perceive and manipulate the external environment (Rumelhart et al., 1986). Broadly, the idea is that patterns in the environment can be internalized, and then function successively so that the pattern in a network on one level affects the next equilibrium state (the next pattern) in some network at another level—which in turn partially constrains the following equilibration of the first network.

For instance, a connectionist computer model has been implemented that uses two mutually influential networks to produce the sequential moves of a game of noughts-and-crosses. The constraints within both networks embody

456

the rules and strategy of noughts-and-crosses, but one network represents "player's move," whereas the other represents "opponent's move." The opponent's moves might be represented only by a *perceptual* network, one reflecting actual events (the opponent's moves) in the outside world; in that case, the player could play the game by repeatedly settling into some equilibrium state in response to the opponent's moves but would be unable to "think" about it, or plan ahead. But if these perceptual patterns can be internalized, they can then be used in the mind to "drive" the equilibration of successive patterns representing the player's own carefully thought-out moves.

An active research area in computer modeling at present concerns "hybrid" computational systems, in which GOFAI and connectionist processes are somehow combined. (An early example was a connectionist system that simulated GOFAI production rules, including general rule schemas that require variable binding; Touretzky & Hinton, 1985.) But the technical problems involved are still highly obscure.

What sort of "combination" actually takes place in the human case is likewise controversial. In other words, the sense in which connectionism provides "Real Foundations" is disputed.

Connectionists who argue that logical properties and syntactic structure can emerge from a PDP base (Smolensky, 1988) are countered by logicists who regard a compositional "language of thought" as an irreducible bedrock of human thought (Fodor & Pylyshyn, 1988). The categories of folk psychology are believed by some to be mere approximations to the underlying psychological reality, much as Newtonian laws are broad generalizations of what happens at the quantum level (Smolensky, 1988); others see them as indispensable aspects of the virtual machine that is the human mind (Clark, 1989). Some claim that our thinking is connectionist through and through, that even the most rigorous conscious thought is at best an approximation to the impossible ideal of conceptual thinking (Cussins, 1990). Others argue that, even though conceptual thought is grounded in, and ultimately derives its semantic content from, connectionist (perceptuomotor) processes, it is (Karmiloff-Smith, in press)—or at least it may be (Clark, in press)—dependent on internal representations of a kind better suited to GOFAI accounts than to connectionist ones; that is to say, the basic architecture is connectionist but the relevant virtual machine is not.

How can connectionist systems be understood?

Quite apart from these general philosophical debates, there is uncertainty about how to explain the performance of a connectionist system once one has got it. A connectionist system that does something interesting may be no more than that: interesting. Beyond its value as a (perhaps largely unintelligible) existence proof, it is illuminating only to the extent that we understand why it does what it does. In this regard, GOFAI often has the edge. The program and/or a specific program trace is explicitly available, and sometimes the abstract "computational-level" theory underlying it is available too. A connectionist system may be much less transparent.

NETtalk, for example, learns how to speak written words, its pronunciation improving with each learning cycle (Sejnowski & Rosenberg, 1986). It does so by mimicking the particular set of pronunciations provided to it, using back propagation: It compares its current output with the correct output, and slightly alters the connection weights if these differ. To learn a new dialect, NETtalk has to be retrained from scratch: One cannot selectively alter certain weights to flatten the vowels, or drop the Hs. [The network has 309 units, linked by 18,629 connections; there are 26 output units, 80 hidden units, and (29×7) input units, which code the target phoneme with its immediate predecessor and successor.]

NETtalk's performance is eerily impressive, evoking the listener's memories of the gradually improving speech of human infants. But even its designers are unclear about just what it is doing, and how.

They suggest three ways of trying to find out: network pathology, records of unit activation, and cluster analysis. The last of these methods identifies the associations that are most often used by the system in partitioning the "space" of its performance. It turns out—to its designer's surprise—that NETtalk develops an implicit hierarchy of (nearly 80) distinctions like those explicitly defined in phonetics: vowels and consonants, voiced and unvoiced consonants, and so on. Network pathology is an approach that involves systematic "lesioning" of the network, either before or after it has learned its task. This method may throw light not only on artificial networks but on clinical neurology too. For instance, when parts of a recent connectionist model of reading are prevented from functioning, the system shows various "dyslexias" that are qualitatively similar to those which afflict human patients (Hinton & Shallice, 1989).

It is not obvious that explanations derived by these sorts of post hoc analysis can fit into the three-tier explanatory hierarchy recommended by Marr. Clark (1990) argued that they cannot. A competence theory may be a useful idealization of what a connectionist system is doing; and, as remarked earlier, it may help the designer to choose the relevant inputs and outputs. But it cannot explain what is really going on, for the network contains neither explicit nor even tacit knowledge of competence constraints. In general, there is no precise mapping between the information processing in connectionist and GOFAI systems performing "the same" task. Connectionists build a network only loosely specified by abstract task constraints, they let it learn to perform the task in question, and only then do they find the high-level principles it has come to embody. In Clark's view, the model's explanatory force lies in those principles, not in the task analysis nor in the set of connection weights.

An important explanatory dimension, or class of dimensions, concerns the computational potential and limits, in principle, of different sorts of connectionist systems. For example, what is the noise level at which a Boltzmann machine becomes impracticable? What classes of problem can be best solved (or solved at all) by back-propagation learning? How can supervised and unsupervised learning be analytically distinguished, and what algorithms suit them best? What is the maximum computational power of connectionist systems having some specific number of units and/or layers? Can anything be said about the optimal relative sizes of the "receptive fields" of neighboring connectionist units whose fields overlap? And to what extent can connectionism benefit from the theoretical results of many years' work in statistical pattern matching? Although some mathematical results, concerning connectionist systems of various types, have been achieved, much work remains to be done.

It is far too early for confidence about either the potential or the limits of the connectionist systems we already have, not to mention those to be defined in the future. And it is far too early to write off traditional AI as a dead end.

Indeed, not all connectionists are as dismissive of GOFAI as the phrase "False Starts" suggests. The high priests of PDP, for instance, believe that "it would be wrong to view distributed representations as an *alternative* to representational schemes like semantic networks or production systems that have been found useful in cognitive psychology and artificial intelligence (Hinton, McClelland, & Rumelhart, 1986, p. 78). They view PDP networks rather as "one way of implementing these more abstract schemas in parallel networks," pointing out that their emergent properties (pattern matching, content-addressable memory, and graceful degradation) provide powerful operations that can be regarded as primitives by psychologists considering more high-level theories implemented in traditional ways.

Conclusion

In summary, GOFAI and connectionism are not "horses of a different color," utterly distinct beasts from rival paradigmatic stables. They have a partly shared pedigree, with common ancestry in the early 1940s. After a period of estrangement, they are approaching each other more closely. They already share common insights, and are thinking about cooperating to produce (non-sterile) hybrids.

To be sure, their differences are real, and important. So if our Hollywood casting director has a lot of money available, he can hire two actors—or better still, a troupe—to play them. But if he needs to save the producer's money, he can do so by hiring only one. The actor chosen must be able to display a range of skills, moods, and preoccupations. But he need work no magical metamorphoses: AI is one beast, like the Wizard's pony.

References

n.a. (1959). *The mechanization of thought processes*. London: Her Majesty's Stationery Office.

Blomfield, S., & Marr, D. C. (1970). How the cerebellum may be used. *Nature, 227*, 1224–1228.

Burns, B. D. (1968). *The uncertain nervous system*. London: Edward Arnold.

Clark, A. J. (1989). *Microcognition: Philosophy, cognitive science, and parallel distributed processing*. Cambridge, MA: MIT Press/Bradford Books.

Clark, A. J. (1990). Connectionism, competence, and explanation. In M. A. Boden (Ed.), *The philosophy of artificial intelligence* (pp. 281–308). Oxford: Oxford University Press.

Clark, A. J. (in press). *Connectionism, non-conceptual content, and representational redescription*. (Research Rep. CSRP 143). University of Sussex, School of Cognitive and Computing Sciences.

Cussins, A. (1990). The connectionist construction of concepts. In M. A. Boden (Ed.), *The philosophy of artificial intelligence* (pp. 368–440). Oxford: Oxford University Press.

Dreyfus, H., & Dreyfus, S. (1988). Making a mind versus modeling the brain: Artificial intelligence back at a branchpoint. In S. R. Graubard (Ed.), *The artificial intelligence debate: False starts, real foundations* (pp. 15–43). Cambridge, MA: MIT Press/Bradford Books. Reprinted in M. A. Boden (Ed.), *The philosophy of artificial intelligence* (pp. 309–333). Oxford: Oxford University Press.

Dreyfus, H., & Dreyfus, S. (in press). Towards a reconciliation of phenomenology and AI. In D. Partridge & Y. A. Wilks (Eds.), *Foundational issues in artificial intelligence*. Cambridge: Cambridge University Press.

Feigenbaum, E. A., & Feldman, J. (Eds.). (1963). *Computers and thought*. New York: McGraw-Hill.

Fodor, J. A., & Pylyshyn, Z. W. (1988). Connectionism and cognitive architecture: A critical analysis. *Cognition, 28*, 3–71.

Graubard, S. (Ed.). (1988). *The artificial intelligence debate: False starts, real foundations*. Cambridge, MA: MIT Press/Bradford Books.

Grossberg, S. (1982). *Studies of mind and brain*. Dordrecht, Holland: Reidel.

Haugeland, J. (1985). *Artificial intelligence: The very idea*. Cambridge, MA: MIT Press/Bradford Books.

Hebb, D. O. (1949). *The organization of behavior: A neuropsychological theory*. New York: Wiley.

Hinton, G. E., McClelland, J. L. & Rumelhart, D. E. (1986). Distributed representations. In McClelland, J. L., Rumelhart, D. E., & the PDP Research Group, *Parallel distributed processing: Explorations in the microstructure of cognition: Vol. 1: Foundations* (pp. 77–109). Cambridge, MA: MIT Press.

Hinton, G. E., & Shallice, T. (1989). *Lesioning a connectionist network: Investigations of acquired dyslexia*. (Tech. Rep. No. CRG-TR-89-3). University of Toronto, Connectionist Research Group.

Karmiloff-Smith, A. (in press). *Beyond modularity: A developmental perspective on cognitive science*. Cambridge, MA: MIT Press/Bradford Books.

Mackworth, A. K. (1973). Interpreting pictures of polyhedral scenes. *Artificial Intelligence, 4*, 121–138.

Mackworth, A. K. (1983). Constraints, descriptions, and domain mappings in computational vision. In O. J. Braddick & A. C. Sleigh (Eds.), *Physical and biological processing of images* (pp. 33–40). New York: Springer-Verlag.

Marr, D. C. (1982). *Vision: A computation investigation into the human representation and processing of visual information*. San Francisco: Freeman.

Minsky, M. L., & Papert, S. (1969). *Perceptrons: An introduction to computational geometry*. Cambridge, MA: MIT Press.

McCulloch, W. S., & Pitts, W. H. (1943). A logical calculus of the ideas immanent in nervous activity. *Bulletin of Mathematical Biophysics, 5*, 115–133. Reprinted in M. A. Boden (Ed.), *The philosophy of artificial intelligence* (pp. 22–39). Oxford: Oxford University Press.

Norman, D. A. (1986). Reflections on cognition and parallel distributed processing. In D. E. Rumelhart & J. L. McClelland (Eds.), *Parallel distributed processing: Explorations in the microstructure of cognition*, Vol. 2: *Psychological and biological models* (pp. 531–546). Cambridge, MA: MIT Press/Bradford Books.

Pinker, S., & Prince, A. (1988). On language and connectionism: Analysis of a parallel distributed processing model of language acquisition. *Cognition, 28*, 73–193.

Pinker, S., & Prince, A. (in press). Rules and connections in human language. *Transactions in the Neurosciences.*

Pitts, W. H., & McCulloch, W. S. (1947). How we know universals: The perception of auditory and visual forms. *Bulletin of Mathematical Biophysics, 9*, 127–147. Reprinted in W. S. McCulloch, *Embodiments of mind*, Cambridge, MA: MIT Press, 1965.

Rosenblatt, F. (1958). The perceptron: A probabilistic model for information storage and organization in the brain. *Psychological Review, 65*, 386–407.

Rosenblatt, F. (1962). *Principles of neurodynamics*. New York: Spartan.

Rumelhart, D. E., Smolensky, P., McClelland, J. L., & Hinton, G. E. (1986). Schemata and sequential thought processes in PDP models. In D. E. Rumelhart & J. L. McClelland (Eds.). *Parallel distributed processing: Explorations in the microstructure of cognition*, Vol. 2: *Psychological and biological models* (pp. 7–57). Cambridge, MA: MIT Press.

Sejnowski, T. J. (1977). Statistical constraints on synaptic plasticity. *Journal of Theoretical Biology, 69*, 385–389.

Sejnowski, T. J., & Rosenberg, C. R. (1986). NETtalk: A parallel network that learns to read aloud. In J. A. Anderson & E. Rosenfeld (Eds.), *Neurocomputing: Foundations of research* (pp. 663–672). Cambridge, MA: MIT Press.

Smolensky, P. (1987). Connectionist AI, symbolic AI, and the brain. *AI Review, 1*, 95–110.

Smolensky, P. (1988). On the proper treatment of connectionism. *Behavioral and Brain Sciences, 11*, 1–74.

Touretzky, D. S., & Hinton, G. E. (1985). Symbols among the neurons: Details of a connectionist inference architecture. *Proceedings of the Ninth International Joint Conference on Artificial Intelligence* (pp. 238–243). Los Angeles, CA.

von Neumann, J. (1945). First Draft of a Report on the EDVAC. In B. Randell (Ed.), *The origins of digital computers: Selected papers* (pp. 355–364). New York: Springer-Verlag, 1973.

von Neumann, J. (1958). *The computer and the brain*. New Haven: Yale University Press.

461

von Neumann, J. (1960). The general and logical theory of automata. In J. R. Newman (Ed.), *The world of mathematics* (pp. 2070–2098), Vol. 4. New York: Random Heights.

Wiener, N. (1948). *Cybernetics, or control and communication in the animal and the machine*. New York: Wiley.

Section 2.2: Developments

42

WAKING UP FROM THE BOOLEAN DREAM, OR, SUBCOGNITION AS COMPUTATION

D. R. Hofstadter

Source: D. R. Hofstadter, *Metamagical Themas: Questing for the Essence of Mind and Pattern*, Basic Books, 1985, pp. 631–65.

Introduction

The philosopher John Searle has recently made quite a stir in the cognitive-science and philosophy-of-mind circles with his celebrated article "Minds, Brains, and Programs", in which he puts forth his "Chinese room" thought experiment. Its purpose is to reveal as illusory the aims of artificial intelligence, and particularly to discredit what he labels *strong AI*—the belief that a programmed computer can, in principle, be conscious. Various synonymous phrases could be substituted for "be conscious" here, such as:

* *think*;
* *have a soul* (in a humanistic rather than a religious sense);
* *have an inner life*;
* *have semantics* (as distinguished from "mere syntax");
* *have content* (as distinguished from "mere form");
* *have intentionality*;
* *be something it is like something to be* (a weird phrase due to T. Nagel);
* *have personhood*;

and others. Each of these phrases has its own peculiar set of connotations and imagery attached to it, as well as its own history and proponents. For our purposes, however, we shall consider them all as equivalent, and lump them all together, so that the claim of strong AI now becomes very strong indeed.

465

At the same time, various AI workers have been developing their own philosophies of what AI is, and have developed some useful terms and slogans to describe their endeavor. Some of them are: "information processing", "cognition as computation", "physical symbol system", "symbol manipulation", "expert system", and "knowledge engineering". There is some confusion as to what words like "symbol" and "cognition" actually mean, just as there is some confusion as to what words like "semantics" and "syntax" mean.

It is the purpose of this article to try to delve into the meanings of such elusive terms, and at the same time to shed some light on the views of Searle, on the one hand, and Allen Newell and Herbert Simon, on the other hand—visible AI pioneers who are responsible for several of the terms in the previous paragraph. The thoughts expressed herein were originally triggered by a paper called "Artificial Intelligence: Cognition as Computation", by Avron Barr. However, they can be read completely independently of that paper.

The questions are obviously not trivial, and certainly not resolvable in a single article. Most of the ideas in this article, in fact, were stated earlier and more fully in my book *Gödel, Escher, Bach: an Eternal Golden Braid*. However, it seems worthwhile to extract a certain stream of ideas from that book and to enrich it with some more recent musings and examples, even if the underlying philosophy remains entirely the same. In order to do justice to these complex ideas, many topics must be interwoven, and they include the nature of symbols, meaning, thinking, perception, cognition, and so on. That explains why this article is not three pages long.

Cognition versus perception: the 100-millisecond dividing line

In Barr's original paper, AI is characterized repeatedly by the phrase "information-processing model of cognition". Although when I first heard that phrase years ago, I tended to accept it as defining the nature of AI, something has gradually come to bother me about it, and I would like to try to articulate that here. Now what's in a word? What's to object to here? I won't attempt to say what's wrong with the phrase so much as try to show what I disagree with in the ideas of those who have promoted it; then perhaps the phrase's connotations will float up to the surface so that other people can see why I am uneasy with it.

I think the disagreement can be put in its sharpest relief in the following way. In 1980, Simon delivered a lecture that I attended (the Procter Award Lecture for the Sigma Xi annual meeting in San Diego), and in it he declared (and I believe I am quoting him nearly verbatim):

> Everything of interest in cognition happens above the 100-millisecond level—the time it takes you to recognize your mother.

466

Well, our disagreement is simple; namely, I take exactly the opposite viewpoint:

> Everything of interest in cognition happens below the 100-millisecond level—the time it takes you to recognize your mother.

To me, the major question of AI is this: "What in the world is going on to enable you to convert from 100,000,000 retinal dots into one single word 'mother' in one tenth of a second?" Perception is where it's at!

The problem of letterforms: a test case for AI

The problem of intelligence, as I see it, is to understand the fluid nature of mental categories, to understand the invariant cores of percepts such as your mother's face, to understand the strangely flexible yet strong boundaries of concepts such as "chair" or the letter 'a'. Years ago, long before computers, Wittgenstein had already recognized the centrality of such questions, in his celebrated discussion of the nonpindownability of the meaning of the word "game". To emphasize this and make the point as starkly as I can, I hereby make the following claim:

> The central problem of AI is the question: *What is the letter* 'a'?

Donald Knuth, on hearing me make this claim once, appended, "And what is the letter 'i'?"—an amendment that I gladly accept. In fact, perhaps the best version would be this:

> The central problem of AI is: *What are* 'a' *and* 'i'?

By making these claims, I am suggesting that, for any program to handle letterforms with the flexibility that human beings do, it would have to possess full-scale general intelligence.

Many people in AI might protest, pointing out that there already exist programs that have achieved expert-level performance in specialized domains without needing general intelligence. Why should letterforms be any different? My answer would be that specialized domains tend to obscure, rather than clarify, the distinction between strengths and weaknesses of a program. A familiar domain such as letterforms provides much more of an acid test.

To me, it is strange that AI has said so little about this classic problem. To be sure, some work has been done. There are a few groups with interest in letters, but there has been no all-out effort to deal with this quintessential problem of pattern recognition. Since letterform understanding is currently an important target of my own research project in AI, I would like to take a moment and explain why I see it as contrasting so highly with domains at the other end of the "expertise spectrum".

Each letter of the alphabet comes in literally thousands of different "official" versions (typefaces), not to mention millions, billions, trillions, of "unofficial" versions (those handwritten ones that you and I and everyone else produces all the time). There thus arises the obvious question: "How are all 'a's like each other?" The goal of an AI project would be, of course, to give an exact answer in computational terms. However, even taking advantage of the vagueness of ordinary language, one is hard put to find a satisfactory intuitive answer, because we simply come up with phrases such as "They all have the same shape." Clearly, the whole problem is that they *don't* have the same shape. And it does not help to change "shape" to "form", or to tack on phrases such as "basically", "essentially", or "at a conceptual level".

There is also the less obvious question: "How are all the various letters in a single typeface related to each other?" This is a grand analogy problem if ever there were an analogy problem. One is asking for a 'b' that is to the abstract notion of 'b'-ness as a given 'a' is to the abstract notion of 'a'-ness. You have to take the qualities of a given 'a' and, so to speak, "hold them loosely in the hand", as you see how they "slip" into variants of themselves as you try to carry them over to another letter. Here is the very hinge-point of thought, the place where one thing slips into alternate, subjunctive, variations on itself. Here, that "thing" is a very abstract concept—namely, "the way that this particular shape manifests the abstract quality of being an 'a'". The problem of 'a' is thus intimately connected with the problems of 'b' through 'z', and with that of stylistic consistency.

The existence of optical character readers, such as the reading machines invented by Ray Kurzweil for blind people, might lead one to believe at first that the letter-recognition problem has been solved. If one considers the problem a little more carefully, however, one sees that the surface has barely been scratched. In truth, the way that most optical character recognition programs work is by a fancy kind of template matching, in which statistics are done to determine which character, out of a fixed repertoire of, say, 100 stored characters, is the "best match". This is about like assuming that the way I recognize my mother is by comparing the scene in front of me with stored memories of the appearances of tigers, cigarettes, hula hoops, gambling casinos, and can openers (and of course all other things in the world simultaneously), and somehow instantly coming up with the "best match".

The human mind and its ability to recognize and reproduce forms

The problem of recognizing letters of the alphabet is no less deep than that of recognizing your mother, even if it might seem so, given that the number of Platonic prototype items is on the small side (26, if one ignores all characters but the lowercase alphabet). One can even narrow it down further—to just a handful. As a matter of fact, Godfried Toussaint, editor of the pattern recognition papers for the *IEEE Transactions*, has said to me that he would like to put up a prize for the first program that could tell correctly, given twenty characters that people easily can identify, which ones are 'a's and which are 'b's. To carry out such a task, a program cannot just recognize that a shape is an 'a'; it has to see *how* that shape embodies 'a'-ness. And then, as a test of whether the program really knows its letters, it would have to carry "that style" over to the other letters of the alphabet. This is the goal of my research: To find out how to make letters slip in "similar ways to each other", so as to constitute a consistent artistic style in a typeface—or simply a consistent way of writing the alphabet.

By contrast, most AI work on vision pertains to such things as aerial reconnaissance or robot guidance programs. This would suggest that the basic problem of vision is to figure out how to recognize textures and how to mediate between two and three dimensions. But what about the fact that although we are all marvelous face-recognizers, practically none of us can draw a face at all well—even of someone we love? Most of us are flops at drawing even such simple things as pencils and hands and books. I personally have learned to recognize hundreds of Chinese characters (shapes that involve neither three dimensions nor textures) and yet, on trying to reproduce them from memory, find myself often drawing confused mixtures of characters, leaving out basic components, or worst of all, being unable to recall anything but the vaguest "feel" of the character and not being able to draw a single line.

Closer to home, most of us have read literally millions of, say, 'u's with serifs, yet practically none of us can draw a 'u' with serifs in the standard places, going in the standard directions. (This holds even more for the kind of 'g' you just read, but it is true for any letter of the alphabet.) I suspect that many people—perhaps most—are not even consciously aware of the fact that there are two different types of lowercase 'a' and of lowercase 'g', just as many people seem to have a very hard time drawing a distinction between lowercase and uppercase letters, and a few have a hard time telling letters drawn forward from letters drawn backward.

How can such a fantastic "recognition machine" as our brain be so terrible at rendition? Clearly there must be something very complex going on, enabling us to *accept* things as members of categories and to perceive *how* they are members of those categories, yet not enabling us to reproduce those things from memory. This is a deep mystery.

In his book *Pattern Recognition*, the late Mikhail Bongard, a creative and insightful Russian computer scientist, concludes with a series of 100 puzzles for a visual pattern recognizer, whether human, machine, or alien, and to my mind it is no accident that he caps his set off with letterforms. In other words, he works his way up to letterforms as being at the pinnacle of visual recognition ability. There exists no pattern recognition program in the world today that can come anywhere close to doing those Bongard problems. And yet, Barr cites Simon as writing the following statement:

> The evidence for that commonality [between the information pro- cesses that are employed by such disparate systems as computers and human nervous systems] is now overwhelming, and the remaining questions about the boundaries of cognitive science have more to do with whether there also exist nontrivial commonalities with informa- tion processing in genetic systems than with whether men and machines both think. Wherever the boundary is drawn, there exists today a science of intelligent systems that extends beyond the limits of any single species.

I find it difficult to understand how Simon can believe this, in an era when computers still cannot do basic kinds of *subcognitive* acts (acts that we feel are unconscious, acts that underlie cognition).

In another lecture in 1979 (the opening lecture of the inaugural meeting of the Cognitive Science Society, also in San Diego), I recall Simon proclaiming that, despite much doubting by people not in the know, there is no longer any question as to whether computers can think. If he had meant that there should no longer be any question about whether machines may *eventually* become able to think, or about whether we humans are machines (in some abstract sense of the term), then I would be in accord with his statement. But after hearing and reading such statements over and over again, I don't think that's what he meant at all. I get the impression that Simon genuinely believes that today's machines are intelligent, and that they really do think (or perform "acts of cognition"—to use a bit of jargon that adds nothing to the meaning but makes it sound more scientific). I will come back to that shortly, since it is in essence the central bone of contention in this article, but first a few more remarks on AI domains.

Toy domains, technical domains, pure science, and engineering

There is in AI today a tendency toward flashy, splashy domains—that is, toward developing programs that can do such things as medical diagnosis, geological consultation (for oil prospecting), designing of experiments in molecular biology, molecular spectroscopy, configuring of large computer systems, designing of VLSI circuits, and on and on. Yet there is no program that has common sense; no program that learns things that it has not been explicitly taught how to learn; no program that can recover gracefully from its own errors. The "artificial expertise" programs that do exist are rigid, brittle, inflexible. Like chess programs, they may serve a useful intellectual or even practical purpose, but despite much fanfare, they are not shedding much light on human intelligence. Mostly, they are being developed simply because various agencies or industries fund them.

This does not follow the traditional pattern of basic science. That pattern is to try to isolate a phenomenon, to reduce it to its simplest possible manifestation. For Newton, this meant the falling apple and the moon; for Einstein, the thought experiment of the trains and lightning flashes and, later, the falling elevator; for Mendel, it meant the peas; and so on. You don't tackle the messiest problems before you've tackled the simpler ones; you don't try to run before you can walk. Or, to use a metaphor based on physics, you don't try to tackle a world with friction before you've got a solid understanding of the frictionless world.

Why do AI people eschew "toy domains"? Once, about ten years back, the MIT "blocks world" was a very fashionable domain. Roberts and Guzmán and Waltz wrote programs that pulled visions of three-dimensional blocks out of two-dimensional television-screen dot matrices; Winston, building on their work, wrote a program that could recognize instantiations of certain concepts compounded from elementary blocks in that domain ("arch", "table", "house", and so on); Winograd wrote a program that could "converse" with a person about activities, plans, past events, and some structures in that circumscribed domain; Sussman wrote a program that could write and debug simple programs to carry out tasks in that domain, thus effecting a simple kind of learning. Why, then, did interest in this domain suddenly wane?

Surely no one could claim that the domain was exhausted. Every one of those programs exhibited glaring weaknesses and limitations and specializations. The domain was phenomenally far from being understood by a single, unified program. Here, then, was a nearly ideal domain for exploring what cognition truly is—and it was suddenly dropped. MIT was at one time doing truly basic research on intelligence, and then quit. Much basic research has been supplanted by large teams marketing what they vaunt as "knowledge engineering". Firmly grounded engineering is fine, but it seems to me that this type of engineering is not built upon the solid foundations of a science, but upon a number of recipes that have worked with some success in limited domains.

In my opinion, the proper choice of domain is the critical decision that an AI researcher makes, when beginning a project. If you choose to get involved in medical diagnosis at the expert level, then you are going to get mired in a host of technical problems that have nothing to do with how the mind works. The same goes for the other earlier-cited ponderous domains that current work in expert systems involves. By contrast, if you are in control of your own domain, and can tailor it and prune it so that you keep the essence of the problem while getting rid of extraneous features, then you stand a chance of discovering something fundamental.

Early programs on the nature of analogy (Evans), sequence extrapolation (Simon and Kotovsky, among others), and so on, were moving in the right direction. But then, somehow, it became a common notion that these problems had been solved. Simply because Evans had made a program that could do some very restricted types of visual analogy problem "as well as a high school student", many people thought the book was closed. However, one need only look at Bongard's 100 to see how hopelessly far we are from dealing with analogies. One need only look at any collection of typefaces (look at any magazine's advertisements for a vast variety) to see how enormously far we are from understanding letterforms. As I claimed earlier, letterforms are probably the quintessential problem of pattern recognition. It is both baffling and disturbing to me to see so many people working on imitating cognitive functions at the highest level of sophistication when their programs cannot carry out cognitive functions at much lower levels of sophistication.

AI and the true nature of intelligence

There are some notable exceptions. The Schank group at Yale, whose original goal was to develop a program that could understand natural language, has been forced to "retreat", and to devote at least a bit of its attention to the organization of memory, which is certainly at the crux of cognition (because it is part of subcognition, incidentally)—and the group has gracefully accommodated this shift of focus. I will not be at all surprised, however, if eventually the group is forced into yet further retreats—in fact, all the way back to Bongard problems or the like. Why? Simply because their work (on such things as how to discover what "adage" accurately captures the "essence" of a story or episode) already has led them into the deep waters of abstraction, perception, and classification. These are the issues that Bongard problems illustrate so perfectly. Bongard problems are idealized ("frictionless") versions of these critical questions.

It is interesting that Bongard problems are in actuality nothing other than a well-worked-out set of typical IQ-test problems, the kind that Terman and Binet first invented 50 or more years ago. Over the years, many other less talented people have invented similar visual puzzles that had the unfortunate property of being filled with ambiguity and multiple answers. This (among other things) has given IQ tests a bad name. Whether or not IQ is a valid concept, however, there can be little question that the original insight of Terman and Binet—that carefully constructed simple visual analogy problems probe close to the core mechanisms of intelligence—is correct. Perhaps the political climate created a kind of knee-jerk reflex in many cognitive scientists to shy away from anything that smacked of IQ tests, since issues of cultural bias and racism began raising their ugly heads. But one need not be so Pavlovian as to jump whenever a visual analogy problem is placed in front of one. In any case, it will be good when AI people are finally driven back to looking at the insights of people working in the 1920's, such as Wittgenstein and his "games", Koehler and Koffka and Wertheimer and their "gestalts", and Terman and Binet and their IQ-test problems.

I was saying that some AI groups seem to be less afraid of "toy domains", or more accurately put, they seem to be less afraid of stripping down their domain in successive steps, to isolate the core issues of intelligence that it involves. Aside from the Schank group, N. Sridharan and Thorne McCarty at Rutgers have been doing some very interesting work on "prototype deformation", which, although it springs from work in legal reasoning in the quite messy real-world domain of corporate tax law, has been abstracted into a form in which it is perhaps more like a toy domain (or, perhaps less pejorative-sounding, an "idealized domain") than at first would appear.

At the University of California at San Diego, a group led by psychologist Donald Norman has been for years doing work on understanding errors, such as grammatical slips, typing errors, and errors in everyday physical actions, for the insights it may offer into the underlying (subcognitive) mechanisms. (For example, one of Norman's students unbuckled his watch instead of his seatbelt when he drove into his driveway. What an amazing mental slippage!) A group led by Norman and his colleague David Rumelhart has developed a radically different model of cognition largely based on parallel subcognitive events termed "schema activations". The reason that this work is so different in flavor from mainstream AI work is twofold: firstly, these are psychologists who are studying genuine cognition in detail and who are concerned with reproducing it; and secondly, they are not afraid to let their vision of how the *mind* works be inspired by research and speculation about how the *brain* works.

Then there are those people who are working on various programs for perception, whether visual or auditory. One of the most interesting was Hearsay II, a speech-understanding program developed at Carnegie-Mellon, Simon's home. It is therefore very surprising to me that Simon, who surely was very aware of the wonderfully intricate and quite beautiful architecture of Hearsay II, could then make a comment indicating that perception and, in general, subcognitive (under 100 milliseconds) processes, "have no interest".

There are surely many other less publicized groups that are also working on humble domains and on pure problems of mind, but from looking at the proceedings of AI conferences one might get the impression that, indeed, computers must really be able to think these days, since after all, they are doing anything and everything cognitive—from ophthalmology to biology to chemistry to mathematics—even discovering scientific laws from looking at tables of numerical data, to mention one project ("Bacon") that Simon has been involved in. However, there's more to intelligence than meets the AI.

Expert systems versus human fluidity

The problem is, AI programs are carrying out all these *cognitive* activities in the absence of any *subcognitive* activity. There is no substrate that corresponds to what goes on in the brain. There is no fluid recognition and recall and reminding. These programs have no common sense, little sense of similarity or repetition or pattern. They can perceive some patterns as long as they have been anticipated—and particularly, as long as the *place* where they will occur has been anticipated—but they cannot see patterns where nobody told them explicitly to look. They do not learn at a high level of abstraction.

This style is in complete contrast to how people are. People perceive patterns anywhere and everywhere, without knowing in advance where to look. People learn automatically in all aspects of life. These are just facets of common sense. Common sense is not an "area of expertise", but a general—that is, domain-independent—capacity that has to do with fluidity in representation of concepts, an ability to sift what is important from what is not, an ability to find unanticipated analogical similarities between totally different concepts ("reminding", as Schank calls it). We have a long way to go before our programs exhibit this cognitive style.

Recognition of one's mother's face is still nearly as much of a mystery as it was 30 years ago. And what about such things as recognizing family resemblances between people, recognizing a "French" face, recognizing kindness or earnestness or slyness or harshness in a face? Even recognizing age—even sex!—these are fantastically difficult problems. As Donald Knuth has pointed out, we have written programs that can do wonderfully well at what people have to work very hard at doing consciously (*e.g.*, doing integrals, playing chess, medical diagnosis, etc.)—but we have yet to write a program that remotely approaches our ability to do what we do *without* thinking or training—things like understanding a conversation partner with an accent at a loud cocktail party with music blaring in the background, while at the same time overhearing wisps of conversations in the far corner of the room. Or perhaps finding one's way through a forest on an overgrown trail. Or perhaps just doing some anagrams absentmindedly while washing the dishes.

Asking for a program that can discover new scientific laws without having a program that can, say, do anagrams, is like wanting to go to the moon without having the ability to find your way around town. I do not make the comparison idly. The level of performance that Simon and his colleague Langley wish to achieve in Bacon is on the order of the greatest scientists. It seems they feel that they are but a step away from the mechanization of genius. After his Procter Lecture, Simon was asked by a member of the audience, "How many scientific lifetimes does a five-hour run of Bacon represent?" After a few hundred milliseconds of human information processing, he replied, "Probably not more than one." I don't disagree with that.

474

However, I would have put it differently. I would have said, "Probably not more than one millionth."

Anagrams and epiphenomena

It's clear that I feel we're much further away from programs that do human-level scientific thinking than Simon does. Personally, I would just like to see a program that can do anagrams the way a person does. Why anagrams? Because they constitute a "toy domain" where some very significant subcognitive processes play the central role.

What I mean is this. When you look at a "Jumble" such as "telkin" in the newspaper, you immediately begin shifting around letters into tentative groups, making such stabs as "knitle", "klinte", "linket", "keltin", "tinkle"—and then you notice that indeed, "tinkle" is a word. The part of this process that I am interested in is the part that precedes the recognition of "tinkle" as a word. It's that part that involves experimentation, based only on the "style" or "feel" of English words—using intuitions about letter affinities, plausible clusters and their stabilities, syllable qualities, and so on. When you first read a Jumble in the newspaper, you play around, rearranging, regrouping, reshuffling, in complex ways that you have no control over. In fact, it feels as if you throw the letters up into the air separately, and when they come down, they have somehow magically "glommed" together in some English-like word! It's a marvelous feeling—and it is anything but cognitive, anything but conscious. (Yet, interestingly, *you* take credit for being good at anagrams, if you are good!)

It turns out that most literate people can handle Jumbles (*i.e.*, single-word anagrams) of five or six letters, sometimes seven or eight letters. With practice, maybe even ten or twelve. But beyond that, it gets very hard to keep the letters in your head. It is especially hard if there are repeated letters, since one tends to get confused about which letters there are multiple copies of. (In one case, I rearranged the letters "dinnal" into "nadlid"—incorrectly. You can try "raregarden", if you dare.) Now in one sense, the fact that the problem gets harder and harder with more and more letters is hardly surprising. It is obviously related to the famous "7 plus or minus 2" figure that psychologist George A. Miller first reported in connection with short-term memory capacity. But there are different ways of interpreting such a connection.

One way to think that this might come about is to assume that concepts for the individual letters get "activated" and then interact. When too many get activated simultaneously, then you get swamped with combinations and you drop some letters and make too many of others, and so on. This view would say that you simply encounter an explosion of connections, and your system gets overloaded. It does not postulate any explicit "storage location" in memory—a fixed set of registers or data structures—in which letters get placed and then shoved around. In this model, short-term memory (and its associated "magic number") is an *epiphenomenon* (or "innocently emergent" phenomenon, as Daniel Dennett calls it), by which I mean it is a consequence that emerges out of the design of the system, a product of many interacting factors, something that was not necessarily known, predictable, or even anticipated to emerge at all. This is the view that I advocate.

A contrasting view might be to build a model of cognition in which you have an explicit structure called "short-term memory", containing about seven (or five, or nine) "slots" into which certain data structures can be fitted, and when it is full, well, then it is full and you have to wait until an empty slot opens up. This is one approach that has been followed by Newell and associates in work on production systems. The problem with this approach is that it takes something that clearly is a very complex consequence of underlying mechanisms and simply plugs it in as an explicit structure, by passing the question of what those underlying mechanisms might be. It is difficult for me to believe that any model of cognition based on such a "bypass" could be an accurate model.

When a computer's operating system begins thrashing (*i.e.*, bogging down in its timesharing performance) at around 35 users, do you go find the systems programmer and say, "Hey, go raise the thrashing-number in memory from 35 to 60, okay?"? No, you don't. It wouldn't make any sense. This particular value of 35 is not stored in some local spot in the computer's memory where it can be easily accessed and modified. In that way, it is very different from, say, a student's grade in a university's administrative data base, or a letter in a word in an article you're writing on your home computer. That number 35 emerges dynamically from a host of strategic decisions made by the designers of the operating system and the computer's hardware, and so on. It is not available for twiddling. There is no "thrashing-threshold dial" to crank on an operating system, unfortunately.

Why should there be a "short-term-memory-size" dial on an intelligence? Why should 7 be a magic number built into the system explicitly from the start? If the size of short-term memory really were explicitly stored in our genes, then surely it would take only a simple mutation to reset the "dial" at 8 or 9 or 50, so that intelligence would evolve at ever-increasing rates. I doubt that AI people think that this is even remotely close to the truth; and yet they sometimes act as if it made sense to assume it is a close approximation to the truth.

It is standard practice for AI people to bypass epiphenomena ("collective phenomena", if you prefer) by simply installing structures that mimic the superficial features of those epiphenomena. (Such mimics are the "shadows" of genuine cognitive acts, as John Searle calls them in his paper cited above.) The expectation—or at least the hope—is for tremendous performance to issue forth; yet the systems lack the complex underpinning necessary.

The anagrams problem is one that exemplifies mechanisms of thought that

AI people have not explored. How do those letters swirl among one another, fluidly and tentatively making and breaking alliances? Glomming together, then coming apart, almost like little biological objects in a cell. AI people have not paid much attention to such problems as anagrams. Perhaps they would say that the problem is "already solved". After all, a virtuoso programmer has made a program print out all possible words that anagrammize into other words in English. Or perhaps they would point out that in principle you can do an "alphabetize" followed by a "hash" and thereby retrieve, from any given set of letters, all the words they anagrammize into. Well, this is all fine and dandy, but it is really beside the point. It is merely a show of brute force, and has nothing to contribute to our understanding of how we actually do anagrams ourselves, just as most chess programs have absolutely nothing to say about how chess masters play (as de Groot, and later, Simon and coworkers have pointed out).

Is the domain of anagrams simply a trivial, silly, "toy" domain? Or is it serious? I maintain that it is a far purer, far more interesting domain than many of the complex real-world domains of the expert systems, precisely because it is so playful, so unconscious, so enjoyable, for people. It is obviously more related to creativity and spontaneity than it is to logical derivations, but that does not make it—or the mode of thinking that it represents—any less worthy of attention. In fact, because it epitomizes the unconscious mode of thought, I think it more worthy of attention.

In short, it seems to me that something fundamental is missing in the orthodox AI "information-processing" model of cognition, and that is some sort of substrate from which intelligence emerges as an epiphenomenon. Most AI people do not want to tackle that kind of underpinning work. Could it be that they really believe that machines already can think, already have concepts, already can do analogies? It seems that a large camp of AI people really do believe these things.

Not cognition, but subcognition, is computational

Such beliefs arise, in my opinion, from a confusion of levels, exemplified by the title of Barr's paper: "Cognition as Computation". Am I really computing when I think? Admittedly, my neurons may be performing sums in an analog way, but does this pseudo-arithmetical hardware mean that the epiphenomena themselves are also doing arithmetic, or should be—or even *can* be—described in conventional computer-science terminology? Does the fact that taxis stop at red lights mean that traffic jams stop at red lights? One should not confuse the properties of objects with the properties of statistical ensembles of those objects. In this analogy, traffic jams play the role of thoughts and taxis play the role of neurons or neuron-firings. It is not meant to be a deep analogy, only one that emphasizes that what you see at the top level need not have anything to do with the underlying swarm of activities bringing it into existence. In particular, *something can be computational at one level, but not at another level.*

Yet many AI people, despite considerable sophistication in thinking about a given system at different levels, still seem to miss this. Most AI work goes into efforts to build rational thought ("cognition") out of smaller rational thoughts (elementary steps of deduction, for instance, or elementary motions in a tree). It comes down to thinking that what we see at the top level of our minds—our ability to think—comes out of rational "information-processing" activity, with no deeper levels below that.

Many interesting ideas, in fact, have been inspired by this hope. I find much of the work in AI to be fascinating and provocative, yet somehow I feel dissatisfied with the overall trend. For instance, there are some people who believe that the ultimate solution to AI lies in getting better and better theorem-proving mechanisms in some predicate calculus. They have developed extremely efficient and novel ways of thinking about logic. Some people—Simon and Newell particularly—have argued that the ultimate solution lies in getting more and more efficient ways of searching a vast space of possibilities. (They refer to "selective heuristic search" as the key mechanism of intelligence.) Again, many interesting discoveries have come out of this.

Then there are others who think that the key to thought involves making some complex language in which pattern matching or backtracking or inheritance or planning or reflective logic is easily carried out. Now admittedly, such systems, when developed, are good for solving a large class of problems, exemplified by such AI chestnuts as the missionary-and-cannibals problem, cryptarithmetic problems, retrograde chess problems, and many other specialized sorts of basically logical analysis. However, these kinds of techniques of building small logical components up to make large logical structures have not proven good for such things as recognizing your mother, or for drawing the alphabet in a novel and pleasing way.

One group of AI people who seem to have a different attitude consists of those who are working on problems of perception and recognition. There, the idea of coordinating many parallel processes is important, as is the idea that pieces of evidence can add up in a self-reinforcing way, so as to bring about the locking-in of a hypothesis that no one of the pieces of evidence could on its own justify. It is not easy to describe the flavor of this kind of program architecture without going into multiple technical details. However, it is very different in flavor from ones operating in a world where everything comes clean and precategorized—where everything is specified in advance: "There are three missionaries and three cannibals and one boat and one river and . . ." which is immediately turned into a predicate-calculus statement or a frame representation, ready to be manipulated by an "inference engine". The missing link seems to be the one between perception and cognition, which I would rephrase as the link between subcognition and cognition, that gap between the sub-100-millisecond world and the super-100-millisecond world.

478

Earlier, I mentioned the brain and referred to the "neural substrate" of cognition. Although I am not pressing for a neurophysiological approach to AI, I am unlike many AI people in that I believe that any AI model eventually has to converge to brainlike hardware, or at least to an architecture that at some level of abstraction is "isomorphic" to brain architecture (also at some level of abstraction). This may sound empty, since that level could be anywhere, but I believe that the level at which the isomorphism must apply will turn out to be considerably lower than (I think) most AI people believe. This disagreement is intimately connected to the question of whether cognition should or should not be described as "computation".

Passive symbols and formal rules

One way to explore this disagreement is to look at some of the ways that Simon and Newell express themselves about "symbols".

> At the root of intelligence are symbols, with their denotative power and their susceptibility to manipulation. And symbols can be manufactured of almost anything that can be arranged and patterned and combined. Intelligence is mind implemented by any patternable kind of matter.

From this quotation and others, one can see that to Simon and Newell, a *symbol* seems to be any token, any character inside a computer that has an ASCII code (a standard but arbitrarily assigned sequence of seven bits). To me, by contrast, "symbol" connotes something with representational power. To them (if I am not mistaken), it would be fine to call a bit (inside a computer) or a neuron-firing a "symbol". However, I cannot feel comfortable with that usage of the term.

To me, the crux of the word "symbol" is its connection with the verb "to symbolize", which means "to denote", "to represent", "to stand for", and so on. Now, in the quote above, Simon refers to the "denotative power" of symbols—yet elsewhere in his paper, Barr quotes Simon as saying that thought is "the manipulation of formal tokens". It is not clear to me which side of the fence Simon and Newell really are on.

It takes an immense amount of richness for something to represent something else. The letter 'I' does not in and of itself stand for the person I am, or for the concept of selfhood. That quality comes to it from the way that the word behaves in the totality of the English language. It comes from a massively complex set of usages and patterns and regularities, ones that are regular enough for babies to be able to detect so that they too eventually come to say 'I' to talk about themselves.

Formal tokens such as 'I' or "hamburger" are in themselves empty. They do not denote. Nor can they be made to denote in the full, rich, intuitive sense of the term by having them obey some rules. You can't simply push around some Pnames of Lisp atoms according to complex rules and hope to come out with genuine thought or understanding. (This, by the way, is probably a charitable way to interpret John Searle's point in his above-mentioned paper—namely, as a rebellion against claims that programs that can manipulate tokens such as "John", "ate", "a", "hamburger" actually have understanding. Manipulation of empty tokens is not enough to create understanding—although it is enough to imbue them with meaning in a *limited* sense of the term, as I stress in my book *Gödel, Escher, Bach*—particularly in Chapters II through VI.)

Active symbols and the ant colony metaphor

So what is enough? What am I advocating? What do I mean by "symbol"? I gave an exposition of my concept of *active symbols* in Chapters XI and XII of *Gödel, Escher, Bach*. However, the notion was first presented in the dialogue "Prelude . . . Ant Fugue" in that book, which revolved about a hypothetical conscious ant colony. The purpose of the discussion was not to speculate about whether ant colonies are conscious or not, but to set up an extended metaphor for brain activity—a framework in which to discuss the relationship between "holistic", or collective, phenomena, and the microscopic events that make them up.

One of the ideas that inspired the dialogue has been stated by E. O. Wilson in his book *The Insect Societies* this way: "Mass communication is defined as the transfer, among groups, of information that a single individual could not pass to another." One has to imagine teams of ants cooperating on tasks, and information passing from team to team that no ant is aware of (if ants indeed are "aware" of information at all—but that is another question). One can carry this up a few levels and imagine hyperhyperteams carrying and passing information that no hyperteam, not to mention team or solitary ant, ever dreamt of.

I feel it is critical to focus on collective phenomena, particularly on the idea that some information or knowledge or ideas can exist at the level of collective activities, while being totally absent at the lowest level. In fact, one can even go so far as to say that *no* information exists at that lowest level. It is hardly an amazing revelation, when transported back to the brain: namely, that no ideas are flowing in those neurotransmitters that spark back and forth between neurons. Yet such a simple notion undermines the idea that thought and "symbol manipulation" are the same thing, if by "symbol" one means a formal token such as a bit or a letter or a Lisp Pname.

What is the difference? Why couldn't symbol manipulation—in the sense that I believe Simon and Newell and many writers on AI mean it—accomplish the same thing? The crux of the matter is that these people see symbols as lifeless, dead, *passive* objects—things to be manipulated by some overlying program. I see symbols—representational structures in the brain (or perhaps someday in a computer)—as *active*, like the imaginary hyper-hyperteams in the ant colony. *That* is the level at which denotation takes place, not at the level of the single ant. The single ant has no right to be called "symbolic", because its actions stand for nothing. (Of course, in a real ant colony, we have no reason to believe that teams at *any* level genuinely stand for objects outside the colony (or inside it, for that matter)—but the ant-colony metaphor is only a thinly disguised way of making discussion of the brain more vivid.)

Who says active symbols are computational entities?

It is the vast collections of ants (read "neural firings", if you prefer) that add up to something genuinely symbolic. And who can say whether there exist rules—formal, computational rules—*at the level of the teams themselves* (read "concepts", "ideas", "thoughts") that are of full predictive power in describing how they will flow? I am speaking of rules that allow you to ignore what is going on "down below", yet that still yield perfect or at least very accurate predictions of the teams' behavior.

To be sure, there are phenomenological observations that can be formal-ized to sound like rules that will describe, very vaguely, how those highest-level teams act. But what guarantee is there that we can skim off the full fluidity of the top-level activity of a brain and encapsulate it—without any lower substrate—in the form of some computational rules?

To ask an analogous question, what guarantee is there that there are rules at the "cloud level" (more properly speaking, the level of cold fronts, isobars, trade winds, and so on) that will allow you to say accurately how the atmo-sphere is going to behave on a large scale? Perhaps there are no such rules; perhaps weather prediction is an intrinsically intractable problem. Perhaps the behavior of clouds is not expressible in terms that are computational *at their own level*, even if the behavior of the microscopic substrate—the molecules—*is* computational.

The premise of AI is that thoughts themselves are computational entities at their own level. At least this is the premise of the information-processing school of AI, and I have very serious doubts about it.

The difference between my active symbols ("teams") and the passive sym-bols (ants, tokens) of the information-processing school of AI is that the active symbols flow and act on their own. In other words, there is no higher-level agent (read "program") that reaches down and shoves them around. Active symbols must incorporate within their own structures the wherewithal to trigger and cause actions. They cannot just be passive storehouses, bins, receptacles of data. Yet to Newell and Simon, it seems, even so tiny a thing as a bit is a symbol. This is brought out repeatedly in their writings on "physical symbol systems".

A good term for the little units that a computer manipulates (as well as for neuron firings) is "tokens". All computers are good at "token manipulation"; however, only some—the appropriately programmed ones—could support active symbols. (I prefer not to say that they would carry out "symbol manipulation", since that gets back to that image of a central program shoving around some passive representational structures.) The point is, in such a hypothetical program (and none exists as of yet) the symbols themselves are acting!

A simple analogy from ordinary programming might help to convey the level distinction that I am trying to make here. When a computer is running a Lisp program, does it do function calling? To say "yes" would be unconventional. The conventional view is that *functions* call other functions, and the computer is simply the hardware that *supports* function-calling activity. In somewhat the same sense, although with much more parallelism, symbols activate, or trigger, or awaken, other symbols in a brain.

The brain itself does not "manipulate symbols"; the brain is the medium in which the symbols are floating and in which they trigger each other. There is no central manipulator, no central program. There is simply a vast collection of "teams"—patterns of neural firings that, like teams of ants, trigger other patterns of neural firings. The symbols are not "down there" at the level of the individual firings; they are "up here" where we do our verbalization. We feel those symbols churning within ourselves in somewhat the same way as we feel our stomach churning; we do not *do* symbol manipulation by some sort of act of will, let alone some set of logical rules of deduction. We cannot decide what we will next think of, nor how our thoughts will progress.

Not only are we not symbol manipulators; in fact, quite to the contrary, we are manipulated by our symbols! As Scott Kim once cleverly remarked, rather than speak of "free will", perhaps it is more appropriate to speak of "free won't". This way of looking at things turns everything on its head, placing cognition—that rational-seeming level of our minds—where it belongs, namely as a consequence of much deeper processes of myriads of interacting subcognitive structures. The rational has had entirely too much made of it in AI research; it is time for some of the irrational and subcognitive to be recognized for its pivotal role.

The substrate of active symbols does not symbolize

"Cognition as computation" sounds right to me only if I interpret it quite liberally, namely, as meaning this: "Cognition is an activity that can be supported by computational hardware." But if I interpret it more strictly as "Cognition is an activity that can be achieved by a program that shunts around meaning-carrying objects called symbols in a complicated way", then I don't buy it. In my view, meaning-carrying objects won't submit to being shunted about (it's demeaning); meaning-carrying objects carry meaning only by virtue of being active, autonomous agents themselves. There can't be an overseer program, a pusher-around.

To paraphrase a question asked by neurophysiologist Roger Sperry, "Who shoves whom around inside the computer?" (He asked it of the cranium.) If some program shoves data structures around, then you can bet it's not carrying out cognition. Or more precisely, if the data structures are supposed to be *meaning-carrying*, representational things, then it's not cognition. Of course, in any computer-based realization of genuine cognition, there will have to be, at *some* level of description, programs that shove formal tokens around, but it's only agglomerations of such tokens *en masse* that, above some unclear threshold of collectivity and cooperativity, achieve the status of genuine representation. At that stage, the computer is not shoving them around any more than our brain is shoving thoughts around! The thoughts themselves are causing flow. (This is, I believe, in agreement with Sperry's own way of looking at matters—see, for instance, his article "Mind, Brain, and Humanist Values".) Parallelism and collectivity are of the essence, and in that sense, my response to the title of Barr's paper is *no*, cognition is *not* computation.

At this point, some people might think that I myself sound like John Searle, suggesting that there are elusive "causal powers of the brain" that cannot be captured computationally. I hasten to say that this is not my point of view at all! In my opinion, AI—even Searle's "strong AI"—is still possible, but thought will simply not turn out to be the formal dream of people inspired by predicate calculus or other formalisms. Thought is not a formal activity whose rules exist *at that level.*

Many linguists have maintained that language is a human activity whose nature could be entirely explained at the linguistic level—in terms of complex "grammars", without recourse or reference to anything such as thoughts or concepts. Nowadays many AI people are making a similar mistake: They think that rational thought simply is composed of elementary steps, each of which has some interpretation as an "atom of rational thought", so to speak. That's just not what is going on, however, when neurons fire. On its own, a neuron firing has no meaning, no symbolic quality whatsoever. I believe that those elementary events at the bit level—even at the Lisp-function level (if AI is ever achieved in Lisp, something I seriously doubt)—will have the same quality of *having no interpretation.* It is a level shift as drastic as that between molecules and gases that takes place when thought emerges from billions of in-themselves-meaningless neural firings.

A simple metaphor, hardly demonstrating my point but simply giving its flavor, is provided by Winograd's program SHRDLU, which, using the full power of a very large computer (a DEC-10), could deal with whole numbers up to ten in a conversation about the blocks world. It knew nothing—at its "cognitive" level—of larger numbers. Turing invents a similar example, a rather sly one, in his paper "Computing Machinery and Intelligence", where he has a human ask a computer to do a sum, and the computer pauses 30 seconds and then answers incorrectly. Now this need not be a ruse on the computer's part. It might genuinely have tried to add the two numbers at the *symbol level*, and made a mistake, just as you or I might have, despite having neurons that can add fast.

The point is simply that the lower-level arithmetical processes out of which the higher level of any AI program is composed (the adds, the shifts, the multiplies, and so on) are completely shielded from its view. To be sure, Winograd could have artificially allowed his program to write little pieces of Lisp code that would execute and return answers to questions in English such as "What is 720 factorial?", but that would be similar to your trying to take advantage of the fact that you have billions of small analog adders in your brain, some time when you are trying to check a long grocery bill. You simply don't have access to those adders! You can't reach them.

Symbol triggering patterns are the roots of meaning

What's more, you *oughtn't* to be able to reach them. The world is not sufficiently mathematical for that to be useful in survival. What good would it do a spear thrower to be able to calculate parabolic orbits when in reality there is wind and drag, the spear is not a point mass—and so on? It's quite the contrary: A spear thrower does best by being able to imagine a cluster of approximations of what may happen, and anticipating some plausible consequences of them.

As Jacques Monod in *Chance and Necessity* and Richard Dawkins in *The Selfish Gene* both point out, the real power of brains is that they allow their owners to simulate a variety of plausible futures. This is to be distinguished from the *exact* prediction of eclipses by iterating differential equations step by step far into the future, with very high precision. The brain is a device that has evolved in a less exact world than the pristine one of orbiting planets, and there are always far more chances for the best-laid plans to "gang agley". Therefore, mathematical simulation has to be replaced by abstraction, which involves discarding the irrelevant and making shrewd guesses based on analogy with past experience. Thus the symbols in a brain, rather than playing out a scenario precisely isomorphic to what actually will transpire, play out a few scenarios that are probable or plausible, or even some scenarios from the past that may have no obvious relevance other than as metaphors. (This brings us back to the "adages" of the Yale group.)

Once we abandon perfect mathematical isomorphism as our criterion for symbolizing, and suggest that symbol triggering-patterns are just as related to their suggestive value and their metaphorical richness, this severely complicates the question of what it means when we say that a symbol in the brain "symbolizes" anything. This is closely related to perhaps one of the subtlest issues, in my opinion, that AI should be able to shed light on, and that is the question "What is meaning?" This is actually the crucial issue that John

Searle is concerned with in his earlier-mentioned attack on AI; although he camouflages it, and sometimes loses track of it by all sorts of evasive maneuvers, it turns out in the end (see his reply to Dennett in the *New York Review of Books*) that what he is truly concerned with is the "fact" that "computers have no semantics"—and he of course means "Computers do not now have, and never will have, semantics." If he were talking only about the present, I would agree. However, he is making a point in principle, and I believe he is wrong there.

Where do the meanings of the so-called "active symbols", those giant "clouds" of neural activity in the brain, come from? To what do they owe their denotational power? Some people have maintained that it is because the brain is physically attached to sensors and effectors that connect it to the outside world, enabling those "clouds" to mirror the actual state of the world (or at least some parts of it) faithfully, and to affect the world outside as well, through the use of the body. I think that those things are *part* of denotational power, but not its crux. When we daydream or imagine situations, when we dream or plan, we are *not* manipulating the concrete physical world, nor are we sensing it. In imagining fictional or hypothetical or even totally impossible situations we are still making use of, and contributing to, the meaningfulness of our symbolic neural machinery. However, the symbols do not symbolize specific, real, physical objects. The fundamental active symbols of the brain represent *semantic categories*—classes, in AI terminology.

Categories do not point to specific physical objects. However, they can be used as "masters" from which copies—instances—can be rubbed, and then those copies are activated in various conjunctions; these activations then automatically trigger other instance-symbols into activations of various sorts (teams of ants triggering the creation of other teams of ants, sometimes themselves fizzling out). The overall activity will be semantic—meaningful— if it is isomorphic, not necessarily to some actual event in the real world, but to some event that is compatible with all the known constraints on the situation.

Those constraints are not at the molecular or any such fine-grained level; they are at the rather coarse-grained level of ordinary perception. They are to some extent verbalizable constraints. If I utter the Schankian cliché "John went to a restaurant and ate a hamburger", there is genuine representational power in the patterns of activated symbols that your brain sets up, not because some guy named John actually went out and ate a hamburger (although, most likely, this is a situation that has at some time occurred in the world), but because the symbols, with their own "lives" (autonomous ways of triggering other symbols) will, if left alone, cause the playing-out of an imaginary yet realistic scenario. [Note added in press: I have it on good authority that one John Findling of Floyds Knobs, Indiana, did enter a Burger Queen restaurant and did eat one (1) hamburger. This fact, though helpful, would not, through its absence, have seriously marred the arguments of the present article.]

Thus, the key thing that establishes meaningfulness is whether or not the semantic categories are "hooked up" in the proper ways so as to allow realistic scenarios to play themselves out on this "inner stage". That is, the triggering patterns of active symbols must mirror the general trends of how the world works as perceived on a macroscopic level, rather than mirroring the actual events that transpire.

Beyond intuitive physics: the centrality of slippability

Sometimes this capacity is referred to as "intuitive physics". Intuitive physics is certainly an important ingredient of the triggering patterns needed for an organism's comfortable survival. John McCarthy gives the example of someone able to avoid moving a coffee cup in a certain way, because they can anticipate how it might spill and coffee might get all over their clothes. Note that what is "computed" is a set of alternative rough descriptions for what might happen, rather than one exact "trajectory". This is the nature of intuitive physics.

However, as I stated earlier, there is much more required for symbols to have meaning than simply that their triggering patterns yield an intuitive physics. For instance, if you see someone in a big heavy leg cast and they tell you that their kneecap was acting up, you might think to yourself, "That's quite a nuisance, but it's nothing compared to my friend who has cancer." Now this connection is obviously caused by triggering patterns possessed by symbols representing health problems. But what does this have to do with the laws of motion governing objects or fluids? Precious little. Sideways connections like this, having nothing to do with causality, are equally much of the essence in allowing us to *place situations in perspective*—to compare what actually *is* with what, to our way of seeing things, "might have been" or might even come to be. This ability, no less than intuitive physics, is a central aspect of what meaning is.

This way that any perceived situation has of seeming to be surrounded by a cluster, a halo, of alternative versions of itself, of variations suggested by slipping any of a vast number of features that characterize the situation, seems to me to be at the dead center of thinking. Not much AI work seems to be going on at present to mirror this kind of "slippability". (There are some exceptions. Jaime Carbonell's group working on metaphor and analogy at Carnegie-Mellon is an example. Some other former members of Schank's Yale group have turned toward this as well, such as Michael Dyer and Margot Flowers at UCLA, and Jerry DeJong at Illinois. I would also include myself as another maverick investigating these avenues. Cognitive psychologists such as Stanford's Amos Tversky and Daniel Kahneman of the University of British Columbia have done some very interesting studies of certain types of slippability, though they don't use that term.) This is an issue that I covered in some detail in *Gödel, Escher, Bach*, under various headings such as "slippability", "subjunctive instant replays", "'almost' situations", "conceptual skeletons and conceptual mapping", "alternity" (a term due to George Steiner), and so on.

If we return to the metaphor of the ant colony, we can envision these "symbols with halos" as hyperhyperteams of ants, many of whose members are making what appear to be strange forays in random directions, like flickering tongues of flame spreading out in many directions at once. These tentative probes, which allow the possibility of all sorts of strange lateral connections as from "kneecap" to "cancer", have absolutely no detrimental effect on the total activity of the hyperhyperteam. In fact, quite to the contrary: the hyperhyperteam depends on its members to go wherever their noses lead them. The thing that saves the team—what keeps it coherent—is simply the regular patterns that are sure to emerge out of a random substrate when there are enough constituents. Statistics, in short.

Occasionally, some group of wandering scouts will cause a threshold amount of activity to occur in an unexpected place, and then a whole new area of activity springs up—a new high-level team is activated (or, to return to the brain terminology, a new "symbol" is awakened). Thus, in a brain as in an ant colony, high-level activity spontaneously flows around, driven by the myriad lower-level components' autonomous actions.

AI's goal should be to bridge the gap between cognition and subcognition

Let me, for a final time, make clear how this is completely in contradistinction to standard computer programs. In a normal program, you can account for every single operation at the bit level, by looking "upward" toward the top-level program. You can trace a high-level function call downward: It calls subroutines that call other subroutines that call this particular machine-language routine that uses these words and in which this particular bit lies. So there is a high-level, global *reason* why this particular bit is being manipulated.

By contrast, in an ant colony, a particular ant's foray is not the carrying-out of some global purpose. It has no interpretation in terms of the overall colony's goals; only when many such actions are considered at once does their statistical quality then emerge as purposeful, or interpretable. Ant actions are not the "translation into machine language" of some "colony-level program". No one ant is essential; even large numbers of ants are dispensable. All that matters is the statistics: thanks to it, the information moves around at a level far above that of the ants. Ditto for neural firings in brains. Not ditto for most current AI programs' architecture.

AI researchers started out thinking that they could reproduce all of cognition through a 100 percent top-down approach: functions calling sub-functions calling subsubfunctions and so on, until it all bottomed out in some primitives. Thus intelligence was thought to be hierarchically decomposable, with high-level cognition at the top driving low-level cognition at the bottom. There were some successes and some difficulties—difficulties particularly in the realm of perception. Then along came such things as production systems and pattern-directed inference. Here, some bottom-up processing was allowed to occur within essentially a top-down context. Gradually, the trend has been shifting. But there still is a large element of top-down quality in AI.

It is my belief that until AI has been stood on its head and is 100 percent bottom-up, it won't achieve the same level or type of intelligence as humans have. To be sure, when that kind of architecture exists, there will still be high-level, global, cognitive events—but they will be epiphenomenal, like those in a brain. They will not in themselves be computational. Rather, they will be constituted out of, and driven by, many many smaller computational events, rather than the reverse. In other words, *subcognition at the bottom will drive cognition at the top.* And, perhaps most importantly, the activities that take place at that cognitive top level will neither have been written nor anticipated by any programmer. This is the essence of what I call *statistically emergent mentality.*

Statistically emergent mentality supersedes the Boolean dream

Let me then close with a return to the comment of Simon's: "Nothing below 100 milliseconds is of interest in the study of cognition." I cannot imagine a remark about AI with which I could more vehemently disagree. Simon seems to be most concerned with having programs that can imitate chains of serial actions that come from verbal protocols of various experimental subjects. Perhaps, in some domains, even in some relatively complex and technical ones, people have come up with programs that can do this. But what about the simpler, noncognitive acts that in reality are the substrate for those cognitive acts? Whose program carries those out? At present, no one's. Why is this?

It is because AI people have in general tended to cling to a notion that, in some sense, thoughts obey formal rules at the thought level, just as George Boole believed that "the laws of thought" amounted to formal rules for manipulating propositions. I believe that this Boolean dream is at the root of the slogan "Cognition as computation"—and I believe it will turn out to be revealed for what it is: an elegant chimera.

Post scriptum

Since writing this diatribe, I have found, to my delight, that there are quite a few fledgling efforts underway in AI that fall squarely under the "statistical emergence" banner. I mentioned the work by Norman and Rumelhart at the Institute for Cognitive Science at the University of California at San Diego. That institute is in fact a hotbed of subversive "PDP" (parallel distributed processing) activity. Paul Smolensky, a PDP researcher there, has developed a theory of perceptual activity directly based on an analogy to the branch of physics known as statistical mechanics, and it includes a mental counterpart to the physical concept of *temperature*. In physics, temperature is a number that measures the degree of random thermal jumbling going on in a system composed of many similar parts. In Smolensky's work, a "computational temperature" controls how much randomness is injected into the system.

Imagine a system that is "looking" at a simple scene. (I mean it has a television camera providing input to a computer.) This system's job is to figure out the most plausible interpretation of what is "out there". Is it the word "READ"? Is it the system's grandmother? Is it Smolensky's dog Mandy? When the system is first faced with a fresh situation, the temperature is high, indicating that the system is in a completely open-minded state, ready to have any ideas activated. As randomly chosen concept fragments (not full concepts) are tried on for size, the system gradually starts developing a sense for what sorts of things "fit". Thus the temperature is lowered a bit, lessening the chances of stray concept fragments floating in and destroying the fragile order that is just beginning to coalesce. As fragments start to fit together coherently, the system continues to turn down its randomness knob.

Gradually, larger conceptual structures begin to form and to confirm each other in a benign, self-reinforcing loop. Furthermore, these high-level structures now bias the probabilities of random activation of lower-level fragments, so that the thermal activity, though still random, is more directed. The system is settling into a stable state that captures, in some internal code, the salient external realities. When it is completely "happy" (or "harmonious", in Smolensky's terminology), then the system's temperature reaches zero: it is "freezing". It is no coincidence that the moment of freezing coincides with the attainment of maximal computational bliss, for the temperature gets lowered only when the system is seen to have made some upward jump in its happiness level.

This idea of stochastically guided convergence to what is called a *globally optimum state* seems to have arisen (as do so many good ideas) in the minds of several people at once, spread around the globe. For all I know, it is an ancient idea (though I will not go so far as to credit the ancient Buddhists with it), but it seems that the atmosphere has to be just right for this kind of spark to "catch". People not involved in AI sometimes have expressed the spirit of this sort of thing very poetically. Here is Henri Poincaré writing in the early part of this century about the genesis of mathematical inspirations:

> Permit me a rough comparison. Figure the future elements of our combinations [full-fledged ideas] as something like the booked atoms of Epicurus. During the complete repose of the mind, these atoms are motionless, they are, so to speak, hooked to the wall; so this complete rest may be indefinitely prolonged without the atoms meeting, and consequently without any combination between them.
>
> On the other hand, during a period of apparent rest and unconscious work, certain of them are detached from the wall and put in motion. They flash in every direction through the space (I was about to say the room) where they are enclosed, as would, for example, a swarm of gnats or, if you prefer a more learned comparison, like the molecules of gas in the kinematic theory of gases. Then their mutual impacts may produce new combinations . . .
>
> Now our will did not choose them at random; it pursued a perfectly determined aim. The mobilized atoms are therefore not any atoms whatsoever; they are those from which we might reasonably expect the desired solution. Then the mobilized atoms undergo impacts which make them enter into combinations among themselves or with other atoms at rest which they struck against in their course. Again I beg pardon, my comparison is very rough, but I scarcely know how otherwise to make my thought understood.

And more recently the biologist Lewis Thomas, in his book *The Medusa and the Snail*, wrote this:

> At any waking moment the human head is filled alive with molecules of thought called notions. The mind is made up of dense clouds of these structures, flowing at random from place to place, bumping against each other and caroming away to bump again, leaving random, two-step tracks like the paths of Brownian movement. They are small round structures, featureless except for tiny projections that are made to fit and then lock onto certain other particles of thought possessing similar receptors. Much of the time nothing comes of the activity. The probability that one notion will encounter a matched one, fitting closely enough for docking, is at the outset vanishingly small.
>
> But when the mind is heated a little, the movement speeds up and there are more encounters. The probability is raised.
>
> The receptors are branched and complex, with configurations that are wildly variable. For one notion to fit with another it is not required that the inner structure of either member be the same; it is

only the outside signal that counts for docking. But when any two are locked together they become a very small memory. Their motion changes. Now, instead of drifting at random through the corridors of the mind, they move in straight lines, turning over and over, searching for other pairs. Docking and locking continue, pairs are coupled to pairs, and aggregates are formed. These have the look of live, purposeful organisms, hunting for new things to fit with, sniffing for matched receptors, turning things over, catching at everything. As they grow in size, anything that seems to fit, even loosely, is tried on, stuck on, hung from the surface wherever there is room. They become like sea creatures, decorated all over with other creatures as living symbionts.

At this stage of its development, each mass of conjoined, separate notions, remembering and searching at the same time, shifts into its own fixed orbit, swinging in long elliptical loops around the center of the mind, rotating slowly as it goes. Now it is an idea.

This poetic passage reminds me of nothing more than my Jumbo system for doing anagrams, which I developed in 1982. There, in what I call the "cytoplasm", letters bash at random into other letters, check each other out a bit, occasionally "mate", then couples continue the search for other compatible couples as well as for more letters they could gobble up to make triples or quadruples. (See Figure 27-3.) Syllables build, sniff at each other's ends, occasionally unite, making word candidates. Then those large "gloms" can undergo internal transformations, break down into their natural subunits or even into elemental smithereens. For instance, "pan-gloss" could become "pang-loss" by *regrouping*, which could then by *spoonerism* become "lang-poss", and so on. Forkerism and kniferism (like spoonerism, only different) are other types of recombination mechanisms, as are sporkerism and foonerism. A typical low-temperature route, meandering through a portion of logological space using these mechanisms, might visit, in sequence, "lang-poss", "lass-pong", "las-spong", "lasp-song", "song-lasp", "son-glasp", and so on. And if, as a consequence of global tension, the temperature rises, the entire bubble may burst apart and we will be left with isolated letters scattered all over the place, with occasional surviving duplets ("ng", maybe) here and there, souvenirs of what it was like before the blast. Sigh . . . Oh, but why suffer pangs of loss? After all, isn't this world, of all possible worlds, the very best?

Given the passages from Poincaré and Thomas, I will not claim that these ideas are totally new—but then, why would I want to? Part of my thesis on creativity is that even the best ideas are simply variations on themes already enunciated, discovered by unconscious and random processes of recombination, filtering, and association. In fact, the "fit" between statistical mechanics and "statistical mentalics" is not yet exact, and it is to be hoped that the collective mental temperature of cognitive scientists is high enough that the jiggling-about of ideas in our brains will finally bring the right ones into contact with each other, thus bringing us closer to an accurate view of the physics-cognition connection, allowing the temperature to go down, bringing us even closer to truth, which will lower the temperature still further—and on and on.

Besides Paul Smolensky, there are many other people sniffing about in roughly the same territory. David Rumelhart (mentioned above), James McClelland, and co-workers in the "PDP" group at San Diego have modeled several types of perceptual and cognitive behavior using a system of this sort. Geoffrey Hinton and Scott Fahlman (like Simon and Newell, at Carnegie-Mellon University) and Terrence Sejnowski (of Johns Hopkins) are exploring, via what they call the "Boltzmann machine", "pseudoneural" models of learning, based on ideas closely resembling those of Smolensky. (The prognosis is good, for "neural" rearranges into "u learn".) J. J. Hopfield of Caltech has studied the statistical properties of neural nets, to see what one can say about the substrate of associative memory. Pentti Kanerva, a highly original and autonomous philosopher-programmer at Stanford, has done related theoretical work aimed at suggesting plausible substrates underlying the fluidity of memory, and his findings dovetail beautifully with recent observations about the anatomical structure of various areas of the brain. This may be a coincidence and it may not, but there is certainly plenty there to speculate about. Related work has been done by T. Kohonen in Finland, and O. P. Buneman and D. Willshaw in England. James Anderson and Stuart Geman at Brown University have developed theories and models of how collective activity of many individual processing units can have emergent character. Jerome Feldman and colleagues at the University of Rochester have developed what they call a "connectionist" theory of perception and cognition, in which neurons can assemble into stable and not-so-stable aggregates called "coalitions". These shifting alliances are presumed to form the subcognitive basis of fluid cognition. And finally, my group's active projects—Jumbo, Seek-Whence, and Copycat—are all thoroughly permeated with an independently conceived vision of a temperature-controlled randomness at the subcognitive level, out of which emerges, at the cognitive level, a fluid but hopefully not wildly meandering train of thought.

Marsha Meredith, who has been working on implementing a Seek-Whence program, seems to really have taken the idea of "fluid" cognition to heart. In writing up what she has implemented so far, she spoke of the cytoplasm of her system:

> The cytoplasm might be viewed as a soup bubbling with gloms, the bubbles which rise to the top being the system's current view of the sequence. If neighboring bubbles have enough mutual attraction

(strong enough bonds) they will combine; otherwise they will either exist independently or burst to permit new bubbles to take their place.

In addition to her cytoplasm, Marsha has created a "Platoplasm" (where Platonic concepts are stored) and a "Socratoplasm" (to mediate between the down-to-earth cytoplasm and the ethereal Platoplasm). Marsha's bubbling, boiling, churning, roiling "Seek-Whence soup" is thus very much like alphabet soup, the only difference being that the good old ABC's have been replaced by 123's.

I think it would be silly to try to attach credit to any one person for these "soup-cognitive" ideas, for they are in the air, as it were, and the time is simply ripe. This is not to say that they are being roundly welcomed by the whole AI and cognitive science community. There are definite "pro" and "con" camps, and some more neutral observers. There are people who cling to the Boolean dream like it was going out of style! Daniel Dennett has recently coined another term for the same concept: "High Church Computationalism", to which he contrasts what he calls "The New Connectionism". I like the vision of orthodoxy implied by the former term, but I think the latter term overstresses the role of neural modeling in the new approaches. A model of thought in the new style need not be based so literally on brain hardware that there are neuron-like units and axon-like connections between them. The essence of the dissenting movement lies, it seems to me, in three notions:

(1) asynchronous parallelism;
(2) temperature-controlled randomness;
(3) statistically emergent active symbols.

Actually, for those who understand this intuition well, line 3 alone says it all. How? Well, the phrase "statistically emergent" clearly implies that collective phenomena are involved, in which many independent uncorrelated microevents, chaotically spread all about in some physical medium, are happening all the time, forming and breaking patterns. This is the imagery attached to lines 1 and 2.

I am reminded, whenever I visualize this kind of thing really clearly, of one fairly old but still influential theory about how water's fluidity emerges out of all the frenetic molecular bumping and banging "down there". This is the theory that goes by the poetic name of *flickering clusters* (referred to also in Chapter 10). The idea is that water molecules can form small and highly ephemeral hydrogen-bonded clusters (with a lifespan even shorter than a mayfly's!). Within microseconds, a group will form and break down again, and its constituent molecules will regroup with other free ones. This is going on, over and over, day and night, second by second, in every tiny drop of water, gadzillions of times. The statistically emergent phenomenon, in that case, is the macroscopic nature of water. In particular, such familiar physical properties of water as its boiling point, density, viscosity, compressibility, and so on are deducible—at least in theory—from such a model.

If one is concerned with minds, however, the phenomena to be explained are less tangible and far more elusive. What seems to most people a primary goal to aim for—and here John Searle and I agree, for once—is that of explaining where *meaning* really comes from, or in other words, a theory of the basis of semantics, or reference. Put in a nutshell, the question is, "What makes mental activity *symbolic?*"

There seems to be a genuine conundrum about how mere matter could possess *reference*. How could a lump of stuff be *about* anything else (let alone about *itself*)? Searle conveniently exempts bio-stuff (or at least neuro-stuff) from this query, assigning to it special "causal powers" that he mysteriously declines to identify but that magically (it would seem) allow brains, or something in them, to refer. This is as thoroughly *ad hoc* as the Boolean dreamers' chutzpah in simply proclaiming that there is no problem at all there, for Lisp atoms *do* refer. The fact of the matter is that an analysis of what reference is has proved a little too tough for both sides so far, and so it degenerates into polemics. Each side already *knows* what "aboutness" is all about, and is most impatient with the other side for its obtuseness. I certainly am just as guilty of this syndrome as any other party, for I too feel I *know* (intuitively and nonverbalizably) just what reference really is, and how it *can* come out of "mere matter" and its patterns. I devoted a very large portion of *Gödel, Escher, Bach* to trying to get across some of those intuitions, and since then I have continued to try to spell them out better (most notably in a paper called "Shakespeare's Plays Weren't Written by Him, But by Someone Else of the Same Name", not co-authored by Gray Clossman and Marsha Meredith but by people of the same names, and in the developing work on roles and analogies, described in Chapter 24 of this book). The questions still seem to stymie the best minds, however.

Does the expression "- -p- -q- - - -" intrinsically mean anything? Does the expression "$(SS0 + SS0) = SSSS0$" intrinsically mean anything? How about "(equals 4 (plus 2 2))" or "$2 + 2 = 4$" or "bpbqd"? What would imbue *one* of them with meaning, if not *all*? If none of these has meaning, then do printed symbols *ever* have meaning? Does an entire set of the *Encyclopaedia Britannica* tumbling out of control in interstellar space have any intrinsic meaning, or is it just an empty lump of nonsymbolic matter? Would it help if we lifted the entire Library of Congress into that selfsame interstellar orbit? If not, why not?

What about a cute little robot that scampers about in your living room, seeking to plug itself into any locatable electric outlet and avoiding banging into furniture? Has it got anything inside it that truly *represents* anything else? If so, why? If not, why not? What about a human-sized robot that roams the world in search of beauty and truth and along the way "emits" strange pieces of weird and garbled "syntactic behavior" such as "This sentence no verb"—might that type of robot possess any shreds of *aboutness*? Or would you have to know precisely what it was made of, down to the most microscopic fibers of its circuitry? What if it objected to such examination? Would your prior knowledge that it was a robot tell you that it was merely "artificially signaling" such objections, and entitle you (as a *bona fide* sentient being) to override its *ersatz* objections without compunction, and to open it up and dissect it?

In a way it is natural but in another way it is curious that most people's threshold for changing their tune on whether or not an organism has a mind and feelings (and "aboutness") seems to lie at just about the point where they can easily identify with the organism. Microbes? "Naah, they're too small." Mosquitos? "Maybe, but they're just mechanical." Mice? "They sure *seem* to experience pain and fear and curiosity." Men? "Well, maybe . . . despite the fact that they don't know what it's like to menstruate."

Such reactions are somewhat natural, but it is curious to me that what seems to be the most convincing is the moving-about in the world, and the perceptual and motor interface. Systems that are not interfaced with our tangible, three-dimensional world via perceptors and motor capacities, no matter how sophisticated their innards, seem to be un-identifiable-with, by most people. I have in mind a certain kind of program that most people would probably find it ludicrous to ever consider conscious: a program that does symbolic mathematical manipulations. Take the famous system called Macsyma, for instance, which can do calculus and algebra problems of a very high order of difficulty. Its performance would have been so unimaginable in the days of Gauss or Euler that many smart people would have gasped and many brilliant people might have worshiped it. No one could pooh-pooh it—but today we do. Today we are "sophisticated". In a way, this is good, but in a way it is bad.

What bothers me is a kind of "hardware chauvinism" that we humans evince. This chauvinism says, "Real Things live in three dimensions; they are made of atoms. Photons bounce off Real Things. Real Things make noises when you drop them. Real Things are material, not insubstantial mental ghosts." The idea that numbers or functions or sets or any other kind of mathematical construct might be Real would provoke guffaws in many if not most intellectual quarters today. The idea that being able to maneuver about in a "space" or "universe" of pure abstractions might entitle a robot to be called "sentient" would be ridiculed to the skies, no matter if the maneuvering in that abstruse high-dimensional space were as supple and graceful as that of the most skilled Olympic ice-skating champion or the greatest jazz pianist.

Speaking of which, the musical universe provides another wonderful testbed. Would a robot able to devise incredibly beautiful, lyrical, flowing passages that brought tears to your eyes be entitled to a bit of empathy? Suppose it were otherwise immobile, its only conception of "reality" being inward-directed rather than something accessible through hands or eyes or ears. How would you feel then?

I personally don't think that such a program could come to exist in actuality, but as a thought experiment it asks something interesting about our conception of sentience. Does access to the "real world" count for a lot? Why should the intangible world of the intellect be any less real than the tangible world of the body? Does it have less structure? No, not if you get to know it. Every type of complexity in the physical world has its mirror image in the world of mathematical constructs, including time. What kind of prejudice is it, then, that biases us in favor of our kind so strongly? As questions of mind and matter grow ever more subtle, we must watch out for tacit assumptions of this sort ever more vigilantly, for they affect us at the deepest level and provide pat answers to exceedingly non-pat questions.

The question that launched this digression was what kinds of entities deserve attribution of genuine meaning, genuine symbolicness. Some people, Searle for one, seem to feel that nothing any computer system might do could ever be genuinely symbolic. It might well capture the "shadows" of symbolic activity, but it would never have the "right stuff", that is, the "causal powers of the brain", whether or not it passed the Turing Test. Now, I don't agree at all with Searle about there being an unbreachable machine-mind gap, but I do agree with his skepticism toward orthodox AI's view that we have just about got to the point where computers are using words and symbols with genuine meanings, in the full sense of the term.

The problem is, as I emphasized in the article, that computers' concepts thus far lack slippability (and therefore, their "aboutness" is very weak). The blurry boundaries between human concepts are not well captured by models that try to do blurring explicitly. Such models range from so-called "fuzzy set theory", in which an unblurry amount of blurriness is inserted into the most precise of logical calculi (actually a rather comical idea), to memory models with concepts strung together in complex kinds of webs, with hierarchical and lateral connections galore, even including explicit "hierarchies of variability". Somehow human fluidity is not even approached, though.

The alternate school's recipe is to build symbolic activity up from non-symbolic activity, rather than presuming that the objects one begins with (Lisp atoms, for instance) can be imbued with all the fluidity one wants by making ever-larger piles of complex rules to push them around in the right ways. I am a strong believer in the idea that symbolicness, like greenness, disintegrates. E. O. Wilson's idea of "mass communication" being "the transfer, among groups, of information that a single individual could not pass to another" seems to me to be at the heart of the idea of statistically emergent active symbols. Somehow, in any genuinely cognitive system, there must be layers upon layers of organization, allowing fluid semantics to emerge at the top level out of rigid syntax at the bottom level. Symbolic events will be broken down into nonsymbolic ones. In the ant-colony metaphor, the top-level hyperhyperteams will be symbolic, hyperteams will be subsymbolic, mere teams will be subsubsymbolic (whatever that means!), and the lowly ants will be totally devoid of symbolicness. Obviously, the number of levels need not be four, but this is enough to make a point: Symbolic events are *not* the primitives of thought.

If you believe in this notion of different layers of collectivity having different degrees of symbolicness and fluidity, then you might ask, "What can we learn from trying to make a system with a small number of such layers?" This is an excellent scientific question. In fact, simply to make a two-layer system in which the upper layer is simultaneously more collective, more symbolic, and more fluid than the lower layer would be the key step—and that is precisely what the statistical-emergence camp is trying to do.

In a way, the AI hope up till recently has been to get away with just one level. This is not dissimilar to the hopes of the brain-research people, who in their own way have wanted to locate everything in just one level: that of neurons. Well, AI people are loosening up and so are brain people, and some meaningful dialogue is beginning. This is a hopeful sign, but some people resent the implications that their long-held views are being challenged. They particularly resent anyone's writing about such matters in a general and philosophical way, full of imagery, meant to stir up the intuitions rather than to present well-known facts dryly and impartially.

My aim in the preceding article, which was solicited expressly for the purpose of interdisciplinary communication (it was published in *The Study of Information: Interdisciplinary Messages*, edited by Fritz Machlup and Una Mansfield), was to spark new intuitions about places where progress is needed—not so much specific new experiments, but new areas for musing and theorizing. I was hoping to stimulate not only AI people but also cognitive psychologists, philosophers of mind, and brain researchers. That is why I used so much imagery and appealed to the intuition.

Allen Newell, whose ideas were criticized in the article, did not take too kindly to it. In his reply (solicited by the book's editors), he dismissed my ideas as nonscientific, despite the fact that all the articles solicited were expressely requested to be personal viewpoints rather than scientific papers. In fact, he treated my article with as much disdain as one would treat a pesky fly that one wanted to swat. I had expected, and would of course have warmly welcomed, a reply discussing the issues in a substantive way.

Fortunately, Newell did spend a page or so doing that kind of thing. He pointed out that in his and Simon's writings, the word "symbol" has always had the meaning of "something that denotes", as distinguished from mere tokens, such as the bits at the bottom level of a computer. He gave several excerpts from articles by Simon and himself, including the following one, referring to the 0's and 1's in a typical computer:

> These entities are not symbols in the sense of our symbol system. They satisfy only part of the requirements for a symbol, namely being the tokens in expressions. It is of course possible to give them full symbolic character by programming an accessing mechanism that gets from them to some data structure.

Newell claims that in my article I have seriously misrepresented his and Simon's well-known views on physical symbol systems. A typical passage where he feels I do so is this one:

> To me ... "symbol" connotes something with representational power. To them (if I am not mistaken), it would be fine to call a bit (inside a computer) or a neuron-firing a "symbol".

Newell comments bluntly: "Hofstadter is indeed mistaken, absolutely and unequivocally." Now here is an opportunity for substantive discussion! I am glad to reply at that level.

Firstly, I plead guilty to one count of misrepresentation of the Newell-Simon view of symbols. I now realize that they place the symbolic level above the bit level; effectively, they place it at the level of Lisp structures. However, I wish to point out that there is a curious vacillation on Newell's part in the paper from which he draws the quote given above. In the first part of the paper, he repeatedly uses the word "symbol" to refer to the 0's and 1's in a Turing machine. In fact, he does it so often that a naïve reader *might* conclude that Newell considers them to *be* symbols. But no! It turns out that after more than a dozen such usages, he turns right around and repudiates any such usage, in the passage quoted above. That, I submit, is hardly clarity in writing, and I would request that it be considered by the jury as constituting mitigating circumstances, possibly providing grounds for a reduced sentence for my client.

But there is a more substantive area of disagreement. Newell repeatedly makes the point that for him, a physical symbol is virtually identical to a Lisp atom with an attached list (usually called its "property list"). He says as much: "That Lisp is a close approximation to a pure symbol system is often not accorded the weight it deserves." And later on, he refers to his paradigmatic physical symbol system as "a garden variety, Lisp-ish sort of beast". (It is no coincidence that the name of one company making Lisp machines is "Symbolics".) Throughout his article, Newell refers to the *manipulation of symbols* by programs (although strangely, he avoids the word "program"). I may have been "mistaken, absolutely and unequivocally" in attributing to Newell and Simon the view that bits are symbols, but I am certainly not mistaken in attributing to them the view that a Lisp atom with attached property list has all the prerequisites of being a genuine symbol, as long as the right program is manipulating it. That much is crystal-clear. And that is the view I was opposing, no less than the view of bits as symbols.

As a sidelight, it is an amusing coincidence that John Searle was quite upset when, in *The Mind's I*, I misquoted him, saying he had said "a few bits of paper" when he had actually said "slips of paper". Now I find myself in a similar situation: I accused someone of having said "bits" when they meant something else. Searle meant "slips"; Newell meant "lisps" (Lisp atoms or lists). And in both cases, although I admit I was wrong in detail, I feel I was entirely right in principle. My arguments remain unchanged even after the misquotation is corrected.

To some, the build-up of atoms from bits might seem to resemble the first layer of emergence of fluid semantics from rigid syntax that I was speaking of earlier. So couldn't a view that sees Lisp structures as slightly more fluid than bits be somewhat consistent with my view? My answer is *no*, and here's why. The rules governing Lisp structures are strictly computational in and of themselves, and implementing a Lisp system in 0's-and-1's hardware adds nothing enriching to the Lisp atoms whatsoever. The logic of a Lisp system does not emerge from the details of levels below it; it is present in full in the written program even without any computer that can run Lisp. In that sense, Lisp programs are Platonic, which is so well demonstrated by Gödel's original "Lisp program", written way back in 1931, before computers existed. In fact, the only distinction between bits and atoms is in number: There are only two types of bit, whereas there can be an arbitrarily large variety of atoms. But as for *fluidity*, nothing is gained by moving from the bit level to the atom level. Either level is 100 percent formal in operation.

What we are looking for, however, in explaining cognition, is *a bridge between the formal and the informal*. Now it may be that Newell does not believe in cognition's informality, and I probably would not be able to convince him of it. Indeed, it would be hard to convince anyone who doesn't see it already that it is reasonable to think of human cognition in those terms, but that is how I see it. And statistical emergence seems to me to be not merely a shot in the dark, but the obvious route to explore. The brain certainly does an immense amount in parallel, with different parts operating completely independently from others. There is known to be a lot of "noise", or randomness, in the brain, and moreover, the world itself is acting on the brain in so many different ways at once that it is like being bombarded simultaneously with the output of a thousand different random number generators. So temperature there's plenty of. All we need to figure out is what kinds of collective entities could evolve in such a rich medium, how they would interact, and how they could be symbolic.

This is the challenge I was posing to Newell and other staunch believers in the Boolean dream. The debate will continue, but meantime research must be done. And there, everyone must be guided by personal intuitions about what the right path is. Newell and Simon have theirs, and I have mine. We both think we're right. As Wanda Landowska, the famous harpsichordist, once remarked, "You play Bach *your* way, and I'll play him *his* way." How can one reply to that? No way. So let the game go on!

Bibliography

Anderson, Alan Ross, ed. *Minds and Machines*. Englewood Cliffs, N.J.: Prentice-Hall, 1964. A classic collection of stimulating articles on the mind-body problem, including Alan Turing's important paper "Computing Machinery and Intelligence", and J.R. Lucas' provocative "Minds, Machines, and Gödel".

Applewhite, Philip. *Molecular Gods: How Molecules Determine Our Behavior*. Englewood Cliffs, N.J.: Prentice-Hall, 1981. A book whose subtitle helped spark my "Careenium" dialogue (Chapter 25).

Atlan, Henri, *Entre le cristal et la fumée: Essai sur l'organisation du vivant*. Paris: Editions du Seuil, 1979. A biologist who views life as the emergence of ordered complexity out of randomness here explains his philosophy.

Axelrod, Robert. *The Evolution of Cooperation*. New York: Basic Books, 1984. A beautifully written account of how mutually beneficial behavior—that is, cooperation—can emerge among purely egoistic organisms that share an environment over time.

Ayala, Francisco José and Theodosius Dobzhansky, eds. *Studies in the Philosophy of Biology: Reduction and Related Problems*. Berkeley: University of California Press, 1974. The proceedings of one of the most fascinating conferences I have ever heard about. Many great biological thinkers were present, and discussed the most fundamental questions about how life and minds can be reconciled with physical law. I wish I had been there!

Bandelow, Christoph. *Inside Rubik's Cube and Beyond*. Boston: Birkhäuser, 1982. A clear and mathematically oriented book about the Cube and its successors. Perhaps the best of all the Cube books in English.

Barr, Avron. "Artificial Intelligence: Cognition as Computation". In *The Study of Information: Interdisciplinary Messages*, edited by Fritz Machlup and Una Mansfield. New York: Wiley-Interscience, 1983. A paper putting forward the orthodox AI dogma: that mental activity is "information processing"—more specifically, that the manipulation of "symbols" (representational data structures) by suitable computer programs is no more and no less than what minds do.

Beck, Anatole and David Fowler. "A Pandora's Box of Non-Games". In *Seven Years of Manifold*, edited by Ian Stewart and John Jaworski. Nantwich, England: Shiva Publications, 1981. An amusing collection of silly pseudo-games with more of a moral than might first meet the eye.

Beckett, Samuel. *Waiting for Godot*. New York: Evergreen, 1954. The classic existential drama in which meaninglessness pervades—and at whose core is the famous nonsensical verbal vomit emitted from the mouth of the sad sack named "Lucky".

Benton, William. *Normal Meanings*. Paducah, Ky.: Deer Crossing Press, 1978. A book of strangely evocative poems, a bit comprehensible in parts, totally incomprehensible in others.

Bernstein, Leonard. *The Joy of Music*. New York: Simon & Schuster, 1959. An exciting medley of ideas by this exuberantly articulate thinker and musician. His dialogues are especially enjoyable.

Biggs, John R. *Letterforms and Lettering*. Poole, England: Blandford Press, 1977. One of the best books on the fluidity of letterforms I have run across. Includes short sections on other languages, such as Hebrew, Chinese, and Arabic.

Blesser, Barry et al. "Character Recognition based on Phenomenological Attributes". *Visible Language* 7, no. 3 (Summer 1973). An early article by researchers who clearly had come to appreciate the depth of the letter-recognition problem.

Bloch, Arthur. *Murphy's Law; Murphy's Law, Book Two; Murphy's Law, Book Three*. Los Angeles: Price/Stern/Sloan, 1977, 1980, 1982. Humorous and cynical observations about the human condition, featuring many self-referential or self-undermining aphorisms.

Boeke, Kees. *Cosmic View: The Universe in 40 Jumps*. New York: John Day, 1957. A book to instill humility and awe in anyone, as well as a vivid sense of the meaning of the term "astronomical number".

Bombaugh, Charles Carroll. *Oddities and Curiosities of Words and Literature*, edited and annotated by Martin Gardner. New York: Dover, 1961. An antique collection of palindromes, acrostics, pangrams, and so on, for wordmongers and people who love the bizarre fringes of language. (Gardner's footnotes at the back are the best part of the book.)

Boole, George. *The Laws of Thought*. New York: Dover, 1961. A reprint of the old classic from the mid-1850's. The hubris of the title is quite remarkable, especially in light of what 130 years' progress has revealed!

Brams, Steven, Morton D. Davis, and Philip Strafin, Jr. "The Geometry of the Arms Race". *International Studies Quarterly* 23, no. 4 (December 1979): 567–88. Looking at international behavior in terms of the iterated Prisoner's Dilemma and similar payoff matrices.

Brilliant, Ashleigh. *I May Not Be Perfect, but Parts of Me Are Excellent; I Have Abandoned My Search for Truth, and Am Now Looking for a Good Fantasy; Appreciate Me Now and Avoid the Rush; I Feel Much Better, Now That I've Given Up Hope*. Santa Barbara, Calif.: Woodbridge Press, 1979–1984. Four books containing many incisive epigrams about life, death, love, relationships, greed, egotism, loneliness, fear, and so on. None is longer than seventeen words.

Bush, Donald J. *The Streamlined Decade*. New York: George Braziller, 1975. Showing how the style of an era permeates its creations in all media. Full of elegant photos. Compare with the books by Loeb and McCall (see below).

Byrd, Donald. "Music Notation by Computer". Ph.D. thesis, Indiana University Computer Science Department. Bloomington, 1984. About the problems of developing a computer program that will have some "understanding" of the subtleties of music notation. The program, SMUT, produced the musical examples in this book.

Chaitin, Gregory. "Randomness and Mathematical Proof". *Scientific American* 232, no. 5 (May 1975): 47–52. An enlightening way of defining the meaning of "random pattern", and the unexpected and deep resonances with Gödel's incompleteness theorem and other metamathematical results.

Charniak, Eugene, C. K. Riesbeck, and Drew V. McDermott. *Artificial Intelligence Programming*. Hillsdale, N.J.: Lawrence Erlbaum Associates, 1980. Sophisticated ways of using Lisp and Lisp-like languages in artificial-intelligence research.

Collet, Pierre and Jean-Pierre Eckmann. *Iterated Maps on the Interval as Dynamical Systems*. Boston: Birkhäuser, 1980. An in-depth study of the iteration of simple smooth functions on the interval [0,1], and the resulting roads to turbulent behavior as parameters are varied.

Compugraphic Corporation. *A Portfolio of Text and Display Type*. Wilmington, Mass.: Compugraphic Corporation, 1982. A collection of many typefaces (mostly book faces), including several extensions to other alphabets of faces originally conceived only for our alphabet.

Conway, John Horton, Elwyn Berlekamp, and Richard K. Guy. *Winning Ways (for your mathematical plays)*. New York: Academic Press, 1982. A two-volume set of remarkable games, some analyzed, some unanalyzed, filled with humorous pictures and an oddball type of creative wordplay that is Conway's hallmark. Included in Volume 2 are discussions of the Cube and Conway's game of Life.

Coueignoux, Philippe. "La reconnaissance des caractères". *La Recherche* 12, no. 126 (October, 1981): 1094–1103. An interesting article about the workings of some computer systems that can read text in a variety of typefaces. The ideas derive from work by Blesser and colleagues (see above). This work is rather practically oriented, and does not come close to giving computers an understanding of letterforms in their full generality.

Csányi, Vilmos. *General Theory of Evolution*. Budapest: Akadémiai Kiadó, 1982. A thorough investigation of the process of simultaneous evolution on both genetic and "memetic" fronts.

Davies, Paul. *God and the New Physics*. New York: Simon & Schuster, 1983. In this book. Davies tackles the biggies of metaphysics: creation, free will, religion, souls, and more. Since he is a good scientist as well as a good writer, his musings are articulate and penetrating.

——. *Other Worlds*. New York: Simon & Schuster, 1980. A popular account, by a highly reliable professional, of the mysteries at the base of quantum mechanics.

Davis, Morton D. *Game Theory: A Nontechnical Introduction*. New York: Basic Books, 1983. An excellent overview of all the main ideas of game theory, including many unresolved issues such as the Prisoner's Dilemma.

Dawkins, Richard. *The Selfish Gene*. New York: Oxford University Press, 1976. A book that views organisms as by-products of a purely molecular-level competition for efficient self-replication. A topsy-turvy, disorienting, yet powerfully revealing viewpoint.

DeLong, Howard. *A Profile of Mathematical Logic*. Reading, Mass.: Addison-Wesley, 1970. A wonderful book on the philosophical and technical issues of logic by someone who knows how to achieve an artistic balance between formalisms and ideas that appeal to the intuition.

Dennett, Daniel C. *Brainstorms: Philosophic Essays on Mind and Psychology*. Cambridge, Mass.: Bradford Books, MIT Press, 1978. A collection of penetrating analyses of problems of mind, brain, and computer models of thought, perception, and sensation. Excellent rebuttals of such figures as B. F. Skinner and J. R. Lucas, and a wonderful "dessert" at the end. Dennett's graceful style and comparative lack of in-references and jargon make this book much more engaging than the average philosophy book.

——. "Can Machines Think?" Unpublished manuscript. A fresh look at the power of the Turing Test, completely in sympathy with my view that the test as originally posed is as valid as ever, despite the doubts of many.

——. "Cognitive Wheels: The Frame Problem of Artificial Intelligence". In *Minds, Machines, and Evolution*. Edited by C. Hookway. New York: Cambridge University Press, 1985. An article about why artificial intelligence is so far from achieving common sense.

——. *Elbow Room: The Varieties of Free Will Worth Wanting*. Cambridge, Mass.: Bradford Books, MIT Press, 1984. One provocative metaphor after another, all building up towards an image of "self-made selves" that enjoy as much free will as it is reasonable to hanker after. Although I resist some of this book's conclusions. I find it the best writing on the subject that I know.

——. "The Logical Geography of Computational Approaches (A View from the East Pole)". Unpublished manuscript. Dennett wittily divides the world of AI approaches into two camps: the orthodox one ("High Church Computationalism"), centered on the "East Pole" (located at MIT), and the unorthodox one ("New Connectionism"), scattered hither and yon.

——. "The Myth of the Computer: An Exchange". *New York Review of Books*. (June 24, 1982): 56. A civil reply to John Searle's biting review of *The Mind's I*.

——. "The Self as a Center of Narrative Gravity". In *Self and Consciousness*, edited by P. M. Cole et al. New York: Praeger, 1985. A wonderful new metaphor for thinking about abstractions such as "I".

Dewdney, A. K. "Computer Recreations: A computational garden sprouting ana-grams, pangrams, and few weeds". *Scientific American* 251, no. 4 (October 1984): 20–27. Includes a description of Lee Sallows' pangram machine, concluding with a public challenge to discover a computer-generated pangram.

DeWitt, Bryce S. and Neill Graham, eds. *The Many-Worlds Interpretation of Quantum Mechanics*. Princeton, N.J.: Princeton University Press, 1973. A well-rounded pre-sentation of one of the most disorienting yet irrefutable ways of thinking about reality yet invented.

Dyer, Michael. *In-Depth Understanding*. Cambridge, Mass.: MIT Press, 1983. A book summarizing a Ph.D. project in language understanding that puts together many recent AI ideas about how memory is organized and how flexible control structures fit into the picture.

Dylan, Bob. *Tarantula*. New York: Macmillan, 1971. The poet-singer lets loose some stream-of-consciousness musings that are sometimes reasonably intelligible and sometimes totally wacko.

Edson, Russell. *The Clam Theater*. Middletown, Conn.: Wesleyan University Press. 1973. Strange and surrealistically written fantasies permeated by a tragic vision of life. To me, the most haunting passage is a description of a human head: "this teetering bulb of dread and dream . . . "

Eidswick, Jack. "How to Solve the $n \times n \times n$ Cube". Mathematics and Statistics Department, University of Nebraska, Lincoln, 1982. A useful manual for those beset by generalized cubic frustration.

Endl, Kurt. *Rubik's Cube Made Simple; The Pyramid; Pyraminx Cube; Impossiball;*

Megaminx; Rubik's Master Cube. Giessen, Germany: Würfel-Verlag GmbH, 1982. These booklets, together with the previous entry, will give you a good reference shelf on Cubology.

Erman, Lee D. et al. "The Hearsay-II Speech-Understanding System: Integrating Knowledge to Resolve Uncertainty". *ACM Computing Surveys* 2, no. 2 (June 1980): 213–53. A review article describing, with a good deal of hindsight, the architecture and performance of what I consider to be the most inspiring work yet done in artificial intelligence.

Evans, Thomas G. "A Program for the Solution of a Class of Geometric-Analogy Intelligence Test Questions". In *Semantic Information Processing*, edited by Marvin Minsky. Cambridge, Mass.: MIT Press (1968): 271–353. Perhaps the first truly large system ever written in Lisp, this impressive project is often pointed to as having "solved" the problem of analogies. How far from the truth that is!

Ewing, John and Czes Kośniowski. *Puzzle It Out: Cubes, Groups, and Puzzles*. New York: Cambridge University Press, 1982. Another lively and mathematically interesting book about the Cube and its variants.

Fahlman, Scott E., Geoffrey Hinton, and Terrence J. Sejnowski. "Massively Parallel Architectures for AI: NETL, Thistle, and Boltzmann Machines". In "Proceedings of the AAAI-83 Conference". Washington, D.C., August, 1983. A comparison of some recent ideas for AI architectures, including ones inspired by physics, in which statistical emergence plays a central role.

Falletta, Nicholas. *The Paradoxicon*. New York: Doubleday, 1983. An excellent collection of paradoxes of all sorts, ranging from Zeno and Epimenides to modern-day voting paradoxes, optical illusions, and antinomies in the philosophies of science and mathematics.

Fauconnier, Gilles. *Espaces Mentaux: Aspects de la construction du sens dans les langues naturelles*. Paris: Les Editions de Minuit, 1984. A probing inquiry into how we make sense of frame-crossing and counterfactual statements of this sort: "If Clark Gable had been a woman, Scarlett O'Hara would have been a man". Full of ideas about reference, identity, slippability, and essence.

Feigenbaum, Mitchell. "Universal Behavior in Nonlinear Systems". *Los Alamos Science* 1, no. 1 (Summer 1981): 4–27. An excellent introduction to the studies of chaos that come from iterating simple functions. Excellent graphics, some of which are reproduced in Chapter 16.

Feldman, Jerome and Dana Ballard. "Connectionist Models and Their Properties". *Cognitive Science* 6, no. 3 (July–September 1982): 205–54. One of several intriguing approaches to computational collectivism currently being investigated in cognitive science. Like most such models, this one is strongly influenced by ideas about human perception.

Feynman, Richard P. *The Character of Physical Law*. Cambridge, Mass.: MIT Press, 1967. The transcripts of five marvelous lectures delivered at Cornell University in 1964 by a physicist who is not only sharp as a nail but also sparkingly witty.

Feynman, Richard P., Robert B. Leighton, and Matthew Sands. *The Feynman Lectures in Physics*. Reading, Mass.: Addison-Wesley, 1965. Lectures given to beginning students, often more suitable for advanced students, filled with the excitement of science and the peppery observations of Feynman.

Franke, H. W. *Computer Graphics—Computer Art*. New York: Phaidon, 1971. By far the best collection of examples and discussion of computers and art I have yet seen, even though it is quite old by now.

Frey, Alexander H., Jr. and David Singmaster. *Handbook of Cubik Math*. Hillside, N.J.: Enslow, 1982. The group-theoretical ideas behind the cube are developed systematically, for possible use in an advanced high-school or college-level course.

Friedman, Daniel P. *The Little LISPer*. Chicago: Science Research Associates, 1974. An engaging and elegant introduction to the recursive ideas of Lisp, by one of its most ardent and accomplished practitioners.

Fromkin, Victoria A., ed. *Errors in Linguistic Performance: Slips of the Tongue, Ear, Pen, and Hand*. New York: Academic Press, 1980. A compendium of articles on how we can infer general mechanisms of thought from observing everyday surface-level quirks that show up ubiquitously in speech, typing, handwriting, listening, and so on.

Frutiger, Adrian. *Type Sign Symbol*. Zurich: Editions ABC, 1980. This book by the creator of Frutiger and Univers, two of today's most popular and elegant sans-serif typefaces, deals with the interaction of technical constraints and artistic creation, and features many beautiful letterforms and styles.

Gablik, Suzi. *Progress in Art*. New York: Rizzoli International, 1976. A heretical theory suggesting that there is a reason why art is where it is today, and that art follows a comprehensible trajectory in some abstract space, even if it is explicable only after the fact.

Gardner, Martin. *Fads and Fallacies*. New York: Dover, 1952. A book that comes about as close as one could hope to being a course on common sense. Many chapters of this classic bunk-puncturer should be part of the cultural education of everyone.

Gardner, Martin. "Mathematical Games: White and brown music, fractal curves, and one-over-f fluctuations". *Scientific American* 238, no. 4 (April 1978): 16–32. A solid introduction to the concepts of fractals and multi-level statistical structures.

Gardner, Martin. *Science: Good, Bad, and Bogus*. Buffalo: Prometheus Press, 1981. Following in the footsteps of *Fads and Fallacies*, this book sharp-swordedly decapitates one dragon of hokum after another—and yet sadly, like a hydra's many heads, they always seem to pop back up again.

Gardner, Martin. *Wheels, Life, and Other Mathematical Amusements*. New York: W. H. Freeman, 1983. Gardner's final collection of his sparkling *Scientific American* columns, showing why mathematics is the ultimate metamagic.

Gebstadter, Egbert B. *Thetamagical Memas: Seeking the Whence of Letter and Spirit*. Perth: Acidic Books, 1985. A curious pot-pourri, bloated and muddled—yet remarkably similar to the present work. This is a collection of Gebstadter's monthly rows in *Literary Australian* together with a few other articles, all with prescripts. Gebstadter is well known for his love of twisty analogies, such as this one (unfortunately not found in his book): "Egbert Gebstadter is the Egbert Gebstadter of indirect self-reference."

Geisel. T. and J. Nierwetberg. "Universal Fine Structure of the Chaotic Region in Period-Doubling Systems". *Physical Review Letters* 47, no. 14 (October 5, 1981): 975–78. An investigation turning up remarkable order deep in the heart of chaos.

Gentner, Dedre. "Structure-Mapping: A Theoretical Framework for Analogy". *Cognitive Science* 7 (1983): 155–70. One in a series of papers attempting to draw guidelines that will help distinguish good analogies from bad.

Gödel, Kurt. *On Formally Undecidable Propositions in "Principia Mathematica" and Related Systems*. Translated by Bernard Meltzer, edited and with an introduction by R. B. Braithwaite. New York: Basic Books, 1962. The fundamental work that opened up worlds to logicians, philosophers, computer scientists, and others.

Golden, Michael. "Don't Rewrite the Bible". *Newsweek* (November 7, 1983): 47. This piece sounds almost like my "Person Paper" in the way it exploits crude mockery of progressive new usages in order to make oppressive old usages sound good. The difference is that Golden is not being sarcastic.

Golomb, Solomon. "Rubik's Cube and Quarks". *American Scientist* 70, no. 3 (May–June 1982): 257–59. In which Golomb puts forth his analogy between twisted corners on the Cube and fractionally charged subatomic particles.

Gonick, Larry and Mark Wheelis. *A Cartoon Guide to Genetics*. New York: Barnes & Noble, 1983. A short and snappy—but most informative and entertaining—overview of molecular biology, genetics, and their human import.

Gould, Stephen Jay. *Hen's Teeth and Horse's Toes*. New York: W. W. Norton, 1983. Written in a lively and engaging way, this book (like its predecessors, *Ever Since Darwin* and *The Panda's Thumb*) relates with great clarity the issues of evolution as illustrated in nature's unbelievable variety of quirks.

Gray, J. Patrick and Linda Wolfe. "The Loving Parent Meets the Selfish Gene". *Inquiry* 23: 233–42. A cogent set of arguments against the pessimistic theses of Louis Pascal, to which he then replies (see below).

Grossman, I. and W. Magnus. *Groups and Their Graphs*. New York: Random House New Mathematical Library, 1975. An excellent visual introduction to group theory, featuring so-called "Cayley diagrams", which lay bare the structure of a group in a marvelously clear way.

Ground Zero. *Nuclear War: What's in It for You?* New York: Pocket Books, 1982. A dispassionate, calmly reasoned discussion for "just-plain folk" of what it means for countries to make and threaten each other with nuclear weapons. The best primer that I have come across on the subject, and one that I wish everyone would read and take to heart.

Guillemin, Victor. *The Story of Quantum Mechanics*. New York: Scribner's, 1968. A thoughtful survey of where quantum mechanics came from and what it has revealed about the physical world, concluding with a long discussion of the philosophical implications of quantum mechanics for such things as free will and causality.

Haab, A., A. Stocker, and W. Hättenschweiler. *Lettera 1* and *Lettera 2*. Arthur Niggli, 1954 and 1961. Some deliciously fanciful alphabets are featured in these books. Books like these ought to make anyone marvel at the fluidity of letters and human perception.

Hachtman, Tom. *Double Takes*. New York: Harmony Books, 1984. Two-in-one caricatures, done in a very satisfying way. It makes one wonder: could a computer ever do this kind of thing?

Hansel, C. E. M. *ESP and Parapsychology: A Critical Re-Evaluation*. Buffalo: Prometheus Books, 1980. A scholar looks at the claims of parapsychologists and finds them wanting.

Hanson, Norwood Russell. *Patterns of Discovery*. New York: Cambridge University Press, 1969. A philosophically rich discussion of how physical concepts progressed by fits and starts through the centuries, culminating in the strange world of elementary particles that we are now finding are not so elementary.

Hardin, Garrett. "The Tragedy of the Commons". *Science* 162, no. 3859 (December 13, 1968): 1243–48. Using the metaphor of shared grazing land that gets ruined by overuse without any specific person being responsible, Hardin argues with great force that people's narrow-minded selfishness will drive us to extinction unless we band together and form strong organizations dedicated to global ecological goals, particularly population control.

Harel, David. "Response to Scherlis and Wolper". *Communications of the ACM* 23, no. 12 (December 1980): 736–37. An amusing list of tricky self-references known to Harel, sporting a footnote claiming to be the first published example of "a reference to the very self-reference being discussed in the very letter being read!"

Hart, H. L. A. "Self-Referring Laws". In *Festskrift Tillägnad Karl Olivecrona*. Stockholm: Kungliga Boktryckeriet, P. A. Norstedt och Söner, 1964. A reply to Alf Ross (see below), in which Hart, perhaps today's leading philosopher of law, claims that self-amending laws are legally possible.

Harth, Erich. *Windows on the Mind: Reflections on the Physical Basis of Consciousness*. New York: William Morrow, 1982. Lively discussions of brain, mind, consciousness, and how they all tie together, by a physicist with a philosophical bent.

Haugeland, John, ed. *Mind Design: Philosophy, Psychology, and Artificial Intelligence*. Cambridge, Mass.: Bradford Books. MIT Press, 1981. A self-proclaimed sequel to Alan Ross Anderson's *Minds and Machines*, now that artificial intelligence has had a couple of decades to develop. This volume is of uneven quality, but it contains many articles sure to provoke thought.

Heiser, Jon F. et al. "Can Psychiatrists Distinguish a Computer Program Simulation of Paranoia from the Real Thing? The Limitations of Turing-Like Tests as Measures of the Adequacy of Simulations". *Journal of Psychiatric Research* 15, no. 3 (1979): 149–62. Researchers who developed the program called "Parry" claim that the Turing Test's validity is cast in doubt because Parry passed a pseudo-Turing Test.

Hinton, Geoffrey and James Anderson, eds. *Parallel Models of Associative Memory*. Hillsdale, N.J.: Lawrence Erlbaum Associates, 1981. A collection of articles exploring different models, all of which are based on the thesis that human perception and memory are statistically emergent phenomena and are best modeled as such.

Hintze, Wolfgang. *Der Ungarische Zauberwürfel*. Berlin: VEB Deutscher Verlag der Wissenschaften, 1982. This is an excellent book about the Cube, including new mathematical results on subgroups. Serious cubists who can read German should obtain this book.

Hobby, John, and Gu Guoan. "A Chinese Meta-Font". Stanford, Calif.: Stanford University Computer Science Department Technical Report STAN-CS-83-974, 1983. A description of a system for creating Chinese characters whose style is "tunable" to some extent. This system is very similar in some ways to Hàn Zì, the variable-style Chinese-character-generation system developed by David Leake and myself at Indiana, at about the same time.

Hodges, Andrew. *Alan Turing: The Enigma*. New York: Simon & Schuster, 1983. The definitive biography of this extremely important figure in mathematics and computer science, written with empathy, insight, and charm.

Hofstadter, Douglas R. *Ambigrams*. Forthcoming in 1985 from the Centre d'Art Contemporain (Geneva, Switzerland). A collection of ambigrams (or "inversions", as Scott Kim prefers to call them) aptly subtitled "A Panoply of Palindromic

Pinwheels". The foreword is by Scott (to whose book I symmetrically wrote the foreword). Also included are a lecture on ambigrams (in French) and an interview (in English).

——. "Analogies and Metaphors to Explain Gödel's Theorem". *Two-Year College Mathematics Journal* 13, no. 2 (March, 1982): 98–114. A collection of simple images and ideas that help to build up one's intuitions to the point where one can fully digest the intricacies of Gödel's clever construction.

——. "The Architecture of Jumbo". In "Proceedings of the Second Machine Learning Workshop", Monticello, Illinois, 1983. A description of the architecture of a biologically-inspired AI system that exploits parallelism and randomness in order to build up "well-chunked wholes" out of isolated parts and then to allow them to seek maximal "happiness" by internally reconfiguring themselves in a manner governed by a computational temperature.

——. "The Copycat Project: An Experiment in Nondeterminism and Creative Analogies". Cambridge, Mass.: MIT Artificial Intelligence Laboratory AI Memo 755, April 1984. A description of ongoing research in my group, first at Indiana, then at MIT, and now at Michigan. The goal is to make a system capable of doing analogies in a tiny domain, but with the insight (and short sight) of humans. Describing how the Jumbo architecture can be adapted to this task is the burden of this paper.

——. "512 Words on Recursion". *Math Bulletin*, Bronx High School of Science (1984): 18–19. A recursively structured article, which quotes a compressed version of itself (in which, of course, a more compressed version is quoted, etc.).

——. *Gödel, Escher, Bach: an Eternal Golden Braid*. New York: Basic Books, 1979. Originally titled "Gödel's Theorem and the Human Brain", this book tries to build up the concepts necessary to show how ideas that arise in Gödel's proof will one day be at the core of explanations of consciousness and the meaning of the word "I". Analogy, humor, and contrapuntal dialogues are essential features of *GEB*.

——. "Gridfonts". Unpublished manuscript, 1984. A still-growing collection of (currently) about 300 skeletal typefaces—that is, distinctive and artistically consistent ways of rendering all 26 letters in a highly confined grid. The purpose is to provide material for discussion of the roots of style and the fluid nature of categories.

——. "On Seeking Whence". Unpublished manuscript, 1982. A discussion of the immense difficulty of extrapolating linear patterns, and its relationship to such deeply human experiences as scientific induction, analogy-making, understanding music, and creativity.

——. "Poland: A Quest for Personal Meaning". *Poland* (May, 1981): 42–47. A compression of a longer piece called "Poland: A Mythical Quest", describing my powerful emotional reactions to Poland on my first visit there, in 1975.

——. "In Search of Essence". Unpublished manuscript, 1983. A discussion of what the "essence" of a written passage is, by way of a description of problems encountered in translating the dialogue *Contracrostipunctus* (from *Gödel, Escher, Bach*) into French.

——. "Simple and Not-So-Simple Analogies in the Copycat Domain". Unpublished manuscript. A collection of 84 analogy problems in the Copycat domain that show how diverse the tiny alphabetic universe can be.

Hofstadter, Douglas R., Gray Clossman, and Marsha Meredith. "Shakespeare's Plays Weren't Written by Him, but by Someone Else of the Same Name". Bloomington: Indiana University Computer Science Department Technical Report 96, 1980. "A study of intensionality in frame-based representation systems" is the subtitle. The paper's main purpose is to discuss the relationship between slots that an entity fills, and that entity's identity. The notion of "Core ID" is presented and explored in an analysis of the title sentence. Closely related to the problems discussed by Fauconnier (see above).

Hofstadter, Douglas R. and Daniel C. Dennett, eds. *The Mind's I: Fantasies and Reflections on Self and Soul*, New York: Basic Books, 1981. Our purpose was to jolt people on all sides of the fence in this anthology of fictional and evocative pieces on the curious fact (or illusion) that something we call an "I" is somehow connected to some hunk of matter floating somewhere and somewhen in some universe.

Holland, John et al. *Induction: Processes of Inference, Learning, and Discovery*. Forth-coming. A wide-ranging study of how learning takes place in genuine human minds, and how aspects of it might be modeled in computer simulations. This pioneering work is by a computer scientist, two psychologists, and a philosopher, and its breadth reflects their diversity.

Hollis, Martin and Steven Lukes, eds. *Rationality and Relativism*. Cambridge, Mass.: MIT Press, 1982. Showing how scholars can get mired in the endlessly circular reasoning that arises when any system of belief tries to provide its own justification. Reminiscent of "Münchhausens Zopf": the quandary of Baron Münchhausen try-ing to pull himself out of a quicksand quagmire simply by tugging on his own braid.

Hopfield, J. J. "Neural networks and physical systems with emergent computational abilities". In *Proceedings of the National Academy of Sciences* 79, Washington, D.C., 1982: 2554–58. A system that makes use of statistics and parallelism to model familiar properties of the mind: reconstructing a full memory from a partial one, generalizing, and so on.

How to Learn Lettering. Hong Kong: Nam San Publisher, n.d. A collection of Chinese characters in modern artistic styles, mostly for the use of advertisers, but also a treasure trove for those interested in the elusive "sameness" we see in wildly different renderings of a single Platonic essence.

Huff, William. "A Catalogue of Parquet Deformations". School of Architecture, State University of New York at Buffalo. Approximately 35 parquet deformations created by students in William Huff's studio, assembled and commented on by Huff.

Hughes, Patrick and George Brecht. *Vicious Circles and Infinity: An Anthology of Paradoxes*. New York: Penguin, 1975. A delightful and provocative collection of paradoxical material and choice epigrams embodying paradoxes of every conceivable sort. Includes lengthy discussions of the paradox of the Unexpected Examination, also known as the "Hangman's Paradox".

Huneker, James Gibbons. *Chopin: The Man and His Music*. New York: Dover, 1966. Originally published around the turn of the century, this romantic biography fea-tures florid prose so rich that it verges on meaninglessness, and yet it is wonderfully evocative.

Jaspert, W. Pincus, W. Turner Berry, and A. F. Johnson. *The Encyclopaedia of Type Faces*. Poole, England: Blandford Press, 1983. An engrossing catalogue of over 1,000 typefaces. One of its unique features is its thorough crediting of designers: the people whose exquisitely developed sense of line and space is far too often completely taken for granted. An index to designers and an index to typefaces are included. This way you can get a sense for the stylistic range of various designers.

Johnson-Laird, P. N. and P. C. Wason, eds. *Thinking*. New York: Cambridge University Press, 1975. A diverse collection of pieces by top-notch authors about nearly all aspects of human thought, including imagery, perception, inference, categories, memory, language, and so on.

Kadanoff, Leo. "Roads to Chaos". *Physics Today* 36, no. 12 (December 1983): 46–53. A good summary of the connection between mathematical approaches to chaos and the physical phenomena to be explained.

Kamack, H. J. and T. R. Keane. "The Rubik Tesseract". Unpublished manuscript, 1982. A companion piece to the one by Eidswick (see above), this discussion of a 3 × 3 × 3 × 3 "Rubik's hypercube" is a *tour de force* in visualization—for its readers almost as much as for its authors!

Kahneman, Daniel and Amos Tversky. "The Simulation Heuristic". In *Judgment Under Uncertainty: Heuristics and Biases*, edited by Daniel Kahneman, P. Slovic, and A. Tversky. New York: Cambridge University Press, 1982: 202–8. In what ways are people inclined to let situations mentally glide into alternate versions of themselves, and how do subtle cognitive pressures modify those tendencies? Two outstanding cognitive psychologists here describe their findings about this sort of slippability or "alternity" in their subjects' minds.

Kanerva, Pentti. *Self-Propagating Search: A Unified Theory of Memory*. Stanford, Calif.: Center for the Study of Language and Information, Technical Report, Stanford University, 1984. A neurocomputational theory of memory: How to make similarity-sensitive, reconstructive software out of statistically robust addressing hardware. This may sound a bit abstruse, but in my opinion Kanerva's elegant work constitutes one of the most important steps toward reconciliation of fluidity and mechanism—mind and brain—that I have seen taken.

Kennedy, Paul E. *Modern Display Alphabets*. New York: Dover, 1974. An excellent collection of visually attractive letterforms in styles of all sorts, and exhibiting all degrees of wildness.

Kim, Scott E. "The Impossible Skew Quadrilateral: A Four-Dimensional Optical Illusion". In *Proceedings of the 1978 AAAS Symposium on Hypergraphics: Visualizing Complex Relationships in Art and Science*. Boulder, Colo.: Westview Press, 1978. Like the work by Kamack and Keane (see above), this article takes a powerful visual imagination to write or to read. The familiar "impossible triangle" is here carried one step further, by a bold process of analogy. The writing style is full of typical Kimian recursive trickery and parallel passages.

——. *Inversions*. Peterborough, N.H.: Byte Books, 1981. A collection of inversions (or "ambigrams", as I prefer to call them) aptly subtitled "A Catalogue of Calligraphic Cartwheels": The foreword is by myself (to whose book Scott symmetrically wrote the foreword). The prose is as full of illusions and tricks of parallelism as the drawings are, although it is not immediately apparent.

——. "Noneuclidean Harmony". In *The Mathematical Gardner*, edited by David A. Klarner. Belmont, Calif.: Wadsworth International/Prindle, Weber, and Schmidt, 1981. A serious treatise on atonal geometry masquerading as a piece of humor. Describes Georg Cantor's important results on supersonic pitches, 2 against 3 correspondence, and uncountable rhythms.

——. "Visual Art: The Creative Cycle". *Response*, no. 1 (December, 1981). Minnesota

Artists Exhibition Program. A short article putting forth a thesis about creative activity, at the heart of which is a loop similar to the one I describe in the *P.S.* to Chapter 12 of this book.

Kirkpatrick, S., C. D. Gelatt, Jr., and M. P. Vecchi. "Optimization by Simulated Annealing". *Science* 220, no. 4598 (May 13, 1983): 671–80. An article describing a new statistical technique for seeking the optimal state of a system with a huge number of degrees of freedom, based on local improvement modulated by occasional local degradation, the amount of which is determined by a "cooling schedule", analogous to the annealing of a metal to strengthen it.

Kleppner, Daniel, Michael G. Littman, and Myron L. Zimmerman. "Highly Excited Atoms". *Scientific American* 244, no. 5 (May 1981): 130–49. A bridge between microscopic quantum-mechanical phenomena and macroscopic classical phenomena is provided by the study of "Rydberg atoms", with which this paper is concerned.

Knuth, Donald. "The Concept of a Meta-Font". *Visible Language* 16, no. 1 (Winter 1982): 3–27. Knuth describes his program, METAFONT, for creating an entire family of typefaces at one fell swoop, by parametrizing all letters of the alphabet with a consistent set of parameters. This is the paper that triggered my response printed as Chapter 13.

——. *TEX and Metafont: New Directions in Typesetting.* Bedford, Mass.: Digital Press, 1979. Knuth describes in detail how to use his programs that facilitate typesetting and letter design.

Kobylańska, Krystyna. *Chopin in His Own Land.* Cracow: Polish Music Publishers, 1956. A collection of hard-to-find Chopiniana, beautifully reproduced in large format.

Koestler, Arthur. *The Act of Creation.* New York: Dell, 1964. The great novelist and amateur psychologist delves into his own mind to come up with interesting but often wrong-headed speculations on humor, creativity, and insight.

——. *The Roots of Coincidence: An Excursion into Parapsychology.* New York: Vintage, 1972. Koestler reveals his belief in the occult, somewhat reminiscent of Arthur Conan Doyle's belief in fairies.

Kolata, Gina. "Does Gödel's Theorem Matter to Mathematics?" *Science* 218 (November 19, 1982): 779–80. An excellent description of how the specification of what today would be considered "large integers" depends on abstruse concepts from mathematical logic.

Koning, H. and J. Eizenberg. "The language of the prairie: Frank Lloyd Wright's prairie houses". *Environment and Planning B*, 8 (1981): 295–323. A description of how pseudo-Frank-Lloyd-Wright houses can be generated from a "shape grammar".

Kripke, Saul. *Naming and Necessity.* Cambridge, Mass.: Harvard University Press, 1972. This theory of extensions, intensions, "rigid designators", and identity is in direct opposition to my views (put forward in the "Shakespeare" paper cited above) that the roots of identity come from patterns of embeddedness in a network.

Kuwayama, Yasaburo. *Trademarks and Symbols, Volume 1: Alphabetical Designs.* New York: Van Nostrand Reinhold, 1973. A celebration of the craziness of letterforms, this collection contains letters to boggle anyone's mind.

Larcher, Jean. *Fantastic Alphabets.* New York: Dover, 1976. The letterforms in Kuwayama's book are highly imaginative, but by comparison, the letterforms in

Larcher's book are downright zany. It just goes to show that a computer program that could deal with letters in their full complexity would be able to deal with the entire world.

Lehninger, Albert. *Biochemistry*, 2d. ed. New York: Worth, 1975. A well-written treatise covering the huge field of biochemistry in a lucid manner.

Lennon, John. *In His Own Write* and *A Spaniard in the Works*. New York: Simon & Schuster, 1964 and 1965. This Beatle had a wonderful sense of silliness, all his own. Stories, pictures, poems—even a little drama or two. Perhaps better than the Beatles' music, if I may venture a heretical opinion.

Letraset, Inc. *Graphic Art Materials Reference Manual*. Paramus, N.J.: Letraset, Inc., 1981. This is the best inexpensive typeface manual available, and is well worth the price. It contains nearly all the common typefaces, as well as many unusual ones. This is a great way to get into typefaces.

Letraset, Inc. *Letraset Greek Series*. Athens: A. Pallis, 1984. This to me is an amazing catalogue of typefaces, because each and every one of them represents a "trans-alphabetic leap". Here we see such faces as Blanchard, Futura Black, Helvetica, Korinna, Optima, Souvenir, University Roman, Zipper, and a number of others— *all in Greek!* All I can say is, "Wow!"

Levin, Michael. "Mathematical Logic for Computer Scientists". Cambridge, Mass.: MIT Laboratory for Computer Science Technical Report LCS TR 131, June, 1974. An unorthodox treatment of logic for those more comfortable with Lisp than with number theory.

Lipman, Jean and Richard Marshall. *Art about Art*. New York: E. P. Dutton, 1978. An amusing annotated collection of self-conscious art, including pieces by Roy Lichtenstein, Andy Warhol, Robert Rauschenberg, Jasper Johns, Robert Arneson, Tom Wesselmann, Larry Rivers, Mel Ramos, Peter Saul, and many others.

Loeb, Marcia. *New Art Deco Alphabets*. New York: Dover, 1975. Showing how some-body can perfectly recreate the spirit of an era in many different ways. These original alphabets all look like they came straight out of the 1930's. Compare with the books by Bush (see above) and McCall (see below).

Lucas, J. R. "Minds, Machines, and Gödel". Reprinted in *Minds and Machines*, edited by Alan Ross Anderson. Englewood Cliffs, N.J.: Prentice-Hall, 1964. The article that launched a thousand rebuttals. Although I find its conclusions totally unjusti-fied, the issues are well raised and deserve to be thought about far more. Closely related to the issues discussed in the book by Webb (see below).

Machlup, Fritz and Una Mansfield, eds. *The Study of Information: Interdisciplinary Messages*. New York: Wiley-Interscience, 1983. A multi-faceted collection of art-icles by high-level scholars about information theory, cybernetics, artificial intelli-gence, cognitive science, librarianship, and more. Many of the pieces are statements of opinion, and conflict with one another. This volume includes the exchange between Allen Newell and myself, which is continued in the *P.S.* to my Chapter 26.

Mandelbrot, Benoît. *The Fractal Geometry of Nature*. New York: W. H. Freeman, 1982. This latest presentation of Mandelbrot's visions is rich in imagery and ideas. Fractal shapes constitute one of the twentieth century's most fertile mathematical playgrounds.

Marek, George R. and Maria Gordon-Smith. *Chopin*. New York: Harper & Row, 1978. One of the many biographies of Chopin in English. I find it to be balanced and well written.

Marx, George, Eva Gajzágó, and Peter Gnädig. "The universe of Rubik's cube". *European Journal of Physics* 3 (1982): 34–43. The implications of extending the concept of entropy to the surface of the Cube are reported on, with the results of several statistical studies done on computer.

Max, Nelson. *Space-Filling Curves*. Chicago: International Film Bureau, Inc., 1974. A marvelous movie done with computer graphics showing the fascination of some of the earliest-discovered fractal curves. The computer-produced music adds extra appeal and eerieness.

May, Robert. "Simple Mathematical Models with Very Complicated Dynamics". *Nature* 261, no. 5560 (June 10, 1976): 459–67. An early review article about the chaos one is led to when one iterates simple functions on the interval [0,1]. Very informative, except for the reversal of two figures!

Maynard-Smith, John. *Evolution and the Theory of Games*. New York: Cambridge University Press, 1982. Showing how new depths of understanding of the mechanisms of evolution can come from modeling the interactions of organisms in a common environment in terms of mathematical game theory.

McCall, Bruce. *Zany Afternoons*. New York: Alfred A. Knopf, 1982. A genius for capturing the flavor of things turns all his talents to recreating the twenties, thirties, forties, and fifties—not only in America but also abroad. This very funny book is an amazing achievement. Compare with the books by Bush and Loeb (see above).

McCarthy, John. "Attributing Mental Qualities to Machines". In *Philosophical Perspectives on Artificial Intelligence*, edited by Martin Ringle, 161–95. Atlantic Highlands, N.J.: Humanities Press, 1979. Under what circumstances does it make sense to speak of machines having desires or beliefs? When to adopt this "intentional stance" is here discussed by one of the pioneers of artificial intelligence.

——. "History of Lisp". In *History of Programming Languages*, edited by Richard L. Wexelblatt, 217–23. New York: Academic Press, 1980. Lisp's genesis as recalled by its inventor.

McCarty, L. T. and N. S. Sridharan. "A Computational Theory of Legal Argument". New Brunswick, N.J.: Rutgers University Computer Science Department Technical Report LPR-TR-13, January 1982. A professor of law and a computer scientist work together to implement "prototype deformation", which they consider the key to computer modeling of argumentation by precedent.

McClelland, James L., David E. Rumelhart, and Geoffrey E. Hinton, eds. *Interactive Activation: A Framework for Information Processing*. Forthcoming. A collection of articles on statistically emergent parallel computation featuring "temperature" as a regulator of randomness.

McKay, Michael D. and Michael S. Waterman. "Self-Descriptive Strings". *Mathematical Gazette* 66, no. 435 (1982): 1–4. A mathematical study of a simple class of sentences that attempt to inventory themselves.

Meehan, James R. "Tale-Spin, an Interactive Program that Writes Stories". In *Proceedings of the 5th International Conference on Artificial Intelligence—1977*, Vol. 1: 91–98. Pittsburgh: Department of Computer Science, Carnegie-Mellon University. One of the funniest (and therefore most sensible) articles ever written on computers and their "understanding" of language. Meehan explains how, in one "mis-spun tale", his program made gravity fall into a river and drown. Meehan's discussions of mis-spun tales in general are among the most illuminating passages I know on that perennial vexation: the fact that AI programs stubbornly resist acquiring common sense, no matter how hard or how often they are spanked.

Miller, Casey and Kate Swift. *The Handbook of Nonsexist Writing for Writers, Editors, and Speakers*. New York: Barnes and Noble, 1980. A first-class book. It is a scandal that this book is not found on every newsman's desk. Thinking about these issues is not only socially important, but challenging and fascinating.

———. *Words and Women*. New York: Doubleday, Anchor Press, 1977. A magnificent and devastating job of showing the absurdity of thinking that women have been dealt a fair hand by our society. If language is the thermometer of society, then this book reveals that collectively, we are gravely ill.

Mills, George. "Gödel's Theorem and the Existence of Large Numbers". Northfield, Minnesota: Mathematics Department, Carleton College, October 1981. Showing how the descriptions of some stupendously large numbers can be obtained via recursive definitions of functions and the process of diagonalization. Repeated jootsing leads to some remarkable destinations!

Minsky, Marvin. "A Framework for Representing Knowledge". In *The Psychology of Computer Vision*, edited by P. H. Winston. New York: McGraw-Hill, 1975. The paper that defined such now-central notions to AI as frames, slots, and default assumptions.

———. "Matter, Mind, and Models". In *Semantic Information Processing*, edited by Marvin Minsky, Cambridge, Mass.: MIT Press, 1968. Some cogent speculations about the meaning of the word "I" in computational terms.

———. "Why People Think Computers Can't". *AI Magazine* (Fall 1982): 3–15. With his usual unusual insight. Minsky tears people apart for not understanding how to think about thinking (or about machines, for that matter).

Mondrian, Piet. *Tout l'Œuvre Peint de Piet Mondrian*. Paris: Flammarion, 1976. For a grand overview of the evolution of the style of one painter. I know of no better book than this, which traces Mondrian from his earliest representational paintings to his most abstract and geometrical ones, revealing the sweep to be continuous and logical, but no less dramatic for that.

Morrison, Philip and Phylis, and the Office of Charles and Ray Eames. *Powers of Ten*. New York: Scientific American Books, 1983. Kees Boeke's inspirational *Cosmic View* (see above) revisited some thirty years later, with considerably more commentary. A charming and worthy successor.

Myhill, John. "Some Philosophical Implications of Mathematical Logic: Three Classes of Ideas". *Review of Metaphysics* 6, no. 2 (December 1952): 165–98. In 1982 I met Myhill and asked him about this paper. He told me he considered it to be a piece of junk. That astonished me, since I consider it to be a thoughtful and important piece of philosophizing making use of mathematical metaphors, something that hardly anyone dares to do. You never know how someone will evaluate their own work 30 years later!

Nagel, Ernest, and J. R. Newman. *Gödel's Proof*. New York: New York University Press, 1958. A gracious and highly accessible introduction to the twists in Gödel's reasoning, as well as to the philosophical issues surrounding his work.

Nakanishi, Akira. *Writing Systems of the World*. Rutland, Vt.: Tuttle, 1980. For a sampling of the many different spirits residing in letterforms, see this book. It features reproductions of newspaper pages showing each writing system in several different styles.

Newell, Allen. "Physical Symbol Systems". *Cognitive Science* 4, no. 2 (April–June 1980): 135–83. A lengthy article putting forth the orthodox dogma on which artificial intelligence has traditionally considered itself founded: the idea that a universal computer embodies all the prerequisites for intelligent behavior.

Norman, Donald. "Categorization of Action Slips". *Psychology Review* 88, no. 1 (January 1981): 1–15. A delightful compendium of types of error that people commit in performing everyday actions such as putting water on to boil, answering the telephone, unbuckling one's seatbelt, driving home from work, and so on. There is remarkable regularity behind the seeming chaos, and Norman's purpose is to chart and exploit that regularity in order to reveal hidden mechanisms of thought.

Nozick, Robert. *Philosophical Explanations*. Cambridge, Mass.: Harvard University, Belknap Press, 1981. A very wide-ranging book on philosophy, intended for lay readers as well as for professionals. It covers matters from personal identity and the meaning of reference to free will and morality, and only occasionally lapses into brief spasms of absolutely inscrutable jargon.

Parfit, Derek. *Reasons and Persons*. Oxford: Clarendon Press, 1984. A very thoughtful treatise on moral dilemmas and ethical behavior, rooted in close consideration of the deepest roots of caring: why do I care about my present and future self? Parfit knows that to make any serious attempt to answer this riddle, one must look long and hard at the meaning of the word "I" in the real world and in many counterfactual ones, which he does with skill and insight.

Pascal, Louis. "Human Tragedy and Natural Selection". *Inquiry* 21: 443–60. Taking up where Garrett Hardin left off (see above), Pascal paints a gloomy picture of a population explosion as the natural outcome of selection itself, something built into the nature of societies just as deeply as the sexual drive is built into individuals.

——. "Rejoinder to Gray and Wolfe". *Inquiry* 23: 242–51. A bitter indictment of the human race's apathy before visibly onrushing catastrophe.

Peattie, Lisa. "Normalizing the Unthinkable". *Bulletin of the Atomic Scientists* 40, no. 3 (March 1984): 32–36. Like Pascal, Peattie is concerned with people's apparent ability to turn off their sensitivities and to focus on the very local to such an extent that great tragedies are allowed to ensue. In a striking analogy, she likens the current public apathy about the arms madness to the inhumanity of collaborators in Hitler's concentration camps.

Pérec, Georges. *La Disparition*. Paris: Editions Denoël, 1969. If anything, writing without 'e's is harder in French than in English, yet here is an entire novel in that bizarre dialect. Naturally enough, its subject is the mysterious disappearance of item number five in a collection of twenty-six objects. It was probably inspired by the 'e' less novel *Gadsby*, written in English by Ernest Vincent Wright in the late 1930's.

Perfect, Christopher and Gordon Rookledge. *Rookledge's International Typefinder*. New York: Frederick G. Beil. 1983. A wonderful (though expensive) compendium of typefaces, indexed in such a way that you can look a typeface up by its features, thus allowing you to home in quickly on an unknown specimen instead of spending hours leafing through catalogues. Lovers of my "horizontal and vertical problems" will delight in this book.

Phillips, Tom. *A Humument: A Treated Victorian Novel*. New York: Thames & Hudson, 1980. Like a child who has covered a wall with colorful crayon drawings, Tom Phillips has completely obliterated the pages of an old novel (*A Human Document* by W. H. Mallock) with his colorful scribblings, and only here and there do traces of the original show through. A droll stunt!

Poincaré, Henri. "On Mathematical Creation". In *The World of Mathematics*, vol. 4, edited by James R. Newman, 2041–50. New York: Simon & Schuster, 1956. A lecture presented to the Psychological Society in Paris in the early part of this century. Anticipating developments in cognitive science some eighty years later, Poincaré speculates on the nature of the events taking place inside his skull as he makes mathematical discoveries.

Pólya, George. *How to Solve It*. New York: Doubleday, 1957. Pólya, like Poincaré a mathematician fascinated by thought processes, attempts here to give recipes for how to attack mathematical problems. The problem with this is that there is—and can be—no failsafe recipe. Even trying to give guidelines is probably futile. The nose that smells the right route is simply rare, and there are no two ways about it.

Post, Emil. "Absolutely Unsolvable Problems and Relatively Undecidable Propositions: Account of an Anticipation". In *The Undecidable*, edited by Martin Davis, 338–443. New York: Raven, 1965. In this paper, Post concludes that mathematicians' thought processes are essentially creative and non-mechanizable. Related to the article by Myhill (see above).

Poundstone, William. *The Recursive Universe: Cosmic Complexity and the Limits of Scientific Knowledge*. New York: William Morrow, 1985. A superlative account of the reductionist miracle: fantastically complex entities—living, self-reproducing organisms—turn out to be vast arrays of very simply interacting parts. Von Neumann's trick of self-reproduction without infinite regress (adapted from Gödel) is one of the main topics explored here, and with the help of Conway's absorbing game of Life, which plays the starring role in his book, Poundstone does a masterful job of explaining how it comes about.

Racter. *The Policeman's Beard Is Half Constructed*. New York: Warner Books, 1984. "Racter" is a program written by Bill Chamberlain and Thomas Etter. *The Policeman's Beard* is a book written by Racter. It is all somewhat tongue-in-check, because Racter does not really know much about half-constructed beards, but what is lovely about Racter's prose is the way it skirts the fringes of meaning, weaving drunkenly across the boundary between sense and senselessness.

Rapoport, Anatol. *Two-Person Game Theory*. Ann Arbor: University of Michigan Press, Ann Arbor Science Library, 1966. A sound treatment of game theory, featuring a most interesting personal discussion on opinions about the meaning of "rationality" in Prisoner's-Dilemma-like situations.

Reps, Paul. *Zen Flesh, Zen Bones*. New York: Doubleday, Anchor Press, n.d. An easily available collection of Zen koans, highly amusing and, perhaps, even enlightening—providing you take it all with sufficiently many grains of salt.

Rogers, Hartley. *Theory of Recursive Functions and Effective Computability*. New York: McGraw-Hill, 1967. A standard reference work on many advanced concepts in metamathematics, including such concepts as "productive" and "creative" sets, referred to in my Chapter 13.

Ross, Alf. "On Self-Reference and a Puzzle in Constitutional Law". *Mind* 78, no. 309 (January 1969): 1–24. A condundrum in the philosophy of law: Can laws modify themselves, or is that paradoxical? Ross' view is that logical inconsistency is unacceptable in law, and therefore that self-amendment is impossible. For a response, see the paper by Hart (above).

Rucker, Rudy. *Infinity and the Mind*. Boston: Birkhäuser, 1982. A book that had to be written. Presenting the most abstruse concoctions of the mind in language that is not abstruse, and connecting it with thoughts about consciousness and the mystery of existence—this is what Rucker excels in.

Ruelle, David. "Les Attracteurs Etranges". *La Recherche* 11, no. 108 (February 1980): 131–44. A good article relating these wispy mathematical clouds to the physics they are supposed to explain, featuring a number of excellent illustrations.

Rumelhart, David E. and Donald A. Norman. "Simulating a Skilled Typist: A Study of Skilled Cognitive-Motor Performance". *Cognitive Science* 6, no. 3 (July–September 1982): 1–36. Anticipating the current "parallel distributed processing" project at the University of California at San Diego, the research described in this article is among the most interesting work on modeling human performance that I have encountered.

Russett, Bruce. *The Prisoners of Insecurity*. New York: W. H. Freeman, 1983. The arms race as an iterated Prisoner's Dilemma, and how we might be able to break out of the deadlock. The last section—"Responsibility"—concludes with this admonition (and how I wish people would take it to heart!): "In a democracy, silence about nuclear issues carries an implication not just of indifference but of acceptance. If we stand silent in the face of an arms race—and the war to which it may lead us—we must share responsibility for the outcome. 'Silence gives consent.'"

Ryder, Frederick, and Company. *Ryder Types*, 2 vols. (with periodic supplements). Chicago: Frederick Ryder and Company. The best catalogue of typefaces I have run across—but it is expensive. Some of the oddest faces I have ever seen are found in the four supplements I own.

Sagan, Carl, ed. *Communication with Extraterrestrial Intelligence*. Cambridge, Mass.: MIT Press, 1973. An entertaining transcript of an international meeting in the days when Russians and Americans spoke to each other. Sagan puts forth his notion of various types of earth-life-based "chauvinisms". A hopeful and intellectually refreshing book—the kind one wishes there were hundreds of.

Sampson, Geoffrey. "Is Roman Type an Open-Ended System? A Response to Douglas Hofstadter". *Visible Language* 17, no. 4 (Autumn 1983): 410–12. Sampson disputes my claim that it is impossible to capture the fluid spirit of letters of the alphabet in parametrized computer subroutines; he suggests that it is possible, if you limit your goals to capturing the spirit of letters suitable for printing serious books in.

Schank, Roger. *Dynamic Memory: A Theory of Reminding and Learning in Computers and People*. New York: Cambridge University Press, 1982. Although I disagree with some of his theorizing. I agree fully with Schank's focus on the types of problems that cognitive science ought to be most concerned with, and I like the examples he uses.

Scherlis, William L. and Pierre L. Wolper. "Self-Referenced Referenced, and Self-Referenced". *Communications of the ACM* 23, no. 12 (December 1980): 736. A humorous short note on papers that cite themselves.

Schrödinger, Ernst. *What Is Life?* and *Mind and Matter*. New York: Cambridge University Press, 1967 (reprint of 1944 edition). This philosophically-minded physicist prophetically speculates on the nature of the hereditary message, before the days when DNA's structure or function were known. Also venturing into the deep waters of consciousness, he comes up with this mystical conclusion: "The over-all number of minds is just one."

Schwenk, Theodor. *Sensitive Chaos*. New York: Schocken, 1976. A book about fluids in the wild and in the laboratory, filled with striking patterns and fantastic photographs strongly suggesting this mystical conclusion: "The over-all number of fluids is just one."

Searle, John. "Minds, Brains, and Programs". *The Behavioral and Brain Sciences* 3 (September 1980): 417–57. Like the Lucas article (see above), this one launched a thousand rebuttals (including two by me). In this, its original setting, it was followed by nearly thirty rebuttals and counter-rebuttals. It is amusing and educational to read them all. I view this article as a litmus test, in the sense that someone convinced by Searle's imagery is almost sure to have a very negative opinion of AI.

——. "The Myth of the Computer: An Exchange". *New York Review of Books* (June 24, 1982): 56–57. Searle portrays Dennett and me as blind advocates of "strong AI"—the notion that "the appropriately programmed computer literally has a mind". He resents the fact that such views are "well financed and backed by prestigious teams of research workers", and tells how he is constantly working toward "the relentless exposure of its preposterousness".

——. "The Myth of the Computer". *New York Review of Books* (April 29, 1982): 3–6. A rather negative review of *The Mind's I* by someone roundly criticized in the book. The one good thing Searle does in this review is to stress the central epistemological problem facing AI: to explain the nature of the fluid reference, or *semanticity*, that mental activity exhibits.

Serafini, Luigi. *Codex Seraphinianus*, Milan: Franco Maria Ricci, 1981. A complete pseudo-encyclopedia, in two volumes. The writing system, the page numbering, the weird diagrams, and especially the wonderful color illustrations are all products of the cryptic mind of Serafini, an Italian architect. Also available in one volume, and more inexpensively, from Abbeville Press in New York, N.Y.

Seuss, Dr. *On Beyond Zebra*. New York: Random House, 1955. Humorous ways of extending the alphabet beyond "z": a metaphor for jumping out of the system ("jootsing").

Simon, Herbert A. "Cognitive Science: The Newest Science of the Artificial". *Cognitive Science* 4, no. 2 (April–June 1980): 33–46. Simon's confident assertion that computers already have what it takes to possess full intelligence: symbol manipulation. In his conclusion, he claims: "Wherever the boundary is drawn, there exists today a science of intelligent systems that extends beyond the limits of any single species."

——. "Studying Human Intelligence by Creating Artificial Intelligence". *American Scientist* 69, no. 3 (May–June 1981): 300–309. This is the lecture in which Simon spoke of the all-important 100-millisecond barrier, below which it is of no interest to cognitive scientists to know what happens (see my Chapter 26). In print he changed "100 milliseconds" to "ten milliseconds", although the point remains the same either way.

Singmaster, David. *Notes on Rubik's "Magic Cube"*. Hillside, N.J.: Enslow, 1981. On its cover, this book proudly boasts: " 'The definitive treatise.'—*Scientific American*." Well, if *Scientific American* says so, who am I to dispute it?

Sloman, Aaron. *The Computer Revolution in Philosophy: Philosophy, Science, and Models of Mind*. Atlantic Highlands, N.J.: Humanities Press, 1978. A book that warns philosophers that they will miss the boat if they don't jump on the AI bandwagon. This a good though somewhat tendentious discussion of the philosophical import of AI.

Smith, Brian C. "Reflection and Semantics in Lisp". Palo Alto, Calif.: Xerox Palo Alto Research Center Report, 1983. A boiling-down of a 500-page Ph.D. thesis into a dozen pages or so, concerning a system capable of reasoning about itself (and reasoning about such reasoning, etc.). This work exemplifies the "meta-meta" style of AI research (see my Chapter 23—especially its *P.S.*).

Smith, Stephen B. *The Great Mental Calculators: The Psychology, Methods, and Lives of Calculating Prodigies*. New York: Columbia University Press, 1983. A set of portraits of very strange yet very human beings whose aberrant minds let them do calculating tasks that we ordinary people—no matter how number-loving—could not conceivably do.

Smolensky, Paul. "Harmony Theory: A Mathematical Framework for Stochastic Parallel Processing". University of California at San Diego Institute for Cognitive Science Technical Report ICS No. 8306. Based on the ideas of statistical mechanics, this project utilizes stochastic parallelism, regulated by a "temperature" that gradually drops to zero, to search most efficiently for the optimal global state of a system.

Smullyan, Raymond. *This Book Needs No Title: A Budget of Living Paradoxes*. Englewood Cliffs, N.J.: Prentice-Hall, 1980. A very humorous collection of observations about the constant intermingling of life and paradox, by a logician whose awareness of paradox is especially keen.

Solo, Dan X. *Sans Serif Display Alphabets*. New York: Dover, 1979. A collection of elegant letterforms whose subdued flair resides exclusively in their gentle curves, stroke taperings, line endings, and the interplay between positive and negative space.

——. *Special-Effects and Topical Alphabets*. New York: Dover, 1978. After you've looked at a book like this, you know why the problem of letterforms is synonymous with the problem of full human intelligence.

Sonneborn, Tracy M. "Degeneracy of the Genetic Code: Extent, Nature, and Genetic Implications". In *Evolving Genes and Proteins*, edited by Vernon Bryson and Henry J. Vogel. New York: Academic Press, 1965. Perhaps the first paper to suggest that there is evolutionary rhyme and reason to the particular match-up between codons and amino acids that exists in the arbitrary-seeming genetic code.

Soppeland, Mark. *Words*. Los Altos, Calif.: William Kaufmann, 1980. A witty collection of words drawn as self-referential pictures: stacks of books whose shapes spell out "books", and so on.

Sorrels, Bobbye. *The Nonsexist Communicator*. Englewood Cliffs, N.J.: Prentice-Hall, 1983. A sizable collection of sexist usages and nonsexist remedies: some of the remedies, however, are needlessly awkward.

Sperry, Roger. "Mind, Brain, and Humanist Values". In *New Views on the Nature of Man*, edited by John R. Platt. Chicago: University of Chicago Press, 1965. The article that asks, and tries to answer, the question "Who pushes whom around in the population of causal forces that occupy the cranium?" My answer is in Chapter 25.

Spinelli, Aldo. *Loopings*. Amsterdam: Multi-Art Points Edition, 1976. A somewhat clumsy realization of a good idea: a book whose pages are all self-inventorying sentences, or close to that. At the end, Spinelli discusses the kinds of locked-in loops and entryways into looping that can arise.

Stanley, H. Eugene et al. "Interpretation of the Unusual Behavior of H_2O and D_2O at Low Temperature: Are Concepts of Percolation Relevant to the 'Puzzle of Liquid Water'?" *Physica* 106a (1981): 260–77. An article that gives a fairly recent picture of the "flickering-cluster" view of water.

Stein, Gertrude. *How to Write.* Craftsbury Common, Vt.: Sherry Urie, 1977. (Originally published in 1931.) Classic volume of absurdities. It would be a nightmare to try to read the whole thing; each page is like a unique grain of sand, but all the pages taken together add up to a rather bland beach. Better to savor it in small bits.

Steiner, George. *After Babel: Aspects of Language and Translation.* New York: Oxford University Press, 1975. This fascinating exploration of the depths of personal meaning is full of obscurities, but it is still one of the best statements on the subtlety of language that I know.

Strich, Christian. *Fellini's Faces: 418 Photographs from the Archives of Federico Fellini.* New York: Holt, Rinehart, and Winston, 1981. A celebration of the remarkable diversity of human physiognomies, as well as their amazing expressivity.

Stryer, Lubert. *Biochemistry.* New York: W. H. Freeman, 1975. An elegantly produced text of biochemistry, on a slightly lower level than Lehninger. The figures—many in color—are especially appealing.

Suber, Peter. "A Bibliography of Works on Reflexivity". Unpublished manuscript, 1984. An extensive collection of pointers to the vast universe of writings on self-modifying laws, self-referring literature, self-fulfilling prophecies, self-replicating machines, self-monitoring computer programs, and on and on.

——. *The Paradox of Self-Amendment: A Study of Logic, Law, Omnipotence, and Change.* Forthcoming. This is the first (and only) book-length study of logical paradoxes in law. It focuses on one family of paradoxes (rules that authorize change being applied to themselves). but eventually tries to address the general problem of how legal reasoning copes with logical paradox. The game of Nomic is featured in an appendix.

Thomas, Dylan. *Collected Poems.* New York: New Directions, 1953. I am the first to admit I don't understand poetry well, but this beguiling collection, with its combination of beautiful language and bewildering opacity, leaves me especially disturbed.

Thomas, Lewis. *The Medusa and the Snail.* New York: Viking, 1979. Short essays on science and life, some of which are very insightful, others of which I find puzzling or just plain silly.

Turing, Alan. "Computing Machinery and Intelligence". Reprinted in *Minds and Machines*, edited by Alan Ross Anderson. Englewood Cliffs, N.J.: Prentice-Hall. 1964. In which the now-infamous "Turing Test" for machine thought is proposed. Lucid and straightforward, this article contains plenty of provocative ideas, even today.

Turner-Smith, Ronald. *The Amazing Pyraminx.* Hong Kong: Mèffert Novelties, 1981. A simple guide to the notation, group theory, and solution of the Pyraminx puzzle.

Ulam, Stanislaw. *Adventures of a Mathematician.* New York: Scribners, 1976. A fascinating account of the intellectual life of a highly innovative and fun-loving mathematician, including some speculations on mind and consciousness.

Vetterling-Braggin, Mary, ed. *Sexist Language: A Modern Philosophical Analysis.* Totowa, N.J.: Littlefield, Adams & Co., 1981. A valuable collection of articles from many perspectives on sexism. Includes one section on the comparison between sexism and racism.

von Neumann, John. *Theory of Self-Reproducing Automata*, edited and completed by Arthur W. Burks. Urbana, Illinois: University of Illinois Press, 1966. Here von Neumann describes how a machine could construct replicas of itself, or even machines more complex than itself, out of raw materials. At the core of this work by von Neumann, however, is Gödel's method of achieving mathematical self-reference—a fact that many people seem to overlook or downplay.

Walker, Alan, ed. *The Chopin Companion*. New York: W. W. Norton, 1966. An excellent collection of articles by composers, performers, and musicologists on Chopin, his music, and its influence.

Watzlawick, Paul. *Change*. New York: W. W. Norton, 1974. A theory of psychological disorder as caused by encounters with paradox in daily living. The suggested therapy is to fight paradox with paradox (if that isn't paradoxical!).

Webb, Judson. *Mechanism, Mentalism, and Metamathematics*. Hingham, Mass.: D. Reidel, 1980. A penetrating scholarly analysis of the import of the most important metamathematical work by Gödel, Church. Turing, Kleene, Tarski, Post, and others. In particular, it seeks to elucidate the relationship of the famous "limitative theorems" applicable to formal systems with attempts to mechanize human mental activity. In essence, its conclusion is that those results strengthen, rather than diminish, the notion that mental activity can in principle be mechanized.

Wells, Carolyn. *A Nonsense Anthology*. New York: Dover Press, 1958. A wonderful collection of strange poems and silly snippets of pseudo-sense.

Wheelis, Allen. *The Scheme of Things*. New York: Harcourt Brace Jovanovich, 1980. A moving story of human and animal attachments, and the emotional resonances of places and scenes. The story hints at many self-references, most notably to another novel called *The Way Things Are*, written by Wheelis' protagonist Oliver Thompson who, like Wheelis himself, is an unorthodox psychiatrist living in San Francisco. Wheelis within Wheelis!

Williams, J. D. *The Compleat Strategyst*. New York: McGraw-Hill, 1954. One of the earliest and clearest books ever written on game theory. It is a very elementary book, with humorous drawings and droll stories to illustrate its points.

Wilson, E. O. *The Insect Societies*. Cambridge, Mass.: Harvard University, Belknap Press, 1971. It is heavy going to read this book, but parts of it are engrossing, as they tell how order at a high level comes from the independent activity of low-level organisms acting without knowledge of one another.

Winston, Patrick Henry. *The Psychology of Computer Vision*. New York: McGraw-Hill, 1975. Although fairly old by AI standards, this collection of six articles is still of considerable interest. One is Minsky's article on frames; another is an article by Winston on learning and recognition; and another is an article by Waltz on economical strategies for vision in the "blocks world".

Winston, Patrick Henry and Berthold Horn. *Lisp*. Reading, Mass.: Addison-Wesley, 1981. A solid textbook on Lisp, starting right at the beginning and going up to AI programming techniques.

Yaguello, Marina. *Alice au pays du language*. Paris: Editions du Seuil, 1981. A French linguist examines the phonetics, syntax, semantics, and gradual shifts of her own language to illuminate the strangeness of human thought. Many of the examples in the book are taken from popular language, slang, or humor, which makes it particularly unstuffy.

——. *Les mots et les femmes*. Paris: Petite Bibliothèque Payot, 1978. On fighting the battle against sexist language in French—but unfortunately, because of the two-gender system of romance languages, eradication of sexism will prove far more difficult in those languages than in English (where it is already ferociously hard).

Zapf, Hermann. *About Alphabets*. Cambridge, Mass.: MIT Press, 1960. A famous contemporary type designer describes his adventures among the alphabets of the world.

43

THE PROSPECTS FOR BUILDING
TRULY INTELLIGENT MACHINES

David L. Waltz

Source: *Daedalus: Journal of the American Academy of Arts and Sciences* 117(1) (1988): 191–212.

Can artificial intelligence be achieved? If so, how soon? By what methods? What ideas from current AI research will in the long run be important contributions to a science of cognition? I believe that AI can be achieved, perhaps within our lifetimes, but that we have major scientific and engineering obstacles to hurdle if it is to come about. The methods and perspective of AI have been dramatically skewed by the existence of the common digital computer, sometimes called the von Neumann machine, and ultimately, AI will have to be based on ideas and hardware quite different from what is currently central to it. Memory, for instance, is much more important than its role in AI so far suggests, and search has far less importance than we have given it. Also, because computers lack bodies and life experiences comparable to humans', intelligent systems will probably be inherently different from humans; I speculate briefly on what such systems might be like.

Obstacles to building intelligent systems

If we are to build machines that are as intelligent as people, we have three problems to solve: we must establish a science of cognition; we must engineer the software, sensors, and effectors for a full system; and we must devise adequate hardware.

Establishing a science of cognition

We have no suitable science of cognition. We have only fragments of the conception, and some of those are certainly incorrect. We know very little about how a machine would have to be organized to solve the problems of intelligence. Virtually all aspects of intelligence—including perception, memory, reasoning, intention, generation of action, and attention—are still mysterious. However, even if we understood how to structure an intelligent system, we would not be able to complete the system because we also lack an appropriate science of knowledge. For some aspects of knowledge, any computational device will be on a strong footing when compared with a person. Machine-readable encyclopedias, dictionaries, and texts will eventually allow machines to absorb book knowledge quite readily. For such understanding to be deep, however, a system needs perceptual grounding and an understanding of the physical and social world. For humans much of this knowledge is either innate or organized and gathered by innate structures that automatically cause us to attend to certain features of our experience, which we then regard as important. It will be extremely difficult to characterize and build into a system the kinds of a priori knowledge or structuring principles humans have.

Engineering the software

Any truly intelligent system must be huge and complex. As Frederick Brooks argues, writing on his experience building the large operating system OS360 at IBM, it is not possible to speed up a software project by simply putting more and more people on it.[1] The optimum team size for building software is about five people. For this reason, and because of the sheer scope of a project of this sort—which dwarfs any that have been attempted in programming to date—hand coding will certainly be too slow and unreliable to accomplish the whole task. Consequently, a truly intelligent system will have to be capable of learning much of its structure from experience.

What structures must be built into a system to allow it to learn? This is a central question for current AI, and the answer depends on issues of knowledge representation: How should knowledge be represented? Out of what components (if any) are knowledge structures built?

Creating the hardware

We must be able to build hardware that is well matched to AI's knowledge representation and learning needs and that compares in power with the human brain. No one should be surprised that the puny machines AI has used thus far have not exhibited artificial intelligence. Even the most powerful current computers are probably no more than one four-millionth as powerful as the human brain. Moreover, current machines are probably at least as deficient in memory capacity: today's largest computers probably have no more than about one four-millionth of the memory capacity of the human brain. Even given these extreme discrepancies, hardware will probably prove the easiest part of the overall AI task to achieve.

I begin with a discussion of traditional AI and its theoretical underpinnings in order to set the stage for a discussion of the major paradigm shifts (or splits) currently under way in and around AI. As an advocate of the need for new paradigms, I here confess my bias. I see no way that traditional AI methods can be extended to achieve humanlike intelligence. Assuming that new paradigms will replace or be merged with the traditional ones, I make some projections about how soon intelligent systems can be built and what they may be like.

Limits of traditional AI

Two revolutionary paradigm shifts are occurring within artificial intelligence. A major force behind the shifts is the growing suspicion among researchers that current AI models are not likely to be extendable to a point that will bring about human-level intelligence. The shifts are toward massively parallel computers and toward massively parallel programs that are more taught than programmed. The resultant hardware and software systems seem in many ways more brainlike than the serial von Neumann machines and AI programs that we have become used to.

For thirty years, virtually all AI paradigms were based on variants of what Herbert Simon and Allen Newell have presented as "physical symbol system" and "heuristic search" hypotheses.[2] (See also the article by Hubert and Stuart Dreyfus in this issue of *Dædalus*.)

According to the physical symbol system hypothesis, symbols (wordlike or numerical entities—the names of objects and events) are the primitive objects of the mind; by some unknown process, the brain mimics a "logical inference engine," whose most important feature is that it is able to manipulate symbols (that is, to remember, interpret, modify, combine, and expand upon them); and computer models that manipulate symbols therefore capture the essential operation of the mind. In this argument it does not matter whether the materials out of which this inference engine is built are transistors or neurons. The only important thing is that they be capable of a universal set of logical operations.[3] The physical symbol system hypothesis in turn rests on a foundation of mathematical results on computability, which can be used to show that if a machine is equivalent to a Turing machine—a simple kind of computational model devised by the pioneering British mathematician Alan Turing—then it is "universal"; that is, the machine can compute anything that can be computed. All ordinary digital computers can be shown to be universal in Turing's sense.*

In the heuristic search model, problems of cognition are instances of the problem of exploring a space of possibilities for a solution. The search space for heuristic search problems can be visualized as a branching tree: starting from the tree's root, each alternative considered and each decision made corresponds to a branching point of the tree. Heuristics, or rules of thumb, allow search to be focused first on branches that are likely to provide a solution, and thus prevent a combinatorially explosive search of an entire solution space.† Heuristic search programs are easy to implement on ordinary serial digital computers. Heuristic search has been used for a wide variety of applications, including decision making, game playing, robot planning and problem solving, natural-language processing, and the classification of perceptual objects. Heuristic search has enjoyed particular prominence, for it is at the heart of "expert systems," AI's greatest commercial success by far.

In retrospect it is remarkable how seriously heuristic search has been taken as a cognitive model. When I was a graduate student in the late 1960s, the standard AI view was that for any intelligent system, the nature of a problem constrains the nature of any efficient solution, and that any system, human or computer, given a problem to solve, tends to evolve a similar, or at least an analogous, internal structure to deal with it. Thus, it was argued, studying efficient problem solutions on computers is a good way to study cognition.[4] Virtually everyone in AI at the time accepted the centrality and immutability of heuristic search machinery unquestioningly and assumed that learning should be accomplished by evolving, adapting, or adding to the heuristics and the knowledge structures of the search space. (The exceptions were the "neural net" and "perceptron" researchers, who had been actively exploring more brainlike models since the early 1950s. More on this later.)

It is now commonly recognized that the nature of the computers and computing models available to us inevitably constrains the problem-solving algorithms that we can consider. (John Backus introduced this idea to the broad computing community in his Turing Award lecture of 1977.[5]) As explained below, it has become clear that traditional AI methods do not scale up well and that new AI paradigms will therefore be needed. Despite this change in attitude, there have been few prospective replacements within AI for heuristic search (or for serial, single-processor digital computers) until very recently.

The reasons AI has focused almost exclusively on the physical symbol system and heuristic search views are deeply rooted in its history and in part reflect the myopic concentration on serial digital computers that has characterized all of computer science. The focus on heuristic search also reflects the influence of the psychological research of the 1950s. AI began at a time when psychologists were much enamored of protocol analysis, a way of examining human behavior by having subjects give accounts of their mental experience while they are solving problems.[6] Such psychological research was interpreted as evidence that the main human mechanism for problem solving is trial and error. AI adapted this model as its heuristic search paradigm. In this paradigm problems are solved by sequentially applying "operators" (elementary steps in a problem solution) and allowing "backtracking," a form of trial and error whereby a program backs up to an earlier decision point and tries new branches if the first ones explored prove fruitless.

It is difficult to see how any extension of heuristic-search-based systems could ever demonstrate common sense. In most AI systems, problem statements have come from users; the systems have not needed to decide what problems to work on. They have had relatively few actions or operators available, so search spaces have been tractable. Real-time performance hasn't generally been necessary. This way of operating will clearly not do in general. Eventually, AI must face the scale-up question: Given the immense range of possible situations a truly intelligent system could find itself in and the vast number of possible actions available to it, how could the system ever manage to search out appropriate goals and actions?

Moreover, as John McCarthy has pointed out, rule-based systems may be inherently limited by the "qualification problem": given a certain general rule, one can always alter the world situation in such a way that the rule is no longer appropriate.[7] For example, suppose we offered the rule:

$bird(x) \rightarrow fly(x)$ (if x is a bird, then x can fly).

Everyone knows that the rule must be amended to cover birds such as penguins and ostriches, so that it becomes:

$not\ flightless(x)\ and\ bird(x) \rightarrow fly(x)$, where "$flightless(x)$" is true of the appropriate birds.

However, we also know a bird cannot fly if it is dead, or if its wings have been pinioned, or if its feet are embedded in cement, or if it has been conditioned by being given electric shocks each time it tries to fly.[8] There seems to be no way to ever completely specify rules for such cases. There are also serious difficulties in formulating rules for deciding which facts about the world ought to be retracted and which should still hold after particular events or actions have occurred. This is known as the "frame problem." "Nonmonotonic logic," which treats all new propositions or rules as retractable hypotheses, has been proposed for dealing with these problems.[9] However, some researchers in this area[10] are pessimistic about its potential, as am I.

By objecting to traditional AI approaches, I am not disputing the notions of universal computation or the Turing machine results, which are established mathematically beyond doubt. Rather, I dispute the heuristic search metaphor, the relationship between physical symbol systems and human cognition, and the nature and "granularity" of the units of thought. The physical symbol system hypothesis, also long shared by AI researchers, is that a vocabulary close to natural language (English, for example, perhaps supplemented by previously unnamed categories and concepts) would be sufficient to express all concepts that ever need to be expressed. My belief is that natural-language-like terms are, for some concepts, hopelessly coarse and vague, and that much finer, "subsymbolic" distinctions must be made, especially for encoding sensory inputs. At the same time, some mental units (for example, whole situations or events—often remembered as mental images) seem to be important carriers of meaning that may not be reducible to tractable structures of words or wordlike entities. Even worse, I believe that words are not in any case carriers of complete meanings but are instead more like index terms or cues that a speaker uses to induce a listener to extract shared memories and knowledge. The degree of detail and number of units needed to express the speaker's knowledge and intent and the hearer's understanding are vastly greater than the number of words used to communicate. In this sense language may be like the game of charades: the speaker transmits relatively little, and the listener generates understanding through the synthesis of the memory items evoked by the speaker's clues. Similarly, I believe that the words that seem widely characteristic of human streams of consciousness do not themselves constitute thought; rather, they represent a projection of our thoughts onto our speech-production faculties. Thus, for example, we may feel happy or embarrassed without ever forming those words, or we may solve a problem by imagining a diagram without words or with far too few words to specify the diagram.

What's the alternative?

Craig Stanfill and I have argued at length elsewhere that humans may well solve problems by a process much more like *lookup* than *search*, and that the items looked up may be much more like representations of specific or stereotyped episodes and objects than like rules and facts.[11]

On the Connection Machine, built by Thinking Machines Corporation,[12] we have now implemented several types of "associative memory" systems that reason on the basis of previous experience.[13] For example, one experimental system solves medical diagnosis problems with "memory-based reasoning": given a set of symptoms and patient characteristics, the system finds the most similar previous patients and hypothesizes that the same diagnoses should be given to the new patient. "Connectionist," or neural net, models, which I shall describe later, solve similar problems, though in a very different manner. While a great deal of research is still required before such systems can become serious candidates for truly intelligent systems, I believe that these architectures may prove far easier to build and extend than heuristic search models. These new models can learn and reason by remembering and generalizing specific examples; heuristic search models, in contrast, depend on rules. It has proved difficult to collect rules from experts—people are generally not even aware of using rules. We do not know how to check sets of rules for completeness and self-consistency. Moreover, a finite set of rules cannot capture all the possible conclusions that may be drawn from a set of examples any more than a set of descriptive sentences can completely describe a picture.

It is important to note, however, that some kinds of knowledge in rule-based systems are hard to encode in our memory-based model. For instance, as currently formulated, our system does not use patients' histories and is unable to figure out that medication dose size ought to be a function of a patient's weight. Recent research strongly suggests that humans reason largely from stereotypes and from specific variations of these stereotypes. Our system does not yet demonstrate such abilities.

Implementing associative memory systems

In the short run, associative memory models can very nicely complement AI models. Associative models have been studied for quite a while but seldom implemented (except for very small problems) because they are computationally very expensive to run on traditional digital computers. One class of associative memory implementation is called the connectionist, or neural net, model. Such systems are direct descendants of the neural net models of the 1950s. In them, thousands of processing units, each analogous to a neuron, are interconnected by links, each analogous to a synaptic connection between neurons. Each link has a "weight," or a connection strength. A system's knowledge is encoded in link weights and in the interconnection pattern of the system. Some units serve as input units, some as output units, and others as "hidden units" (they are connected only to other units and thus cannot be "seen" from either the input or the output channels).

Such networks display three interesting abilities. The first is *learning*. Several methods have now been devised that enable such a system, upon being given particular inputs, to be taught to produce any desired outputs. The second interesting ability is *associative recall*. Once trained to associate an output with a certain input, a network can, given some fraction of an input, produce a full pattern as its output. The third interesting property is *fault tolerance*: the network continues to operate even when some of the units are removed or damaged. In short, connectionist computing systems have many of the properties that we have associated with brains; these systems differ significantly from computers, which have traditionally been viewed as automatons with literal minds, able to do only what they are programmed to do.[14]

These networks can now be implemented efficiently on such massively parallel hardware as the Connection Machine system or by using custom chips. While associative memory systems have been simulated on traditional serial digital computers, the simulations have been very slow; a serial computer must simulate each of the computational units and links in turn and must do so many times to carry out a single calculation. A massively parallel machine can provide a separate small processor for each of the units in the associative memory system and can thus operate much more rapidly.

Stanfill and I have been exploring a functionally similar massively parallel method called memory-based reasoning. In this type of reasoning, a Connection Machine is loaded with a large data base of situations. Each situation in the data base contains both a set of attributes and an outcome. In a medical data base, for instance, the attributes would be symptoms and a patient's characteristics, and the outcome would be a diagnosis or a treatment. Each item in the data base is stored in a separate processor. When a new example to be classified is encountered, its properties are broadcast to all the processors that hold situations; each of these processors compares its situation with the input situation and computes a score of nearness to the input. The system then finds the nearest matches to the input example and, provided they are sufficiently close, uses the outcomes of these matching items to classify the new example.

Memory-based reasoning systems also have many desirable characteristics. They are fault tolerant; they can generalize well to examples that have never been seen in their exact form before; they give measurements of the closeness of the precedents to the current example, which can serve as measures of confidence for the match. If there is an exact match with a previous example, the systems can give a decision with certainty. It is easy to teach such systems: one simply adds more items to their data bases.

The complicated part of memory-based reasoning systems is the computation of nearness. To calculate the similarity of any memory example to the pattern to be classified, each memory item must first find the distance, or difference, between each of its attribute values and the attribute values of the pattern to be classified. These distances in turn depend on the statistical distribution of attribute values and on the degree of correlation between each attribute value and the outcomes with which it simultaneously occurs. All the distances for each attribute must then be combined for each memory item to arrive at its total distance from the item to be classified. Thus, computing the nearness score involves a great deal of statistical calculation across all records in the data base.[15]

What is the role of associative memory systems in traditional artificial intelligence? While they can substitute for expert systems under certain circumstances, connectionist and memory-based reasoning systems are better viewed as complements to traditional AI than as replacements for it. In one very useful mode, associative memory systems can be used to propose or hypothesize solutions to complex problems, and traditional AI systems can be used to verify that the differences between the problems that are currently being attacked and examples in the data base are unimportant. If such differences are important, the associative memory systems can propose subgoals to attempt. Thus, the associative memory process can provide a very powerful heuristic method for jumping to conclusions, while traditional AI can be used to verify or disconfirm such conclusions. Such hybrid systems could help AI models avoid the problems of searching combinatorially large spaces. Because of the computational resources required, the bulk of the computing power in an AI system of this sort would probably reside in the associative memory portion.

In the long run, however, such models are still unlikely to provide a satisfactory explanation for the operations of human thought, though I suspect they will come much closer than AI has. To my mind, the best exposition on the ultimate architecture required is Marvin Minsky's "society of mind."[16] Minsky argues persuasively, using a very wide range of types of evidence, that the brain and the mind are made up of a very large number of modules organized like a bureaucracy. Each module, or "demon," in the bureaucracy has only limited responsibilities and very limited knowledge; demons constantly watch for events of interest to themselves and act only when such events occur. These events may be external (signaled by sensory units) or purely internal (the result of other internal demons that have recognized items of interest to themselves). Actions of demons can either influence other demons or activate effectors and can thereby influence the outside world. One can make a simple analogy between a society of mind and associative memory models: in memory-based reasoning each data base item would correspond to an agent; in a connectionist model, each neural unit would correspond to an agent.

Logical reasoning

I believe logical reasoning is not the foundation on which cognition is built but an emergent behavior that results from observing a sufficient number of regularities in the world. Thus, if a society of demonlike agents exhibits logical behavior, its behavior can be described by rules, although the system contains no rules to govern its operation. It operates in a regular fashion because it simulates the world's regularities.

Consider a developing infant. In the society-of-mind model, the infant first develops a large number of independent agencies that encode knowledge of the behavior of specific items in the physical world: when a block is dropped, it falls; when the child cries, its parent comes to attend; when the child touches a flame, it feels pain. Each of these examples is handled initially by a separate small bureaucracy of agents. Each bureaucracy represents the memory of some specific event. A particular agency becomes responsible for an episode because of the initial "wiring" of the brain; shortly after an agency is first activated, it changes its synaptic weights, so that any new event that activates any part of the agency will cause the entire agency to be reactivated. When similar events reactivate these agencies, new bureaucracies encoding the similarities and differences between the new and the old events are constructed out of previously unused, but closely connected (hence activated), agents. After many such incremental additions to the society of agents, a child eventually develops agents for abstract categories and rules; cuts, pinches, and burns all cause pain, and thus other agents that happen to be activated in these cases become associated with the concept of pain. Eventually, the concepts of the constant conjunction of pain with its various causes become the specialty of particular "expert" agents responsible for certain regularities in the world. Ultimately, these agents become part of the bureaucracy for the concept of causality itself. Thus agents come to reason about very general categories, no longer necessarily rooted directly in experience, and can understand abstract causal relationships. Take pain in the abstract, for example: if one breaks a law and is apprehended, one knows one will probably be punished; if one does not keep promises, one understands that other people may be angry and may retaliate; and so on.

On the surface it might seem that what is being proposed is to replace a single expert program with many expert programs, arranged in a hierarchy. However, each of the expert agents is extremely simple, in the sense that it "knows" only about one thing. The experts are connected to a perceptual system and to each other in such a way that they are triggered only when the conditions about which they are expert are actually satisfied.

While this may be a satisfactory description of the composition of the mind, it is not yet sufficiently precise to serve as a design for a very large-scale program that can organize itself to achieve intelligence. Programs that operate on the principles of the society of mind may well be the end point of many steps in the evolution of the design of intelligent systems. I believe that hybrids of associative memory and traditional AI programs for logical reasoning show the greatest promise in the near term for AI applications. It is possible that they will also prove to be useful models of cognition.[17]

Limits of traditional computer hardware

Researchers' suspicion that current AI models may not be extensible to systems with human-level intelligence is not the only force driving the paradigm shift toward massively parallel computing models. Economic considerations, which transcend AI concerns, are another. Today's serial computers have begun to reach limits beyond which they cannot be speeded up at reasonable cost. For a serial, single-processor computer to operate more rapidly than at present, its processor must execute each instruction more rapidly. To accelerate processing, manufacturers have brought new, faster-acting materials into use. They have also shrunk circuits to smaller and smaller sizes so as to shorten signal paths, since internal communication speeds, and therefore overall processing rates, are limited by the speed of light. The smaller the computer, the faster its internal communications. Because each component generates heat, and because dense chips produce more heat than others, ultradense chips of exotic materials often require the addition of elaborate and expensive cooling systems. All this means that doubling the power of a serial machine usually increases its cost by more than a factor of two—sometimes much more.

In contrast, parallel designs promise the possibility of doubling power by simply doubling the number of processors, possibly for less than two times the cost, since many system components (disk storage units, power supplies, control logic, and so on) can be shared by all processors, no matter how numerous. For example, the Connection Machine system contains up to 65,536 processors. Even in its initial version, the Connection Machine is very inexpensive in terms of the number of dollars it costs per unit of computation; its cost in relation to its performance is about one-twentieth that of serial supercomputers.‡ Moreover, the cost of highly parallel processors is likely to drop dramatically. Initially, any chip is expensive because of low yield (only a fraction of usable chips results from initial production) and the need to recover research, design, and development costs. The price of chips follows a "learning curve," a drop-off in cost as a function of the number of chips fabricated. Memory is the prime example: the cost per bit of memory storage has dropped by a factor of ten every five years for thirty-five years running, yielding a cost that is one ten-millionth that of the 1950 price—one one-hundred millionth after adjustment for inflation! Since the processors of a massively parallel computer are mass-produced, as memory chips are, the cost of a given amount of processing power for parallel machines should drop as rapidly as the cost of memory—that is, very rapidly indeed.

The cost of computer systems involves, of course, both hardware and software. How is one to program a machine with tens of thousands or perhaps millions of processors? Clearly, human programmers cannot afford the time or the money to write a program for each processor. There seem to be two practical ways to program such machines. The first, which has been in most use to date, is to write a single program and have each processor execute it in synchrony, each processor working on its own portion of the data. This method is "data-level parallelism." A second way is to program learning machines that can turn their experiences into a different code or data for each processor.

Research in machine learning has grown dramatically during the last few years. Researchers have identified perhaps a dozen distinctly different learning methods.[18] Many massively parallel learning schemes involve the connectionist, or neural net, models mentioned earlier. Connectionist systems have usually been thought with some form of supervised learning: an input and a desired output are both presented to a system, which then adjusts the internal connection strengths among its neuronlike units so as to closely match the desired input-output behavior. Given a sufficiently large number of trials, generally on the order of tens of thousands, such systems are able to learn to produce moderately complex desired behavior. For example, after starting from a completely random state and being trained repeatedly with a 4,500-word data base of sample pronunciations, a system called NETtalk was able to learn to pronounce novel English words with fairly good accuracy.[19]

The central problem to be solved in connectionist and society-of-mind learning research is the "credit assignment problem," the problem of apportioning simple rewards and punishments among a vast number of interconnected neuronlike computing elements. To show the relevance of this problem to the ultimate goals of AI, I will couch the problem in terms of the "brain" of a robotic system that we hope will learn through its experiences.

Assume a large set (perhaps billions) of independent neural-like processing elements interconnected with many links per element. Some elements are connected to sensors, driven by the outside world; others are connected to motor systems that can influence the outside world through robotic arms and legs or wheels, which generate physical acts, as well as through language-production facilities, which generate "speech acts." At any given time a subset of these elements is active; they form a complex pattern of activation over the entire network. A short time later, the activation pattern changes because of the mutual influences among processing elements and sensory inputs.

Some activation patterns trigger motor actions. Now and then rewards or punishments are given to the system. The credit assignment problem is this: which individual elements within the mass of perhaps trillions of elements should be altered on the basis of these rewards and punishments so the system will learn to perform more effectively—that is, so the situations that have led to punishments can be avoided in the future and so the system will more often find itself in situations that lead to rewards?

The credit assignment problem has at least two aspects. The simpler is the *static* credit assignment problem, in which rewards and punishment occur shortly after the actions that cause them. Such systems receive instant gratification and instant negative feedback. The static credit assignment problem has been found reasonably tractable: units that are active can be examined, and those that have been active in the correct direction have their connections with action systems strengthened, while those that have been inappropriately active have their connection strengths reduced. If the reward or punishment occurs substantially after the fact, however, we have a *temporal* credit assignment problem, which is significantly more difficult. To solve this problem, a system must keep memories of the past states through which it has passed and have the capacity to analyze and make judgments about which earlier states were responsible for the rewards and punishments. Progress on the temporal credit assignment problem has been promising, but much remains to be done before it can be considered solved.[20]

In my estimation, these learning methods will only be suitable for producing modules of an overall intelligent system. A truly intelligent system must contain many modules. It seems very unlikely that the organization of an entire brain or mind could be automatically learned, starting with a very large, randomly interconnected system. Infants are highly organized at birth. They do not, for instance, have to learn to see or hear in any sense that we would recognize as learning. Their auditory and visual systems seem already organized to be able to extract meaningful units (objects, events, sounds, shapes, and so on). Elizabeth Spelke and her research associates have found that two-month-old infants are able to recognize the coherence of objects and that they show surprise when objects disappear or apparently move through each other.[21] At that age they cannot have learned about the properties of objects through tactile experience. It is not too surprising that such abilities can be "prewired" in the brain: newborn horses and cattle are able to walk, avoid bumping into objects, and find their mother's milk within minutes of birth. In any case, the necessity for providing intelligent systems with a priori sensory organization seems inescapable. On what other basis could we learn from scratch what the meaningful units of the world are?[22]

The future of artificial intelligence

Any extrapolation of current trends forces one to conclude that it will take a very long time indeed to achieve systems that are as intelligent as humans. Nevertheless, the performance of the fastest computers seems destined to increase at a much greater rate than it has over the last thirty years, and the cost/performance figures for large-scale computers will certainly drop.

The effect of a great deal more processing power should be highly significant for AI. As claimed earlier, current machines probably have only one four-millionth the amount of computing power that the human brain has. However, it is quite conceivable that within about twenty-five years we could build machines with comparable power for affordable prices (for the purposes of this argument, let an affordable price be $20 million, the cost of today's most expensive supercomputer).

The Connection Machine system, currently probably the fastest in the world, can carry out the kinds of calculations we think the brain uses at the rate of about 3.6×10^{12} bits a second, a factor of about twenty million away from matching the brain's power (as estimated by Jack Schwartz in his article in this issue of *Dædalus*). One may build a more powerful Connection Machine system simply by plugging several of them together. The current machine costs about $4 million, so within our $20 million budget, a machine of about five times its computing power (or 1.8×10^{13} bits per second) could be built. Such a machine would be a factor of four million short. The stated goal of the DARPA (Defense Advanced Research Projects Agency) Strategic Computing Initiative is to achieve a thousandfold increase in computing power over the next ten years, and there is good reason to expect that this goal can be achieved. In particular, the Connection Machine system achieves its computation rates without yet using exotic materials or extreme miniaturization, the factors that have enabled us to so dramatically speed up traditional computers. If a speedup of one thousand times every ten years can be achieved, a computer comparable in processing power to the brain could be built for $20 million by 2012.

Using Schwartz's estimates, we find that the total memory capacity of the brain is 4×10^{16} bytes. The current Connection Machine can contain up to two gigabytes (2×10^9 bytes). In today's computer world, two gigabytes of memory is considered a large amount, yet this is a factor of twenty million short, or a factor of four million short for a system with five Connection Machines.

At today's prices, two gigabytes of memory costs roughly $1 million, so to buy enough memory to match human capacity would cost on the order of $20 trillion, roughly ten times our current national debt. Given its long-term price decline of roughly a factor of ten every five years, the cost of 4×10^{16} bytes of memory will be in the $20 million range within thirty years, so that the time at which we might expect to build a computer with the potential to match human intelligence would be around the year 2017.§ As suggested earlier, however, building the hardware may be the easiest part; the need to untangle the mysteries of the structure and functioning of the mind, to gather the knowledge both innate and learned, and to engineer the software for the entire system will probably require time that goes well beyond 2017. Once we have a piece of hardware with brain-level power and appropriate a priori structure, it still might take as long as the twenty years humans require to reach adult-level mental competence! More than one such lengthy experiment is likely to be required.

What could we expect the intelligence of such powerful machines to be like? Almost certainly they will seem alien when compared with people. In some ways such machines will eclipse maximum human performance, much as pocket calculators outperform humans in arithmetic calculation. The new machines may have perfect recall of vast quantities of information, something that is not possible for people. (While humans apparently have vast amounts of memory, we are quite poor at the literal memorization of words, images, names, and details of events.) Unless deliberately programmed in, such machines would not have a repertoire of recognizable human emotions. Nor would they have motivation in any ordinary human sense. Motivation and drive seem to be based on innate mechanisms developed over eons of evolution to ensure that we make species-preserving decisions—to avoid pain, continue to eat and drink, get enough sleep, reproduce, care for our young, act altruistically (especially towards relatives and friends)—without requiring that we understand that the real reason for carrying out these actions is species preservation.[23] (It is, however, quite possible that it will prove useful to endow machines capable of problem solving and learning with the ability to experience some analogues of frustration, pleasure at achieving a goal, confusion, and other such emotion-related attitudes toward emergent phenomena in order that they can generate useful abstractions for deciding when to abandon a task, ask for advice, or give up.)

AI researchers can grasp the opportunity to build human-level intelligent machines only if they find ways to fill prodigious quantities of memory with important material. They will be able to do so only if AI can produce adequate sensory systems (for hearing, vision, touch, kinesthesia, smell, and taste). With sensory systems, AI systems will for the first time be able to learn from experience. Such experience may initially be little more than rote memory—that is, storing records of the partially digested sensory patterns seen by the system. Yet, as argued earlier, the storage of vast amounts of relatively literal material may be a key to intelligent behavior. The potential for artificial intelligence depends on the possibility of building systems that no longer require programming in the same sense that it is now required. Then we could overcome the tendency of systems development to be very slow because of software engineering difficulties.

There is also the question of what kind of "body" such an intelligence must be embedded in for it to really understand rather than to merely simulate understanding. Must the machine be wired to have emotions if it is to understand our human emotional reactions? If a machine were immortal, could it understand our reactions to our knowledge of our own mortality? Intelligent machines might be cloned by simply copying their programming or internal coding onto other identical pieces of hardware. There is no human analogue to a machine that would have experience as a unitary entity for an extended period and then, at some point during its "lifetime," suddenly become many separate entities, each with different experiences. Exactly what kind of intelligence this would be is therefore an open question.

Summary

We are nearing an important milestone in the history of life on earth, the point at which we can construct machines with the potential for exhibiting an intelligence comparable to ours. It seems certain that we will be able to build hardware that is a match for human computational power for an affordable price within the next thirty years or so. Such hardware will without doubt have profound consequences for industry, defense, government, the arts, and our images of ourselves.

Having hardware with brain-level power will not in itself, however, lead to human-level intelligent systems, since the architecture and programs for such systems also present unprecedented obstacles. It is difficult to extrapolate to future effects from the rate of progress that has been made to date. Progress has been very slow, in part because the computational models that have been used have been inappropriate to the task. This inappropriateness applies most critically to the problem of learning. Without learning, systems must be handbuilt. We don't know how closely we must match human brain details to foster appropriate learning and performance. With the right architectures, it is likely that progress, both in the building of adequately powerful hardware and in programming such hardware (by teaching), will accelerate. I believe that the construction of truly intelligent machines is sufficiently likely to justify beginning study and policy planning now. In that way we can maximize their benefits and minimize their negative effects on society.

Notes

* There is perhaps one critical aspect in which all computers fail to match a Turing machine: the Turing machine includes an infinite tape, from which it reads its programs and onto which it writes its results. All computers (and presumably humans) have finite memories.

† Combinatorially explosive problems are problems in which the computational costs of solving each slightly more difficult problem grow so rapidly that no computer will ever be able to solve them; that is, even a computer with as many components as there are electrons in the universe and an instruction execution time as short as the shortest measurable physical event might require times greater than the age of the universe to consider all possible problem solutions.

‡ The cost/performance figure is the cost per standard computing operation. The typical standard computing operation is either a fixed-point addition or a floating-point multiplication. Fixed-point performance is measured in millions of instructions per second (MIPS). Floating point performance is measured in millions of floating operations per second (MFLOPS—pronounced "megaflops"). Cost/performance is measured in dollars per MIPS or dollars per MFLOPS.

§ Well before the 2017 date, however, mass storage devices (disk units and other storage media) will certainly be capable of storing this much material at an affordable price.

1 Frederick P. Brooks, *The Mythical Man-Month: Essays on Software Engineering* (Reading, Mass.: Addison-Wesley, 1974).

2 Allen Newell and Herbert Simon, *Human Problem Solving* (Englewood Cliffs, N.J.: Prentice-Hall, 1972).

3 The Boolean operations AND, OR, and NOT constitute a universal set. NAND (NOT AND) also is universal by itself, as is NOR (NOT OR). For a derivation of this result see Marvin L. Minsky, *Computation: Finite and Infinite Machines* (Cambridge: MIT Press, 1967).

4 Herbert A. Simon, *The Sciences of the Artificial* (Cambridge: MIT Press, 1965).

5 John Backus, "Can Programming Be Liberated from the von Neumann Style? A Functional Style and its Algebra of Programs," *Communications of the ACM* 21 (8) (August 1978):613–41.

6 George A. Miller, Eugene Galanter, and Karl Pribram, *Plans and the Structure of Behavior* (New York: Holt, Rinehart, and Winston, 1954).

7 John McCarthy, "Epistemological Problems in Artificial Intelligence," in *Proceedings of the Fifth International Joint Conference on Artificial Intelligence* (Los Altos, Calif.: Morgan-Kaufman, August 1977), 1038–44.

8 Example from Marvin Minsky, personal communication.

9 John McCarthy, "Circumscription—A Form of Nonmonotonic Reasoning," *Artificial Intelligence* 13 (1) (1980):27–39; and Drew V. McDermott and Jon Doyle, "Nonmonotonic Logic 1," *Artificial Intelligence* 13 (1) (1980):41–72.

10 Steve Hanks and Drew V. McDermott, "Default Reasoning, Nonmonotonic Logics, and the Frame Problem," in *Proceedings of the Fifth National Conference on Artificial Intelligence* (Los Altos, Calif.: Morgan-Kaufmann, August 1986), 328–33.

11 Craig Stanfill and David L. Waltz, "Toward Memory-Based Reasoning," *Communications of the ACM* 29 (12) (December 1986):1213–28.

12 W. Daniel Hillis, *The Connection Machine* (Cambridge: MIT Press, 1986).

13 David E. Rumelhart, James L. McClelland, and the PDP Research Group, eds., *Parallel Distributed Processing: Explorations in the Microstructure of Cognition*, vols. 1, 2 (Cambridge: MIT Press, 1986).

14 For extended treatment of such systems, see Rumelhart and McClelland, *Parallel Distributed Processing*, and the special issue on connectionist models of *Cognitive Science* 9 (1) (1985).

15 For details, see Stanfill and Waltz, "Toward Memory-Based Reasoning."

16 Marvin L. Minsky, *The Society of Mind* (New York: Simon and Schuster, 1986); *The Hedonistic Neuron: A Theory of Memory, Learning, and Intelligence*, by A. Harry Klopf (Washington, D.C.: Hemisphere, 1982), presents a compatible neural theory.

17 There is also a fairly extensive literature on learning and knowledge acquisition. It is based on the heuristic search and physical symbol system paradigms. Broadly speaking, these learning algorithms fall into three categories. The first type is statistical and uses a large number of processors to find patterns or regularities in data bases of examples—in medical diagnosis, weather forecasting, and decision making, for example. Three systems that fall into this category are the ID3 system of Ross Quinlan and the systems built by Ryszard Michalski, both of which are described in Ryszard S. Michalski, Jaime Carbonell, and Thomas Mitchell, eds., *Machine Learning: An Artificial Intelligence Approach* (Los Altos, Calif.: Tioga Publishing Company, 1983), and the "memory-based reasoning" system of Craig Stanfill and David Waltz (see Stanfill and Waltz, "Toward Memory-Based Reasoning"). A second type of learning algorithm uses "production rules" (sometimes termed "if-then rules") and learns by adding to and modifying an existing set of such rules. The rules are changed by providing "experience," which may include "rewards and punishments." Such systems can also be taught by giving them correct examples from which they can learn rules by rote. Two systems of this sort are the genetic algorithms of John Holland (see John H. Holland, *Adaptation in Natural and Artificial Systems: An Introductory Analysis with Applications to Biology, Control and Artificial Intelligence* [Ann Arbor: University of Michigan Press, 1975]) and the SOAR system of Allen Newell and Paul Rosenbloom (see John E. Laird, Paul S. Rosenbloom, and Allen Newell, "Chunking and SOAR: The Anatomy of a General Learning Mechanism," *Machine Learning* 1 [1] [1986]:11–46). The third branch is "explanation-based learning" (see Gerald F. DeJong and Raymond A. Mooney, "Explanation-Based Learning: An Alternative View," *Machine Learning* 1 [2] [April 1986]:145–76). An explanation-based learning system attempts to build causal structures, or "schemata," as explanations of new phenomena and as elements for building new schemata.

18 One of the most successful learning methods is the centerpiece of McClelland and Rumelhart's *Parallel Distributed Processing*. Other systems include Stephen Grossberg's, Andrew Barto's, and Geoffrey Hinton's. See Stephen Grossberg, "Competitive Learning: From Interactive Activation to Adaptive Resonance," *Cognitive Science* 11 (1) (January–March 1987):23–64; Andrew G. Barto, "Learning by Statistical Cooperation of Self-Interested Neuron-like Computing Elements," *Human Neurobiology* 4 (1985):229–56; and Geoffrey Hinton, "The Boltzmann Machine," in Geoffrey E. Hinton and John A. Anderson, eds., *Parallel Models of Associative Memory* (Hillsdale, N.J.: Lawrence Erlbaum Associates, 1981).

19 Terrence J. Sejnowski and Charles R. Rosenberg, "NET talks: A Parallel Network that Learns to Read Aloud," Technical Report JHU/EECS-86–01 (Baltimore,

Md.: Johns Hopkins University, Electrical Engineering and Computer Science, 1986).

20 Ronald J. Williams, "Reinforcement-Learning Connectionist Systems: A Progress Report" (unpublished manuscript, College of Computer Science, Northeastern University, November 1986).

21 Elizabeth Spelke, "Perceptual Knowledge of Objects in Infancy," in Jacques Mehler, Edward C. T. Walker, and Merrill Garrett, eds., *Perspectives on Mental Representation: Experimental and Theoretical Studies of Cognitive Processes and Capacities* (Hillsdale, N.J.: Lawrence Erlbaum Associates, 1962).

22 In the *Critique of Pure Reason* Immanuel Kant argues essentially this point: that "the innate forms of human perception and the innate categories of human understanding impose an invariant order on the initial chaos of raw sensory experience." This is quoted from Paul M. Churchland in *Matter and Consciousness* (Cambridge: MIT Press, 1984), 84.

23 See Isaac Asimov, *I, Robot* (New York: The New American Library of World Literature, 1950), 6, for an early exploration of the need for a kind of ethics for robots, embodied in three laws of robotics:

> 1. A robot may not injure a human being, or, through inaction, allow a human being to come to harm; 2. A robot must obey the orders given it by human beings except where such orders would conflict with the First Law; 3. A robot must protect its own existence as long as such protection does not conflict with the First or Second Law.

Ironic, alas, for the first highly intelligent mobile robot will probably be embedded in tanks and fighter aircraft.

44

CONNECTIONISM AND THE FOUNDATIONS OF AI

Paul Smolensky

Source: D. Partridge, *The Foundations of Artificial Intelligence: A Sourcebook*, Cambridge University Press, 1990, pp. 306–326.

There are few principles on which nearly all practitioners of AI will agree. One of them is that intelligence is the formal manipulations of symbols. This nearly unanimous consensus is being systematically challenged by an approach to AI that models intelligence as the passing of numerical *activation values* within a large network of simple parallel processors. In this *connectionist* approach to AI, intelligence is an *emergent property* of the network's processing: each individual processor has no intelligence, and the messages they exchange – real numbers – participate only in very simple numerical operations. Input to the network is coded as a set of numerical activity values on the input processors, and after this activity has propagated through the connections in the network, a pattern of activity appears on the output processors: this pattern encodes the system's output for the given input. Each connection between processing units has a numerical strength or *weight*; each unit typically computes its activity by using these weights to form the weighted sum of the activity of all the units giving it input, and passing this weighted sum through a non-linear response function such as a threshold or sigmoid curve.

This paper addresses the sense in which intelligence is supposed to "emerge" in these connectionist systems, and the relation that this implies between the connectionist and traditional approaches to AI. The characterization I will formulate for a connectionist approach to AI is controversial in certain respects, and is *not intended as a consensus connectionist view*. A sample of connectionist research that by and large fits with the framework I will describe can be found in the books, *Parallel Distributed Processing: Explorations in the Microstructure of Cognition* (Rumelhart, McClelland, and the PDP Research Group, 1986; McClelland, Rumelhart, and the PDP Research Group, 1986).

A few comments on terminology: I will refer to the traditional approach to AI as the *symbolic paradigm*, intending to emphasize that in this approach, cognitive descriptions are built of entities that are *symbols* both in the semantic sense of referring to external objects and in the syntactic sense of being operated upon by "symbol manipulation." The connectionist approach I will formulate will be called the *subsymbolic paradigm*; the term "subsymbolic" is intended to suggest cognitive descriptions built up of *constituents* of the symbols used in the symbolic paradigm; these fine-grained constituents might be called *subsymbols*. Entities that are typically represented in the symbolic paradigm by symbols are typically represented in the subsymbolic paradigm by a large number of subsymbols. Along with this semantic distinction comes a syntactic distinction. Subsymbols are not operated upon by "symbol manipulation": they participate in numerical – not symbolic – computation. Operations that in the symbolic paradigm consist of a single discrete operation (e.g. a memory fetch) are often achieved in the subsymbolic paradigm as the result of a large number of much finer-grained (numerical) operations.

Most of the foundational issues surrounding the connectionist approach turn, in one way or another, on the *level of analysis* adopted. Since the level of cognitive analysis adopted by the subsymbolic paradigm for formulating connectionist models is lower than the level traditionally adopted by the symbolic paradigm, for the purposes of relating these two paradigms it is often important to analyze connectionist models at a higher level; to amalgamate, so to speak, the subsymbols into symbols. While the symbolic and subsymbolic paradigms each have their preferred level of analysis, the cognitive models they offer can each be described at multiple levels. It is therefore useful to have distinct names for the levels: I will call the preferred level of the symbolic paradigm the *conceptual level* and that of the subsymbolic paradigm the *subconceptual level*. These names are not ideal, but will be further motivated in the course of characterizing these levels. A primary goal of this paper is to articulate a coherent set of hypotheses about the subconceptual level: the kind of cognitive descriptions that are used, the computational principles that apply, and the relations between the subconceptual and conceptual levels.

The choice of level greatly constrains the appropriate formalism for analysis. Probably the most striking feature of the connectionist approach is the change in formalism relative to the symbolic paradigm. Since the birth of cognitive science and AI, *language* has provided the dominant theoretical model. Formal cognitive models have taken their structure from the syntax of formal languages, and their content from the semantics of natural language. The mind has been taken to be a machine for formal symbol manipulation, and the symbols manipulated have assumed essentially the same semantics as words of English.

The subsymbolic paradigm challenges both the syntactic and semantic role of language in AI. Section 1 formulates this challenge. Alternative fillers are described for the roles language has traditionally played in AI, and the new role left to language is delimited. The fundamental hypotheses defining the subsymbolic paradigm are formulated, and the question is considered of whether it can offer anything fundamentally new. Section 2 briefly discusses the preferred level of the subsymbolic paradigm, the subconceptual level, and its relation to the neural level. Section 3 elaborates briefly on the computational principles that apply at the subconceptual level. Section 4 discusses how higher, conceptual-level descriptions of subsymbolic models approximate symbolic models (under their conceptual-level descriptions).

There is not space here to consider a number of important issues: the characterization of what makes a system *cognitive* at the subconceptual level; the implications of the subsymbolic paradigm for explanations of cognitive behavior, for semantics, for rationality, and for the constituent structure of mental states; the subsymbolic approach to modeling the conscious use of rules. For treatment of these issues, the reader is referred to Smolensky (1988).

In this paper I have tried to typographically isolate concise formulations of the main points. Most of these numbered points serve to characterize the subsymbolic paradigm, but a few define opposing points of view; to avoid confusion, the latter have been explicitly tagged: *to be rejected.*

1 Formalization of knowledge

1.1 Cultural knowledge and conscious rule interpretation

What is an appropriate formalization of the knowledge cognitive agents possess and the means by which they use that knowledge to perform cognitive tasks? As a starting point, we can look to those knowledge formalizations that predate AI and cognitive science. The most formalized knowledge is found in sciences like physics that rest on mathematical principles. Domain knowledge is formalized in linguistic structures like "energy is conserved" (or an appropriate encryption), and logic formalizes the use of that knowledge to draw conclusions. Knowledge consists of axioms, and drawing conclusions consists of proving theorems.

This method of formulating knowledge and drawing conclusions has extremely valuable properties:

(1) a. *Public access*: the knowledge is accessible to many people.
   b. *Reliability*: different people (or the same person at different times) can reliably check whether conclusions have been validly reached.
   c. *Formality; bootstrapping, universality*: the inference operations require very little experience with the domain to which the symbols refer.

These three properties are important for science because science is a *cultural activity*. It is of limited social value to have knowledge that resides purely in one individual (1a). It is of questionable social value to have knowledge formulated in such a way that different users draw different conclusions (e.g. can't agree that an experiment falsifies a theory) (1b). For cultural propagation of knowledge, it is helpful if novices with little or no experience with a task can be given a means for performing that task, and thereby a means for acquiring experience (1c).

There are other cultural activities besides science with similar requirements. The laws of a nation and the rules of an organization are also linguistically formalized procedures for effecting action which different people can carry out with reasonable reliability. In all these cases, the goal is to create an abstract decision system that resides outside any single person.

Thus *at the cultural level* the goal is to express knowledge in a form that can be executed reliably by different people, even inexperienced ones. We can view the top-level conscious processor of individual people as a *virtual machine* – the *conscious rule interpreter* – and we can view cultural knowledge as a program that runs on that machine. Linguistic formulations of knowledge are perfect for this purpose. The procedures different people can reliably execute are explicit, step-by-step linguistic instructions. This is what has been formalized in the theory of *effective procedures*. Thanks to property (1c), the top-level conscious human processor can be idealized as *universal*: capable of executing any effective procedure. The theory of effective procedures – the classical theory of computation – is physically manifest in the von Neumann computer. One can say that the von Neumann computer is a machine for automatically following the kind of explicit instructions that people can fairly reliably follow – but much faster and with perfect reliability.

Thus we can understand why the production system of computation theory, or more generally the von Neumann computer, has provided a successful model of how people execute instructions (e.g. models of novice physics problem-solving such as Larkin, McDermott, Simon and Simon, 1980). In short, when people (e.g. novices) consciously and sequentially follow rules (e.g. that they have been taught), their cognitive processing is naturally modeled as the sequential interpretation[1] of a linguistically formalized procedure. The rules being followed are expressed in terms of the consciously accessible concepts with which the task domain is conceptualized. In this sense, the rules are formulated at the *conceptual level* of analysis.

To sum up:

(2) a. Rules formulated in natural language can provide an effective formalization of cultural knowledge.

   b. Conscious rule application can be modeled as the sequential interpretation of such rules by a virtual machine called the conscious rule interpreter.

    c. These rules are formulated in terms of the concepts consciously used to describe the task domain – they are formulated at the conceptual level.

1.2 Individual knowledge, skill, and intuition in the symbolic paradigm

But the constraints on *cultural knowledge formalization* are not the same as those on *individual knowledge formalization*. The intuitive knowledge in a physics expert or a native speaker may demand, for a truly accurate description, a formalism that is not a good one for cultural purposes. After all, the individual knowledge in an expert's head does not possess the properties (1) of cultural knowledge: it is not publicly accessible, is not completely reliable, and is completely dependent on ample experience. Individual knowledge is a program that runs on a virtual machine that need not be the same as the top-level conscious processor that runs the cultural knowledge. By definition, conclusions reached by intuition do not come from conscious application of rules, and intuitive processing need not have the same character as conscious rule application.

What kinds of programs are responsible for behavior that is not conscious rule application? I will refer to the virtual machine that runs these programs as the *intuitive processor*. It is (presumably) responsible for all of animal behavior, and a huge portion of human behavior: perception, practiced motor behavior, fluent linguistic behavior, intuition in problem-solving and game-playing – in short, practically all of skilled performance. The transference of responsibility from the conscious rule interpreter to the intuitive processor during the acquisition of skill is one of the most striking and well-studied phenomena in cognitive science (e.g. Anderson, 1981). An analysis of the formalization of knowledge must consider both the knowledge involved in novices' conscious application of rules and the knowledge resident in experts' intuition, as well as their relationship.

An appealing possibility is this:

    (3) a. The programs running on the intuitive processor consist of linguistically formalized rules that are sequentially interpreted. (*To be rejected.*)

This has traditionally been the assumption of cognitive science. Native speakers are unconsciously interpreting rules, as are physics experts when they are intuiting answers to problems. Artificial intelligence systems for natural-language processing and problem-solving are programs written in a formal language for the interpretation of symbolic descriptions of procedures for manipulating symbols.

To the syntactic hypothesis (3a) there corresponds a semantic one:

(3) b. The programs running on the intuitive processor are composed of elements – symbols – referring to essentially the same concepts as are used to consciously conceptualize the task domain. (*To be rejected.*)

This applies to production-system models in which the productions representing expert knowledge are complied versions of those of the novice (e.g. Anderson, 1983; Lewis, 1978) and to the bulk of AI programs.

Hypotheses (3a) and (3b) together comprise

(3) **The unconscious rule interpretation hypothesis:** (*To be rejected.*)
The programs running on the intuitive processor have a syntax and semantics comparable to those running on the conscious rule interpreter.

This hypothesis has provided the foundation for the symbolic paradigm for cognitive modeling. Cognitive models of both conscious rule application and intuitive processing have been programs constructed of entities which are *symbols* both in the syntactic sense of being operated on by "symbol manipulation" and in the semantic sense of (3b). Because these symbols have the conceptual semantics of (3b), I will call the level of analysis at which these programs provide cognitive models the *conceptual level*.

1.3 The subsymbolic paradigm and intuition

The hypothesis of unconscious rule interpretation (3) is an attractive possibility which a connectionist approach to cognitive modeling rejects. Since my purpose here is to formulate rather than argue the scientific merits of a connectionist approach, I will not argue against (3) here. I will point out only that in general, connectionists do not casually reject (3). Several of today's leading connectionist researchers were intimately involved with serious and longstanding attempts to make (3) serve the needs of cognitive science.[2] Connectionists tend to reject (3) because they find the consequences that have actually resulted from its acceptance to be quite unsatisfactory, for a number of quite independent reasons, for example:

(4) a. Actual AI systems built on hypothesis (3) seem too brittle, too inflexible, to model true human expertise.
b. The process of articulating expert knowledge in rules seems impractical for many important domains (e.g. common sense).
c. Hypothesis (3) has contributed essentially no insight into how knowledge is represented in the brain.

What motivates pursuit of connectionist alternatives to (3) are hunches that such alternatives will better serve the goals of cognitive science. Comprehensive empirical assessment of these hunches is probably at least a decade away.

One possible alternative to (3a) is

(5) **The neural architecture hypothesis:** (*To be rejected.*) The intuitive processor for a particular task uses the same architecture that the brain employs for that task.

Whatever appeal this hypothesis might have, it seems incapable in practice of supporting the needs of the vast majority of cognitive models. We simply do not know what architecture the brain uses for performing most cognitive tasks. There may be some exceptions (like vision and spatial tasks), but for problem-solving, language, and many others, (5) simply cannot now do the necessary work.

These points and others relating to the neural level will be deferred to section 2. For now the point is simply that viably characterizing the level of analysis of connectionist modeling is not trivially a matter of identifying it with the neural level. While the level of analysis adopted by most connectionist models is not the conceptual level, it is also not the neural level.

The goal now is to formulate a connectionist alternative to (3) that, unlike (5), provides a viable basis for cognitive modeling. A first, crude cut at this hypothesis is:

(6) The intuitive processor possesses a certain kind of connectionist architecture (which abstractly models a few of the most general features of neural networks). (*To be elaborated.*)

Postponing the parenthetical remark to section 2, we now consider the relevant kind of connectionist architecture.

The kind of connectionist model I will consider can be described as a network of very simple processors, *units*, each possessing a numerical *activation value* that is dynamically determined by the values of the other processors in the network. The *activation equation* governing this interaction has numerical parameters which determine the direction and magnitude of the influence of one activation value on another; these parameters are called the *connection strengths* or *weights*. The activation equation is a differential equation (usually approximated by the finite difference equation that arises from discrete time slices; the issue of discrete approximation is taken up in section 3.1). The weights modulate the behavior of the network: they constitute the "program" for this architecture. A network is sometimes programmed by the modeler, but often a network programs itself to perform a task by changing its weights in response to examples of input/output pairs for the task. The *learning rule* is the differential equation governing the weight changes.

The knowledge in a connectionist system lies in its connection strengths. Thus for the first part of our elaboration on (6) we have the following alternative to (3a):

(7) a. **The connectionist dynamical system hypothesis:** The state of the intuitive processor at any moment is precisely defined by a vector of numerical values (one for each unit). The dynamics of the intuitive processor are governed by a differential equation. The numerical parameters in this equation constitute the processor's program or knowledge. These parameters may change according to a learning equation.

This hypothesis states that the intuitive processor is a certain kind of dynamical system, with the same general character as dynamical systems traditionally studied in physics. The special properties that distinguish this kind of dynamical system – *a connectionist dynamical system* – are only vaguely described in (7a), and a more precise specification is needed. It is premature at this point to commit to such a specification, but one large class of subsymbolic models is that of *quasi-linear dynamical systems*, explicitly discussed in Smolensky (1986b) and Rumelhart, Hinton, and Williams (1986). Each unit in a quasi-linear system computes its value by first calculating the weighted sum of its inputs from other units, and then transforming this sum with a non-linear function. An important goal is to characterize the computational properties of various kinds of connectionist dynamical systems (such as quasi-linear systems) and to thereby determine which kinds provide models of various types of cognitive processes.

The connectionist dynamical system hypothesis (7a) provides a connectionist alternative to the syntactic hypothesis (3a) of the symbolic paradigm. We now need a semantic hypothesis compatible with (7a) to replace (3b). The question is: What does a unit's value *mean*? The most straightforward possibility is that the semantics of each unit is comparable to that of a natural-language word; each unit represents such a concept, and the connection strengths between units reflect the "degree of association" between the concepts.

(8) **The conceptual unit hypothesis:** (*To be rejected.*) Individual intuitive processor elements – individual units – have essentially the same semantics as the conscious rule interpreter's elements – words of natural language.

But (7a) and (8) make an infertile couple. Activation of concepts spreading along "degree of association" links may be adequate for modeling simple aspects of cognition – like relative times for naming words in various contexts, or the relative probabilities of perceiving letters in various contexts – but it cannot be adequate for complex tasks like question-answering or grammaticality judgments. The relevant structures cannot even be feasibly represented in such a network, let alone effectively processed.

Great computational power must be present in the intuitive processor to deal with the many cognitive processes that are extremely complex when described at the conceptual level. The symbolic paradigm, based on hypothesis (3), gets its power by allowing highly complex, essentially arbitrary, operations on symbols with conceptual-level semantics: simple semantics, complex operations. If the operations are required to be as simple as those allowed by hypothesis (7a), we cannot get away with a semantics as simple as that of (8).[3] A semantics compatible with (7a) must be more complicated:

> (7) b. **The subconceptual unit hypothesis**: The entities in the intuitive processor with the semantics of conscious concepts of the task domain are *complex patterns of activity over many units*. Each unit participates in many such patterns.

(See Hinton, McClelland, and Rumelhart, 1986, and several of the papers in Hinton and Anderson, 1981; the neural counterpart is associated with Hebb, 1949 and Lashley, 1950, about which see Feldman, 1986.) The interactions between *individual units* are simple, but these units do not have conceptual semantics: they are *subconceptual*. The interactions between the entities with conceptual semantics – interactions between complex patterns of activity – are not at all simple. Interactions at the level of activity patterns are not directly described by the formal definition of a subsymbolic model; they must be computed by the analyst. Typically, these interactions can be computed only approximately. There will generally be no precisely valid, computable formal principles at the conceptual level; such principles exist only at the level of the units – the *subconceptual level*.

> (7) c. **The subconceptual level hypothesis**: Precise, formal descriptions of the intuitive processor are generally tractable not at the conceptual level, but only at the subconceptual level.

Hypotheses (7a-c) can be summarized as

> (7) **The subsymbolic hypothesis**: The intuitive processor is a subconceptual connectionist dynamical system that does not admit a precise formal conceptual-level description.

This hypothesis is the corner-stone of the subsymbolic paradigm.[4]

1.4 The incompatibility of the symbolic and subsymbolic paradigms

I will now show that the symbolic and subsymbolic paradigms, as formulated above, are incompatible – the hypotheses (3) and (7) about the syntax and semantics of the intuitive processor are not mutually consistent. This issue requires care, since it is well known that one virtual machine can often be implemented in another, that a program written for one machine can be translated into a program for the other. The attempt to distinguish subsymbolic and symbolic computation might well be futile if each can simulate the other. After all, a digital computer is in reality some sort of dynamical system simulating a von Neumann automaton, and in turn digital computers are usually used to simulate connectionist models. Thus it seems possible that the symbolic and subsymbolic hypotheses (3) and (7) are *both* correct: that the intuitive processor can be regarded as a virtual machine for sequentially interpreting rules on one level *and* as a connectionist machine on a lower level.

This possibility fits comfortably within the symbolic paradigm, under a formulation such as

> (9) Valid connectionist models are merely implementations, for a certain kind of parallel hardware, of symbolic programs that provide exact and complete accounts of behavior at the conceptual level. (*To be rejected.*)

However (9) contradicts hypothesis (7c), and is thus fundamentally incompatible with the subsymbolic paradigm. The symbolic programs that (3) hypothesizes for the intuitive processor could indeed be translated for a connectionist machine, but the translated programs would not be the kind of subsymbolic program that (7) hypothesizes.

What about the reverse relationship, where a symbolic program is used to implement a subsymbolic system? Here it is crucial to realize that the symbols in such programs represent the activation values of units and the strengths of connections. By hypothesis (7b), these do not have conceptual semantics, and thus hypothesis (3b) is violated. The subsymbolic programs that (7) hypothesizes for the intuitive processor can be translated for a von Neumann machine, but the translated programs are *not* the kind of symbolic program that (3) hypothesizes.

These arguments show that unless the hypotheses of the symbolic and subsymbolic paradigms are formulated with some care, the substance of the scientific issue at stake can easily be missed. It is well known that von Neumann machines and connectionist networks can simulate each other. If one cavalierly characterizes the approaches *only syntactically*, using (3a) and (7a) alone, then indeed the issue – connectionist or not connectionist – appears to be "one of AI's wonderful red herrings."[5] It is a mistake to claim that the connectionist approach has nothing new to offer cognitive science. The issue at stake is a central one: *Does a complete formal account of cognition lie at the conceptual level?* The answer offered by the subsymbolic paradigm is: *No – it lies at the subconceptual level.*

2 The subconceptual and neural levels

Hypothesis (7b) leaves open important questions about the semantics of subsymbolic systems. What kind of subconceptual features do the units in the intuitive processor represent? Which activity patterns actually correspond to particular concepts?

Each individual subsymbolic model has adopted particular procedures for relating patterns of activity – activity vectors – to the conceptual-level descriptions of inputs and outputs that define the model's task. The vectors chosen are often vectors of values of fine-grained features of the inputs and outputs, based on some pre-existing theoretical analysis of the domain. For example, for the task studied in Rumelhart and McClelland (1986b), transforming root phonetic forms of English verbs to their past-tense forms, the input and output phonetic strings were represented as vectors of values for context-dependent binary phonetic features. The task description at the conceptual level involves consciously available concepts such as the words "go" and "went," while the subconceptual level employed by the model involved a very large number of fine-grained features such as "roundedness preceded by frontalness and followed by backness." The representation of "go" is a large pattern of activity over these features.

Substantive progress in subsymbolic cognitive science requires that systematic commitments to vectorial representations be made for individual cognitive domains. The vectors chosen to represent inputs and outputs crucially affect a model's predictions, since the generalizations the model makes are largely determined by the similarity structure of the chosen vectors. Unlike symbolic tokens, these vectors lie in a topological space, in which some are close together and others far apart.

It might seem that the mapping between patterns of activity and conceptual-level interpretations ought to be determined by neuroscience. This brings us back to the parenthetical comment in (6) and the general issue of the relation between the subconceptual and neural levels. Space does not permit the investigation of this issue here; in Smolensky (1988), the salient features of neural computation are compared to those of typical connectionist AI models, leading to the following conclusions:

(10) a. Unlike the symbolic architecture, the subsymbolic architecture possesses a number of the most general features of the neural architecture.

b. However, the subsymbolic architecture lacks a number of the more detailed but still quite general features of the neural architecture: the subconceptual level of analysis is higher than the neural level.

c. For most cognitive functions, neuroscience cannot now provide the relevant information to specify a cognitive model at the neural level.

d. The general cognitive principles of the subconceptual level will likely be important contributors to future discoveries of those specifications of neural computations that we now lack.

In other words, the study of subsymbolic computational principles is a research program that is likely to inform and be informed by neuroscience, but its value as exploration of a new computational framework for AI stands quite independently of neuroscience.

3 Computation at the subconceptual level

Hypothesis (7a) offers a brief characterization of the connectionist architecture assumed at the subconceptual level by the subsymbolic paradigm. In this section, I consider the computational principles implicit in that hypothesis.

3.1 Continuity

According to (7a), a connectionist dynamical system has a continuous space of states and changes state continuously in time. I would like first to motivate this continuity condition, reconcile it with some apparent counterexamples, and point out some of its implications. Within the symbolic paradigm, the basic, uncomplicated descriptions of a number of cognitive processes assume a quite discrete nature:

(11) a. Discrete memory locations, in which items are stored without mutual interaction.

b. Discrete memory storage and retrieval operations, in which an entire item is stored or retrieved in a single, atomic (primitive) operation.

c. Discrete learning operations, in which new rules become available in an all-or-none fashion.

d. Discrete inference operations, in which new conclusions become available in an all-or-none fashion.

e. Discrete categories, to which items either belong or do not.

f. Discrete production rules, with conditions that are either satisfied or not, and actions that either execute or do not execute.

Cognitive behavior often shows much less discreteness than this. Indeed, cognition seems to be a richly interwoven fabric of continuous and discrete processes. One way to model this interplay is to posit separate discrete and continuous processors in interaction. This approach has a number of theoretical problems: it is difficult to introduce a hard separation between the soft and the hard components of processing. An alternative is to adopt a fundamentally symbolic approach, but to soften various forms of discreteness by hand. For example, the degree of match to conditions of production rules can be given numerical values, productions can be given strengths, interactions between separately stored memory items can be put in by hand, and so on (e.g. see Anderson, 1983).

The subsymbolic paradigm offers another alternative. All the discrete features of (11) are neatly swept aside in one stroke by adopting a fundamentally continuous framework. Then, when the continuous system is analyzed at a higher level, various aspects of discreteness emerge naturally. These aspects of hardness are intrinsically embedded in a fundamentally soft system.

It may appear that the continuous nature of subsymbolic systems is contradicted by the fact that it is easy to find in the literature models that are quite within the spirit of the subsymbolic paradigm but which have neither continuous state spaces nor continuous dynamics: for example, models having units with binary values that jump discretely on the ticks of a discrete clock (e.g. the Boltzman machine, Hinton and Sejnowski, 1983b, Ackley, Hinton and Sejnowski, 1985; harmony theory, Smolensky, 1983, 1986a). I will now argue that these models should be viewed as discrete simulations of an underlying continuous model, considering first discretization of time and then discretization of the units' values.

Dynamical systems evolving in continuous time are nearly always simulated on digital computers by discretizing time. Since subsymbolic models have almost always been simulated on digital computers, it is no surprise that they too have been so simulated. The equations defining the dynamics of the models can be more easily understood by most cognitive scientists if the differential equations of the underlying continuous dynamical system are avoided in favor of the discrete-time approximations that actually get simulated.

When subsymbolic models employ binary-valued units, these values are best viewed not as symbols like T and NIL that are used for conditional branching tests, but as numbers (not numerals!) like 1 and 0 that are used for numerical operations (e.g. multiplication by weights, summation, exponentiation). These models are formulated in such a way that they are perfectly well-defined for continuous values of the units. Discrete numerical unit values is a simplification that is sometimes convenient.

Some dramatic historical evidence for the view that subsymbolic computation should be viewed as fundamentally continuous is a case where switching from discrete to continuous units enabled a revolution in subsymbolic learning theory. In their classic, *Perceptrons*, Minsky and Papert (1969) exploited more or less discrete mathematical methods that were compatible with the choice of binary units. They were incapable of analyzing any but the simplest learning networks. By changing the discrete threshold function of perceptions to a smooth, differentiable curve, and thereby defining continuously-valued units, Rumelhart, Hinton, and Williams (1986) were able to apply continuous analytic methods to more complex learning networks. The result has been a major advance in the power of subsymbolic learning.

The final point is a foundational one. The theory of discrete computation is quite well understood. If there is any new theory of computation implicit in the subsymbolic approach, it is likely to be a result of a fundamentally different, continuous formulation of computation.

It must be emphasized that the discrete/continuous distinction is not to be clearly understood by looking at simulations. Discrete and continuous machines can of course simulate each other. The claim here is that the most analytically powerful descriptions of subsymbolic models are continuous ones while those of symbolic models are not.

The continuous nature of subsymbolic computation has profound significance because it implies that many of the concepts used to understand cognition in the subsymbolic paradigm come from the category of continuous mathematics, while those used in the symbolic paradigm come nearly exclusively from discrete mathematics. Concepts from physics, from the theory of dynamical systems, are at least as likely to be important as concepts from the theory of digital computation. And analog computers, both electronic and optical, provide natural implementation media for subsymbolic systems (e.g. Anderson, 1986; Cohen, 1986).

3.2 Subsymbolic computation

An important instance of the continuous/discrete mathematics contrast that distinguishes subsymbolic and symbolic computation is found in inference. A natural way to look at the knowledge stored in connections is to view each connection as a *soft constraint*. A positive ("excitatory") connection from unit a to unit b represents a soft constraint to the effect that if a is active, then b should be too. A negative ("inhibitory") connection represents the opposite constraint. The numerical magnitude of a connection represents the strength of the constraint.

Formalizing knowledge in soft constraints rather than hard rules has important consequences. Hard constraints have consequences singly; they are context-independent rules that can be applied separately, sequentially, irrespective of whatever other rules may exist. But *soft constraints have no implications singly*; any one can be overridden by the others. It is only the *entire set* of soft constraints that has any implications. Inference must be a cooperative process, like the parallel relaxation processes typically found in subsymbolic systems. Furthermore, adding additional soft constraints can repeal conclusions that were formerly valid. Subsymbolic inference is fundamentally non-monotonic.

One way of formalizing soft constraint satisfaction is in terms of statistical inference. In certain subsymbolic systems, the soft constraints can be identified as statistical parameters and the activation passing procedures can be identified as statistical inference procedures (Hinton and Sejnowski, 1983a; Geman and Geman, 1984; Smolensky, 1986a; see also Shastri, 1985; Pearl, 1985). This identification is usually rather complex and subtle, and is usually not simply a matter of identifying the strength of the connection between two units with the correlation between their activity. An important goal is to determine how statistical and other formal theories of continuous (as opposed to logical) inference can be employed to mathematically elucidate the inference found in other subsymbolic systems.

To sum up:

(12) a. Knowledge in subsymbolic computation is formalized as a large set of soft constraints.

b. Inference with soft constraints is fundamentally a parallel process.

c. Inference with soft constraints is fundamentally non-monotonic.

d. Certain subsymbolic systems can be identified as employing statistical inference.

4 Conceptual-level descriptions of intuition

The previous section concerned computation in subsymbolic systems analyzed at the subconceptual level, the level of units and connections. In this final section I consider analyses of subsymbolic computation at the higher, conceptual level. I focus on subsymbolic models of intuitive processes, and my conclusion will be this: conceptual-level descriptions of aspects of subsymbolic models of intuitive processing roughly approximate symbolic accounts. The picture that emerges is of a symbiosis between the symbolic and subsymbolic paradigms: the symbolic paradigm offers concepts for better understanding subsymbolic models, and those concepts are in turn illuminated with a fresh light by the subsymbolic paradigm.

4.1 The Best Fit Principle

The notion that each connection represents a soft constraint can be formulated at a higher level:

(13) **The Best Fit Principle:** Given an input, a subsymbolic system outputs a set of inferences that, as a whole, give a best fit to the input, in a statistical sense defined by the statistical knowledge stored in the system's connections.

In this vague form, this principle can be regarded as a desideratum of subsymbolic systems. But it is exactly true in a precise sense, at least in an idealized limit, for the class of connectionist dynamical systems that have been studied in harmony theory (Riley and Smolensky, 1984; Smolensky, 1983, 1984a, 1984b, 1986a, 1986c).

To render the Best Fit Principle precise, it is necessary to provide precise definitions of "inferences," "best fit," and "statistical knowledge stored in the system's connections." This is done in harmony theory, where the central object is the harmony function H which measures, for any possible set of inferences, the goodness of fit to the input with respect to the soft constraints stored in the connection strengths. The set of inferences with the largest value of H, i.e. highest harmony, is the best set of inferences, with respect to a well-defined statistical problem.

Harmony theory basically offers three things. It gives a mathematically precise characterization of the prediction-from-examples goal as a statistical inference problem. It tells how the prediction goal can be achieved using a connectionist network with a certain set of connections. And it gives a procedure by which the network can learn the correct connections with experience, thereby satisfying the prediction-from-examples goal.

The units in harmony networks are stochastic units: the differential equations defining the system are stochastic. There is a system parameter called the *computational temperature* that governs the degree of randomness in the units' behavior: it goes to zero as the computation proceeds. (The process is *simulated annealing*, as in the Boltzmann machine: Ackley, Hinton, and Sejnowski, 1985; Hinton and Sejnowski, 1983a, 1983b, 1986. See Rumelhart, McClelland, and the PDP Research Group, 1986, p. 148, and Smolensky, 1986a, for the relations between harmony theory and the Boltzmann machine.)

4.2 Productions, sequential processing, and logical inference

A simple harmony model of expert intuition in qualitative physics was described in Riley and Smolensky (1984) and Smolensky (1986a, 1986c). The model answers questions like "what happens to the voltages in this circuit if I increase this resistor?" Higher-level descriptions of this subsymbolic problem-solving system illustrate several interesting points.

It is possible to identify *macro-decisions* during the system's solution of a problem; these are each the result of many individual micro-decisions by the units of the system, and each amounts to a large-scale commitment to a portion of the solution. These macro-decisions are approximately like the firing of production rules. In fact, these "productions" "fire" in essentially the same order as in a symbolic forward-chaining inference system. One can measure the total amount of order in the system, and see that there is a qualitative change in the system when the first micro-decisions are made: the system changes from a disordered phase to an ordered one.

It's a corollary of the way this network embodies the problem domain constraints, and the general theorems of harmony theory, that the system, when given a well-posed problem, and infinite relaxation time, will always give the correct answer. So under that idealization, the *competence* of the system is described by *hard* constraints: Ohm's Law, Kirchhoff's Law. It's as though it had those laws written down inside it. However, as in all subsymbolic systems, the *performance* of the system is achieved by satisfying a large set of *soft* constraints. What this means is that if we go outside of the ideal conditions under which hard constraints seem to be obeyed, the illusion that the system has hard constraints inside is quickly dispelled. The system can violate Ohm's Law if it has to, but if it doesn't have to violate the law, it won't. Thus, *outside the idealized domain of well-posed problems and infinite processing time, the system gives a sensible performance.* It isn't brittle the way that symbolic inference systems are. If the system is given an ill-posed problem, it satisfies as many constraints as possible. If it is given inconsistent information, it doesn't fall flat, and deduce anything. If it is given insufficient information, it doesn't just sit there and deduce nothing. Given finite processing time, the performance degrades gracefully as well. So the competence/performance distinction can be addressed in a sensible way.

We can sum this up neatly using a physics-level analogy, in which subsymbolic theory corresponds to quantum mechanics and symbolic theory corresponds to classical mechanics. The subsymbolic inference system just described is a "quantum" system that appears to be "Newtonian" under the proper conditions. A system that has, at the micro-level, soft constraints, satisfied in parallel, *appears* at the macro-level, under the right circumstances, to have hard constraints, satisfied serially. But it doesn't *really*, and as soon as we step outside the "Newtonian" domain, we see that it's really been a "quantum" system all along.

4.3 Conceptual-level spreading activation

According to the subconceptual unit hypothesis (7b), the concepts we use to consciously represent problem domains correspond in subsymbolic systems to patterns of activity over many network units. A situation in which many concepts occur corresponds to an activity pattern that incorporates the sub-patterns corresponding to the relevant concepts, all suitably superimposed in a way not yet fully understood. Using the mathematics of the superposition operation, it is possible to approximately analyze connectionist dynamical systems at the conceptual level. If the connectionist system is purely linear (so that the activity of each unit is precisely a weighted sum of the activities of the units giving it input), it can easily be proved that the higher-level description obeys formal laws of just the same sort as the lower level: the computation of the subconceptual and conceptual levels are *isomorphic*. Linear connectionist systems are, however, of limited computational power, and most interesting connectionist systems are non-linear. However, most of these are in fact *quasi*-linear: each unit combines its inputs linearly even though the effects of this combination on the unit's activity is non-linear. Further, the problem-specific *knowledge* in such systems is in the combination weights, i.e. the *linear part* of the dynamical equations; and in learning systems it is generally only these linear weights that adapt. For these reasons, even though the higher level is not isomorphic to the lower level in non-linear systems, there are senses in which the higher level *approximately* obeys formal laws similar to the lower level. (For details, see Smolensky, 1986b.)

The conclusion here is a rather different one from the preceding section, where we saw how there are senses in which higher-level characterizations of certain subsymbolic systems approximate productions, serial processing, and logical inference. What we see now is that there are also senses in which the laws approximately describing cognition at the conceptual level are *activation-passing laws* like those at the subconceptual level, but operating between units with individual conceptual semantics. Such semantic-level descriptions of mental processing (which include *local* connectionist models; see note 3) have been of considerable value in cognitive science. We can now see how these "spreading activation" accounts of mental processing fit into the subsymbolic paradigm.

4.4 Schemata

The final conceptual-level notion I will consider is that of the *schema* (e.g. Rumelhart, 1980). This concept goes back at least to Kant (1787/1963) as a description of mental concepts and mental categories. Schemata appear in many AI systems in the forms of frames, scripts, or similar structures: they are prepackaged bundles of information that support inference in stereotyped situations.

I will very briefly summarize work on schemata in connectionist systems reported in Rumelhart, Smolensky, McClelland, and Hinton (1986; see also Feldman, 1981, and Smolensky, 1986a, 1986c). This work addressed the case of schemata for rooms. Subjects were asked to describe some imagined rooms using a set of 40 features like has-ceiling, has-window, contains-toilet, and so on. Statistics were computed on this data and these were used to construct a network containing one node for each feature, and containing connections computed from the statistical data.

This resulting network can perform inference of the same general kind as that carried out by symbolic systems with schemata for various types of rooms. The network is told that some room contains a ceiling and an oven; the question is, what else is likely to be in the room? The system settles down into a final state, and the inferences contained in that final state are that the room contains a coffee cup but no fireplace, a coffee pot but no computer.

The inference process in this system is simply one of greedily maximizing harmony. To describe the inference of this system on a higher level, we can examine the global states of the system in terms of their harmony values. How internally consistent are the various states in the space? It's a 40-dimensional state space, but various 2-dimensional subspaces can be selected and the harmony values there can be graphically displayed. The harmony landscape has various peaks; looking at the features of the state corresponding to one of the peaks, we find that it corresponds to a prototypical bathroom; others correspond to a prototypical office, and so on for all the kinds of rooms subjects were asked to describe. There are no units in this system for bathrooms or offices: there are just lower-level descriptors. The prototypical bathroom is a pattern of activation, and the system's recognition of its prototypicality is reflected in the harmony peak for that pattern. It is a consistent, "harmonious" combination of features: better than neighboring points like one representing a bathroom without a bathtub, which has distinctly lower harmony.

During inference, this system climbs directly uphill on the harmony landscape. When the system state is in the vicinity of the harmony peak representing the prototypical bathroom, the inferences it makes are governed by the shape of the harmony landscape there. This shape is like a "schema" that governs inferences about bathrooms. (In fact, harmony theory was created to give a connectionist formalization of the notion of schema; see Smolensky, 1984b, 1986a, 1986c.) Looking closely at the harmony landscape we can see that the terrain around the "bathroom" peak has many of the properties of a bathroom schema: variables and constants, default values, schemata embedded inside of schemata, and even cross-variable dependencies, which are rather difficult to incorporate into symbolic formalizations of schemata. The system behaves as though it had schemata for bathrooms, offices, etc., even though they are not "really there" at the fundamental level: these schemata are strictly properties of a higher-level description. They are informal, approximate descriptions – one might even say they are merely metaphorical descriptions – of an inference process too subtle to admit such high-level descriptions with great precision. Even though these schemata may not be the sort of object on which to base a formal model, nonetheless they are useful descriptions that help us understand a complex inference system.

4.5 *Conclusion*

The view of symbolic structures that emerges from viewing them as entities of high-level descriptions of dynamical systems is quite different from the view provided by the symbolic paradigm.

(14) a. Macro-inference is not a process of firing a symbolic production but rather of qualitative state change in a dynamical system, such as a phase transition.

    b. Schemata are not large symbolic data structures but rather the potentially quite intricate shapes of harmony maxima.

    c. Categories (it turns out) are attractors in connectionist dynamical systems: states that "suck in" to a common place many nearby states, like peaks of harmony functions.

    d. Categorization is not the execution of a symbolic algorithm but the continuous evolution of the dynamical system, the evolution that drives states into the attractors, to maximal harmony.

    e. Learning is not the construction and editing of formulae, but the gradual adjustment of connection strengths with experience, with the effect of slowly shifting harmony landscapes, adapting old and creating new concepts, categories, schemata.

The heterogenous assortment of high-level mental structures that have been embraced in this section suggests that the conceptual level lacks formal unity. This is just what one expects of approximate higher-level descriptions, which, capturing different aspects of global properties, can have quite different characters. According to the subsymbolic paradigm, the unity underlying cognition is to be found not at the conceptual level, but rather at the subconceptual level, where relatively few principles in a single formal framework lead to a rich variety of global behaviors.

Notes

I am indebted to a number of people for very helpful conversations on these issues: Rob Cummins, Denise Dellarosa, Jerry Fodor, Zenon Pylyshyn, and Georges Rey. Dave Rumelhart's ideas have been extremely influential on the view argued for here, although I of course bear full responsibility for the formulation.

This research has been supported by National Science Foundation grant IST-8609599 and by the Department of Computer Science and Institute of Cognitive Science at the University of Colorado, Boulder.

A considerably revised and much expanded version of this paper appeared in *The Behavioral and Brain Sciences*, vol. 11, no. 1, March 1988; I am most grateful to the Editor for permission to reprint portions of that paper here.

1   In this paper, when "interpretation" is used to refer to a process, the sense intended is that of computer science: the process of taking a linguistic description of a procedure and executing that procedure.

2   Consider, for example, the connectionist symposium at the University of Geneva held September 9, 1986. The advertised program featured Feldman, Minsky, Rumelhart, Sejnowski, and Waltz. Of these five researchers, three were major contributors to the symbolic paradigm for many years: consider Minsky, 1975; Rumelhart, 1975, 1980; and Waltz, 1978, for example.

3   This is an issue that divides connectionist approaches. "Local connectionist models" (e.g. Dell, 1985; Feldman, 1985; McClelland and Rumelhart, 1981; Rumelhart and McClelland, 1982; Waltz and Pollack, 1985) accept (8), and often deviate significantly from (7a). This approach has been championed by the Rochester connectionists (see Feldman, Ballard, Brown, and Dell, 1985). Like the symbolic paradigm, this school favors simple semantics and more complex operations. The processors in their networks are usually more powerful than those allowed by (7); they are often rather like digital computers running a few lines of simple code. ("If there is a 1 on this input line then do X else do Y," where X and Y are quite different little procedures; e.g. Shastri, 1985.) This style of connectionism, quite different from the subsymbolic style, has much in common with the branch of traditional computer science that "parallelizes" serial algorithms by decomposing them into routines that can run in parallel, often with certain synchronization points built in. The grain size of the Rochester parallelism, while large compared to the subsymbolic paradigm, is small compared to standard parallel programming: the processors are allowed only a few internal states and allowed to transmit only a few different values (Feldman and Ballard, 1982).

4   As stated in the introduction, a large sample of research that by and large falls under the subsymbolic paradigm can be found in the books, Rumelhart, McClelland and the PDP Research Group (1986), *Parallel Distributed Processing: Explorations in the Microstructure of Cognition*, and McClelland, Rumelhart and the PDP Research Group (1986), *Parallel Distributed Processing: Explorations in the Microstructure of Cognition*. While this work has come to be labelled "connectionist," the term "PDP" was deliberately chosen to distinguish it from the localist approach which had previously adopted the name "connectionist" (Feldman and Ballard, 1982).

5   The phrase is Roger Schank's, in reference to "parallel processing" (Waldrop, 1984). Whether he was referring to connectionist systems I do not know; in any event, I don't mean to imply that the grounds for his comment are addressed here.

45

LOGICAL VS. ANALOGICAL OR SYMBOLIC VS. CONNECTIONIST OR NEAT VS. SCRUFFY

Marvin Minsky

Source: P. H. Winston and S. A. Shellard (eds), *Artificial Intelligence at MIT, Expanding Frontiers*, Vol. 1, MIT Press, 1990, pp. 218–43.

Engineering and scientific education conditions us to expect everything, including intelligence, to have a simple, compact explanation. Accordingly, when people new to AI ask "What's AI all about," they seem to expect an answer that defines AI in terms of a few basic mathematical laws.

Today, some researchers who seek a simple, compact explanation hope that systems modeled on neural nets or some other connectionist idea will quickly overtake more traditional systems based on symbol manipulation. Others believe that symbol manipulation, with a history that goes back millennia, remains the only viable approach.

Minsky subscribes to neither of these extremist views. Instead, he argues that Artificial Intelligence must employ many approaches. Artificial Intelligence is not like circuit theory and electromagnetism. There is nothing wonderfully unifying like Kirchhoff's laws are to circuit theory or Maxwell's equations are to electromagnetism. Instead of looking for a Right Way, Minsky believes that the time has come to build systems out of diverse components, some connectionist and some symbolic, each with its own diverse justification.

Minsky, whose seminal contributions in Artificial Intelligence are established worldwide, is one of the 1990 recipients of the prestigious Japan Prize—a prize recognizing original and outstanding achievements in science and technology.

Why is there so much excitement about Neural Networks today, and how is this related to research on Artificial Intelligence? Much has been said, in the popular press, as though these were conflicting activities. This seems exceedingly strange to me, because both are parts of the very same enterprise. What caused this misconception?

The symbol-oriented community in AI has brought this rift upon itself, by supporting models in research that are far too rigid and specialized. This focus on well-defined problems produced many successful applications, no matter that the underlying systems were too inflexible to function well outside the domains for which they were designed. (It seems to me that this happened because of the researchers' excessive concern with logical consistency and provability. Ultimately, that would be a proper concern, but not in the subject's present state of immaturity.) Thus, contemporary symbolic AI systems are now too constrained to be able to deal with exceptions to rules, or to exploit fuzzy, approximate, or heuristic fragments of knowledge. Partly in reaction to this, the connectionist movement initially tried to develop more flexible systems, but soon came to be imprisoned in its own peculiar ideology—of trying to build learning systems endowed with as little architectural structure as possible, hoping to create machines that could serve all masters equally well. The trouble with this is that even a seemingly neutral architecture still embodies an implicit assumption about which things are presumed to be "similar."

The field called Artificial Intelligence includes many different aspirations. Some researchers simply want machines to do the various sorts of things that people call intelligent. Others hope to understand what enables people to do such things. Yet other researchers want to simplify programming; why can't we build, once and for all, machines that grow and improve themselves by learning from experience? Why can't we simply explain what we want, and then let our machines do experiments, or read some books, or go to school—the sorts of things that people do. Our machines today do no such things: Connectionist networks learn a bit, but show few signs of becoming "smart;" symbolic systems are shrewd from the start, but don't yet show any "common sense." How strange that our most advanced systems can compete with human specialists, yet be unable to do many things that seem easy to children. I suggest that this stems from the nature of what we call *specialties*—for the very act of naming a specialty amounts to celebrating the discovery of some model of some aspect of reality, which is useful despite being isolated from most of our other concerns. These models have rules which reliably work—so long as we stay in that special domain. But when we return to the commonsense world, we rarely find rules that precisely apply. Instead, we must know how to adapt each fragment of "knowledge" to particular contexts and circumstances, and we must expect to need more and different kinds of knowledge as our concerns broaden. Inside such simple "toy" domains, a rule may seem to be quite "general," but whenever we broaden those domains, we find more and more exceptions—and the early advantage of context-free rules then mutates into strong limitations.

AI research must now move from its traditional focus on particular schemes. There is no one best way to represent knowledge, or to solve problems, and limitations of present-day machine intelligence stem largely from seeking "unified theories," or trying to repair the deficiencies of theoretically neat, but conceptually impoverished ideological positions. Our purely numerical connectionist networks are inherently deficient in abilities to reason well; our purely symbolic logical systems are inherently deficient in abilities to represent the all-important *heuristic connections* between things—the uncertain, approximate, and analogical linkages that we need for making new hypotheses. The versatility that we need can be found only in larger-scale architectures that can exploit and manage the advantages of several types of representations at the same time. Then, each can be used to overcome the deficiencies of the others. To do this, each formally neat type of knowledge representation or inference must be complemented with some "scruffier" kind of machinery that can embody the heuristic connections between the knowledge itself and what we hope to do with it.

Top-down vs. bottom-up

While different workers have diverse goals, all AI researchers seek to make machines that solve problems. One popular way to pursue that quest is to start with a "top-down" strategy: begin at the level of commonsense psychology and try to imagine processes that could play a certain game, solve a certain kind of puzzle, or recognize a certain kind of object. If you can't do this in a single step, then keep breaking things down into simpler parts until you can actually embody them in hardware or software.

This basically reductionist technique is typical of the approach to AI called heuristic programming. These techniques have developed productively for several decades and, today, heuristic programs based on top-down analysis have found many successful applications in technical, specialized areas. This progress is largely due to the maturation of many techniques for representing knowledge. But the same techniques have seen less success when applied to "commonsense" problem solving. Why can we build robots that compete with highly trained workers to assemble intricate machinery in factories—but not robots that can help with ordinary housework? It is because the conditions in factories are constrained, while the objects and activities of everyday life are too endlessly varied to be described by precise, logical definitions and deductions. Commonsense reality is too disorderly to represent in terms of universally valid "axioms." To deal with such variety and novelty, we need more flexible styles of thought, such as those we see in human commonsense reasoning, which is based more on analogies and approximations than on precise formal procedures. Nonetheless, top-down procedures have important advantages in being able to perform efficient, systematic search procedures, to manipulate and rearrange the elements of complex situations, and to supervise the management of intricately interacting subgoals—all functions that seem beyond the capabilities of connectionist systems with weak architectures.

Short-sighted critics have always complained that progress in top-down symbolic AI research is slowing down. In one way this is natural: in the early phases of any field, it becomes ever harder to make important new advances as we put the easier problems behind us—and new workers must face a "squared" challenge, because there is so much more to learn. But the slowdown of progress in symbolic AI is not just a matter of laziness. Those top-down systems are inherently poor at solving problems which involve large numbers of weaker kinds of interactions, such as occur in many areas of pattern recognition and knowledge retrieval. Hence, there has been a mounting clamor for finding another, new, more flexible approach—and this is one reason for the recent popular turn toward connectionist models.

The bottom-up approach goes the opposite way. We begin with simpler elements—they might be small computer programs, elementary logical principles, or simplified models of what brain cells do—and then move upwards in complexity by finding ways to interconnect those units to produce larger scale phenomena. The currently popular form of this, the connectionist neural network approach, developed more sporadically than did heuristic programming. In part, this was because heuristic programming developed so rapidly in the 1960s that connectionist networks were swiftly outclassed. Also, the networks need computation and memory resources that were too prodigious for that period. Now that faster computers are available, bottom-up connectionist research has shown considerable promise in mimicking some of what we admire in the behavior of lower animals, particularly in the areas of pattern recognition, automatic optimization, clustering, and knowledge retrieval. But their performance has been far weaker in the very areas in which symbolic systems have successfully mimicked much of what we admire in high-level human thinking—for example, in goal-based reasoning, parsing, and causal analysis. These weakly structured connectionist networks cannot deal with the sorts of tree-search explorations, and complex, composite knowledge structures required for parsing, recursion, complex scene analysis, or other sorts of problems that involve *functional parallelism*. It is an amusing paradox that connectionists frequently boast about the massive parallelism of their computations, yet the homogeneity and interconnectedness of those structures make them virtually unable to do more than one thing at a time—at least, at levels above that of their basic associative functionality. This is essentially because they lack the architecture needed to maintain adequate short-term memories.

Thus, the present-day systems of both types show serious limitations. The top-down systems are handicapped by inflexible mechanisms for retrieving knowledge and reasoning about it, while the bottom-up systems are crippled by inflexible architectures and organizational schemes. Neither type of system has been developed so as to be able to exploit multiple, diverse varieties of knowledge.

Which approach is best to pursue? That is simply a wrong question. Each has virtues and deficiencies, and we need integrated systems that can exploit the advantages of both. In favor of the top-down side, research in Artificial Intelligence has told us a little—but only a little—about how to solve problems by using methods that resemble reasoning. If we understood more about this, perhaps we could more easily work down toward finding out how brain cells do such things. In favor of the bottom-up approach, the brain sciences have told us something—but again, only a little—about the workings of brain cells and their connections. More research on this might help us discover how the activities of brain-cell networks support our higher level processes. But right now we're caught in the middle; neither purely connectionist nor purely symbolic systems seem able to support the sorts of intellectual performances we take for granted even in young children. This essay aims at understanding why both types of AI systems have developed to become so inflexible. I'll argue that the solution lies somewhere between these two extremes, and our problem will be to find out how to build a suitable bridge. We already have plenty of ideas at either extreme. On the connectionist side we can extend our efforts to design neural networks that can learn various ways to represent knowledge. On the symbolic side, we can extend our research on knowledge representations, and on designing systems that can effectively exploit the knowledge thus represented. But above all, at the present time, we need more research on how to combine both types of ideas.

Representation and retrieval: structure and function

In order for a machine to learn, it must represent what it will learn. The knowledge must be embodied in some form of mechanism, data-structure, or *representation*. Researchers in Artificial Intelligence have devised many ways to do this, for example, in the forms of:

- Rule-based systems.
- Frames with default assignments.
- Predicate calculus.
- Procedural representations.
- Associative data bases.
- Semantic networks.
- Object-oriented programming.
- Conceptual dependency.
- Action scripts.
- Neural networks.
- Natural language.

In the 1960s and 1970s, students frequently asked, "Which kind of repre-sentation is best," and I usually replied that we'd need more research before answering that. But now I would give a different reply: "To solve really hard problems, we'll have to use several different representations." This is because each particular kind of data-structure has its own virtues and deficiencies, and none by itself seems adequate for all the different func-tions involved with what we call "common sense." Each have domains of competence and efficiency, so that one may work where another fails. Fur-thermore, if we rely only on any single "unified" scheme, then we'll have no way to recover from failure. As suggested in section 6.9 of *The Society of Mind*, "The secret of what something means lies in how it connects to other things we know. That's why it's almost always wrong to seek the *real meaning* of anything. A thing with just one meaning has scarcely any meaning at all."

In order to get around these constraints, we must develop systems that combine the expressiveness and procedural versatility of symbolic systems with the fuzziness and adaptiveness of connectionist representations. Why has there been so little work on synthesizing these techniques? I suspect that it is because both of these AI communities suffer from a common cultural-philosophical disposition: they would like to explain intelligence in the image of what was successful in Physics—by minimizing the amount and variety of its assumptions. But this seems to be a wrong ideal; instead, we should take our cue from biology rather than from physics. This is because what we call "thinking" does not emerge directly from a few fundamental principles of wave-function symmetry and exclusion rules. Mental activities are not the sorts of unitary or "elementary" phenomenon that can be described by a few mathematical operations on logical axioms. Instead, the functions performed by the brain are the products of the work of thousands of different, special-ized sub-systems, the intricate product of hundreds of millions of years of biological evolution. We cannot hope to understand such an organization by emulating the techniques of those particle physicists search in the simplest possible unifying conceptions. Constructing a mind is simply a different kind of problem—of how to synthesize organizational systems that can support a large enough diversity of different schemes, yet enable them to work together to exploit one another's abilities.

To solve typical real-world commonsense problems, a mind must have at least several different kinds of knowledge. First, we need to represent goals: what is the problem to be solved. Then the system must also possess adequate knowledge about the domain or context in which that problem occurs. Finally, the system must know what kinds of reasoning are applicable in that area. Superimposed on all of this, our systems must have manage-ment schemes that can operate different representations and procedures in parallel, so that when any particular method breaks down or gets stuck, the system can quickly shift over to analogous operations in other realms that may be able to continue the work. For example, when you hear a natural language expression like

"Mary gave Jack the book"

this will produce in you, albeit unconsciously, many different kinds of thoughts (see *The Society of Mind*, section 29.2)—that is, mental activities in such different realms as:

- A visual representation of the scene.
- Postural and tactile representations of the experience.
- A script-sequence of a typical script-sequence for "giving."
- Representation of the participants' roles.
- Representations of their social motivations.
- Default assumptions about Jack, Mary, and the book.
- Other assumptions about past and future expectations.

How could a brain possibly coordinate the use of such different kinds of processes and representations? Our conjecture is that our brains construct and maintain them in different brain-agencies. (The corresponding neural structures need not, of course, be entirely separate in their spatial extents inside the brain.) But it is not enough to maintain separate processes inside separate agencies; we also need additional mechanisms to enable each of them to support the activities of the others—or, at least, to provide alternative operations in case of failures. Chapters 19 through 23 of *The Society of Mind* sketch some ideas about how the representations in different agencies could be coordinated. These sections introduce the concepts of:

- *Polyneme*—a hypothetical neuronal mechanism for activating corresponding slots in different representations.
- *Microneme*—a context-representing mechanism which similarly biases all the agencies to activate knowledge related to the current situation and goal.
- *Paranome*—yet another mechanism that can apply corresponding processes or operations simultaneously to the short-term memory agents' *pronomes* of those various agencies.

It is impossible to summarize briefly how all these mechanisms are imagined to work, but section 29.3 of *The Society of Mind* gives some of the flavor of our theory. What controls those paranomes? I suspect that, in human minds, this control comes from mutual exploitation between:

- A long-range planning agency (whose scripts are influenced by various strong goals and ideals; this agency resembles the Freudian superego, and is based on early imprinting).

568

- Another supervisory agency capable of using semi-formal inferences and natural-language reformulations.
- A Freudian-like censorship agency that incorporates massive records of previous failures of various sorts.

Relevance and similarity

Problem-solvers must find relevant data. How does the human mind retrieve what it needs from among so many millions of knowledge items? Different AI systems have attempted to use a variety of different methods for this. Some assign keywords, attributes, or descriptors to each item and then locate data by feature-matching or by using more sophisticated associative data-base methods. Others use graph-matching or analogical case-based adaptation. Yet others try to find relevant information by threading their ways through systematic, usually hierarchical classification of knowledge— sometimes called *ontologies*. But, to me, all such ideas seem deficient because it is not enough to classify items of information simply in terms of the features or structures of those items themselves. This is because we rarely use a representation in an intentional vacuum, but we always have goals—and two objects may seem similar for one purpose but different for another purpose. Consequently, we must also take into account the functional aspects of what we know, and therefore we must classify things (and ideas) according to what they can be used for, or which goals they can help us achieve. Two armchairs of identical shape may seem equally comfortable as objects for sitting in, but those same chairs may seem very different for other purposes, for example, if they differ much in weight, fragility, cost, or appearance. The further a feature or difference lies from the surface of the chosen representation, the harder it will be to respond to, exploit, or adapt to it—and this is why the choice of representation is so important. In each functional context we need to represent particularly well the heuristic connections between each object's internal features and relationships, and the possible functions of those objects. That is, we must be able to easily relate the structural features of each object's representation to how that object might behave in regard to achieving our present goals. This is further discussed in sections 12.4, 12.5, 12.12, and 12.13 of *The Society of Mind*.

New problems, by definition, are different from those we have already encountered; so we cannot always depend on using records of past experience. Yet, to do better than random search, we must still use what we have learned from the past, no matter that it may not match perfectly. Which records should we retrieve as likely to be the most relevant?

Explanations of "relevance," in traditional theories, abound with synonyms for nearness and similarity. If a certain item gives bad results, it makes sense to try something different. But when something we try turns out to be good, then a similar one may be better. We see this idea in myriad forms, and whenever we solve problems we find ourselves employing metrical metaphors: we're "getting close" or "on the right track;" using words that express proximity. But what do we mean by "close" or "near." Decades of research on different forms of that question have produced theories and procedures for use in signal processing, pattern recognition, induction, classification, clustering, generalization, etc., and each of these methods has been found useful for certain applications, but ineffective for others. Recent connectionist research has considerably enlarged our resources in these areas. Each method has its advocates—but I contend that it is now time to move to another stage of research. For, although each such concept or method may have merit in certain domains, none of them seem powerful enough alone to make our machines more intelligent. It is time to stop arguing over which type of pattern classification technique is best—because that depends on our context and goal. Instead, we should work at a higher level of organization, discover how to build managerial systems to exploit the different virtues, and to evade the different limitations, of each of these ways of comparing things. Different types of problems, and representations, may require different concepts of similarity. Within each realm of discourse, some representation will make certain problems and concepts appear to be more closely related than others. To make matters worse, even within the same problem domain, we may need different notions of similarity for:

- Descriptions of problems and goals.
- Descriptions of knowledge about the subject domain.
- Descriptions of procedures to be used.

For small domains, we can try to apply all of our reasoning methods to all of our knowledge, and test for satisfactory solutions. But this is usually impractical, because the search becomes too huge—in both symbolic and connectionist systems. To constrain the extent of mindless search, we must incorporate additional kinds of knowledge—embodying expertise about problem-solving itself and, particularly, about managing the resources that may be available. The spatial metaphor helps us think about such issues by providing us with a superficial unification: if we envision problem-solving as "searching for solutions" in a space-like realm, then it is tempting to analogize between the ideas of similarity and nearness: to think about similar things as being in some sense near or close to one another.

But "near" in what sense? To a mathematician, the most obvious idea would be to imagine the objects under comparison to be like points in some abstract space; then each representation of that space would induce (or reflect) some sort of topology-like structure or relationship among the possible objects being represented. Thus, the languages of many sciences, not merely those of Artificial Intelligence and of psychology, are replete with attempts to portray families of concepts in terms of various sorts of spaces equipped with various measures of similarity. If, for example, you represent things in terms of (allegedly independent) properties then it seems natural to try to assign magnitudes to each, and then to sum the squares of their differences—in effect, representing those objects as vectors in Euclidean space. This further encourages us to formulate the function of knowledge in terms of helping us to decide "which way to go." This is often usefully translated into the popular metaphor of "hill-climbing" because, if we can impose on that space a suitable metrical structure, we may be able to devise iterative ways to find solutions by analogy with the method of hill-climbing or gradient ascent—that is, when any experiment seems more or less successful than another, then we exploit that metrical structure to help us make the next move in the proper "direction." (Later, we shall emphasize that having a sense of direction entails a little more than a sense of proximity; it is not enough just to know metrical distances, we must also respond to other kinds of heuristic differences—and these may be difficult to detect.)

Whenever we design or select a particular representation, that particular choice will bias our dispositions about which objects to consider more or less similar to us (or, to the programs we apply to them) and thus will affect how we apply our knowledge to achieve goals and solve problems. Once we understand the effects of such commitments, we will be better prepared to select and modify those representations to produce more heuristically useful distinctions and confusions. So, let us now examine, from this point of view, some of the representations that have become popular in the field of Artificial Intelligence.

Heuristic connections of pure logic

Why have logic-based formalisms been so widely used in AI research? I see two motives for selecting this type of representation. One virtue of logic is clarity, its lack of ambiguity. Another advantage is the pre-existence of many technical mathematical theories about logic. But logic also has its disadvantages. Logical generalizations apply only to their literal lexical instances, and logical implications apply only to expressions that precisely instantiate their antecedent conditions. No exceptions at all are allowed, no matter how "closely" they match. This permits you to use no near misses, no suggestive clues, no compromises, no analogies, and no metaphors. To shackle yourself so inflexibly is to shoot your own mind in the foot—if you know what I mean.

These limitations of logic begin at the very foundation, with the basic connectives and quantifiers. The trouble is that worldly statements of the form, "For all X, $P(X)$," are never beyond suspicion. To be sure, such a statement can indeed be universally valid inside a mathematical realm—but this is because such realms, themselves, are based on expressions of those very kinds. The use of such formalisms in AI have led most researchers to seek "truth" and universal "validity" to the virtual exclusion of "practical" or "interesting"—as though nothing would do except certainty. Now, that is acceptable in mathematics (wherein we ourselves define the worlds in which we solve problems) but, when it comes to reality, there is little advantage in demanding inferential perfection, when there is no guarantee even that our assumptions will always be correct. Logic theorists seem to have forgotten that any expression like $(\forall X)(PX)$, in actual life—that is, in a world which we find, but don't make—must be seen as only a convenient abbreviation for something more like this:

"For any thing X being considered in the current context, the assertion PX is likely to be useful for achieving goals like G, provided that we apply in conjunction with certain heuristically appropriate inference methods."

In other words, we cannot ask our problem-solving systems to be absolutely perfect, or even consistent; we can only hope that they will grow increasingly better than blind search at generating, justifying, supporting, rejecting, modifying, and developing "evidence" for new hypotheses.

It has become particularly popular, in AI logic programming, to restrict the representation to expression written in the first order predicate calculus. This practice, which is so pervasive that most students engaged in it don't even know what "first order" means here, facilitates the use of certain types of inference, but at a very high price: that the predicates of such expressions are prohibited from referring in certain ways to one another. This prevents the representation of meta-knowledge, rendering those systems incapable, for example, of describing what the knowledge that they contain can be used for. In effect, it precludes the use of functional descriptions. We need to develop systems for logic that can reason about their own knowledge, and make heuristic adaptations and interpretations of it, by using knowledge about that knowledge—but these limitations of expressiveness make logic unsuitable for such purposes.

Furthermore, it must be obvious that in order to apply our knowledge to commonsense problems, we need to be able to recognize which expressions are similar, in whatever heuristic sense may be appropriate. But this, too, seems technically impractical, at least for the most commonly used logical formalisms—namely, expressions in which absolute quantifiers range over string-like normal forms. For example, in order to use the popular method of "resolution theorem-proving," one usually ends up using expressions that consist of logical disjunctions of separately almost meaningless conjunctions. Consequently, the *natural topology* of any such representation will almost surely be heuristically irrelevant to any real-life problem space. Consider how dissimilar these three expressions seem, when written in conjunctive form:

AVBVCVD ABVACVADVBCVBDVCD ABCVABDVACDVBCD

The simplest way to assess the distances or differences between expressions is to compare such superficial factors as the numbers of terms or sub-expressions they have in common. Any such assessment would seem meaningless for expressions like those above. In most situations, however, it would almost surely be useful to recognize that these expressions are symmetric in their arguments, and hence will clearly seem more similar if we re-represent them—for example, by using S_n to mean "n of S's arguments have truth-value T"—so that then they can be written in the form S_1, S_2, and S_3. Even in mathematics itself, we consider it a great discovery to find a new representation for which the most natural-seeming heuristic connection can be recognized as close to the representation's surface structure. But this is too much to expect in general, so it is usually necessary to gauge the similarity of two expressions by using more complex assessments based, for example, on the number of set-inclusion levels between them, or on the number of available operations required to transform one into the other, or on the basis of the partial ordering suggested by their lattice of common generalizations and instances. This means that making good similarity judgments may itself require the use of other heuristic kinds of knowledge, until eventually—that is, when our problems grow hard enough—we are forced to resort to techniques that exploit knowledge that is not so transparently expressed in any such "mathematically elegant" formulation.

Indeed, we can think about much of Artificial Intelligence research in terms of a tension between solving problems by searching for solutions inside a compact and well-defined problem space (which is feasible only for prototypes)—versus using external systems (that exploit larger amounts of heuristic knowledge) to reduce the complexity of that inner search. Compound systems of that sort need retrieval machinery that can select and extract knowledge which is "relevant" to the problem at hand. Although it is not especially hard to write such programs, it cannot be done in "first order" systems. In my view, this can best be achieved in systems that allow us to use, simultaneously, both object-oriented structure-based descriptions and goal-oriented functional descriptions.

How can we make *logic* more expressive, given that its fundamental quantifiers and connectives are defined so narrowly from the start. This could well be beyond repair, and the most satisfactory replacement might be some sort of object-oriented frame-based language. After all, once we leave the domain of abstract mathematics, and free ourselves from those rigid notations, we can see that some virtues of logic-like reasoning may still remain—for example, in the sorts of deductive chaining we used, and the kinds of substitution procedures we applied to those expressions. The spirit of some of these formal techniques can then be approximated by other, less formal techniques of making chains, like those suggested in chapter 18 of *The Society of Mind*. For example, the mechanisms of defaults and frame-arrays could be used to approximate the formal effects of instantiating generalizations. When we use heuristic chaining, of course, we cannot assume absolute validity of the result, and so, after each reasoning step, we may have to look for more evidence. If we notice exceptions and disparities then, later, we must return again to each, or else remember them as assumptions or problems to be justified or settled at some later time—all things that humans so often do.

Heuristic connections of rule-based systems

While logical representations have been used in popular research, rule-based representations have been more successful in applications. In these systems, each fragment of knowledge is represented by an *If-Then* rule so that, whenever a description of the current problem-situation precisely matches the rule's antecedent *If* condition, the system performs the action described by that rule's *Then* consequent. What if no antecedent condition applies? Simple: the programmer adds another rule. It is this seeming modularity that made rule-based systems so attractive. You don't have to write complicated programs. Instead, whenever the system fails to perform, or does something wrong, you simply add another rule. This usually works quite well at first— but whenever we try to move beyond the realm of "toy" problems, and start to accumulate more and more rules, we usually get into trouble because each added rule is increasingly likely to interact in unexpected ways with the others. Then what should we ask the program to do, when no antecedent fits perfectly? We can equip the program to select the rule whose antecedent most closely describes the situation—and, again, we're back to "similar." To make any real-world application program resourceful, we must supplement its formal reasoning facilities with matching facilities that are heuristically appropriate for the problem domain it is working in.

What if several rules match equally well? Of course, we could choose the first on the list, or choose one at random, or use some other superficial scheme—but why be so unimaginative? In *The Society of Mind*, we try to regard conflicts as opportunities rather than obstacles—an opening that we can use to exploit other kinds of knowledge. For example, section 3.2 of *The Society of Mind* suggests invoking a *principle of non-compromise*, to discard sets of rules with conflicting antecedents or consequents. The general idea is that whenever two fragments of knowledge disagree, it may be better to ignore them both, and refer to some other, independent agency. In effect this is a managerial approach in which one agency can engage some other body of expertise to help decide which rules to apply. For example, one might turn to case-based reasoning, to ask which method worked best in similar previous situations.

Yet another approach would be to engage a mechanism for inventing a new rule, by trying to combine elements of those rules that almost fit already. Section 8.2 of *The Society of Mind* suggests using K-line representations for this purpose. To do this, we must be immersed in a society-of-agents framework in which each response to a situation involves activating not one, but a variety of interacting processes. In such a system, all the agents activated by several rules can then be left to interact, if only momentarily, both with one another and with the input signals, so as to make a useful self-selection about which of them should remain active. This could be done by combining certain present-day connectionist concepts with other ideas about K-line mechanisms. But we cannot do this until we learn how to design network architectures that can support new forms of internal management and external supervision of developmental staging.

In any case, present-day rule-based systems are still are too limited in ability to express "typical" knowledge. They need better default machinery. They deal with exceptions too passively; they need censors. They need better "ring-closing" mechanisms for retrieving knowledge (see section 19.10 of *The Society of Mind*). Above all, we need better ways to connect them with other kinds of representations, so that we can use them in problem-solving organizations that can exploit other kinds of models and search procedures.

Connectionist networks

Up to this point, we have considered ways to overcome the deficiencies of symbolic systems by augmenting them with connectionist machinery. But this kind of research should go both ways. Connectionist systems have equally crippling limitations, which might be ameliorated by augmentation with the sorts of architectures developed for symbolic applications. Perhaps such extensions and synthesis will recapitulate some aspects of how the primate brain grew over millions of years, by evolving symbolic systems to supervise its primitive connectionist learning mechanisms.

What do we mean by *connectionist*? The usage of that term is still evolving rapidly, but here it refers to attempts to embody knowledge by assigning numerical conductivities or weights to the connections inside a network of nodes. The most common form of such a node is made by combing an analog, nearly linear part that "adds up evidence" with a nonlinear, nearly digital part that "makes a decision" based on a threshold. The most popular such networks today, take the form of multilayer perceptrons—that is, of sequences of layers of such nodes, each sending signals to the next. More complex arrangements are also under study; these can support cyclic internal activities, hence they are potentially more versatile, but harder to understand. What makes such architectures attractive? Mainly, that they appear to be so simple and homogeneous. At least on the surface, they can be seen as ways to represent knowledge without any complex syntax. The entire configuration-state of such a net can be described as nothing more than a simple vector—and the network's input-output characteristics as nothing more than a map from one vector space into another. This makes it easy to reformulate pattern-recognition and learning problems in simple terms—for example, finding the "best" such mapping, etc. Seen in this way, the subject presents a pleasing mathematical simplicity. It is often not mentioned that we still possess little theoretical understanding of the computational complexity of finding such mappings—that is, of how to discover good values for the connection-weights. Most current publications still merely exhibit successful small-scale examples without probing either into assessing the computational difficulty of those problems themselves, or of scaling those results to similar problems of larger size.

However, we now know of quite a few situations in which even such simple systems have been made to compute (and, more important, to learn to compute) interesting functions, particularly in such domains as clustering, classification, and pattern recognition. In some instances, this has occurred without any external supervision; furthermore, some of these systems have also performed acceptably in the presence of incomplete or noisy inputs— and thus correctly recognized patterns that were novel or incomplete. This means that the architectures of those systems must indeed have embodied heuristic connectivities that were appropriate for those particular problem-domains. In such situations, these networks can be useful for the kind of reconstruction-retrieval operations we call *ring-closing*.

But connectionist networks have limitations as well. The next few sections discuss some of these limitations, along with suggestions on how to overcome them by embedding these networks in more advanced architectural schemes.

Limitation of fragmentation: the parallel paradox

In our Epilogue to *Perceptrons*, Papert and I argued as follows:

> "It is often argued that the use of distributed representations enables a system to exploit the advantages of parallel processing. But what are the advantages of parallel processing? Suppose that a certain task involves two unrelated parts. To deal with both concurrently, we would have to maintain their representations in two decoupled agencies, both active at the same time. Then, should either of those agencies become involved with two or more sub-tasks, we'd have to deal with each of them with no more than a quarter of the available resources! If that proceeded on and on, the system would become so fragmented that each job would end up with virtually no resources assigned to it. In this regard, distribution may oppose parallelism: the more distributed a system is—that is, the more intimately its parts interact—the fewer different things it can do at the same time. On the other side, the more we do separately in parallel, the less machinery can be assigned to each element of what we do, and that ultimately leads to increasing fragmentation and incompetence. This

is not to say that distributed representations and parallel processing are always incompatible. When we simultaneously activate two distributed representations in the same network, they will be forced to interact. In favorable circumstances, those interactions can lead to useful parallel computations, such as the satisfaction of simultaneous constraints. But that will not happen in general; it will occur only when the representations happen to mesh in suitably fortunate ways. Such problems will be especially serious when we try to train distributed systems to deal with problems that require any sort of structural analysis in which the system must represent relationships between substructures of related types—that is, problems that are likely to demand the same structural resources."

(See also section 15.11 of *The Society of Mind*.)

For these reasons, it will always be hard for a homogeneous network to perform parallel *high-level* computations—unless we can arrange for it to become divided into effectively disconnected parts. There is no general remedy for this—and the problem is no special peculiarity of connectionist hardware; computers have similar limitations, and the only answer is providing more hardware. More generally, it seems obvious that without adequate memory-buffering, homogeneous networks must remain incapable of recursion, so long as successive "function calls" have to use the same hardware. This is because, without such facilities, either the different calls will side-effect one another, or some of them must be erased, leaving the system unable to execute proper returns or continuations. Again, this may be easily fixed by providing enough short-term memory, for example, in the form of a stack of temporary K-lines.

Limitations of specialization and efficiency

Each connectionist net, once trained, can do only what it has learned to do. To make it do something else—for example, to compute a different measure of similarity, or to recognize a different class of patterns—would, in general, require a complete change in the matrix of connection coefficients. Usually, we can change the functionality of a computer much more easily (at least, when the desired functions can each be computed by compact algorithms); this is because a computer's "memory cells" are so much more interchangeable. It is curious how even technically well-informed people tend to forget how computationally massive a fully connected neural network is. It is instructive to compare this with the few hundred rules that drive a typically successful commercial rule-based Expert System.

How connected need networks be? There are several points in *The Society of Mind* which suggest that commonsense reasoning systems may not need to increase in the density of physical connectivity as fast as they increase the complexity and scope of their performances. Chapter 6 argues that knowledge systems must evolve into clumps of specialized agencies, rather than homogeneous networks, because they develop different types of internal representations. When this happens, it will become neither feasible nor practical for any of those agencies to communicate directly with the interior of others. Furthermore, there will be a tendency for newly acquired skills to develop from the relatively few that are already well developed and this, again, will bias the largest scale connections toward evolving into recursively clumped, rather than uniformly connected arrangements. A different tendency to limit connectivities is discussed in section 20.8, which proposes a sparse connection-scheme that can simulate, in real time, the behavior of fully connected nets—in which only a small proportion of agents are simultaneously active. This method, based on a half-century old idea of Calvin Mooers, allows many intermittently active agents to share the same relatively narrow, common connection bus. This might seem, at first, a mere economy, but section 20.9 suggests that this technique could also induce a more heuristically useful tendency, if the separate signals on that bus were to represent meaningful symbols. Finally, chapter 17 suggests other developmental reasons why minds may be virtually forced to grow in relatively discrete stages rather than as homogeneous networks. Our progress in this area may parallel our progress in understanding the stages we see in the growth of every child's thought.

If our minds are assembled of agencies with so little inter-communication, how can those parts cooperate? What keeps them working on related aspects of the same problem? The first answer proposed in *The Society of Mind* is that it is less important for agencies to co-operate than to exploit one another. This is because those agencies tend to become specialized, developing their own internal languages and representations. Consequently, they cannot understand each other's internal operations very well—and each must learn to exploit some of the others for the effects that those others produce—without knowing in any detail how those other effects are produced. For the same kind of reason, there must be other agencies to manage all those specialists, to keep the system from too much fruitless conflict for access to limited resources. Those management agencies themselves cannot deal directly with all the small interior details of what happens inside their subordinates. They must work, instead, with summaries of what those subordinates seem to do. This too, suggests that there must be constraints on internal connectivity: too much detailed information would overwhelm those managers. And this applies recursively to the insides of every large agency. So we argue, in chapter 8 of *The Society of Mind*, that relatively few direct connections are needed except between adjacent "level bands."

All this suggests (but does not prove) that large commonsense reasoning systems will not need to be "fully connected." Instead, the system could consist of localized clumps of expertise. At the lowest levels these would have to be very densely connected, in order to support the sorts of associativity required to learn low-level pattern detecting agents. But as we ascend to higher levels, the individual signals must become increasingly abstract and significant and, accordingly, the density of connection paths between agencies can become increasingly (but only relatively) smaller. Eventually, we should be able to build a sound technical theory about the connection densities required for commonsense thinking, but I don't think that we have the right foundations as yet. The problem is that contemporary theories of computational complexity are still based too much on worst-case analyses, or on coarse statistical assumptions—neither of which suitably represents realistic heuristic conditions. The worst-case theories unduly emphasize the intractable versions of problems which, in their usual forms, present less practical difficulty. The statistical theories tend to uniformly weight all instances, for lack of systematic ways to emphasize the types of situations of most practical interest. But the AI systems of the future, like their human counterparts, will normally prefer to satisfy rather than optimize—and we don't yet have theories that can realistically portray those mundane sorts of requirements.

Limitations of context, segmentation, and parsing

When we see seemingly successful demonstrations of machine learning, in carefully prepared test situations, we must be careful about how we draw more general conclusions. This is because there is a large step between the abilities to recognize objects or patterns (1) when they are isolated and (2) when they appear as components of more complex scenes. In section 6.6 of *Perceptrons* we see that we must be prepared to find that even after training a certain network to recognize a certain type of pattern, we may find it unable to recognize that same pattern when embedded in a more complicated context or environment. (Some reviewers have objected that our proofs of this applied only to simple three-layer networks; however, most of those theorems are quite general, as those critics might see, if they'd take the time to extend those proofs.) The problem is that it is usually easy to make isolated recognitions by detecting the presence of various features, and then computing weighted conjunctions of them. Clearly, this is easy to do, even in three-layer acyclic nets. But in compound scenes, this will not work unless the separate features of all the distinct objects are somehow properly assigned to those correct "objects." For the same kind of reason, we cannot expect neural networks to be generally able to parse the tree-like or embedded structures found in the phrase structure of natural-language.

How could we augment connectionist networks to make them able to do such things as to analyze complex visual scenes, or to extract and assign the referents of linguistic expressions to the appropriate contents of short term memories? This will surely need additional architecture to represent that structural analysis of, for example, a visual scene into objects and their relationships, by protecting each mid-level recognizer from seeing inputs derived from other objects, perhaps by arranging for the object-recognizing agents to compete to assign each feature to itself, while denying it to competitors. This has been done successfully in symbolic systems, and parts have been done in connectionist systems (for example, by Waltz and Pollack) but there remain many conceptual missing links in this area—particularly in regard to how another connectionist system could use the output of one that managed to parse the scene. In any case, we should not expect to see simple solutions to these problems, for it may be no accident that such a large proportion of the primate brain is occupied with such functions.

Limitations of opacity

Most serious of all is what we might call the problem of *Opacity*: the knowledge embodied inside a network's numerical coefficients is not accessible outside that net. This is not a challenge we should expect our connectionists to easily solve. I suspect it is so intractable that even our own brains have evolved little such capacity over the billions of years it took to evolve from anemone-like reticulae. Instead, I suspect that our societies and hierarchies of sub-systems have evolved ways to evade the problem, by arranging for some of our systems to learn to "model" what some of our other systems do (see *The Society of Mind*, section 6.12). They may do this, partly, by using information obtained from direct channels into the interiors of those other networks, but mostly, I suspect, they do it less directly—so to speak, behavioristically—by making generalizations based on external observations, as though they were like miniature scientists. In effect, some of our agents invent models of others. Regardless of whether these models may be defective, or even entirely wrong (and here I refrain from directing my aim at peculiarly faulty philosophers), it suffices for those models to be useful in enough situations. To be sure, it might be feasible, in principle, for an external system to accurately model a connectionist network form outside, by formulating and testing hypotheses about its internal structure. But of what use would such a model be, if it merely repeated, redundantly? It would not only be simpler, but also more useful for that higher-level agency to assemble only a pragmatic, heuristic model of that other network's activity, based on concepts already available to that observer. (This is evidently the situation in human psychology. The apparent insights we gain from meditation and other forms of self-examination are genuine only infrequently.)

The problem of opacity grows more acute as representations become more distributed—that is, as we move from symbolic to connectionist poles—and it becomes increasingly more difficult for external systems to analyze and reason about the delocalized ingredients of the knowledge inside distributed representations. It also makes it harder to learn, past a certain degree of complexity, because it is hard to assign credit for success, or to formulate new hypotheses (because the old hypotheses themselves are not "formulated"). Thus, distributed learning ultimately limits growth, no matter how convenient it may be in the short term, because "the idea of a thing with no parts provides nothing that we can use as pieces of explanation" (see *The Society of Mind*, section 5.3).

For such reasons, while homogeneous, distributed learning systems may work well to a certain point, they should eventually start to fail when confronted with problems of larger scale—unless we find ways to compensate the accumulation of many weak connections with some opposing mechanism that favors toward internal simplification and localization. Many connectionist writers seem positively to rejoice in the holistic opacity of representations within which even they are unable to discern the significant parts and relationships. But unless a distributed system has enough ability to crystallize its knowledge into lucid representations of its new subconcepts and substructures, its ability to learn will eventually slow down and it will be unable to solve problems beyond a certain degree of complexity. And although this suggests that homogeneous network architectures may not work well past a certain size, this should be bad news only for those ideologically committed to minimal architectures. For all we know at the present time, the scales at which such systems crash are quite large enough for our purposes. Indeed, the *Society of Mind* thesis holds that most of the "agents" that grow in our brains need operate only on scales so small that each by itself seems no more than a toy. But when we combine enough of them—in ways that are not too delocalized—we can make them do almost anything.

In any case, we should not assume that we always can—or always should—avoid the use of opaque schemes. The circumstances of daily life compel us to make decisions based on "adding up the evidence." We frequently find (when we value our time) that, even if we had the means, it wouldn't pay to analyze. Nor does the *Society of Mind* theory of human thinking suggest otherwise; on the contrary it leads us to expect to encounter incomprehensible representations at every level of the mind. A typical agent does little more than exploit other agents' abilities—hence most of our agents accomplish their job knowing virtually nothing of how it is done.

Analogous issues of opacity arise in the symbolic domain. Just as networks sometimes solve problems by using massive combinations of elements each of which has little individual significance, symbolic systems sometimes solve problems by manipulating large expressions with similarly insignificant terms, as when we replace the explicit structure of a composite Boolean function by a locally senseless canonical form. Although this simplifies some computations by making them more homogeneous, it disperses knowledge about the structure and composition of the data—and thus disables our ability to solve harder problems. At both extremes—in representations that are either too distributed or too discrete—we lose the structural knowledge embodied in the form of intermediate-level concepts. That loss may not be evident, as long as our problems are easy to solve, but those intermediate concepts may be indispensable for solving more advanced problems. Comprehending complex situations usually hinges on discovering a good analogy or variation on a theme. But it is virtually impossible to do this with a representation, such as a logical form, a linear sum, or a holographic transformation—each of whose elements seem meaningless because they are either too large or too small—and thus leaving no way to represent significant parts and relationships.

There are many other problems that invite synthesizing symbolic and connectionist architectures. How can we find ways for nodes to "refer" to other nodes, or to represent knowledge about the roles of particular coefficients? To see the difficulty, imagine trying to represent the structure of the Arch in Patrick Winston's thesis—without simply reproducing that topology. Another critical issue is how to enable nets to make comparisons. This problem is more serious than it might seem. Section 23.1 of *The Society of Mind* discusses the importance of "Differences and Goals," and section 23.2 points out that connectionist networks deficient in memory will find it peculiarly difficult to detect differences between patterns. Networks with weak architectures will also find it difficult to detect or represent (invariant) abstractions; this problem was discussed as early as the Pitts-McCulloch paper of 1947. Yet another important problem for memory-weak, bottom-up mechanisms is that of controlling search: In order to solve hard problems, one may have to consider different alternatives, explore their sub-alternatives, and then make comparisons among them—yet still be able to return to the initial situation without forgetting what was accomplished. This kind of activity, which we call "thinking," requires facilities for temporarily storing partial states of the system without confusing those memories. One answer is to provide, along with the required memory, some systems for learning and executing control scripts, as suggested in section 13.5 of *The Society of Mind*. To do this effectively, we must have some *insulationism* to counterbalance our *connectionism*. Smart systems need both of those components, so the symbolic-connectionist antagonism is not a valid technical issue, but only a transient concern in contemporary scientific politics.

Mind-sculpture

The future work of mind design will not be much like what we do today. Some programmers will continue to use traditional languages and processes. Others programmers will turn toward new kinds of knowledge-based expert systems. But eventually all of this will be incorporated into systems that exploit two new kinds of resources. On one side, we will use huge pre-programmed reservoirs of commonsense knowledge. On the other side, we will have powerful, modular learning machines equipped with no knowledge at all. Then what we know as programming will change its character entirely—to an activity that I envision as more like sculpturing. To program today, we must describe things very carefully, because nowhere is there any margin for error. But once we have modules that know how to learn, we won't have to specify nearly so much—and we'll program on a grander scale, relying on learning to fill in the details.

This doesn't mean, I hasten to add, that things will be simpler than they are now. Instead we'll make our projects more ambitious. Designing an artificial mind will be much like evolving an animal. Imagine yourself at a terminal, assembling various parts of a brain. You'll be specifying the sorts of things that we've only been described heretofore in texts about neuro-anatomy. "Here," you'll find yourself thinking, "We'll need two similar networks that can learn to shift time-signals into spatial patterns so that they can be compared by a feature extractor sensitive to a context about this wide." Then you'll have to sketch the architectures of organs that can learn to supply appropriate inputs to those agencies, and draft the outlines of intermediate organs for learning to suitably encode the outputs to suit the needs of other agencies. Section 31.3 of *The Society of Mind* suggests how a genetic system might mold the form of an agency that is predestined to learn to recognize the presence of particular human individuals. A functional sketch of such a design might turn out to involve dozens of different sorts of organs, centers, layers, and pathways. The human brain might have many thousands of such components.

A functional sketch is only the start. Whenever you employ a learning machine, you must specify more than merely the sources of inputs and des-tinations of outputs. It must also, somehow, be impelled toward the sorts of things you want it to learn—what sorts of hypotheses it should make, how it should compare alternatives, how many examples should be required, and how to decide when enough has been done; when to decide that things have gone wrong, and how to deal with bugs and exceptions. It is all very well for theorists to speak about "spontaneous learning and generalization," but there are too many contingencies in real life for such words to mean anything by themselves. Should that agency be an adventurous risk-taker or a careful, conservative reductionist? One person's intelligence is another's stupidity. And how should that learning machine divide and budget its resources of hardware, time, and memory?

How will we build those grand machines, when so many design constraints are involved? No one will be able to keep track of all the details because, just as a human brain is constituted by interconnecting hundreds of different kinds of highly evolved sub-architectures, so will those new kinds of thinking machines. Each new design will have to be assembled by using libraries of already developed, off-the-shelf sub-systems already known to be able to handle particular kinds of representations and processing—and the designer

583

will be less concerned with what happens inside these units, and more concerned with their interconnections and interrelationships. Because most components will be learning machines, the designer will have to specify, not only what each one will learn, but also which agencies should provide what incentives and rewards for which others. Every such decision about one agency imposes additional constraints and requirements on several others—and, in turn, on how to train those others. And, as in any society, there must be watchers to watch each watcher, lest any one or a few of them get too much control of the rest.

Each agency will need nerve-bundle-like connections to certain other ones, for sending and receiving signals about representations, goals, and constraints—and we'll have to make decisions about the relative size and influence of every such parameter. Consequently, I expect that the future art of brain design will have to be more like sculpturing than like our present craft of programming. It will be much less concerned with the algorithmic details of the sub-machines than with balancing their relationships; perhaps this better resembles politics, sociology, or management than present-day engineering.

Some neural-network advocates might hope that all this will be superfluous. Perhaps, they expect us to find simpler ways. Why not seek to find, instead, how to build one single, huge net that can learn to do all those things by itself. That could, in principle, be done since our own human brains themselves came about as the outcome of one great learning search. We could regard this as proving that just such a project is feasible—but only by ignoring the facts—the unthinkable scale of that billion year venture, and the octillions of lives of our ancestors. Remember, too, that even so, in all that evolutionary search, not all the problems have yet been solved. What will we do when our sculptures don't work? Consider a few of the wonderful bugs that still afflict even our own grand human brains:

- Obsessive preoccupation with inappropriate goals.
- Inattention and inability to concentrate.
- Bad representations.
- Excessively broad or narrow generalizations.
- Excessive accumulation of useless information.
- Superstition; defective credit assignment schema.
- Unrealistic cost/benefit analyses.
- Unbalanced, fanatical search strategies.
- Formation of defective categorizations.
- Inability to deal with exceptions to rules.
- Improper staging of development, or living in the past.
- Unwillingness to acknowledge loss.
- Depression or maniacal optimism.
- Excessive confusion from cross-coupling.

Seeing that list, one has to wonder, "Can people think?" I suspect there is no simple and magical way to avoid such problems in our new machines; it will require a great deal of research and engineering. I suspect that it is no accident that our human brains themselves contain so many different and specialized brain centers. To suppress the emergence of serious bugs, both those natural systems, and the artificial ones we shall construct, will probably require intricate arrangements of interlocking checks and balances, in which each agency is supervised by several others. Furthermore, each of those other agencies must themselves learn when and how to use the resources available to them. How, for example, should each learning system balance the advantages of immediate gain over those of conservative, long-term growth? When should it favor the accumulating of competence over comprehension? In the large-scale design of our human brains, we still don't yet know much of what all those different organs do, but I'm willing to bet that many of them are largely involved in regulating others so as to keep the system as a whole from frequently falling prey to the sorts of bugs we mentioned above. Until we start building brains ourselves, to learn what bugs are most probable, it may remain hard for us to guess the actual functions of much of that hardware.

There are countless wonders yet to be discovered, in these exciting new fields of research. We can still learn a great many things from experiments, on even the very simplest nets. We'll learn even more from trying to make theories about what we observe in this. And surely, soon, we'll start to prepare for that future art of mind design, by experimenting with societies of nets that embody more structured strategies—and consequently make more progress on the networks that make up our own human minds. And in doing all that, we'll discover how to make symbolic representations that are more adaptable, and connectionist representations that are more expressive.

It is amusing how persistently people express the view that machines based on symbolic representations (as opposed, presumably, to connectionist representations) could never achieve much, or ever be conscious and self-aware. For it is, I maintain, precisely because our brains are still mostly connectionist, that we humans have so little consciousness! And it's also why we're capable of so little functional parallelism of thought—and why we have such limited insight into the nature of our own machinery.

Note

This research was funded over a period of years by the Computer Science Division of the Office of Naval Research.

References

Minsky, Marvin, and Seymour Papert [1988], *Perceptrons*, (2nd edition) MIT Press.
Minsky, Marvin [1987a], *The Society of Mind*, Simon and Schuster.

Minsky, Marvin [1987b], "Connectionist Models and their Prospects," Introduction to Feldman and Waltz Nov. 23.

Minsky, Marvin [1974], "A Framework for Representing Knowledge," Report AIM-306, Artificial Intelligence Laboratory, Massachusetts Institute of Technology, Cambridge, MA.